The

NEW YORK

REVISED EDITION

Editor & Chief Restaurant Critic
Edward Guiliano

Managing Editor
Robert C. Fisher

Editorial Director
Jim Burns

Contributing Editors
Jonathan Burton,
Colette Rossant (restaurants),
Lisa Sternlieb, Tina Traster

Associate Editor
Catherine Jordan

Prentice Hall Press Editor
Amit Shah

Operations
Alain Gayot

Directed by
André Gayot

PRENTICE
HALL
PRESS

New York ■ London ■ Toronto ■ Sydney ■ Tokyo ■ Singapore

Other Gault Millau Guides Available
from Prentice Hall Press

The Best of Chicago
The Best of France
The Best of Hong Kong
The Best of Italy
The Best of London
The Best of Los Angeles
The Best of New England
The Best of Paris
The Best of San Francisco
The Best of Washington, D.C.

 Published by Prentice Hall Press
A division of Simon & Schuster Inc.
15 Columbus Circle
New York, NY 10023

Please address all comments regarding
The Best of New York to:
Gault Millau, Inc.
P.O. Box 361144
Los Angeles, CA 90036
(213) 965-3529

Please address all advertising queries to:
Mr. Geoffrey Gropp, Vice President
Welsh Publishing Group, Inc.
300 Madison Avenue
New York, NY 10017
(212) 687-0680

Library of Congress Cataloging-in-Publication Data

The Best of New York /editor and chief critic, Edward Guiliano ;
    contributing editors, Jonathon Burton . . . [et. al.]. — New and rev.
      p. c.m.
    ISBN 0-13-068255-1 : $16.95
    1. New York—Description—1981- —Guide-books.
  I. Guiliano, Edward. II. Burton, Jonathon.
F128.18.B43 1990
917.47'10443—dc20   89-26493

Special thanks to the staff of Prentice Hall Press, Travel Books, for their invaluable
aid in producing these Gault Millau guides.

Ton G

CONTENTS

INTRODUCTION

OF APPLES AND APES

Impressed by the magnitude of the Empire State Building and by the World Trade Center's twin towers? You haven't seen anything yet! These monuments are Lilliputian compared to the piles of envelopes delivered to New York City's residents each year, which, if accumulated—even without the assistance of NASA—would reach an altitude of three-and-a-half-billion feet. That's a bundle of paper. Figures haven't been made available to us, but there is little doubt that the waste products coming out of this metropolis would, if compressed, suffice to erect a bridge from Battery Park to the planet Mars.

In the (temporary) absence of this bridge, be prepared to glide into a paracosmic dimension, to meet supernovas of superlatives and galaxies of numbers beyond the imagination. "Super," "mega," "macro"—the ceiling on our vocabulary falls just short of our needs when it comes to defining and describing the Big Apple. It's the only place on Earth where a humble fruit (the apple, of course) and a primate could have been blown up to such gigantic proportions, even if the Big Apple and King Kong *are* only in the imagination. Only in New York could an ape have grown so big that pest control was handed over to the U.S. Air Force. But the reality of this city is no monkey business: all of the problems here are the size of King Kong. One-tenth of the American population—approximately 25 million human beings—dwells or, sadly, camps out in the greater New York City area. Add to that the twenty million guests a year who stay at the 500-plus hotels in New York, the millions of other visitors accommodated by friends or family, and you have a resident/transient population the size of England's.

Indeed, New York is a very particular and unique "nation": poured into the American mold, anchored to the American soil, the city remains open to the people, ideas, cultures, political currents, religions and products not only of Europe, as it was in the past, but of the entire world. With all this evolving at the lightning speed of communications today, the result is an electronic Babylon, a nouvelle-American melting pot. With ever-changing ingredients and lots of spice, this stew can be a bit hard to swallow sometimes, and could become the prefiguration of the world tomorrow.

Let's keep an attentive watch on what's happening to this great city. It's a captivating show for sure, even if you come to hate it because of the not-so-well-kept streets, the rundown sidewalks, the semi-abandoned neighborhoods. You may be disconcerted by the constant shift from riches to rags, and by the vast discrepancies between the chic set and its marble palaces and the have-nots, living in the shambles of a Third World–like setting.

But what energy, what dynamism, is contained in these contradictory patterns, and how to sort it all out? That's where we come in. Our team of critics has tasted, prodded, coaxed and sampled the best that New York has to offer, for this new edition of *The*

Best of New York. A lot has changed since we published our first guide to New York in 1981, and it is with understandable pride that we present you with our most recent findings—which we present after years of meticulously combing the city. Need the perfect restaurant, the nattiest hotel, a stellar night on the town? Just turn to the appropriate pages—we're confident that you will find your answer.

Here's hoping that you enjoy New York as much as we do. Super, mega, macro—Big Apple, you're a lot more than mere boasting and bravura.

André Gayot

A DISCLAIMER

Readers are advised that prices and conditions change over the course of time. The restaurants, hotels, shops and other establishments reviewed in this book have been reviewed over a period of time, and the reviews reflect the personal experiences of the reviewers. The reviewers and publishers cannot be held responsible for the experiences of the reader related to the establishments reviewed. Readers are invited to write the publisher with ideas, comments and suggestions for future editions.

RESTAURANTS

INTRODUCTION

THEATER OF THE 1990s

Anyone who follows the theater knows there are good seasons and bad seasons, brilliant new plays and dismal fiascos. Another opening, another show, is the rallying cry for the eternal optimism of the American theater. Anyone who follows the restaurant scene knows that these establishments increasingly have become a sort of theater in our generation, and nowhere more so than in America's stage capital, New York. There are openings and closings to be sure; there are stars—in the kitchens, in the front room, on the banquettes and at the tables; there are stunning new stage sets. People used to dress for Broadway shows in New York; now they don their finest wear for its top restaurants.

Professional theater critics see beyond a single play or season and note patterns and trends. Similarly, as professional restaurant critics, we have noted in the past few decades the revolution in American tastes and attitudes. Healthier and lighter foods, fish and increasingly diverse produce and types of preparations have all been embraced. New Yorkers have become increasingly discriminating and demanding, and the overall quality of restaurants has risen sharply. The restaurant scene in New York retains its unmatched vibrancy and diversity, reflecting the richness and high energy of this city that never sleeps. The trends we noted in our previous edition have continued: more Asian restaurants and influences; more bistro fare; and more fusion cuisine built upon French classics and techniques and incorporating Italian, Asian, Californian and Southwestern cooking. Some notable new trends, however, have emerged in recent years.

When the stock market crashed in October 1987, restaurants were booming like never before. Expense accounts knew no limits, two-income families were rewarding themselves (out of both desire and necessity) with meals out several nights a week, people were entertaining not at home but in restaurants, and tourists were visiting restaurants not just to eat but as part of their sightseeing and theater agenda. The market crash did not put an end to all this, but it did instill fiscal caution and, thus, set off a restaurant recession. At the quality restaurants of the sort we write about, business dropped about twenty percent from their precrash highs. Some places were hurt; some hopes and dreams were dashed; and yet other places reverberated with the kind of success for which New York is famous. And as always, there are yet new openings and unspoiled dreams.

One notable trend that will carry through the early nineties is toward stable, even lower prices. Tabs barely have risen in the past few years, and a number of upscale restaurants have either cut their prices or introduced a fixed-price lunch or dinner option that can be a real bargain. Another trend is to larger, brasserie-style restaurants aspiring to good (not outstanding) quality, offering moderate prices and anticipating profits by sheer volume of business.

The culinary landscape of New York is also undergoing some striking remodeling. Much of the excitement in the past few years has been in lower Manhattan, at least from

23rd Street south. Chelsea and TriBeCa, in particular, have emerged as restaurant destinations to go along with already thriving Greenwich Village and SoHo. Midtown and the Upper East Side are holding their own, and the enigmatic Upper West Side continues in singing its restaurant woes. For quality, innovation and trend-setting excitement, the arrows are pointing south.

Modern Gotham is a culinary crossroads where people, products and ideas travel en masse and often in style. Staying au courant of its ever-changing scene is easier said than done, and a nightmare for anyone publishing a book such as this, with a lag of a few months between the finalizing of text and publication. We have done our best to be timely and accurate, and trust our readers will understand the inevitable ravages of time.We hope you will find this a truthful guide that will help you explore and enjoy the restaurants of New York.

ABOUT THE REVIEWS

Gault Millau ranks restaurants in the same manner French students are graded, on a scale of one to twenty, with twenty being unattainable perfection. While thousands of satisfying New York restaurants rate below a ten, with an eight or nine still a passing grade, for *The Best of New York* we have selected restaurants rated ten or higher; these are restaurants that for one or more reasons we can recommend. The rankings reflect *primarily the quality of the cooking*, decor, service, welcome and atmosphere are explicitly commented on within the reviews. Restaurants that are ranked thirteen and above are distinguished with toques (chef's hats) according to the following table:

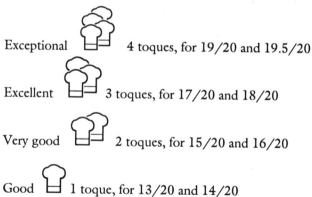

Exceptional — 4 toques, for 19/20 and 19.5/20

Excellent — 3 toques, for 17/20 and 18/20

Very good — 2 toques, for 15/20 and 16/20

Good — 1 toque, for 13/20 and 14/20

These ranks are *relative*. One toque for 13/20 is a good but modest ranking for a highly reputed restaurant, yet is highly complimentary for a small place without much culinary pretension.

Unless otherwise noted, the prices given are for a complete meal for two persons, including an appetizer, main course and dessert for each person, and a bottle of wine. Naturally the prices are approximations; they have been checked and rechecked, but over time will have a tendency to rise. Menus and dishes we've described are also subject to the winds of change. Note well that *prices do not include tax and tip.* In New York City, a sales tax of 8.25 percent is added to every bill. Tipping, which constitutes the bulk of the service staff's wages, and thus should not be considered wholly optional, averages 15 percent to 20 percent, and in special circumstances and for special service, is more. Many diners find it convenient to double the sales tax to arrive at a 16.5 percent gratuity. The number and quality of wines and beverages ordered, as well as the type of main course selected, will significantly affect the bottom line of your check. Bear that in mind when reviewing our average prices, adjust accordingly, and add the tax and tip (say, another 25 percent) to come up with a more individual and useful estimate. Remember, too, that reservations are always suggested and often essential.

TOQUE TALLY

19.5/20

Le Cirque

19/20

Le Bernardin

18/20

The Quilted Giraffe
Restaurant Lafayette

17/20

Chanterelle
Montrachet

Le Périgord
San Domenico

16/20

Arcadia
Aureole
Bouley
Cellar in the Sky
Le Cygne
Lutèce
The Sign of the Dove

15/20

Adrienne
Allison
Arizona 206
Duane Park Café
Felidia
The Four Seasons
Gotham Bar & Grill
La Grenouille
Harlequin
Hubert's
Le Madri

Manhattan Ocean Club
Mitsukoshi
Mondrian
Nippon
Parioli Romanissimo
Petrossian
The Polo
Le Régence
La Réserve
Tai Hong Lau
Umeda
Union Square Café

14/20

Acquavit
An American Place
Amerigo's
Arqua'
Aurora
Il Cantinori
La Caravelle
The Carlyle Restaurant
Cavaliere
Cent' Anni
Le Chantilly
Chelsea Central
Chez Louis
Chikubu
Chin Chin
China Grill
La Colombe d'Or
La Côte Basque
Dawat
Eze
"44"
Hatsuhana
Jane's Bar & Grill
Kuruma Zushi
Lola
Malvasia

La Métairie (*Upper East Side*)
Mezzogiorno
Michael's
Il Mulino
Il Nido
Orso
Palio
Pamir
Paola's Restaurant
Park Bistro
Periyali
Primavera
Prunelle
Quatorze
Raphäel
Remi
The River Café
Rosemarie's
Sandro's
Scarlatti
Shun Lee Palace
Sistina
Sofi
Sparks Steakhouse
TriBeCa Grill
La Tulipe
The Village Green

13/20

Adele
Alcala
Anatolia
Andiamo
Auntie Yuan Restaurant
The Ballroom
Barocco
Barrow Street Bistro
Bellini by Cipriani
Bice
Bombay Palace

Brandywine
Bukhara
Café de Bruxelles
Café des Artistes
Café Luxembourg
Café Pierre
Café Rakel
Canton
Chelsea Trattoria Italiano
Chez Jacqueline
The Coach House
Coastal
Darbar
Da Silvano
Da Umberto
L'Escale
Ferrier
Fu's
Gage & Tollner
Gallagher's
La Gauloise
The Gibbon
Indochine
Jane Street Seafood Café
John Clancy's Restaurant
King Fung
Lello
Lusardi's
Madeline's
Manducati's
Manhattan Chili Co.
Maxim's
Memphis

La Métairie (*Greenwich Village*)
Mezzaluna
Mie
Moreno Ristorante
The Nice Restaurant
Oriental Pearl
Oyster Bar & Restaurant
Le Pactole
Peter Luger
Poiret
Positano
Primola
Provence
Le Refuge
René Pujol
La Ripaille
The Russian Tea Room
Sabor
San Giusto
Seryna
Sfuzzi
Smith & Wollensky
Terrace Restaurant
Tommasso's
Tommy Tang's
Toscana
Trastevere
I Tre Merli
"21" Club
Vanessa
Water's Edge
Wilkinson's Seafood Café
Zarela

BY CUISINE

AFGHAN

Pamir

AMERICAN

Adele

The American Harvest Restaurant
An American Place
Arcadia
Arizona 206
Aureole
The Barclay
Barrow Street Bistro

Bridge Café
B. Smith's
Café Luxembourg
Carolina
Chelsea Central
Claire
The Coach House
Coastal
The Dolphin
Duane Park Café
"44"
Gage & Tollner
Gallagher's
Garvin's
Gloucester House
Gotham Bar & Grill
Jane's Bar & Grill
Jezebel
Keen's
Lola
Madeline's
Manhattan Chili Co.
Manhattan Ocean Club
Man Ray
Memphis
Michael's
Mondrian
Nightfalls
The Odeon
Oyster Bar & Restaurant
The Palm
The Polo
The River Café
Rogers & Barbero
Sam's Café
Santa Fe
The Sea Grill
Sidewalkers
The Sign of the Dove
Smith & Wollensky
Sparks Steakhouse
Sylvia's
Tenbrooks
TriBeCa Grill
"21" Club

Union Square Café
Village Atelier
The Village Green
Ye Waverly Inn
Wilkinson's Seafood Café

BELGIAN

Café de Bruxelles

BRAZILIAN

Cabana Carioca

CAJUN

Memphis

CARIBBEAN

Devon House Ltd.
Lola

CHINESE

Auntie Yuan Restaurant
Canton
Chin Chin
Fu's
King Fung
The Nice Restaurant
Oriental Pearl
Panda Garden
Pig Heaven
Say Eng Look
Shun Lee Palace
Tai Hong Lau
20 Mott Street Restaurant
Wong Kee

CONTINENTAL

Adrienne
Cellar in the Sky
Devon House Ltd.

Mortimer's
One If By Land, Two If By Sea
The Rainbow Room
Sammy's Roumanian Restaurant
The Stanhope Dining Room
Water's Edge
Windows on the World Restaurant

CUBAN

Sabor

ECLECTIC

China Grill
The Four Seasons
The Gibbon
Greene Street Café
Hubert's
Island
150 Wooster
The Quilted Giraffe
Tavern on the Green

ETHIOPIAN

Abyssinia
Blue Nile

FRENCH

Allison
Aurora
Le Bernardin
Bistro Bamboche
The Black Sheep
La Bohême
La Boîte en Bois
Bouley
Brandywine
Café Crocodile
Café des Artistes
Café de Bruxelles
Café du Parc
Café Loup
Café Luxembourg

Café Pierre
Café Rakel
Capsouto Frères
La Caravelle
The Carlyle Restaurant
Chanterelle
Le Chantilly
Chez Jacqueline
Chez Josephine
Chez Louis
Chez Ma Tante
Le Cirque
La Cité
La Colombe d'Or
La Côte Basque
Le Cygne
L'Escale
Eze
Ferrier
La Gauloise
The Gibbon
La Grenouille
Hulot's
Lutèce
Man Ray
Maxim's
La Métairie (*Greenwich Village*)
La Métairie (*Upper East Side*)
La Mirabelle
Mondrian
Montrachet
Nicole Brasserie de Paris
Le Pactole
Park Bistro
Le Périgord
Petrossian
Poiret
Provence
Prunelle
Quatorze
Raoul's
Raphaël
Le Refuge
Le Régence
Le Relais

René Pujol
La Réserve
Restaurant Lafayette
La Ripaille
Terrace Restaurant
Au Troquet
La Tulipe
Vanessa
Le Veau d'Or

GREEK

Periyali

INDIAN

Akbar
Bombay Palace
Bukhara
Darbar
Dawat

ITALIAN

Alo Alo
Amerigo's
Andiamo
Arqua'
Baci
Barbetta
Barocco
Bellini by Cipriani
Bice
Bravo Gianni
Café du Parc
Il Cantinori
Cavaliere
Cent' Anni
Chelsea Trattoria Italiano
Contrapunto
Da Silvano
Da Umberto
Dieci Ristorante
Dominick's
Elio's
Ennio & Michael Restaurant

Erminia
Felidia
Frank's
Lattanzi
Lello
Lusardi's
Le Madri
Malvasia
Manducati's
Manganaro's
Mezzaluna
Mezzogiorno
Moreno Ristorante
Il Mulino
Il Nido
Orso
Palio
Paola's Restaurant
Paper Moon
Parioli Romanissimo
Petaluma
Pietro-Vanessa
Pinnochio
Positano
Primavera
Primola
Quaglino by Tino Fontana
Rao's
Remi
Rosemarie's
Rosolio
San Domenico
Sandro's
San Giusto
Sant Ambroeus
Scarlatti
Sfuzzi
Siracusa
Sistina
Sofi
Tommasso's
Toscana
Trastevere
I Tre Merli
Tre Scalini

Il Valletto
Vucciria

JAPANESE

Chikubu
The Gibbon
Hatsuhana
Hyotan-Nippon
Inagiku
Kuruma Zushi
Mie
Mitsukoshi
Nippon
Omen
Seryna
Tatany Village
Umeda

JEWISH

Lattanzi
Sammy's Roumanian Restaurant

MEDITERRANEAN

Eze

MEXICAN

Cinco de Mayo
Rosa Mexicano
Santa Fe
Zarela

MIDDLE EASTERN

Cedars of Lebanon

MOROCCAN

Café Crocodile

PERUVIAN

The Ballroom

RUSSIAN

The Russian Tea Room

SCANDINAVIAN

Acquavit

SEAFOOD

Le Bernardin
Claire
The Dolphin
Gloucester House
Jane Street Seafood Café
John Clancy's Restaurant
Manhattan Ocean Club
Oyster Bar & Restaurant
The Sea Grill
Sidewalkers
Water's Edge
Wilkinson's Seafood Café

SOUL FOOD

Jezebel
Sylvia's

SPANISH

Alcalà
The Ballroom
El Faro
Harlequin
Paradis Barcelona
El Rincón de España

STEAKHOUSE

Frank's

Gallagher's
The Palm
Peter Luger
Smith & Wollensky
Sparks Steakhouse

SWISS

Chalet Suisse

THAI

Bangkok House
Thailand

Tommy Tang's
Toon's

TURKISH

Anatolia

VIETNAMESE

Cuisine de Saigon
Indochine
Saigon Restaurant

BY AREA

BELOW HOUSTON STREET

Abyssinia
Allison
The American Harvest Restaurant
Arqua'
Barocco
Bouley
Bridge Café
Café Rakel
Canton
Capsouto Frères
Cellar in the Sky
Chanterelle
Cinco de Mayo
Duane Park Café
Greene Street Café
King Fung
Madeline's
Mezzogiorno
Montrachet
Il Mulino
The Nice Restaurant
The Odeon
Omen
150 Wooster

Oriental Pearl
Le Pactole
Pietro-Vanessa
Provence
Raoul's
El Rincón de España
Rosemarie's
Saigon Restaurant
Sammy's Roumanian Restaurant
Say Eng Look
Tai Hong Lau
Tenbrooks
Thailand
Tommy Tang's
I Tre Merli
TriBeCa Grill
20 Mott Street Restaurant
Vucciria
Windows on the World Restaurant
Wong Kee

GREENWICH VILLAGE

Barrow Street Bistro
The Black Sheep

La Bohême
Café de Bruxelles
Café Loup
Il Cantinori
Cent' Anni
Chez Jacqueline
Chez Ma Tante
The Coach House
Cuisine de Saigon
Da Silvano
Ennio & Michael Restaurant
El Faro
Garvin's
La Gauloise
Gotham Bar & Grill
Harlequin
Indochine
Jane Street Seafood Café
John Clancy's Restaurant
Manhattan Chili Co.
La Métairie
Mie
One If By Land, Two If By Sea
La Ripaille
Rosolio
Sabor
Siracusa
Tatany Village
Toon's
Au Troquet
La Tulipe
Vanessa
Village Atelier
The Village Green
Ye Waverly Inn

14TH STREET TO 42ND STREET

An American Place
The Ballroom
Brandywine
Café du Parc

Cedars of Lebanon
Chelsea Central
Chelsea Trattoria Italiano
Claire
La Colombe d'Or
Da Umberto
The Dolphin
L'Escale
Eze
Frank's
Keen's
Lola
Le Madri
Manganaro's
Man Ray
Moreno Ristorante
Park Bistro
Periyali
Positano
Quatorze
Rogers & Barbero
Sofi
Umeda
Union Square Café

MIDTOWN EAST (E. 42nd Street to E. 59th Street)

Akbar
Aurora
The Barclay
Bice
Bukhara
Chalet Suisse
Le Chantilly
Chez Louis
Chikubu
Chin Chin
La Côte Basque
Le Cygne
Dawat
Felidia

The Four Seasons
Gloucester House
La Grenouille
Hatsuhana
Inagiku
Lello
Lutèce
Mitsukoshi
Mondrian
Il Nido
Nippon
Oyster Bar & Restaurant
The Palm
Paper Moon
Paradis Barcelona
Le Périgord
Prunelle
The Quilted Giraffe
Restaurant Lafayette
Rosa Mexicano
Sandro's
San Giusto
Scarlatti
Seryna
Shun Lee Palace
Smith & Wollensky
Sparks Steakhouse
Toscana
Tre Scalini
Zarela

MIDTOWN WEST
(W. 42nd Street to W. 59th Street)

Acquavit
Adrienne
Barbetta
Bellini by Cipriani
Le Bernardin
Bombay Palace
B. Smith's
Cabana Carioca

La Caravelle
Carolina
Chez Josephine
China Grill
La Cité
Darbar
"44"
Gallagher's
Jezebel
Kuruma Zushi
Lattanzi
Manhattan Ocean Club
Michael's
Nicole Brasserie de Paris
Orso
Palio
Petrossian
The Rainbow Room
Raphaël
Remi
René Pujol
La Réserve
The Russian Tea Room
San Domenico
The Sea Grill
"21" Club

UPPER EAST SIDE

Alo Alo
Anatolia
Arcadia
Arizona 206
Auntie Yuan Restaurant
Aureole
Bangkok House
Bistro Bamboche
Bravo Gianni
Café Crocodile
Café Pierre
The Carlyle Restaurant
Le Cirque
Contrapunto

Devon House Ltd.
Dieci Ristorante
Elio's
Erminia
Ferrier
Fu's
The Gibbon
Huberts
Hulot's
Hyotan-Nippon
Island
Jane's Bar & Grill
Lusardi's
Malvasia
Maxim's
La Métairie
Mezzaluna
Mortimer's
Pamir
Panda Garden
Paola's Restaurant
Parioli Romanissimo
Petaluma
Pig Heaven
Pinnochio
The Polo
Primavera
Primola
Quaglino by Tino Fontana
Rao's
Le Refuge
Le Régence
Le Relais
Sam's Café
Sant Ambroeus
The Sign of the Dove
Sistina
The Stanhope Dining Room
Sylvia's
Trastavere
Il Valletto
Le Veau d'Or
Wilkinson's Seafood Café

UPPER WEST SIDE

Alcala
Andiamo
Baci
Blue Nile
La Boîte en Bois
Café des Artistes
Café Luxembourg
Cavaliere
Coastal
Memphis
La Mirabelle
Poiret
Santa Fe
Sfuzzi
Sidewalkers
Tavern on the Green
Terrace Restaurant

OTHER BOROUGHS

Adele (*Brooklyn*)
Amerigo's (*the Bronx*)
Dominick's (*the Bronx*)
Gage & Tollner (*Brooklyn*)
Manducati's (*Queens*)
Nightfalls (*Brooklyn*)
Peter Luger (*Brooklyn*)
The River Café (*Brooklyn*)
Tommasso's (*Brooklyn*)
Water's Edge (*Queens*)

Note that in the following chapter, average prices given do not include tax (which is a whopping 8.25 percent in New York), or gratuity. You can figure on adding roughly 25 percent to each of the prices quoted here, for your final bill.

BELOW HOUSTON STREET

10/20 Abyssinia
  35 Grand St. (Thompson St.)
  226-5959

ETHIOPIAN
Open Mon.-Fri. 6 p.m.-11:30 p.m., Sat.-Sun. 1 p.m.-midnight. Cards: AE.

Ah, traditional Ethiopian cuisine in SoHo. Talk about competition! Owner Araya Selassie has had a solo field since opening this still busy oasis in 1982. Talk about quintessential New York! Where else would restaurant goers support themselves on three-legged stools, eat with their hands and take lessons in African table etiquette in a room dressed in grasscloth wallpaper and filled with African handcrafts, folk paintings and musical instruments? Is ersatz Africa as good as the real thing? At Abyssinia, it's good enough.

The menu is divided into four categories: vegetarian, fish, poultry and lamb. Everything is served on very thin, spongy, white pancakes called injera, which are used to pick up the food, replacing forks and knives. (You will probably end up licking your fingers.) Doro wot is marinated chicken served in a thick, fiery red-pepper sauce called berbère (you'll need plenty of beer to soothe your burning throat). The equally spicy beef stew has a nice touch of ginger, and the lamb dish, ye'beg alitcha, by far the best on the menu and the restaurant's most popular dish, is served in the same red sauce, but this time with the addition of turmeric, onions and exotic African spices. All the dishes are well prepared, even if the chef skimps on the meat. The Ethiopian version of steak tartare is delightful, coupled with azefa wot, a lentil salad reminiscent of French bistro fare. Vegetables are sadly overcooked, and the fish dishes relatively unencumbered constitute an alternative for those who are not fond of hot and spicy cuisine. For dessert, stick to fruit unless you succumb to the "darkest Africa" chocolate-chip cake (made with zucchini). Enjoy a sweet glass of Ethiopian honey wine instead, a perfect touch to end the evening. A meal with beer costs $40 for two, plus tax and tip.

Allison
  38 Dominick St.
  (Varick & Hudson Sts.)
  727-1188

FRENCH
Open Mon.-Wed. noon-2:15 p.m. & 6:15 p.m.-11 p.m., Thurs.-Fri. noon-2:15 p.m. & 6:30 p.m.-11:30 p.m., Sat. 6:30 p.m.-11:30 p.m. All major cards.

Allison Price, for whom this restaurant is named, plays it safe with simple decor: a long, white room with banquettes, photographs on the walls and black drapery hiding the kitchen. She takes risks, however, with the southwestern French cuisine in this TriBeCa restaurant, opened in 1989. Ms. Price, also the owner, will greet you at the door, and you can wait for your table at the long, crowded bar. Guests are from the neighborhood: relaxed and unassuming. Hot sourdough rolls and sweet butter are handed to diners along with a short menu. Best among the appetizers is a portion of tender, homemade smoked duck served with roasted barley and tender mixed greens in a light vinaigrette. Also excellent is a transparent tomato consommé garnished with white beans, a few wild mushrooms and a leek cleverly stuffed with seafood and tomato. The ragoût of mussels with white beans, wild mushrooms and artichokes is hearty and warming. Among the salads, try one of beets with a tangy vinaigrette. Also, Allison recommends the marinated mackerel or the smoked salmon roulade.

Chef Thomas Valenti's strength lies in his broth-cooked dishes. A sautéed sea bass swims in a tomato broth flavored with tarragon and black olives and is served with artichoke hearts over a light, fluffy couscous; a tender squab is coupled with lentils. The latter is poached in poultry broth so that its slightly gamey taste is accentuated. The roast guinea hen (one of the best sellers), tried once, is surprisingly bland, although its accompaniment of creamy thyme risotto is unusual and perfectly executed. The lamb shank is recommended.

Desserts sound enticing, but don't live up to

their descriptions: the dough is too heavy on a pistachio-and-fig tart; the powerful cinnamon ice cream overpowers a delicate pear-and-walnut tart and the grapefruit sauce topping a terrine of orange and grapefruit is insipid. Waiters are attentive without being obtrusive and diners are served quickly. A wine list of about 60 offerings provides reasonably priced French wines with a smattering of California picks. If it's still available, try the Rully Clos St. Jacques 1986 at $22. Reservations, made a few days in advance, are necessary at this deservedly popular restaurant, poised to become an admired feature on the New York restaurant scene. Dinner for two, with wine, runs about $120.

12/20 The American Harvest Restaurant

Vista International Hotel,
3 World Trade Center
938-9100

AMERICAN

Open Mon.-Fri. 7 a.m.-10 a.m., noon-2:30 p.m. & 6 p.m.-10 p.m.; closed last 2 weeks before Labor Day weekend. All major cards.

They try hard at this Hilton restaurant, opened in 1981 on the plaza level of the Vista Hotel. We give it an American salute for its concept, which is announced by the harvest table at the entrance: "to present the freshest of foods at their peak of flavor in American dishes." Thus, the menu changes monthly; for instance, in August, when locally grown sweet corn comes to market, Martha's Vineyard green-corn pudding is featured. (Speaking of corn, we recommend the Tennessee corn soup.) In February, citrus fruits from Florida and Texas are featured. Gimmicks aside, the menu that executive chef Walter Plendner has been supervising since the restaurant opened is straightforward. But, then it's hard to put the gimmicks aside. Indeed, a perfectly sound baked red snapper comes, in February, with lemon-orange sauce. Ditto for the tasty charcoal-broiled salmon unnecessarily bombarded with juniper berries, or the broiled salmon served with lemon mayonnaise. For starters, the ocean-fresh Blue Point oysters always satisfy. Try the seafood sausage with lime-butter sauce. Wisconsin lake trout with golden mushrooms makes for a good main course as does the crisply roasted duckling with Casselman plum sauce. Seasonal vegetables usually

are prepared properly and are a bonus. The staff's recommended desserts include the blackberry cream puff and the open plum tart.

The all-American theme permeates the restaurant's five dining rooms, which are quiet and intimate. Floor-to-ceiling glass vitrines featuring a specially commissioned folk-art collection by William Accorsi separate the rooms. The extensive wine list is heavily American, and the restaurant hosts a winemaker's dinner series. Lunch averages $60 for two, and dinner is $100 or more, with a modest wine, plus tax and tip.

Arqua'
281 Church St. (White St.)
334-1888

ITALIAN

Open Mon.-Thurs. noon-3 p.m. & 5:30 p.m.-11 p.m., Fri. noon-3 p.m. & 5:30 p.m.-11:30 p.m., Sat. 5:30 p.m.-11:30 p.m. Cards: AE.

When Venice was a republic, the Doges periodically repaired to Arqua' Petrarca, a village near Padua, to discuss matters of state in a relaxing atmosphere. Arqua' was also the home of the Renaissance poet Petrarch and, more recently, of Leonardo Pulito, this restaurant's chef and co-owner (with wife Antoinette). The decor—in what must have once been a nondescript industrial space before its 1986 transformation into a fine, friendly restaurant—has cleverly been kept minimal, with little within the soaring Venetian pink walls to distract you from the serious business of eating. The lighting is kind and the tables unusually well spaced. Arqua' has a tight focus—the food of the Veneto. The hallmarks are seafood, fresh pasta, polenta, simple preparation, relatively little fat and the freshest of ingredients.

The small, well-edited menu features, to start, the classic Venetian marinated mackerel in a light sweet-and-sour sauce spiked with onion; a good stuffed artichoke; fresh pickled sardines with onions; grilled sea scallops and many good homemade pastas, especially the pappardelle dei dogi with ricotta and radicchio, lamb-stuffed half-moon pasta, airy agnolotti filled with spinach in a light tomato sauce and the mattonella d'Arqua', pasta layered with artichoke purée and brought together with béchamel. When they are available, the whole baby octopuses are delicious. Various risottos are offered, most nota-

18

bly the famous Venetian black-ink risotto, which you can get when seppie, tiny inkfish, are available from Italy. Main courses, on the whole, come off less well than the starters; the kitchen seems overtaxed at peak hours. The sometimes curt service, occasionally overcooked fish (just a piece of fish on a plate), and inordinately long waits between courses bear out this theory. Poached red snapper in red-pepper-tomato sauce with polenta is a popular fish dish. Pollo al prosecco, chicken braised in the slightly sparkling wine of the Veneto with a paste of olives, mushrooms and sweet peppers, is a good main course choice. Also try the tender sautéed veal chop with sage and shallots. If you like liver, it's delicious here, served thinly sliced with sautéed onions and triangles of polenta. As for dessert, with tiramisu on every Italian menu in town, one can afford to be picky. The desserts at Arqua' aren't special, except for its lemony cheesecake. Of course, there's a supremely rich chocolate cake for votaries. Strawberries or a raspberry tart are options. Prices are moderate; about $80 for two for dinner.

Barocco
301 Church St. (Walker St.)
431-1445

ITALIAN

Open Mon.-Sat. 6:30 p.m.-11:30 p.m., Sun. 6:30 p.m.-10:30 p.m. All major cards.

Noisy, convivial Barocco attracts Bohemians with money and the people who subsidize them: publishers, gallery owners and parents. You'll have better luck with the appetizers and pastas instead of the entrées; the portions are skimpy; and turnover, at least on weekends, is strongly encouraged. (Those who don't dig in their heels to slow down the pace will find themselves back on the street faster than you can say pappardelle al coniglio.) Still, Barocco remains popular for very good reasons. It bills itself as a trattoria, and it effortlessly achieves an ambience that is warm and relaxed, but still electric with the excitement of people who know they are in the right place at the right time—and having a good time and a good meal to boot. Everyone's packed into a single room on the ground floor of a turn-of-the-century loft building. Typical of many warehouse-turned-restaurants, the room has high ceilings and is punctuated by tall, iron Corinthian columns. The decor is minimal and the food simply prepared. And when the kitchen is under pressure, it's best to stick with preprepared or especially simple dishes.

The house bread, a crusty homemade Tuscan loaf, is one of the best in town. They dress this up with garlic, call it fettunta, and give you two slices for $2, which would qualify as petty larceny were the dish not so delicious. Every other appetizer sampled was equally tasty, from grilled eggplant, zucchini and red peppers, to a refreshing salad of fennel with Parmigiano, to carpaccio of beef with arugula and shards of Parmigiano. We'd happily argue in favor of any of the homemade pastas, from the aforementioned pappardelle al coniglio (with rabbit, black olives and sun-dried tomatoes), fettuccine with tomatoes and artichokes, to delicate spinach ravioli (its ricotta-spinach filling is tinged with nutmeg; its light, fresh tomato sauce topped with shreds of fresh basil). Entrées fare less well. Whole roasted snapper with herbs and garlic can be dry and bland. Roast pork—paper-thin slices of meat, served at room temperature and fanned out around a pile of broccolirab (rape)—is somewhat better, but not a meal you eat with gusto. The à la carte roast potatoes, however, topped with deep-fried sage leaves and rosemary, are terrific. Try the roast rabbit with polenta. For dessert, there are good renditions of the standards—tiramisu and ricotta cheesecake as well as homemade ice cream. The serviceable wine list offers mostly Italian. Plan on spending $80 for two, with wine.

Bouley
165 Duane St.
(Hudson & Greenwich Sts.)
608-3852

FRENCH

Open Mon.-Fri. noon-3 p.m. & 6 p.m.-11 p.m., Sat. 6 p.m.-11 p.m. All major cards.

It still takes an eternity between courses here, but the wait now ends in rejoicing at the arrival of consistently excellent dishes. A couple of years after opening Bouley, chef David Bouley deserves to proudly display his name above his magnificent front door. A carved, curvilinear wood construction, it opens off Duane Square (a triangular slice of TriBeCa) and into a strikingly handsome cloister of a restaurant. The setting has the feel of a European inn. Beige walls, vaulted ceilings, paintings, tiles, antiques, sunset lighting, Christofle forks, Limoges china—this table stage set evokes the inspirational countryside of Provence, with unintentional hints of southern Germany. Service and setting go black-tie all the way.

Bouley worked in France for lauded chefs Bocuse, Girardet, Lenôtre and Vergé, and in New York at Le Cirque, before helping to establish and becoming the first chef for the very fine Montrachet. At Bouley, however, the dishes sometimes sound better than they taste. What can be recommended without hesitation for a starter is the warm crabmeat with asparagus-and-leek vinaigrette, the simple fresh tuna cured gravlax style and served with a three-radish salad (Bouley loves to offer things in threes). To continue, have the roasted pigeon, one breast served with a slice of grilled foie gras, the other stuffed into a cabbage leaf, and accompanied by wild mushrooms and baby yellow zucchini. The spit-roasted duckling with nine spices also is recommended, as are a number of salad appetizers, including a stimulating assortment of three, named a panache of salads. Also try the fricassee of clams and oysters and the venison with red-wine-and-black-pepper sauce. On the eight-course tasting menu, the only dish that used to be consistently underwhelming was the tiny rack and loin of lamb, but its revival is emblematic of the greater control in and out of the kitchen.

Meals begin with complimentary and generally tasty finger foods and end with a complimentary and a generally so-so platter of petits fours. Desserts are distinguished by their striking presentations and their busy, ambitious and usually successful combinations. Crowned by soufflés and sorbets, the pistachio opera cake with chocolate-ganache terrine served with a bitter-chocolate sorbet is dark, deep and luscious. The mostly French wine offerings are sound, but wildly overpriced. This place is pitched to the Wall Street crowd for lunch and the uptown taxi and limousine crowd for dinner. If prices were closer to Earth, we could get more excited about this romantic, maturing restaurant. Jacket and tie are required for men. For dinner, expect to pay $200 or more for two, plus tax and tip.

11/20 Bridge Café
279 Water St. (Dover St.)
227-3344
AMERICAN
Open daily 11:45 a.m.-midnight. All major cards.

A brick-red structure built in 1801 houses this cozy restaurant. Huddled in the shadow of the Brooklyn Bridge, it greets the eye like a candle in the wilderness. Located a few blocks north of the South Street Seaport, it is the one sign of life in another kind of wilderness—the only bona fide restaurant anywhere near the theme park that Rowse built. Inside the warm and relaxing room, a bar spans one wall, and a dozen or so tables with red-and-white checked cloths fill the balance of the space without overcrowding it. An air of old New York that never goes out of style hangs here. Today, it attracts neighborhood families and couples for dinner, and Wall Streeters and city workers for weekday meals and drinks (the roster of which includes seven wines by the glass).

A number of chefs have waltzed in and out of the kitchen at the Bridge Café during its ten years, but the current keeper of the title, John Hesse, has stabilized things. He's not daring, but steers a steady course over basically American waters that never varies much from an acceptable direction. Soft-shell crabs in shallot butter with a range of vegetables on the side is the dish to order (and the restaurant's best-seller) when it's available. Fish fares a bit better than fowl. Duck in green-peppercorn sauce is gussied up and overcooked; chicken tastes dried out. Grilled Norwegian salmon served with Belgian endive, tomato and balsamic vinegar is, on the other hand, cooked perfectly and is a good bet. Go with the corn chowder for a starter. Desserts, such as apple-nut cake served with a warm rum sauce, or pear-and-ginger tart, or pecan pie, are homey, hearty and filling. The American/European wine list is a good one, with a range of good choices and modest, attractive prices (mostly in the teens and twenties). Consider the Bridge café for brunch. The food is predictable (such as omelets, banana-buckwheat pancakes, sautéed flounder) but the setting is appealing. Dinner, with wine, averages about $90 for two.

Café Rakel

231 Varick St. (Clarkson St.)
929-1630

FRENCH

Open Mon.-Fri. noon-2:15 p.m.& 6:30 p.m.-11 p.m., Sat. 6:30 p.m.-11 p.m. All major cards.

The "kel" of Rakel, talented chef and partner Thomas Keller, is gone, and the "Ra" of Rakel, partner Serge Raoul, has lowered the prices, mainstreamed the cuisine and added the word "café" to the name. Yet, despite these highly publicized changes in 1989, the dining experience here feels much the same as it did when Keller helped launch the restaurant. And it surely belies the appellation "café."

The handsome, high-ceilinged room with a large bar area and a raised dining space is still downtown-style elegant. Diners more often than not come in jacket and tie or evening dress, and the formal service staff wear familiar faces; their performance remains occasionally lamentable. Some of the art and live video is gone. As for the bill, it's not so much lower than in yesterday's. Gone are the wonderful complimentary *amuse-gueules* of Keller days, as well as some of Keller's more ambitious sauces and cuisine marriages. Some of the expensive produce items are gone from the menu, but on the whole, expect a combination of old Rakel with the bistro fare of nearby Raoul's, Serge's nearby restaurant. The wine list remains the same as in the past, and you'll have no problem selecting from the reasaonably extensive offerings. Expect to pay $80 per couple, plus tax and tip.

Canton

45 Division St.
(Market St. & The Bowery)
226-4441, 226-0921

CHINESE

Open Wed.-Fri. & Sun. noon-10 p.m., Sat. noon-11 p.m. Closed mid-July through mid-Aug. No cards.

The trick here is to ignore the menu and let Eileen (Mrs. Leang, co-owner with her chef-husband, Larry) order. You will eat very well. She's a great hostess, equally fluent in English and Chinese, and attracts as many trusting non-Asians and upscale Chinese as her husband's cooking. If not exactly chic, Canton's decor is a far cry from that of most Chinatown restaurants. It has a simple, up-town, Western-style interior. The sea is Canton's decorative theme, and fish and sea-food dishes are also the strength of the kitchen. You will eat consistently well-prepared food here, whether you are a regular or not, but especially if you do not order from the uninspired English menu. Larry devotedly prepares his specials from ingredients found at the market the same day.

No, this is not your typical Chinatown restaurant. No, the cuisine is not Cantonese via Hong Kong. In fact, Larry learned to cook in Chinatown, and cites refined French and Italian cuisines as continuing influences on his own. Stir-fried cooking is not the only rule here. To start, try a hand roll of lettuce, stuffed variously with either squab, chicken or vegetables. The steamed dumplings are also very good. Consider a main dish of boneless and herbed chicken with scallions, or a simple and excellent roast duck, cut into pieces that you can manage easily with chopsticks. The stuffed duck—a command performance—is lovely. Lobster in a black-bean sauce is recommended, but if you can get Larry to fix you a fish specially, get ready for a treat. He prepares a sublime pike; its skin is removed and its meat served as light quenelles. Carp, that soft-finned freshwater fish, is something of a specialty and comes as light as air and as tasty as can be. Sea bass is also tamed by a master. Neither wine nor liquor is served, but plenty of people bring their own. Many people consider Canton to be tops; at worst, it surely is a good and appealing place to try. Dinner averages between $50 and $70 for two.

12/20 Capsouto Frères

451 Washington St. (Watts St.)
966-4900

FRENCH

Open Sun. noon-3 p.m. & 6 p.m.-11:30 p.m., Mon. 6 p.m.-11:30 p.m., Tues.-Thurs. noon-3 p.m. & 6 p.m.-11:30 p.m., Fri.-Sat. noon-3 p.m. & 6 p.m.-12:30 p.m. All major cards.

It is not easy to find this place. Even the local TriBeCa police officers are liable to mis-direct you. But it is worth finding, even for brunch on the weekend (there's an outdoor terrace). The 1891 landmark building–the former Fleming Smith warehouse–with its high ceilings, red brick walls, soaring columns, ceiling fans and slices of Hudson River views all speak for the kind of urban restoration and reclamation one expects in Seattle, Baltimore or even Boston rather than New York. The spacious multi-level dining room is warm and countrylike. The food, too, is French country. The three Capsouto brothers have been doing a nice job since opening in 1980, advertising their existence regularly in *The Wall Street Journal* and pioneering what is now the hottest new restaurant area on the East Coast.

For starters, the grilled-mushroom special, when available, is excellent. The terrine Provençale (layered eggplant, roasted peppers and goat cheese) is recommended, while the gravlax and smoked salmon (the latter served with caviar on an iced plate) do not always taste as if they were the highest quality fish and can be bland and fatty. The poached salmon as a main course, served with warm fresh-herb vinaigrette, remains a sound choice, and the roast duckling with ginger and a black-currant sauce is okay, as are the beets and carrots that are sometimes served with it. Dessert choices include soufflés, fresh fruit and an assortment of pies and pastries. The wine list is good and moderately priced. Sam Capsouto tries to cover all geographic regions, concentrating on France and California, and keeps a learned eye out for better vintages. However, the waiters could keep a better eye out for their customers. Figure $100 for dinner for two, plus tax and tip.

 Cellar in the Sky
One World Trade Center, 107th Fl.
938-1111
CONTINENTAL
Open Mon.-Sat. 7:30 p.m. (one seating). All major cards.

The breathtaking view of Manhattan at night from the 107th floor of the World Trade Center will put anyone in the mood for being pampered at dinnertime. The Cellar's dining room has an intimate feel, with its small wooden tables in a darkened room lined with wine bottles. The fixed price, six-course menu is designed around five wines. While guests dine, solicitous and professional waiters glide among the tables, whispering the names of the different wines, replenishing glasses, offering detailed, knowledgeable explanations of the dishes served. For the most part, the pairing of wines and courses is successful; the wines

are chosen with care and represent a balance among French, Italian and California vintages.

A typical fall menu begins with Veuve Clicquot brut Champagne colored by a drop of homemade cassis, served with the chef's canapés: light, little tarts of flaky pastry, filled with tender morsels of seafood. Hawaiian prawns are juicy and moist, surrounded by sautéed chanterelle mushrooms, and a soft, sweet baked pumpkin filled with crème fraîche is enhanced by a sprinkle of crunchy pepitas. A light, dry Bonny Doon Chardonnay is paired with an uninteresting poached lobster médaillon on a bed of pasta overwhelmed by basil. A Château Mouton Baronne Philippe, a rich, 1986 red, is served with a plump, glazed breast of squab with a powerful ginger compote: a perfect marriage. The creamy, but bitter, raddichio salad must fight with a heady Fourme D'Ambert. Dessert, a small timbale of hot, sweet ricotta cheesecake enveloping tasty vanilla ice cream, is delightful with its partner of golden Muscat. The helpful staff serves port with ordinary petits fours and weak American coffee.

In this concept restaurant, where there's one menu that changes every two weeks, one seating and one price, you entrust yourself to fate, as well as to the good professionals on hand, since you can't make on-the-spot selections and often have to book well in advance, not knowing what will be on the menu (though you can ask). Some wines are better than others, some dishes and preparations are better than others, some marriages of food and wine are better than others, so, naturally, some weeks the Cellar in the Sky is better than others. The range of dining experience runs from good (say a 13 on our scale), to excellent (say a 17). When making reservations at the Cellar, be ready to give a credit-card number for the deposit ($77 per person). Dinner for two, then, will be $154, plus tax and tip.

 Chanterelle
2 Harrison St. (Hudson St.)
966-6960
FRENCH
Open Tues.-Sat. 6 p.m.-10:30 p.m. Closed July and the 1st week in Jan. All major cards.

When your cozy restaurant is widely admired as one of the city's finest, you're taking a risk moving pots and pans from your SoHo storefront to one in TriBeCa. The aging kids from the Bronx who took that risk, David and Karen Waltuck, must ponder the merits of their defacto invitations to critics and customers to look closely again at what they are doing. Not all the comments have been favorable—the new room, location, prices and the food have, by someone or other, all been lambasted. We still admire the couple and the restaurant, which remains one of our favorites. Its kitchen, however, has not yet settled down to the day-in, day-out consistency and assuredness of its days before the move. Can it be the added meals chef David Waltuck is turning out every evening, or the pressure of having to be bold and inventive to recapture the attention of a fickle city of diners and reviewers? David Waltuck, trained at the Culinary Institute of America and a student of restaurants in France, is a strong talent, and we expect this restaurant only to get better. He is sensitive to the market, to freshness and to new gustatory marriages. Not everything he does works to perfection, but he constantly experiments—the menu changes every few weeks—and we have seen some stunning new items added in the year since the move. What emerges, as it does at all great restaurants, is a personal cuisine.

The bigger space seats 60 comfortably, and there's a small lounge, where you can enjoy a drink while waiting for your table. As in SoHo, David and Karen—she minds the front masterfully—have camped their grand restaurant in a reverse chic, relatively rundown area of warehouses and lofts. As before, the dining room is elegant and minimalist. Here, with its high ceilings, yellow/beige color, cleanly ornamental polished-wood walls and columns, gray carpet, huge windows on two sides facing out on a dreary street, comfortable chairs and finely appointed tables, there is a starkness cut only by the sensational, grand flower bouquets. One of our fellow diners, who was visiting from France, remarked that the room is the sort British Army officers sought out for dinner during World War II. The civilized service is highly professional and faultless (and you must know how rare that is in America or anywhere). The dinners are elaborate, with little extras appearing at each table like magic.

Of the two or three *amuse-gueules* that arrive even before you place your order, you can count on at least one being outstanding, such as a perfect miniature onion quiche or sensational fried calamari. The warm, hard roll that arrives early weakens your will power to resist, in order to have the space and desire for what is to come. The grilled seafood sausage with a vinaigrette sauce is a long-time favorite appetizer at Chanterelle. The lobster and bouillabaisse aspic with edible flowers is sensational to look at and pretty good to eat, too. A lot is done with edible flowers, and the visual appeal of most dishes is superb. An elaborate, yet simple, starter we've enjoyed is the shellfish fricassee: pairs of oysters, clams and mussels in a cream sauce. The various dumpling appetizers (usually shrimp) are okay, but a bit less successful. The foie-gras terrine accompanied with delicious toasted bread is always good. Soups are refined and complex.

Fish dishes are currently a great strength of the chef. Among the hundreds of restaurants in New York offering salmon, none delivers a better prepared and presented dish than Chanterelle—its sublime, thick, moist Norwegian salmon comes in a beet sauce with beurre blanc and champagne vinegar. Sensational! The swordfish steak, in a lime sauce with crispy beet chips, is perfection. Among the meat and fowl dishes we have enjoyed recently are the popular squab and black truffles, served with rice and spinach, a rabbit "chop," and the beef filet with red wine and marrow. The cheese tray is extraordinary and includes French, Italian and American cheeses offered as part of the fixed-price meal. We've never been great fans of the French/American wine list, with its obscure estate-bottled Burgundies—even though we love estate-bottled Burgundies—and less known appellations from the Rhône. Now that the list has grown substantially and many of the wines come of age, Michael Bilunas, the studious maître d' and sommelier, deserves credit for shaping an impressive and distinctive list. There are good values to be found—let him steer you to some discoveries under $40 (you can spend $400 a bottle if you like, though)— and when in the future some of the wines aging in the cellar, including some Italian ones, appear on the list, it will be a distinguished one.

Desserts are one of the areas where the restaurant is not as consistently strong as it could be. Although some desserts are excellent, overall, they're not up to what precedes them. We have had an extraordinary wild-blueberry pie here, but one time the chocolate ice cream is fabulously dark, rich and creamy, the next time it is merely dark and somewhat bitter. Sorbets have never been strong, nor have the petits fours. The fallen chocolate soufflé cake is a safe and popular choice. A strong digestif list provides a grand opportunity for ending the meal. Such elaborate meals may require more than one wine, and with only fixed-priced menus ($68 and $92), it is difficult getting away with spending less than $250 for two, plus tax and tip.

12/20 Cinco de Mayo
349 W. Broadway (Broome St.)
226-5255

MEXICAN

Open daily noon-midnight. All major cards.

This is not a one-sauce-fits-all, mediocre, unauthentic Mexican eatery, as is so common in New York. Cinco de Mayo offers good and often unusual cuisine, elegant and airy surroundings, and professional service. It's just not as good as it was a few years ago. José Hurtado Prud'homme, the chef since 1982, was raised in Mexico and trained at his grandmother's knees. Maybe he needs to be spanked. Nevertheless, on Friday and Saturday nights, customers are willing to wait a half or three-quarters of an hour for a table and a chance at his queso fundido, misiotes or guacamole for starters, and his fajitas de la casa or pechuga con rajas poblanas to follow. The restaurant is divided among three very different spaces: a crowded front room with a bar, an intimate back room and a second floor balcony to escape the din of the crowd. Daily specials always include one or two soups and interesting additions to the entrées on the menu. Appetizers are delightful; even the ubiquitous guacamole has a creamy, chunky texture and a fresh, spicy taste. Don't shy away from taquitos de moronga, soft corn tortillas filled with minced blood pudding and fresh coriander; they are excellent, and as authentic as you can get without flying east of Mexico City, where chef Prud'homme was born. The enchiladas are freshly made and happily lack the overdose of sour cream and bean mush that has made the dish famous (and infamous). Try anything with mole. Cinco de Mayo's rich, delicious version of this classic Mexican sauce would dress up the most pedestrian dish. Another dish seldom touched

by American taste buds is a stew of tripe, chiles and bits of vegetable called menudo norteño. Entrées from the grill are uneven; while the steak is tasty, the skewered shrimp served with dull rice lack flavor. Desserts are homemade but quite American, except for the flan de chocolate, a flourless, extremely dense chocolate cake flavored with Kahlúa and served with whipped crème fraîche. Cinco de Mayo has separate lunch and brunch menus, lighter in fare and in price. The wines here are reasonably priced and mainly hail from Spain and California. The Mexican beers are highly recommended, as are the frozen margaritas. About $60 for two, with drinks, for dinner.

Duane Park Café
157 Duane St. (W. Broadway & Houston Sts.)
732-5555

AMERICAN

Open Mon.-Fri. noon-3 p.m. & 6 p.m.-11 p.m., Sat. 6 p.m.-11 p.m. All major cards.

The top pick on what is becoming the restaurant row of TriBeCa, Duane Park Café is a most appealing medium-size restaurant staffed by professionals. It wins honors as one of the best new restaurants in the past couple of years, and by extending ourselves a bit to award it two toques, we hope to encourage the people working there to fully realize their talents. The cuisine is the so-called New American. Curiouser and curiouser, the owner is a Japanese chef, Seiji Maeda. He has, however, worked at K Paul's in New Orleans and at Hubert's in New York, and he has hired American Jim Littman as executive chef, and Joan Winters, who worked at Arcadia, as pastry chef.

The handsome, square dining room is subdued: fabric and veneer walls, wood floors and black chairs and tables, are supplemented by a stylish, well-trained staff. The menu is less subdued, a mixture of Italian, Californian, Cajun and Japanese interpretations. The agnolotti (ravioli) with eggplant and zucchini is excellent. Sweetbreads are lovely, though the accompanying polenta is not. Pan-fried Cajun rib-eye is very good and comes with tasty roast potatoes. The homemade agnolotti are filled with butternut squash and served with a sauce of melted Mascarpone and toasted almonds, and is delicious. The seafood risotto is very nice, as is the skate with ponzu, a complex dipping sauce that adds much excitement to the crisply cooked fish. Also, the osso buco, which is generally flawed around this city, is popular and outstanding. Did we say this was an Italian restaurant? It's not, but for dessert, the biscotti pudding with espresso-custard sauce stands out. The tarts—such as the seasonal fresh-fig-and-raspberry tart—are fine. For chocolate freaks, there is a strong chocolate soufflé. The American/French/Italian wine list is fine, but a bit young. It has been carefully chosen, as have the vintage ports and single-malt Scotches. Dinner for two, with wine, is a reasonable $100.

12/20 Greene Street Café
101 Greene St. (Prince & Spring Sts.)
925-2415
ECLECTIC
Open Tues.-Thurs. 6 p.m.-11:30 p.m., Fri.-Sat. 6 p.m.-12:30 a.m., Sun. noon-8:30 p.m. All major cards.

This enormous SoHo loft with brick walls, a jungle look and showy lighting continues to be an area favorite. A lively place, it attracts locals, who meet here for a drink at the bar and to listen to live music (light jazz—solo piano during the week and duos and trios on weekends) and, of course, to sample Asian chef Pang's fare, which displays a fondness for New York nouvelle cuisine and, of course, a bit of Asia.

The excellent chicken consommé with enoki mushrooms has an unusually strong, rich chicken flavor. The lobster sausage, served with artichokes in an herb mayonnaise, is delicious. The escalope of salmon is broiled lightly and perfectly complimented by its vinegar-and-herb sauce. Unfortunately, you will still find a lot of the same old standbys, such as goat-cheese salad and seafood ravioli—indeed, the lobster ravioli is one of the favored appetizers. Try the salad of sliced artichoke hearts if you desire something green, or the filet mignon carpaccio if you wish to start off with meat. Entrées also have an often sadly "déjà vu" quality to them: red snapper (don't New York restaurants know any other fish? Yes, grilled yellow-fin tuna), loin of lamb and/or double-cut rack of lamb (very good), and a breast of chicken with roasted garlic (too dry). Yet the filet of salmon with three caviars is inspired, and the sirloin steak with roasted

carrots and potatoes, juicy.

Desserts are good, especially the excellent fruit tarts; the fresh fruits are beautifully served. Most popular, however, is the chocolate marquis. Also try the gelato sundae with warm chocolate sauce. The wine list merits special kudos; it is well rounded, with some European wines, as well as those from Australia and California. The selection has considerable depth, with a reserve list of over 100 wines, helping it win *The Wine Spectator's* Award of Excellence in 1989. Thirteen wines are offered by the glass. Prices are reasonable. Dinner for two, with a drink, will run about $100.

King Fung
20 Elizabeth St. (Canal St.)
964-5256/57
CHINESE
Open daily 8 a.m.-11 p.m. All major cards.

Although King Fung was once among the few well-designed Chinese restaurants in New York, now it looks sad. Some of the windows literally are boarded up, and the facade has not aged well. Yet King Fung is a favorite with the well-to-do Chinese community for wedding and christening receptions. As a matter of fact, there is a wedding reception almost every evening; surprisingly, the food does not suffer in the least.

The menu is longer than it was two years ago, and the additions smack of Hong Kong cuisine. Squab, Hong Kong's favorite bird, is served steamed, glazed, roasted and fried. A steamed squab with ham in a delicate, creamy sauce and served with bright green Chinese cabbage, is succulent, tender and moist. Seafood is excellent here: a delicate steamed flounder is deliciously light, and fried filets come not in the least bit greasy on their bed of shredded lettuce, served with an unusual vinegar sauce. Unfortunately, King Fung has given in to mayonnaise! Lobster and large prawns drown in the sweet, thick emulsion: avoid them at all costs. Stay away, too, from the so-called "Hong Kong–style" sizzling steak. Desserts include refreshing sliced oranges, red bean paste with lotus seed and a heavenly tapioca soup with coconut and balls of ripe honeydew melon. Beer is available. Dinner for two will cost about $60.

Madeline's
177 Prince St.
477-2788

AMERICAN

Open Tues.-Sat. 9 a.m.-midnight, Sun. 9 a.m.-9 p.m. Cards: AE.

Unobtrusively tucked between a butcher shop and a Catholic parish, Madeline's is the now-grown-up pastry shop serving full meals that was known for a decade as Café Lanciani. Madeline Lanciani is a superb pastry chef, so it's not surprising that exquisite cakes are shown off in a glass-enclosed case by the bar. Walls are painted pale peach, and from the high ceiling of the rectangular dining room hangs an artfully draped fiberglass curtain. The result is unusual and elegant.

Madeline and James Kang, her chef, have put together an ecletic menu, reflecting Madeline's attention to detail and Kang's Asian background. Lunch is informal—no tablecloths—and consists of hearty fresh soups, omelets with fresh vegetables, homemade biscuits and hamburgers with their usual trappings. Sandwiches, however, are interesting: one is stuffed with grilled shiitake mushrooms and roast peppers; another, grilled vegetables with a homemade lemony mayonnaise. Fresh pasta dishes are well prepared, but not too new; salads are lively. Among the entrées, try the steamed Japanese ravioli, stuffed with veal, ginger and scallions in a fragrant duck broth (served as an appetizer at dinner and highly recommended), or the medallion of lotte, lightly sautéed with thick segments of lemon on bitter greens. Dinner is a more formal affair (with nothing less than pink tablecloths), and with a much more elaborate menu—from the confit of duck to the delicate, warm oysters served with balsamic vinegar and butter sauce. Lamb marinated with rosemary is tender and sweet, while the grilled tuna is served with a pungent, garlicky eggplant caviar. You won't find high-calorie sauces here, just incredibly fresh ingredients and a light hand. Also recommended are the sliced breast of rare duck with raspberry-and-pecan sauce and the filet of salmon in a pistacchio crust. Desserts, on the other hand, are sinfully rich, such as the bitter-sweet chocolate cake in the form of ribbons, moist, New Orleans–style beignets, and mouth-watering fruit tarts. If desserts are your passion, head for this place and feast at a

level above the competition. Put to the test, Madeline recommends the boule noire and the biscotto di Saronno. There's an interesting wine list, with a selection of Californian and French wines at modest markups. Lunch for two will run about $35, dinner about $70, with a bottle of wine.

Mezzogiorno
195 Spring St. (Sullivan St.)
334-2112

ITALIAN

Open daily noon-3 p.m. & 6 p.m.-1 a.m. No cards.

More than a café, but less than a full-blown restaurant, this handsome establishment, with its glass and terra-cotta facade, quietly opened two years ago. The owners of the uptown Mezzaluna, Roberto Bozzi and Romano Molfetta, turned to Florentine architect Roberto Magries to design their new venture. A large marble bar dominates the long, airy room, and a brick pizza oven burns brightly at noon and late into the evening, giving the restaurant a feeling of warmth and hospitality. Small marble-topped tables (without tablecloths) are set well apart and are occupied by a mostly young, chic clientele. Waiters are young, handsome, Italian and just a little bit snooty, in an amusing way.

Among the antipasti is an excellent cold veal, thinly sliced and served with a pungent tuna sauce. The insalate (salads) are unusual, complex and very good: the salad bearing the restaurant's name is composed of celery, mushrooms and artichokes and topped with paper-thin slices of Parmigiano. The trouble is that olive oil and vinegar are brought to the table with a pretentious flourish and you must make your own dressing, difficult on the small tables. Pasta is no less than divine: homemade, light and beautifully sauced. Shaved white truffles (when they're in season) top the thin spaghetti, and squid-ink linguine is bathed in a piquant, thick tomato sauce redolent of garlic and pepper. Other pasta staples are a springlike farfalle with zucchini and parsley and a hearty, rustic whole-wheat pasta with leeks. Best among the carpaccios is a plate of barely seared, almost transparent, slices of beef, with a dressing of olives and tomatoes. Lunchtime and a late supper bring a delightful individual pizza, with a thin crust and simple, fresh toppings. Desserts are ordinary, apart from a melon mousse with kiwi, pineapple and strawberries and an outstanding tiramisu. The functional wine list is pure Italian, save for two Champagnes. Lunch runs about $65 for two; dinner, with wine, about $90.

Montrachet
239 W. Broadway (White St.)
219-2777

FRENCH

Open Mon.-Thurs. 6 p.m.-11 p.m., Fri. noon-3 p.m. Cards: AE.

Falstaffian owner and restaurateur par excellence, Drew Nieporent is the downtown counterpart to Le Cirque's Sirio Maccioni. Nieporent is shrewd and savvy, committed to quality, broadly knowledgeable, personable and obsessed by restaurants, especially his. He also pulled a fast one a few years ago. When his chef left, he quietly promoted *sous*-chef Debra Ponzek, kept her in the kitchen and did not mention there had been a change; on the contrary, he kept giving out the name of the former chef. The food was better than ever, and we and some others credited the old chef, and the customers did not miss a service. After six months of the charade and a portfolio of unretractable praise, he let slip that Debra had been doing the cooking and the old chef now lived in California. We really can't complain. Debra Ponzek is talented and was named one of America's Ten Best Young Chefs for 1989 by a respected national magazine, so she is getting her due. By raising our rating of Montrachet to the upper-echelon 17/20 (three toques), we're putting Nieporent on notice that we expect him to keep the restaurant a satisfying step ahead of us and not let his stage-managing proprietorship for buddy Robert DeNiro at the TriBeCa Grill sap his commitment to excellence. Who knows, maybe our promotion will convince him it's time to trade in those cat-burglar costumes his staff wears for some other outfits.

Despite the false impression its expensive name provides, Montrachet doesn't look like a great restaurant and need not be expensive. Established in 1985 in a TriBeCa industrial space, it can be a little tricky for uptowners and out-of-towners to find the first time around. Its low-key, storefront entrance is a bit inconspicuous and certainly doesn't suggest the large restaurant beyond: a high-ceilinged, rectangular dining room with a mahogany-and-onyx bar that leads into another spacious, square dining room, which leads into yet another high-ceilinged dining room, this one used often for private parties. Soft colors—pale pinks and greens—and soft lights contribute to the comfortable, open, unpretentious feeling of the dining spaces.

Ordering is easy if you choose one of the three fixed menus, at $25, $29 or $45. The first is a bargain and an almost sure bet, featuring a flawlessly roasted duck and closing on a high note with a terrific crème brûlée. The other menus also feature roasted birds, such as quail and squab. There are always specials and plenty of temptations on the à la carte list. The bow-tie pasta with foie gras and truffle juice is a meltingly irresistible appetizer. The parsley soup with belon oysters never disappoints, and the salad of roast pigeon and baby corn is sensational. Lobster au pistou is also recommended. For a main course, try the pigeon with raisins and Madeira or the coq au Riesling. Additionally, the red snapper with roasted peppers and lemon is cooked ever so well; the skin is slightly crisp and the meat is moist, tender and as flaky as you can imagine. The baby pheasant with orzo and olives is both an interesting and successful combination, as well as being a standout dish. If you like kidney, the roast kidney with Chiroubles wine (a light, fruity Beaujolais) is sensational.

Nieporent certainly knows the trick for sending his customers off smiling and contented. One dessert after the next is excellent—we love the fig tart with créme fraîche, and there are good digestifs and after-dinner drinks for anyone who desires a coup de grâce. Wines merit special mention, as this is certainly a wine-destination restaurant. Sommelier Daniel Johnnes is eager to help and has been developing an increasingly sophisticated and unusual list—one that lacks some breadth, but makes up for it with unusual bottles and pleasant drinking wines in vintages not highly esteemed. The 150 selections focus on the great appelations of Burgundy, the Loire and the Rhône, with notable California and Champagne offerings. Trust Daniel or Drew for a recommendation. Book well in advance. About $100 for two, with a modest wine (but, the bill can easily mount to $200), plus tax and tip.

Il Mulino
86 W. Third St. (Sullivan &
Thompson Sts.)
673-3783

ITALIAN

*Open Mon.-Fri. noon-2:30 p.m., 5 p.m.-11 p.m.
& Sat. 5 p.m. to 11 p.m. Cards: AE.*

There's a comforting earnestness about this place. With its well-spaced tables and chairs, one exposed brick wall playing off papered walls, and a row of tall, stately plants that serve as a room divider, Il Mulino typifies the next generation (what is it now . . . second, third or fourth?) of Italian-American restaurants in the Village-SoHo area. The streets are pretty grim, but inside, a sort of understated elegance has taken hold. Lighting, pleasant, rosey and atmospheric, is often so low you barely can read the menu. What you can read, you can be sure is good.

The place can be crowded with aficionados, and reservations are taken lightly—you may have to join the jam at the bar, where the noise level approaches that of a large cocktail party. Once you're seated, however, flagging spirits will be revived quickly by the wonderful fried zucchini, crisp and greaseless, or the bruschetta/panzanella, a tasty tomato-garlic toast that will be sped to your table. Other nights, it's salami or chunks of Parmigiano. From there, you can go on to the addictive bocconcini, moist balls of buffalo mozzarella, flecked with roasted sweet peppers. Be sure to check out the pasta specials, such as pappadelle (a broad ribbony pasta) in a gorgeously robust fresh tomato (or sometimes a game) sauce, or the unusual carbonara, or the classic spaghettini alla bolognese, or perhaps a more trendy capellini all' arrabbiata. Salmon with balsamic vinegar-slicked porcini mushrooms is a good main course choice, as is the veal chop fragrant with rosemary, or sautéed with cheese and wild mushrooms. Some

We're always interested to hear about your discoveries, and to receive your comments on ours. Please feel free to write to us, and do state clearly exactly what you liked or disliked.

entrées come quite naked, so ask if you need to order a veggie or two. Il Mulino's fresh orange slices, marinated in Grand Marnier and rasberries, are just right as a dessert, ditto the poached pear with white wine and grappa; or enjoy the fresh berries with a fine zabaglione. About $110 for two for lunch or dinner.

The Nice Restaurant
35 E. Broadway
406-9776

CHINESE

Open daily 8 a.m.-10:30 p.m. Cards: AE.

Located on the second floor of a building clothed in pink marble, The Nice restaurant is a great favorite of large Chinese families sharing some of the best dishes in Chinatown. The immense dining room is filled with tables that accommodate at least ten people, so it's the perfect place to bring your entire family–from a tiny tot (no one will mind if she runs around) to a great-grandmother who likes her rice extra hot and fresh (it is). The decor is typical Hong Kong–style: a chartreuse ceiling lit by an imitation crystal chandelier and a back wall featuring gold dragons with red light-bulb eyes. The weirder dishes on the extensive menu may amuse—fish cheeks with scallions, sea slug sautéed with garlic—but they are very serious and very good. A little book of photographs of specialties of the house, updated every year, may help you to understand the menu better and to be adventurous. If you are stuck, ask for Mr. Shing Chan, one of the managers. His English is quite good and he'll be able to explain the more exciting dishes. Seafood with fresh abalone, black mushrooms and moss is extraordinary, contrasting textures and flavors; and bean curd, stuffed with tender pork and fresh vegetables is refreshingly simple and tasty. After tasting eggplant with pungent cilantro and chopped pork, you'll never eat Chinese eggplant any other way. The succulent roast suckling pig is served on top of sweet-cooked soy beans; try, too, a wondrous Peking duck, crisp and tender, to roll into tiny soft pancakes with scallions. Avoid casserole dishes; they tend to be overcooked or oversauced. A meal here ends with the usual sliced oranges unless you insist upon the cold tapioca soup with honeydew melon, the best in Chinatown. Beer is available. An average meal is a reasonable $35 for two.

CHATEAU CARIGNAN

PREMIÈRE CÔTE DE BORDEAUX

A.O.C.

GRAND VIN DE BORDEAUX

MIS EN BOUTEILLES AU CHATEAU

CHATEAU CARIGNAN

PREMIÉRE COTE DE BORDEAUX

APPELLATION PREMIERE COTE DE BORDEAUX CONTROLÉE

PRODUCE OF FRANCE **1985**

G.F.A. A. Philippe Pieraerts

12 % vol   Propriétaire à Carignan de Bordeaux (Gironde)

750 ml

SA DI MA 17130

The best ratio quality/price

TERROIR ET TRADITION

Château Carignan

CARIGNAN-DE-BORDEAUX

33360 LATRESNE (FRANCE)

Téléphone 33.56.21.21.31

CHAMPAGNE

Veuve Clicquot Ponsardin
MAISON FONDÉE EN 1772
REIMS
FRANCE

*"Une seule qualité:
la toute première"*

*"One quality...
the very finest"*

Madame Veuve Clicquot Ponsardin

12/20 **Odeon**

145 W. Broadway (Thomas St.)
233-0507

AMERICAN

Open Mon.-Thurs. noon-2 a.m., Fri.-Sat. noon-4 a.m., Sun. noon-3 p.m. & 7 p.m.-2 a.m. All major cards.

Let's not argue with success. This art-deco cafeteria, catering to the young and fashionable late-late-night crowd, is now in its second decade. It's not what it used to be, when the crowd at the long bar with its tubular lights and neon-rimmed clock, was six-deep, and when every table was crammed with artists, designers, writers, punk rockers, local judges, thrill-seeking Wall Streeters and just-off-the-plane movie stars, but it's not too far from its old self. The neighborhood has grown up around it, and competition has moved in. Odeon now offers Sunday brunch, and live music late at night has maintained some of the excitement. The late-night supper is an institution, and the food has its moments. Of course, the waiters and waitresses are as spacey as ever.

What should you order? For starters, the fried calamari is fine; the salmon gravlax, safe; the herbed goat-cheese ravioli passable; the fennel, white-bean and tomato salad refreshing. Chef Stephen Lyle and his crew grill salmon well and serve it with lentils and a parsley vinaigrette. We like the mahi-mahi with lime, coriander and soy vinaigrette, too. Calf's liver with glazed shallots is recommended. The radiator pasta with artichokes and olivada is an okay entrée. The burgers aren't half bad for lunch or supper. For dessert, the triple-chocolate pudding is touted, though we prefer the warm berries in puff pastry. The wine list is priced moderately, with a steady scale starting at $9 and working up to $150 per bottle. Figure $50 to $60 for lunch and $80 to $90 for dinner, in each case for two.

12/20 **Omen**

113 Thompson St. (Prince St.)
925-8923

JAPANESE

Open Tues.-Sun. 5:30 p.m.-10:30 p.m. Cards: AE, DC.

As at its esteemed family-owned counterpart in Kyoto, people come to Omen for the specialty dish of the same name, an elaborate mating of assorted vegetables (spinach, scallions, burdock root, kelp) in a broth with dried flakes of bonito, ginger, sesame seeds and udon noodles. At $8.80, it's a meal in itself, and a must for first-timers. We respect Omen, which has a different feel than most Japanese restaurants in New York—a more rustic, friendly feeling. There's a nonreverential approach to Japanese eating, and the portions are enormous. Opened in 1981, it's a virtual old-time Japanese restaurant in New York. The casual dining room, up one flight of metal stairs from the street, is long and narrow, with brick walls and wooden floors, and with a tatami room at the back.

The menu is extensive, and everything is tasty, from tuna sashimi or a specially marinated chicken, to a potpourri of pickles and relishes. Try the mussels in miso, the tuna steak with ginger, the fried soba noodle, and the steamed acorn squash, stuffed with tofu and vegetables. Vegetables continue to be a strength, tempura a relative weakness (though it need not be avoided). If you order more than the signature Omen, your bill will average about $60 for two, with beer or saké.

12/20 **150 Wooster**

150 Wooster St. (Houston St.)
995-1010

ECLECTIC

Open nightly 6:30 p.m.-11:45 p.m. All major cards.

Scene one, fall, 1989: Entering 150 Wooster is like opening stage door left. Faces turn, from the unobtrusive, jam-packed bar and the twenty or so tables in the narrow, rectangular room, necks crane and often recognition sets in like a domino effect. There are double kisses all around, little waves, glasses held in toast. Women are beautiful, in red or black; men, with hair fashionably long, are gallant. New York needs a handful of restaurants such as 150 Wooster to serve as backdrops for people-watching. Too bad the food isn't better. Brian McNally, who also owns Indochine, could do better. The potato ravioli, sauced with a strange mix of olives and red wine, is so soft it becomes pasty in the mouth; the delicate flavor of a duck mousse studded with escargots is muffled by tomato-butter sauce. A grilled T-bone steak comes cooked just the way you order it, matched with tasty potatoes and crisply fried shallots. The roast chicken with wild mushroom polenta (a touch rubbery) and grilled red onions is simple and fragrant. Fish, generally, are grilled to underdoneness, which is fine, but the accompanying sauces lack finesse. (The staff recommends the tournedo of tuna with Cognac, mustard and green-peppercorn demiglaze.) A happy break from brown food is a green salad of baby lettuces tossed with a very French vinaigrette. Diners clap their hands over the desserts, which are too sweet, but very pretty. The prettiest is a ball of vanilla ice cream nestled in a lacy gaufrette cup, napped with orange sauce and garnished with a delicious slice of preserved orange.

Scene two, summer, 1990: The trendiness, crowds, Rollses and Jags are gone, as are a couple of chefs. The place has settled into a neighborhood spot, and may be on precarious footing near extinction. For the summer, Jeffrey Zakarian (formerly of "44" in The Royalton, Maxwell's Plum and elsewhere) is looking after the kitchen and offering a French-oriented menu, while he waits to open a new restaurant in SoHo with downtown restaurant empressario McNally.

Scene three, 1991: Anyone's guess, but people will still be talking about when 150 Wooster was the hottest place in town . . . and how it burned itself out. Wines are fairly priced and good—for a white, consider the Rully from Domaine de la Folie ($28); the espresso is excellent. Dinner for two, with a modest wine, will run about $115, plus tax and tip.

Oriental Pearl
103-105 Mott St.
(Hester & Canal Sts.)
219-8388
CHINESE
Open daily 8 a.m.-11 p.m. No cards.

Let's face reality: people are not treated evenhandedly in Chinatown's restaurants, so we can't single out Oriental Pearl for criticism. If you are served fried wonton by an indifferent waiter, send it back straightaway and ask for the delicious pickled vegetables that come to the tables of Asians, thus putting your waiter on notice that you are serious about eating well. You can eat very well here, but again, the reality is that the dining experience may range from no toques (say an 11/20) to two toques (15/20). We've had both. If you look around this enormous, clean, modern restaurant seating hundreds, you will always see Chinese groups celebrating something in partitioned areas of the dining room. With so many restaurants to choose from, you can bet they know where to eat very well. Here.

The dining room looks as if it were a sparkling 1930s cafeteria with greater ambitions. All the ceramic animals and colored lights and dragons don't help on that score, only adding to the loud-party atmosphere. What does set the kitchen of this Hong Kong–style restaurant apart is the quality of the produce, which is maintained by weekly shipments from that British colony. Eat Chinese-style and fill the table with dishes. Some we like include the deep-fried shrimp, the crispy chicken and the steamed sea bass. Remember to order vegetables separately, and when available (not listed on the menu) try the snow-pea leaves. What is absolutely extraordinary—if you can coax the staff to part with something that is in limited quantity and reserved for special customers—is the goose cooked in a pot. Ditto for a special dessert. We all know about desserts being afterthoughts in Asian restaurants; well, you'll change your mind after tasting a traditional Hong Kong summer treat: chilled tapioca with honeydew balls and coconut in a delicious sauce. Prices can range from $40 to $80 for two for dinner.

Le Pactole
2 World Financial Center (Vesey St.)
945-9444
FRENCH
Open Mon.-Sat. noon-11 p.m., Sun. noon-9 p.m. All major cards.

One of the most strikingly handsome restaurants opened in 1990, Le Pactole is upstairs in Manhattan's wonderful and new marbled-and-palm-treed Winter Garden. With its large bar, marble floors and plush carpets, two long and elegant dining rooms, two private party rooms and window walls exposing drop-dead views of the Hudson River, the marina and New York Harbor, palatial Le Pactole has a lot going for it. Run by two seasoned restaurateurs and partners, Romeo Gobbi (formerly of Le Cirque) out front and Willy Kraus (Perigord Park) in the kitchen. The shakedown cruise for this complex restaurant may take some time, but we already recommend it for a drink, a weekday business lunch, a weekend brunch or for a wedding or other private party.

The menu looms enormous (about 50 French entrées, with a smattering of Italian) and uneven. If you want the cuisine of twenty years ago—30, 40, 50 years ago, head here. One of the menu selections is even titled "Les Preparations Retro." While there is some evidence of a lighter touch than twenty years ago, there's too much going on here for the kitchen to handle it all well, and some of it should be left to rest in peace. Oysters in a seawater gelée are a good cold appetizer; hot oysters with leeks and a delicious dish of sautéed wild mushrooms with mache make good warm alternatives. Rabbit in a white-wine sauce with herbs, diced vegetables and beans tastes good as a main course, better than the mediocre steak filet. Desserts are okay: try the good bread pudding or the chocolate sampler plate. The wine list needs time to develop, and could ease up on the preponderance of French wines produced by Prosper Maufoux. No way out of here for less than $120-$150 per couple, unless you go for brunch that starts with a $21.50 fixed price (plus drinks), tax and tip.

12/20 Pietro-Vanessa
23 Cleveland Pl.
(Lafayette & Spring Sts.)
226-9764
ITALIAN
Open Mon.-Fri. noon-11 p.m., Sat. 4 p.m.-11 p.m., Sun. 4 p.m.-10 p.m. Cards: AE, MC, V.

Students of restaurant management should look carefully at how Pietro-Vanessa violates every rule of the Restaurant Handbook. Note the address: isolated SoHo location, nowhere near the area's trendy galleries and dance spots. Note the reservations policy: there isn't one. Note the decor: no design award here. And be sure to note the friendly service, crowded tables and long lines: perfect proof that perhaps the handbook can be thrown away; this small unpretentious place is doing something right. Probably it's the diverse and creative food, which seldom depresses the palate or the pocketbook.

Nothing on this trattoria's menu is more than $10. A small artichoke stuffed with breading and garlic makes a good appetizer for intimate friends to tear apart. Delicious stracciatella brims with tender spinach and egg, and an attractive salad pomodoro offers tomatoes with onions and red peppers. Pastas

are generally excellent. Linguine alle vongole is served with a tasty red or white clam sauce; spaghetti filleto combines tomato, prosciutto and onion. The accommodating kitchen will mix pastas and sauces on request. Perhaps the best choices are not on the menu, including seafood fra diavolo, a family-size portion of fresh clams, mussels, shrimp and calamari, served over pasta in a spicy tomato sauce. A beautifully done salmon steak with fresh vegetables (when available) is another specialty. Summer is a pleasant time to linger at a backyard outdoor table. The wine list is small, reasonable and Italian, but you can bring your own bottle. Dinner without wine will cost about $50, for two.

Provence
38 MacDougal St.
(Houston & Prince Sts.)
475-7500
FRENCH
Open Tues.-Sun. noon-3 p.m. & 6 p.m.-midnight. Cards: AE.

The intoxicating smell of garlic lets you know you are in the right place. One of New York's inspirational restaurant success stories since opening on Bastille Day 1986, this handsome SoHo Provençal bistro continues to fit the trendy and not-so-trendy like a glove. While the food is satisfactory, the surroundings are congenial, and the prices stunningly modest. It works . . . and works . . . and so do Patricia and Michel Jean, the owners of this pleasant evocation of sun-drenched Provence, where the couple briefly owned a small inn near his hometown of Salon-de-Provence. Expansive French windows, bordered in blue, look out onto MacDougal Street; pale-yellow walls, dried flowers, handsome brass chandeliers and a garden out back seating 40, all contribute to an attractive country feeling. People don't complain about being crowded in the two indoor dining areas.

We like the caviar d'aubergines (eggplant purée) and the morue St. Tropez (cod, tomatoes and potatoes with saffron) as appetizers, and from an extensive handwritten menu and wine list, patrons can order large bowls of a hot and powerful fish soup, reminiscent of the kind that you'd drive miles to the Marseilles waterfront to experience. On Fridays, there's bouillabaisse that also recalls the Riviera. Of course, there is pissaladière, the Provençal onion-and-anchovy tart, for a starter. As a main course, you can have poached seafood with aïoli, a garlic mayonnaise, or perhaps skate "wings" with a caper-and-olive-oil sauce. Rabbit is prepared nicely here, both in terrine as an appetizer and as a paillard with mustard for a main course. As you might expect from a good bistro, you can get a decent roast baby chicken washed in garlic, or a decent steak with french fries. For lunch, there's a good range of omelet and poached-egg dishes. The sorbets and fruit tarts are okay desserts, and a so-so crème Catalane and a sinful chocolate marquise are the top sellers. There are some good wines from Provence on the all-French list (Château Vignelaure is one suggestion for red, and a Bandol for a rosé). With wine, dinner averages $90 for a couple.

11/20 Raoul's

180 Prince St.
(Sullivan & Thompson Sts.)
966-3518

FRENCH

Open Sun.-Thurs. 6:30 p.m.-11:30 p.m., Fri.-Sat. 6:30 p.m.-midnight. Cards: AE, MC, V.

They wouldn't dare change a thing about what is as close to an authentic neighborhood French bistro as you'll find in New York. When Serge Raoul opened the restaurant in 1974, people in the neighborhood started dropping in nightly for dinner. Many preferred eating at the bar. Nowadays, there's also a trendier crowd. Wall Streeters and uptowners who arrive in hired cars and pay with expense accounts are here, but the locals still drop by and expect to get a table. One of their tricks is to eat out back in the "garden" dining area (a glassed-in conservatory dining room popular for private parties), which requires walking through the kitchen (and having a chat with the gregarious chef). This place doesn't try to look good, but it is warm and hosts a friendly crowd. The decor is classic New York storefront, a long and narrow room with a bar up front, tin ceilings, a personal collection of photos and prints, as well as booth seating. The seven booths are in great demand; there are also six banquette tables facing the bar.

The blackboard menu changes daily. Nothing is going to send you into gastronomic ecstasy, but neither are you going to go away hungry or with heartburn. Alain Quirin has been running the kitchen since 1982 and turns out a pungent country pâté, a nice celery rémoulade, a sweetbread salad, and regularly has oysters on hand as standard appetizers. There's a decent and popular house foie gras d'oie. Steak au poivre is a standard, of course, and there's a duck breast with green peppers. Desserts are good, especially the gratin aux fruits and the regular fruit tarts. Profiteroles with chocolate are one of the "in" desserts in New York just now, and though Raoul's version doesn't rival the best in France, it is at least up to most efforts served in New York. As well as plenty of drinkable Bordeaux and Burgundy wines, the restaurant has added a large variety of California and other American wines; consider the Kistler Chardonnay at $37, the Eyrie Pinot Noir at $34, or, while it lasts, a best-buy bottle of Château Latour Haut-Brion 1979 at $38. With a bottle of one of these wines, dinner runs about $120 for two.

10/20 El Rincón de España

226 Thompson St.
(Bleecker & W. 3rd Sts.)
475-9891

SPANISH

Open Sun.-Thurs. noon-3 p.m. & 5 p.m.-11 p.m., Fri.-Sat. noon-3 p.m. & 5 p.m.-midnight. All major cards.

A fixture since 1966, this small, intimate and dark restaurant is owned by Carlos Ventoso, a Spanish chef who makes a wonderful octopus dish (pulpo a la Carlos) that will send you reeling with its pungent taste of garlic. It's the sort of place best frequented when you're in a group and wish to be entertained with Spanish and American songs by a strumming guitarist in front of your table. The appetizers are disappointing; stay far away from entremeses variados, a mishmash of salty tuna, cold tomatoes, rigid and tasteless shrimp and other nondescript tidbits. If you must begin with something, order the chorizos, a spicy Spanish dried sausage, or the jamón con melón, a hearty country ham with melon. Any seafood entrée with salsa verde, a garlicky green herb sauce, is very good, but avoid the white sauce. Entrées come with a mediocre Spanish rice and an almost inedible iceberg-lettuce salad. Most dishes here, as you might have gathered, are flavored with garlic; if you desire a bit of purity, try the tender grilled lamb chops or the grilled filet of beef. Now for the specialties: yes, the paellas are good. They are chock-full of fresh seafood (and chicken in the paella valenciana), well seasoned, and authentic. After the paellas, arroz con pollo, arroz con camarones and the camarones a la Carlos are best-sellers. With a swig of Rincón's very good Spanish red wines, you will be well satisfied. Desserts are ordinary, although the flan is homemade and pleasantly refreshing. The coffee tastes as it ought to: strong, robust, with a true Spanish spirit. Price for two, with wine, is $70, lunch or dinner.

 Rosemarie's
145 Duane St.
(W. Broadway & Church St.)
284-2610
ITALIAN
Open Mon.-Fri. noon-3 p.m. & 5:30 p.m.-10:30 p.m.; Sat. noon-3 p.m. & 5:30 p.m.-11 p.m. All major cards.

This quiet little Italian place in TriBeCa, with its large, brick-walled dining room behind a long bar, and its ceiling painted with *faux* clouds-cum-sky, is truly a trattoria, where food and wine are enjoyed and lingered over in an unpretentious setting. Tables are set far apart so the guests, a pleasant mix of young and less young, are comfortable and relaxed. Background music is subdued, and the waiters are easy-going and friendly.

The menu, devised by chef Jamie Bergen, is simple, yet original. Appetizers include a delicious terrine of roasted eggplant and goat cheese with a smokey, rich flavor; another appetizer worth trying is veal sausage and lentil salad, fragrant with fresh thyme. Unfortunately, the lentils are undercooked. Among the pastas, pappardelle con funghi is by far the best. Homemade pasta is topped with a light sauce made from pungent porcini mushrooms, tomato and cream. Tender, tasty gnocchi are served with shrimp cleverly trimmed to resemble the gnocchi, and spiced with a bit of saffron. Chef Bergen shines when it comes to fish: a seared salmon steak with radicchio sauce and a hint of balsamic vinegar is superb. The baked sea bass, cooked perfectly, is served with tender braised baby artichoke, sun-dried tomatoes and a mound of crisp fried leeks. A roast loin of lamb comes pink, juicy and smelling of basil, but the grilled

goat cheese overpowers the delicate meat. Avoid the duck breast altogether. Salads are clumsy: enormous, thick-cut orange slices overwhelm a fennel-and-arugula salad. Desserts include an acceptable cheesecake and the usual tiramisu. A reasonably priced wine list offers decent California and Italian vintages. Dinner costs about $85 for two, with a bottle of wine, plus tax and tip.

11/20 Saigon Restaurant
60 Mulberrry St. (Bayard St.)
227-8825
VIETNAMESE
Open Sun.-Thurs. 11:30 a.m.-10:30 p.m.; Fri.-Sat. 11:30 a.m.-11 p.m. Cards: AE, MC, V.

This subterranean Chinatown fixture may be the only place in the United States to display a wall clock shaped like Vietnam, and it also may be the last restaurant in Manhattan that offers $2 bottles of beer. (Please don't point this out to management.) You should ask for a menu with photographs of wonderfully exotic Vietnamese dishes and point at what looks good. It's hard to go far wrong, as the constant crowds here will attest. Vietnamese is, of course, a refined cuisine, with unique flavors of lemon grass and curry in its dishes. It's certainly not Chinese. When Saigon is on target, which is usual, it delivers with style, if not always elegance and refinement.

Order Vietnamese spring rolls, lightly fried meat-and-vegetable dumplings that you wrap in cool lettuce leaves and dip in a seafood sauce. A discriminating choice is the shrimp and pork roll, which tastes better than it sounds. Sometimes called imperial roll, it is a combination of shrimp, pork, vegetables and green onion, wrapped in a thin rice-paper coating, served cold, and accompanied by a rich peanut sauce. Other top Saigon offerings are chicken with lemon grass, jumbo shrimp fried in salt and pepper, and seafood with flat rice noodles. But shrimp cooked in beer was lackluster and a great-looking barbecued whole fish could have been more meaty. As in most Asian restaurants, dessert is not an attraction, but do have coffee, Vietnamese style. A small filter covers the top of a glass, the bottom of which is filled with condensed milk. Hot water drips through the filter and strong coffee mixes with milk for a sweet sensation. Dinner with beer will cost not much more than a modest $40 for two.

11/20 Sammy's Roumanian Restaurant

157 Chrystie St. (Delancey St.)
673-0330
CONTINENTAL/JEWISH
Open Sun.-Fri. 4 p.m.-10 p.m., Sat. 4 p.m.-2 a.m. All major cards.

Sammy's only *looks* like it has been there forever. It opened in 1975 in a run-down section of the Lower East Side, and ever since has attracted crowds, who come for the quintessential melting pot, old–New York Jewish ambience and food: chopped eggs and onions, chicken soup with noodles, chopped chicken livers, stuffed derma (kishka), sliced brains, Rumanian beef sausages (karnatzlach), grilled meats with chopped garlic, potato pancakes, cholesterol, huge portions, schmaltz. Yes, there's still a container of milk, a jar of Fox's U-Bet chocolate syrup and seltzer on every table, so you can make your own egg cream. You can forget kosher here. You can forget Rumanian, too. The fare—filling and honest, but uneven and undistinguished—is generally Central European Jewish cooking.

The storefront restaurant with low ceilings and dark walls is a collection of chairs and tables, as well as people against a backdrop of noise and live singing, as well as piano playing—assorted Jewish songs in English or Yiddish, with an occasional Broadway tune for a surprise. This could be a tourist version of how things were, but for the moment it is still the real thing. In 1988, owner Stanley Zimmerman added a party room, so the crazy bar-mitzvah atmosphere is more prevalent than ever. If you aren't too stuffed, there's strudel and the like to finish you off. There's a full bar, too. Try the Rumanian wines, Premiat cabernet sauvignon and Premiat blanc, both selling for $15.95. Tabs can be very low here, but for the full show, count on $76 for two.

12/20 Say Eng Look

5 E. Broadway
(adjacent to Chatham Square)
732-0796
CHINESE
Open Sun.-Thurs. 11 a.m.-10 p.m., Fri.-Sat. 11 a.m.-11 p.m. All major cards.

Established in 1964, and still one of the better choices in Chinatown, Say Eng Look doesn't operate at the frenetic pace of most Chinatown establishments, and is a particularly good spot to gather six or eight friends around a table. The phrase "say eng look" means "four, five, six," a winning combination in mah-jong, and this Shanghai cuisine restaurant does indeed have a reputation for preparing winners. In general, the level of sophistication here stands a notch above its neighbors, though still well removed from most uptown standards.

All the food served inside the red-and-black pagoda-theme dining room is sound and consistent, with sauces more elegant than the surroundings. Fried wonton and cold noodles with sesame (bland) are standard appetizers, as are the Shanghai spring rolls and various dumplings. Filet of eel, scallops with crab, and king sea cucumber with shrimp seeds (a slimy delicacy) are usually available, though perhaps the nod for fish goes to fried roll fish with bean-curd sheet, firm and moist inside, with a crisp light-golden crust. About a dozen pieces of the roll fish are served in a dish bordered partly with a strip of salt, which lends an extra dimension to the dish. Tai-chi chicken remains a staple here, as is the sesame chicken (and sesame shrimp), and the chunk chicken in spiced sauce with watercress and mushrooms is excellent. If you shy away from hot foods, this dish may still appeal to you; it's not too spicy. The orange-flavored beef is a favorite; the sautéed watercress is sensational. There are a good many flops among the 122 dishes on the menu, but the roasted whole carp or sea bass are other reliable choices. You can finish with an Italian tortoni or spumoni, much better than the scoop of industrial ice cream usually served in Chinese restaurants. The offering makes sense if you remember that Chinatown borders Little Italy: perhaps gelato can be considered Marco Polo's way of saying thanks. Say Eng Look also has an assortment of inexpensive wines, and you must try the one Chinese wine featured. Lunch can

We're always interested to hear about your discoveries, and to receive your comments on ours. Please feel free to write to us, and do state clearly exactly what you liked or disliked.

be had for $24 to $30 for two, and an elaborate dinner, with wine, will cost from $40 to $50, plus 20 cents for every bowl of rice you eat.

Tai Hong Lau
70 Mott St.
(Canal & Bayard Sts.)
219-1431
CHINESE
Open daily 11 a.m.-11 p.m. No cards.

For a while, Tai Hong Lau, one of the best restaurants in Chinatown, had lost its touch. The food was mediocre because Cindy Wo, harbinger of good taste and innovation from Hong Kong, had left. But now she's back, to everyone's delight. Below street level and behind a simple, stainless-steel facade, the elegant dining room is noisy and warm. No egg rolls here, and no fried noodles or sweet-and-sour soup.

The kitchen expertly prepares delicate minced clams and pork, sprinkled with cashew nuts and served with a mound of crisp lettuce, and a halved pineapple stuffed with tasty fried rice speckled with ham, pineapple chunks, tiny pieces of roast duck, crabmeat and vegetables. Cindy brought other wonders from Hong Kong, too: crisp, light, bean-curd skins wrapped around tender shrimp and scallops; al dente asparagus with tiny oysters; airy fish balls with a spicy ginger-and-scallion sauce; crab, sautéed with ham, scallions and fermented beans; and a salt-baked squab, juicy and succulent. Tai Hong Lau's renowned hot peanut soup, sweet and mysterious, can cap a satisfying meal, or try a sweetened red-bean soup and traditional slices of orange. On a cold winter's day, you can ask for a seafood soup from the small take-out shop just above the restaurant, also owned by Tai Hong Lau. No wine is served, but beer is available. Count about $60 for two, with beer.

12/20 Tenbrooks
62 Reade St.
(Broadway & Chambers Sts.)
349-5900
AMERICAN
Open Mon.-Fri. noon-10:30 p.m. All major cards.

Durability, indulgence without extravagance and an enthusiasm for freshness and new produce have driven this restaurant well through the 1980s, as daytime regulars from the government and financial communities and evening folk from the growing TriBeCa neighborhood enjoyed themselves here. Of course, it doesn't hurt to have Mama Klein there, and she usually is. Mama Klein is a trim, elegant, no-nonsense, energetic lady of "a certain age." She's called "Mama" by the highly professional staff, but she really is mama to Peter Klein, the co-owner and executive chef for the restaurant and its booming catering business. Mama keeps a keen eye on the 50-seat dining room-cum-art gallery (gray rug, Formica tables and a couple of rows of banquettes) and works the room like a pro. Eight to twelve art shows deck the walls each year, representative of diverse contempoary idioms and media.

The daily soup, pasta and market fish are always good, and for a basic and inexpensive lunch, there are good omelets and hamburgers. The kitchen, however, is also up to more ambitious things. Try the jalapeño-corn pancakes with sour-cream-and-chive sauce as an appetizer, or the grilled fennel sausage with mustard fruits; these deserve to remain the most popular choices. The menu and the wine list are updated seasonally, but tender, spicy crabcakes served with wild rice and, usually, broccoli, are always to be found as a main course. Lamb Louisiana with chili, garlic and fennel is also a good bet, as is the steamed ginger fish with aromatic vegetables. Duck salad with roasted peppers and cashews is a good main course for lunch. If you have room for dessert, Mama recommends the triple-layer cheesecake, seasonal strudels or her own Mama Rose's homebaked pies, which must be reserved. The 30-odd-bottle wine list is split between California and French wines, with a bottle or two of Australian or Italian thrown in; all land in the $12-to-$40 range and reflect careful quality and price selectivity. A half bottle of Guigal Côte du Rhône at $8 can't be faulted, nor can any of the wines by the glass. Reservations at lunch are helpful. Figure about $70 for two, though it is possible to enjoy lunch with a glass of wine for $40, again for two people.

10/20 Thailand
106 Bayard St. (Baxter St.)
349-3122
THAI
Open daily 11:30 a.m.-11 p.m. Cards: AE.

Too many Thai restaurants in New York remind us of Italian restaurants in Bangkok. At its roots, Thai food is, of course, an alluring blend of fiery spices and delicate, cooling sauces, though too few restaurants get it right. In a gritty Chinatown location, Thailand boasts a campy Tiki Punch decor.

An attractive menu features the seafood, beef and whole-fish courses that good Thai chefs use with flair; but overall, this lively, crowded restaurant fails to please. Tom kah gai, the classic chicken-and-coconut-milk soup, is an excellent starter. If only several main courses held up! When we dined here last, an eye-catching shrimp cooked in lime juice was spiced so extremely, the dish was virtually inedible, even for palates accustomed to hot foods. A similar, but less-shocking, fate befell an order of sautéed chicken with a good, thick peanut sauce. Perhaps the biggest disappointment was a plate of much-heralded pad Thai noodles, another culinary test, seemingly overcooked and overly starchy. Nonetheless, being able to eat dinner out in New York for less than $30 for two is itself a recommendable and exotic experience.

Tommy Tang's
323 Greenwich St. (Duane St.)
334-9190
THAI
Open Mon.-Thurs. 11:30 a.m.-3 p.m. & 6 p.m.-11 p.m., Fri. 11:30 a.m.-3 p.m. & 6 p.m.-midnight, Sat. 6 p.m.-midnight. All major cards.

We've got to give Hollywood's Tommy Tang's credit for succeeding with this New York outpost, when many thought it would fail. The emergence of the neighborhood, with its influx of hungry professionals, helped, as have Keith Sutha and Lucky Tang's cooking. From the looks of things at this funky Thai restaurant where the champagne flows, investment bankers are here in full force, as are the young artists and neighborhood folk (the two occasionally coincide, since the neighborhood is TriBeCa). The high-energy, loud, cavernous room, with a bar up front and a raised dining area in the rear, has been snazzied up with bed sheets painted in ab-

stract turquoise and pink patterns. Out-of-town guests take a fancy to this place.

Spicy, curry-flavored fried wontons are delicious, as is Thai toast, deep-fried circles of bread topped with minced pork and shrimp. If a dish sounds sweet, watch out: striking the sweet-savory balance seems a problem here. The original wings are popular starters (boneless chicken wings stuffed with shiitake mushrooms, bamboo shoots and onions). Fish are done well. Try the chili fish (fresh fish of the day with cayenne, black pepper, garlic powder and Thai red peppercorns, pan-fried in unsalted butter and topped with Serrano chiles, fresh ginger and garlic sauce). Thai pasta, a cold noodle dish with garlic, black-bean sauce, three peppers, cilantro and shreds of chicken breast, sounds delicious but lacks a certain freshness of taste and is oversweet. The original Tommy duck is a better main course option. Its honey-plum sauce is sweet, too, but the duck itself—steamed, baked, and deep-fried—is succulent and delectable. If you haven't overdosed on sweetness, a good bet for dessert is the banana-ice-cream sundae, but hold the chocolate sauce. The 25-item list of California wines plus French Champagnes is a good one. Expect to pay about $80 per couple for dinner with drinks, $60 or so per couple for lunch.

I Tre Merli
463 W. Broadway
(Houston & Prince Sts.)
254-8699
ITALIAN
Open Sun.-Thurs. noon-1 a.m., Fri.-Sat. noon-2 a.m. All major cards.

Beams of white light cut the harsh darkness of a deconstructivist, open SoHo warehouse space, and music blares from speakers poised near the towering ceilings. Hundreds of wine bottles line one side of an exposed brick wall; on the other is a long, crowded bar. A split-level area at the back breaks up the room and offers a sweeping view of the cavernous main floor. Pretty waitresses in short black skirts and white blouses weave among tables that are filled with the brave faces of attractive investment bankers, artists, models and downtown scene-makers. I Tre Merli is Italian for "the three blackbirds," but at first glance there's a strong temptation to change the name to "It's Merely Trendy."

Then the food comes, and proves that first impressions are often misleading. A basket of steamy fresh focaccia bread is a special order, and worth every bite. A unique appetizer of large and small fresh mushrooms is served over sculptured, rich polenta. It looks beautiful and tastes even better. Marinated seafood salad with shrimp, squid, scallops and rosemary, presented on a bed of radicchio lettuce, is another inviting starter. Delicious pastas are carefully prepared, and the kitchen will make half orders. Tender homemade gnocchi, small potato-pasta dumplings, comes with a choice of either tomato, pesto or a white gorgonzola-cheese sauce. Linguine al pesto is simple and balanced. Fazzoletti is luscious, flat ravioli filled with riccotta cheese and basil and served in a light tomato sauce. Among the best main courses is a finely sautéed tuna steak, simmered with tomatoes, onions, capers and olives. For a dessert experience, don't miss zuccotto, a tremendous wedge of dark, chocolate-frosted cake, filled with fluffy chocolate-and-hazelnut mousse. Much of the serviceable wine list carries the house label, I Tre Merli, and those same bottles line the brick wall. Some surprisingly good red wine selections are a 1986 Nebbiolo d'Alba and a 1987 Dolcetto d'Alba. Those well-chiseled waitresses, by the way, are generally attentive. At the end of a fine meal, you will be given a bill of about $110.

TriBeCa Grill

375 Greenwich St. (Franklin St.)
941-3900
AMERICAN
Open Mon.-Fri. noon-3 p.m., Mon.-Sat. 6 p.m.-10:45 p.m. All major cards.

The winner of the 1990 trend-o-mat of the year award, TriBeCa Grill opened in April 1990, following much anticipation and advance publicity, and for months its telephones peeled like the bells of St. Peter's announcing a new pope. Even managing partner and restaurateur par excellence Drew Nieporent admits his place is a crazy scene, and he doesn't know what the future will bring.

This is a big restaurant, and not all those people are showing up to catch a glimpse of partner Robert DeNiro and friends (a rarity). What they do see is Robert DeNiro Sr.'s paintings on the brick walls of this industrial-size and imaged space, and the big old four-

side art-deco (legendary singles) bar from Maxwell's Plum in the middle of the main dining room. There's a back dining room and a big upstairs space for private parties. The outside of this corner space and the main dining area have an authentic TriBeCa look—loading platforms, metal stairs, exposed brick, barbershop tiles, celing tiles and other warehouse accoutrements dressed up with some nice carpeting and comfortable chairs, booths and tables with white linen.

The food is better than it needs to be, at least during the relatively early days with Nieporent on the scene regularly eyeing the dishes, and the menu prepared by a big team that includes young veterans out of The River Café and other successful New York spots. Nieporent, of course, is nursing this child and leaving his older one, Montrachet, in the hands of its established team a few blocks away. Among the bistro fare, try the duck salad to start, or the tomato soup or a pasta. Various fish in a handful of preparations are available as a main course (roasted snapper is delicious) and among the standout meat and fowl entrées is a simply grilled chicken over vegetables, squab over lentils and big, moist veal chop. Don't miss the delicious potatoes "Vonnas" as an à la carte vegetable—light yet rooty pancakes. Among desserts, the rice pudding is memorable and the rich chocolate cake vibrant. The wine list is okay, though we hope in time it becomes stronger. Count on $80 for two.

12/20 20 Mott Street Restaurant

20 Mott St.
(Bowery & Chatham Square)
964-0380
CHINESE
Open daily 8 a.m.-midnight. Cards: AE, MC, V.

Welcome to the dim sum circus. At lunchtime or earlier (8 a.m. to 3 p.m.), Chinese waitresses circle the floors of this bright, three-tiered restaurant featuring trolleys packed with inviting dishes. Some offerings are familiar, such as spring rolls (Chinese mushrooms, pork and tofu in thick golden deep-fried rolls), or wonton soup (here virtually a dish of ravioli in brodo, with many soft, stuffed wontons filling the soup bowl). Be on the lookout for golden-fried crab claws, but consider carefully before ordering the steamed beef; in spite of the oiliness inside, the three meatballs often stick together and to the dish. The women wielding the carts barely speak English, so when an unfamiliar dish goes by, ordering can become low-stake gambling. The waiters aren't much help, either. It takes technique to break up the conversation they're usually holding among themselves; you may get a dour, single word response, if any, to questions. In short, the service here on most days leaves a lot to be desired. The food—be it dim sum or the more elaborate fare off the regular menu—is a better bet, and it all arrives promptly, which are two of the reasons that people line up outside. The menu isn't much use. Every Chinese dish imaginable seems to be on it, either poorly described or not at all, and what comes out of the kitchen is often a surprise—a pleasant surprise. The Chinese regulars seem to know how to order, so if you point to their dishes, you may do very well. In general, try the off-the-menu specials. However, you will certainly not suffer if you order duck, especially roast duck. Recommended starters include melon soup and deep-fried assorted seafood rolls. The lightly battered fried oysters are also distinguished; they reflect the kitchen's mastery of the ancient salt-cooking technique, culminating in either hot-oven baking or deep-frying. Try the shrimp in a shell for another good example. Seafood in a basket makes a good main dish, as does black fish with black-pepper sauce. There's beer to get you through the meal, as well as a plum wine that is better than a dessert. Everything is inexpensive; $30 a couple will set you in play and bring you to the cashier nicely; $40 to $50 per couple will keep you at it indefinitely.

11/20 Vucciria
422 W. Broadway (Broom St.)
941-5811

ITALIAN
Open Mon.-Thurs. noon-midnight, Fri.-Sat. noon-1 a.m., Sun. noon-11:30 p.m. Cards: AE.

We were lucky on our last visit, since we were able to observe from a distance the pop/jazz combo (with drums) performing near the entrance. We could almost enjoy our meal, except the food wasn't that enjoyable. If you should visit and if you're lucky, the loud music will be banished and the kitchen will get back to the higher level of performance that marked it when the restaurant opened a short while ago. Here on the main street of

artsy/touristy SoHo, in a rectangular space with one exposed brick wall, warm yellow walls, a painted ceiling of blue-and-white clouds, and a decorative catwalk overhead, is that most unchic of restaurants, a southern Italian trattoria. It's Sicilian, to be exact, as the many photographs of old Palermo testify. SoHo has a way, however, of transforming the formerly unchic into something trendy.

The offerings of antipasti, pastas, grilled fish and meats are filling and sound. When we dine here, all around us, people are starting with vegetables, such as roasted peppers or grilled radicchio or endives, or quartered-and-fried artichokes. A few, like us, enjoy a reasonably good carpaccio, bathed in olive oil and showered with Parmigiano shards. The earthy pastas are recommended: the anelletti in a dense Sicilian meat sauce with chunks of tomato is special. Fish appear as daily specials and are generally dressed with olive oil and grilled; a slice of salmon or a whole red snapper most regularly are offered. Palermo chicken is a good peasant dish—chunks of chicken with mushrooms and sausage and garlic. The veal chop is an alternative. The Sicilian cheesecake, with its creamy ricotta base, makes a choice dessert, and the Vucciria's version of the ubiquitous tiramisu is fine as well. So is the Italian wine list. Figure on $70 per couple, without tax and tip, but with free live music.

12/20 Windows on the World Restaurant
One World Trade Center, 107th Fl.
938-1111

CONTINENTAL
Open Mon.-Sat. 5 p.m.-10 p.m., Sat. noon-3 p.m., Sun. noon-7:30 p.m. All major cards.

Why do all good things have to end? This grand tourist restaurant is beginning to act like a tourist restaurant, with food and service not what they could be, or what they were five years ago. However, this place is tops, literally, if not gastronomically. A quarter of a mile above lower Manhattan, the view takes the triteness out of the word "spectacular." Heady and sensational vistas of the Manhattan skyline and waters make you a winner here before you pick up a menu. A huge, 350-seat restaurant, Windows on the World has been designed to afford intimacy and serenity. The large professional staff is skilled at seeing that

nothing intrudes into your dining experience.
In addition to a full à la carte menu, six
four-course dinners (prix-fixe by your choice
of the entrée) are good values ($35-39).
We've also enjoyed the weekend buffet, where
the choices are many and the portions unlimited. For weeknight dining, we always enjoy
oysters on the half shell to start, but the lobster
salad with corn and fried oysters is hard to
resist. The smoked sea scallops with baby
lettuce is a fine and simple opener. The mushroom ravioli in duck broth with scallions is a
viable alternative. For a main course (which
tends to be contemporary without being
trendy), the whole lobster in star anise broth
and vegetables with garlic croutons is recommended, as is the sautéed fresh venison with
wild mushooms and ginger potatoes. There is
the always reliable rack of young lamb prepared in the manner of, and named after,
James Beard. For a spectacular ending, try the
warm bread pudding with apples topped with
caramel sauce, or the hazelnut dacquoise with
raspberry coulis, or the warm blueberry pudding (without the chocolate sauce).
As well as being a top tourist destination,
Windows on the World is a mecca for wine
aficionados (and is also the site of a celebrated
wine school). The wine offerings are justly
famous for both their breadth—though the
strength of the list is Californian, then
French—and reasonable prices. There are ac-

DANDY SALADS

If a recent trend persists, dandelions
soon will earn their rightful place of
honor, alongside nasturtiums, in the
Unusual Salad Greens Hall of Fame. In
New York, a growing number of restaurants, including Le Cirque, Lutèce
and "21," have dandelions on their
menus. During the 1980s, sales of
commercially grown dandelions tripled, but as with any food fad, we
predict its demise later in the nineties.
Meanwhile, watch for small golden
flowers in your food.

tually two lists. So not to confuse or overwhelm anyone, a captain's list of 130 selections and featuring dozens of wines priced
under $30, is presented. More intrepid souls
may request the list of about 800 (!) offerings.
If you don't overindulgew, expect to spend
$120 per couple, ordering à la carte.

12/20 Wong Kee
113 Mott St. (Canal & Hester Sts.)
966-1160

CHINESE
Open daily 11 a.m.-9:45 p.m. No cards.

At lunch, you can be in and out of this
agreeable spot comfortably in fifteen minutes.
It's unlikely you'll be disappointed at Wong
Kee, although neither we nor the restaurant
claim the food will send you anywhere in
particular. You will certainly get your money's
worth at this popular Cantonese-style restaurant. Beyond a handsome stainless-steel facade lies a bright, colorful dining room that
seats about 100. Canisters of chopsticks and
forks grace the green-Formica tables and,
through a window-case of hanging Peking
ducks, you can also see the kitchen.
We recommend for appetizers the roast
pork, roast duck or barbecued spare ribs—all
cold cut. For a main course, try the chicken in
sizzling platter or the Wong Kee spiced
chicken or pork. The chicken is cubed,
breaded and mixed with black beans, fresh
garlic, hot pepper and a sweet and pungent
sauce. Or, try hong shiu chicken, which the
menu describes as "one of the most wonderful
dishes in the house. Fresh cut spring chicken
meat fried to a golden brown crispness topped
with shredded bamboo shoots, Chinese
mushroom and Chinese vegetables." Order
the mong kee steak, the specialty of the house,
and choice strips of steak come sizzling out of
the kitchen, sautéed Cantonese-style. The
tender, skillfully cooked meat is served with
broccoli and a thick sauce that displays overtones of both hot spice and sweetness. No
beer or wine is served here, though you can
bring your own. No desserts either, which can
be taken as an admirable sign of purity and
integrity. You are, more or less, in Little Italy,
so Italian pastries and ice creams are just
around the bend. The service is friendly, helpful and hopping in this busy restaurant. Meals
average $26 per couple for dinner, with wine,
and for a little more ($36), two can overdose.

GREENWICH VILLAGE

12/20 Au Troquet
328 W. 12th St.
(Hudson & Washington Sts.)
924-3413

FRENCH

Open daily 6 p.m.-11 p.m. Cards: AE, V, DC.

Count this as one of those secret, out-of-the-way restaurants people enjoy discovering. It's in the far West Village, on a dull corner where you wouldn't expect to find a restaurant, but look into the lace-curtained windows and you'll see a lovely, romantic room with fourteen tables. Antiques and flowers, in addition to the oil paintings and watercolors, enhance the blue and yellow decor. French charm oozes everywhere, including from the Edith Piaf tapes that play on the sound system.

Don't expect to be overly charmed by the menu and dishes. They are predictable and palatable—good and hearty, not elegant and flashy. It is one step up from bistro fare, though. The handwritten menu changes periodically. The fresh salmon marinated with basil is a very good appetizer, cool and flavorful. Snails with garlic butter and anise-flavored Ricard works well. There's usually an okay endive salad with Roquefort and a real soup that tastes as if it had been to school in France and had been at work all day in the kitchen. Among the ten or so main courses, nothing is irresistible, but the chicken breast with mustard sauce is ever so reliable. The rabbit dish is prepared well, but rabbit in New York just doesn't taste like rabbit does in Europe. Spinach, carrots and potatoes dauphinoise (nicely crusted on top with potato slices, cream, and nutmeg beneath) are passable side vegetables. Grilled meats, fowl or fish continue to be generally safe bets. For dessert, enjoy the daily tart. The wine list of mostly French and a few American wines deserves special mention; it's incredible, depressingly so. A wine list without vintages or even the name of the producer is a rarity in New York in the 1990s. It doesn't speak well for the restaurant. Count on $90 for two, with a bottle of wine.

Barrow Street Bistro
48 Barrow St.
(Bedford St. west of Seventh Ave.)
691-6800

AMERICAN

Open Mon.-Thurs. 6 p.m.-11 p.m., Fri.-Sat. 6 p.m.-midnight; Sun. 5 p.m.-10 p.m. Cards: AE, MC, V.

Open-kitchen, New American cuisine is taken to an extreme here. You literally must walk through the working kitchen to reach the main dining room. Situated two steps down from street level in a Greenwich Village brownstone, the Barrow Street Bistro has a dark, low-ceilinged, crowded front dining room with a bar, a mid-restaurant kitchen, and a makeshift back "garden" dining room, replete with green Astroturf, tented ceiling and various garden fixtures. The low-budget decor focuses your attention on what's on the plate, solidly in the Californian and Southwestern traditions of grilling, cross-cultural dishes and imaginative treatment of vegetables.

Early in 1990, owner and host Lee Friedman changed the name (formerly it was Melrose) and lowered the prices when chef and ex-partner Richard Krauss left to open an even less expensive restaurant. We expect the quality to remain the same, but to see less expensive ingredients, a simpler menu and less frills on the plate. Currently, the kitchen team grills up a storm, such as the chicken served in the summmer with cool ratatouille, browned butter, blanched garlic and crisp shoestring potatoes; or loin of veal, grilled salmon, the rare charred blue tuna steak, or the perfectly prepared red snapper. We liked the duck with crisp potato slices and mushrooms, but for starters, we trust the wonderful potato pancakes topped with crème fraîche and three caviars (sturgeon, salmon, and whitefish). Some fans love the ginger crêpe with lobster and duck. In winter, the chunky vegetable soup surely hits the spot, as does the blackbean soup. In summer, try a refreshing salad of assorted organic mixed greens. The wine choices, approximately 120 selections, come mostly from California and cost in the $25-to-$45 range. The raspberry tart is the day-in, day-out winner among desserts; the chocolate-chip ice-cream sandwich a crowd pleaser. Figure $70 for two for dinner.

12/20 The Black Sheep
344 W. 11th St. (Washington St.)
242-1010
FRENCH

Open Mon.-Thurs. 6 p.m.-11 p.m., Fri.-Sat. 6 p.m.-midnight, Sun. noon-4 p.m. & 6 p.m.-10:30 p.m. All major cards.

It seems incredible that the 1990s mark the third decade we'll be heading agreeably to The Black Sheep, which we continue to recommend as a good, steady restaurant for dinner, or a quaint spot for Sunday brunch. French country bistro is its calling, and although it has barely changed since it opened (when it was a hot, fine outpost hidden in the far West Village), it need not. Black Sheep has mastered the formula that in the past few years dozens of New York restaurants have tried to learn. The five-course menu is a top value, the waiters are friendly and concerned (and talk about the theater) and the decor is beguiling, and to many, romantic. With the incredible development of the far West Village around it, the Black Sheep is flourishing as a neighborhood bistro and weekend mecca.

The prix-fixe menu (priced according to the entrée) begins as it has from day one, with a rustic table portion of crudités. Soup, pâté or the daily appetizer special follow. A hot soup of two types of squash is simple and pure. Vegetables (eggplant, zucchini) on a hot pastry-dough crust surrounded by a tomato coulis taste like a good French apple tart in vegetable drag. Main courses range from pastas and grilled striped bass to leg of lamb Provençal or chicken stuffed under the skin with tarragon. The last is superb—moist, luscious and well seasoned. The pasta of the day is uneven, but can be outstanding. If you are there for brunch, try the curried-chicken salad with dill, raisins and toasted almonds served in a croissant, or superb Amaretto whole-wheat french toast (made from Zito's bread) served with fresh berries. Desserts are very good. The wine list merits praise. It's extensive, with well-chosen French and American wines and a few from elsewhere, all bearing

reasonable prices—and there's a very good selection of quality wines offered by the glass. Dinner will run about $90 for two, with a modest bottle of wine. A ten-percent discount is given to customers paying cash.

11/20 La Bohême
24 Minetta Ln. (Sixth Ave.)
473-6447
FRENCH

Open Tues.-Sat. 5:30 p.m.-midnight, Sun. noon-11 p.m. Cards: AE.

With its wood-fired pizza oven, its white stucco walls and its Provençal pottery and fabrics, La Bohême would look quite at home in Arles—except maybe the light fixtures, which are made of painted colanders that scream New York to us. While students, tourists and off-Broadway theatergoers flock to this place, designed by Sam Lopata and opened in 1985, La Bohême is really a spot for Villagers. A convivial place in which to chat, or to enjoy a light supper or a full-fledged meal, La Bohême serves forth food that is as good as it needs to be.

Some regulars subsist on pizzas with a "side" of fries. The pizzas, in fact, are the best way to start a meal, the most popular choices: vegetarian, La Bohême (with capers and anchovies), or Gitane (with snails). Steak frites is fine, featuring good beef cooked to order and topped with a pat of herb butter. Specials, too, can be satisfying, particularly the thin slices of medium-rare leg of lamb arranged around a mix of goat cheese and spinach, or the salmon en croûte in a light, basil-scented sauce. The 25-item wine list is serviceable if you don't mind ordering without knowing the vintage or the producer's name (neither of which are listed), and is reasonably priced. If we could, we'd shape up the casual service, and perhaps pay a bit more attention to cleanliness and maintenance. Dinner, with wine, costs about $70 for two.

Café de Bruxelles
118 Greenwich Ave. (13th St.)
206-1830
BELGIAN/FRENCH

Open Tues.-Sat. noon-3 p.m. & 5 p.m.-11 p.m., Sun. noon-10:30 p.m. Mon. 5 p.m.-11 p.m. All major cards.

Don't let the name, the array of Belgian beers or the waterzooï de poissons and other daily Belgian specialities fool you: this is a charming French bistro, owned and operated since October 1987 by the very French and endearing Thierry and Patricia Moity. Bubbly, petite Patricia is the able maitre d' and Thierry the chef (he won praise for La Gauloise when he manned its ovens). This sophisticated café, with starched lace curtains and walls lacquered in essence-of-bistro beige, is located on an odd triangle where Greenwich Avenue meets 13th Street; the restaurant is approximately the same shape, its small, cozy but crowded bar (with an excellent bar menu) joined by a long narrow space to a proper-size room.

Mussels, a Belgian passion, appear here as moules marinière, plump, steamed beauties in a delectable, garlicky white-wine broth, portions large enough to feed two, easily. The bouillabaisse, chock-full of perfectly cooked shrimp, mussels, lobster and shellfish, remains one of the town's best renderings, rich and winey, with accents of Pernod and garlic. Other Belgian specialties include the aforementioned waterzooï, a lemony, leek-fragrant stew (excellent in both the chicken and the fish version) and carbonnade à la flamande, tender chunks of beef flavored with onions and a smoky note of beer. For a first course or luncheon dish, try the salade liégeoise of string beans, red onions, potatoes and bacon, or moules (mussles) au garlic. If you're not planning to have the fine steak pommes frites for a main course, you will probably still receive those crisp golden fries on the side (the Belgians claim authorship of this way of cooking potatoes and go crazy when you call the fries French). Placed on your table in a cone of paper, they are meant to be dipped, in the Belgian manner, in mayonnaise. For dessert, we love the fabulous Belgian waffle with a scoop of vanilla ice cream and bittersweet hot Belgian-chocolate sauce. It seems that only a trencherman could manage it after the hearty

We're always interested to hear about your discoveries, and to receive your comments on ours. Please feel free to write to us, and do state clearly exactly what you liked or disliked.

cooking and generous portions of this restaurant. The wine list is more than adequate, and the service friendly and attentive. On Friday and Saturday nights, you'd better reserve. Figure $70 for two for dinner, sharing a modest bottle of wine.

12/20 Café Loup
105 W. 13th St. (Sixth Ave.)
255-4746
FRENCH
Open daily noon-midnight. Cards: AE, DC.

Owners Roxanne and Bruce Bethany moved their small bohemian Village bistro two blocks west in 1989, but they still cater to publishing types from Farrar, Straus & Giroux, *Forbes*, *The Village Voice* and *Womens Wear Daily*. Chef (since 1979) Lloyd Feit came with them and must like his bigger kitchen. The simple, and generally French, bistro food is more satisfying than ever. The new 100-seat room, with tables adorned with paper tablecloths but linen napkins, is adorned with photos and eclectic gimcrackery. The walls are, for the most part, exposed brick, and there is a long, busy bar (with a short, good menu) up front at this deep, large restaurant.

Along with the move came the addition of pasta, french fries and ice creams to the short and classic menu (mussels rémoulade, escargots, saucisson, steak au poivre, calf's brains, tournedos, liver, lamb chops with Provence herbs and one or two fish dishes). The snails and mussels are recommended for starters, the roast duck entrée and calf's brains (with brown butter and capers) for main courses. The half chicken (from Bell & Evans) is always prepared to a moist perfection. The fish specials are okay, though we don't fancy the soft-shell crab when it's offered, and the vegetables—mostly rice, spinach, carrots, Swiss chard—are fine. The desserts have an American look and include Key lime pie and Mississippi mud cake. The service is friendly and the wine list attractive. Someone here knows what he or she is doing. The Château Meyney 1983 at $20 or the Talbot 1979 at $28 cannot be faulted. Try the Penfold's Cabernet Sauvignon/Shiraz Hununga Hill 1986 for $16, or one of the other unusual wines that represent good values. The markups are reasonable, at least by uptown standards. Figure $40 per couple for lunch with a drink and $80 at dinner with a bottle of wine.

Il Cantinori

32 E. 10th St.
(University Pl. & Broadway)
673-6044

ITALIAN

Open Mon.-Thurs. noon-3 p.m. & 6 p.m.-11:30 p.m., Fri. noon-3 p.m. & 6 p.m.-midnight, Sat. 6 p.m.-midnight, Sun. 5 p.m.-11 p.m. Cards: AE, DC.

This spacious Village restaurant serves the real thing, true Italian food conceived, as was the modern Italian language, in Tuscany. This relatively casual "rustic" restaurant has a staff that is knowledgeable about Italian food and wine. For a serious Italian (Tuscan) meal, Il Cantinori rarely disappoints, and when it does, it is because the enthusiastic staff becomes overambitious and attempts more than they can handle. You'll enjoy browsing through the huge list of specials, in addition to the already substantial regular menu. Overall, the service and food may have slipped some in the past few years, but the restaurant still commands considerable and deserved respect.

When you enter the front room with its stucco walls, you are treated to a lavish and colorful presentation of cold antipasti that may tempt you to decide on your first course before you take off your coat. The offerings range from marinated mushrooms and zucchini with capers to more unusual and elaborate preparations. The art and fashion crowds that have made Il Cantinori one of their clubhouses seem to prefer the special assortment of grilled vegetables for a starter. Of course, risotto or pasta dishes (six regular ones plus usually about four specials) entice; they can be ordered as appetizers or main courses. The pastas are a bit uneven, but can be very good. Consider the spaghetti with beans and mussels, or the rigatoni al buristo (blood sausage) or a classic puttanesca. Actually, you will do extremely well if you simply ask for spaghetti with tomato sauce, or the roasted quail with polenta and tomato as a nice entrée. Pheasant comes a bit dry by design and won't appeal to most—try the osso buco, instead. For dessert, ask for the fine tiramisu, or you may opt for a dessert wine by the glass—vin santo or even picolit—with some traditional dry biscuits. The Italian wine list has been constructed by people who care about small vineyards, pro-

ducers and high quality. Try the Barbaresco Martinenga. Dinner runs about $98 for two.

Cent' Anni

50 Carmine St.
(Bleecker & Bedford Sts.)
989-9494

ITALIAN

Open Mon.-Fri. noon-2:30 p.m. & 5:30 p.m.-11 p.m., Sat.-Sun. 5:30 p.m.-11 p.m. Closed last 3 weeks in July. Cards: AE.

Don't worry, it's as good as ever. The food remains straightforward and flavorful—still a lusty mix of old and new Florentine fare—the portions gleefully too large, and the staff engagingly ethnic. Cent' Anni means "one hundred years," as in "You should live to be a hundred," or "You should eat and live well for the next century." Good feelings abound in this small, bustling storefront restaurant, with fifteen tables usually occupied by serious and fashionable folks in their 30s, 40s, 50s and 60s.

Your waiter will invariably propose "a nice appetizer," which inevitably turns out to be an assortment of offerings that are indeed nice, such as the combination of warmed radicchio with melted Taleggio cheese, bocconcini (little mouthfuls of stewed veal), fagioli (white beans), and uccelletti (small birds). The cold seafood salad is a highly recommended opener. We like the zuppa ortolana, or "greengrocer's soup," a striking, baked soup of beans, cabbage, leeks, toast, cheese and pancetta. Try a half-order of pasta, if you wish, or ask for a combination plate with several varieties. Among the outstanding choices (and the house favorite), the cappellini con aragosta (angel hair pasta in a light tomato sauce with lobster meat and clams) and the pappardelle al coniglio (a broad noodle with a rabbit-and-game sauce) remain favorites. You might also consider the veal chop salvia, a monstrous double-cut chop of top-quality veal, which is broiled, then sautéed in wine and fresh sage. We have savored in the past such entrées as the calamari con aglio (squid sautéed in oil, garlic, tomato and spices) and the pollo alla diavola (broiled game hen marinated in oil, garlic, basalmic vinegar and rosemary), not to mention the roast loin of pork Florentine style (when it's not overcooked). For dessert, stick to fruit or cheese, or possibly the satisfying cold, homemade zabaglione with berries. Chocolate-lovers won't mind the chocolate cake. The wines, mostly Italian, are sound, and the list has grown impressively, to about 100 offerings, including some from California and Australia—most at generally modest prices, with plenty of choices in the $20-to-$30 range. Lunch averages $60 to $70 for two, and dinner $80 to $90 with wine.

Chez Jacqueline
72 MacDougal St.
(Bleecker & Houston Sts.)
505-0727

FRENCH
Open Sun.-Thurs. 6 p.m.-11 p.m., Fri.-Sat. 6 p.m.-11:30 p.m. Cards: AE.

If you lived in a modest *arrondissement* of Paris, a restaurant not unlike Chez Jacqueline would no doubt be your *bistro du coin*, the place you'd fall into at night when you didn't want to prepare your own meal, confident you'd get the same French home cooking you'd known all your life. Customers wander into this (what else?) lace-curtained bistro wearing everything from business suits to jeans, and, occasionally, toting their baby along. Everyone is greeted like a friend, which is exactly what most of the customers are. The tables are small, the decor pleasantly nonexistent. Jacqueline Zini and her brother, Titou Quiquerez, the owners and chefs, are Niçois, which explains the touches of the cuisine of the sun (and the fading photograph of Nice in 1910).

With your glass of wine, you'll be offered pieces of feather-light, addictive pissaladière (a kind of pizza with onions, olives and anchovies). Ask for the brandade de morue, an airy whip of salt cod, garlic, olive oil and potato purée, probably the best in town. Pâté de campagne, a menu cliché elsewhere, presents beautifully balanced flavors here, as does the fish soup, heady and soul-stirring. That hard-to-find French Sunday dinner standby, blanquette de veau à l'ancienne, absolute perfection as made here, melts tenderly in the mouth, the sauce not too gussied up with cream and egg yolk. A real buy, it comes with a timbale of rice. Gigot d'agneau (leg of lamb), happily paired with flageolets and garnished with a small mound of gratin dauphinoise and a grilled tomato niçoise, was well seasoned and rare, as requested. The small, well-chosen menu includes veal kidneys

in a creamy Dijon-mustard sauce with Cognac; basquaise chicken prepared with tomatoes, green peppers and onions; and the winey beef stew, daube niçoise. For liquid accompaniment, sample from the inexpensive list one of the Provence wines, say the red or rosé of Château Requier. If you go on a night when there's the buttery apple tart, don't miss it. Dinner about $60 for two.

11/20 Chez Ma Tante
189 W. 10th St. (Bleecker St.)
620-0223

FRENCH
Open Sun.-Thurs. 6 p.m.-11:30 p.m., Fri. 6 p.m.-12:30 a.m.; Sat. noon-3 p.m. & 6 p.m.-12:30 a.m., Sun. noon-3 p.m. Cards: AE, MC, V.

This open-air storefront bistro beckons passersby with its pretty interior and the heady smell of garlic. You won't go far wrong if you succumb. Yes, it can be crowded and noisy (especially in winter when the wall of doors is closed), too pretty, and the service can be off-putting—Lutéce, it is not.

Since you can't eat the white walls, wood floor, tangerine-colored ceiling and the moving picture of Village characters passing by—except with your eyes—stick to basic bistro fare. The fish soup, flavored with spicy rouille and tomato, is okay, as is the poussin and the standard steak frites combination. The latter selection seemingly suffers from a glandular condition—the servings are enormous. The other classics arrive sometimes passable, sometimes not. The crème brûlée is a decent choice of dessert, often arriving still warm, with a properly crusty top. The wines are a disappointment, the predictable choices of one major supplier. Still, all things considered, the dining experience is pleasant here. Figure about $78 for two for dinner with a reasonable wine, plus tax and tip.

The Coach House
110 Waverly Pl. (off Washington Square West)
777-0303

AMERICAN
Open Tues.-Sun. 5:30 p.m.-10:30 p.m. All major cards.

An institution, they call it an institution. Perhaps museum is a better word. You can come here to learn what James Beard and

Craig Claiborne ate in the 1960s, when they raved about the place and built its reputation. Not much has changed since then, lending it a "folkloric" charm. The brick walls, the red-leather banquettes, the oil paintings of hunting scenes and still lifes of food, look just the way they always have. This restaurant is housed in a building constructed 150 years ago as a coach house for the Wanamaker family, and the fashionable French who reserve here have come to taste the vintage setting as well as the hefty portions of prime rib, the thick black bean soup and the corn sticks, all of which have served owner Leon Lianides well over the past 40 years and have (not without criticism) become the stuff of legend. The Coach House has always been a place to bring parents, grandparents, aunts and uncles—a place to impress recruiters from white-shoe law firms. It also attracts a young business crowd, Greek expatriates and food writers on their day off.

They come for owner-chef Leon Lianides's production at its best—which means sitting downstairs (and not in the converted hayloft) for cosseting Old World service, for the good crabcakes and for "Continental" selections such as salmon served with a court bouillon in which it has been perfectly poached, Grand Marnier Bavarian cream, chocolate mousse cake, dacquoise and a wine list that is extensive, reasonably priced and thoughtfully put together. Of course, there are down sides: some find Lianides chilly; at peak hours, service can be hurried; and the chicken pot pie tastes as if it were chicken à la king made from a can of soup, leftovers and store-bought pastry cups. But if you're wondering where to celebrate your grandmother's birthday, your search is over. Expect to pay $118 per couple for dinner, with wine.

11/20 Cuisine de Saigon
154 W. 13th St.
(Sixth & Seventh Aves.)
255-6003
VIETNAMESE
Open Mon.-Thurs. 5 p.m.-11 p.m., Fri. 5 p.m.-11:30 p.m., Sat. 5:30 p.m.-11:30 p.m., Sun. 5 p.m.-10:30 p.m. All major cards.

In a town not blessed with good Vietnamese restaurants, Cuisine de Saigon weighs in as a respectable middleweight. Some of the offerings are merely of journeyman quality, but there are some jabs at excellence. Leo Tran is usually out front to greet you as you enter the pleasant and separate bar of this long and narrow ground floor restaurant in a Village brownstone. He leads you through a passageway surrounded by the kitchen, where Marie Tran is responsible for the authentic Vietnamese cooking, and into the dining room. Peach walls, gray wall-to-wall carpeting, ceiling fans, original paintings by a Vietnamese artist—the room is pleasant enough and fills up with locals and groups out for a modestly priced, modestly exciting meal.

Spring rolls are touted as a house specialty, but this Vietnamese staple turns out to be unmemorable. The kindred shrimp roll on occasion turns out to be dominated by bean sprouts rather than shrimp, and, like most of the appetizers, may be greasier than you'd like. Steamed dumplings stuffed with pork and shrimp are all right, but soups are probably a better choice for a starter. The real temptation, however, is to get some of the good entrées on the table right away, and dig in Asian-style. Shrimp-wrapped sugar cane (chao tom) is broiled shrimp fixed to a sugar-cane stalk and served with rice paper, lettuce and vegetables. You fashion a hand roll that is seasoned with accompanying sweet hoisin sauce. All of the broiled dishes come out fine, as does the steamed fish. Pasta via Saigon (bahn cuon) is an intriguing and excellent noodle dish. Light ravioli-like shells are stuffed with minced pork and mushrooms and served with a light, flavorful sauce that is the best of the three or four sauces served. Both the chicken and the shrimp crêpes are dependable, if undistinguished; the crêpes themselves are prepared well. For meat eaters, lemongrass beef—strips of beef sautéed with lemon grass (a delicious, thin, scallionlike herb) served with a peanut-curry sauce—is recommended, as are the boneless stuffed chicken and the aromatic duck. Steamed (and gooey) banana cake is available for dessert, though desserts are an afterthought at Vietnamese restaurants. Consider an espresso and dessert at one of the nearby Village pastry shops. There's a handful of beers to choose from, and the balanced wine list includes about 25 generally inexpensive, but sound, wines—consider the Simi Chardonnay at $18. Reserve ahead on weekends. Dinner runs about $54 for two, with wine.

Da Silvano

260 Sixth Ave.
(Bleecker & Houston Sts.)
982-2343

ITALIAN

Open Mon.-Thurs. noon-3 p.m. & 6 p.m.-11:30 p.m., Fri. noon-3 p.m. & 6 p.m.-midnight, Sat. 6 p.m.-midnight, Sun. 5 p.m.-11 p.m. Cards: AE.

We don't know what it is about Tuscan restaurants in New York (along with Da Silvano, Il Cantinori and Le Madri are on our mind), but first, the list of specials is often nearly as long as the menu—eighteen might be an average number—and second, the specials are not all written down, but are recited in their entirety, table by table. At Da Silvano, this can slow otherwise good service down to a crawl when the place is crowded. The size of the small tables at this rustic and attractive eatery may be conducive to intimate conversation, but you're always wondering what will end up on the floor.

Go for the antipasto giardiniera del giorno, especially the tiny, braised Italian artichokes, cooked in olive oil with lots of garlic. We find the carpaccio ordinary, but the panzella—a cold-bread salad with roasted peppers, tomatoes, cucumbers and onions—with its well-seasoned vinaigrette, tastes delightful, as does the insalata di mare, a salad of calamari and mussels in the same vinaigrette. You'll want lots of bread to soak up the sauce. We like the homemade pasta, though the sauces disappoint. The spaghettini puttanesca lacks pungency and differs little from one of the specials, tagliatelle checa, prepared sparingly with whole tomatoes and mozzarella. At a recent dinner, a pasta special with fresh porcini mushrooms seemed overly buttery to our taste. Among the main courses, the calf's liver with sage nearly drowned in a heavy wine sauce, but the accompanying polenta saved the day. We found the roast suckling pig overly salty. The short wine list features good Italian bottles at reasonable prices. Among desserts, we adore the tiramisu—here it is very good, not too sweet and infused with a pleasing coffee flavor. You'll pay $110 per couple, with a modest wine, plus tax and tip.

12/20 Ennio & Michael Restaurant

504 LaGuardia Pl.
(Bleecker & W. 3rd Sts.)
677-8577

ITALIAN

Open daily noon-11 p.m. Cards: AE.

Ennio Sammarone and Michael Savarese moved their restaurant in 1989 more or less diagonally across the street. Their new spot is equally sleek and elegant as was their former home, the size is about the same or maybe just a touch smaller, the room squarer and with some art-deco overtones, but they've added a welcome front deck for fine weather dining. The restaurant is set back from the street, and in summer the outdoor space is one of the most pleasant around. Giulio Castro, the chef since 1981, found his way across the street as well, so the reasonably refined Italian-American cuisine has not changed much.

If you pull Ennio or Michael over, either can probably crank the kitchen up a point or two for you, but we haven't tried. The fried zucchini (in thin strips) are light and addictive (thankfully, the plate is well stacked). Stuffed artichoke or spiedini alla romana also get the nod as appetizers, as does the simple spiedini al salmone. Hearty rigatoni alla matriciana is one of the better bets for pasta, as is the fusilli alla Ennio. The spaghetti puttanesca is tame and the pasta primavera is anemic (a few peas and some zucchini). For a main course, the scaloppine alla Sorrentia (veal sautéed with wine and topped with eggplant and mozzarella) is one of the most popular dishes. It's palatable, but the veal tends to be very thinly sliced and bland. Chicken all'arrabbiata (golden-brown pieces of chicken in a spicy garlic-and-vinegar sauce, without a hint of oiliness) is another favorite and is more successful. The wine list has improved, but could still use some work, though most of Italy is represented and there are good special bottles to be found. Order the Montepulciano d'Abruzzo by Casal Thaulero, at $17 the best red-wine value offered. Desserts are ever so sweet. Consider Michael's special—slivers of dark chocolate covered with hazelnut ice cream topped with marinated strawberries, and a cold zabaglione, all served in a wine glass. However, we prefer Michael's grandmother's cheesecake, moist and delicious. Dinner costs about $80 per couple, plus tax and tip.

10/20 El Faro
823 Greenwich St. (Horatio St.)
929-8210
SPANISH
*Open Sun.-Thurs. 11 a.m.-midnight, Fri.-Sat.
11 a.m.-1 a.m. All major cards.*

El Faro celebrated its 30th anniversary in 1989, so you know they must be doing something right, and, indeed, this culinary institution gets points for having been around so long. Its dark murals of flamenco dancers, its raffish decor and the aroma of garlic give this out-of-the-way spot a spicy ambiance. There's a big downside—the place is jammed with tourists, which makes the wait for tables interminably long (no reservations accepted), and the food is mediocre. Still, people flock here.

Whether or not the fare can be called authentically Spanish is open to question. It is, however, authentically Greenwich Village Spanish, from wilted salad and chorizos to mariscada (mixed seafood) in green sauces (parsley, onions, garlic and olive oil), as well as paella and chicken Villarroy (béchamel sauce separates the chicken breast from the baked breading). Veal a la coruñesa (with tomato, sherry and butter) is a popular dish, as is the crabmeat with green sauce. Perhaps best is the side order of fried potatoes. Of course, order the flan for dessert. Most diners drink sangría by the pitcher, and there is a short list of Spanish wines—the white Monopole at $18.50 is an excellent choice. Dinner costs about $56 for two with wine, plus tax and tip.

10/20 Garvin's
19 Waverly Pl. (Green & Mercer Sts.)
473-5261
AMERICAN
Open Mon.-Fri. 5 p.m.-11 p.m., Sat.-Sun. 11 a.m.-11 p.m. All major cards.

Richard Garvin has put together a handsome, romantic dining room with a 1900s look: there are tapestries, antiques, objets d'art, a baby-grand piano, high ceilings and a 28-foot bar (where you can order most dishes). It's a good place to stop by for a drink. He also does good business out of his three private rooms, including using them for the wine courses taught by The New School. William Billias has been Garvin's chef since 1984 and turns out American fare with Continental overtones. It's okay, sort of.

We like to follow one rule here: keep it simple when ordering. The sun-dried tomato salad with warm, smoked mozzarella makes a good appetizer, as does the seafood terrine of scallops and lobster. There are some pasta options as starters or as main courses, but you're on your own with them. The grilled tournedos with madiers and green-peppercorn-and-braised-shallot sauce and the sautéed medallions of veal with morel mushrooms, brandy and crème fraîche are popular, but you might safely stick with the grilled swordfish steak, which is overdressed with fresh basil, tomato and Dijon-mustard butter. A large display of desserts, to satisfy at least your eyes, is always available; all are baked on the premises. Prices are reasonable here, especially for the 50 or so French, California and Australian wines. There's also a $17.95 pretheater dinner, served from 5 p.m. to 7 p.m. (opt for the mesquite-grilled boneless breast of chicken entrée). Figure $80 for two for dinner.

 La Gauloise
502 Ave. of the Americas
(12th & 13th Sts.)
691-1363
FRENCH
Open daily noon-3 p.m. & 5:30 p.m.-11 p.m. All major cards.

Established in 1978 and thus one of the first of the new wave of chic French brasseries to hit New York, La Gauloise is a trusted Village restaurant, serving hearty meals of exemplary honesty and regularity. Owner Jacques Allimann has created a handsome establishment decorated with art-deco lamps, mahogany-bordered mirrors and the obligatory banquettes, in which he delivers true bistro fare made from products of high quality. Onion soup, oysters, escargots bourguignon, pâté de campagne, choucroute, bouillabaisse, grilled chicken, entrecôte béarnaise and another dozen or so dishes one would expect to find in Paris at a good neighborhood bistro, are there on the menu. Hearty portions attract customers who don't complain that, now and again, the chicken is dry and the veggies are only so-so, or that the saumon paillard with basil sauce is a little bland. We like the lighter fare on the summer menu, and think the $19.50 prix-fixe dinner (Tuesday through Friday from 5:30 p.m. to 6:45 p.m.) is a good value. Typically French bistro, the service seems sometimes charming and stunningly efficient, and at other times indifferent. The range of desserts should cement a solid meal, especially the lemon tart and crème brûlée. You'll find a good selection of wine, with good years; mostly French, with a handful of American offerings, the bottles are all attractively priced. Dinner, with wine, averages $96 for two, lunch about $60 for two.

Gotham Bar & Grill
12 E. 12th St.
(Fifth Ave. & University Pl.)
620-4020

AMERICAN

Open Mon.-Thurs. noon-2:30 p.m. & 6 p.m.-10:45 p.m., Fri. noon-2:30 p.m. & 6 p.m.-11:15 p.m., Sat. 6 p.m.-11:15 p.m., Sun. 5:30 p.m.-9:30 p.m. All major cards.

Not a whole lot has changed here since talented and seriously trained Alfred Portale (Culinary Institute of America, Maximin, Guérard, Troisgros) took over the kitchen in March 1985 and made what appeared on the plates at least the equal of the restaurant's splendid architectural design. Winner of the 1984 Restaurant and Hotel Design award for postmodern setting, the restaurant is a breathtaking transformation of some 5,000 square feet of formerly raw warehouse space (a half block deep), with palatial ceilings. Gotham takes the "see and be seen" excitement of restaurant-going to the "nth" degree: everyone can make an entrance worthy of a prima ballerina. The feel of the place, with its chintz-covered banquettes, parachute-cloth-swaddled fixtures and aqua trim, exudes contemporary and urban allure.

The size of the room and the number of dinners served make us nervous. Plenty must be prepared in advance, and Portale cannot eagle-eye everything coming out of the kitchen. (Nor can he be there all the time; we've had some Sunday night fiascos.) That explains the occasional flop, but you will not find a better seafood salad than the one here: opalescent slices of squid, scallop, hunks of lobster, and mussels dressed in a vibrant vinaigrette are served with chunks of avocado, a perfect counterpoint in both flavor and tex-

ture. We loved the house-smoked duck breast with lettuce, rice and an apricot-pear chutney as an appetizer. Expect everything to be presented stunningly and to bear, perhaps, only slight similarity to the description on the menu. We remember fondly a grilled tuna, expertly cooked and lovely when served with a delicious homemade lemon-basil pasta. For an outstanding fish dish, try the sautéed black bass. Squab, cooked rare, has a gamey richness. Its garnishes include wild mushrooms and Swiss chard, but once again, the pasta steals the show: homemade Spätzle, tossed in mustard butter, is so good you want to eat it every night. While we like the free-range chicken, the grilled rack of lamb spells perfection. For a dessert, consider the warm chocolate cake with brandied-cherry ice cream or the peach Melba coupe. In summer, try the good lemon-mint ice, refreshing and sweet. The active wine-by-the glass program includes three whites, three reds, two sparkling and four dessert wines. The wine list of 130 selections is balanced and well priced, and the wine itself is kept at the proper temperatures and served graciously. In general, service here is highly professional. Book ahead and expect to pay about $118 per couple for dinner, with wine, plus tax and tip.

Harlequin
569 Hudson St. (W. 11th St.)
255-4950

SPANISH

Open daily noon-3 p.m. & 5:30 p.m.-11 p.m. All major cards.

Harlequin remains a revelation. Dedicated to *alta cocina española*, it is easily the finest Spanish restaurant in New York City, and probably in the United States. Since opening Harlequin in 1985, the husband and wife team of Ileana and (chef) José Bárcena have pledged themselves to offering "superbly prepared food in an 800-year-old Spanish tradition of warm hospitality." They are in a fix, however, because New Yorkers aren't ready for a top Spanish restaurant. When they think of Spanish, they want bargain prices and paella, not uptown prices, ambitious and refined dishes and gentility. They should appreciate that some of the finest and most admired cooking in Europe is coming out of Spain's top restaurants.

The chef's food stops conversation, or at least it has on the many occasions we've revealed this charming restaurant to the unsuspecting. Some dishes are arrestingly magnificent. Consider as a must the brilliant rendition of brandada de bacalao (salt cod with potatoes, olive oil and garlic), served hot in a small baking dish, textured as if it were a firm vegetable purée, with all the flavors asserting themselves subtly and harmoniously. The shrimp on a bed of two creams of garlic (one mild, one heavy) was memorable, as were the soups and the boquerones (fresh anchovy filets in vinaigrette). Although not listed on the menu, angulas are often available, so if you have the stomach for these sizzling spaghettilike white eels, order without hesitation. We thought them sensational, prepared in the traditional manner in an earthenware crock and cooked with olive oil and chopped garlic (and even the traditional wooden forks are provided). Chef Bárcena has a light touch, but he can be firm when necessary. His handling of meats and desserts has improved markedly in the past two years. If you must, order the paella, generally acknowledged as the best in the city and a bargain. The paella's yellow rice, with its saffron, garlic, tomato and chicken-stock flavors, cooked perfectly, joins a cavalcade of seafoods—lobster, shrimp, crayfish, clams, mussels—and a medley of sausage, pork and chicken in an exciting and hearty rendition of this popular Spanish dish. Meats, including game, are equally lusty. We especially enjoyed the zortziko de pescados, the Basque fish stew, and the boneless duck with Chinchón liqueur and grapes. Better yet, let one of the professional waiters order for you, and don't be shy about trying one of the specials. The wine offerings merit special kudos. The comprehensive listing of Spanish wines has been shrewdly and lovingly assembled. You'd have to go to a top restaurant in Madrid to find its equal. There are old and great wines, as well as fresh offerings of great value and modest prices. We suggest the CUNE Monopole as an excellent white wine choice. Lunch averages $58 per couple; dinner, $78, though with a bottle of Vega Sicilia, the "Spanish Petrus," the bill will be much higher.

Indochine
430 Lafayette St. (Astor Pl. & 4th St.)
505-5111
VIETNAMESE
Open daily 6 p.m.-12:30 p.m. All major cards.

Indochine takes you back to the era of expatriates lolling in the palm-strewn lobby of a sultry hotel, while white-robed natives serve them icy gin with lots of lime. This large, well-lit, elegant restaurant sports painted palm fronds on the walls, such real exotic flowers as birds of paradise and anthuria, and dark-green banquettes set against pure white tablecloths. Although contrived, it works. And so does the food, which is authentically Vietnamese. Located right across the street from the Public Theater on Lafayette Street, Indochine draws young actors (how do they afford it?) as well as theatergoers and New York "Euro-brats." Owner and downtown restaurant impresario Brian McNally manages to attract the late-night celebrity crowd that keeps this big place hopping.

Efficient waitresses (beautiful, unemployed actresses?) will suggest that you order by number, which is an amusing request considering the sophistication of the restaurant. But you'll soon understand why, if you dare try to pronounce the names of any of the 40-plus dishes featured on the menu (which hasn't changed at all in the past several years). We love the rich and satisfying soups, especially the fish soup, a deep broth flavored with lemon grass and full of delicate noodles. Be forewarned about the spicy appetizers that are not marked as such; they are excellent and even refreshing, but are know to burn the tongue, so eat them after the milder dishes you order. Tender tongues will enjoy the steamed shrimp with fresh mint and lemon grass, highly seasoned but not hot, or the large, tender and delightfully fresh shrimp. We've also enjoyed a refreshing salad of fresh pineapple and shrimp. We also sampled the steamed ravioli, delicate and filled with minced pork; and a variety of superb spring rolls, especially goi cuon, rice paper filled with shrimp, vermicelli and bean sprouts. Although very peppery, the beef salad may be your best bet for an appetizer—the thinly sliced beef is succulent and well-complemented by sliced shallots, lemon grass and a vinegary sauce.

The staff serves main courses Chinese-style, so you may taste several dishes in one evening. We found highlights to be the steamed whole fish with ginger, flaky and delicate, and the enormous, boneless chicken wings, stuffed with vermicelli and chopped chicken breast, and flavored with lemon grass. Although lemon grass figures in many of the dishes, each dish is distinct in flavor, and redolent with many other seasonings. Consider the brochette of filet of beef and the brochette of tamarind-glazed chicken. We found the brochettes of prawns and swordfish delightfully simple, while the frogs' legs in coconut had a more complex, sweeter taste. Sticky rice is a must; the tasty brown rice, flavored with tiny bits of pork, offsets the clean bite of the spicier dishes. To cool off, most diners at dessert time go for the exotically flavored sorbets. The short wine list is reasonably well-chosen and -priced, but cold beer goes just as well with this cuisine. Dinner is about $76 per couple.

can hit any mark or pace you desire, and smile the whole time. The grainy and crisp Italian bread has always been very good here, and arrives straightaway at your table with some complimentary coleslaw, carrots and the like—all crunchy and well-matched, with a creamy dressing. We thought the Manhattan clam chowder fine—chunky and spicy—but not great. The fried oysters, however, are very good, crispy on the outside and fresh and lush on the inside. We urge you to sample any of the sole dishes—for example, broiled with slices of fresh tomato, herbs and Parmesan cheese; or Portuguese-style, sautéed in garlic, butter, herbs, fresh tomatoes and mushrooms, flambéed with sherry and served on a bed of brown rice. There are about 86 choices of wine to wash that down, most of them good and reasonably priced. For dessert, try the not overly sweet vanilla cheesecake or the chocolate truffle cake. Figure $70 for two sharing a modest bottle of wine.

Jane Street Seafood Café
31 Eighth Ave. (Jane St.)
242-0003, 243-9237

SEAFOOD

Open Mon.-Thurs. 5:30 p.m.-11 p.m., Fri.-Sat. 5:30 p.m.-midnight, Sun. 4 p.m.-10 p.m. All major cards.

Now in its second decade, this casual, New England–style fish house on the corner of one of Greenwich Village's most charming residential streets, still adheres to its no-reservations policy, and still has folks lining up nightly for some of the freshest finny fare around, prepared reliably in a range of styles, priced moderately and served efficiently and with good fellowship. The list of fish available and noted on the chalkboard has grown, and some trendy preparations occasionally make the list of daily specials. On the whole, there are few surprises. The staples remain, such as linguine with mussels or clams, which you can always see on a nearby table.

The long, cozy room features brick walls, old wooden floors, a working fireplace, a nineteenth-century tin ceiling, and bare wood tables with small candles. The staff—both male and female—dresses in jeans and rugby shirts, pony tails being popular with both genders. Like the good actors they probably are, they

John Clancy's Restaurant
181 W. 10th St. (Seventh Ave. South)
242-7350

SEAFOOD

Open Mon.-Sat. 6 p.m.-11 p.m., Sun. 5 p.m.-10 p.m. All major cards.

Once one of the city's most reliable and best seafood restaurants, John Clancy's Restaurant (no longer owned by John Clancy, but by Samuel Rubin) appears to have dropped down a notch, although everything still looks the same, and you'll still eat everything unless you are overwhelmed by the enormous portions. Why our most recent meals have not been up to the old standards is a puzzle—Melissa Lord has been the executive chef and Richard Glavin the pastry chef since 1987. Can they be tired already? Occupying two floors of a century-old townhouse, John Clancy's deserves credit for being the first place in New York to introduce mesquite-grilled seafoods and for continuing to show trendy others how it should be done. The downstairs, with its low ceiling and candlelit tables, is colored with quiet tones of gray and white—white brick walls (bearing garden posters), a gray carpet and white or gray bentwood chairs. Upstairs, the attractive dining room is more intimate.

Gravlax with crème fraîche and caviar makes

a silky cold appetizer. For a hot appetizer, try the wild mushrooms ragoût or broiled oysters. When available as a special, you should order the mussels steamed with spicy tomato-and-leek broth, though the mussels at times move beyond plumpness into obesity. Half of the entrée offerings come from the mesquite grill, and thus arrive enhanced with a light baptism of woody smoke. The grilled swordfish on a skewer more than justifies the visit, as do the barbecued jumbo Ecuadorian shrimp. Accompanying vegetables, usually a broccoli purée, potatoes and/or rice, can be good, but won't occupy your attention. Desserts are huge and all-American, with a heavy dose of chocolate (often, four out of six possibilities). A lemon-meringue tart appears regularly, and a huge, multilayer English trifle is a staple. The computerized wine list is a gem. You won't have any difficulty choosing from the approximately 75 reasonably priced offerings (the majority whites) from Australia, America and France, starting at $14. (Also, experiment with good choices by the glass.) Expect to pay $110 per couple for dinner.

Manhattan Chili Co.

302 Bleecker St.
(Seventh Ave. & Grove St.)
206-7163

AMERICAN

Open Mon.-Thurs. noon-midnight, Fri.-Sat. noon-1 a.m., Sun. noon-11 p.m. All major cards.

"Wish I had time for just one more bowl of chili." Allegedly the dying words of Kit Carson, these words are printed on the cover of the Manhattan Chili Co.'s menu. Had Carson time for one more bowl, he might well have chosen this engaging Village restaurant. Since chili inspires fanaticism, we would be asking for trouble to claim that one place serves the best in the city. Suffice it to say that Manhattan Chili Co. is on anyone's short list of Manhattan's best chili purveyors (you can also get burgers, sandwiches, soups and salads and a range of Southwestern entrées). Its roster of chilis, however, ranges from the Real McCoy (no beans, no tomatoes, no bull) to Cincinnati-style (with lamb and hominy), and from vegetarian to the two most popular—Numero Uno and Texas Chain Gang (which gets its fire from jalapeños). When William Altamirano joined as chef in 1989, he added

high-plains turkey chili with hominy and corn. The kitchen explores other Southwestern themes as well. Ask for appetizers such as the chunky guacamole with lots of red onion, tomato and cilantro, or the zippy salsa, either plain (with tortilla chips) or with chèvre. A side order of calico corn muffins, made with buttermilk, corn, jalapeños and red peppers, makes for a delectable meal in itself. Entrées other than chili that might convert even Carson include the chicken fajitas (grilled strips and onions served with salsa, guacamole and warm flour tortillas) and the chicken tortilla pie. Side orders usually taste as good as the dishes they accompany—particularly the mustardy coleslaw and the rice salad with green and red peppers, olives, corn, kidney beans and scallions.

The setting matches the cooking. It mixes the collegiate informality of Austin, Texas, with the colors of Taos (turquoise, pink and adobe) and a kind of tongue-in-cheek playfulness manifested by the neon jalapeño in the window and Elvis, the armadillo, on a counter by the bar. A small backyard patio for warm-weather dining makes the place one of the nicest brunch options in town. The restaurant offers a number of wines by the glass. Its beer selection, however, is even longer as is its roster of frozen margaritas (six flavors), which go, oh-so well, with the truckstop 501 nachos and Chico's special chicken wings. Dinner, with wine or drinks, costs about $56 for two

La Métairie

189 W. 10th St. (W. 4th St.)
989-0343

FRENCH

Open daily 6 p.m.-11:30 p.m. Cards: AE, MC, V.

This charming place has to be seen to be believed. It seats twenty in cramped quarters, and looks as if Laura Ashley had been set loose in a chicken coop: candles flicker on teeny tables; a pitchfork is angled on a stuccoed wall; a caged dove coos; Provençal paisleys cover tightly wedged banquettes; decorative dark-wood beams give a rustic timbered look, as do the white shutters and Dutch door opening onto 10th Street. You expect Snow White to come out of the kitchen. The food, however, is elemental and boldly flavored, particularly the couscous, a vivid and substantial dish, as it should be. With grains on one side of the platter, you have a mix of muttony chunks of lamb, merguez (lamb sausage), chicken, carrots and zucchini crowding the other. Ask for the harissa and use it with respect: it roars with garlic and heat. Garlic-lovers will want to work up to the couscous along with an appetizer of snails with vegetables (carrots, turnips) served with aïoli (addictive garlic mayonnaise). Ask to keep the gravy boat. You'll finish the aïoli with the very good rolls served here. Other recommended appetizers include the boudin (sausage) of fruits de mer and the feuillantine de courgettes (zucchini) with ginger. For timid palates, La Métairie takes a sweeter approach with citified selections such as pompano marinated and sautéed with balsamic vinegar. Look into the bouillabaisse and the cassoulet, also. Food-lovers plan well ahead for those twenty seats, so remember to reserve. Dinner, with a mediocre French wine (the place still could use a better and broader selection of red Rhônes), comes to about $100 for two. And if you love this place, also pay visit to La Métarie's more upscale sister on the East Side (see page 135).

Mie
196 Second Ave. (12th & 13th Sts.)
674-7060

JAPANESE

Open Tues.-Sun. 5:30 p.m.-12:30 p.m. All major cards.

Hidden in the basement of a Second Avenue tenement in the East Village, Mie stands out as an oddity among the other ethnic Village restaurants, insofar as it remains true to its roots. You'll enter down a "landscaped" stone path, past rocks and a semblance of a garden, just like many Tokyo restaurants. You'll find much of the Mie clientele Japanese, plus a few diehard Western aficionados. Small tables surround the sushi bar, with a larger room for parties of four or more. Pleasant tranquility reigns in all the rooms, discreetly decorated with wood benches and delicate wall lanterns. The menu offers several dinners typical of most second-rate Japanese restaurants around the city, including suki-yaki, tempura and teriyaki—avoid these. But if you choose à la carte, the chef will know you're serious, and you will profit accordingly.

The sushi and sashimi are excellent, freshly prepared by an imaginative chef. If you sit at the sushi bar and befriend him, you'll be in for a treat. Yakiniku, thin slices of beef broiled with garlic and sancho peppers, come tender and rare, and will remind you of tuna. We liked the fish teriyaki, marinated in soy sauce and spices, then lightly broiled and served with kombu sauce. Mie has several udon-noodle dishes: one, which features thick wheat noodles in a casserole along with vegetables, large, barely-cooked shrimps, roast pork and egg, is the only dish on the menu that will satisfy a hearty appetite. We think Mie's side dishes to be just wonderful: there's yudofu, airy, silken bean curd served in a hot, tasty broth with excellent seaweed, or, in the summer, the same bean curd served cold in a bowl of ice water with shaved bonito and sliced fresh ginger. We love chawan-mushi, the best egg custard served in New York, filled with tiny pieces of chicken, vegetables, shrimp and gingko nuts—a sheer delight. If you must have dessert, try the green-tea ice cream or bean paste. The service is always pleasant. About $40 to $50 for two, with beer or saké.

12/20 One If By Land, Two If By Sea
17 Barrow St.
(Seventh Ave. & W. 4th St.)
228-0822

CONTINENTAL

Open Sun.-Thurs. 5:30 p.m.-midnight, Fri.-Sat. 5:30 p.m.-1 a.m. All major cards.

What a setting! This place looks sensational, and is surely one of the most attractive and romantic restaurants in Manhattan. It is in a restored eighteenth-century carriage house, and features bilevel dining, lots of space, some exposed brick walls, handsome paintings and furnishings (including red-velvet banquettes and chairs and a warm patterned carpet) and a pretty garden in a courtyard. The humble street entrance doesn't prepare you for the interior: a pianist seated at a grand piano near the door greets you and entertains throughout the evening; regulars chat comfortably at a long bar, a few diners await their guests while having a drink at a low table near the fireplace, while friendly waiters in black tie move suavely about. It is hard to imagine a date, a relative or an out-of-town business guest who would not be flattered by a dinner here.

For that dinner, which might be considered an accessory to the atmosphere, the coquilles St. Jacques is a tasty appetizer. The soups, shrimp cocktail, pâtés and salads all go down without much trouble—or impression. An individual beef Wellington is something of a house specialty as an entrée, and as it is not seen that often in New York, it merits attention—but don't expect the finest pastry wrapped about perfectly cooked beef. You won't go wrong with the simple charcoal-grilled meats. The veal chop is especially good, and grilled to perfection. The waiters push the Long Island duck, which is okay, but expect a big portion accompanied by some version of a sweet sauce. Vegetables are simply steamed, nicely undercooked, crunchy and innocuous. The desserts look all right and taste all right, but are nothing special. The anemic wine list, however, still needs a good transfusion. One If By Land is open for drinks from 4 p.m. to 4 a.m. Figure on $120 per couple, plus tax and tip.

La Ripaille
605 Hudson St.
(12th & Bethune Sts.)
255-4406
FRENCH
Open Mon.-Sat. 5:30 p.m.-11:30 p.m. All major cards.

Behind an undistinguished facade on a dreary strip of Hudson Street, across from Abingdon Square, lies this appealing French restaurant that has been attracting West Villagers and pilgrims from uptown since it opened in 1979. The pleasant, somewhat rustic decor remains unchanged: a tiny bar, bare-brick walls and stucco, lovely fresh flowers, an ancient grandfather clock, well-executed reproductions of medieval tapestries, and huge cross beams overhead. All this adds up to a cozy and charming room that seats 45. But while the food and ambience are good, both have slipped a little over the years. Brothers and co-owners Patrick and Alain Laurent from Metz, France, made the restaurant, and have opened a successful second restaurant, L'Escale. Nephew Alain Laurent (who studied three years in France and worked in Strasbourg and Paris) has handled the kitchen for the past few years. The large menu here changes daily, which is a tip-off that this kitchen is sincere in its claims to be sensitive to what's fresh and available on the market. Much of the strictly French fare comes in the classic style, but always with nouvelle touches.

The light mousse of broccoli with lemon butter usually heads the list of appetizers. We also like the creamy and flavorful fettucine with smoked salmon. The escargots come bathed in a tomato-and-basil cream. Vegetarians will like the cold vegetable salad or the wild mushrooms, featured as appetizers. For the main course, priced from $14.95 to $21.50, try the salmon steak (served on a bed of endives) or the grilled, nicely seasoned lamb chops. Rack of lamb arrives grilled and seasoned predictably but effectively, with thyme and rosemary. We also liked homemade ravioli and chicken with mushrooms, not to mention a dish of frogs' legs in a sauce of garlic, parsley and tomato. For dessert, we love the classic crème caramel with a touch of orange or the lemon tart. You can forget the bombe glacée pralinée and the profiteroles. Most people don't pass up the white chocolate mousse, however. The French wine list (with some California wines for good measure) can pass scrutiny—it has grown in breadth in recent years. Figure about $80 per couple for dinner, plus tax and tip.

12/20 Rosolio
11 Barrow St. (Seventh Ave.)
645-9224
ITALIAN
Open Tues.-Thurs. noon-3 p.m. & 6 p.m.-11 p.m., Fri.-Sat. noon-3 p.m. & 6 p.m.-11:30 p.m., Sun. 6 p.m.-11 p.m. Cards: AE, DC, V.

The neighborhood, the dining room and the menu are a kind of New York Italian fusion, covering generations and regions, yet yielding a charming little Northern Italian eatery. This storefront restaurant with yellow-gold walls, clay-tile floor, eighteen tables with white linen, and a high ceiling made of brick tends toward being crowded and noisy. Take the people waiting outside for a table as a good sign.

The balanced menu is always supplemented by enticing specials. Among the appetizers, the crostini with baby octopus or the piadina bread with prosciutto, mozzarella and arugula are recommended. The pastas are all freshly made on the premises and can be excellent and unusual. The orecchiette with broccoli and fresh tomatoes; the stracci (literally, "rags") of fresh pasta with chicken, string beans and tomatoes; and the ravioli with ricotta and Pecorino cheeses might serve as excellent entrées or as a first course, if you skip the antipasti. Among the good assortment of meat and fish, we haven't been pleased with the osso buco, a bit too timidly handled, but we cannot say we were disappointed, at least not as much as we have been with the overly bland polenta. The simple lamb paillard with fresh herbs is fine; the veal scaloppine with zucchini and scamorza cheese is pleasant. For fish, the grilled mixed seafood is a safe bet to offer some things you will enjoy. Of course for dessert, there's tiramisu (okay, not special). The Italian wine list, however, is solid, if a bit short. For white, consider the Tokay by Livio Felluga ($24) and for red, the Chianti classico from Castello di Rampolla. We like this restaurant, but it's a timid hand away from its first toque. Figure $80 for two for dinner.

Sabor
20 Cornelia St.
(W. 4th & Bleecker Sts.)
243-9579
CUBAN
Open Sun.-Thurs. 6 p.m.-11 p.m.. Fri.-Sat. 6 p.m.-midnight. Cards: AE, MC, V.

Havana has its problems, too. This American-made, unpretentious storefront of a Cuban restaurant has been having some difficulties with consistency, but when it's "on," the inspired cooks dish up some of the best Cuban food around. Any of the escabeches—raw fish or shellfish "cooked" from marinating in lime juice, then garnished with onions, celery and capers—make pleasant starters, as do plump, briny mussels in tomato sauce, spicy squid and the frituras de malanga, a deep-fried starchy tuber served with two sweet-hot sauces that set you pleasantly afire. For the main course, you can't do better than the perfectly baked whole red snapper or succulent sautéed shrimp, both dishes blanketed in Sabor's outstanding salsa verde. Beef dishes include carne estofada, a pot roast with overtones of orange, and ropa vieja, chewy shredded beef exotically spiced with hints of cloves and cinnamon. The classic accompaniments, rice and black beans, are fresh and blessedly unmushy. To round things out, be sure to ask for fried sweet plantains. For eight or more, Sabor will do a feast around a moist-meated, crisp-skinned, roast sucking pig. Dessert freaks will love the custardy Key lime pie, the coco quemado (a tart of freshly grated coconut, sherry and cinnamon served warm), and the homemade ice creams. The coffee is excellent, and great fresh-fruit dark-rum daiquiris will get you in the mood. Neighborhood folk treat Sabor as a drop-in place, and it's small, so definitely reserve seats. Dinner runs about $70 for two.

12/20 Siracusa
65 Fourth Ave. (9th & 10th Sts.)
254-1940
ITALIAN
Open Mon.-Thurs. noon-3 p.m. & 5:30 p.m.-11 p.m., Fri. noon-3 p.m. & 5 p.m.-11:30 p.m., Sat. 5 p.m.-11:30 p.m. Cards: AE.

Don't let the front counter and groceries mislead you; there's an attractive and simple restaurant in the back that serves a pleasing menu of native Sicilian dishes. Siracusa attracts a generally upscale and downtown crowd—actors from the nearby Public Theater, as well as neighborhood artists, designers, writers and architects. The antipasto misto is an excellent starter, with a delicious caponata with vivid flavors of eggplant, capers and peppers. The soft and tasty mozzarella topped with sun-dried tomatoes is a fine addition, but the fried zucchini makes a limp accompaniment to an otherwise noteworthy dish. As for the rest of the menu, with the occasional exception of the triglia, a Mediterranean fish, each of the limited number of main courses is a pasta dish. Mezzaluna is large, crescent-shaped raviolis filled with ricotta, spinach and mushrooms, served with a rich tomato sauce. At $18, it ought to contain more than two raviolis. There is also a bow-tie pasta with fresh artichokes, fava beans and peas in a light tomato sauce. Tagliarini with crabmeat is adequate, but nothing special, as has been the much-touted homemade pasta with sardines. A bold red Gattinara ($25) goes nicely with your food, but why not try the fine Sicilian wines made by Regaleali? For dessert, the choice is homemade gelati. Try a sampling of three—say, ricotta, espresso and hazelnut. In summer, skip the restaurant offering and go next door to the quaint Gelateria Siracusa for even more dynamic (and less expensive) flavors. Take a pint home; it's $6, well spent.

Be prepared for the cafeteria-style setting of this engaging take-out shop/wine bar/restaurant. Moreover, there is one point about Siracusa that has always disturbed us. For the price, and the small but quality portions of food, service can be irregular and downright rude. None of the staff seems to care if something isn't right. This doesn't appear to bother a loyal patronage—perhaps they expect nothing more. But New York is a place where attitude is delivered free of charge every day; here, you'll easily spend $90 per couple on dinner, plus tax and tip, for more of it.

12/20 Tatany Village
62 Greenwich Ave. (Seventh Ave.)
675-6195
JAPANESE
Open Mon.-Fri. noon-2:30 p.m. & 5:30 p.m.-10:30 p.m., Sat.-Sun. 5:30 p.m.-10:30 p.m. Cards: AE, V.

This casual but elegant duplex restaurant, occupying a landmark brownstone on one of the Village's busy streets, turns out first-rate sashimi, sushi and tempura to an increasingly sophisticated clientele. At the tables, the dishes and combination platters are predictable and good, with cool, fresh fish and ethereally light deep-frying. There are no uptown banquet-style meals offered, but the standard items are done well. If you want magic, sit at the sushi bar and win the confidence of one of the sushi chefs. Utilizing the pick of the freshest fish—which are often top local catches—and an artistry learned as an apprentice in Japan, he will expand your horizons. The chefs have learned English and how to accommodate New Yorkers. When they have a calm moment, a rarity at a frenetic sushi bar, they will delight in entertaining and educating your palate. Drink tea or Japanese beer with your meal (though you can order Champagne here), and expect a sweet plum wine to leave you with a pleasant aftertaste. There's an equally good and reliable Tatany under the same ownership on Third Avenue between 27th and 28th streets. Expect to pay $40 to $60 for two, with saké.

12/20 Toon's
417 Bleecker St. (Bank St.)
924-6420, 243-9211
THAI
Open Mon.-Thurs. 5 p.m.- 11:30 p.m., Sat. 5 p.m.-midnight, Sun. 4 p.m.-11 p.m. Cards: AE, MC, V.

For moderately priced Thai food, spiffy and reliable Toon's is a good Village option. The entrance and bar are on Bank Street, but unless the restaurant is very crowded, you'll dine in the front room, with huge windows looking out on Bleecker and Bank streets, surrounded by plants and dramatically illuminated stalks of purple orchids. Tables are very close together, so if you haven't come with friends, you may end up making some new ones.

For starters, the shrimp fritters are good, though on occasion a bit oily, and ditto for the addictive zucchini fritters. The nuur satay is excellent; these strips of thinly sliced steak, marinated in coconut milk and Thai herbs, are charboiled and served on thin wooden skewers. The peanut sauce on the side is a yummy dressing. Good frogs' legs are available with sauces such as garlic and pepper or basil leaf or chili pepper, along with a red curry. You can get a nicely deep-fried whole fish here and a decent curry chicken (kang kai). Less fiery choices are the honey duck or the mee krob—crisply fried rice-stick noodles—mixed with tamarind sauce and topped with shrimp and ocean sprouts. This ubiquitous Thai dish seems to taste different at every Thai restaurant, and here it is a bit sweet. Though many Thai dishes border on the violently hot, none here are lethal. A Thai beer helps. There's a second branch in TriBeCa. The tab runs only about $50 for two with beer.

La Tulipe
104 W. 13th St. (Sixth Ave.)
691-8860
FRENCH
Open nightly 6:30 p.m.-closing. All major cards.

For those who crave a little refinement, a moment of French savoir-faire, a cozy tête-à-tête, La Tulipe, housed in a charming Greenwich Village townhouse, is the place to go—and has been since its loftier days, a few years back. Down a few steps and across the period threshold, the tiny bar and three marble café tables welcome diners to an almost perfect replica of a "bon petit restaurant" in provincial France. The small dining room's dark-mauve walls, soft lighting from tulip-shaped lamps and comfortable banquettes suggest solidity and old-world confidence. The menu echoes this sentiment.

Imagination and inspiration do not live in La Tulipe's kitchen, although each dish is dependably well prepared and the wine list is varied and enticing. We couldn't love a fish soup, ladeled atop a few nuggets of lobster and served with an ordinary rouille, though it was delicate, because it tasted a bit flat. On the other hand, nothing is flat about the Parmesan soufflé, light, creamy and complemented by a paper-thin, buttery crust. A favorite, blini with caviar and smoked salmon, looks pretty, but doesn't impress as much as a more original chef's creation might. We like the toasted brioche, filled with wild mushrooms and too much cream, especially when it's cold outside. We found the most successful dish among the entrées to be a filet of fresh cod surrounded by a whipped brandade de morue and enveloped in a crusty, browned layer of thinly sliced potatoes. It tasted rich, satisfying and delightfully simple. Stay away from the pretentious lobster tail atop a mealy tomato; try, instead, the breast of squab, red and succulent, served with a refreshingly light braised cabbage. We would have liked the tender lamb chops more had the chef not marred the presentation with an ordinary stuffed tomato. Do not forego the green salad served at meal's end, a tribute to the glory of a purist's vinaigrette that will cleanse the palate in preparation for dessert. Of the desserts (all made on the premises), we loved the airy, not-too-sweet apricot soufflé, which must be ordered in advance. The buttery French fruit tart vies in flavor with the best. Small portions and big prices have been known to make people blink here. The prix-fixe dinner is $62 a person; a meal for two, with a modest bottle of Côte du Rhône, will run about $170.

Vanessa

289 Bleecker St. (Seventh Ave. South)
243-4225
FRENCH
Open Thurs.-Fri. noon-3:30 p.m. & 5: 30 p.m.-midnight, Sat. noon-5 p.m.; Sun. 12:30 p.m.-3 p.m. & 5:30 p.m.-10 p.m., Mon.-Wed. 5:30 p.m.-midnight. All major cards.

Will the real Vanessa please stand up? This handsome restaurant has had its ups and downs and is now coasting through one of its middle periods; however, it's still a notch up from a few years back. Although the turn-of-the-century decor and grandiose floral arrangements haven't changed in years, its owners and chefs have; the owner and hostess

are Japanese, and the current chef, Thomas Lisch, is American. Perhaps he's the reason the food has become steadier since the departure of the French-trained Japanese chef who preceded him. It must be said, however, that the food is relatively ordinary and predictable. Go with something simple or with pasta as a starter. We have enjoyed the rich and thick duck ravioli as an appetizer.

The entrée choices include the usual suspects, what you expect to find in any restaurant of this caliber: broiled swordfish, red snapper, medallion of veal or Long Island duck. Indeed, this is your throwback French/Continental menu. We loved the lamb en croûte. Desserts do not excite, but suffice. When we've eaten well here, it has been when we've cultivated the waiter's opinions and recommendations. The wine list is short but good, and reasonably priced. However, we suspect a storage problem—red wines come to the table on the warm side, and taste tired or cooked. You can have a pleasant dining experience in this attractive and romantic restaurant, and we love the live guitar music. Vanessa is now open for Sunday brunch. Dinner here runs $100 for two, with wine, and some people resent it.

12/20 Village Atelier

436 Hudson. St. (Morton St.)
989-1363
AMERICAN
Open Mon.-Fri. noon-3 p.m. & 5:30 p.m.-11:30 p.m., Sat. 5:30 p.m.-11:30 p.m. Cards: AE.

Why not Midwestern farmhouse cooking in Greenwich Village? Wasn't the Village once farmland? We like this cozy, rustic storefront opened in 1989 by owner-chef Craig Bèro and his mother (and co-owner), Charlotte Marie Bèro. The quaint room, decorated with American country antiques (circa 1890) from the family farm in northern Wisconsin, can be a bit noisy and the service a bit innocent, but you could not ask for a friendlier place, and the food is good and the menu interesting.

The delicious banana bread and whole-wheat breads that come straightaway can become a meal in themselves. That would be too bad. You'd miss the roast wild American mushrooms with garlic and lemon-thyme appetizer or the nice Atelier green salad. The fruitwood-grilled North Atlantic salmon with wild rice, hazelnuts and Grand Marnier butter is a good fish dish, but we've also enjoyed the red snapper, although the accompanying vegetables can be weak. Go for the venison when available, or the roast poussin with wild fruit and maple glaze (stuffed with apple, prunes and venison sausage–very nice, and sweet from the glaze). For dessert, the top choices are the Wisconsin lattice montmorency cherry pie or the angel food cake. The wine list is short but interesting, focusing on American wines from small vineyards. Lunch runs $50 and dinner $76, for two.

 ### The Village Green
531 Hudson St. (Charles St.)
255-1650
AMERICAN
Open Mon.-Sat. 5:30-11:30 p.m. All major cards.

From the outside, you'd never know this long-established, warm-and-cozy West Village restaurant has had a tumultuous five years. It closed in 1986 and re-opened in June 1987 under new ownership, only to change owners and chefs again in May 1989. The place always has looked inviting and currently so is the food. This handsome spot, nestled in an 1827 townhouse, looks just like it always did. Upstairs, the bar and lounge with its fireplace and grand piano, beckon. A pianist arrives at 8:30 p.m. to play at the upstairs bar. Downstairs, the intimate brick-and-wood decor dining room seats 30. Some would call this a romantic spot, and perhaps it is, if you do your romancing with your eyes alone. The room is small and the tables are sufficiently close together that you can pick up any conversation at will.

The chef does his romancing, of course, on the plates, with contemporary American fare, but you must be careful not to spoil your appetite by eating too many of the delicious, warm sourdough rolls. Two fixed-price menus offer plenty of choices, one at $45 and a tasting menu at $75. That's steep, but we hope the new owners and chef Steven Levine (formerly of Aureole and the River Café) find a steady following. We love the pan-fried oysters in the shell with foie-gras butter and caramelized onions to start. Other safe choices for an appetizer include yellowfin tuna car-

paccio and the crisp roulade of chicken and prosciutto. For fish, we're drawn again to the sourdough, here battered over pompano and served with a miso vinaigrette. For a main course, we adored the pan-roasted squab with roast-garlic-and-potato pie. The desserts change regularly. We have tried the crème brûlée and the cinnamon-apple tart and liked them, but the ice cream is only so-so. The wine selection passes with very high marks. Figure on at least $120 for two, but we find it tough to get out for less than $150.

10/20 Ye Waverly Inn
16 Bank St. (Waverly Pl.)
929-4377, 243-9396
AMERICAN
Open Mon.-Thurs. noon-2 p.m. & 5:15 p.m.-10 p.m., Fri. noon-2 p.m. & 5:15 p.m.-11 p.m., Sat. 5:15 p.m.-11 p.m., Sun. noon-3:30 p.m. All major cards.

Talk about a Village institution! Is it three generations, or four, that have enjoyed eating here? The two chefs at this Greenwich Village tribute to colonial Americana, William Thompson and William McDow, have been reporting to work since 1945 and 1955, respectively. Both prepare simple, honest fare which is perhaps a bit heavy, overcooked, and even overseasoned by current standards. But what is most important to remember about this charming landmark is that customers continue to go away satisfied.

Chicken pot pie is a house specialty and merits consideration, along with entrées of Yankee pot roast, Southern fried chicken and a barbecued rack of ribs. Plenty of seafood specials are offered daily. The price of a dinner is a revelation: between $12.25 and $21.75, depending upon the main course, will bring you a cup of soup, a choice of entrée, one vegetable, a salad, homemade dessert and coffee or tea. That must impart as much satisfaction as does the pecan pie. Situated on the corner of one of the West Village's handsomest residential streets, the restaurant has four small dining rooms just below street level in an old townhouse; they sport low ceilings and wooden booths, and there are two working fireplaces. In summer, there are also tables in an outdoor garden. An à la carte dinner, with wine, will run about $50 for two.

14TH STREET TO 42ND STREET

An American Place
2 Park Ave. (32nd St.)
684-2122

AMERICAN

Open Mon.-Fri. 11:45 a.m.-2:30 p.m. (bar menu 3 p.m.-7 p.m.) & 5:30 p.m.-10 p.m., Sat. 5:30 p.m.-10 p.m. All major cards.

The room is huge, with its high-ceilinged, Provençal-yellow walls adorned with large works of art, wood floors with scattered carpets, wooden armchairs and lots and lots of tables with white linen—it shouldn't be difficult getting a table. Quite a contrast to the restaurant's more intimate uptown digs of the 1980s. This grand café has been operating in its larger space since 1989, and although it has taken some time to settle down, our most recent meals have suggested the kitchen has returned to its former level.

At the least, An American Place will offer you an intellectual dining experience, grounded in history and culture. The menu celebrates Americana in a unique style. You'll find unusual dishes, whose roots master chef Larry Forgione has traced to colonial times, as well as regional dishes. Forgione has a supersleuth's eye for American ingredients, and a surgeon's hands for sewing things together. A poet's imagination is at work here as well, but sometimes the results are failed verses. You'll find the friendly staff serious about the food and the exclusively American wines offered. No question will receive less than a full and thoughtful response. This was all relatively exciting a few years ago when Forgione began to raise people's consciousness about a new style of American cuisine. Others have caught up to (and some have surpassed) Forgione, but what he has that few others can claim, excepting great chefs, is a distinctive personal cuisine (albeit one marked by some incoherence on the plate). But let's not be misleading, today others are executing that kind of cuisine for Forgione, namely, the working chef at An American Place, Richard D'Orazi, and his understudy, Mark Meyer. What few other restaurants can match, how-

ever, will be the extra-carefully selected, extraordinary American produce used here.

For starters, if you try the peanut-barbecued Gulf shrimp with chayote and red-pepper salad, you'll find it only fair. In our experience, the peanut flavor barely is noticeable. We prefer the baked oysters and sea urchins with chive sauce, though we find that the sea urchin and the butter sauce overpower the taste of the oysters. Best of all, the Pennsylvania Dutch potato pancakes with grilled, lightly smoked salmon rated high marks. Unfortunately, you only get two little coins of pancakes with three tasty strips of salmon; you could eat a dozen. In our opinion, the pasta dishes generally deliver more looks than taste, but why would you go here for pasta anyway? If you want carbohydrates, indulge in the sensational and varied bread basket. Among entrées, we love the grilled free-range chicken with tarragon and mixed herbs, served with mashed potates and another vegetable (usually grilled morel mushroooms or French green beans when in season). Herbs dominate the moist chicken breast, and the mashed potatoes fit in nicely. Friends of ours who have dined here have liked the sautéed soft-shell crab with sherry on a bed of greens and thin sliced Smithfield ham, and there have been cheers for a surprisingly good charred Black Angus steak, marinated in beer and fresh thyme. On the lighter side, we have played with the grilled tuna steak—it tends to be dry, but is served with a gazpacho sauce and deep-fried leeks. There's an emphasis on seasonal produce, which means the call of wild game. The best of that is the breast of wild duck, glazed with molasses and black pepper, accompanied by apples and sweet potatoes.

For dessert, we adore a chocolate devil's food cake that is 50-percent fudge, as well as the banana betty and chocolate pudding. On the wine list, you'll see mostly California items, plus a few New York and Washington State wines, with a lot of sound selections in the $20 to $40 range. With wine and coffee, figure at least $120 for two, plus tax and tip, for dinner.

The Ballroom

253 W. 28th St.
(Seventh & Eighth Aves.)
244-3005

SPANISH/PERUVIAN

Open Tues.-Fri. noon-1 a.m., Sat. 4:30 p.m.-1 a.m. All major cards.

The talented Peruvian chef, Felipe Rojas-Lombardi, runs The Ballroom as a multifaceted restaurant-cabaret. The large front room has an enormous bar and small café tables where you can sit from 4 p.m. on, eating tapas ($2.50 to $12.50 each, so they can add up) and drinking wine. This chef's imagination knows no limits; you can make a dinner of tapas by choosing a careful combination of dishes. We tried snails and red beans, and crunchy and spicy pigs' ears with pearl onions. On other occasions, we had the roast suckling pig and the Ballroom empanadas, stuffed with meat or fish and spicy sausage, which we think are some of the best in New York. Follow them with some succulent roasted kid and then perhaps yucca or braised morels. For dessert, the tapas bar (and restaurant proper) offers several flans, fruit tarts and cold compotes. Try the crema catalana, a wonderful, nutty-tasting flan.

The restaurant offers a more sedate, short menu, neither Spanish nor Peruvian, but ersatz Continental, and uneven much too often. We have enjoyed, however, three different kinds of paella, the broiled rack of lamb, the grilled duck with figs and the grilled Norwegian salmon. The duck can be dry on occasion. For good value ($25), try the buffet lunch of tapas and special entrées. The Ballroom has an extensive wine list with Spanish, California and French wines fairly priced. Average price for dinner for two is $98.

Brandywine

274 Third Ave. (21st St.)
353-8190

FRENCH

Open Mon.-Fri. 11:30 a.m.-2:30 p.m. & 5 p.m.-10:30 p.m., Sat. 5 p.m.-10:30 p.m. Cards: AE, MC, V.

Never mind that there must be some secret reason for having kept the misleading Brandywine (a place name in the Pennsylvania, Maryland and Delaware horse country) as a moniker for this posh and authentic Alsatian restaurant. Wood paneling, dark banquettes, beamed ceiling, French wall sconces and a real, cast-iron street lamp in the guise of a woman that dwarfs the already small room, all evoke Strasbourg, not Manhattan. Tables are so close that waiters have a hard time laying dishes on them—especially awkward here, because dishes are presented theatrically in their earthenware crocks before being dished onto a plate.

In 1990 Michael Mandato became the full-time chef, and he is following the Alsace-steakhouse route. The menu is slightly confusing: on the left side are the Alsatian specialties, from a rich foie gras enveloped in brioche to a typical Backeoffe. On the right side, the Brandywine side, dishes are not tied to any particular regions, and include such things as a light mushroom soup studded with fragrant rabbit sausage and a classic filet mignon. Although heavier, the Alsatian dishes are more fun. We adore the tarte flambée, a flat circle of pastry covered with creamy fromage blanc, melting onions and crisp, smokey bacon, finding it unctuous and perfectly executed (better than a quiche Lorraine). On the other hand, the mussels bathed in Riesling are sweet and tender, but bland. Finally, we love pigs' cheeks—little breaded circles of tender pork—light and tasty, served with an understated but delicious lukewarm potato salad. For a real kick, try the piquant, oniony, marinated herring. On the Brandywine side, we find the the best appetizer to be the innovative braised squid, tender and fresh and surrounded with a pool of liquid polenta.

Among the Alsatian entrées, try the tripe. It's cut into thin strips, simmered until tender with carrots and Riesling, and served with homemade melt-in-your-mouth Spätzle. Forget the roast pheasant—rather tough and dry, despite its wine-laced, gamey sauce and delicate sauerkraut accompaniments. Our favorite Alsatian dish is the goose stew, layered with creamy mashed potatoes and fragrant red cabbage: rich, satisfying and full of regional flavors, such as juniper, Riesling and good fat. The Brandywine entrées are less interesting, except for the swordfish infused with anchovies and napped with a glorious herb sauce. A short dessert menu features a popular chocolate mousse served in pastry cupcakes with hazelnut ice cream, and an unusual beer sorbet with broiled gingerbread. Stick with a Riesling wine if the Alsatian menu is your choice. Dinner for two will run about $100 to $120, with wine.

11/20 Café du Parc

106 E. 19th St. (Park Ave. & Irving Pl.)
777-7840
FRENCH/ITALIAN
Open Mon.-Fri. noon-3 p.m. & 5 p.m.-10 p.m., Sat. 5 p.m.-10 p.m. Closed 2 weeks in Aug. All major cards.

The name may be French, and the menu may be in French, and owner De Nicola (since 1988) and chef Cicillini may call it a French restaurant, but this is an Italian restaurant, and not a terribly good one, though it is cozy. A narrow room with visually tempting desserts on a two-tiered cart as you enter, Café du Parc's romantic tone is created by exposed brick walls, etched glass partitions, candles, flowers and tables spaced far enough apart to permit—even promote—conversation among the well-heeled neighborhood clientele. They lean back and take their time over dinner.

Dinner might begin with a good fettucine with shrimp and leeks, or okay oysters with spinach, or a sound fish salad, or formaggio aiello. Antelope is brought in twice a week from Texas and may be the best choice to follow, although what are billed as medallions turn out, on ocassion, to be a scaloppine. (They're big on scaloppine here.) The duck (from France) with plum sauce (which turned out to be strawberry, ugh) was tough and dry. Grilled chicken with wild rice and grilled eggplant is nothing special, but is a safe choice. Desserts are awful. The homemade peach ice cream is glutinous. The poached pear and ice

Note that average prices given in this chapter do not include tax (which is a whopping 8.25 percent in New York) or gratuity. You can figure, then, on adding roughly 25 percent to each of the prices quoted here, for your final bill.

cream is popular. Ask for fruit. The serviceable wine list contains mostly French, with some American wines. Château Coufran at $20 is appropriate with the cooking here. Expect to pay $90 for two for dinner and about half that for lunch.

11/20 Cedars of Lebanon

39 E. 30th St.
(Madison & Park Aves.)
679-6755, 725-9251
MIDDLE EASTERN
Open daily noon-11 p.m. All major cards.

Not much changes at this Middle Eastern restaurant that has been around for more than 30 years. To some extent, it lives off of a long-established reputation, built during its more exciting years as the only Middle Eastern restaurant in Manhattan. Owners François and Antonio Hossri feature their authentic Lebanese cuisine in ambient, lively surroundings, with scenes of old Lebanon on the walls and belly dancing to live music on the weekend. Those biblical cedars in the restaurant's name are described on the cheery menu as "one of Lebanon's most precious possessions." Another, by implication, is Lebanese cooking, which the brothers Hossri attempt to serve up with a thorough, enjoyable pride. The restaurant, a rectangular room with silver wallpaper (an unsuccessful attempt at modernity), traditional red lights, chandeliers and archetypical white arches, has a dinerlike atmosphere. As you sit down, a waiter will bring you small chunks of crunchy, sour, pickled turnips, along with a plate of hot chilis; don't try them before ordering your beer, or your mouth may burn forever. The menu features more than a dozen appetizers. The hummus (mashed garbanzos with sesame sauce), flavored with cumin, is creamy. The baba ghanouj, mashed eggplant, has a marvelous smoky taste but a trifle too much tahine (a paste of crushed, raw sesame seeds). Falafel (more garbanzos, this time deep fried) here is perfect, tender and soft inside, with lots of parsley and a golden crust; but the stuffed vine leaves run a close second, with their slightly lemony filling of rice and a bit of lamb. If you're feeling adventurous, try the authentically Lebanese kibby nayeh, raw chopped lamb spiced with cumin and garlic, mixed with cracked wheat. Salads are refreshing and sometimes unusual, such as sliced brains in a lemony sauce; fava beans served hot with a lemon vinaigrette and pickles; and tabouli, cracked wheat with an equal amount of chopped parsley and chopped tomatoes. Among the three soups on the menu, only the yogurt soup is worth a try; it exudes a very strong aroma of garlic and a touch of cumin and mint.

The main course offerings tend to be less satisfying. The shish kebab is often overcooked, the rice watery, and the vegetables (a non-Lebanese addition) have a watery, frozen taste. The same is true for the baked kibby, large chunks of ground stewed lamb, served with cracked wheat and pine nuts. Your best bets are the stuffed vegetables, because the stuffing of rice, chopped lamb, cumin and mint has a pleasant texture and a lively flavor. The desserts are a welcome surprise. The homemade baklava is filled with chopped nuts, and the crisp layers of phyllo are doused with just the right amount of honey and syrup. Other Lebanese desserts are just as good. Turkish and Lebanese coffees are delicious, but the American coffee is weak and the tea isn't freshly brewed. Drink beer with dinner, as a quality wine list is not on hand. Expect to pay $24 for two at lunch and $52 for dinner.

Chelsea Central
227 Tenth Ave. (23rd & 24th Sts.)
620-0230

AMERICAN
Open daily noon-midnight. Cards: AE, MC, V.

This American bistro-tavern has come into its own in the past few years, being a reliable place to eat simply and well. The restaurant has an early twentieth-century look, though once an unpretentious saloon. Notice the mahogany bar up front, the projection television, tables scattered all over the place, above, a stamped-tin ceiling and well-worn wooden wainscoting. In the back main dining areas there are tulip-shaped brass lights. In September, you can still catch glimpses of last season's Christmas decorations.

Lots of good American bistro fare can be had here, right through the day. We've enjoyed very good crabcakes and also mussels as starters. Look for oysters or a vegetable tart served with a tomato coulis. You could also taste the hearty black-bean soup, but for a more elegant appetizer, try the butternut-squash ravioli.

For a meat course, we liked the roast duck, the roast leg of lamb and the veal chop with wild mushrooms. Grilled swordfish tops the recommended fish dishes. Among the no-nonsense desserts, we liked the flourless chocolate cake. You'll appreciate, as we did, the list of first-rate wines, especially for a restaurant of this class. Among the French and American wines, consider the Sterling Vineyards Chardonnay ($25) for a white wine and a Domaine Rougeot Pommard for a red ($29). With one of these bottles, dinner for two will cost about $90.

Chelsea Trattoria Italiano
108 Eighth Ave. (16th St.)
924-7786

ITALIAN
Open Mon.-Fri. noon-midnight, Sat. 5 p.m.-midnight. All major cards.

What's not to like? This is a friendly, attractive and casually elegant place serving good pasta and more-than-acceptable entrées, a place where you are treated like an adult and pay reasonable prices. They don't take many risks at the Chelsea Trattoria Italiano, nor, in turn, will you. Just don't expect anything flashy. The long narrow dining room has brick-and-whitewashed walls and a bar up front, off to one side. The maitre d' in tuxedo greets you as if you were a regular, entering some high-priced uptown wonder.

We liked, for appetizers, the carpaccio of beef with Parmigiano shavings and olive oil, shrimps with beans, and herbed and smoked tuna, but you should consider the specials or a soup such as the Florentine bean soup or a lusty minestrone. Maybe you should also try a dish of mussels in a flavorful broth as an opener. With such fine pastas, however, you may opt for a half portion of the pappardelle with diced vegetables, the tortellini alla bolognese, linguine with clam sauce, agnolotti (stuffed pasta) filled with cheese and spinach served with a pesto sauce, or penne all'arrabbiata with a properly spicy tomato sauce. Indeed, the chef has a sure hand with seasoning. We can't eliminate the excellent fish risotto (squid, clams, shrimp, crabmeat) or the daily risotto special from consideration, either. If you don't choose pasta as a main course, you'll still have plenty of options: the mixed grilled vegetables, the T-bone steak fiorentina, the squid with its natural ink, and the red snapper in foil; even the chicken breast sautéed in white wine with sausage, mushrooms and garlic. For a dessert, try the ricotta cake, unless you must have a tiramisu. The wine list is fine. The tab for two is even finer, about $78, with a good bottle of wine.

12/20 Claire
156 Seventh Ave. (19th & 20th Sts.)
255-1955
AMERICAN/SEAFOOD
Open daily noon-4 p.m. & 5:30 p.m.-12:30 a.m. All major cards.

Claire is a restaurateur's sleight of hand: the illusion of Key West on an unpicturesque strip of Seventh Avenue in Chelsea. Inside it's restaurant as theater, with a handsome, artfully laid out set by the great stage designer, Robin Wagner: blond wood floors; walls in pastel blues, greens and pinks; light wooden lattice room dividers and ceiling overhangs; mirrors; dramatic lighting; stunning flower arrangements and plants; plus a team of lazily turning tropical ceiling fans that create a breezy and continually fresh Gulf environment. The staff is at once both laid back and efficient. All of this would be pretentious, of course, if the food weren't legitimately good, but it is that, although not quite as reliable and good as it has been. Danny Choladda is still the chef (he opened the place in 1982), but what may have happened is that the restaurant has become a victim of its own steady success. In a developing neighborhood, there is often a crowd waiting to get in. This not only makes it a noisy, flamboyant spot, but puts the kitchen to a test it does not handle all that well.

Danny's Thai background comes to the fore in several dishes—for example, broiled fish "Thai style" with coconut-curry sauce—and his bold handling of spices regularly reveals his culinary roots. Most appetizers are interesting: squid salad is chewy and sharply flavorful served in oil, garlic and lime juice, and seasoned with bits of red pepper. Steamed mussels are very good in an onion-infused broth, as is ceviche of fresh tuna, Gulf-style. The softshell Louisiana crawfish and rock shrimp and the barbecued alligator ribs are also recommended appetizers. There's a list of fifteen or so tempting fish and seafood main courses variously broiled, pan-fried or blackened— two of which have a strong and deserved following here: blackened redfish New Or-

leans–style, and a Claire specialty, blackened bluefish, which is extra spicy. Swordfish teriyaki with stir-fried vegetables is a popular dish. Vegetables are nothing to get excited about, but there are a few laudable meat entrées to balance the menu. The wine list has been shrewdly developed with an eye on the cost. Everything on the menu is reasonably priced, including the wines; most run in the teens. At $15, the Chardonnay Wyndham Estate Bin 222 from Hunter Valley, Australia, is recommended. It's hard to pass up dessert here: fresh Key lime pie jumps off the menu and is fine; Mississippi mud cake with whiskey sauce is appealing, as well. About $46 for two, with wine, for lunch, $76 for dinner.

 ## La Colombe d'Or
134 E. 26th St.
(Lexington & Third Aves.)
689-0666; Fax 689-2952
FRENCH
Open Mon.-Fri. noon-2:30 p.m. & 6 p.m.-11 p.m., Sat. 6 p.m.-11 p.m. All major cards.

Attractive Colombe d'Or, maintained with consistency by owners George and Helen Studley, moved up in class when chef Wayne Nish appeared on the scene in 1988. Nish is gone, and chef Mark May, once Nish's second-in-command, now runs the kitchen, delivering fare in the same tradition. Now well into its second decade, it has never been better. Comprising the ground floor of two brownstones, the restaurant sports two dining rooms and a bar. The long rooms with brick walls, tin ceilings, paintings and provincial-print banquettes continue to be at once rustic and inviting.

For openers, we loved the house smoked salmon with tomato and cucumber or the fish soup, although the delicious bread brought in from Tom Katz's bakery in Queens might addict you the minute it hits the table. A very good tapenade (an olive-paste spread) arrives early on. Ratatouille also merits consideration as a first course, for this warm Provençal vegetable stew with eggplant, zucchini, onion, herbs and garlicky tomato, is vibrant, as is the soup (perhaps the only *must* on the menu). The chef prepares his bouillabaisse with a tomato-sauce topping. We have also liked, as entrées, a straightforward chicken with olives and a braised and sautéed squab with black figs, honey and thyme. Instead of the usual fish choice (who doesn't serve grilled salmon or tuna these days?), go for the cod with lima beans, tomato, parsley and sage. We die for the desserts here, especially the gâteau victoire or the raspberry tart with Mascarpone cream, and, definitely, the ginger custard. George has found some pleasant regional French wines with prices from $12 to $55, and he lays it on the line by starring his favorites. For an inexpensive white, he'd recommend a 1988 Muscadet St. Fiacres ($12.50), and for a red, a 1983 Château Simone from Provence ($25). You can count on professional service here. Figure on about $66 for two for lunch and $96 per couple for dinner.

Da Umberto
107 W. 17th St. (Sixth Ave.)
989-0303
ITALIAN
Open Mon.-Thurs. noon-3 p.m. & 5:30 p.m.-11 p.m., Fri.-Sat. noon-11:30 p.m. Cards: AE.

This bright-and-spiffy Tuscan trattoria, on an unattractive Chelsea street, continues to be popular beyond reason. It's good to be sure, but why do so many people single this restaurant out, and not others, when, on the plate, they are more or less its equal? Could it be the atmosphere and room? It's fresh, modern, casual and authentically Italian. A high-ceilinged front room with wooden floor and white walls opens into a back room with a red-tile floor, which ends with a window on the kitchen. Up front, notice the green-marble bar, and a big, colorful and tempting display of foodstuffs, notably antipasti and desserts. The tables, surrounded by black bentwood chairs, sport white linen. The noise, complex food smells, and the people add color to a reasonably simple, white dining room.

If you enjoy vegetables, especially grilled vegetables with olive oil, you'll feast here on the extensive antipasti. When available, you can overdose on grilled porcini (or have it over risotto). You'll be able to sample a garlicky seafood salad from the jumble of displayed appetizers. In general, the fare is hearty, including the pasta dishes. Chef Franco Migliorini hails from Genova, not Florence, and his linguine alla viareggina proves it. We hail the rigatoni fagiolata, tubes of pasta in a strong tomato sauce with white beans, and the gnocchi with a spicy arrabbiata sauce. For a fish course, we suggest the special sting ray

with a Pernod-cream sauce, served with zucchini when available. Owner Umberto Assante worked at another fine Tuscan restaurant, Cent' Anni, and he brought along that restaurant's signature dish—a big, thick, pink, luscious veal chop. We've enjoyed the rabbit and the suckling pig here as well, despite oversalting. For dessert, try the moist ricotta cheesecake. Good wines can be found, but the list doesn't thrill us. Some items don't even include vintages, and if you order a bottle of Champagne, you are served your bubbly in a dreadful, "anti-champagne" glass. Service can be slow and inattentive—surprising for a relatively small and busy place with plenty of waiters. Figure $96 for two for dinner.

12/20 The Dolphin
227 Lexington Ave.
(33rd & 34th Sts.)
689-3010
AMERICAN/SEAFOOD
Open Mon.-Fri. noon-3 p.m. & 5 p.m.-11 p.m., Sat. 5 p.m.-11 p.m., Sun. 5 p.m.-10 p.m. Cards: AE, MC, V.

Opened and operated by Elio Rugova, an Albanian chef with an Italian background, The focus of The Dolphin's menu, as the restaurant's name suggests, is on fresh fish. The large dining room, simply decorated, but with garish paintings on the *faux*-brick walls, should be as pure and fresh as the fish. Although the service is slow, once you do get the waiter's attention, he will wheel out a table piled high with fresh seasonal fish, from which you will choose your meal; it may be red snapper, turbot, salmon, blowfish, halibut, sole, tuna, flounder, trout, bass or whatever else can be purchased fresh from the market. The fish will then be cooked to order, fileted or whole, broiled or sautéed. The broiling is faultless, and among the best fish on the menu is the superb broiled whole flounder. Marinated first in Provençal herbs, shallots and garlic, it is lightly broiled and moist. The red snapper, or poached turbot or salmon, are also good choices, all come with an excellent hollandaise sauce. All the fish are served with two vegetables and rice or potatoes.

Don't neglect the appetizers, however. The escargots bourguignon are fat and juicy, and filled with garlic in a hot-butter sauce. The mussels, cooked in a light tomato sauce, are fresh tasting and well seasoned. The Dolphin offers a wide selection of clams and several kinds of oysters, all refreshing in their sparkling purity. The scungilli-and-calamari salad (an Italian marvel) is excellent—tender pieces of octopus are marinated in a pungent vinaigrette and served on a fresh green salad with thinly sliced onions. The New England clam chowder is rich, but too starchy, and the clams are hard to find. It is a good idea to finish dinner with a salad; desserts are nothing special. The house salad, a fresh mixture of watercress, Boston and romaine lettuce, plus some endive and arugula, is tossed in an excellent Italian dressing. The Dolphin has a good and reasonably priced, if ordinary, wine list. Dinner for two runs about $86.

L'Escale

43 E. 20th St.
(Park Ave. South & Broadway)
477-1180
FRENCH
Open Mon.-Fri. noon-3 p.m. & 4 p.m.-11 p.m.,
Sat. 6 p.m.-11 p.m. All major cards.

This port-of-call (the meaning of the restaurant's name) in the Flatiron district beckons mostly to the increasing number of local artsy business types at lunch and a mix of the area's new residents and local workaholics at dinner. Patrick Laurent, owner of La Ripaille, opened this pleasant bistro in 1986. In an informal (the walls are decorated with French movie posters from the 1940s) and intimate atmosphere, you can meet friends and talk around a good bottle of wine without being disturbed. The food here is always good, never great.

We think the menu true bistro, ranging from rabbit stew to cassoulet, couscous on certain nights, and the traditional steak pommes frites which will instantly transport you to Paris. We liked the well-seasoned Lyon saucisson, served with boiled potatoes doused in fruity olive oil, and salads, with leeks and fresh artichokes tossed in a piquant vinaigrette. Try the terrine d'aubergine, chef Marcel Lattoni's own invention, an unusual pâté of eggplant accompanied by hot chèvre, or the duck with fresh figs and wine sauce. Chef Lattoni's ris de veau (sweetbreads) with port and capers has the distinct flavor of Normandy cooking. On Friday and Saturday, L'Escale serves an excellent

bouillabaisse, generous with its chunks of fish and seafood, and served with a strong, traditional rouille. For dessert, go for the favorites, those found in Paris: a chestnut dessert with ice cream, a good apple pie, and a lip-puckering lemon tart. L'Escale has a well-balanced wine list, reasonably priced, and most wines are French. Reservations at lunch are especially important. Average price per couple, with wine, is about $84 for dinner, $50 per couple for lunch.

Eze

254 W. 23rd St.
(Seventh & Eighth Aves.)
691-1140
FRENCH/MEDITERRANEAN
Open Tues.-Sat. 6 p.m.-10:15 p.m. Closed Aug.-
Labor Day. All major cards.

It takes a leap of imagination to conjure up images of the sublime Riviera hilltop village of Eze when contemplating a restaurant on West 23rd Street. Once inside this handsome townhouse, however, chef/owner Gina Zarrilli's Provençal-Mediterranean cuisine can transport you with its smell of fresh produce and poignant herbs. Indeed, when you enter the L-shaped dining room, the subtle aroma of garlic welcomes, reassuring and transformational. In this starkly elegant restaurant of about 40 seats, concentrate on the food. A highly professional staff, discrete and calm, makes this a perfect place to spend an evening, enjoying flavorful, refined food, to linger over an after dinner drink and to enjoy precious tête-à-tête dining, so atypical of New York. The $49 fixed-price menu (plus $5 for an added salad course or $7 for a cheese course) changes weekly or biweekly, depending on the market. You can expect a choice of about five appetizers, six main courses and four desserts. Among starters, try the cream of ratatouille soup and the pastas (fettucine with a powerful pesto, or pasta with salmon and tarragon). When fresh sardines are available, Ms. Zarrilli—who worked in the kitchens at Chanterelle, The Quilted Giraffe, Glorious Foods and Roxanne— will grill them with olive oil and herbs. Delicious, but be forewarned that on your plate of three sardines, there's likely to be a seven-inch number that defies preconceived notions of how a sardine ought to look.

Among the fine main courses, at least two stand out: the semi-signature dish of a whole braised red snapper (for two), cooked in white wine and laced with saffron, surrounded and bedded with couscous and a red-pepper purée and saffron-cream sauce; and the perfectly prepared rack of lamb, with sweet-garlic-and-onion jam. If you need a third option, then consider the halibut with marjoram. The wine list is fitting and includes some nice, uncommon wines produced near the Côte d'Azur. For dessert, ask about the flourless chocolate cake, the puff pastry with fresh figs and the pear-and-red-wine tart, just three of the excellent choices. Expect to pay $130 for two, with a single bottle of wine, plus tax and tip.

12/20 Frank's
431 W. 14th St.
(Ninth & Tenth Aves.)
243-1349
ITALIAN/STEAKHOUSE
Open Mon.-Thurs. 10 a.m.-3 p.m. & 5 p.m.-10 p.m., Fri.-Sat. 10 a.m.-11 p.m. All major cards.

The waiters here pretend not to notice you beckoning, even when you display your most blatant semaphore techniques. Established in 1912, this old-fashioned restaurant in the meat-packing district on the verge of becoming a co-op city has a soul that remains pure—pastas, steak, casual service, good prices and food the way it used to taste (to the degree that ingredients taste the way they used to). The downstairs dining room looks the same, too—old tile floors, long bar, pressed tin ceiling, a lazy fan and sawdust on the floor. George Molinari Jr., who received his training at the Culinary Institute of America, runs the place now, greeting diners at the door and ambling from table to table with his blackboard of specials. What would grandma say? *"Mangia."*

For dinner, consider an appetizer-portion of good, fresh pasta. Give serious attention to the catch of the day and the meat specials, but don't neglect the prime shell steak (unremarkable vegetables on the side), red snapper cooked Livornese-style, or a broiled veal chop. The meats are top quality, including tripe and sweetbreads, but it's the pastas and steaks you'll remember. For pasta, the tagliarini puttanesca is appropriate. Puttanesca (a sauce

of tomatoes, capers, garlic, black olives and anchovies) translates literally as "prostitute-style," and, appropriately, out the front window of Frank's, you can glimpse some of the "wild West" Village ladies of the night and transvestites. Wine has long been a tradition at Frank's, and the low markup on popular Italian and French wines (and a few familiar California ones) encourages consumption. In 1990, a 1978 Giacosa Barbaresco sells for $33. For the whole show, meaning lots of food on your plate, expect to pay about $100 for two for dinner.

12/20 Keen's
72 W. 36th St. (Fifth & Sixth Aves.)
947-3636
AMERICAN
Open Mon.-Fri. 11:45 a.m.-3 p.m. & 5:30 p.m.-11 p.m., Sat. 5 p.m.-11 p.m. Closed week before Labor Day through Labor Day weekend. All major cards.

Ninety-thousand pieces of memorabilia—including clay churchwarden pipes, theater posters and programs, photographs, early American prints and paintings, and front pages of turn-of-the-century newspapers—give this restaurant an early 1900s air. It's opening (1885) predates that, in fact. There are numerous dining rooms, upstairs and down. A garment-center institution, Keen's does steady lunch-hour business (reservations are a must), and the private rooms are very active, as is the street-level tap room at noon and at 5 p.m.

The mutton chop for which Keen's is known continues to be larger than life—thick and flavorful, accompanied by its juice with just the right touch of mint. The rack of lamb is very good, as is the broiled veal chop with wild mushrooms. Steaks are making a comeback here under new general manager Cheryl To. She especially recommends the Keen's classic, aged prime porterhouse steak ($29.50), and the T-bone steak with sautéed spinach. Fish and fowl balance the meat-and-potatoes offerings. Consider the jumbo-shrimp scampi or the simple, boneless half chicken. All the fare is hearty and filling, but you'll want an appetizer—perhaps a bowl of chowder or steamed mussels. Fresh oysters are also available. Desserts include English puddings and the usual

New York cheesecake. You might try the roasted pear with aged Stilton and plum purée. The wine offerings are more than sound. There are daily specials by the glass, and the 130 items on the list include examples from Spain, Italy, France and the U.S.; many are priced attractively in the teens and twenties. About $56 for two at lunch and $84 per couple for dinner, with wine, plus tax and tip.

Lola
30 W. 22nd St. (Fifth & Sixth Aves.)
675-6700
AMERICAN/CARIBBEAN
Open Mon.-Thurs. noon-3 p.m. & 6 p.m.-midnight, Fri. noon-3 p.m. & 6 p.m.-1 a.m., Sat. 6 p.m.-1 a.m., Sun. noon-4 p.m. Cards: AE.

Now, if you're just hankering for a Sunday "Gospel" brunch, head on down to Lola's place. Come and see her and many beautiful people as well as the Gospel musicians performing at 1 p.m. and 3 p.m. on Sundays. Weeknights, you can hear good live music at 9 p.m. Surrounding its clients with minimal decor, Lola's should be an appealing setting for meeting a friend for drinks or dinner. Better yet, you don't have to worry about a cover or minimum. While sipping an excellent margarita (or indulging in some exotic concoction) at a small table near the handsome bar, try the cayenne-laced ribbon onion rings, threadlike, transparent and crisp, or the deep-fried calamari with green-chile sauce, another excellent hors d'oeuvre.

Back in the dining room, with its trompe l'oeil courtyard filled with flowers, pale salmon-pink walls bearing original art with food themes, and upholstered banquettes and chairs, you may choose from a menu that offers dishes from the Caribbean as well as South America, with a touch of Portuguese, and Lola's own version of American cuisine. Steven Stinnet has been the chef since 1989 and has kept to what works well here. On the menu are "small plates" (appetizer-size) and "large plates" (geared toward a full course). We loved especially, among the large plates, the crispy, skinned duckling, served with braised red cabbage and pumpkin polenta. The restaurant serves its island-style shrimp-and-chicken curry, hot but not burning, with tasty wild rice waffles to soak up the sauce. For

those who long for good fried chicken, the kind usually found only in the South, Lola's 100-spices Caribbean-fried chicken, with deep-fried parsnips, can transport you straight out of the city. Lola also serves grilled fish and meats, each prepared very originally. Friends liked the blackened salmon paillard with a sweet-corn-and-bell-pepper relish. The menu changes a lot, so you'll have to return to decide on favorites. We thought Lola's atmo-

THE TOQUE, CIRCA 1700

Have you ever wondered about the origin of that towering, billowy (and slightly ridiculous) white hat worn by chefs all over the world? Chefs have played an important role in society since the 5th century B.C., but the hats didn't begin to appear in kitchens until around the 18th century A.D. The toque is said to be of Greek origin: many famous Greek cooks, to escape persecution, sought refuge in monasteries and continued to carry on with their fine art. The chefs donned the tall hats traditionally worn by Orthodox priests but, to distinguish themselves from their fellows, they wore white hats instead of black. The practice eventually was adopted by chefs from Paris to Peking.

sphere a bit noisy, full of fun, right for both the young and the not-so-young. Among the scrumptious desserts, we liked a chocolate-toffee torte with pecan crust and layers of fudge, brown sugar toffee and white-chocolate mousse—so rich you'll have to diet for a week. When it's available, ask for the simple homemade vanilla ice cream that tastes of the vanilla bean. The compact French and American wine list is shrewdly chosen and very well priced, with almost all offerings in the $18-to-$35 range. Average price will run about $90 per couple for dinner, $50 for two persons at lunch.

Le Madri

168 W. 18th St. (Seventh Ave.)
727-8022

ITALIAN

*Open daily noon-3 p.m. & 6 p.m.-12:30 p.m.
Cards: AE.*

So 1990s Italian, and one of the newest of New York's chic Italian restaurants, Le Madri has an unassuming entrance, but you soon feel the air of sophistication, elegance and toniness. Near the front bar stands an attractive hostess, who greets diners with a warm smile. On the way, you'll pass a colorful and beguiling cornucopia of vegetables and antipasti. Take in the large main dining room, with a gently vaulted ceiling, Tuscan-yellow walls with Italian engravings, tables set well-apart and a wood-burning pizza oven. Clothed in pinstriped shirts and khakis, the waiters—handsome, youthful Italians all—take up relaxed, attentive poses and charming (or disarming?) stares. The management has adorned the simply set tables with a small basket of vegetables (heads of garlic, mostly) with some almonds glued on. The clientele, sedate and quietly chic (tie required for men), spends its time people- and fashion-watching in this spot, in the shadow of Barney's. Le Madri was created by Pino Luongo, the Florentine who is the founder and co-owner of the still-successful Il Cantinori on East 10th Street, as well as one of the Hamptons's best restaurants.

You'll find Le Madri's dinner menu a mixture of country dishes from Tuscany and classic Italian dishes from other regions. If diners want to be educated by Pino Luongo about true regional cuisine, they won't get any help from the menu, with its lack of explanation. For an appetizer, try the simple *fritto di calamari e prezemolo*: the small, crisp and tender rings of fried squid and miraculously intact fried parsley will melt in your mouth. Forget the *carpaccio di tonno con ricci di mare*, paper-thin slices of raw tuna, strangely bland. Ask for a dish of homemade pasta with mushrooms and baby artichokes, as close to perfection as country dishes can come. You can gamble on complex ravioli filled with quail meat, quail eggs and Swiss chard, flavorful one time then sorely undercooked on one occasion, yet another time overly dry. Waiters recite a huge list of specials, rattled off at breakneck speed, but without giving prices. It's tough to get a reservation at this restaurant that serves 300 to 350 dinners nightly, and the waiters could not speak any faster, but if the ten-minute recitation routine were cut, who knows, you might see your first dish in reasonable time and the restaurant could turn over even more tables. Among the more memorable special dishes we've eaten at Le Madri, we recall with fondness an appetizer consisting of four zucchini flowers stuffed with buffalo mozzarella and sardines lightly fried and served on a tomato base.

Luongo sends out mixed messages with his main-course dishes. At a recent dinner, we loved a curve of barely cooked skate (the menu uses the term "filet"; for the record, skate has no filet), authentically accented with fresh-chopped tomatoes and fava beans. Friends liked pan-fried liver, glazed with an unusual mixture of honey and balsamic vinegar, then served with light "pellets" of polenta. Grilled tuna, a special of the day, sweet, rare and delicately charred, finds its complement in a circling of finely shredded marinated fennel. We thought the selection of roasted meats disappointing. Tough, ungainly morsels of lamb, liver and venison prove that, even with "mamas" (or, in Italian, *le madri*) in the kitchen, you can't import all of Italy without breaking something. No dinner is complete without a forkful of insalata di carciofini crudi, thinly sliced, crisp baby artichokes with Parmigiano in a delightful oil-and-lemon sauce. Enchanting! Much here can be. Headily flavorful dishes make it one of our favorite New York City destinations for true Italian food. However, when the crowded room fills up, the service and the food suffer significantly, especially in warm weather, when a patio is open. For fine dining, try lunchtime. Forget the desserts, hardly worthy of discussion: an indecently heavy chocolate cake, raspberries in an overly sweet zabaglione, and a mediocre Italian-style cheesecake are but three examples. If you have ice cream, avoid the espresso-fig concoction. The Italian wine list is excellent. Dinner for two runs about $100 to $150, depending on your choice of wine.

10/20 Manganaro's

488 Ninth Ave. (37th St.)
563-5331, 563-7748

ITALIAN

Open Mon.-Sat. 8:30 a.m.-7 p.m. All major cards.

Maybe this only belongs in our Quick Bites chapter, but this glorified, blue-collar Italian deli (opened in 1893) is an experience you should know about and may want to try. The food is pretty good, the kind you can taste at lots of low-key catered affairs, and there is a love here of good ingredients. If one of the old women serving the hot food likes you, she may give you the best rice ball, some extra Parmesan, or the freshly sliced, rather than recycled, bread. But if you hesitate between gnocchi and fettucine, off with your head! The capriciousness of the short, buxom, razor-eyed Italian cooks in baggy print dresses has probably held sway in this family-owned restaurant since Grandmother Nina's time. Let's hope it stays that way. The Convention Center two avenues away and designer lofts up the ratty side streets threaten higher prices, tablecloths, maybe even waiters. So far, the Dell' Orto family has held out. The kids in contemporary garb are honing their cantankerousness, but dad stays up front supervising the old-world store with its cold cuts, olive oils and pastas. In back, at the tavola calda, timing is everything. Arrive before or after lunch and you breeze through the "cold" line for terrific heroes, good pasta salads, marinated mushrooms, roast peppers, mozzarella-and-tomato salad and the like. At those hours, you can also pause, without threat of the guillotine, to decide between hefty portions of the aforementioned gnocchi, meatballs, lasagne (regular or vegetarian), polenta, sausages and various things "Parmigiana." Arrive at the height of lunch hour and the wait is similar to that for a first-run movie. There are few seats at the communal tables, either counterside or upstairs in the less hectic but no less minimally decorated dining rooms, each of which is filled with about as good a cross section of New York as the U.S. Census Bureau could ever hope to find. The cannoli here are still a buck, and you can get a half bottle of decent Chianti Classico for $6.95. A full meal, with mineral water, beer or wine, costs about $30 to $40 per couple.

12/20 Man Ray

169 Eighth Ave. (18th & 19th Sts.)
627-4220

FRENCH/AMERICAN

Open Mon.-Thurs. & Sun. 11:30 a.m.-3:30 p.m. & 5:30 p.m.-11 p.m., Fri.-Sat. 11:30 a.m.-3:30 p.m. & 5:30 p.m.-1 a.m.) Cards: AE.

This handsome bistro—a study in back and white next to the Joyce Theater—opened, then closed, then opened again under the management of the Brian McNally organization. Named after the American-born artist Man Ray who spent much of his life in Paris, this noisy bistro, nevertheless, is all New York. In its current incarnation, some of the black-and-white photographs are out, lots of colorful flowers are in and Chef Matthew Tivy (formerly of the Canal Bar, a defunct Brian McNally restaurant) supervises the reasonably priced menu. Pizza and pasta and even hamburgers await, but most of the dishes are familiar appetizers and entrées in the new New York/European vein. We've recently enjoyed the chicken soup, fried calamari, duck with couscous and the lamb shank. Thumbs down on the french fries. Desserts suffice, and the short wine list reads well at this showy bilevel dining spot on upcoming Chelsea's restaurant row. Expect to pay $50 to $70 for two.

Moreno Ristorante

65 Irving Place (18th St.)
673-3939

ITALIAN

Open Mon.-Fri. noon-3 p.m. & 5 p.m.-midnight, Sat. 5 p.m.-midnight, Sun. 2 p.m.-midnight. All major cards.

The folks in the Gramercy Park neighborhood and beyond took to this place like garlic to olive oil. Clearly, they were starved for a decent place to eat after work or for a reliable, casual meal on weekends. Though the restaurant serves good contemporary Italian food, we don't consider that the key to the place's success; any good bistro would have done as well—and this place has done very well since opening in 1988. Moreno, of the restaurant's name, co-owner and maitre d', supervises the entire kitchen. Out front, he will guide you to a cozy table in the bright, yellow-colored room or to a corner one dedicated to nonsmokers. In warm weather, sought-after tables are set on the sidewalk outside of this street-corner restaurant with big picture windows.

Though a different salad appears on the menu every day, people come here for the pasta. We consider delicious the homemade spinach ravioli with pesto sauce and the home-made fettucine with lobster. If you choose a pasta for a main course, you can start with one of the lovely antipasti—perhaps homemade mozzarella with yellow and red roast peppers or an assortment of fresh mushrooms sautéed with garlic and oil (funghi trifolati). Also try the dried beef from northern Italy, served with goat cheese and endive (rollatini di bresaola). We've also enjoyed the penne with tomato, smoked salmon and a vodka sauce. We can vouch for the salmon with mustard sauce and the swordfish alla milanese, as well as the veal chop, but consider the scaloppine only fair (to make it worse, the latter was accompanied by slices of unripe tomato). For an outstanding dessert, ask for the chocolate zuccotto. Good Italian wines highlight a list that has grown to between 150 and 200 offerings. Four wines can be ordered by the glass and change daily. Figure about $60 per couple for lunch and $90 for dinner.

busy kitchen in the rear.

If we say we've not eaten well here, it's meant as a compliment, sort of. We've had overly salted and rubbery lamb, rubbery shrimp, fair chicken, okay rabbit, and soft, undistinguished bread. It made us thinkingly of Nice or Lyon. When there's a mob scene, what can you expect? We have, of course, eaten much better here than is necessary for a successful French bistro. The food served in the quieter surroundings, around the corner in the restaurant's private dining room in a brownstone (lots of corporate action there), makes you appreciate how much talent works in the kitchen. We like any dish with a Provençal connection: starters include a sardine sandwich (garlic, olive oil, onion, tomato) and anything presented with goat cheese and herbs, such as the wonderful goat-cheese-and-potato tart. Entrées include rabbit roasted in the Provençal style or a leg of lamb with garlic and flageolets (legumes resembling green kidney beans). For a fish dish, try the grilled mackerel, cooked in the Greek style, or the skate seasoned with parsley and herbs. For dessert, go for one of the fruit tarts here. The wine list is short, with low-priced, unusual wines from small producers. Figure $80 per couple.

Park Bistro

414 Park Ave. South
(28th & 29th Sts.)
689-1360

FRENCH

Open Mon.-Fri. noon-3 p.m. & 6 p.m.-11 p.m., Sat.-Sun. 6 p.m.-11 p.m. Cards: AE, DC.

You won't find a more authentic bistro in New York, or in Paris, for that matter. You'd have to head for Lyon's rue Mercière to match the archetypal perfection of this wildly popular New York spot that opened in 1986, but exploded on the culinary map of the city in 1989 with the arrival of chef Jean-Michel Diot and his able front-room cohort, Max Bernard (joining the original owner, Philippe La-Jaunie). We're not talking grand food, we're talking crowded, cramped, noisy, frenetic and wonderful bistro. The room is "studied authentic"—Burgundy banquettes, mirrors, lace curtains, French photos on the walls—but has a fascinating window that looks into the

Periyali

35 W. 20th St. (Fifth & Sixth Aves.)
463-7890

GREEK

Open Mon.-Thurs. noon-3 p.m. & 6 p.m.-11 p.m., Fri. noon-3 p.m. & 6 p.m.-11:30 p.m., Sat. 6 p.m.-11:30 p.m. Cards: AE, MC, V.

If you've always thought that New York needs a first-rate, authentic Greek taverna, keep on thinking, or start prowling around Astoria. We think Periyali qualifies for the gentrified Greek-American title, however, with a serious commitment to quality. Although intended to look like a taverna, it comes across like something that would be featured in *Architectural Digest*, replete with designer name-dropping. To their credit, owners and experienced restaurant creators (Il Cantinori, Aureole) Steve Tzolis and Nicola Kotsoni have created a wonderful theater—white walls, tiled floor, dark beams and a tented ceiling of billowing white cloth (like all tavernas in Greece?). The good wine list is half Greek, so be sure to order a bottle of Greek white. Much of the food has Greek names (the chef Charles Bowman doesn't), but in the end we found the food mostly more of the usual— nicely done, nevertheless. We liked the paidakia thendrolivano, for example, very good lamb chops grilled over charcoal and seasoned with fresh rosemary.

Sure, they serve phyllo pastry here. Order the phyllo-wrapped cheese-and-spinach pies. For appetizers, we love the charcoal-grilled octopus or the white beans with garlic sauce. For an entrée, you will do well with fish, say, the grilled whole black sea bass with olive oil, lemon and herbs; or, if you want to think about Greece, delve into a plate of moussaka, the layered casserole of eggplant and ground lamb with a béchamel sauce. As for desserts, try the baklava for quality and the lemon-semolina cake for curiosity. Drachmas are not accepted, but about $80 per couple for dinner is.

Positano
250 Park Ave. South (20th St.)
777-6211
ITALIAN
Open Mon.-Thurs. noon-3 p.m. & 5:30 p.m.-11:30 p.m., Fri. noon-3 p.m. & 5:30 p.m.-12:30 a.m., Sat. 5:30 p.m.-12:30 a.m. All major cards.

A cavernous former industrial space in an old neo-Gothic building was converted cleverly in 1984 by knowing Italian hands into an airy pink, white and green restaurant-as-theater. Now, noise and bustle and hip, attractive, young people fill the place, and it continues in the 1990s to serve good, contemporary Italian food. The room has three levels: the upper-dining tier, a mid-level tier devoted to the bar (which becomes ever more animated as neighborhood offices empty out), and the ground-floor perimeter, set up with booths and twosomes by the windows. As the big room fills, the hubbub increases. If dining is your aim, isolate yourself in one of the spacious and comfortable booths on the ground level.

For a choice opener, we liked the battered, fried artichoke hearts with mozzarella, served with a tomato sauce, and the simply grilled vegetables (when available). Sautéed mussels

(be wary of overcooking) in tomato sauce with croutons come in a flavorsome broth that begs to be dipped in, and sautéed baby calamari with fresh tomato, parsley and olive oil were divine. Over the years, the polenta has tended to be tasteless, with a gummy hunk of fontina on top, not redeemed by tasty nubbins of sautéed mushrooms. Main-course offerings include rack of lamb with potatoes and mushrooms, grilled veal chop with roast potatoes and vegetables, and a tasty boneless chicken sautéed with pancetta and onions in a light white-wine sauce.

For desserts, we suggest the custard cake or the gelati, but not the tiramisu. Always amiable, but casual and sometimes slow, one of the the staff may give you a fork with a bowl of raspberries. You can order wines by the glass from the cruvinet or by the bottle. About $60 per couple at lunch, $90 per couple at dinner.

Quatorze
240 W. 14th St.
(Seventh & Eighth Aves.)
206-7006; Fax 727-8048
FRENCH
Open Mon.-Fri. noon-2:30 p.m. & 6 p.m.-11:30 p.m.; Sat. 6 p.m.-11:30 p.m., Sun. 5:30 p.m.-11 p.m. Cards: AE.

We keep returning to Quatorze, both the most reliable bistro in town, and an authentic Alsatian brasserie. You won't be hit by any attitudes here; the plates are simple, the portions large and the food very good. Owners Peter Meltzer and Mark DiGiulio, students of French bistros, both of whom travel to France regularly, have gone to some lengths to replicate a typical bistro decor, down to the Fernet Branca posters, *Le Figaro* in the newspaper rack, and a classic yellow menu card with "service non compris" printed on the side. Take note of the long, narrow, bright room with its red banquette, tile-and-wood floors, and a bar up front. The place is always crowded, busy and crushingly noisy, but has a friendly *joie de vivre*. You can order from the entire menu at the bar, even if the tables aren't full. (For Upper East Siders who don't want to taxi downtown, a second bistro, Quatorze Bis, opened in 1990 at 323 East 79th Street, with the same winning formula.)

You can get any staple French-bistro fare at Quatorze. You might start with a chicory salad with a warm bacon vinaigrette dressing, grilled boudin blanc with béarnaise sauce, or an Alsatian onion tart. For a primary plate, try the sautéed calf's liver in a shallot sauce, roast duck in a green-peppercorn sauce, cassoulet (in fall and winter), very fine Alsatian sauerkraut with pork and sausages (choucroute garnie), flounder filet (grilled or meunière), superbly grilled and seasoned salmon, an enviable grilled half chicken with herbs or, of course, a steak with french fries. Desserts, generous and not bad, include an apple tart and a properly baked crème caramel. The individual French apple tart, done to order, has developed a wide reputation and following. The wine list offers about three-dozen French selections, ranging in price from $14 to $70, all nicely appropriate to the food. With a restaurant that succeeds so well with its good formula, why not give it a rating of *quatorze*, or fourteen? Expect to pay about $76 per couple for dinner.

12/20 Rogers & Barbero

149 Eighth Ave. (17th & 18th Sts.)
243-2020; Fax 691-0695
AMERICAN
Open daily noon-midnight. Cards: AE, MC, V.

Along the revitalized stretch of Eighth Avenue, between 14th and 23rd streets, that's becoming a restaurant row, this is one of the most pleasant and reliable eateries. Pat Rogers and Robert Barbero, who established their restaurant near the Joyce Theater in 1983, take their work seriously, and succeed with a casual yet elegant place that works well within its sensible limits. They've always been sensitive to price, and their current fixed-price dinner at $19.95 is making the neighborhood folk, who call it home, smile. The clean, modern dining room is simple, yet dramatic: it took on a more Mediterranean than cool urban look when the original designers, but most noticeably David Gropman, freshened up the look in 1989.

The cuisine is imaginative, but based upon traditional fare. Sometimes it misses, but the basics are pretty solid. The terrine of roasted eggplant and red peppers is a recommended starter, as are the salmon cakes with dill sauce. There's a daily pasta special, which has never been our favorite, but we really can't complain about the angel-hair preparations. For a main course, you might go for the grilled chicken

breast with avocado and arugula or a flank steak marinated in ginger, garlic and beer. Steak is good here, as are the hamburgers, which are available on the lunch, brunch and dinner menus. Various fish and seafood dishes are offered, and if they have yet to distinguish themselves, they need not be avoided. There are plenty of choices, and the menu changes several times a year. Among the good desserts, the apple-bread pudding with bourbon sauce is excellent, and the "seriously chocolate cake" is serious. There is an intelligently planned and affordable list of American, French and Italian wines ($12.50 to $90), with an assortment of wines by the glass, including ports and dessert wines. Expect to pay as little as $30 per couple for lunch or brunch and up to about $70 to $80 for two for full à la carte dinners.

 Sofi

102 Fifth Ave. (15th St.)
463-8888
ITALIAN
Open Mon.-Fri. noon-2:30 p.m. & 6 p.m.-10:30 p.m., Sat. 6 p.m.-10:30 p.m. All major cards.

We've always enjoyed Sofi, a solid success of fine food and stylish interior in the nouveau-chic, South-of-Flatiron neighborhood. You get restaurant-as-theater, with a stage setting that creates a strong first impression. You'll be impressed by the theater, a huge high-flying affair with five giant *faux* marble columns including Corinthian crowns, a narrow balcony, dark floors, embroidered chairs and a patterned carpet, as well as an elegant, raised living room at the entrance near the bar. The cast has been assembled by co-owner Richard Lavin (of Lavin's, a private lunch club), and to our great delight now includes Georgine Cavaiola in the kitchen.

We lamented the demise of Cavaiola's own restaurant—once the best by far in Little Italy—but now she has the chance to please a larger audience. She has tossed out Sofi's eclectic former menu of contemporary Americans songs with French, Italian and Asian overtones, and replaced it with a strictly contemporary Italian opera. Her crisp calamari is lovely, and we remember ever so well her grilled littleneck clams, sweet with garlic and parsley, and the grilled eggplant with a note of mint, served on a bed of arugula with shards of pecorino cheese. Her pastas taste terrific.

We recently enjoyed penne all' arrabbiata and farfalle alla putanesca, and recall with pleasure her ravioli and tagliolini. For a main course apart from pasta, we've enjoyed the grilled boneless quail with fennel, Tuscan beans and olive oil. Lavin's shrewdly constructed wine list peaks at $50 and is picking up more Italian offerings. Figure on $80 for two.

Umeda
102 E. 22nd St.
(Park & Lexington Aves.)
505-1550

JAPANESE

Open daily noon-2:30 p.m. & 6 p.m.-1 a.m. Cards: AE, MC.

When Hubert's restaurant moved out of its digs on East 22nd Street, Umeda moved in. Owned by chef Normiro Miyake, who arrived in New York in 1988 and speaks little English, Umeda resembles a Japanese country inn, paneled in blond wood. The saké bar—a first in New York—sports a pagoda-style roof and serves about one-hundred different sakés. A list with descriptions of the sakés educates diners. We like dry saké with broiled fish or sushi and sweeter saké with vegetable dishes or dessert. Both are served either hot or cold. The tables, placed slightly too close for a Westerner's comfort, sport rustic Japanese napkins. The one tatami room seems furnished with little thought to serenity.

You can experience adventurous dining at Umeda; many of the menu's offerings come across as unusual, especially the seafood preparations. Try a delicately poached fish stuffed with soba (Japanese buckwheat noodles), topped with grated mountain potato and doused with a fragrant broth, for example. We also liked the fluke, grilled and sauced with briny sea urchin, and sashimi crab marinated in saké. Also try the toro (the most tender, fattiest part of fresh tuna), seared and served with a vinegar-based sauce. Chef Miyake's steamed vegetables, including shiitake mushrooms, Japanese pumpkin and spongy bean curd, evoke the season with their unadulterated, essential flavor. The earthy, artichoke flavor of sautéed burdock makes the traditional sweet omelette—part of most sushi platters—more complex and interesting. Among the desserts, we liked best the poached, sweet fresh fig floating in ice water. The waiters, although inexperienced, are

pleasant. The remarkably beautiful "Japanese" porcelain comes from Great Barrington, Vermont. Dinner for two, including saké, will be about $120.

Union Square Café
21 E. 16th St.
(Fifth Ave. & Union Square West)
243-4020

AMERICAN

Open Mon.-Thurs. noon-3 p.m. & 6 p.m.-11 p.m., Fri. noon-3 p.m. & 6 p.m.-midnight, Sat. 6 p.m.-midnight. All major cards.

Smart young owner Danny Meyer was prescient enough in 1985 to snag for his restaurant the name that would come to define the "new" neighborhood. Both the neighborhood and the restaurant have prospered in the years since then. The Union Square Café has become so well known and respected, Meyers and crew (and some willingly hip foodniks) casually refer to it as USC, and there's no doubt in their minds that the initials are sufficient (What? You mean there are other institutions using the same initials?). When you're packed, and when your customers continue to go away smiling and raving, you develop a certain, let's say, assuredness. Meyer was also savvy enough to design his several rooms to be both smart and comfortable. Stop by the bar, an inviting place to sample the wines offered by the glass, or to try the variety of fresh oysters or a casual meal. In the three dining areas (the most popular being the main room, several steps below the bar), all with their cherry wood floors, hunter green wainscoting, and ample space between tables, the servers remain attentive without being obtrusive.

The kitchen used to have its weaknesses. But since 1988, with talented Michael Romano (formerly the chef at La Caravelle) in charge, all arrows are pointing upwards here. In any event, the food can be very good, or, on occasion, excellent. (At lunch, for example, you can get one of the best hamburgers in town, and the "sides" of garlic cottage fries and mashed turnips with crisped shallots are not to be missed.) Though a classically trained and experienced French chef, Michael Romano has taken a turn lately toward the Italian. Mouthwatering starters include sheep's-milk-cheese ravioli with black-pepper-and-sage butter; bombolotti "al modo mio" with sweet-fennel sausage, Cognac and cream; and a warm, white-bean-and-seafood salad with shrimp, scallops, calamari and mussels. We loved the grilled, marinated filet mignon of tuna. It's not for everyone, though, being a gargantuan slab of tuna, seared on the outside, sushi-raw within—its sheer size overwhelms. More restrained options include grilled rabbit (fine but never thrilling, which may be a function of the quality of available rabbit); a moist and perfectly roasted chicken with creamy polenta, and tomato-and-sourdough panzanella; grilled veal lombatina with a zucchini, eggplant and Parmigiano tortino. Among dishes we don't regularly see on the changing menu, we've enjoyed a very good lamb paillard with eggplant; and a roast suckling pig with rosemary and garlic, served with sautéed field greens and herb-roast potatoes. Meyer is also a wine buff and prides himself on his ambitious, ever-changing, reasonably priced list that wins awards. They know wines at this place, so ask for help, especially if you are interested in unique ones from small producers. A long list of dessert wines by the glass accompanies the list of mostly American-style desserts. We've found the raspberry crème brûlée cold and more like a gratin with too much sugar on top, and the special short cake with blueberries (or plums) and ice cream too dry, but thoroughly enjoyed the sour-cherry crisp tart with lemon curd. Generally, we prefer the homemade hazelnut-dipping biscotti and one of the dessert wines. Expect to pay $110 per couple for dinner, with wine, $70 for two for a simpler lunch, plus tax and tip.

MIDTOWN EAST
(E. 42nd Street to E. 59th Street)

12/20 Akbar

475 Park Ave. (57th & 58th Sts.)
838-1717

INDIAN

Open Mon.-Sat. 11:30 a.m.-2:45 p.m. & daily 5:30 p.m.-10:45 p.m., Fri.-Sat. 5:30 p.m.-11:30 p.m. All major cards.

Akbar has been satisfying questing palates in search of reliable northern Indian cuisine since 1976. Its success resulted in a second Akbar outpost in 1988, at 256 E. 49th Street (755-9100), so you should always be able to get a table in order to satisfy your vegetarian cravings (a dozen vegetarian entreés highlight the menu). Handsome Akbar on Park has a subtly lit, low-key interior with airy white fretwork and well-spaced tables. Service, sometimes lackadaisical, tends toward uncommunicative, and the piped-in sitar music after a while becomes monotonous, but you can put together quite a decent meal here if you order well. If you're interested in a vegetarian meal, ask about the day's special thali, a large metal plate which contains smaller bowls of three vegetables plus the spiced sautéed lentil staple (dal), a samosa (a spiced vegetable-stuffed pastry) served with rice pilaf, raita (a yogurt-and-cucumber side dish), and the Indian bread, naan. You will be hard put to finish this good and reasonably priced dish, especially if you order as an accompaniment the onion kulcha (naan stuffed with onions). Perhaps you'd like to compose your own meal: aloo gobi, spiced cauliflower and potatoes, and the spicy okra called bhindi are the best choices (though on occasion excessively oily). Any of the vegetable dishes eaten with the banarasi pilaf—made with saffron-infused basmati rice, vegetables and nuts—make a filling, meatless meal with complete proteins. We like tandoori chicken, marinated in yogurt and spices with a pleasant charred flavor (from the heat of the tandoor, a clay oven), tender and moist. There is also boti kebab, skewered chunks of marinated lamb, or a chicken ginger kebab, and an unremarkable, but pleasant, Mogul dish of curried chicken with rice. For weight-watchers, there's a special low calorie menu at $20.95. If you must have a dessert, go for the mango ice cream. An average lunch for two is $44; dinner $60 per couple.

Aurora
60 E. 49th St.
(Madison & Park Aves.)
692-9292

FRENCH

*Open Mon.-Thurs. noon-2:30 p.m. & 5:30 p.m.-
10 p.m., Fri.-Sat. noon-2:30 p.m. & 5:30 p.m.-
11 p.m., Sun. 1 p.m.-9 p.m. Closed Sun.in
summer. All major cards.*

This posh and expensive eatery enters the
1990s with Andrew Wilkinson in charge of the
kitchen. He cooks "contemporary Continental," and over time he will modify the menu,
but we see no changes since the recent management turnover, except for a very modest
reduction in the super-high prices. So, if $38
for a top entrée seems just too much, but $35
sounds better, you're in luck.

Once you pass under the postmodern canopy, you will find yourself in a comfortable,
wood-paneled dining room with large leather
armchairs, elegant table settings and delicate,
tasteful flowers. The crowd reflects the clubby
atmosphere: middle-aged businessmen with
their clients and their dolled-up wives, young
couples from Wall Street and an occasional
bohemian, just to take the edge off things. We
like the horseshoe-shaped bar in the middle,
a good place for a person alone to enjoy a
meal. We have had very uneven meals here,
but have enjoyed the following: for starters,
the curried oyster soup with asparagus tips,
the tart of wild mushrooms and lobster,
sautéed foie gras, and tartar of fresh and
smoked salmon. We've adored the halibut
steak and the broiled lobster, the roasted
squab with marinade, cured duck leg in broth
with vegetables and duck breast with port
sauce.

You should enjoy dessert. Perhaps try the
granite of Zinfandel or Pinot Noir (whatever's
up that day) with berries; for a heartier sweet,
go for a warm tart or a simple baked apple
infused with apricot sauce. Chocolate-lovers
will find that the chocolate torte brings them
to their knees. For the curious, we suggest the
lavender ice cream, when available. The wine
list is intelligently thought out, with many
intriguing bottles beckoning. Now, if only the
bill were not so special—it, too, can take away
your breath (at those heights, perhaps it's the
lack of oxygen that does it). Figure $160 per
couple, plus tax and tip, plus the price of
exploring beyond the basics of the wine list.

12/20 The Barclay
Hotel Inter-Continental,
111 E. 48th St.
(Park & Lexington Aves.)
421-0836

AMERICAN

Open daily 7 a.m.-11:30 p.m. All major cards.

You could be anywhere in the world, in any
good hotel. The expensive decor—clublike
America, circa 1900, with striking portraits,
plus a semiprivate dining area on an upper
level near a marble fireplace—is rather
gloomy. This excellent hotel chain often features fine restaurants, but here in New York,
the competition overwhelms the Barclay's sincere efforts. The menu, notable for its light
fare and seafood, is nourishing but not memorable. Lunch is livelier than dinner; at night,
the restaurant is mainly inhabited by lonely
guests or people here on business and indifferent about what they eat. Alexander Feher,
executive chef since 1983, is not an indifferent
man. One thing he insists on is that his kitchen
pursue produce both market-fresh and seasonal.

The menu changes regularly, often daily
(thanks to computers and laser printers), and
will scare no one. It also stars numerous dishes
that are designed with lower sodium and cholesterol levels. Among the appetizers, the
cured duck "ham" with cranberry relish and
kiwi shines. When available, try the smoked
lobster sausage with braised cabbage. The
goose liver with leeks and truffles is heavy, but
good, if you want to go that route. The salads
belong in a cafeteria: iceberg lettuce, romaine
and the likes (the Caesar salad is prepared
tableside), but we recently have enjoyed an
arugula-and-endive salad at lunchtime. The
menu offers several soups. Among the fish,
choose the sautéed baby angler fish with Pinot
Noir sauce and pearl onions. We haven't had
luck with the steak (which is tasteless), but
recommend the medallions of venison served
on apples and black currants. For dessert,
people seem to enjoy the raspberry black-for-
est cake and the chocolate-truffle cake with
strawberry coulis. So much for a low-calorie,
low-cholesterol meal. The wine list has 145
selections (40-percent American) and a good
inventory; although markups are high, there

are 27 half bottles offered. Without a bottle of Lafite, expect to pay about $110 per couple for dinner, less if you go before 7 p.m. for the fixed-price pretheater meal ($36).

Bice
7 E. 54th St. (Madison & Fifth Aves.)
688-1999; Fax 752-1329

ITALIAN

Open daily noon-3 p.m. & 6 p.m.-11:30 p.m. Closed Sun. in July & Aug. Cards: AE, MC, V.

Bice hasn't exactly slowed down or calmed down since its trendsetting opening in 1987. There's no arguing with success, and if the kitchen is a little uneven, write it off to the number of meals they must turn out. The couture crowd and associated made-up faces and hot celebs still pack themselves into big and handsome Bice (pronounced bee-tchay) and give it an identity. The large, sleek room bespeaks snappy Milan design as well—a long curved bar with white Italian marble, multi-level seating, expensive wood chairs, striped banquettes, deep-green-and-beige plaid carpeting, bright lighting and exquisite flower arrangements. The earthy Italian color scenes and the lighting create an upscale sense of vitality. Bice teems with vitality—everybody rushes around, including, sometimes, the staff.

We admire the talent and cooking of Marta Pulini, who shares the job of chef. When she hits top form, her pastas and risottos soar. The long and comprehensive menu changes daily. We like the Tuscan bean-and-pasta soup, when available, garlicky and beguilingly bracing. All those models seem to enjoy the various salad antipasti, though the components, from avocado, hearts of palm, Parmigiano, tomato and basil, too often lack deep and pure flavors. Also, when olive oil is doled out, it seems to arrive either in floodgate quantities or in a mere trickle. Among salads, we liked the lobster and arugula version. Friends adored the various risottos (with seafood, or black with baby squids, or with arugula, radicchio and bacon, for some examples). We found the homemade pasta offerings a bit more problematic, the sauces sometimes not up to the dough. We thought the best of the lot the homemade macaroni with radicchio and bacon, and the light lobster ravioli. For a main course, consider the salmon in a poppy crust or lamb tenderloin. Of the desserts, we

like the ricotta cheesecake with pine nuts and raisins, and the apple pie with homemade gelati. The 180-item wine list has interesting and reasonably priced Italian offerings to help one while away the time between courses. Or, you can spend the time, like many others, smiling and nodding at familiar faces across the room. Just don't think about the bill. About $140 per couple for dinner; $90 for lunch for two, plus tax and tip.

Bukhara
148 E. 48th St.
(Lexington & Third Aves.)
838-1811

INDIAN

Open daily noon-3 p.m. & 6 p.m.-11 p.m. All major cards.

Bukhara, with cuisine described as "frontier" food of northwest India, is a little hard to find, since it hides behind the facade of the Helmsley Middletowne Hotel. You'll be impressed by the large, attractive dining room, done in Indian country style—plaster walls with lots of beaten brass and colorful woven wall hangings. Don't look for the usual Indian fare at this Indian equivalent of a grill. The cooking style, said to originate with semi-migrant tribes in Peshawar (now Pakistan), revolves around charcoal-grilling or roasting food that has been marinated in yogurt and spices. Every entrée on the limited menu reflects this, many made in the tandoor ovens which you can see behind a glass partition. Don't look for silverware either (though they will produce it if you ask), for here you are meant to eat with your fingers or use your bread to scoop up the delicious dal. Actually, it can be fun, rather like a barbecue, especially if you are with a group of friends all doing the same thing. You prepare yourself by using the hot, moist handtowels handed around after you're seated, as well as the gigantic checkered cotton bib-*cum*-napkin you next receive. The latter will really come in handy; ask for a second one for your lap.

The tandoor chefs produce some terrific breads, including the astounding bukhara naan, which is meant for your whole party to rip into; as big as a table, it arrives sprinkled with tasty onion seeds, and should be used for scooping, wrapping, dipping and everything else you do when you don't have a knife and fork. Also try the khasta roti, a whole-wheat flatbread with toasted cumin seeds. One irresistible nan resembles a pizza; it's a flat bread loaded with garlic, tomatoes and cheese. Instead of one of the appetizers on the newly expanded menu, nibble on the fabulous breads, perhaps dipped into the mint-ginger chutney you will find on your table. For the best-entrée award, we choose the chicken Bukhara, a whole bird marinated in yogurt, chili, garlic and ginger, then roasted in the tandoor so it is meltingly tender, yet moist. It is cut into parts, so four can share this dish nicely with, say, dal as a side dish. We've also enjoyed the roasted leg of lamb (peshawari boti), the lamb kebabs (seekh kebab) and the tiger prawns Bukhara, jumbo shrimp marinated in an ajwain-flavored yogurt, blended with Asian spices and toasted in the shell. Drink beer (Indian or domestic) as the ideal beverage for this food, although you could choose from the small, serviceable wine list. Service is congenial, if not always sharp. For the best and most appropriate dessert, ask for a frozen orange crème served in a scooped-out orange shell (for this, you get a spoon.) Lunch and dinner menus are the same; ordering à la carte, you will average about $50 per couple for lunch, $70 for dinner for two.

11/20 Chalet Suisse

6 E. 48th St. (Fifth Ave.)
355-0855

SWISS

Open Mon.-Fri. noon-2:30 p.m. & 5 p.m.-9:30 p.m. Closed Aug. All major cards.

If you're hankering for a fondue or for a nostalgic glimpse of folkoric Swiss costumes (modeled by the waitresses), head straight for this flagbearer of traditional Swiss cuisine that has become agreeably stuck in time, say 1967. Chalet Suisse is tucked away on 48th Street with an entrance that's difficult to find. The dark interior is dramatically defined by heavy white arches, and Swiss folk items adorn the walls.

Among the appetizers is a very good cervelat salad, quite vinegary. Marinated herring is just as tasty, and authentically prepared. Steer clear of the heavy onion pie and the bland pâté maison. The entrées represent a mixture of French and Italian-Swiss cuisine, and the fish dishes are the best—try the red snapper, freshly prepared with a piquant, rather than sweet, dill sauce. Each entrée comes with a

choice of Rösti, Spätzle or rice. Choose the Spätzle, a small, irregular noodle which goes well with some of the heavier dishes. On the à la carte side, a wonderful appetizer is Bündnerfleisch, very fine slices of dried beef. Bratwurst and liver, and kidney à la Swiss in a wine sauce, are both recommended. On a cold winter's night, try a cheese fondue, a pleasant, simple dish to have after the movies or the theater. Desserts are what you'd expect them to be: Swiss apple tart, carrot cake, mousse au chocolat and ice cream. Try, instead, a plate of Swiss cheeses, excellent if someone has remembered to take them out of the refrigerator for at least an hour before dinner. There's a fair listing of wines on the expensive side. Average price per couple, with wine, is $90.

Le Chantilly

106 E. 57th St.
(Park & Lexington Aves.)
751-2931

FRENCH

Open Mon.-Fri. noon-3 p.m. & 5:30 p.m.-10 p.m., Sat. 5:30 p.m.-11 p.m. All major cards.

Early in 1990, when Le Chantilly was about to make a move on the top-rank French restaurants by bringing in talented André Gaillard, that young chef who brought La Réserve to prominence died tragically. So, Le Chantilly's well-heeled clients will continue ordering luxury-liner comforts of classical French cooking at this long-established restaurant. Proprietor Camille Dulac signed up Bruno Chemel as chef in the summer of 1990, so things may be looking up. The old-world dining room works: misty murals of the château of Chantilly seem to blend into dulcet, pale-green walls. Banquettes and chairs, upholstered in hunter-green tapestry with a floral pattern, contribute to the graceful, feminine tone. In the past, the kitchen's output arrived with sound predictability—from terrine of duck foie gras and ravioli stuffed with diced snails, tomato and shiitake mushrooms, to noisettes of lamb sautéed with dill and green peppercorns. Popular trends have lightened the menu somewhat, and now you can order raw marinated salmon, red tuna and bass with dill-and-endive salad as an appetizer, or a red snapper sautéed with sesame oil and served with crisped vegetables. We've also enjoyed the Maine lobster broiled with Thai herbs. We look forward fully to the arrival of some new dishes. Mocha layer cake, strawberry tart and St-Honoré are among the long-standing desserts. Figure $130 per couple for dinner, with wine.

Chez Louis
1016 Second Ave. (53rd & 54th Sts.)
752-1400

FRENCH
Open Mon.-Fri. 11:45 a.m.-3 p.m. & 6 p.m.-midnight, Sat. 6 p.m.-midnight, Sun. 5 p.m.-10 p.m. All major cards.

Karen and David (as in David's Cookies) Liederman run one of the better bistros in a suddenly bistro-mad city. Established a few years back, this straightforward, low-frills (by design) eatery was given its name in frank homage to deceased Antoine Magnin's legendary Paris bistro, L'Ami Louis. The name wears well in this comfortable and casual place. Though seemingly dedicated to serving hearty French-bistro fare, they really concentrate here on large portions of roasted and grilled foods, and, as of late, low-cholesterol options. Will that be the bistro of the 1990s? As appropriate in a true bistro, posters adorn the walls, though here the walls are painted in red lacquer, giving it the look of a simple bistro in front and Chinese bordello in back.

For starters, have one of the best onion soups you'll ever eat, gratinéed, a bit sweet, rich, and supremely satisfying. We declare as another highlight the increasingly well-known crusty chicken for two, Chez Louis's signature dish, a deceptively simple item never easy to find at all on the restaurant circuit, let alone this good. He serves it with an outrageously rich-and-buttery potato pie—a thick, crisp pancake (when it's not too greasy) with bits of garlic and parsley strewn on top. We also loved the roast poussin, or squab chicken, which came the same way, though more diminutive, and with addictive angel-hair-thin fried onion rings, which many tables order to nibble with drinks. Other trencherman dinner offerings include roast suckling pig, veal rib with roast vegetables, and roast prime rib steak. But how's the cassoulet? This is touted to be a bistro, after all! Well, the cassoulet tastes mostly of garlic. A changing variety of mostly French and American wines comes by the glass as well as by the bottle, most well-chosen and fairly priced. Lunch averages $50

to $60 per couple; dinner will run between $80 and $100 for two, unless you overindulge.

Chikubu
12 E. 44th St.
(Fifth & Madison Aves.)
818-0715

JAPANESE
Open Mon.-Fri. 11:30 p.m.- 2 p.m. & 5:30 p.m-10:30 p.m., Sat. 5:30 p.m.-10:30 p.m. Cards: AE, DC.

Cleanly modern, if austere, Chikubu aims for the Japanese community, specializing in the cuisine of Kyoto (including broiled fish and casseroles). You can sit at the tables and order any number of dishes from a regular menu (in English as well as Japanese), or sit at the counter, where the chef creates a meal for you if you say "omakase, kudasai," meaning "the chef's choice, please." Then relax and enjoy. You can enjoy traditional kaiseki cuisine, or banquet meal, in the four tatami rooms upstairs or in the long, sleek dining room, though it helps ordering if you speak Japanese.

Among the things that might appear when you say the magic word, "omakase," are a delicious whole raw fish, its flesh chopped tartar-fashion with scallions and horseradish, and reassembled minus the skin; miso soup with bits of poached chicken; morsels of octopus; an exquisite steamed dish of freshwater eel with burdock, lightly bound with egg white; a small, grilled whole river fish with a green-vinegar sauce; a tempura dish of shrimp balls and lotus root with mysterious and delicious batter-dipped flowers; fried bean curd in mirin broth; and a windup of delicious rice steamed with shrimps, clams, scallops and pickled vegetables. You may also order regular sushi and sashimi, both at the counter and at the table (at lunch), but the surprise and inventiveness of "omakase" should be the real reason for coming here. Other dishes we've enjoyed include steak cooked on a hot stone, fried pork cutlets and broiled eel. If you insist on dessert, try the pumpkin pudding. Anticipate communication gaps. Prices run a huge gamut, from about $40 per couple at lunch to $80 to $150 for two at dinner, if you let the chefs fully exercise their talents.

Chin Chin
216 E. 49th St.
(Second & Third Aves.)
888-4555

CHINESE

Open Mon.-Fri. 11:30 a.m.-11:30 p.m., Sat.-Sun 5 p.m.-11:30 p.m. All major cards.

We can't vouch for the culinary authenticity of this new-wave Chinese restaurant, but we can attest to its genuine merits and charms as a westernized midtown-east quality establishment. The Chin duo (Jimmy and Wally), who give their names to the restaurant, are savvy, professional owners and hosts. Chef Chin Hin Kuen offers imaginative Taiwanese fare that respects the traditional dishes, but includes on the menu other contemporary interpretations such as vegetable-duck pie and veal with spicy peppercorn sauce. The place doesn't look like a standard Chinese restaurant, either, but rather a Californian bistro. Sepia-tone photographic portraits of the extended Chin family provide the unifying decorative detail in the three dining rooms, done mostly in clean wood tones and peach colors.

An excellent wine list, carefully chosen to marry well with the menu, also sets Chin Chin apart. Divisions of the extensive and readable menu include the usual categories and Peking duck dinner (recommended at $26 per person). For appetizers, we love the shrimp dumplings, shredded roast-duck salad (on a bed of rice noodles), and snails with coriander-and-garlic broth. Crispy sea bass (with a powerful glaze), crisped orange beef and country chicken with spinach get the nod among many sound, if not scintillating, entrées. If you want desserts, try the usual ice cream, sorbet or fruit. Figure $80 a couple for the whole show, with wine, plus tax and tip.

La Côte Basque
5 E. 55th St. (Fifth & Madison Aves.)
688-6525

FRENCH

Open Mon.-Sat. noon-2:30 p.m. & 6 p.m.-10:30 p.m. All major cards.

A once-elegant enclave of French dining that has lost its charm, La Côte Basque, by failing in its culinary output, risks becoming something of a dinosaur. If it were a new restaurant, we would simply call it a good, old-fashioned—okay, let's say 1950s/1960s-style classic French restaurant—but we're talking about a New York institution, with devoted and aging regulars who think they are eating well, but who observe the large portions or the pretty room rather than the sameness of sauces or other troubling signs on the plate. The interior, recreating the outdoor scenes of a harbor village in the Basque country with the help of colorful murals and rustic post beams, still brings a sense of gaiety to the restaurant, but the sloppiness and flippant manner of the waiters dims the light. A guest is lucky if his waiter rattles off the specials of the day; luckier still if he proffers the wine list. And the wait for a first course that was most likely composed, in large or full part, hours before, seems interminable.

If you can pay more than the prix fixe, you'll find the foie gras delightfully rich and satisfying, but a promising ratatouille with seafood, also costly, tastes cold from the refrigerator and the thick vinaigrette that surrounds the crab and lobster seems too sweet. We found the most successful appetizer, by far, to be an innovative fan of delicately poached skate served at room temperature on airy tomato coulis. We also loved the soups, created with a kind hand, especially a sprightly lobster bisque and creamy fresh pea soup, both unpretentious and hot. Not so with one of the restaurant's "signature" main courses: chef Rachou's cassoulet. He provides you with insipid beans, lacking complexity and goose fat, surrounded by indistinguishable pieces of stringy meat and sausage, serving the whole thing tepid. Uninspired, too, is the oft-ordered English grilled sole—its mustardy sauce has an overly eggy base—just boring, albeit very fresh. The kitchen smothers sweetbreads in a brown hunter-type sauce with pungent morels and other wild mushrooms. Unfortunately, its accompaniment of peas and carrots formed into a little timbale and called "Maintenon de Petites Légumes," is flavorless. When we recently ordered the steak au poivre, which is supposed to be flambéed with Armagnac, it came, bigger than a brick, almost burned. You may have to wait a precious minute or two for your steak knife and the steak's creamy sauce; we tasted Armagnac in there, somewhere, raw and unpleasant. At dessert time, waiters arbitrarily decide which desserts they will present to which tables. You might therefore miss out on an excellent opera cake and be stuck with a cloyingly sweet, heavy chocolate mousse. The staff puts the desserts on the plates with nonchalance and serve up anything-but-delicate petits fours with the coffee. Espresso, full-bodied, steaming-hot and delicious, fills a triple-size demi-tasse. The cost for dinner for two may surprise; although the prix-fixe sets you back only $55 per person (lunch, $32), the showy wine list is extremely expensive, and, with a bottle of Chambolle Musigny, you'll end up spending about $220 for two, including tax and tip.

 ## Le Cygne
55 E. 54th St. (Madison Ave.)
759-5941

FRENCH

Open Mon.-Fri. noon-2:30 p.m. & 6 p.m.-10:30 p.m., Sat. 6 p.m.-11 p.m. Closed Aug. All major cards.

Now into its third decade, a goodly period for a New York restaurant, Le Cygne keeps up with the times admirably well, and satisfies loyal clientele with ever-increasing quality. Owners Michel Crouzillat and Gérard Gallian have steered their restaurant to a new level, thanks to the recruitment of a top chef in 1988. A couple of years earlier, they took care of the look of their restaurant by moving to the brownstone next door to the original place, and expanding into three dining rooms over two floors. If you want serenely postmodern—muted lighting and toned-down peach-and-gray walls, misty wildflower murals and bountiful bouquets—ask for the main room. Upstairs, the macho executive wine room retains a medieval feel with its wood beams, clay-tiled floors and brick walls.

Chef Jean-Michel Bergougnoux, who joined in 1988 from Lutèce (and worked prior to that as chef of La Régence), has infused a rather stodgy menu with new life, adding fine seafoods and game, and contemporary and subtle preparations. On one of our many dinners here, we liked the tartar of raw salmon and sea bass with truffled oil dressing for a cool and clean starter, as well as the oysters on the half shell, served with a special dressing. Even better, we thought, was the hot and cold rabbit with mushroom mousse, a more challenging opener. For a fish course, we've found the turbot very good, and recommend both the brandade of cod with crisp potatoes and thyme, and the fresh salmon with lentils and

parsley. We can rave about the boned pigeon, glazed with honey vinegar and served with a buckwheat crêpe and a sour-cream flan. For meat, consider rabbit or venison when available, but we point first to a simple veal chop, sautéed in light white-wine sauce and served with glazed vegetables. Friends also liked the sliced duck breast with sweet-and-sour spices, and heavenly mashed potatoes with sesame.

Do save some room for dessert, though we find it a notch below the rest of the offerings. The restaurant is known for its soufflé au citron (a $12.50 supplement for two), in which a sweet, dark raspberry sauce subdues the lemon. Some of us find that sauce too sweet. Although the apple tart is touted, we find it a bit bland, and nothing special compared with what's available elsewhere. In the past, we have enjoyed the rich, dark chocolate cake, which is served with a nicely tart orange sauce. Le Cygne has an extensive wine collection, developed over the years, with an assortment of fairly priced Bordeaux and Burgundies. Ever-popular with the well-suited (jacket and tie obligatory for men), Le Cygne not only requires reservations, but "gladly appreciates cancellations, even on short notice." Lunch has a fixed price of $35 and dinner $58, but with all the supplements, plus wine and coffee, expect to pay $100 per couple for lunch, and $140 for two at dinner, plus tax and tip.

 ## Dawat
210 E. 58th St.
(Second & Third Aves.)
355-7555

INDIAN

Open Mon.-Thurs. 11:30 a.m.- 3 p.m. & 5:30 p.m.-11 p.m., Fri.-Sat. 11:30 a.m.-3 p.m. & 5:30 p.m.-11:30 p.m. All major cards.

The word "dawat" means "an invitation to a feast" in Urdu, and that is the operative phrase at this airily attractive Indian restaurant, with pretty, pale turquoise-and-peach lacquered walls, discreet lighting and comfortable banquettes. A glass-enclosed tandoor kitchen occupies one back corner, where a cheerful chef produces nans, rotis, kulchas, parathas and other tandoori dishes. Well-known cooking teacher/food writer/actress Madhur Jaffrey has designed the appealingly diverse menu, which includes a sprinkling of the tried-and-true—mulligatawny soup, samosas and the like—and then a number of dishes with extraordinary flavor levels. The chances are overwhelmingly good that you will have a very good meal, though we find this esteemed Indian restaurant a notch off its former standard of cooking and service since the opening of its surburban outpost in Westchester, and the dining room's charms have faded some.

Read the provocative menu, best done leisurely over a drink, while you nibble on the welcoming plate of airy pappadums, dipped in the accompanying savory mint chutney. Starters include beautifully executed samosas and Jaffrey's baghari jinga, moist shrimp flavored with garlic, mustard seeds and the highly aromatic curry leaves. Don't miss the dahi aloo poori, a mouthwatering mixture of small homemade crisps, diced potatoes and chickpeas in a light yogurt-and-tamarind sauce. We especially enjoy the bhaja, crisp light fritters made with whole spinach leaves and potato skins. We find outstanding the reshmi kebab, meltingly tender cubes of chicken that have been marinated in yogurt and ginger, then roasted in the tandoor, so that they arrive sizzling at your table. If you have a hard time deciding, order the mixed grill, so you can taste a lot of meats, but be forewarned: it's uneven in quality. Rather choose the excellent goat with rice. Jaffrey's Parsee-style patra-ni-machhi, salmon smothered in a sublime fresh coriander chutney and steamed in a banana leaf, is positively super. For a tasty, yet mild, dish, try keema matar, ground lamb with peas, ginger and browned onions. Vegetarians will love the imaginative dishes here, such as the deliciously smooth sarson ka sag, a buttery purée of mustard greens, a Punjabi winter dish meant to be scooped up with the traditional flat cornmeal bread that comes with it. Or order the unusual moong dal of yellow peas, cooked with spinach and flavored with fennel seeds; or bhindi masala, okra flavored with browned onions and dried mango; or superlative baked eggplant, with the elusive sweet-sour note of tamarind sauce. For a side dish, order the vegetable biryani, rice baked with nubbins of vegetables, raisins and nuts, a wonderful complement to all these dishes. Dawat offers some very good desserts, including coconut or mango ice cream; the traditional Indian ice cream, kulfa; sweet cottage cheese dumplings and a nice rice pudding. Though

beer is usually the call with Indian food, it can be bloating, and with the refined preparations here, wine goes very well. A refreshing cup of Darjeeling may be all you need. Dinner averages $76 per couple, considerably less for the lunch special, one of the better buys in the city.

Felidia
243 E. 58th St. (Second Ave.)
758-1479

ITALIAN

Open Mon.-Fri. noon-2 p.m. & 5:30 p.m.-11 p.m., Sat. 5 p.m.-11 p.m. Closed 1st 3 weeks in July. All major cards.

Enthusiasm reigns over everything here, from proprietors Lydia and Felix Bastinach's love of food, to the mouth-watering descriptions of the day's special pasta recited by them or the maître d'. We think it funny how things come together in New York to make a longstanding, good Italian restaurant. Lydia and Felix hail not from Italy proper, but from Istria, in the Yugoslavian-Italian border region, and their everyday chef bears the name Edgar Torres. We find the dining room in this two-story restaurant, with exposed brick walls and hanging plants, an abrupt, but winning combination of rustic and elegant. For many, this is a wine destination, with over 700 Italian wines, many of them displayed along the brick walls.

To begin, octopus with warm potatoes in a vinaigrette sets the stage for a challenging and rewarding meal. We like, among the many excellent appetizers, pastas and risottos, broiled fresh porcini on a bed of polenta, unequaled in its earthy, authentic flavor. Our taste buds declare the fuzi with broccoli di rape or with a pheasant sauce, and the papardelle integrale alle verdure (large flat pasta with vegetable sauce) toothsome wonders. Return to try the pasutice all' Istriana (diamond-shaped pasta with seafood). The extensive and intriguing menu offers such specialties as roasted baby goat with fresh peas, tender calf's liver in a delicate wine sauce with lots of onion, Florentine tripe in a succulent fresh tomato sauce, saltimbocca alla romana and feather-light fried calamari. Some think Lydia's veal chops, stuffed with savory broccoli di rape, so thick they look like steak, and taste like veal fed on cream rather than on milk. Be forewarned, however, that the kitchen can be a bit inconsistent, and the food, in general, on the heavy side. We liked the zuppa di pesce, light without being briny, and filled generously with chunks of fish and seafood. Try the red snapper with polenta or the monkfish with mustard sauce, both hearty and fresh-tasting. We recently enjoyed the homemade-style roast chicken (casalinga) with crisp skin and herbs, tossed with fried potatoes and onions, and ringed with red peppers. We liked many desserts here, as well as choosing one of the excellent, though expensive, Barolo wines with some bottle age. For lunch, expect to pay about $100 to $120 per couple, and for dinner $120 to $140 for two, plus tax and tip and the potential to spend much more on wine.

The Four Seasons

99 E. 52nd St.
(Park & Lexington Aves.)
754-9494, 754-1027

ECLECTIC
Open Mon.-Sat. noon-2:30 p.m. & 5 p.m.-11:30 p.m. All major cards.

At The Four Seasons, the elegant restaurant located in New York's only Mies van der Rohe building, the food is usually good (though, on occasion, we've found the food to be dreadful, we'll not comment beyond that). We've found the service always superb, and the spot perennially popular and respected as a culinary institution exuding power and maintaining high standards. At lunch, financial and political power brokers dining at the grill decide the city's fate, and publishers decide what you'll read next. The spectacular dining room around the pool, with its atmosphere of luxurious discretion, has not changed in years, but still makes a good impression. The menu changes every season, if not every day (the menu bears the date), and some of the creations of chefs Stefano Battistini and Christian "Hitsch" Albin are superb, such as crisped shrimp with mustard fruit or the soup of watercress and black-eyed peas. The crayfish ravioli is as light as air, but the delicate cream sauce falls flat, uninspired. If you go for the Spa Cuisine, featuring dishes such as grilled fennel, leeks and radicchio salad, or mussels with mango-and-cilantro salsa, or veal escalope or grilled swordfish, you'll not find it as enjoyable as the classic menu. Even if you are on a diet, we suggest splurging for one night and indulging, for example, in the superb calf's liver with braised Maui onions, or a succulent pink roasted rack of lamb with tarragon. Perhaps, choose the crabmeat cakes with mustard sauce and fried capers. We found the Dover sole meunière exceptionally fresh-tasting, and the côte de boeuf for two, a thick, juicy rib roast, as tender as can be. Vegetables and salads of the highest quality arrive beautifully prepared. If you're having the crisp farmhouse duck au poivre, you should insist on tender, braised endives for an accompaniment. They're big on tableside preparation here. It may show off the staff's skills, but we think that old practice is simply better left to the professional hands in the kitchen these days. It makes for a good show, maybe once, to see steak tartare prepared by the captain (at The Four Seasons, we trust the ingredients sight unseen), but who needs it? We want to eat the stuff, not bless it.

Those of you with sweet tooths will love the Four Seasons' desserts, one of its greatest strengths. The chocolate cake cannot be bettered in preparation and richness. If you don't go for luscious fresh fruit, such as raspberries with cream, try the raspberry soufflé. Prices for the wine offerings, international and reasonably extensive, range from $15 to $500 with steep markups and, too frequently, they've run out of what we order. The pretheater dinner averages $120 for two and is a good value. For lunch, expect to pay $140 to $150 per couple, and for dinner, $200 for two at this big-league establishment.

12/20 Gloucester House

37 E. 50th St.
(Madison & Park Aves.)
755-7394

AMERICAN/SEAFOOD
Open Mon.-Fri. noon -3 p.m. & 5:30 p.m.-10 p.m., Sat. noon-10 p.m. All major cards.

Gloucester House stands like a fortress on 50th Street. Not much changes at this bastion for male executives entertaining their male clients; it is almost as if it was suspended in time. The house motto still seems to be "Fine Ingredients at Astronomical Prices." The decor remains "Cape Cod," as imagined by a city restaurant designer years ago: captain's chairs at bare wood tables, and nautical motifs adding "atmosphere"; all this is wears a bit thin in these "contemporary" times, but this place doesn't change for the sake of change. If you order judiciously, you can have a fine meal. The soups (bisques, chowders and broths) are not really up to snuff, so you'll do better by sticking to raw clams or oysters as appetizers. They are as fresh as you'll find, as is all the fish and seafood. Red snapper, striped bass, Dover sole, flounder and their relatives are broiled to perfection, and if they were not served with overcooked vegetables (spinach is the exception), you'd forget the price. To accompany your meal, you'll have to get by with a selection from an unremarkable list of American and French wines. At meal's end, the American desserts (such as apple pie, strawberry shortcake and so on) tend to be overly sweet, and are served in portions big enough for two. The pecan pie, served with a sugarless whipped cream, will, however, surely satisfy any sweet tooth. Expect to pay $110 per couple, plus the obligatory tax and tip.

La Grenouille

3 E. 52nd St. (Fifth & Madison Aves.)
752-1495

FRENCH

Open Tues.-Sat. noon-2:30 p.m. & 6 p.m.-11:30 p.m. Closed Aug.-Labor Day. All major cards.

Having dinner in a French restaurant in the 1950s and early 1960s was the be-all, and usually end-all, of nighttime New York romance. La Grenouille will send you back to that era with panache. Its pretty dining room has hardly changed since the restaurant opened in 1962. Banquettes in—what else?—red velvet line the walls of this small, flower-filled and stolid restaurant. (Famous for its sensational flower bouquets, La Grenouille has set the standard for other restaurants in this matter.) We felt the tables too close to each other, close enough that you might be tempted to pick a morsel from your neighbors' plate or participate in the discussion about their latest merger. The elegant, aging clientele feels noticeably at home in this bourgeois setting, comforted by a menu of classics, with an occasional surprise or two. *Amuse-gueules*, which on one visit were small squares of golden, flaky dough served with drinks, prove irresistible. You may find yourself gobbling a couple of freshly baked rolls, too, while you wait for your first course.

Excellently prepared ravioli arrive stuffed with chunks of toothsome lobster, but a bland tomato coulis fails to stand up to the lobster's intensity. Called a gâteau, delicate leaves of stewed cabbage, flavored with truffles, envelop a buttery, thick slice of foie gras—truly superb. Less inspired is a bundle of asparagus topped with flaky pastry and sauced with a piquant vinaigrette. Consider also the corn crêpe with chicken livers. For entrées, try the grilled sole, napped with an exquisite mustard sauce, sweet tasting and fresh. We also love the tender, stewed oxtails, abundant in their dark pool of wine sauce and served with buttery mashed potatoes. Friends swear by lamb, served rare with crisp, seared edges and a sprightly melange of Provençal herbs, but its accompaniment, a soggy, undercooked potato pancake, almost crawls in shame to the edge of your plate. We also rate highly the frogs' legs with garlic butter and tomatoes, and the salmon roasted in a meat sauce, as well as the pike dumplings done in the Lyon style. A finger bowl of lemon-water placed in front of each guest is a nice touch after the main course. Avoid the unimpressive cheese tray.

Dessert lovers will like the homemade sorbets and ice cream, but not the heavy île flottante, which doesn't float in its skimpy pool of overly sweet vanilla sauce. Instead of a standard Napoleon in a raspberry coulis, try the light Grand Marnier and chocolate soufflés. We declare the supreme dessert here, however, to be the tourte chaude au chocolat, a small round cake surrounded with delicious pure-chocolate sauce, served lukewarm. You'll find the wine list impressive and, on the whole, reasonably priced. A steady restaurant of this age has an inventory of French and American wines with considerable bottle age. Consider, for example, a Château L'Angelus 1978 ($60). With the prix fixe dinner at $68 (lunch prix fixe is $37.50), figure on spending about $195 for two, with wine and espresso.

Hatsuhana

17 E. 48th St.
(Madison & Park Aves.)
355-3345

JAPANESE

Open Mon.-Fri. 11:45 a.m.-2:30 p.m. & 5 p.m.-10 p.m., Sat. 5 p.m.-10 p.m. All major cards.

With the acceptance of raw fish and the rest of the Japanese diet by Americans, Hatsuhana went a bit commercial, opening a second restaurant and serving throngs at lunch. Long admired for presenting the freshest and finest of sushi, Hatshuhana's sushi bar (the bright restaurant has a long sushi bar on each of its two floors) remains one of the best destinations in New York, though gone are the days when you could relax, take your time and trust the sushi chef to lead you through an incredible experience—eating chopped tuna inside mountain potato, or small squares of seaweed still dotted with minuscule eggs. Gone today is the imaginative menu that listed dishes you'd never heard of; we now find everything here predictable, fast-paced and high priced.

However, if you are familiar with Japanese cuisine, can pronounce the names of dishes that you would like to have (that don't appear on the menu, such as uni—sea urchin—served on a shiso leaf), and have established a relationship with the sushi chef, you may still be surprised at how good Hatsuhana can be. Lots of Japanese enjoy and indulge themselves here. Worth tasting are the oshitashi (broiled fresh spinach prepared in a sesame-soy sauce), the avocado salad with salmon caviar, the vegetable sushi and the broiled eel wrapped in paper-thin cucumber served with a sweet sauce. Also, if at a table, order the teriyaki of salmon or a tempura. Makizushi from California, with its fake, rubbery "crab", should be avoided at all costs. If you don't feel like thinking, order the deluxe dinner ($34) for the works, but expect no surprises or special thrills. You don't eat desserts most of the time in Japanese restaurants, but if you insist, ask for the standard green-tea or red-bean ice cream with fresh fruit and yokan, a sweet paste. Hatsuhana has a full bar; saké followed by Japanese tea is *de rigueur*. Dinner will run about $90 per couple. (The other branch is at 237 Park Avenue, at 45th Street; 661-3400.)

12/20 **Inagiku**
Waldorf-Astoria Hotel,
111 E. 49th St.
(Park & Lexington Aves.)
355-0440
JAPANESE
Open Mon.-Fri. noon-2:30 p.m. & 5:30 p.m.-10 p.m., Sat. 5:30 p.m.-10 p.m. All major cards.
Inagiku is a Japanese restaurant that recalls a fifteenth-century shrine, but without the

grace of an open-air garden or the beauty of flowering plum trees. The golden walls bring some life to this rather dull and heavy-handed dining room, located in the basement of the Waldorf-Astoria. The tokonoma (the alcove found in all Japanese homes) boasts a skillful flower arrangement and a magnificent lacquered box. Waitresses in lovely blue-and-red kimonos glide silently among the noisy tables, attentive to your slightest wish. Inagiku is primarily a tempura restaurant, and at the central tempura bar, a crowd of chefs in superb maroon *happi* coats and black straw hats fry seafood, vegetables, and even flowers with amazing dexterity.

In the main restaurant, where you can see elegant Japanese businessmen entertaining, dinner may be chosen from a sample of three suggested menus: A, B and C. "A" is the one worth trying, as it offers choices of both sashimi and sushi, plus tempura or tender steak cooked on a large, red-hot stone. However, if you feel secure, it would be much better to switch to à la carte, or to go for the kaiseki dinner, a ten-course meal composed around the season, the chef's mood, and your waiter's judgment. If you have convinced him that you are fearless, you are in for an exciting experience.

For appetizers, try the satsuma-age (minced fish and crabmeat mixed with vegetables, lightly steamed and then deep-fried), or the very delicate chawan-mushi (egg custard with tiny morsels of fish, chicken and gingko nuts). The beef tataki (thin slices of tender beef quickly seared) is served with a tasty ponzu sauce. Another good appetizer is hirame usuzukuri, paper-thin slices of fluke served with soy sauce and grated pink radish. The tempura Inagiku is excellent, as is the very popular ishiyaki steak, cooked on a large stone with vegetables and bean curd. Dessert is what you'd expect in a New York Japanese restaurant: melon, oranges or green-tea ice cream. Dessert in the kaiseki dinner is usually a delightful, small cake of sweet azuki bean, wrapped in transparent, sweet seaweed jelly. The restaurant has a small, but fairly representative, wine list, plus Kirin beer, and two excellent sakés, one quite dry and one medium dry. Lunch will run around $60 for two, dinner around $90 per couple, plus tax and tip.

Lello

65 E. 54th St.
(Madison & Park Aves.)
751-1555

ITALIAN

Open Mon.-Fri. noon-3 p.m. & 5:30 p.m.-10:30 p.m., Sat. 5:30 p.m.-10:30 p.m. All major cards.

If you want a posh midtown restaurant, with comfortable northern and southern Italian offerings that won't confuse you, this is it. Velvet walls, banquettes, chandeliers, mirrors, subdued (dark?) lighting, formal tableware, tacky adornments, businessmen—you know the setting. You know the menu, too (which is almost identical to that of Lello's sister restaurant, Scarlatti). Yes, it can be boring, and the specials are nothing to get excited about, but once in a while, this is just the right spot. Good service and reliable cooking (now entering a second decade) gets our attention and respect.

Carpaccio makes a fine starter, and the fresh clams are superior to the tired baked-casino rendition. We think the kitchen tends to overcook the meats and vegetables, so try to get in a word with your waiter about it. We liked scampi ribelli (baked in mozzarella) and most of the seafood sauces. Try a grilled fish with oil and garlic. Friends thinks the desserts are serious, and there are plenty of Italian wines that will please you. However, prices and pretenses can run pretty high at what, in the end, is simply a good restaurant. Expect to pay at least $80 per couple for lunch and $110 for two at dinner, plus tax and tip.

Lutèce

249 E. 50th St.
(Second & Third Aves.)
752-2225, 752-2226

FRENCH

Open Tues.-Fri. noon-2 p.m. & 5:30 p.m.-9:45 p.m., Mon. & Sat. 5:30 p.m.-9:45 p.m. Closed Aug. All major cards.

The great André Soltner (and we do mean great) never leaves his restaurant. Whether out of pride, stubbornness or necessity, he is always there. Lutèce is closed for lunch on Saturdays, but call at 10:30 in the morning, and he's there answering the telephone. If we could have one culinary wish in New York, it would be to take chef Soltner out to dinner a dozen times in the coming year. He has been offering the same menu for years and could use some new ideas; he just hasn't eaten around enough to see and taste what has been going on in the exciting, contemporary culinary scene of the past couple of years. And we are certain that whatever we would find, he could do it better. That caveat aside, Lutèce is doing fine. You still have to book weeks, if not months, ahead to get a reservation, and most people walk away from Lutèce nodding their approval. That approval is fairly remarkable, considering that this favored temple of haute cuisine is a relatively modest restaurant. Lutèce is not very big, not very fancy, not really intimate or exciting; it is simply a fine restaurant that works, and works again.

What we are hearing more and more frequently about dining at Lutèce is that the food is very good, often excellent, but just not that memorable. The kitchen has had a few problems in recent years, and those seemingly have led to some inconsistency. First, Soltner's longtime aide-de-camp, chef de cuisine Christian Bertrand, left to open his own suburban restaurant, but talented chef Jean-Michel Bergougnoux came on board to replace him, only to decamp prematurely himself, in 1988, for Le Cygne. He has not been replaced at time of writing. Sweet and gentle Soltner cracks every whip in this restaurant, from running the kitchen and ordering the wine, to working in his chef's regalia as mâitre d'. It's amazing, but he pulls it off. He also secures the finest ingredients that can be had. As king of the hill, Soltner, with a huge network of suppliers, has first dibs on the finest produce available. Someone in Washington state calls when the first wild berries are ready, rare oysters are sent from three different spots in the Pacific, fish is shipped from the Paris market, as is foie gras from upper New York state and so on. Everything is prepared at the last possible moment.

Over the years, we have eaten remarkably well in the spruced-up, downstairs garden dining room (with slate floors and white latticework), as well as upstairs (in the more formal little dining room), and relatively affordably—the $38 prix-fixe lunch and the $60 dinner are good values. The superb bread and the Alsatian specialties remain compelling. The onion tart at lunch, the foie gras en brioche, snails à l'alsacienne, choucroute (blond sauerkraut) with pork and sausages, fresh trout in a cream sauce, dishes accompanied by noodles (also an Alsatian specialty), all define the genre. Hot saucisson en croûte (at lunch) continues to be light, and would be a find in Lyon; our only caveat with this—and other dishes—is that its presentation on a heavy white plate reminds us of a cafeteria meal. For great appetizers, we like the marinated salmon and the cold shrimp terrine. Order the special crab-and-potato pancakes, if they're available, and you'll know what all the fuss has been about. We declare the light, flavorful mussel soup something of a miracle, and we've rejoiced with the fish-and-crab soup. For an appetizer, also try the artichoke stuffed with mushrooms and saffron. If salmon mousse reminds you of cream cheese, lox and bagels, order Soltner's salmon with mousse of mustard for a revelation.

The kitchen manages fish deftly, so take your pick—perhaps the salmon or bass (for four) en croûte, or the special feuilleté of the day, any one of which is beyond the range of most restaurants. The puff pastry is perfection. Keep an eye open for scallop preparations as well, and when pigeon is a special, go for it. Perhaps the proof of the kitchen's excellence is the simple, bistro-style, baby chicken with herbs. We love the sweetbreads with capers and the standout spring lamb, braised and slowly simmered with garlic cloves, carrots, onions, tomatoes, turnips, celery and bay leaves, and served with irreproachable noodles. We've always had outstanding potatoes and side vegetables here. We've also been well pleased with the veal médaillons with morels and the heavier filet mignon with foie gras. Portions are human-size, not under- or overwhelming.

The old-time French service staff performs soundly, but is smug. Since we criticized the all-French wine list as being arrogantly below standard, it has been revised for the first time in twenty years. It's better, but still flawed in places, and now includes three American wines (for visiting French) among its 250 French offerings. Soltner seemingly doesn't care about vintages, because they are often wrong or on his short list, or simply not there. Desserts go a long way toward sending diners off in gastronomic bliss. The tarte tatin is a classic, and other worthy temptations include luscious and ever-changing fresh berries from around the world, fruit pies, hot and cold soufflés, ice cream, sorbet and a satisfying and moist chocolate cake, highlighted with orange. You can pay $100 per couple for lunch, and get away with $150 for two at dinner (plus tax and tip), but since this is one of the temples where you should worship without inhibition, expect to pay about $200 or more, per couple, at dinner.

 Mitsukoshi
461 Park Ave. (57th St.)
935-6444

JAPANESE
Open Mon.-Sat. noon-2 p.m. & 6 p.m.-10 p.m. All major cards.

Mitsukoshi has, for many years, remained the bastion of classic Japanese cuisine in New York, with the best sushi and sashimi in the city. Located beneath an elegant clothing store, the dining room's decor duplicates an old-fashioned eatery in Japan, allowing the clientele, Japanese tourists and businessmen, to feel at home. A sushi bar seats only about ten guests, so it's hard to get a seat without reservations; if you do, get to know one of the sushi chefs, and he'll treat you to slightly more playful fare, like fan-cut giant clam and sea urchin. The two dining areas are lit softly and are pleasant. Some of the top-quality seafood is flown in daily, direct from Japan. At lunchtime, shakodo bento, the traditional Japanese lunch box, changes every day; however, its elements are uninteresting. For something better, order a light, crisp tempura or kabayaki, imported eel broiled to perfection.

Dinner offerings include a grilled fish of the day, moist and fresh-tasting; shabu-shabu, a delightful and amusing dish consisting of simmering broth, in which diners dip paper-thin slices of beef and fancifully cut vegetables; and tempura. Of course, connoisseurs make a dinner out of the superb sushi, asking one of the chefs for his recommendations. The service is gracious and efficient. You'll probably spend about $90 for two for dinner.

Mondrian

7 E. 59th St. (Fifth & Madison Aves.)
935-3434

FRENCH/AMERICAN

Open Mon.-Fri. noon-2:30 p.m. & 6 p.m.-10:30 p.m., Sat. 6 p.m.-10:30 p.m. All major cards.

Everything is so perfect—the room, the artwork, the menu, the presentation, the service—but is it real? This elegant, and fine, restaurant, opened in 1988, named after the Dutch painter, Piet Mondrian, who lived (in the 1940s) in the building that houses the restaurant. Alas, the restaurant lacks a soul! That must explain why it hasn't yet caught on in a big way, because, otherwise, all the individual elements are there. Occupying the old Playboy Club space, Mondrian was designed, elegantly, by Philip George with a small bar up front and three dining areas, one leading into the next. There's plenty of oak on the walls, leather on the chairs, and art on the walls (Henry Moore, Joan Miró). The business types at lunch give the room more of a corporate air than it needs.

Though self-described as a French restaurant, a fusion of American, French and Italian cuisine takes place here, and chef Tom Colicchio's renditions of what is being called New American cooking are innovative and effective. He likes to layer contrasting flavor upon flavor, leaning toward light seafood preparations. Representative appetizers on the fixed-price luncheon ($34) and dinner ($56) menus include a tasty black-pasta ravioli with fresh-water prawns, a ceviche of oysters with a potato-caraway terrine, and a tuna-and-salmon tartare with a sea-urchin vinaigrette. Unlike the usual tartare, the latter consists, rather, of slices of intertwined tuna and salmon on top of a salad doused with the sea-urchin sauce. We also liked as an opener the room temperature terrine of leeks and oysters with truffle juice. Our friends like main courses such as the salmon with porcini crust and mushrooms "à la grecque," seared tuna with white beans and lemon confit, roasted lobster with coral-butter sauce and the saddle of lamb. You should try also the venison with barley-and-sweet-potato feuilleté with apples, or the absolutely super halibut special, sautéed with vegetables.

We have enjoyed great desserts here, such as the banana tart with coconut ice cream, Flor-entines and caramel sauce. Absolutely tops! The chocolate-hazelnut dacquoise is not to be sneezed at, either. The French and American wine list contains nearly 200 wines, from $13 to $165. The Burgundy selection (about 80 wines), in particular, is enticing. They charge $3.50 for an espresso and $4 for a cappuccino on top of the fixed price, but you'll probably need a digestif as well, so be prepared to pay no less than $100 to $120 per couple at lunch and $160 for two at dinner.

Il Nido

251 E. 53rd St.
(Second & Third Aves.)
753-8450

ITALIAN

Open Mon-Sat. noon-2:30 p.m. & 5:30 p.m.-10:30 p.m. All major cards.

We like many things about ten-year-old and reliable Il Nido. One of the first Manhattan restaurants to serve northern Italian food in a serious setting, Il Nido still appeals to the diner with its Tuscan country decor of plaster walls and half timbering, comfortable banquettes and thick carpeting. The 250-item wine list still excites, and so does the thoughtful service. We think the food and prices rank high, although we can't feel thrilled with the static quality of the encyclopedic menu. One of the nicest things about Il Nido is that you can ask to be fed well, and the owner, Addi Giovanetti, and his capable staff, notably maître d' Tony Rossini, will suggest a meal strategy, making a genuine effort to work around how you feel. And if how you feel is not on the menu, they'll make anything within reason for you, a kind of personal service found in few restaurants today. Il Nido has always served the best ravioli malfatti (literally "badly made ravioli," a lenten dish so-called for having no outer pasta), feather-light dumplings of cheese and spinach in a fresh tomato sauce. A half-portion makes a good starter. The carpaccio (a combination of beef, raw salmon and artichokes) has the best green sauce around, but would do nicely without the artichokes. We liked the crostini di polenta with mushrooms and nubbins of chicken liver, and the capelli d'angelo, angel-hair pasta with seafood. You can also order the risotto Nido (an assortment) for a starter. For main courses, rely on any of the fish dishes or simply grilled meats, such as the fine veal chop. Perhaps indulge in the fritto misto for two (sweet-breads, veal, lamb, brains, liver) or opt for the simpler veal scallops with prosciutto, spinach and white wine. We've enjoyed the broiled scampi with anchovies and capers. For dessert here, do try and save some room for the excellent homemade gelati, served with a knockout sauce of wild cherries—the tantalizing bittersweet chocolate and the coconut especially good. We feel it worth fasting a day for an airy creation of mocha, almonds and crushed meringue. Ditto for fresh raspberries and zabaglione, offered when good berries are available. The lunch and dinner menus look essentially the same, prices being about ten-percent higher at dinner. You must reserve. Figure $120 per couple at dinner.

Nippon

155 E. 52nd St. (Lexington Ave.)
758-0226

JAPANESE
Open Mon.-Thurs. noon-2:30 p.m. & 5:30 p.m.-10 p.m., Fri. noon-2:30 p.m. & 5:30 p.m.-10:30 p.m., Sat. 5:30 p.m.-10:30 p.m. All major cards.

Fugu is the famed fish that Japanese gourmets crave, but which can kill if improperly prepared. Also known as puffer or blowfish, the varieties of fugu are prized in sashimi for the delicacy of their translucent white flesh. In 1989, for the first time ever, fugu was exported from Japan, following extensive import and export certifications. The fish was airfreighted to Nippon, once again confirming its stature among Japanese restaurants. Opened in 1963, Nippon and its owner, Nobuyoshi Kuraoka, are trailblazers. Though the restaurant may have lost its uniqueness, and even attractiveness, as glitzy Japanese restaurants proliferated in the city, it still represents the best of traditional Japanese establishments (in spite of its decor and its frantic lunchtime commercialism).

A tatami-lined floor in a quiet room, silk cushions around a black-lacquered table, whispering waitresses in traditional kimonos: this is the setting of one of the private rooms at the Nippon restaurant. We think Nippon rates among the city's finest eating places, at its best with Japanese ceremonial dinners, such as a traditional seven-course kaiseki menu. Mr. Kuraoka has imported the finest sushi and sashimi chefs from Japan, including his current masters, Haruo Shibata and Katsuyoshi Isobe. The pleasure of sitting at the cypress sushi bar, in front of a chef whose dexterity will transform a piece of cucumber into a well, filled with yamakake (chopped raw tuna mixed with grated mountain potato and wasabi, and garnished with salmon caviar), defies description. The beauty of the dish simply hints at its extraordinary taste. We also adore chimmi, another wonder—seaweed, imported from Japan with the roe still attached to its briny tendrils.

Hot appetizers include shishamo, small broiled smelts, and sake kawayaki, smoked salmon skin soaked in saké, then broiled until delicately crisp; both are superb. Another appetizer worth trying is composed of slivers of sautéed duck breast, served with a light soy sauce and tender broiled scallions, which will make you wonder why you ever ate duck any other way. We also delight in stuffed steamed shrimp flavored with shiso. We also liked transparent slices of raw fluke, arranged like the petals of a pink anemone, with vinegared grated ginger and fennel, delicate and fresh tasting. Fresh tuna, Norwegian smoked salmon, and yellow-tail set on small black trays can be followed by exquisite tempura tsutsumiage—deep-fried bay scallops wrapped in a small purse of diaphanous dough and served with fried burdock and gingko nuts. The Nippon's chefs invented a superb and widely imitated roast-beef salad: thin slices of roast beef, barely cooked, served on a bed of Japanese greenery in a sesame vinaigrette. Mr. Kuraoka also introduced New York to the kobachi: six small dishes to eat while drinking saké. The dishes depend on the chef's mood and the season. The soups here are delicate and unusual; among them, we vote for homasui, a clam consommé with sculptured vegetables, seaweed strands and clams. We never fail to order una-ju, broiled eel kabayaki, served in a lacquered box over rice and with a piquant sauce, a Japanese fantasy. Try something unusual for dessert—the small, round Japanese cake made of rich marzipan; inside, you will find a slightly tart, glazed green plum. Nippon's saké collection compares favorably to those of other Japanese restaurants. This restaurant's ambitious formal dinners propel it a rank above the city's several superb sushi- and sashimi-based establishments. Expect to pay $100 per couple.

Oyster Bar & Restaurant

Grand Central Terminal (lower level),
42nd St. & Vanderbilt Ave.
490-6650, 490-6653 (saloon)
AMERICAN/SEAFOOD
*Open Mon.-Fri. 11:30 a.m.-9:30 p.m. All major
cards.*

Must everything that rises fall? The Oyster
Bar in Grand Central is still an amazing place,
but the food and service no longer amaze; they
disappoint. The staff has managed an unbe-
lievable "I don't give a damn" attitude, and
the kitchen manages to send out dishes such
as a simple filet of sole swimming in an un-
identifiable concoction. And even though it is
billed as Dover sole, it sure looks like American gray sole to us. Nevertheless, the fish is as
fresh as can be, and this place still has to be
seen to be believed.

The cavernous main dining room, in Grand
Central Station just off a main entrance to the
train tracks, boasts acres of tables under a
colossal vaulted ceiling of sand-colored tiles.
A couple of thousand meals are served here
each weekday, a mere level away from the
comic frenzy of dashing commuters and thun-
dering trains of Grand Central Station. This is
New York with all of its extremes. The rather
long menu is redone daily in order to include
the day's catch, which averages about 30 types
of creatures fished out of the sea, stream, lake
or river: grouper, lotte, mahi-mahi, pompano,
sturgeon, tilefish, wolf fish, just name it. A
dozen or so varieties of oyster appear for sale
by the piece—all as fresh as can be, and generally make exquisite appetizers. You come
here for oysters, really, and that's what you
should have, to be sure you'll eat well. The
milky New England clam chowder gets the
nod over the Manhattan version, with Maryland she-crab soup for the curious. With fish
this fresh, a simple preparation (grilled, fried,
meunière) often flatters the fish most and gets
our vote. You'll enjoy any of the pan-roasted
shellfish, cooked following the Oyster Bar's
classic preparation, but perhaps the panfried
filet of Florida pompano with rum raisins gets
the first nod. Also consider the broiled, "har-
pooned" blue-fin tuna steak with fresh coriander salsa, the fried Point Judith baby squids
with mustard-fruit mayonnaise and the
broiled filet of Chincoteague sea bass with
fresh ginger and scallions.

The all-American list of 150 wines offers
plenty of excellent, nicely priced choices, including, say, a Congree Springs Chardonnay
1986 at the low-to-mid price of $24.50, and
the Mayacamas Vineyards Chardonnay 1984
toward the high end, at $54. The good, hefty
desserts weigh in as all-American, too: apple
pies and tarts, cheesecake, carrot cake, rice
pudding, fresh fruits and the obligatory assortment of chocolate concoctions (as in
mousse cake). Try the Key lime pie. If the
fast-paced, noisy playing fields of the main
dining room bother you, try the separate den
called the Saloon, with a nautical motif, a tad
less noisy and on a slightly more human scale.
Solitary diners can eat along the oyster bar
counters and watch the cooks shucking oysters and preparing the stews. As odd as it may
sound for a place of this size, reservations are
a necessity for lunch. Dinner for two is $90.

11/20 The Palm

837 Second Ave. (44th St.)
687-2953
AMERICAN/STEAKHOUSE
*Open Mon.-Fri. 11:30 a.m.-11:30 p.m., Sat. 5
p.m.-11:30 p.m. All major cards.*

What can we do? People like this place; we
just don't. Walking across the sawdust-strewn
floor of this macho steakhouse, you will feel
you are in an aggressively staged scene from
the 1950s that never was. There is no menu.
The waiters, who behave as if they belonged
to some union requiring rude-and-crude be-
havior, rattle off only the most traditional
dishes, such as lobsters (boiled, broiled),
steaks and rib roast. This place deals in the
basics. If you want something else, you must
then ask for more information. You might
hear about the veal chops (very good) or
double lamb chops. Vegetables are represented solely by a dish of creamed spinach, as
watery as it used to be twenty years ago. If
ordered broiled, the four-pound lobsters are
too often dry; boiled, they are a moist, fresh
sea feast. Sirloin? Large and tender, but not
always very flavorful. On the other hand, rib
roast, about three inches thick, is magnificent,
with its deep-roasted, brown outside, and er-
ubescent inside—by far the best dish on the
menu. Stale, overdone fried potato chips,
served with fried onions, is the traditional side
order here. A salad made from oil-drenched
iceberg lettuce and soapy tomato wedges is to

be avoided. "Just like it always was," is the explanation. After the rib roast, guess what you can order for dessert? Right, okay cheesecake and a rich chocolate mousse cake. There is a full bar, with a short wine list (California wines and some not-too-great French ones). Good beer can be had on tap. Palm Two, across from The Palm on the east side of Second Avenue, is a faithful replica. Price per couple, with drinks, $120 to $130.

12/20 Paper Moon
39 E. 58th St.
(Fifth & Madison Aves.)
758-8600

ITALIAN

Open daily noon-3 p.m. & 6 p.m.-midnight. All major cards.

For a glorious individual pizza and an authentic Italian salad, Paper Moon fits the bill; thereafter, much on the menu needs refining, and the atmosphere could use a puff of fresh air. Established late in 1989, Paper Moon is the newest in a chain of Milanese restaurants, based upon the original Paper Moon in Milan, and more or less replicated as far away as Tokyo. Tables (manufactured in Italy, like the chairs, bar, tablecloths and place settings) in the spacious dining room, unfortunately, are lined up in rows like soldiers, so that intimacy is impossible. The starkness of the peach walls and heavy black pizza bar in the rear makes us feel as if we were in a high-tech executives' prison mess hall. That feeling is intensified by the waiters, constantly strolling the aisles, surveying every table.

To begin a meal, a good choice would be the insalata Paper Moon, with arugula, celery, hearts of palm and paper-thin slices of excellent Parmesan, tossed in a vinaigrette made with pungent olive oil. We're surprised the pastas we've tasted tended to be overdone and soggy. Pappardelle alla Paper Moon was perhaps the only expertly prepared pasta dish (out of about fifteen), with smokey pancetta and light tomato-cream sauce. Penne with a simple tomato and basil sauce had fresh flavor, but the farfalle al salmone was drenched in cream, and the smoked salmon was cut so chunky, we might as well have been eating lox on a bagel. Meats are pleasant, albeit overpriced: the grilled veal kidney and liver is particularly tasty, with a hint of reduced balsamic vinegar. The carpaccio (paper thin slices

of raw beef) are no less than smothered with the various toppings offered and, therefore, all you taste are toppings.

Now for the restaurant's forte: the pizzas are delectable, with a thin crust and honest, fragrant toppings, such as ricotta cheese with sage-infused sausage, arugula with mozzarella and porcini mushrooms with tomato and basil. All the wines at Paper Moon are Italian, and reasonably priced. Dessert offerings are the classics: a superbly light tiramisu, gelati drenched in liqueur and several pastries. Count on spending about $100 for two for a full meal, with a bottle of young Barolo, $70 for a lighter meal built around pizza.

11/20 Paradis Barcelona
145 E. 50th St.
(Lexington & Third Aves.)
754-3333

SPANISH

Open Mon.-Fri. noon-3 p.m.& 6 p.m.-midnight, Sat. 6 p.m.-midnight, Sun. noon-midight. All major cards.

The success of several Paradis restaurants in Barcelona and Madrid encouraged the chain to open in Manhattan, and the result is an elegant and intimate dining room, with large, elaborate mirrors and rich dark-wood furniture. Oil paintings by contemporary Spanish artists adorn the walls. Near the front, a clear glass partition separates hundreds of racked wine bottles that comprise the attractive Spanish wine list. That's the good news.

If only it were possible to pay homage to the Catalonian food here! The enticing and exotic menu doesn't always deliver, and occasionally disappoints. At first, all is well. A plate of crusty bread, drenched in olive oil and topped with bits of tomato, is brought immediately to the table. Oddly, however, the waiter will not offer it again for the rest of the meal. Among the best hot appetizers is butifarra, a mouth-watering Catalan sausage, served with tender white beans and eggplant. Sautéed spinach is given a pleasant twist, with a liberal spicing of raisins and pine nuts. A cold appetizer of marinated swordfish and roasted peppers sounded promising, but the small, sculpted mound of swordfish and peppers that appeared, surrounded by an erratic array of nouvelle-style vegetables, was completely uninviting. Rescue by the main courses was not forthcoming. A paella of boneless meat, fish and poultry was flavorless, abundant with squid and heavy with olive oil. A black rice pilaf with squid and shrimp looked majestic on the plate, the rice turned dark with squid ink; on the palate, it was much less. Salted-cod filet with dried-red-peppercorn sauce seemed to miss even the salt. Its blandness was vaguely reminiscent of a basket of fish-and-chips.

The waiters make up with imagination what they sometimes lack in efficiency. A chocolate truffle cake was served over a completely unexpected, pale-green liquid that two waiters insisted was mint sauce. Not so. Its taste was rather akin to confectioners sugar. More care, seemingly, has been given to an extensive wine list. Some of the better reds include a marvelous 1978 Cune Vina Real Reserva for $28 and a more forward 1985 Gran Coronas Reserva, also $28. Expect to pay about $120 for two.

Le Périgord
405 E. 52nd St. (First Ave.)
755-6244

FRENCH

Open Mon.-Sat. noon-3 p.m. & 5:30 p.m.-10:30 p.m. All major cards.

Antoine Bouterin is a great chef, perhaps the finest working in New York today. He lacks, however, a platform to show off his talents, the kind that Daniel Boulud has at Le Cirque, that André Soltner has at his own Lutèce, and that even Jean-Georges Vongerichten (to exhaust our short list of culinary equals) at Lafayette has. Le Périgord is a very good restaurant, with good service, but it is getting old. Having passed its 25th anniversary, its low-ceilinged room seems more claustrophic than ever. That's why the dowager's summer-of-1990 facelift was a welcome sign of renewed lust for culinary life. Le Périgord's Sutton Place, far east, location takes some effort to reach in traffic, and its well-heeled but aging clientele are used to the historic Périgord, with its old-school, French haute-cuisine. Eager for daring new dishes, they are not. A grilled filet of sole with a slice of lemon is just fine with them, thank you.

Too bad. Bouterin can do it all; he is even so bold as to add, when you aren't looking, a dab of mustard butter to the sole. This guy deserves a place where he can let loose.

We love one memorable opener: a light vegetable tart in a sheer lime-perfumed beurre blanc. We think the foie gras and apple sauce,

served cold or hot, with capers, outstanding. Soupe au pistou, a delicious and satisfying country soup, which almost never appears on menus here, shares billing with a sublime fish soup. For appetizers we also like the sweetbread crêpe and the special pancake stuffed with crabmeat in lobster sauce. Our vote for one of the headiest dishes on the menu: alluring, smoky grilled lobster with a counterpoint of pleurottes (meaty oyster mushrooms) on a chiffonnade of green cabbage, surrounded by a sheer fumet of wild mushrooms. We love the quenelles of snapper with lobster sauce and the curry of lotte (monkfish) with apple. Bouterin's Provençal rendition of soft-shell crabs on a bed of delicious rataouille is thrilling and unforgettable. This is one of the rare places you still can get a classic beef stew, cooked country-style to perfection. We prefer, however, the boneless quails stuffed with vegetables. Dieting could be painless with the low-calorie itmes on the menu: steamed filet of halibut or salmon with mussels.

You'll love the old-fashioned dessert cart, still in evidence here. If you see something on it with lemon, order it, if you have not already ordered ahead a lemon soufflé (which comes with a raspberry sauce). We also think the lemon meringue tart is tops. The wine list is good but unexciting, with big-name producers and one importer dominating, and prices that make you blink, though you can order decently in the $40 range per bottle. Still, we'd recommend more exciting bottles and prices if this place is going to keep pace with the top restaurants in town. Although the fixed-price menu reads $32 for lunch and $55 for dinner, there are so many supplements, expect to spend at least $90 per couple for lunch and $150 for two at dinner, plus tax and tip. Better yet, why not count on $200, and order wines that match Bouterin's cooking?

Prunelle
18 E. 54th St. (Fifth Ave.)
759-6410

FRENCH

Open Mon.-Fri. noon-3 p.m. & 5:30 p.m.-11 p.m., Sat.-Sun. 5:30 p.m.-11 p.m. All major cards.

This heavyweight, with chic decor and serious clientele, will never be the champion, but it slugs it out willingly with the big boys of French cuisine in New York. Lately, it has been losing more than it should. Prunelle is owned and operated by two seasoned professionals who hail from France: skier, sailor and New York restaurant-network organizer Jacky Ruette, and chef Pascal Dirringer. An efficient staff, which actually seems happy, works one of the prettiest dining rooms in town. Its stunning art-deco design, gorgeous flower arrangements and subdued lighting help create an atmosphere of low-key elegance. When the restaurant opened in 1983, its pricey fixed lunch and dinner menu convinced people they were paying, literally, for the decor. Today, the $38 lunch or $58 dinner doesn't raise many eyebrows.

Instead of the hardly inspired smoked fish and the gravlax of salmon as appetizers, try the crabcakes or the salad of chicken scallops and wild mushrooms. Concentrate on the light lobster ravioli, the sweetbreads with leeks or the tasty snails with basil. Among the entrées, we declare seafood a clear winner—monkfish, Dover sole, swordfish and lobster especially, all being served with various baby vegetables and light but flavorful sauces. We've enjoyed the salmon with lemon vinaigrette and a wonderful and unusual luncheon entrée, a moist cheese soufflé with dried tomatoes. We like the perfectly cooked rack of lamb, the buttery Black Angus steak and the crisp duck confit for meat dishes—all served in big, old-fashioned portions. Though the dessert cart looks appealing, albeit not overly imaginative, we like the apple tart and most other fruit tarts, as well as the lemon selections (soufflé, meringue tart) and the rich chocolate cake. Lately, we've enjoyed a delicious caramel mousse. You'll find the essentially French wine list extensive and expensive. Men must wear a jacket and tie. Even with one of the less expensive wines, prepare to pay $90 to $100 per couple at lunch and $140 to $160 for two at dinner, plus tax and tip.

The Quilted Giraffe

AT&T Building,
550 Madison Ave. (55th & 56th Sts.)
593-1221

ECLECTIC

Open Tues.-Fri. noon-2:30 p.m.& 5:30 p.m.-10 p.m., Sat. 5:30 p.m.-10 p.m. All major cards.

Are we getting mellow, or did the humbling experience of the failed Casual Quilted Giraffe and the trying move of The Quilted from its

lovely brownstone home to the arcade of the A T & T building inspire Barry and Susan Wine to calm reassessment and careful growth? (The new location struck us, at first, as looking like a designer cookie shop.) Whatever, we've grown to enjoy The Quilted Giraffe, and admire what Barry Wine has done. His restaurant has never been better—even the all-too-busy gray-and-black postmodern dining room (with mezzanine) seems a bit more restrained under new lighting.

To its credit, there is nothing else like The Quilted Giraffe in New York; it is more an experience than it is cuisine. Executive chef Wine pioneered the use of Japanese produce and techniques (in non-Japanese restaurants), and has increasingly created a fusion of Japanese, French and American styles. He prepares everything to order, and he believes in quick preparations that maintain the fresh integrity of produce. Look around the dining room, and you will, no doubt, see Japanese admirers of his work. Peek into his kitchen, and you will see Japanese chefs scouting his latest. The Japanese influence has extended here to a custom "kaiseki" tasting menu ($125), a very popular choice. And speaking of influence, the proof of The Quilted Giraffe's greatness lies not only in its intellectual pursuit of culinary refinement and its willingness to experiment and change, but also in the extent to which its innovations have been copied. The menu has inspired other restaurants in New York to develop a fusion cuisine, and its kitchen—and this is too often overlooked—has served as a training ground for many successful chefs in the city and beyond. To that end, only Le Cirque surpasses it, and as of late, Chanterelle approaches it.

Did we say that the food is excellent? What should you order? Perhaps the renowned wasabe pizza with sashimi tuna for a starter, or the house smoked salmon with ginger and cucumber. We've never been devotees of the famous beggar's purses, consisting of a dollop of fine beluga caviar dropped into a little sack that looks just like a moneybag. You should try this appetizer once, but thereafter, ask for the sautéd sweetbreads with caramel soy and chips. It's sensational.

Inventiveness prevails where the entrées and desserts are concerned, as well, and few could ever fault Wine for lack of originality. We love the Norwegian salmon grilled with sweet hot mustard, the rack of lamb with Chinese mustard (accompanied by wonderful mashed potatoes), and the duck confit on sweet-potato pancakes. We also fancy the Japanese-style beef sirloin, sautéed 60 seconds on one side. For dessert, consider bypassing the tempting cheese cart, even though it comes with the $75 dinner menu package, and head for the delectable pecan squares, or warm fruit tart with ginger ice cream . . . or, for a $10 supplement, the grand dessert, which consists of a little of seven or eight different offerings of the evening. You may need a stiff after-dinner drink to help you digest after that, and there are superb offerings to be had, especially among Cognacs and ports. You'll enjoy browsing in the computerized, and daily updated, outstanding wine list, which displays depth, breadth, shrewd selections and Tiffany-like price tags. You must reserve for dinner, the sooner the better. Gentlemen must wear jacket and tie at all times, except Saturday lunch. Expect to pay $140 per couple for lunch and $200 to $300 for two at dinner, plus tax (8.25 percent) and tip (18 percent automatically added on).

Restaurant Lafayette
Drake Hotel,
65 E. 56th St. (Park Ave.)
832-1565
FRENCH
Open Mon.-Fri. noon-2:30 p.m. & 6:00 p.m.-10:30 p.m. Closed July 20-Aug. 20. All major cards.

The cuisine of this elegant restaurant is nothing less than revolutionary. Since Jean-Georges Vongerichten took over the reins from his mentor and consulting chef, Louis Outhier, there is no stopping him. His talent is prodigious, his imagination boundless and his menu anything but traditional. Diners choose from two fixed-price menus, at $65 and $85, which change with the seasons. The menus come divided into four parts: Bouillons (simmered vegetable broths), Vinaigrettes (delicately balanced citrus juices, vinegars and oils), Huiles Parfumées (oils infused with herbs, spices and vegetable reductions) and Jus de Légumes (fresh vegetable extracts). Each section has its hors d'oeuvres and its entrées, although one is not bound to stay in a single section. Gone are ostentatious garnishes; dishes are served with simplicity, and the brilliant hues of Jean-Georges' fresh sauces harmonize beautifully.

Jean-Georges has staked his reputation on his revolutionary sauces. He has every reason to. A tiny, flaky tart topped with tangy fromage blanc and garnished with caramelized onion threads is enhanced by a pungent onion consommé, flavored with cumin and coriander. Soft polenta swims in a lyric vegetable broth, garnished with sticks of fried polenta and tiny stewed squid. A biting vinaigrette brings a frisée salad with delicate fried calamari to life. Ingredients never cease to surprise: a daring dish of crisp, corn-breaded pork cheeks paired with moist sautéed foie gras comes arranged on a bed of black beans, while roasted sweetbreads arrive topped with chestnuts and dabbed with chestnut vinaigrette. We think the most triumphant dish an open ravioli made with Swiss-chard pasta squares hovering over a spicy confit of rabbit, garnished with a sprig of thyme and lightly sauced with red-pepper oil. You should also try a tender breast of pheasant, crowning a purée of beets, topped with paper-thin fried beets.

Happily, desserts here easily match the standards set by the rest of the menu. Besides the homemade sorbets and a classic chestnut mousse cake, offerings include a compote of dried fruit served with pain d'épices ice-cream and topped with razor-thin, toasted slices of pain d'épices (Jean-Georges hails from Alsace where pain d'épice is king), and an extraordinary dish of fresh dates, filled with white-chocolate mousse nestled atop an espresso aspic.

We have never liked the look or feel of the dining room. If you like to eat up a room, head for La Côte Basque or any of the snazzy new designer eateries. Sometimes we wish Vongerichten would, too: he deserves the absolutely best surroundings. Big and plush in the international-hotel mode, the dining room boasts shades of salmon, feels spacious and comfortable, but has an overall heaviness that we forgot as soon as the glorious food arrived. The restaurant seems to succeed better at lunch, with businesspeople, than in the evening, when the hotel guests join prospecting gastronomes. An extensive—and expensive—wine list offers some highly drinkable California wines and some notable dessert wines, as well as the expected fine French bottlings. Depending on the menu chosen, figure about $200 to $250 for dinner for two.

Champagne DELABARRE

19, rue Dom Pérignon - 51200 EPERNAY
Tél. 26 54 78 57 - Télécopie 26 51 06 66

12/20 Rosa Mexicano

1063 First Ave. (58th St.)
753-7407

MEXICAN

Open daily noon-3:30 p.m. & 5 p.m.-midnight. All major cards.

This upscale Mexican eatery, with pink stuccoed walls and arches, machine-carved wood chairs and an open grill in the front room (the livelier of the two dining areas), could be located in Anywheresville, U.S.A. Generally considered one of the best Mexican restaurants in the city—which may be damning with faint praise—Rosa Mexicano often promises a tad more than it delivers. The menu, which hasn't changed in years, introduced such dishes as menudo (a spicy tripe stew) and pozole (a stew based on pork and hominy), not usually seen around town, and fuels expectations.

But for all its potential, Rosa Mexicano can be disappointing. Even the made-to-order guacamole is an anticlimax. Though it still is made tableside from separate bowls of crinkly skinned avocados, chopped onions, chiles, cilantro and tomatoes, it is fine, but no longer stellar, and the waiters seem to ignore requests for "spicy," as opposed to "mild." However, one of the tastiest appetizers, taquito de tinga poblana, shows what the kitchen is capable of doing. Coarse tortillas, with the distinctive taste of masa harina, enwrap a fiery blend of shredded pork, smoked chipotle chile, onions and tomatoes. We like the corn-dumpling soup, and the enchiladas filled with chicken are a notch above average, due to a mole sauce that is more subtle than the one-note, fudgy moles usually encountered in New York. Mixiote de Tlaxcala, a traditional method of cooking meats in agave leaves, is here accomplished with parchment. Chicken or lamb is coated with chiles, spices and beer, placed in the parchment, and oven-braised. Much ado about nothing, it seems, for the chicken thigh is often as dry as terry cloth—but when it is moist, it is good. We have liked the budín azteca (layers of tortilla bearing shredded chicken, white cheese and poblano-chile sauce, served casserole style), the baked filet of grouper and the marinated pork chops. Coconut ice cream with a raspberry sauce or a so-so flan end the meal on a sweet note. The small wine list is largely ignored in favor of Mexican beers, classic margaritas and the house margarita with pomegranate juice. Dinner for two, with beer or drinks, comes to about $90.

Sandro's

420 E. 59th St.
(First Ave. & Sutton Pl.)
55-5150; Fax 751-9380

ITALIAN

Open Mon.-Sat. 5:30-11 p.m. All major cards.

Established in 1985, Sandro's—a Roman style trattoria—has already taken on the feel and reputation of a great old standby. Sandro Fioriti, co-owner, chef, namesake and sometime maître d', inspires confidence. This tall, robust chef of Rabelaisian proportions and appetite, has limitless energy in the kitchen (and elsewhere, it seems, since by his own account he has had six wives). Brought to Manhattan from his restaurant in Castelli, near Roma, by restaurant impresario Tony May (San Domenico, La Camelia), Sandro is the perfect emissary to win hearts and minds to the gastronomic specialties of the Roman kitchen. Certainly, you come here to savor his uncompromising renditions of that lusty cuisine.

Start with carciofi alla giudia (artichokes Jewish-style). We like these they way the kitchen prepares them, deep-fried in corn oil, until they flower like roses, finding them delicious and addictive. Just as much, we liked the fried ricotta. Moist and creamy on the inside, it boasts a crisp and greaseless egg-and-breadcrumb coating and a fresh, light tomato sauce for a zingy accompaniment. Pungent salads of puntarelle clear the palate for hearty stews and roasts. We declare the ravioli, filled with sea-urchin roe, with a sauce of baby scallops and tomato, a winner, as we do the baccalà (salt cod) with tomatoes, onions and potatoes. In the past, we have enjoyed roast pork Roman-style, seasoned with wild fennel, garlic and fresh rosemary, and doused with olive oil (so delectable it could be banned by the Vatican), and oxtail stew with celery, carrots, onions and pancetta. Recently, we've enjoyed the butterflied Cornish hen, crisply fried, and the lamb chops, nicely flavored with balsamic vinegar. You'll find plenty of attractive Italian wines (and a few California) to wash all this down agreeably, from a simple Pinot Grigio by Marco Felluga ($18) to one of many red wines with considerable bottle age on the special reserve wine list, including a Biondi Santi Brunello di Montalcino 1967 ($720). We think the top dessert award goes to the cream of polenta with raspberry sauce; it costs only $6.50.

Now for the downside: location, and, to a lesser degree, tariff. First, Sandro's is located on the ground floor of a high-rise both unfortunate in its look (anonymous) and in its location (way, way east). As for the prices, $16 for a plate of pasta and $23.50 for sausages with broccoli, seems daunting. In a perfect world, Sandro's rustic and handpainted plates and mugs, the communal table (a fabulous, if underutilized, concept), and his homemade grappas (they're actually sweet, and flavored with fruits such as pear, strawberry and banana) would be more centrally located. Dinner, with a moderately priced wine, averages $120 per couple, plus normal tax and tip.

San Giusto
935 Second Ave. (49th & 50th Sts.)
319-0900

ITALIAN
Open Mon.-Fri. noon-3 p.m. & 5 p.m.-11 p.m., Sat. noon-3 p.m. & 5 p.m.-11:30 p.m. All major cards.

Pleasurable San Giusto was born of two Italians: a chef, Gino Martincich, and a maître d', Bruno Viscovich. Both come from the same Italian enclave in Yugoslavia, and both have not only a great love of fine cuisine, but a desire to see their guests enjoy the food. Jovial Bruno seems everywhere at once in this elegant restaurant with excellent service. We suggest ordering best by putting yourself in his hands and letting him decide for you—including the wine. He believes strongly that high-priced wines generally aren't worth it, and touts quality, low-priced Friuliano whites and Tuscan Chiantis. He may start you off with prosciutto e pepperoni gialli, delicious homemade prosciutto served with marinated yellow peppers that melt in your mouth; or with airy mozzarella fritta; or, when in season, carciofo ripieno, a whole stuffed artichoke, redolent of garlic and Parmesan cheese, with strong olive oil. Gino has mastered the risotto, several of which appear on the menu. We liked the risotto with mushrooms (or white truffles), creamy and rich, with the flavor of earthy fungi. The gnocchi with meat ragoût or with fresh tomato sauce brings cries of sheer delight

from the customers, though we prefer the ravioli among many pleasing pastas. You pick the noodle and match it with a sauce. Gino will also fix you up with a combination of any three for an appetizer or main course. Among the fish and seafood dishes, we believe the best are the broiled, whole red snapper, the large, tender, broiled shrimps in a garlic butter with some sherry, and a poached salmon coated with fresh tomato coulis. If you are in the mood for meat, the veal chop with butter and sage gets an early vote. A friend loved the sweet Italian sausages cooked with porcini mushrooms and polenta, a hearty combination that takes you back to the Italian countryside. Instead of heavy Italian desserts, ask for the sorbets or the fresh fruit. Price per couple, with wine, is about $100.

Scarlatti
34 E. 52nd St.
(Madison & Park Aves.)
753-2444

ITALIAN
Open Mon.-Thurs. noon-3 p.m. & 5:30 p.m.-10:30 p.m., Fri. noon-3 p.m. & 5:30 p.m.-midnight, Sat. 5:30 p.m.-midnight. All major cards.

This place serves up grand opera, rather than the music of Scarlatti. It's posh, formal, well run, pretentious and safe. The kitchen can crank it up and get it out for you, and can enchant with specials.

You'll notice specialties from many Italian regions on the large menu: the familiar antipasti, soups, pastas, rice dishes, fish, chicken, veal or other meat dishes, as well as grilled meats. You might start with crostini di mozzarella, the luscious seafood salad (cool slivers of squid and shrimp and other seafood items), or a half portion of a good pasta, perhaps the malfatti con carciofi (artichokes). We have enjoyed veal medallions with garlic, tomato and mushrooms, something of a house specialty, as a main course. We can also suggest a good scampi ribelli (baked in mozzarella), or a healthy veal chop as alternatives. Decent, if unremarkable, wines go along with all this, and good desserts include a zabaglione prepared at your table by a captain who separates the eggs, whisks them over a flame and delivers the hot froth to you. If you ask Ernest Cavalli, the maître d' since Lello Arpaia opened this spot in 1984, he'll probably recommend the tiramisu. We fear this opulent place appears, in large part, as little more than theater, with steady, and sometimes sensational, cuisine and Broadway prices. Lunch will run at least $76 per couple and dinner $100 for two.

Seryna
11 E. 53rd St. (Madison Ave.)
980-9393

JAPANESE

Open Mon.-Fri. noon-2 p.m.& 5:30 p.m.-10 p.m., Sat. 6 p.m.-10 p.m. All major cards.

Japanese businessmen pack this discreetly planted spot (in one of Madison Avenue's high-rises), their American clients and advertising executives watching their weight. At night, we find the restaurant quieter and the service more pleasant. Although this eatery has a good sashimi bar, it only serves sashimi and sushi as an appetizer or an afterthought. The restaurant's forte is steak of the highest quality, cut paper-thin and served raw, accompanied by a delicate dipping sauce made with soy, garlic and apples. We think ishiyaki steak, tender filet mignon sizzled on a hot stone that absorbs all the fat, even better. The superb meat comes with two dipping sauces, a hot chili sauce or a garlic-soy sauce—but in small portions, so it's advisable to order a soup and an appetizer as well, or you may find yourself wanting pizza an hour after you finish dinner.

Shabu-shabu, a dish served in most Japanese restaurants, has panache here. More paper-thin slices of beef, plus various vegetables and noodles, come to the table arranged next to a copper pot of steaming hot broth. You poach the beef to your taste and dip it in sesame sauce; the vegetables are then added to the broth with the noodles and dipped in a soy-and-lime sauce. Among the appetizers, the chawan mushi, a lightly steamed egg custard filled with delicious chunks of chicken, shrimp and gingko nuts, should not be missed. The crab kohra-age is also good—a huge crab shell, stuffed with crabmeat in a light white sauce, then fried. The crab, like most dishes on the menu, comes with a tangy sauce. We thought delicious one of the nicest side dishes, shiso rice, steamed rice which has been spiced with salted Japanese plums, sesame seeds, crushed bonito and chopped shiso leaves (a very fragrant member of the mint family). There's not much variety for dessert; you can stick to melon and ice cream. The restaurant

offers several sakés and a short, expensive wine list. Dinner for two, with wine, runs $100 to $120.

Shun Lee Palace
155 E. 55th St.
(Third & Lexington Aves.)
371-8844

CHINESE

Open Sun.-Thurs. noon-11 p.m., Fri.-Sat. noon-11:30 p.m. Cards: AE, DC.

The spacious dining room is packed tightly with tables, its walls covered with ancient Chinese motifs and beautiful paintings. The table is set European-style and the maître d' wears evening clothes. The menu even lists tiramisu and profiteroles for dessert. The food can be excellent, with reliable nightly specials reflecting both Cantonese and Szechuan cuisine.

We think the cold appetizers more interesting than the hot. Start with crunchy honey-glazed walnuts, followed by slices of lean-and-smoky cold duck, served with a pungent Hunan sauce. Next, order wontons floating in a rich duck broth, light and tasty. The hot-and-sour soup belongs in a cafeteria, however. Shun Lee Palace has a few unusual dishes, such as stir-fried sweetbreads with hot peppers, and frogs' legs with black Chinese mushrooms and scallions in a ginger sauce with black beans (similar to the French version, and you won't miss the garlic). The Szechuan tripe with scallions and pork is served in a hot-and-peppery sauce with a faint touch of vinegar. The menu offers several well-prepared, standard Chinese dishes of poultry and fish, and a few noodle dishes—among them, go for the Peking duck (first rate), the prawns Szechuan style and the orange-flavored beef. Among other interesting, and recommended, dishes, we favor Western-leaning Norwegian salmon in rice wine, and a house favorite, a smoked duck that has a caramelized skin, accompanied by scallion pancakes.

You'll find an extensive wine list at this 20-year-old East Side establishment. If you insist on having a Western dessert, skip the so-so tiramisu and profiteroles and opt for the honey-apple fritters, dusted with sesame seeds. One reservation: with all the waiters rushing about, it's hard to imagine why the service is slow. The overall high quality and ambience have their justifiable price: here, it averages about $80 per couple for dinner, $56 for two at lunch.

Smith & Wollensky

201 E. 49th St. (Third Ave.)
753-1530
AMERICAN/STEAKHOUSE
Open Mon.-Fri. 11:45 a.m.-midnight, Sat.-Sun. 5 p.m.-midnight. All major cards.

Counting the two dining rooms and the saloon, this brass-and-wood barn of a steakhouse can probably seat 500 people. People who don't enjoy sawdust under their shoes, but who probably savor locker rooms, frequent this place and eat like real men. What do they eat? Surprise, surprise—the shrimp or the crab or the lobster cocktail, followed by steak, or, maybe now that we're in the lighter-and-healthier nineties, the fish of the day. Certainly, for steak and chops, Smith & Wollensky is fine, and you can always get humongous lobsters. The grilled fish is all right, too. You have to order hashed browns, onion rings, cottage fries or zucchini as vegetables on the side.

The wine list distinguishes S&W. It seems that people who order $29.50 steaks don't drink cheap wines. There are great old vintages and big bottles here from France and California. Desserts have improved some, but if you're an occasional visitor, no doubt you'll order the cheesecake. We think it better to go for the maple-pecan pie and the hot deep-dish apple pie with vanilla sauce. For dinner, expect to pay $110 or so per couple, without a rare wine, somewhat less for lunch.

Sparks Steakhouse

210 E. 46th St.
(Second & Third Aves.)
687-4855; Fax 557-7409
AMERICAN/STEAKHOUSE
Open Mon.-Fri. noon-3 p.m. & 5 p.m.-11 p.m., Sat. 5 p.m-11:30 p.m. All major cards.

When some primordial monster inside us cries "meat"—big, red, juicy, unadorned meat—we think old-time steakhouse. Among New York's old reliables, Sparks remains tops (or should we say prime?). Last decade, when mobster Paul Castellano was rubbed out on the street in front of Sparks, it was not a bad thing for business. If anything, it added to the macho, larger-than-life image of this big joint. The large dining rooms continue to be filled with he-man business types, doing some serious eating here at lunch and dinner.

In terms of fine dining, this is not it. But we can't fault the unadorned prime sirloin or the juicy filet mignon, the lamb chops (three doubles), or the charred veal chop. Recently, there has been more than a lip-service commitment here to fish, as well. You can now always choose between a half dozen fish filets. We like the grilled-swordfish and tuna steaks, as well as the red snapper and trout. Moreover, you can order lobster, which comes in three sizes that could be dubbed not-so-small, big and man-eating. Appetizers are pretty standard, with the broiled shrimp with lemon butter or the warm lump crabmeat and bay scallops the top choices. The meats come unadorned, so you have to order vegetables as side dishes. Unlike the usual steakhouse, Sparks has learned to handle vegetables, from al dente broccoli and crumbly, hash brown potatoes to cooked fresh asparagus in a vinaigrette. Naturally, you eat cheesecake for dessert, or perhaps walnut-pecan pie à la mode. The award-winning wine list is enormous, and even if you don't subscribe to *The Wine Spectator*, you'll be able to spot familiar and inviting names and vintages. This place believes in serving wines when they are ready to drink, so the 1978 Bordeaux, for example, are available in 1990 in volume . . . and you can get two bottles here for practically what you'd pay for one at most other places. Expect to pay $120 or so per couple.

Toscana

200 E. 54th St.
(Second & Third Aves.)
371-8144
ITALIAN
Open Mon.-Sat. noon-3 p.m. & 5:30 p.m.-10:30 p.m. All major cards.

This 7,700-square-foot, architecturally exciting restaurant in the "lipstick" building is an enigma. It looks so good, starts with fine produce and seemingly tries so hard, but, ultimately, it never quite lives up to expectations. The good news, however, is that the kitchen has improved considerably, since young chef Paolo Casagranda arrived from Borgo-Valsugana in Trento. High Milanese style defines the dining room's floor of curvilinear pearwood and Carrara marble, its walls of imitation gray slate, a lofty skylight decorated with undulating blue-green glass strips and asymmetrical (and uncomfortable) chairs made of burlwood and black leather. The room is asymmetrical as well. Up front, you'll find a bar and grill that features light Tuscan fare, but for the whole show, you have to go to the dining room in back.

The house-smoked swordfish with herbs, the warm duck breast with balsamic vinegar, and the traditional, thick and hearty Tuscan bean soup make for good appetizers. Pastas really reign supreme here. We like the ravioli with zucchini flowers, available as a half portion for a starter, as are the other pastas. Friends adored the paglia e fieno (green and white flat noodles in a sauce of tomatoes, scallions and green peppers). Risotto honors go to the risotto with Gorgonzola and walnuts. For fish, we prefer the steamed filet of snapper with leeks (warn the waiter that you do not want your fish overcooked) or the sea bass in red wine (though an admittedly inferior imitation of what Le Cirque has made so popular in this city), and for meat, either the pheasant with wild mushrooms, the lamb tartelette or the sliced rabbit saddle with artichokes. The strips of rabbit (with rosemary rescuing the somewhat bland meat) fan across the plate, the baby artichokes placed alongside. We like the strong list of Italian wines, including some splendid Brunellos and Barolos that are opened ahead of time and go beautifully with the great selection of Italian cheeses available here. Have a dessert wine with one of the homemade biscotti. Price runs $110 per couple, and more with one of those high-priced red wines.

12/20 Tre Scalini

230 E. 58th St.
(Second & Third Aves.)
688-6888

ITALIAN
Open Mon.-Fri. noon-3 p.m. & 5:30 p.m.-midnight., Sat. 1 p.m.-midnight, Sun. 1 p.m.-11 p.m. All major cards.

When you enter this long, narrow dining room with mirrors, hanging plants and big bouquets of flowers, and walk past an old-fashioned "gourmet" display of antipasti and whatnot, you know what to expect: an Italian menu of the old school. And that's what you

get. On this street of many Italian (and other) restaurants, Tre Scalini stands out for delivering reliable, if unexciting, meals, and for providing what the clientele seemingly wants.

Mario Bodolo has been in the kitchen since the day the restaurant opened in 1978, so not all that much has changed, though there are occasional forays into the world of contemporary Italian cooking. After all, with 25 different pastas, what's another dollop of this or slice of that? The carpaccio is tender and served, as is traditional, with thin slices of excellent Parmesan. Bresaola, thin slices of air-dried beef, is delicious with the restaurant's Italian bread, and the ginestrata (soup of shrimp, eggs and spinach) is flavorful and bracing. The risotto verde is highly recommended. As you can imagine, there are plenty of ordinary pastas on the list, but the gnocchi stuffed with spinach and ricotta and the spaghetti with celery, tomato, balsamic vinegar and olive oil are fine. Fish are not the way to go here. Try the game in season—the wild duck with Marsala wine and chestnuts or the regularly available roasted pheasant with truffles. A top dish is the veal nuggets with chiodini mushrooms. Chicken cacciatore is good, if not spectacular. In general, things need to be lightened up a bit, though the steady flow of clientele suggests that diners here don't notice, or don't care. They enjoy their cigars and order one of the heavy desserts (the not-too-sweet zabaglione still gets the nod). The wine list is extensive, but the staff deals in the usuals. Figure $90 per couple for lunch and $110 for dinner for two.

Zarela

953 Second Ave. (50th & 51st Sts.)
644-6740

MEXICAN
Open Mon.-Thurs. noon-3 p.m. & 5 p.m.-11:30 p.m., Fri. noon-3 p.m. & 5 p.m.-midnight, Sat. 5 p.m.-midnight, Sun. 5 p.m.-10 p.m. Cards: AE, DC.

Mexican food, unfortunately, has never been New York's strongest draw. Zarela Martínez is doing her best to change that, and we wish her success. Judging by the young, well-heeled crowd that fills both levels of her attractive and lively East Side restaurant with a party atmosphere, she doesn't need our promotion. You will need a reservation. Perhaps to its credit, Zarela can't be held to typical Mexican restaurant standards. Its food is not the bloating fare found in college hangouts and downtown dives. Zarela works because it pointedly avoids such common items as tacos and burritos. Instead, the lighter and more sophisticated cuisine of Mexico's coastal regions is featured. The most well-known offerings may be enchiladas and tamales, served only as appetizers, and, even then, both are filled with chicken and prepared in an eclectic, delicious brown mole sauce with a subtle chocolate flavor. Another good starter, thinly rolled fried tortillas called flautas, stuffed with chicken and served with cool and tasty guacamole, should be on everyone's list.

From here, familiarity ends for most residents north of the border. Don't panic. Order camarones al ajillo, salty shrimps sautéed in olive oil and garlic. You don't often find fish on Mexican menus, but this one offers tuna in mole sauce, grilled salmon with mayonnaise and cucumber relish and grilled trout with onion and cilantro. Zarela could do better with its pollo borracho, a half chicken, cut up and cooked in a sauce of tequila and white vinegar and garnished with green olives, raisins and almond shavings. The sauce has the taste of heavy corn starch, and the salty olives don't blend well with the sweet raisins. Zarela also offers obligatory steak fajitas, grilled and served with salsa and guacamole. Main dishes come with refried black beans and rice. Mexican beer goes best with this food. We should mention another distinction between this and other Mexican restaurants: the price. Expect to spend $70 for dinner for two, with drinks.

MIDTOWN WEST
(W. 42nd Street to W. 59th Street)

Acquavit
13 W. 54th St. (Fifth & Sixth Aves.)
307-7311; Fax 265-8584
SCANDINAVIAN
Open Mon.-Fri. noon-2:30 p.m. & 5:30 p.m.-10:30 p.m., Sat. 5:30 p.m.-10:30 p.m. All major cards.

You step down into an old building—the former townhouse of Nelson Rockefeller—come upon a modern Scandinavian bar, informal restaurant and gourmet take-out, then descend a flight of stairs and emerge in a startling dining room: a waterfall tumbles gracefully, and the eight-story glass atrium is filled with kitelike mobiles, tall birch trees and slick black leather-and-chrome chairs. Top notch Scandinavian design and food returns to New York in this building. Scandinavian cuisine has less to do with technique and preparation than with special ingredients imported from Sweden, Norway, Finland and Denmark, such as smoked or raw Arctic venison, smoked or raw salmon and herring, snow grouse, hazel grouse, Swedish blueberries, Arctic brambleberries, lingonberries and cloudberries. Chef Christer Larson prepares it all simply, elegantly and with reverberations of his French training.

The fixed-price menu downstairs is $55 ($32 at lunch), with plenty of supplements, and, naturally, stresses fish. A smörgåsbord appetizer plate provides an engaging gustatory experience with four versions of herring, two versions of salmon and a heap of orange roe plus some pâté and a taste of mild Västerbottenost cheese. Most of these items can be ordered separately as starters and get our nod over the tartar of salmon and belon oysters that is okay, but a bit lost in mustard flavors. We liked the salmon and Dover sole fish courses, treated simply and presented with butter sauces. We thought the game dishes more unusual, and the snow grouse engaging, though they both can turn up a bit too bloody and gamey. They come with very good potato pancakes and mushrooms. We also liked the loin of Arctic venison with apple-juniper sauce. With all those imported berries, desserts are tempting, especially the blueberry clafoutis. Also, consider the brambleberry sorbet and the Swedish pancakes with raisin ice cream. What to drink with all of this? To start, a shot of one of the many aquavits offered. Try one of the French or American white wines that work well through several courses, and you can return to Scandinavia, figuratively speaking, for a Finnish liqueur at the end of the meal. Ties are required for men downstairs, and regardless of sex, count on paying $140 or more per couple for dinner, plus tax and tip.

Adrienne
Peninsula Hotel,
700 Fifth Ave. (W. 55th St.)
903-3918

CONTINENTAL

Open Mon.-Fri. noon-2:30 p.m. & 6 p.m.-10:30 p.m., Sat. 6 p.m.-10:30 p.m., Sun. noon-3 p.m. All major cards.

You should be able to get a table. One Friday night when we couldn't get into any of a half dozen good places at the last minute, we had our pick of tables here. We entered this luxurious and vast art-deco formal dining room, two flights up in the Peninsula Hotel, and watched two captains standing side-by-side, hands clasped behind their backs, chatting. Seated in the half-filled dining room, we gave our order to a waiter. As the menu is solely in French, we ordered in French. He said, "excuse me?" We repeated. He said, "excuse me?" We looked at one another in blank confusion. All we were saying was "huîtres," as we were starting with the oyster dish. On the third try, he must have figured out we were ordering in French, because this time he replied that he was sorry, but he did not speak French. So much for the dining room. Meanwhile, chef Gray Kunz and a highly professional team cook their hearts out in the kitchen. Several meals confirm exciting and first-rate food. Given a better platform upon which to show his wares, the 34-year-old Swiss chef who trained with Freddy Girardet and worked at the Hong Kong Regent Hotel, would be the talk of the town.

We finally succeeded in ordering the gently warmed oysters with confetti of shallots and sesame seeds in a chervil sauce. Everything was gratinéed before being served. Delicious! The chef's Asian experience is ever present, including in the crispy ravioli starter, filled with leeks and ginger in a vegetable broth with cream, served with extra sautéed leeks on the side. We savored the perfumes of Asia on every dish. This master with vegetables puts them through preparations not seen elsewhere. How about a lovely crab bisque with raviolini

stuffed with tarragon? We thought the pompano perfect, fried on one side only and served moist and nearly raw with ribbons of daikon in red-wine vinegar and diced vegetables wrapped in a tiny cabbage ball. We also loved sweetbreads with asparagus, as well as the braised salmon with watercress-butter sauce. For a meat dish, try the lamb with eggplant—mignonettes of meat spread over an eggplant ragoût in a light cream sauce.

The mostly French wine list boasts bottles in all price ranges. We found the desserts lovely surprises—where else in New York can you find chrysanthemum soup with a garnish of nougat ice cream? (We liked it.) We enjoyed the semolina soufflé with a Sauternes-and-vanilla reduction, but be alert and order it at the begining of the meal (it takes 25 minutes to prepare). We liked the fruit tarts and the *petits fours* with coffee. For dinner, expect to pay $140 per couple.

10/20 Barbetta
321 W. 46th St.
(Eighth & Ninth Aves.)
246-9171

ITALIAN

Open Mon.-Sat. noon-2 p.m. & 5 p.m.-midnight. All major cards.

Aged Barbetta continues to seduce, though not always via her culinary charms. One of the theater district's longest-running restaurants (since 1906), it turns out dish after dish of northern Italian standards, many featuring the cuisine of the Piedmont, to a receptive and not-too-demanding audience. The place, comprised of townhouses dating from 1874 and 1881, has an individual style about it. Owner Laura Baiolglio furnished each room opulently (brocade-upholstered chairs, drapes, crystal chandeliers), but we think the restaurant's biggest success the charming garden, with its century-old trees and rainbow flowers. In fine weather, ask for one of the wrought-iron tables covered with linen.

These days, the food has improved, but you'll still find heavy, old-world fare at contemporary high prices. The "grande antipasto piemontese" on the menu lets you start off with a huge assortment of cold dishes, some worth trying. In the fall, when the white truffles are in season, you can have fettucine topped with shaved truffles or fonduta con tartufi; otherwise, the risotto piemontese is a good choice and one highly recommended by the waiters. We like the pasta primavera here, as well as the pesto sauce, which accompanies trenette (narrow, flat noodles). In summer, ask for the cold minestrone soup, hearty and refreshing. Our favorites include the passable fish dishes (such as the old, standard, broiled Dover sole), and nice, attractive game dishes in season. The more standard the item, generally the more standard the taste. For dessert, the chocolate mousse, the zuppa inglese or fruit are all right. The wine list has some appealing choices—though the list is still not well-maintained and vintage dates are wrong too often. Try some of the Piedmont wines (Gavi, Barbaresco, Barolo) from the hundreds of choices available. The staff has a long-established haughtiness that abets their nonchalance, though it makes for a pretheater show. Lunch averages $70 per couple; dinner averages $98 for two.

Bellini by Cipriani
777 Seventh Ave. (50th & 51st Sts.)
265-7770

ITALIAN
Open Mon.-Sat. noon-3 p.m. & 5:30 p.m.-11:30 p.m., Sun. 5:30 p.m.-9 p.m. All major cards.

Now that some of the chi-chi crowd and controversy have moved on to other haunts, Bellini has settled in as a good restaurant for pre- and post-theater dining in a district without top competition. You'll find here an attractive Venetian menu with the famed bean-and-noodle soup (so-so with an overdose of cheese), and a wonderful calf's liver with onions and polenta. We found the pastas and, especially, the risottos (try one topped with arugula) very good. Try to sit upstairs at one of the tiny tables. When crowded, this elbow-to-elbow bright rectangle of a place with marble floors can be very noisy.

Everyone starts with a glass of Champagne or the namesake Bellini, the peach liqueur concoction with sparkling wine that on neutral turf would lose every time in a shootout with Champagne, but evokes memories of Bellini's sister restaurant, Harry's Bar, in Venice. We feel the food fits the Cipriani style of simple home-cooking. We approve the appetizer of spinach ravioli with butter and herbs and the simple asparagus vinaigrette; we love the baked green taglioni. Spinach-and-potato

gnocchi can be overly dry and pasty. We think you should try the reigning risottos, which change regularly, as a main course. If you want fish, try the sea bass alla Carlina with rice pilaf and the salmon in wine sauce with zucchini. Friends liked the chicken, done either in veneto or romana style by chef Alfredo del Peschio. We thought the desserts very good, from a special rendition of lemon meringue to a dark-chocolate cake that is rich, dense and dependable. There's a good wine list with plenty of affordable bottles, though this place ain't cheap. Lunch is slightly less expensive than dinner, for which you should expect to pay $100 for two.

Le Bernardin
155 W. 51st St.
(Sixth & Seventh Aves.)
489-1515

FRENCH/SEAFOOD
Open Mon.-Thurs. noon-2:15 p.m. & 6 p.m.-10:15 p.m., Fri.-Sat. noon-2:15 p.m. & 5:30 p.m.-10:45 p.m. Cards: AE, MC, V.

This is the place that taught American fish to speak French fluently and, in doing so, raised the standards of fish preparation at many of this country's fine restaurants. That is no small accomplishment! When it opened in 1986, Le Bernardin earned breathless praise rife with flowery adjectives, slavering adulation and critical fireworks and stars, and had the boulevardiers of the world panting for tables. Let's say, also, that Le Bernadin earned quite a bit of media hype. Did it deserve all this? Its kitchen did raise the consciousness of a city of smug gourmets as to what can be done with fish. People were stunned by the layers of flavor in simply done food, and in one burst, Le Bernardin spurred other top New York restaurants to new heights of awareness and performance. Still, too much came to it, too soon. Why have we just now edged up our already high rating of Maguy and Gilbert Le Coze's restaurant? Two words explain our reasoning: consistency and influence. We found much to admire in the past about the restaurant's dishes, but there were flaws as well. Now we walk away in culinary bliss ever so frequently. An irony here is that the greatly talented Gilbert Le Coze is probably doing as little cooking as he has since boyhood. Executive chef Eberhard Mueller deserves credit for delivering the flawlessly prepared fish dishes, day in and day out. There's consistency out front, as well. Richard Hollocou has been deftly managing the restaurant since its opening, along with the Le Cozes, but the staff seems more assured and less laden with attitude now. As for influence: that is the extra dimension only the rarest of restaurants has, and if you see a sea-urchin dish or sauce, or a preparation of skate, on a menu in America, you can thank Le Bernardin. Ditto for a half dozen other simple innovations.

When you enter Le Bernardin, it speaks grand luxe at once. Its walls covered in muted blue-and-gray paisley fabric, its streetside windows draped with filmy cream curtains, its table lamps and floral displays and its glass and wood-frame partitions sectioning the open room into discrete dining and drinking areas, make it feel as if it were the lobby of a genteel, conservative and fabulously expensive hotel. (It's a setting that some adore, and others find cold.) The tables, spaced well apart from one another, are, in midtown Manhattan, the ultimate luxury. Only the oils of fishing scenes suggest Le Coze's less-ritzy background (his grandfather was a fisherman in Brittany) and the restaurant's seafood theme. We used to be turned off by the seemingly strictly-businessman types filling the restaurant's plush seats at lunchtime and paying with fat expense accounts. Now an attractive mix of women customers is utilizing the fish knives as well.

The food truly follows the market. The menu has not changed much in recent years, but the availability of fish has, thus expanding the options and extending the daily specials. The quality of the fish and seafood is always superb, and the preparations often brilliant. Sushi lovers will adore the carpaccio of tuna, as well as the slivers of black bass with basil and coriander leaves; oyster hounds justifiably go nuts over oysters cooked with truffles and artistically arranged on a bed of seaweed. We find pounded tuna a fascinating and delicious opener, as it is indeed pounded paper thin, almost to the size of a round plate, then drizzled with olive oil and served with toasted French bread. We love baked sea urchins, perhaps the restaurant's most famous dish, with a nuanced and sensuous blend of sea urchin and butter. On our last visit, friends found the sea urchin soup worth exploring,

and the seafood chowder and the fish soup set oh-so-high standards. We also liked the roast monkfish with savoy cabbage and chunk bacon, a terrific combination of perfectly cooked fish, contrasting nicely with the earthiness of the cabbage and the bacon. Salmon rouelle—two slices rolled up into one another, then sautéed and served with a fresh fennel sauce and julienne of fennel and bits of tomato—is excellent. We liked the successful and satisfying, if not quite worth all the ballyhoo, preparation of poached skate in brown butter. One noticeable change since opening has been a reduction in the saltiness of many dishes; apparently, the kitchen has, thankfully, succumbed a bit to the American palate.

Desserts have become even more spectacular. Theme desserts such as a half dozen variations on "pear"—offering sorbets, mousses and tartlets—work best. We adore the chocolate-mousse cake and pretty chocolate millefeuille with pistachio cream and chocolate sauce. Friends have found the caramel dessert plate sensational, ditto the changing palette of fresh-fruit sorbets. Discouragingly high-priced, the wine list does seem well-chosen, and now includes an increased range of California wines and older French wines. The restaurant has been criticized for its high prices. If you forget the rent, and just consider the quality of produce, the extensive team in the kitchen, the spectacular and expensive tableware, the crystal glassware, the nineteenth-century paintings, the doting service and so on, you may have to concede that Le Bernardin is, in fact, a tad underpriced, as are some of the other top restaurants in New York City. No doubt Maguy and Gilbert Le Coze would argue that's true. Book well in advance. The fixed price at lunch is $80 per couple; dinner is $130 for two, but your tab (with tax and tip) will run much higher than that.

Bombay Palace
30 W. 52nd St. (Fifth & Sixth Aves.)
541-7777
INDIAN
Open Mon.-Sat. noon-3 p.m. & 5:30 p.m.-11 p.m., Sun. noon-3 p.m. & 5:30 p.m.-10 p.m. All major cards.

They aim to please at this long-established, sugar-coated Indian eatery, and they do, mostly with their $9.95 all-you-can-eat lunch. A turbaned doorman still sweeps you out of your car as if he were ushering you into the Raj. We think Punjabi or Mughlai food more delicate than the usual run-of-the-mill Indian chow; ghee (clarified butter) rather than oil is the cooking medium, and complex, elusive tastes rather than fiery hotness the hallmark. We can't testify to the absolute authenticity of Bombay Palace on all points, but it generally appears to score well. The food reveals personal, inventive touches, though it raises the issue of authenticity versus good eating and evolving cuisine. Flavors come through as they are meant to, allowing you to appreciate the complex taste levels and contrasts characteristic of this cuisine.

We love mattar panir, a fine vegetarian dish of squares of chewy homemade cottage cheese, braised with peas, onion and tomato. The Indian bread, onion kulcha, which is often sodden and doughy elsewhere, comes out light and puffy here. At a recent feast, friends loved the rogan josh (mildly spiced lamb curry with yogurt), one of the most popular dishes, as well as the tandoor chicken, lamb or prawns, carried aloft on a sizzling platter to the table. Chicken makhani or butter chicken (shredded tandoori chicken in a buttery tomato sauce with hints of ginger and garlic, garnished with chopped coriander), and the jhinga masala (spicy shrimp) were outstanding. We learned that many dishes, like the flavorsome keema mattar (ground meat with peas) are garnished with crispy fried caramelized onions, adding an extra delicious note. Do start with a drink as an excuse to nibble on the delicious samosas, pakoras and spicy pappadum. The Indian kitchen generally offers a very limited range of desserts, sweets being eaten by Indians rather as snacks throughout the day. For diehards, however, there is kulfi, the Indian "ice cream," made with condensed milk and chopped almonds and pistachios. Or you can try mango ice cream or, if you have room, Indian rice pudding with almonds and rose water. Beer or a light white wine goes well with Indian food. On hot days, try the lassi, a cooling yogurt drink which you may have in any desired degree of sweetness, as well as salted or plain. At lunchtime, the free-for-all buffet of salads, curries and grills is set out on the second floor.

For two, lunch averages about $30, dinner about $60.

12/20 B. Smith's
771 Eighth Ave. (47th St.)
247-2222

AMERICAN
Open daily noon-midnight. All major cards.

The bad news first. You know the food isn't all that good when, on two successive visits, different waiters warn you off two different dishes. The up side? At least you know that the waiters are honest; and if you make your 6:30 p.m. reservation, they'll absolutely get you out in time for your show. More good news is that this is an attractive, upbeat place with a lively bar (expect noise) and good jazz into the night. All things considered, this is one of the better spots in the theater district.

The dinner menu is divided usefully into eight columns: appetizers, soups, salads, light plates, seafood, meats and poultry, pasta and desserts. The homemade bread comes warm, but the carrot soup has too much cream and the carrot flavor is lost. Opt instead for the gulf shrimp steeped in Chardonnay with garlic and herbs for a starter, though the shrimp are rubbery occasionally. The shrimp scampi, by the way, is not a good choice—it's bland, and it comes with a bad mango purée. The spinach linguine is okay, and no more. Ditto the soft-shell crab special, which is overly garlicky. The lobster ravioli is a best-seller here. The ravioli are served in a shellfish bisque with a warm Mascarpone cheese. The hot grilled-salmon-filet salad with wild mushrooms, roast potato and greens is recommended, as is the flash-roast salmon with chervil and tarragon in a tomato bisque.

B. Smith, the former black model and current co-owner, offers an individual-size rendition of her grandmother's sweet-potato pie with pecans for dessert. Our experience with the gratin of fresh seasonal fruits and berries with hazelnut crème anglaise has been one of watery sweetness and semi-cooked fruit. The medium short wine list is fine, with all reliables and no surprises. Expect to pay $80 per couple for dinner and about $50 for two at lunch.

12/20 Cabana Carioca

123 W. 45th St.
(Sixth & Seventh Aves.)
581-8088

BRAZILIAN

Open daily noon-11 p.m. All major cards.

This folkloric Brazilian restaurant in the theater district delivers exuberant good food at low prices, and a fun evening. A seeming bright spot on one of the seedier streets in midtown, its facade is lemon-yellow, and, inside, the banister of a shabby staircase is painted in vibrant primary colors. The second-floor dining room is jammed with the broadest cross section of New Yorkers to be found outside of the U.N. The small bar is lined with regulars downing massive portions of mixed grill, feijoada (Brazil's national dish), pork and steak. A caipirinha, a Brazilian cocktail made from cachaça (local rum), lime juice and sugar, is a fine way to whet the appetite. Move on to a traditional soup such as caldo verde, a thick potato-based broth with collard greens and sausage disks. Sopa a alentejana is a watery but vividly garlicky soup, made more substantial by the egg that has been poached in its broth, and the slices of bread that have absorbed its savory juices. Feijoada, the best entrée, is offered nightly: a substantial bucket is filled with beans, rich sausage, beef ribs and whatever other meat comes up in the ladle. Rice is served alongside, as well as a number of condiments, including sliced oranges; a sharp relish made of tomato, vinegar and onions; and manioc flour, which looks and tastes like finely ground stale bread crumbs. Brahma, the Brazilian beer, is rather boring. Opt for one of the Portuguese wines or the caipirinha. Dinner with drinks comes to about $48 for two, plus tax and tip.

La Caravelle

33 W. 55th St. (Fifth & Sixth Aves.)
586-4252

FRENCH

Open Mon.-Fri. noon-2:30 p.m. & 5:30 p.m.-10:30 p.m., Sat. 5:30 p.m.-10:30 p.m. Closed last week in Aug.-1st week in Sept. All major cards.

This 30-year-old quintessential New York French restaurant—the kind you used to see in 1960s movies with Jack Lemmon—looks the same, but its spirit and dedication have soared since André Jammet took over full ownership in 1988. Inside, you can expect serious European waiters with impeccable manners, white tablecloths and dim lights, china and the glimmering silverware and the Henry Pagès postwar murals of Paris. The red/pink velvet banquettes are among several items that show the room's age, but the dinnerware and what's on it have taken a more contemporary turn. So has the clientele, which used to be almost exclusively old, monied regulars. When talented chef David Ruggiero left in 1990, he was replaced by Frank Champely, formerly executive chef at The Regency Hotel. Champely is an able fellow, but he has been told by Jammet to bring back some of the La Caravelle cuisine of ten years ago. This retro-cuisine is well-done, but a recent meal left us longing for the revitalized dishes we sampled here in 1989. Let's hope Champely is given more latitude to express his own talents.

Salmon with fennel works well as an *amuse-gueule* while you contemplate an improved wine list with a huge selection of French wines, from inexpensive to very expensive, as well as increasing numbers of American wines. Among many very good appetizers, we liked crab ravioli, a not-too-creamy pumpkin soup with lots of nutmeg, a vegetable terrine with aspic, wild quail sautéed with mushrooms, and snails in a Pernod sauce with couscous. Among fish entrées, the sea bass with potato crust (not wrapped, but with a "slice" on top) is our first recommendation, and the sea scallops in a light chive sauce the second. The Caravelle classic quenelles are attractive: ground pike, crabmeat and truffle dumplings are first poached, then put into a closed cassoulet with chopped lobster and lobster sauce. The sauce boils and the fragrant steam expands the quenelles. By the time the dish is brought to the table and its cover opened to release the sweet steam, the dumplings have become as light and airy as a soufflé. We found the mignon of veal with crayfish in a crayfish sauce one main course that was only okay. We loved the roast duck with cranberries, well-done and appearing with a crispy skin.

Among the top dessert tarts and tartlets, soufflés and mousses, we go for the chocolate or the anisette-with-coffee-grains soufflé. Their floating island is weak—the egg whites are heavy and the créme-anglaise sauce too watery. Lunch, pretheater dinner and dinner are prix fixe at $32, $35 and $57 per person respectively, so figure on $100 to $150 per couple for dinner with wine, plus tax and tip.

11/20 Carolina

355 W. 46th St.
(Eighth & Ninth Aves.)
245-0058

AMERICAN

Open Mon. noon-3 p.m. & 5:30 p.m.-9 p.m., Tues.-Fri. noon-3 p.m. & 5:30 p.m.-11:30 p.m., Sat. 5:30 p.m.-10:30 p.m., Sun. 5 p.m.-9 p.m. Closed Sun. in summer. Cards: AE, MC, V.

It's been said before, including by us, that something could be finer at Carolina, notably the food, which wavers at various levels within an acceptable range. A trendsetting restaurant that opened early in the 1980s, Carolina now plays its regional American repertoire half-heartedly for a convention crowd and people with their minds on the show they are trying to make, rather than for a savvy New York audience. The restaurant's location—on the theater district's restaurant row—is the key to its survival. Speaking of keys, the one absolute draw here is the tart Key lime pie. Appetizers demonstrate the kitchen can hit its mark and get you in and out in a New York minute (no doubt there's plenty of pre-preparation).

There are satisfied customers here, and presumably they are happy with the most popular items on the menu—corn chowder, Hell's Kitchen chili, hot smoked barbecued ribs and swordfish grilled over a wood fire (not bad). Indeed, go for soup and a grilled fish. Cornbreads fill you up, too. Mud cake and apple crisp head the list of desserts. Opt for the romantic, candle-lit back room, with its mirrors and skylight—you'll enjoy eating the atmosphere, too. Dinner comes to about $90 per couple, with wine or beer.

12/20 Chez Josephine

414 W. 42nd St.
(Ninth & Tenth Aves.)
594-1925

FRENCH

Open Mon.-Sat. 5 p.m.-midnight. Cards: AE, MC, V.

Ambience, and not the decent home-cooking, is the reason you head for this flamboyant bistro that recalls Paris's Montmartre and New York's Harlem of the 1920s and 1930s. It is dedicated to Josephine Baker, the world-renowned chanteuse and star of *La Revue Nègre*, and owned by one of her "rainbow tribe" of thirteen adopted children. Jean-Claude Baker, one of the warmest and most endearing hosts around, pays homage to Josephine's early years in Paris (1925–1930) with numerous vintage posters and paintings of the singer (in various stages of artistic undress) from the Folies Bergères and Casino de Paris. The hundred-year-old grand piano was once used by Miss Baker for rehearsals in Harlem; Jean Claude has restored it and splendid pianists now entertain on it during dinner and late into the night (see Nightlife chapter, page 223).

The cooking is hearty, a blend of Paris bistro fare with the down-home cooking of Miss Baker's early years. Jean-Claude Teulade has been heading the kitchen since 1988, but we have hardly noticed a difference over his predecessors, and we continue to enjoy ourselves at every meal. The Chinese ravioli with roasted pignoli, fresh dill and goat cheese has long been a pleasant appetizer, though it is a bit chewy and dry, and the dill is only a sprig on the side. The leeks in a warm tomato vinaigrette stands out as an appetizer. The boudin noir (blood sausage) with red cabbage, onions, apples and french fries is first-rate, except that the french fries (like the sweet-potato fries) have been oily on every one of our visits for years. Seared Black Angus strip steak is tasty and cooked to perfection; it comes with excellent julienned vegetables and french fries. Lobster cassoulet, with shrimps, scallops, black beans and seafood sausage, also is recommended. Desserts are okay: fruit tarts, crème caramel and a chocolate ganache called "La Délice Josephine." The wine list is balanced and affordable, with a couple of good half bottles. Dinner averages about $70 to $80 per couple.

China Grill

52 W. 53rd St. (Sixth Ave.)
333-7788, 956-7062

ECLECTIC

Open Mon.-Thurs. noon-2:30 p.m. & 5:30 p.m.-11 p.m., Fri.-Sat. noon-2:30 p.m. & 5:30 p.m.-midnight, Sun. 6 p.m.-10 p.m. Closed Sun. from July 4-Labor Day. All major cards.

You'll find China Grill a high-energy, high-quality, oversize brasserie and culinary knock-off of Los Angeles's Chinois on Main, featuring Californian/French fare with Asian accents. It works, at least for us and the bicoastal crowd that packs it. The huge, slickly elegant restaurant is carved out of a space in the CBS building previously occupied by four separate restaurants. A postmodern study in black and white, with high ceilings painted in black, white moon-shield lights overhead, black walls, bleached-white-wood floors and white tablecloths, the restaurant has two halves—each side of the restaurant runs from 52nd Street to 53rd Street, a mirror image of the other. Each half contains two dining areas, one raised slightly, and a long bar where you can be served a complete meal. The dining areas, seating about 200 in all, hinge in the middle at an open kitchen. Pulsating, upbeat, modern music fills the room, where a young service staff of both sexes dances the kitchen's wonders to your table.

In the past, we have found crackling calamari salad with potato crisps and sweet-and-sour sauce superb, and the Confucius chicken salad only good. However, we adore another appetizer, tempura sashimi—tuna quickly battered, then deep fried, sliced, and served with a Champagne-and-sea-urchin sauce—subtle and lovely. We love just looking at the grilled quail appetizer, served in a nest of crispy noodles. The always-artful presentations add to the excitement of the meal. Dishes are generally served Chinese-style, so you can sample plate after plate around the table with either the chopsticks or knife and fork provided. We think they handle vegetables and side dishes superbly here, and like the way garlic is liberally used in many dishes. We've also enjoyed Chardonnay steamed mussels in black beans and saké.

Main courses range from sizzling whole fish with ginger served with ponzu sauce and grilled free-range chicken with toasted garlic and grilled mushrooms to an excellent grilled, dry-aged Szechuan beef dish. We think the desserts freshly inviting (certainly also stunning to look at, arriving on *faux*-marble plates), including a curious cream-cheese mousse with a five-fruit coulis. We also liked warm noodles in honey cream with sautéed apples and golden raisins, as well as an ever-changing array of fruits and pastries. The wine list is superb, though not enormous, containing only top-quality wines in top vintages from Europe and California, and including many scarce wines. About $120 per couple for dinner.

11/20 La Cité
120 W. 51st St.
(Sixth & Seventh Aves.)
956-7100
FRENCH
Open Mon.-Fri. noon-midnight, Sat.-Sun. 5 p.m.-midnight. All major cards.

This is supposed to be like a French brasserie, but only the name measures up. The place reminds us nothing at all of the wonderful Parisian brasseries, such as Chez Flo or La Coupole. La Cité's decor is—let's say—different; the food, so-so; and the service so cute and robotlike, we become nostalgic for a haughty French waiter. Prices? Don't ask, and don't think brasserie. Our first meal was totally unmemorable. On our second visit, we brought along a couple of colleagues from Paris. They love brasseries, but were disappointed to the point of amusement by this rococo, art-deco showplace in cream, yellow and black formality, with bilevel dining rooms as well as a less expensive grill room. Waiters wear traditional costume: black jackets and long white aprons.

Appetizers are passable; the winners are the potato-and-sausage tart and the fresh shellfish. The mustard-coated chicken breast entrée was moist, but three fish dishes were dry. The swordfish special looked as if it were a shoe sole in the middle of our dish (we're translating from one of our French colleagues). Steamed mushrooms were okay, as, on one occasion, was the grilled salmon with a dill vinaigrette. La Cité wants to be known for hearty dishes—petit salé of duck, choucroute and the likes—but even on a cold day, the sight of the open silver cart trolleying around is a turnoff. Perhaps the best thing to do here is to order oysters on the half shell to start, followed by a very good steak and french fries. Desserts did not fare much better, whether American (say, the rice pudding) or French (say, the profiteroles, which tasted stale, and the tarte tatin, which didn't look or taste like the real thing). Still, if you must, go for the banana ice cream with coconut cookies. With its quality/price problems, we wonder how long the curious will fill the place. Figure $100 per couple, plus tax and tip.

Darbar

44 W. 56th St. (Fifth & Sixth Aves.)
432-7227

INDIAN

Open Mon.-Thurs. noon-2:30 p.m. & 5:30 p.m.-
10:30 p.m., Fri. noon-2:30 p.m. & 5:30 p.m.-
11:30 p.m., Sat 5:30 p.m.-11:30 p.m. All major
cards.

With so many mediocre Indian restaurants in Manhattan effectively making one avoid the food altogether, Darbar is a rare pleasure. This elegant midtown find scores first with an eye-catching decor of elaborate plaques, intricate tapestries and copper trays that hang from velvet-covered walls. A spiral staircase leads to a second level, with tables tucked romantically alongside tall picture windows. We liked the most intimate seating, behind carved wood screens on the first floor.

The art compares favorably with the craftwork of an excellent kitchen that delivers with style and doesn't compromise for inexperienced Western palates. Start with anguri samosa, greaseless fried dumplings filled with lightly spiced vegetables, or onion bhujia, a tangled web of thinly sliced onions, deep-fried in a flour batter. Channe ki chaat is a combination of cold chickpeas, potatoes and onions. Appetizers come with an array of condiments, including a cooling mint sauce, a sweet-and-sour tamarind sauce, and chunks of spicy marinated vegetables. Among the best main courses, we loved murgh tikka masala, tender white-meat chicken pieces broiled in a charcoal clay tandoor oven and added to a rich sauce of tomato, onion and butter. Gosht vindaloo blends lamb or beef with potatoes in hot curry.

The more adventuresome will enjoy murgh madras, a southern Indian speciality that mixes chicken with lemon, cinammon and an unforgettable spicy pepper sauce. Vegetarian choices include bayngan bhurta, a puréed eggplant mixture with tomatoes and a hint of onion, and a savory dish of seasoned chickpeas, onions and tomatoes called channa masala. They counter the more potent dishes, as does patiala pillau, a basic offering of scented white basmati rice. An alternative to rice is a simple naan bread, stone-white and cooked quickly on the sides of the tandoor, that complements any dish. We thought more elaborate the fried whole-wheat poori, puffed

into a golden-crusted balloon, and the onion kulcha, a flatbread stuffed with onions. This spicy food requires Indian beer such as Taj Mahal, which comes in a bottle big enough for two, or a standard-size bottle of Kingfisher. Dinner runs about $80 for two.

"44"

Royalton Hotel,
44 W. 44th St. (Fifth Ave.)
944-9415, 944-9416

AMERICAN

Open Mon.-Fri. 7 a.m.-midnight, Sat.-Sun. 8
a.m.-1 a.m. All major cards.

This place is better than it needs to be, and it should get even better. Situated at the raised upper end of the long, long futuristic lobby of the Royalton Hotel, "44" is a convenient spot for a business lunch, pre- or post-theater dinner or for people-watching. This Philippe Starck–designed landscape is home turf to visiting Europeans on the prowl for a contemporary scene and the hip downtown crowd. Note the fashions, note the hairdos, note the nubile bodies and good looks. And that's only the staff.

The cuisine of Joseph Manzare, formerly of PosTrio in San Francisco, gently rearranges reliable international standard items, giving them new life and a pronounced American accent. We've enjoyed the simple anise-cured salmon to start, as well as the delicious sweetbread salad with mixed greens and walnuts. Grilled sardines with tabouli are okay We thought we'd like the tempting offering of wild mushrooms with polenta soup, and while not quite a disappointment, we found the mushroooms overpowering. Pasta specials work well as a first course. For a main course, go for the exceptional pigeon, the roasted chicken with lentils or a grilled salmon with cucumber. The veal chop turns out to be breaded, and was overcooked, but flavorful. We liked the fish-and-chips (halibut and french fries), a safe and filling upscale version of the classic, which shows the chef has a sense of humor, not extending, thank goodness, to serving it in a newspaper cone. For a dessert, we loved the banana baklava—phyllo dough and banana cream—sweet but good, reminding us of glorified baby food. Our first choice among the desserts, however, is the lemon and yogurt trifle. You can always satisfy yourself with the *petits fours* alone or with coffee. We think the wine list selective and good. This hotel dining room does triple duty, and breakfast is served daily on its well-spaced tables surrounded by comfortable chairs. A popular and satisfactory café is adjacent, and is open all sorts of hours. For dinner for two, count on $100.

Gallagher's
228 W. 52nd St.
(Broadway & Eighth Ave.)
245-5336
AMERICAN/STEAKHOUSE
Open daily noon-midnight. All major cards.

There has been no news out of Gallagher's for years, affirming that the old adage, "If it ain't busted, don't fix it," also applies to New York steakhouses. They just keep feeding satisfied customers the same fare, done in the same way, and served in the same huge portions as it was 50 years ago. You'll still find sawdust on the floors, and red tablecloths. This theater district stalwart proudly packs in businesspeople at lunch and the Broadway crowd at night. Entering this former speakeasy, you'll pass by a glass-enclosed aging refrigerator, where more than 600 prime sirloin strips can be viewed, and arrive in the large wood-paneled dining room, its walls covered with photos of famous New York politicians, athletes and actors—vintage New York nostalgia—and a now-important collection of photographs by C. C. Cook.

You won't have to look at the menu to know that clams or oysters on the half shell make a good starter, though many prefer the oxtail soup or marinated herring in cream sauce to begin. There's an open kitchen, with a charcoal broiler where meat, fish and poultry cook over hickory logs; you might try your oysters grilled. You can order a jumbo shrimp cocktail so truly jumbo that it would be a parody of the appetizer, except that this is the original. You can have lobster if you want to pass on meat, or a nicely grilled swordfish steak. There's roast prime rib of beef, too. But face it, you came here to experience the gluttony of a serious, monstrous steak. Order a simple baked potato on the side or perhaps some French fried onion rings, expect overcooked greens if you insist on ordering beans or spinach, and finish up with a hefty piece of cheesecake or strawberry shortcake. You'll be ready for a return visit in a couple of years. The wine

list contains highly selected, limited offerings of acceptable American wines to wash this all down—perhaps a Jordan ($32), Stag's Leap ($47.50) or Heitz Cellar's Martha's Vineyard ($85) Cabernet. Per ounce of food, the tab here isn't that high: about $70 per couple for lunch and $100 for two for dinner, without tax or tip and with a modest wine.

11/20 Jezebel
630 Ninth Ave. (45th St.)
582-10450
AMERICAN/SOUL FOOD
Open Mon.-Sat. 5:30 p.m.-midnight. Cards: AE.

You're paying for the packaging, that is, the setting and the scene, but soul food—ribs, ham hocks, chicken and sausage—does have its followers. Dinner here is theater. And in the theater district, playing to a theater crowd, dinner—not what's on your plate, but what's around you—had better be one helluva show. The performance starts at the nondescript entrance, with only a small, well-camouflaged plaque saying "Jezebel." But inside, the decor is New Orleans bordello out of *Pretty Baby*, with seven-foot-high palms, orange birds of paradise in antique vases, white wicker furniture, crystal chandeliers, lawn swings, settees, antique shawls draped from the ceilings, mirrored columns, movie posters, jelly glasses for water and zombie waitresses who seem part of some cabalistic order (headed by Jezebel?), though the piano player seems lively enough. They tell you seatings are at 6 p.m. and 9 p.m., which is for outsiders. Regulars may arrive whenever. If forced, opt for 9 p.m.; that's when things start to swing. The crowd is dominated by actors, directors and large groups of acting students who take turns in the lawn swings, table-hop, and sing along to the Berlin, Ellington and Fats Waller tunes. The scene is worth the price of the meal.

Whether the result of ritual or management, service is slo-o-o-w and the timing unpredictable, which can make the pretheater crowd, shall we say, nervous. Popular appetizers include rib bits and shrimp sautéed in garlic, either of which might be handed out free in a bar during happy hour. The corn bread is delicious, so you don't have to worry about leaving hungry, and, with portions fit for heavy laborers, the contrary is the concern anyway. For main courses, the fried chicken, smothered chicken, pork chops, curried goat and the like are akin to versions served at less artifical places, and the complete package includes yams, greens, black-eyed peas and okra. The deep-fried whole fish have a following, as do the spicy shrimp dishes. For dessert, the bread pudding has it over most choices, including a strawberry shortcake that inexplicably ranges from lamentable to laudatory. Expect to pay $90 per couple for dinner, sharing an overpriced bottle of cheap wine.

Kuruma Zushi
18 W. 56th St. (Fifth & Sixth Aves.)
541-9039

JAPANESE
Open Mon.-Sat. noon-2:30 p.m. & 5:30 p.m.-10 p.m. All major cards.

Admittedly for serious devotees of raw fish who are oblivious to raw decor, Kuruma Zushi is a restaurant we patronized when it was the best "secret" sushi address in town, situated over a noodle parlor and almost impossible to find. Now well-established at yet another location, the restaurant is doing what it does best—serving first-rate sushi, sashimi and simple Japanese dinners. The restaurant has a plain Japanese-style decor with an ample sushi bar in back, a few tables and a private tatami room into which are carried possibly the most ravishingly beautiful sushi platters ever seen. The chefs bellow greetings, farewells and calls for the bill in tones that would do the Old Vic proud.

Perhaps no other Japanese restaurant in town offers the variety of fish found here—the sushi menu lists about 40 items, including all the usual fish, though, of course, not all may be available on any one day. We watched all the sushi and sashimi items cut well and presented simply, with a minimum of razzle-dazzle. The rice in the sushi has a slightly sweet presence that is very agreeable. At the tables, you may have chicken or beef teriyaki or broiled fish. Sushi items are priced by the piece; dinner will run about $100 per couple without drinks, depending, of course, on one's appetite, with a $20 dinnertime minimum per person at the counter. Expect to spend $40 per couple for lunch at the counter, or take advantage of the three fixed-price soup-and-sushi lunches offered under $20.

12/20 Lattanzi
361 W. 46th St.
(Eighth & Ninth Aves.)
315-0980

ITALIAN/JEWISH
Open Mon.-Thurs. noon-2:30 p.m. & 5 p.m.-11 p.m., Fri. noon-2:30 p.m. & 5 p.m.-midnight, Sat. 5 p.m.-midnight. Cards: AE.

A snug spot with a low ceiling, brick walls, cloth-covered hanging lamps and piped-in opera, Lattanzi may not exude charm, but offers some enjoyable dishes at reasonable prices for midtown, and a reasonably sound spot to dine in the theater district. Everything is prepared to order, even during the pretheater crunch, by a kitchen staff that makes sure you will be out on time. The regular menu offers such simple, well-prepared dishes as homemade fettuccine Lattanzi with peas and mushrooms in cream (occasionally under- or overdone), spaghetti with white-clam sauce, roasted half-chicken with fresh rosemary and garlic (sometimes overly dry) and veal chop with fresh mushrooms. After 8 p.m., a small transformation takes place: a second menu featuring classic Roman Jewish food is offered also (and at lunchtime). This second menu is simple, straightforward food, the best-known dish probably being artichokes Jewish-style, peeled, flattened and deep-fried in boiling olive oil laced with garlic cloves, and seasoned with salt and pepper. In Italy, special large artichokes, tender and chokeless, are used for this ancient preparation: they emerge as totally edible bronze flowers. Because American globe artichokes are too fibrous, Lattanzi uses baby ones, which imitate the taste, if not the appearance, of the originals. An interesting opener on the Jewish menu is caponata ebraica, which is an unusual combination of the marinated eggplant dish, mozzarella in carrozza, and a deep-fried ball of rice with tomato sauce. The caponata, with its elusive sweet edge, is the secret recipe of manager Vittorio Lattanzi's Aunt Maria, and may just be the best you have ever tasted anywhere. Fish is done reasonably well. Ask for the fish of the day, which may be red snapper with shrimps, clams and mussels in a fragrant, thick, red-tomato sauce. On the Jewish menu, the red snapper with raisins and vinegar harkens back to the old Venetian sweet-sour fish preparations. Simply grilled lamb chops and veal chops are recommended. Desserts are all homemade and okay, with the cassola (containing ricotta and eggs), the napoleone and, especially, the chocolate tartuffo recommended; the house wine is a pleasant Chianti and the remaining Italian wines on the list are all serviceable, such as a Chianti Classico from Antinori ($20) or, for a top choice, a Barolo 1978 from Pio Cesare ($65). Service can be nonchalant and gruff, so be forewarned. Dinner for two averages $84 on the regular menu, $78 on the Jewish menu; figure $70 per couple at lunch, plus tax and tip.

 Manhattan Ocean Club
57 W. 58th St. (Fifth & Sixth Aves.)
371-7777
AMERICAN/SEAFOOD
Open Mon.-Fri. noon-midnight; Sat.-Sun. 5 p.m.-midnight. All major cards.

The Manhattan Ocean Club, which takes pride in its loyal clientele and fresh fish, has given a boost to its once uninspired menu with the addition of a new chef, Jonathan Parker. The food is dramatically improved, the dining room the same, and the prices still sky-high. The dining room gives guests the vague feeling that they're on the Hollywood set of a Roman gladiator movie, but it's still a safe place to bring your parents or a new friend of the opposite sex. Downstairs, Picasso plates adorn the walls (no one seems to look at them), while upstairs, Picasso paintings look down upon a younger crowd, which doesn't mind climbing the metal staircase with its cruise-ship look. To the regular menu of fish dishes—broiled, roasted or sautéed—chef Parker has added several very original preparations.

Among the cold appetizers, the big surprise is the chilled tuna-and-eggplant terrine, prepared in a checkerboard pattern. The soft, broiled eggplant has a smoky, burnt flavor which complements the tender, clean-tasting tuna. A crab-and-parsley terrine, fresh and delicate, came with a spicy, lemony mayonnaise. We found the ceviche tangy, and served on a bed of chopped tomatoes, fragrant with coriander. For a restaurant that caters to an older crowd, these dishes seem daring. If you love seafood, you can choose freshly shucked Hog Island or Malpeque oysters, clams, even sea urchins or crab, when in season, served on a large platter with thin slices of fresh pumpernickel bread. We found the plate of crab cakes,

spicy and moist, a pleasant alternative to the simply prepared fish entrées, and we loved the swordfish au poivre, a thick, tender filet spread with crushed peppercorns and served with refreshing shredded cucumbers. A seared tuna steak, pink inside, comes served with grapefruit segments and deep-fried leeks. Don't miss the shoestring potatoes, but avoid the salads, which swim in dressing. Finish off your meal with a cup of good espresso and some cookies; most of the desserts seem too heavy and sweet. The computerized wine list here is intelligently composed, and contains some good California wines and some fairly good French ones, including red wines for a "red wine with fish" experience. If you're dining alone, the very friendly waiters will make your meal pleasant; otherwise, their friendliness can be "de trop." A final note: if you happen to want a car service to pick you up, the restaurant will provide one at no charge. First come, first served, but what a way to dine! The average price for two at dinner, with wine, is about $150.

 Michael's
24 W. 55th St. (Fifth & Sixth Aves.)
767-0555
AMERICAN
Open daily noon-2:30 p.m. & 6 p.m.-11 p.m. All major cards.

Native New Yorker Michael McCarthy finally has delivered the New York City restaurant he has been promising since his wonderful and influential Santa Monica eatery helped put Californian cuisine on the world map. A handsome and friendly chap who knows his business extremely well, he took his show successfully on the road, first to Denver and then to Washington, D.C., before trying to make it in New York. So far, so good. This huge place has been packed since it opened late in 1989. As Michael notes, "we know everybody, and they're dropping by."

The cuisine is not cutting-edge any longer. Indeed, the museum-quality contemporary art adorning the china white walls (Jasper Johns and friends) has a more up-to-date feel than what's on the plate. Expect plenty of grilling, and produce with state names attached. For us, Michael, with his slicked back hair and broad-shouldered 1930s custom-made suits, is more memorable than what we've eaten. If you're in the mood for a salad,

Michael's should be a top consideration, with its lush greens and separate section of listings on the appetizer side of the menu. The warm lamb salad, the curly endive with bacon salad, the grilled quail salad, join a host of other combination salad plates, ranging from seafood to mushrooms. We like the pastas: our favorite is the fettucine with salmon and tomatoes, married with a range of cheeses. The grilled swordfish is fine (no better than at lots of places), but the grilled chicken served with french fries is special, as is the grilled duck.

We like some of the desserts, though some are too sweet, even cloying. The Heath Bar torte will catch your eye, but doesn't stand up to its name. Wines, on the other hand, are enticing, with, as can be expected, some lovely offerings from California, to go with good bottles from all the other major wine areas. Be sure to sit in the back, with the garden view, or the front room of this redone defunct Italian pavilion. In the middle, the ceiling is low, and the heat and air conditioning blow to the extremes of temperature. Expect to pay about $100 per couple, plus the 15-percent gratuity that is automatically added to your bill.

11/20 Nicole Brasserie de Paris

Omni Park Central Hotel,
870 Seventh Ave. (56th St.)
765-5108

FRENCH
Open Mon.-Sat. 11:30 a.m.-3:30 p.m.& 5:30 p.m.-midnight, Sun. noon-3 p.m. & 5:30 p.m.-midnight. All major cards.

Though it cannot boast a top kitchen, Nicole still has a lot going for it. The handsome decor here is Alsatian brasserie via Paris: art-nouveau designs, and accoutrements such as an antique bar and pastry cart, four-color marble floor, *faux* marble and trompe l'oeil walls and bentwood chairs. The open kitchen is a nod to California. The location is superb. You can see the back of Carnegie Hall from your seat, and Lincoln Center, the theater district, Rockefeller Center and Fifth Avenue shopping are within easy walking distance. So with its location, appealing atmosphere and wide-open hours, Nicole is a good choice for pre- or postconcert or theater meals, or light meals at odd hours, as well as all-out lunches or dinners. But then there is the food.

We had reasonably high hopes for it when the restaurant opened, but hotel restaurants are a contrary lot. Unlike most new restaurants, which take months to iron out wrinkles and years to build up a clientele, restaurants owned by hotels tend to open in all their glory—no doubt with the highly paid executive chef and outside consultant eagle-eyeing everything and everyone—and then fall off lazily. That appears to be what has gone on here. If you choose well, you can eat well, although some dishes vary from visit to visit. The traditional brasserie dishes are usually sound. Consider the cassoulet (lamb, duck and garlic sausage stewed with white beans and tomatoes) or the old reliable entrecôte (sirloin steak) with french fries. Among the bistro fare items, the onion soup has proven uneven: once it is excellent, hot, flavorful and crowned with cheese gratinée crust that must be broken with a spoon; the next time, the topping is an anemic floating cheese cross, and the broth a bit undernourished. The couscous is minor league as well. It looks good, and the portion is large, but the grains have not been worked well. Salads are very large, and make a good meal if you handle the dressing yourself; if not, you wind up with something resembling flavored industrial mayonnaise. The veal paillard is a sound, simple and reliable choice, as is the Dover sole—nothing extraordinary, but nothing regrettable. There's a general inconsistency in cooking pasta. Though hardly a staple in either Alsace or Paris, the crabcakes with curried tomatoes or Louisiana sauce is an attractive main course. The desserts are so-so, though they look appealing. As you would expect in a good European brasserie, there is a nice range of beers, and the wine list, featuring French and California wines, is fine, with a number of bottles priced in the teens plus nine premium wines offered by the glass. Price for lunch is about $50 for two, and for dinner, $76.

Orso

322 W. 46th St.
(Eighth & Ninth Aves.)
489-7212

ITALIAN
Open Sun.-Tues. & Thurs.-Fri. noon-ll:45 p.m., Wed. & Sat. ll:30 a.m.-ll:45 p.m. Cards: MC, V.

This place gets an extra point for probably being the top spot to eat in the theater district, and, anyway, there has got to be a lot right about a restaurant that serves good food, with amiable service, in a pleasant setting where you can eat, drink and philosophize late into the night. The people-watching's not bad, either; since opening in 1985, Orso has become a theatrical hangout for actors, critics, producers and the groupies. The action takes place in the bar and in two small dining rooms, the last of the latter with a skylight and an open kitchen. Mottled mauve, cream and gray walls come cluttered with photos of the known (D.H. Lawrence, Olivier) and the unknown. Handpainted Italian china and pitchers by Vietri make artistic backdrops for the fresh and satisfying food.

For a light meal, you can't beat the small pizzas—salads, actually—with crusts more brittle and thinner than matzos. The copious toppings generally fall off, but the ingredients make for tasty eating. We love pizza alla Siciliana, for example, a cornucopia of roasted peppers, raw Paris mushrooms, black olives, tomatos, onions, garlic and fresh basil. Pastas change daily, and such preparations as tagliatelle (flat noodles) with peppers, leeks, mushrooms, butter and Parmesan cheese, make more substantial and equally savory meals. For a truly hefty repast, try the densely packed homemade sausages of veal and lamb, distinctively flavored with anise. You'll find seafood and fish the best choices—from the grilled shrimp appetizer to the required grilled tuna with black olives and tomato. We loved for dessert the gelati and chocolate-mousse layer cake. The wine list is more than reasonably priced, and there's not an unappealing selection. In all, this is a truly inviting, genial and engaging trattoria. Reserve well ahead. A leisurely dinner, including a moderately priced bottle of wine, will run about $88 a couple.

Palio
151 W. 51st St.
(Sixth & Seventh Aves.)
245-4850

ITALIAN

Open Mon.-Fri. noon-2:30 p.m. & 5:30 p.m.-11 p.m., Sat. 5:30 p.m.-11 p.m. All major cards.

The Palio, the name of the famed horse race through the streets of Siena, comes depicted in an extraordinary mural surrounding the marble and stainless-steel bar of the restaurant

bearing its name. Upstairs, the dining room's decor presages the kind of cuisine the restaurant serves: it has a cold, corporate feeling, punctuated by a contingent of businesspeople, theatergoers and an occasional tourist. Palio's menu is so long that it takes diners about twenty minutes just to read through the choices, which include a series of fixed-price menus (a theater menu, a hunter menu, a monthly menu, a farmer's menu and a fisherman's menu). We watched the indifferent waiters watching us as the maitre d' assigned to our section walked around with his hands behind his back, looking bored. A basket containing several breads arrived at the table with drinks; except for a pungent, pleasant olive-oil loaf, you can forget the breads. We're sorry that this attempt at a grand Italian restaurant so rarely lives up to its potential. Chef Andrea Hellrigel, who recently purchased the restaurant from former partner Tony May, has great talent, but some piece in his restaurant always seems out of whack in the total dining experience.

When we dined here last, we found the potato-stuffed ravioli—swimming in melted butter and sprinkled with Parmesan cheese—bland without the shaved white truffles they are supposed to nobly bear, according to the menu. At $32 a portion, anyone could do better than that. Although tender, the marinated, roast squab seemed cloyingly sweet, despite a faint taste of wine vinegar. The addition of cinnamon mars otherwise deliciously light pumpkin ravioli, tossed in butter and fresh Parmesan cheese. While a rich chicken broth bears perfectly cooked, fresh tortellini, a fisherman's soup, with an abundance of seafood, including shrimp, lobster, mussels and clams, lacks depth. It's hard to believe that the chef doesn't use food coloring to make its broth so red, or is it scarlet? On the other hand, we thought the maccheroni all' amatriciana (fresh tomato-and-sweet-pepper sauce) perfect, and suggest you go for the house special, spaghetti alla chitarra—fresh pasta gone through a guitar-shaped cutter to make it square, half black from cuttlefish ink—with excellent seafood in a red sauce. Executive chef Theo Schoenegger also offers a tasty marinated eel in balsamic vinegar, served with lentil salad as a tempting appetizer.

Among the entrées, we found a gamey hare drowned in a rich, winey sauce set off by red cabbage, sweet and heavy. We loved the monkfish with vegetables (pieces of fish are topped with sautéed yellow peppers and zucchini). Also consider the rollatine of salmon, with black olives and sun-dried tomatoes. We thought the desserts uninspiring unless you're a fan of creamy gelatins or heavy chocolate cakes, though the pine-nut ice cream is, at least, unusual. Instead, end the meal with a crisp, fresh radicchio salad with artichoke hearts in a wine vinaigrette or a mixed salad of fresh greens garnished with endive. The wine list is like the menu, extensive and expensive, but it has extensive offerings of brunellos, Barolos and barbarescos at formidable prices. We saw a few reasonably priced California wines, but the only French ones are Champagnes—the most expensive cuvées only. Prices here are high, though there is a $35, three-course luncheon menu and a $70, five-course dinner menu. Nevertheless, with wine, expect to pay around $190 for a dinner for two.

Petrossian
182 W. 58th St. (Seventh Ave.)
245-2214
FRENCH
Open Mon.-Sat. 11:30 a.m.-3:30 p.m. & 5:30 p.m.-midnight, Sun. 11:30 a.m.-3:30 p.m. & 5:30 p.m.-10 p.m. Also cold bar daily 3:30 p.m.-5:30 p.m. All major cards.

This is one place that doesn't worry about restaurant reviews. What's to worry when you serve the finest caviar around, superb North Atlantic salmon, and fine foie gras you raise and prepare? The place knows why people come, and, generally delivers. In the small dining room, in an establishment synonymous with the finest caviar, the black, gray and pink art-deco decor seems to be the decorating equivalent to caviar: gray mink-and-kid-leather banquettes, Erté etched mirrors, Lalique appointments and a long, long Angolan and Finnish granite bar running the length of the back wall?) Here, with a flute of Champagne in hand (or a glass of chilled vodka), you feel like a welcome extra on the set of *Lifestyles of the Rich and Famous.*

True aficionados of those fragile fish eggs enjoy the superb beluga, osetra and sevruga caviars at Petrossian au naturel, without chopped onions, eggs or sour cream. Ditto for the salmon and for the foie gras. You can, of course, order some variations on their themes, such as raviolis of smoked salmon in a Champagne sauce, or a fantastic green salad with foie gras. Among the more conventional (some would say classic French) offerings, the roasted breast of duck with honey and fresh raspberries is fine, as are the medallions of lamb sautéed with sprigs of fresh rosemary. We loved the thickly sliced, seared fresh tuna, and consider the pick of the à la carte selections to be the classic red snapper with julienne of vegetables. If you want to go all out, Petrossian offers Babette's Feast ($90), the six courses recreated from the Oscar-winning film based on Isak Dinesen's novel. Under chef Michel Attali's hand, the menu garnered Petrossian considerable publicity and praise. Attali is now the consulting chef (could he have gotten tired of counting all those grams of fish eggs?), but we've not noticed the slightest drop-off in quality. Top honors among the desserts—all done on the premises—go to the apple or pear tarts, unless you are a chocolate freak, in which case the rich chocolate cake prevails. Chocolate doesn't go overly well with Champagne, but everything else on the menu does, and the wine list is filled with top bubbles as well as a broad selection of quality still wines. You get a taste of the basics on the reasonably priced pre- and post-theater ($35) menus. And should you crave more, there's always the Petrossian gourmet boutique, adjacent to the dining room. Lunch runs $80 per couple and dinner about $120, though those little eggs can rocket a bill to the stratosphere in a hurry.

12/20 The Rainbow Room
30 Rockefeller Plaza, 65th Fl.
(49th & 50th Sts.)
632-5100
CONTINENTAL
Tues.-Sat. 5:30 p.m.-midnight, Sun. noon-2 p.m. & 5:30 p.m.-10:30 p.m. Cards: AE.

"Rainbow, rainbow, rainbow/and I let the fish go," poet Elizabeth Bishop wrote. Here, they serve up the fish reasonably well and consistently cooked, considering the substantial numbers being served in the dining and private rooms. Everything aside from the so-so fare is indeed rainbows at this refurbished art-deco emporium. Renowned restaurateur Joe Baum (Windows on the World, Aurora) and designer Milton Glaser have recreated this

1930s nightspot and breathed new life into it. It's now the sort of touristy spot that works—with its exceptional views, nostalgia, romance, and its dancing to a live orchestra.

You don't choose the Rainbow Room for its food (which, by 1930s standards, is pretty good). Lobster thermidor, tournedos Rossini and oysters Rockefeller recall the 1930s and 1940s. With oysters or a shellfish appetizer, you can't go far wrong—though Champagne and caviar capture the room's spirit. Rack of lamb (for two) is fine, and do order the pommes soufflé, the delicate ballooned potato crisp that is a house specialty and an increasing rarity around town. If you are stepping back in time for the evening, then by all means, after a swing or two around the dance floor, choose the baked Alaska for dessert. The wine list is excellent, and there are plenty of those cocktails of yesteryear. Book well in advance. pretheater dinner for two runs $77 and brunch $69 per couple, without wine. A late-night supper for two averages $110, and dinner $150 per couple, with a bottle of wine.

Raphaël
33 W. 54th St. (Fifth & Sixth Aves.)
582-8993
FRENCH
Open Mon.-Fri. noon- 2:30 p.m. & 6 p.m.-10 p.m., Sat. 6 p.m.-11 p.m. Closed Sat. during Aug. All major cards.

Dusted off, polished up and reopened after a 1989 fire, Raphaël is back to the ways that for more than a dozen years has earned it a solid reputation and following, especially among the French business community. Occupying the narrow ground floor of a midtown townhouse, Raphaël seats only about 40 people in a rustic, château-like setting. One wall is brick, with a cozy fireplace, and the back wall opens onto a pretty little garden. In this comfortable, sedate setting, owners Mira and Raphaël (thus the name) Edery supervise a small but steady team of French professionals, which has included a number of talented chefs who came and went amiably.

Because of the chef changes, the menu has been freshened up a bit with some contemporary fare. Like the room and the staff, the menu (in French) seems relatively petit—one typed page of offerings changes every few weeks to exploit the seasonal market, but the bulk of the menu never varies radically. For starters, we've enjoyed the ravioli of Saint Jacques with zucchini and thyme, as well as simple oysters or the salmon gravlax with an olive oil vinaigrette. We also like canard Apicius, with a purée of dates and apples. The smoked and roasted lobster with herbs is marvelous, and the simple veal paillard, grilled and served with a lemon sauce, one of the best around. For desserts, try the classic apple tart or a special raspberry millefeuille. The wine list is in harmony with the menu. It contains about 90 selections, mostly French, but with an increasing assortment of American wines, and runs from $19 (a Louis Jadot St. Amour) to the low hundreds. A few good bottles are listed, but there are too many off vintages and too many predictable wines from big importers and producers. About $80 per couple at lunch and $100 for two at dinner, with wine, plus tax and tip.

Remi
145 W. 53rd St. (Sixth & Seventh Aves.)
581-4242
FRENCH
Open daily noon-2:30 p.m. & 5:30 p.m.-11:30 p.m. All major cards.

Architect/designer/restaurateur Adam Tihany and chef/partner Francesco Antonnuci are savvy, smart, ambitious and ever-so-talented fellows. They opened their first Remi to great success on the Upper East Side and surprised everyone when they closed it. They thought they knew best; they wanted a bigger space and a luncheon clientele. A year later they reopened, drawing crowds on West 53rd Street, a midtown area still lacking a choice of very good restaurants. (Tihany and Antonucci are also partners in the new Remi in Santa Monica, California, and are planning more Remi outposts—the venture is obviously a good investment.)

What the twosome offers on 53rd Street and elsewhere are strikingly handsome design, solid northern Italian cuisine (Milanese and Venetian for the most part), excellent selections of Italian wines and grappas, and reasonable prices (most entrées priced in the teens, to a top of $24). The wines are listed in novel fashion: three price categories of $16 to $25, $26 to $36 and "Remi Selections," which run from $40 to $130.

Antonucci prepares his cuisine with a light

touch, and he offers eleven antipasti, nine pastas and risottos, and eleven fish and meat entrées, plus specials made very much in the style of the former Remi. The risotto tastes stronger than it has been in the past, and the pasta is good, though the shellfish variety we ate recently was only passable (opt for the seafood risotto), ditto the grilled vegetables (awash in garlic-flavored olive oil), a longtime and colorful favorite of ours at the old Remi. Perhaps you'll need to keep an eye on what produce is seasonal or local to fully enjoy the dish. The tasty beef carpaccio topped with arugula and Parmesan continues to be an excellent and light starter. Grilled snapper pleased our palates and in the past we've enjoyed rack of lamb as a main course.

Desserts continue to look better than they taste, though the tiramisu is better than par; it will probably take months after opening, however, to train the waitstaff to deliver coffee after dessert. After all, this is supposed to be an authentic Italian restaurant, isn't it? Expect to pay $75 for two with a modest wine, plus tax and tip.

René Pujol
321 W. 51st St.
(Eighth & Ninth Aves.)
246-3023

FRENCH
Open Mon.-Fri. noon-3 p.m. & 5 p.m.-11:30 p.m., Sat. 5 p.m.-11:30 p.m. Closed July. All major cards.

With the promotion in 1989 of Jean Charles Michel, the *sous*-chef for four years, to chef, this good, conservative French restaurant in the theater district made its first menu change in years. Don't worry, this solid place continues to deliver on all fronts, and to attract hordes of theatergoers, as well as tourists looking for a not-too-too-expensive, authentic French meal to eat. René delivers, along with his family, notably daughter Nicole Franques and wife Monique Pujol. They run the show out front in the appealing French country dining room (stucco and brick walls, false-wood beams, copper pots and bric-a-brac), made more cozy in winter by the glowing fireplace.

Under the new chef, the restaurant has seemingly lost some of its traditional bourgeois dishes (like boeuf bourguignon, though you can still get escargots bourguignon) and

found more contemporary fare and a fixed price dinner ($30, plus plenty of supplementary options). From the extensive menu, you won't have difficulty finding a good dish to order. Among good, but ordinary, appetizers, the lobster ravioli stands out for quality, as does the julienne of vegetables with smoked chicken. We think entrée winners include the sea scallops with Belgian endive, the veal tenderloin with sweetbreads sautéed and served with a truffle sauce, and a very nice roast leg of lamb. We loved, for dessert, the marquise au chocolat, which has long sent away satisfied customers (the place opened in 1970), but try the feuilletée tiède with apples and raisins. The wine list (and cellar) is a very good one, and has received an award of excellence by *The Wine Spectator*. Beyond a modest, yet serviceable, offering of California wines, you'll find a large and comprehensive French assortment at reasonable prices, with especially strong Burgundies. Unlike so many New York restaurants that serve wines right off the truck, at René Pujol the inventories have been built up carefully over the years, so that properly aged wines at civilized prices are offered. A comfortable bar and dining room upstairs hosts private parties of up to 50 persons. Lunch averages $58 for two, dinner $116, à la carte with wine, plus tax and service.

La Réserve
4 W. 49th St. (Fifth Ave.)
247-2993

FRENCH
Open Mon.-Sat. noon-3 p.m. & 5:30 p.m.-10:30 p.m. Closed July. All major cards.

What will it mean? André Gaillard, the young Burgundian chef who joined owner Jean-Louis Missud in 1985 and built La Réserve into a fine restaurant (greatly admired by critics, though not as fully endorsed by the public), left in January 1990, weeks before his sudden and premature death. A couple of chefs have done the waltz before at this handsome café, opened in 1983, and then Gaillard came in and brought the kitchen to the verge of greatness. So, Monsieur Missud knows all too well the difference that a chef makes. He has replaced Gaillard with Dominique Payraudeau, the former chef and partner at La Promenade in Closter, New Jersey, who also cooked in Manhattan previously at The Terrace Restaurant. Our current rating, therefore, is a provisional one. The challenge to the Missud-Payraudeau team will be compounded by the additional loss of a talented French pastry chef, brought in by Gaillard and shrewdly taken by him to Le Chantilly. Nothing has changed in the restaurant's two dining rooms (featuring attractive, fabric-covered banquettes, comfortable chairs, large paintings of waterfowl and beautiful chandeliers) as well as the private-party rooms, nowadays filled with a range of relaxed and serious diners. Not much has changed on the wine list, though it has grown to 175 wines, including 30 from California. It's still tough, however, to find a decent Burgundy here. We wish the owner would hire a consultant and stop using a major distributor and supplier to formulate his list, which includes too many off vintages and lesser wines. The kitchen, of course, has begun its slow transition, but the range of offerings is the same, and all meals are prix fixe—$30 for lunch, $39 for pretheater, and a comparatively low $48 for dinner. Among the dishes we have recently enjoyed are the cannelloni of salmon appetizer and the rosace de St-Jacques. The salad of grilled quail with hazelnut vinaigrette comes with one perfectly grilled and largely deboned quail on a bed of greens, and with three soft-boiled quail eggs surrounding the nest. The foie de canard flavored with passion fruit works, with its fresh sautéed New York State foie a sure-fire hit. We have always enjoyed the magret of duck with roasted quail and the sweetbreads with asparagus and truffles. The service is veteran European professional, and the desserts are good, including the tarte tatin and the dacquoise. With wine and an occasional supplement, you'll be up to about $130 per couple for dinner, plus tax and tip.

 The Russian Tea Room
150 W. 57th St.
(Sixth & Seventh Aves.)
265-0947
RUSSIAN
Open daily 11:30 a.m.-11:30 p.m. All major cards.

In fickle New York, where "in" dining places change with the hemlines, the Russian Tea Room has a record for longevity and popularity that is the envy of its competition. Since its early days, when homesick Russian ballet dancers, hungry for blinis and sour cream, formed the nucleus of its patrons, its show-biz clientele has been one of the RTR's biggest attractions. The best time to people-watch is at lunch or after the theater, but make sure you have a reservation, or you may be dining peacefully in Siberia upstairs. In the days when the Russian Tea Room was a quiet little restaurant, the waiters were all Russian, and you could always get a table. But that was before the power lunch and the $75 theater ticket. Now the waiters have first names such as Ahmed and Pedro, and the restaurant caters to two clearly different clienteles. There are the regulars—movers and shakers of show business, who inhabit their assigned tables day after day and order appetizers for lunch that get computed onto their monthly bills—and a constant flow of intimidated out-of-towners, who wait patiently in line.

The decor is pleasant and idiosyncratic—deep green walls, red banquettes, brightly shining antique samovars, the RTR art collection on the walls, and Christmas decorations that got left up longer and longer each year, until they became part of the decor. The food remains as good as it has been in years. French chef Jacques Pepin was hired as a consultant to gradually introduce "lighter, more contemporary fare" to complement the old standbys, and since 1988, chef Jerry Reiner has been seeing to the ovens here. You'll like the streamlined menu and fixed prices. You can trust the house specialties: the mainstay peasant soups like borscht (cold in summer, hot in winter), or zakuska for an appetizer. We like the unctuous eggplant orientale, a puréed merger of eggplant, onions, green peppers and tomato, zesty and filling, and best eaten with black bread. Of course, you could try the Swedish matjes herring, smoked salmon and the like. And where better to enjoy the great choice of caviar and blini with one of the twenty vodkas offered? Crêpes appear in many guises. Main courses include the marinated and skewered lamb karsky shashlik (supreme!), the côtelette à la Kiev, luli kebab (ground lamb patties broiled on skewers), and a beef Stroganoff, too rich for some people's tastes. The best entrée may be the moistly buttery chicken cutlet Kiev. For dessert try kissel, a sweetened cranberry purée served with cream and sugar. The international selection of wines has many familiar names, fairly priced. Dinner begins with a fixed price menu at $39.50, so with wine, figure at least $110 per couple, plus tax and tip; lunch, about $58 for two.

San Domenico
240 Central Park South (east of Columbus Circle)
265-5959

ITALIAN

Open Mon.-Sat. 11:45 a.m.-2:30 p.m. & 5:45 p.m.-11 p.m., Sun. 5:45 p.m.-10 p.m. All major cards.

Italian restaurateurs in New York think the critics have it in for them. Most of the top-rated restaurants are French, with only a few American-style places gaining equal kudos. There's been nary an Italian eatery in the top ten or twenty. Prejudice? Hardly. New Yorkers hope each year for a great Italian eatery. And Tony May keeps trying to build that great Italian restaurant. This is his finest attempt. He teamed up with the owner of one of Italy's most renowned culinary spots, the celebrated San Domenico, in Imola (near Bologna). Its very talented young chef, Valentino Marcattilii (who apprenticed with the Troisgros in France) came to New York to cook regularly, and together they opened this super-premium restaurant in mid-1988. Talented chef Paul Bartolotta is the man regularly on the scene. Some days the food is super, and if we have one criticism, it is that they are trying to do too many things on the plate to impress. With some dishes, you wish they'd take one ingredient away and double the portion. If we had a second criticism, it would be consistency, but that's all-too-frequently a problem at top restaurants; still, we're ready to take a leap of faith and count San Domenico among New York's elite.

We love the original menu; many of its dishes made their first appearance in New York with the opening of San Domenico. We consider the pastas a quantum level above others around town. Go for one of the raviolis, say the seafood in a broccoli, olive oil, garlic and white-wine sauce, or the potato-filled spinach ravioli in a pesto sauce. Marcattilii is renowned for his single, large ravioli filled with a runny egg yolk. Try it. We think other winners include the boneless stuffed quail with asparagus-and-hazelnut sauce, and sensational pan-roast medallions of sweetbreads, scented with garlic. We love the lobster fricassée with sliced artichoke hearts—it's destined to become a classic here. We like the guinea hen braised with savoy cabbage and mushrooms, as well as the risotto with beef glaze, sliced roasted sirloin of beef with porcini mushrooms, and veal medallion in smoked-bacon-and-cream sauce. A pricey, but princely, 900-item list of Italian and American wines can make for interesting food and wine marriages, if you can afford to experiment. In true Italian style, the best dessert may be fresh fruit. Alternatively, go for the nice sorbets and brandy-soaked fruits, or other unctuous concoctions. The 130-seat room with imported terra-cotta floors, marble columns and orange tablecloths bespeaks barrels of lire and helps explain why this place makes the top ten in price. There's a $32.50 prix-fixe lunch and a $65 dinner, but figure $200 per couple à la carte.

12/20 The Sea Grill
Rockefeller Plaza, 19 W. 49th St. (Fifth & Sixth Aves.)
246-9201

AMERICAN/SEAFOOD

Open Mon.-Sat. noon-3 p.m. & 5:30 p.m.-11 p.m. All major cards.

While skaters twirl in winter around Rockefeller Center's skating rink, you can be sipping a glass of sparkling wine behind the glass wall of this seafood restaurant, watching the pirouettes. The Sea Grill's elegant, spacious dining room is a pleasant haven after a morning of shopping. The large tables are set far apart, allowing room for conversation without being overheard. Don't expect great cuisine, just very fresh fish and seafood, an ample selection of wines and respite from the bustle of New York.

Among the cold appetizers, the fresh oysters and clams need but a squeeze of lemon; they are of excellent quality. The chilled snow-pea soup with sweet, buttery Kumamoto oysters is delicately seasoned but the tender asparagus on a bed of red oak leaves is overpowered by white-truffle oil. The hot appetizers are, on the whole, unsuccessful. The Maryland crabcakes, served tepid instead of piping hot, leave an aftertaste of bread crumbs instead of ocean-fresh crab. Lobster, served with an uninspiring chive sauce, is rubbery. Best among the entrées are broiled fish and grilled langoustine. The pristine Dover sole is ruined by an overcooked crayfish stew that tastes as if it had been made weeks before. The spiced monkfish medallions with oyster mushrooms are cloaked in a heavy port-wine sauce that puts a clamp on what would otherwise be a complex, refined dish. A real treat is the grilled yellowfin tuna, beautifully seared on hardwood coals, moist and tender. Certain meat dishes are well-prepared here, surprisingly enough; a sautéed filet of veal is served with a smooth, authentic polenta and a simple brown butter sauce. However, avoid steaks drowning in heavy sauces.

Dessert is predictable: chocolate cakes (one named Prometheus is probably the richest chocolate cake ever), mousses, tarts and a dreadful cappucino flan. A tangy, rich Key lime pie makes a nice ending to a seafood dinner. The all-American wine list offers excellent choices and is reasonably priced. The same menu is offered for lunch and dinner. Dinner is about $160 for two, with a bottle of wine.

"21" Club

13

21 W. 52nd St. (Fifth & Sixth Aves.)
582-7200

AMERICAN

Open Mon.-Fri. noon-3 p.m. & 5:30 p.m.-midnight, Sat. 5:30 p.m.-midnight. All major cards.

They'll be telling the story for years: early in 1987, the new owners of this legendary club closed the 60-odd-year-old restaurant down for a couple of months of cleaning and renovation, fired some of the old staff, and hired some hot-shot chefs. Some $9.5 million later, the place looked better—cleaner and more plush, like a museum. The expensive art added to the already fine American collection justifies the notion. The irony is that despite the high-price chefs and consultants, the food still wasn't very good. Now, three years later, those chefs are gone and the menu and repu-

tation are back to their pre-renovation days, except that hardworking chef Michael Lomonaco is shrewdly taming the kitchen. The classics are back, as mediocre as ever, but his newer offerings bode well for the future.

Prices still seem absurdly high here, but the pretheater ($37.50) and late-night supper menus that have been added to bolster business at least are of this world, and provide an opportunity to case the former speakeasy. What should you order? Keep it simple, and go for the legendary dishes: Maryland crabcakes or, perhaps, oysters on the half shell or a salad to start, and a "21" burger with french fries or chicken hash to follow. We also like the pepper tuna steak or roasted chicken. Chef Lomonaco has added a trim menu and has been coming up with such winning combinations as roasted fennel with grilled lake trout and fennel ratatouille with grilled Alaskan silver salmon. On the even less trim side is venison with currant sauce as a special. The currants reputedly are flown in from New Zealand, a fact that might make for trivial dinner conversation. Also for the end-of-the-year holiday period, he offered cioppino, an Italian fish stew traditionally eaten on Christmas eve, as well as the traditionally English entrée of roast goose with chestnut dressing (though a number of other European countries could claim that classic as well). We like the wine list, with Bordeaux and Burgundies aged and purchased in a bygone era at "21" and shrewdly updated and maintained. Dinner à la carte, with wine, is way up there, at between $150 and $200 per couple.

> *Note that average prices given in this chapter do not include tax (which is a whopping 8.25 percent in New York) or gratuity. You can figure, then, on adding roughly 25 percent to each of the prices quoted here, for your final bill.*

UPPER EAST SIDE

12/20 Alo Alo
 1030 Third Ave. (61st St.)
 838-4343
ITALIAN
Open daily noon-midnight. All major cards.
  The circular bar in this slightly chic, glass-walled corner restaurant serves as a backdrop for young shoppers from Bloomingdale's, who need some refreshment after dealing with the crowds and the credit cards. The diners, dwarfed by the theatrical kitsch (a Dino De Laurentiis production) of the airy but somewhat noisy dining room, are a more sedate and serious polyglot crowd of young and old Europeans, South Americans and Upper East Siders. The space is big enough so that seating is not a problem, and Alo Alo is an easy, cheerful kind of a place to fall into. One of its best traits is the daylight that pours in through the soaring windows that face, in back, a vest-pocket park, complete with a waterfall of sorts.
  The cuisine at Alo Alo (the accent is on the second word) is sprightly, and sometimes surprisingly good, under the guidance of co-chefs Saulo Fernandes and Protassio Marques, who joined in 1986. Antipasti include a recommended bresaola, a thinly sliced air-cured beef served with arugula and seasoned with mustard. The carpaccio, served with arugula and thin shavings of Parmesan, is delightful. Its mix of sweet, delicate beef, salty cheese and tart greenery works exceptionally well. For a salad, try the endives with New York State goat cheese. There's a daily risotto, and another special might be fennel salad with mandarin sections, also refreshing. As for entrées, the pastas are serviceable, from the simple, al dente spinach gnocchi in a tomato-and-cream sauce to the farfalle (butterfly pasta) primavera. If you're not in the mood for pasta, try the calf's liver. It is tender and pink inside, and served with sautéed leeks and delicious timbales of polenta imbued with a sauce redolent of sage. The grilled swordfish with tomatoes, capers and endive is also worth a try. The breaded-and-pounded veal chop served with grilled endive is palatable for those who like their veal breaded. Service here includes pushy actor-types, young, often friendly, but not the

most attentive or professional. Desserts include raspberry or apple tart and a luscious St-Honoré. The Italian/California wine list is short, but nicely affordable, with bottles ranging from $17 to $36. A pasta lunch, with a glass of wine, will run about $50 per couple, before taxes and tip; dinner for two, with a bottle of wine, about $84.

 Anatolia
 1422 Third Ave. (81st St.)
 517-6262
TURKISH
Open Mon.-Sat. noon-2:30 p.m. & 5:30 p.m.-11:30 p.m., Sun. 5 p.m.-10:30 p.m. Closed Sun. in July & Aug. All major cards.
  At last, we have the gourmand's dream: a restaurant where one can, if so inclined, make a meal of dish after dish of delicious appetizers. Restaurant addicts won't be able to resist the appealing simplicity and freshness of tomatoes, red onions, olives, lemon, garlic, feta, dill, leeks, eggplants and yogurt in dozens of combinations and permutations. Loosen your tie (or better, wear none) and *eat!* The Turks claim to know a thousand ways of preparing eggplant, and the offerings here prove it—the soguk memzeler (cold appetizers) include pan-fried eggplant disks with a tangy garlic-and-yogurt sauce; sublime patlikan ezme, a garlicky, parsley-dotted purée of grilled eggplant (which is delicious, though not as smoky as we'd like); and the imam bayeldi, roasted baby eggplant stuffed with tomato, garlic and onion. We loved the hot version, stuffed with ground beef, peppers and tomatoes, and the prices are so easy we tried them all. Don't miss the Turkish bean salad, piyazi, firm white beans tossed with olives, tomatoes and onions in a light lemony dressing; and surely don't miss the cacik, chilled cucumber-yogurt soup, laced with mint. Outstanding hot appetizers include the pan-fried cubes of liver topped with spiced red onions and the zucchini "pancakes" oozing feta, dill and scallions. If you can restrain yourself, eat just one or two of the appetizers, and select a main course, such as lamb shank with lemon sauce; skewers of grilled swordfish; skewers of grilled quail in grape leaves, served with a currant-and-pine-

nut-studded pilaf; shish kebab; or stuffed Cornish game hen. If you still have room for an excellent dessert (the Turkish palate is known for its attention to sweets), a lovely tray will be brought out (or you will be escorted up to shop the big tray), from which you can select various types of baklava, a yogurt cake with sour-cherry sauce or rice pudding. The Turkish coffee will make you sit up straight; tell the server in the gold-bullioned jacket how you like it—very sweet or medium.

Note the modern tavern decor: marble-topped tables, garden chairs, improbable gold-touched Corinthian columns, and a touch of neon here and there. The banquette arrangement makes seating a bit cheek-to-jowl. You'll like the attentive and pleasant service staff, the more so as food arrives with astonishing promptness. You can order five wines by the glass, or from the inexpensive wine list (plenty of choices in the teens), mostly California and, to a lesser degree, French. The Clos du Bois cabernet sauvignon at $19.50 makes for a fine accompaniment. Dinner, before tax and tip, averages $50 or so per couple.

 Arcadia
21 E. 62nd St.
(Fifth & Madison Aves.)
223-2900

AMERICAN

Open Mon.-Fri. noon-2 p.m. (two sittings, noon and 1:45 p.m.) & 6 p.m.-10 p.m., Sat. 6 p.m.-10 p.m. All major cards.

Welcome back, Anne! Chef and proprietor Anne Rosenzweig, that is—which means the return of a very, very good kitchen. Though small and narrow, Arcadia boasts a soothingly sylvan mural by artist Paul Davis, which gives airiness and dimension to this popular place. (The elbow near to you can often be connected to a face you usually see on televison.) Diminutive chef Rosenzweig essentially developed her very personal, consistently superb renderings of essentially down-home food here, which is why patrons are celebrating her return after a heavy involvement in the "21" Club. The low ceiling and cheek-by-jowl banquette arrangement can produce a fair din when clients pack the restaurant, which it almost always the case. The menu, small and select, changes seasonally and has been miraculously edited of clinkers; everything on it

seems familiar, yet with an unexpected twist. In Rosenzweig's thoughtful, complex renderings, flavors may be repeated like musical themes, building in intensity. For an elegant opener, corn cakes, a takeoff on blini, accompany dabs of osetra and golden whitefish caviars and crème fraîche. In cold weather, don't miss the spicy, grilled duck sausages, surrounded by roasted chestnuts and sautéed apple slices. We declare a meltingly good, grilled, wild-mushroom sausage on toasted barley a winner, as well as the fricassée of mussels with fava beans and saffron.

You'll discover that the lunchtime star—a substantial lobster club sandwich with bacon, tomato and lettuce in a French brioche—is appealing as a concept, but hard to eat gracefully. And with a food like lobster, where delicacy should prevail, the point is lost in the hearty company of bacon and thick bread. At dinner, we loved the moist, sweet chimney-smoked bites of lobster served with crusty Chinese noodle cakes. The chef removed the meat, with a tantalizing hint of smoke, from the shell, cut, then replaced for ease in eating. The kitchen also pairs flawless duck breast filets punctuated by cracklings with savoy cabbage and kasha. We also liked roasted loin of veal with stewed tomatoes and onions, accompanied by scalloped potatoes, and the grilled salmon on tomato sabayon with couscous of spring garlic and peas, as well as the molasses-roasted quail on dandelions with rhubarb sauce, served with wonderful sweet-potato fries.

We love the irresistible desserts, from the house specialty (billed as chocolate bread pudding, but really a rich, warm, chocolate-permeated brioche cake, served in brandy-custard sauce), to the lemon-curd tart swathed in raspberry sauce (it has just the right degree of astringency). Or try a simple plate of perfect fruit, enhanced by an intense grapefruit sorbet; an opulent tuile filled with lemon curd mousse; or the pear timbales, dressed with caramel sauce and served with homemade sugar cookies. The wine list, while small, is nicely varied and fairly priced. When you reserve, which you must do as far ahead as possible, specify the main room; the tables added to the front bar room are continually grazed by the passing parade. Jacket and tie are required. A prix-fixe dinner plus wine is about $125 for two; lunch costs about $60 per couple.

Arizona 206
206 E. 60th St. (Third Ave.)
838-0440

AMERICAN

Open Mon.-Thurs. noon-3 p.m. & 6 p.m.-11 p.m., Fri.-Sat. noon-3 p.m. & 6 p.m.-11:30 p.m., Sun. 6 p.m.-11 p.m. Café: Mon.-Sat. noon-midnight, Sun. 5 p.m.-11 p.m. All major cards.

All's well in Arizona, at least on 60th Street. The blasé bartender still clangs the Soleri "designer" bell to signal the waitress to pick up her frozen margaritas, and astonishingly, the bell can be heard above the blaring rock. The waitress (in pink oxford shirt and khaki pants) responds, elbowing her way through the three-deep crowd of Burberry coats and tooled leather jackets at the bar. More Soleri bells hang, strategically placed, in the small après-ski-style lounge area, where diners with reservations usually have to wait for a solid half hour for their tables. Still, the bells instantly evoke the American Southwest—the magic touch needed to transform a former Austrian dining room into Tucson, Phoenix or Anywhere, Arizona.

In 1988, when Brendan Walsh left, his longtime second, Marilyn Frobuccino, took charge as chef. As often happens, the pupil surpassed the teacher. The food has never been better, more refined or more consistent at Arizona 206. Our perennial favorite here, blue-corn-coated oysters with cabernet shallots and Serrano-lime butter, should be your choice of appetizer, or the Southwestern Peking duck with plum mole or the barbecued foie gras and cactus-pear salad. We love the quail with polenta and the roasted baby chicken with mashed potatoes and rutabagas. Also among entrées, try the pistachio-crusted tenderloin of rabbit with mole and creamed collards or the pan-seared Louisiana shrimp and crabmeat gumbo. What impresses here are the natural, true flavors and the assertive seasonings. If you love corn, then order the grilled salmon with corn pudding.

The wines (mostly American) and the desserts pass muster. The apple cranberry crisp hits the spot . . . the tiny spot left in your stomach after such a good meal. Ask the highly professional staff about a wine, and you'll get as long a dissertation as you'd like

on marrying various wines with the unusual items on the changing menu. Arizona 206 has space next door at Number 204 for a café serving tapa-size portions of selected items. Dinner for two in the restaurant costs about $120, with wine. Lunch for two will run about $90.

Auntie Yuan Restaurant
1191A First Ave. (65th St.)
744-4040

CHINESE

Open daily noon-11:30 p.m. Cards: AE, CB, DC.

This is definitely not your usual Chinese restaurant. Conspicuously absent, for one thing, are Asian customers, that unerring benchmark of other good Chinese restaurants. Though the food preparation at Auntie Yuan remains Chinese, many of the ingredients (such as quail, salmon and mussels) seem Western, as are many of the waiters. Instead of the usual garish (or nondescript) decor and bright lights, this tranquil dining room comes sleekly black, with overhead pinlights illuminating a flower here, a snow-white tablecloth there. The captains, in black tie, assist you in planning the meal you'd like; no columns A and B here.

We love two welcoming giveaways, a chili-pepper dressing with julienned carrots and white radishes, and shredded Chinese cabbage in a coriander-sesame-oil vinaigrette, but you must force yourself to save room for appetizers such as dumplings (vegetable, seafood and pork) or the honey baby spare ribs and, perhaps, above all, barbecued quail. Although the kitchen has slipped some, the Peking duck remains one of the city's best, with shiny, brittle skin and moist, sweet meats that you eat sandwiched with a scallion-and-hoisin sauce in a rice pancake.

They handle seafood particularly well, especially the steamed salmon or flounder with fermented black beans and ginger. Other good bets: shrimp with ginger and garlic, and the not-too-sweet orange beef. Vegetarians can have a field day with the pan-fried vegetables with noodles and the homestyle eggplant. Champagne or a spicy wine from Alsace could elevate your dining experience—both can be had from the list of 25 or so American and French wines offered. You'll find only one dessert on the menu, sherbet, the apple flavor especially good. Figure on $80 per couple for dinner and perhaps slighly less for lunch.

Aureole

34 E. 61st St. (Madison & Park Aves.)
319-1660

AMERICAN

Open Mon.-Thurs. 11:30 a.m.-2:30 p.m. & 5:30 p.m.-10:30 p.m., Fri.-Sat. 11:30 a.m.-2:30 p.m. & 5:30 p.m.-11 p.m. Cards: AE, MC, V.

Big, brawny, hardworking, young, committed and exceedingly talented, chef Charles Palmer leads this splendid new restaurant to the top of the New York charts. In 1989, it emerged as one of the few clear successes, at a time when the restaurant business was well off pace. We find minor inconsistencies and other lapses, but this place and chef will be watched and encouraged. Aureole's rapid rise means a challenge to grow and continue to please with its all-around high level of performance. With partners Nicola Kotsoni and Steve Tzolis (Il Cantinori, Periyali) lending experience, and with Palmer (formerly the chef at the River Café) always in the kitchen, there's an enviable level of professionalism in this handsome restaurant duplex in a restored brownstone. A huge picture window, beige walls with slick birds in bas relief, blond wood floors, well-spaced and -appointed tables, a bar on the first level and the kitchen on the second, set the stage for Palmer's food. (One drawback: the narrowness of the dining areas, so head for the back of the main floor if you like more space.) Incredible displays of flowers flank the entrance, but you may want to head for the garden in season.

The chef, who trained at the Culinary Institute of America, won't call his offerings "nouvelle" or characterize them as American or even French. "My dishes are just good basic ideas, based on seasonal things and done in a very pure and natural way." Ever so market sensitive, he can change the daily menu (produced on the premises) up to twenty minutes before the first service begins. Accordingly, specific recommendations have only a slim chance of reappearing on a given day. Such pre-appetizers as a tiny monkfish roll, or bits of salmon or tuna carpaccio, lead to standout appetizers like duck cracklings with artichoke, sweetbread terrine, sea scallops sandwiched in crispy potato crust and citrus juices, or terrine of foie gras and hickory-smoked chicken. Roasted monkfish with sweet garlic cloves and a crisp potato tart, or any variation on duck (a passion of the chef) will satisfy as a main course. Also consider the fricassée of sea bass with herb-smoked bay shrimp, or the wood-grilled lamb chops with curry noodles. We picked this place for a Thanksgiving dinner, and were not disappointed. An excellent, medium-size wine list proffers notable candidates for marriage to the food, including several Bonny Doon wines from California in the $20 to $40 range. Pastries and other desserts are good, sometimes excellent, sometimes disappointing. A special triple-layer tangerine concoction, with multilayers of flaky pastry and vanilla cream, brought back satisfying childhood memories. We thought the blueberry tartlet with lemon verbena light and lovely. A $50 fixed-price menu with coffee (espresso extra) tells only part of the tale; figure on $160 per couple, à la carte, with wine.

12/20 Bangkok House

1485 First Ave. (78th St.)
249-5700

THAI

Open daily 5 p.m.-11 p.m. All major cards.

Manhattan still seeks its first great Thai restaurant, where fans of Chinese and Indian cuisine can go wacky over Thai flavors, endlessly new combinations and stellar preparation. Bangkok House doesn't fit that bill, but satisfies Upper East Siders, who have few alternatives, in any case. Bangkok House has a solid reputation. Comfortable captain's chairs, spacious tables with glass tops, pretty batik squares, attractive drawings, fresh flower arrangements and good lighting (supplemented by votive candles) are pleasing, though in need of some freshening. The place is pleasant and relaxed, in spite of the fact that it can be noisy when very full. Soothing deep purple walls and dark carpeting make the narrow space appear deceptively small; actually, the main room is almost half a block long, and there's a nice smaller room annexed as well, so seating is rarely a problem (except on Saturday nights).

The gentle staff is charming, and your meals will arrive with alacrity, but don't expect too much help in choosing what to eat. Do plan to eat as the Thai do, sharing as you would in a Chinese place. Appetizers to try include bamboo-skewered, marinated, lean beef satays, served with the traditional cucumber salad; tiny, delicate Thai spring rolls; and the outstanding peek-gai, lightly fried chicken wings (stuffed with a savory mixture of ground pork, black mushrooms and scallions), which you dip in plum sauce. Pla-pa-muok, a citrusy salad of squid with red onion and lemon grass, or pla-koong, shrimp similarly prepared, are excitingly hot and flavorsome.

Don't miss a specialty "for Thai people," not on the menu, steamed mixed seafood or a steamed fish, the foil packet cut open under your nose to release smells so tantalizing that two adjacent tables will sit up and sniff the air. When available, try hoi-pad-king, stir-fried sea scallops tossed with ginger and scallions. Gang-gai is an interesting sautéed sliced chicken breast with coconut milk and bamboo shoots in a fiery red curry. Whatever else you have, don't miss pad Thai, a deeply satisfying tangle of rice noodles stir-fried with shrimp and scallions with the intriguing note of ground peanuts. For a further example of Thai talent with noodles, try the addictive mee krob, sweet crisp noodles with shrimp, pickled garlic and tamarind sauce. The diversified nine-page menu is nicely balanced between dishes that are mild and flavorful, very hot and spicy, or absolutely incendiary, all helpfully flagged on the menu. Singha (the light Thai beer) and plain rice will brake the burn. The house white wine goes nicely with this food, too. Three desserts are offered: a custard, green-tea ice cream or red bean ice cream, and, in deference to American tastes, chocolate mousse, totally inappropriate to this cuisine. As sweet notes appear in many dishes, consider finishing with Thai salad—lettuce, cucumber and bean sprouts in an intriguing peanut dressing. Reservations accepted for parties of four or more. Average price per couple, when two or more share dishes, is between $42 and $56.

11/20 Bistro Bamboche

1582 York Ave. (83rd & 84th Sts.)
249-4002
FRENCH
Open Mon.-Sat. 6 p.m.-11 p.m.. Cards: AE.

New York has everything, including a friendly Polish couple running a pleasing little French bistro; Yocanta, the wife, is the cook, and Gregory Warankow, the husband, maître d'. Bistro Bamboche, your regular little neighborhood restaurant, offers no surprises (even though the à la carte menu has been recently expanded) and food that, most of the time, is good. The long rectangular room has only about fifteen closely packed tables covered with flowered tablecloths, exposed brick walls and lovely etchings. There are specials every night. Among the appetizers, the sorrel soup is excellent, slightly bitter and rich. The fresh leaf salad has a pleasant dressing. The mousse of coquilles St-Jacques (scallops) and the ballotine of duck are also recommended openers.

Among the entrées, it used to be that you'd have better luck with the fish and seafood than with the meat and poultry, but our recent visits negate that belief. The food seems consistent across the menu. The papillote of salmon with vegetable tastes very fresh and fine. The poulet farci, however, tastes more like a first-class airplane meal, and the sweetbreads are overcooked. Go for the ris de veau with sauce Nantua or the duck, or the butterflied veal chops with asparagus—superb. Bistro Bamboche's forte is the apricot soufflé: light, tart, magnificent. The other desserts, a tulipane and a tarte aux pommes, are not worth writing to Paris about. Bistro Bamboche has a limited, but quite good, wine list, reasonably priced and equally divided between French and California. Price per couple is about $110.

12/20 Bravo Gianni

230 E. 63rd St.
(Second & Third Aves.)
752-7272
ITALIAN
Open Mon.-Fri. noon-2:30 p.m. & 5:30 p.m.-midnight, Sat. 5:30 p.m.-midnight. All major cards.

This is the story: if you know Gianni and the staff, you are treated well. Take it or leave it. Lots of people take it, and thereafter, their experience is fine. The ritual here starts when top-gun Gianni either welcomes you or ignores you, and everyone else in the restaurant (mostly a middle-aged, well-dressed group) follows suit. The first time you come here, you'll wonder why you're being shunned, but if you keep returning anyway, one evening owner Gianni will do a characteristic about-face and come to the door to greet you personally. Then the reception in the dining room will be a lot different, too.

The generally northern Italian food here is always satisfactory, and sometimes very good—classic, lusty and made with good produce. People come here for the clubbiness and the spectacle as much as for the food. The pastas can be good. Try the tortellini in cream sauce, or the tiny raviolis (pansoti) in a walnut sauce that's cut with garlic (and just in time, too). The house's light tomato sauce, fragrant with herbs, is good on almost anything. But, for the most part, the entrées lack luster. The red snapper, served with capers, is notable, as is the squid in white-wine sauce. The scampi looks healthy—huge prawns swimming in garlic butter—but, to our taste, is overdone. The veal is best as a chop topped with vegetables, which liven up the taste. For dessert, be swank and order zabaglione—far superior to the regulation cheesecake and chocolate mousse—and espresso. Joining this film-premiere crowd for dinner will cost you about $110 per couple.

11/20 Café Crocodile
354 E. 74th St. (First & Second Aves.)
249-6619
FRENCH/MOROCCAN
Open Mon.-Sat. 5:30 p.m.-11:00 p.m. Cards: AE.

Once upon a time, only a couple of years ago in fact, this small restaurant, on the ground floor of an Upper East Side town house, served up delightful Mediterranean food in an unpretentious atmosphere. Recently, Mme. Andrée Abramoff, chef and owner, gave the decor a face-lift and flipped the cuisine to mainly Provençal fare. The dining room is now lighter, more comfortable, more serene. The food is now forgettable, except for an occasional dish. Oh, well.

The menu changes every other week, save for a few dishes. Appetizers here are far better than the entrées; you may even want to make a meal of them. A popular and decent, if not inspirational, choice is the Alexandria quartet, usually consisting of well-made taramosalata, eggplant caviar, tabouli and three excellent dolmas (stuffed vine leaves). The linguine, topped with a spicy eggplant-tomato sauce, is earthy and satisfying. A rather bland salmon

terrine comes to the table too cold, although its lemony mayonnaise with capers has a delightful bite and is very fresh. Strangely enough, the entrées that remain on the menu miss the mark completely. Rough chunks of flavorless fish sit atop a mound of couscous, garnished with undercooked pieces of red and green pepper, a handful of chickpeas and a few limp slices of quince, and the sauce offered on the side is so peppery, it drowns out what taste is left to the dish. A tender, pink baby rack of lamb is almost ruined by a too-thick crust of garlic and parsley; its accompaniments—sautéed potatoes and a melange of Mediterranean vegetables—save this simple dish from oblivion. A better bet is the seared tuna, a large slab of rare-cooked, very fresh fish. Desserts, although supposedly seasonal, are problematic. The clafouti is icy cold and pasty, and the chocolate mud-type cake has no finesse. Espresso and regular coffee are good, and the service is truly pleasant. The wine list is all right, and modestly priced. Dinner for two can run up to about $100.

 Café Pierre
Hotel Pierre, 2 E. 61st St. (Fifth Ave.)
940-8185
FRENCH
Open Mon.-Sat. 7 a.m.-10:30 a.m., noon-2:30 p.m. & 6 p.m.-11:30 p.m.; Sun. 7 a.m.-10:30 a.m., noon-3 p.m. & 6 p.m.-11:30 p.m. All major cards.

Café Pierre evokes the grand old style of the 1930s and 1940s. The walls of the long and sleek room are covered in satin, and roomy tables abound—a combination of mirrored-modern and tearoom baroque. The piano player isn't bad.

The place is brightest at lunch, when some local power moguls drop in, and when you can start with a warm breast of chicken with crushed black peppercorns and follow it with a panache of seafood on a pasta leaf with basil butter. The menu changes seasonally. The lasagne of lobster with spinach and basil is a good appetizer at dinner, the terrine of foie gras is fair; ditto the ragoût of wild and reconstituted mushroooms. We have liked the honey-duck salad with walnuts. There's always a lamb preparation for two, a loin of lamb, medallions or a nice individual rack of lamb with stone-ground mustard and turnip gratin. The desserts are neither to be shunned, nor are they memorable. The wine list is excellent, featuring more than 350 wines— good French and California offerings, including those of all the top properties, and some other countries and regions as well. Lunch for two, will come to about $90 and dinner $130, plus tax and tip.

The Carlyle Restaurant
35 E. 76th St. (Madison Ave.)
744-1600

FRENCH

Open daily 7 a.m.-10:30 a.m., noon-3 p.m. & 6 p.m.-11 p.m. All major cards.

Oh, so ve-e-e-ry elegant . . . and why not? If you are in the mood for luxury, head for this most attractive and comfortable dining room of the superb Carlyle Hotel. Beautifully decorated in the classic Georgian style, with tête-de-nègre linen, velvet upholstered walls, discreet chinoiserie touches, a thick carpet, comfortable chairs, and a center banquette surmounted with a fabulous flower arrangement, it manages to be both elegant and cozy. Light comes from well-placed spots, softened by pink-shaded wall sconces. Consider eating breakfast in this lovely setting, with its buffet laden with fruit, all kinds of breads, muffins and rolls, scrambled eggs in a chafing dish, bacon, sausages and so on. Coffee comes discreetly, but nonstop. At all three meals, the clientele looks like it belongs in the room.

We find the food at lunch and dinner, thankfully, much better than it needs to be in such a lavish hotel. On the essentially classic French/Continental menu, you'll find some nouvelle overtones in presentation and garniture, but that doesn't prevent some dishes from being extremely rich, so order carefully, and ask questions about sauces. Unless you are fluent in restaurant French, you'll have to do a lot of asking, anyway, because the menu is pretentiously presented only in French. We've enjoyed the quail appetizer with sautéed foie gras on canapés with grapes, as well as the médaillons of lobsters and chanterelles. At lunch in the past, we've delighted in the beautifully poached cold Norwegian salmon and the pristine Dover sole. We found the pastas okay—fettucine done any way you like it and, on occasion, rich and delicious ravioli with wild mushrooms and shrimp or crab. At both meals, hearty eaters will like the saddle of lamb with truffles and a vegetable torte or the

sautéed veal chop with braised endives, and weight watchers the veal medallions with finely julienned vegetables on lettuce leaves. Other dinner offerings include a fine breast of duck with apple, potato and raisin gâteau. We love the soufflées for dessert (raspberry, chocolate or Grand Marnier); otherwise, you can have yet another crème brûlée. The mostly French and American wine list is extensive, and an award winner, with a good range of prices from moderate to expensive (for the rarities). Consider the Simi Chardonnay, which comes in full or half bottles, for a white ($28 and $15), or perhaps the 1979 Château La Tour Haut-Brion at an attractive $45, for a red. You must dress up for the impeccable service. Expect to pay $140 per couple at dinner, plus tax and tip, and $90 for two at lunch; there is a prix-fixe of $35 for Sunday brunch.

Le Cirque
58 E. 65th St.
(Park & Madison Aves.)
794-9292

FRENCH

Open Mon.-Sat. noon-2:30 p.m. & 6 p.m.-10:30 p.m. Closed 1st 3 weeks in July. Cards: AE, DC.

What now? What do you do when you are Sirio Maccioni, owner and ringmaster of this megawatt circus, and after sixteen years of constant striving, you have brought your restaurant to where it is now—when people look at Le Cirque and see its food, wine, ambience, influence and fame, and deem it all extraordinary? For years, a myth was propagated that the crowd here was more interesting than the food, but the arrival of Daniel Boulud, and his brilliant Cambodian *sous*-chef, Sottha Khunn, have ensured that nobody can say this now.

So, what *do* you do if you are owner Maccioni (born in Italy—Tuscany, he would say)? Well, what Sirio, as the legendary restaurateur is known to hordes of regulars, *is* doing is sparing no expense or effort to make the place even better. Since Le Cirque opened, the desserts have been unfailingly superb, in their own way doing as much as the glitterati to give the restaurant its personality. In 1989, Sirio went out and hired a stupendous new pastry chef, Frenchman Jacques Torres, one of the youngest winners ever of the prestigious title "Meilleur Ouvrier de France." Then a few months later, he built Torres a new pastry department. Today, when it comes to desserts, no restaurant in the world does it better. Simply sensational! Torres can fill every inch of your table, day after day, with different desserts, one better than the next—from the restaurant's signature crème brûlée to Torres's signature petit piano "Opera." Apparently not being able to figure out in 1990 how to significantly improve what goes on the plates at Le Cirque, Sirio did the next best thing: he changed the actual plates themselves. We thought he already had the most striking plates around (the kitchen regularly matches the color and pattern of the plate to the food going on it for maximum visual appeal), but Sirio had Limoges china create a new line of custom-designed dishes for him, and hundreds of these plates, at $75 a pop, are now in the kitchen's arsenal, joining the superb crystal glassware Sirio previously designed and commissioned.

Monkey murals provide a touch of circus whimsy to the elegant, grand room, which is filled with excesses, including people—Europeans, Latin Americans and New Yorkers buzz about. Mind you, the glitter, frenzy and electricity of this place is not for everyone: many high-level business types find it tough to unwind here after a hectic day, and resent the elbow-to-elbow conditions (even if one of those elbows leads to a face that stops traffic). On the other hand, Le Cirque (French for "the circus") is the ultimate pick-me-up for legions of well-coiffured and bejeweled ladies, and despite inevitable power surges, it's often a thrilling experience for the rest of us. Superb bouquets adorn the room (Le Cirque employs a full-time florist on the premises). If there is something in the room to criticize (if you accept the close quarters), it's probably the service. Always proper, always courteous, never condescending, nevertheless it can get a bit frantic and seemingly inattentive to small, and sometimes not-so-small, details. This, of course, drives Sirio crazy—just watch him walking the floors, eyeing patrons and staff, himself a bundle of worry, checking that all is well. When he stops worrying, you'll know Le Cirque has peaked and is on its way down. Watch his face light up when someone offers a tribute at the end of a meal, and watch him kiss the hand of a parting lady, sharing some of the room's electricity and making her feel like a princess.

There are ever-changing specials; one of the restaurant's most popular dishes, pasta primavera, does not even appear in print. We advise you to order generally what's in your head (they have it) or better, let Sirio, chef Boulud, Benito (the manager) or one of the captains do the ordering for you. French? Italian? American? Asian? Fish? Fowl? Game? Meat? Bistro? Haute cuisine? It's all there for the asking.

THE TOQUE, CIRCA 1700

Have you ever wondered about the origin of that towering, billowy (and slightly ridiculous) white hat worn by chefs all over the world? Chefs have played an important role in society since the 5th century B.C., but the hats didn't begin to appear in kitchens until around the 18th century A.D. The toque is said to be of Greek origin: many famous Greek cooks, to escape persecution, sought refuge in monasteries and continued to carry on with their fine art. The chefs donned the tall hats traditionally worn by Orthodox priests but, to distinguish themselves from their fellows, they wore white hats instead of black. The practice eventually was adopted by chefs from Paris to Peking.

Relentless experimentation goes on in the kitchen, and new and exciting dishes fly into the dining room with breathtaking regularity. We declared Boulud's sea scallops black tie the hit of the eighties: unforgettably moist, poached scallops dressed to the hilt with thin slices of black truffles sandwiched inside each scallop and grated on top. The sweetness and texture of the scallop proves a fine companion for the usually overpowering truffle. The 1990s got off to a grand and innovative start with one of the simplest and greatest offerings we've had, another truffle dish: a baked potato on a bed of salt—open the potato (sliced in half) and discover the insides mashed and mashed with a fork, oozing butter and showered with grated white truffles.

We have found other remarkable dishes such as the carpaccio of red snapper; the otherworldly pasta with white truffles; variations on a sublime fresh New York State foie gras—sautéed and served with black pepper and grapes or in a terrine with sweet Lipari wine; lobster ravioli on a bed of spinach; spicy butterfly pasta with squid; skate with ginger; and fresh tuna with lemon, olive oil, garlic toast and diced salad. The roasted rack of lamb with a nine-vegetable cake and potato gratin makes a superb offering for two; and when in season—and Le Cirque gets the first and the finest—the salmon carpaccio with white truffles is a lovely, innovative offering. The list can go on.

Influence, as well as originality, is one of the characteristics of a great restaurant, and here, too, Le Cirque distinguishes itself. No one had heard of pasta primavera until Maccioni concocted it. Former Le Cirque employees now own or work in many outstanding restaurants and have brought with them a piece of Le Cirque. It's clear, too, that Le Cirque's legendary dessert, crème brûlée, inspired the vast proliferation of that old Catalan standard in New York City, across America, and over to Europe and Japan. A few years back, Le Cirque was the first restaurant in America to offer the lovely Italian dessert wine, Malvasia del Lipari. Now, that, too, can be found all across the city and country.

Speaking of wine, in recent years Le Cirque has become a destination for its offerings. More than 500 wines appear on the list (60-percent French, 25-percent American, 15-percent Italian), and many more lie aging among the 50,000 bottles in the cellar. You can close your eyes and point, and be sure you'll hit a quality wine. Prices are good for a restaurant of this class, with more than 150 wines priced in the teens, twenties, or thirties. On the other hand, if you just closed a million- or billion-dollar deal and want to splurge, head directly here. You'll be able to order great and rare Bordeaux and Burgundies in top vintages going back to the nineteenth century. And, of course, Champagne flows at Le Cirque like sparkling water. You must reserve, and men must wear jacket and tie. We believe the $33 fixed-price lunch a remarkable

value, but for dinner, don't inhibit yourself: expect to spend $200 per couple.

12/20 Contrapunto
200 E. 60th St. (Third Ave.)
751-8616
ITALIAN
Open daily noon-midnight. All major cards.

The knee bone's connected to the thigh bone. And in the corporate body of the admirable Santo group (Dr. Joe Santo also owns Sign of the Dove), Contrapunto, the second-story pastaria on 60th and Third, is connected to Santo-owned Yellowfingers (ground floor), which is connected to Arizona 206 (the fourth member of the group, located one door east). Like Bloomingdale's, across the street, the Santo complex offers a series of adjoining boutiques, each exploiting a different contemporary gastronomic fashion in an atmosphere as frenzied, noisy and crowded as the subway at rush hour—albeit somewhat cleaner, brighter and more cheerful.

Something just feels right about an American restaurant ridden by chef Jesse James (as of June 1989) and specializing in pasta and gelati. The long list, divided into imported and fresh pastas, includes unusual dishes (though not that unusual, or contrapuntal), but they're fine, making this outpost a pleasant option for the Bloomie's shoppers and Third Avenue moviegoers who wait in the corridor for tables to open up as docilely as they'd line up to pay for a Tahari dress or to buy tickets for Woody Allen's latest.

If your tastes run to the rustic, choose the focaccia bread, a thick bready rendition topped with roasted peppers and tomatoes. Slightly wilted braised hearts of radicchio gain nothing by cooking but, abetted by strips of fresh mozzarella and strands of arugula, make a satisfying appetizer. Simpler is better when it comes to the twenty-plus selections of pasta. Cansonsei tre herbe, large pasta pockets filled with spinach, parsley, ricotta and Parmesan and tinged with nutmeg, are fresh and delicious when served with a basil-butter sauce. Capelli bergino, on the other hand, is a hodgepodge of ingredients and flavors, comprising sun-dried tomatoes, fresh artichokes, diced scallions, slightly cooked domestic mushrooms, chives, Parmesan and butter, all showered over angel-hair pasta. Less would be more. Fusilli/Ciccoria piccante is a favorite—

corkscrew pasta with arugula, dandelions, chopped tomatos, fennel, garlic, jalapeños, butter and Parmesan cheese. Ditto for three more dishes, the pappardelle/boscaiola, the tagliarini/Francesco and the Malfatti/granchio. In all, there are 21 pastas and four nonpasta dishes as main courses. The gelati for dessert—chocolate, banana, vanilla–is so-so, but the house red is just fine, as is the rest of the short, but *au courant*, French and Italian wine list. Expect to pay about $60 per couple for dinner, with house wine, plus tax and tip.

12/20 Devon House Ltd.

1316 Madison Ave. (93rd St.)
860-8294
CONTINENTAL/CARIBBEAN
Open Mon.-Sat. 6 p.m.-11 p.m. Cards: AE, MC. V.

Established in 1981, Devon House gets points for trying, and for sticking to its guns. And if time heals all wounds, then the high prices charged here no longer seem so out of line, especially with all the highly leveraged new designer restaurants around town providing diners with stunning bills that resemble cash withdrawal slips at the end of a meal. What Mrs. Yvonne Scherrer's restaurant has going for it are sincerity, good intentions, pretty flower arrangements, a glass of port with the cheese course and an iffy premise— the attempt to create the fantasy of "dining out" in the home of English gentry. Devon House Ltd. occupies the ground floor of a lovely brownstone. Diners ring the front door bell to gain admittance. Inside, there are two small dining rooms with a half dozen or so tables apiece. The rooms look as if they were in a private home—or a doctor's posh office— right down to the coffee-table books angled on window sills and the bowl of dried flower petals on the mantel of the fireplace. In this setting, the presence of so many separate tables seems artificial, a feeling underscored by the fact that diners feel obliged to whisper to their companions, rather than disturb the near-silence that prevails. And therein lies the rub. There's no sense of occasion here. You're not at home; you're not in someone else's home; and you don't feel you're in a restaurant, either. The experience is recommended either one time or many times (the latter so that you would feel at home).

Otherwise, the premise would need fabulous food to bring it to life, but none of the Continental fare with Jamaican overtones served here is fabulous—not the snails Madagascar in somewhat soupy cream sauce, not the pheasant in brown sauce flavored with rosemary and sage, not the popular Jamaican-style salmon, which tastes as if it were brushed with some sort of calypso sauce. Worthy of consideration are the sweetbreads in puff pastry, the rack of lamb, the breast of chicken stuffed with shrimp and leeks and flavored with Pernod, and loin of pork stuffed with guava, mango and Jamaican spices. Fish are specials of the market of the day, which usually translates to nothing extraordinary—perhaps trout, Dover sole, salmon and soft-shell crabs. Desserts appear brought in from a good bakery. Wine options are fine, if you are prepared to pay $40 or $50 a bottle. Your dinner check will average between $120 and $150 per couple, without tax or tip, and can run up with added or expensive wines.

11/20 Dieci Ristorante

568A First Ave. (81st St.)
628-6565
ITALIAN
Open daily 5:30 p.m.-11:30 p.m. Closed Sun. in July &Aug. All major cards.

Walking into Dieci is like walking into an exclusive club. Here, the membership consists mostly of neighborhood regulars, but the smugness is the same. The kitchen, though prolific, sometimes has trouble dealing with delicate foods, but the guys are nice guys at this classic Italian restaurant (established in 1985), with its cozy feel, peach-colored walls, oak, brick, brass and colorful flowers. Noteworthy are the George Hurrell photos of Hollywood stars, collectors' items worth $4,500 to $60,000 apiece.

The best appetizers are those left somewhat unadulterated: grilled mushrooms, mozzarella served with roast peppers, prosciutto with melon. Among pastas, it's safe to stick with linguine with clam sauce (white or red), or the capellini (angel hair) with vegetables. Caviar served with the heavy penne is completely wasted; nevertheless, this is one of the house specialties. Instead, go for another specialty, the pasta cartoccio with assorted seafood. Keep to the simple entrées as well. Grilled swordfish steak with anchovies, garlic and capers comes with a red sauce on the side so you can protect the fish from its intrusion. Veal chops giardino are another specialty—done Milanese-style and topped with tomatoes, arugula, endives, radicchio and sweet onions. Filet mignon, grilled to your liking, is fine, but boneless baby pheasant, served for two, is slightly overcooked, and you'll wish they'd just let you do it yourself. The roasted and grilled baby goat, when available, is worthy of your attention, as it is not commonly offered in New York, and is prepared well here.

Desserts are what you'd expect. The baked peach with zabaglione is attractive, and merits first consideration, except when pure fresh fruit is at its vine-ripened best. When you order wine, no doubt you will pass on the aged Brunello di Montalcino Biondi Santi for $7,500; there's enough to choose from in a lower price range, starting at $17. This is the sort of place that decants every red wine. You can eat dinner here for $100 a couple (without the Biondi Santi).

12/20 Elio's
1621 Second Ave. (84th & 85th Sts.)
777-2242
ITALIAN
Open daily Mon.-Sat. 5:30 p.m.-midnight. All major cards.

With its welcoming globe lights, wood paneling and wainscoting, pretty flower arrangements and animated crush of patrons, Elio's is like a neighborhood gathering spot, an "in" place in which to see and be seen, people-watch and table hop. The people-watching is pretty good, with plenty of big-name television types on hand; the wait for a table can be pretty bad. Elio Guaitolini used to be a partner at Parma, and the menus of the two restaurants greatly resemble each other. Here, the bill of fare is, by and large, predictable, but good. You will eat well, if not grandly.

Trendy tuna carpaccio is a good opener; there are the usual clams, raw or oreganante, and for weight-watching, on-air television types, the raw mushroom salad with Parmesan and fennel is fine. Seafood risotto is good, and the staff claims that all ten of the pastas are good. Well, from what we've tasted, they're not bad. But listen to the specials (if you can—the noise level is such that unless your waiter shouts, you may not hear them). They

can be quite superior, one notable example being the eggplant rollatini appetizer. Main courses include veal in all expected guises (scaloppine, piccata and Marsala)—a decent chop, nice quality, well executed. A cut above is the popular noisette of veal with sage. Tasty Cornish hen al mattone merits serious consideration. Fish, which varies from day to day, is cooked with respect, and saffroned zuppa di pesce with lobster is satisfying.

Service is brisk and efficient. The wine list has been given a lot of thought, and offers a good selection of popular, well-priced Italian wines, with a few French and California offerings. Desserts fare better than in the usual Italian restaurant, thanks to the fine hand of Elio's partner, Anne Isaak. The vanilla cheesecake is very good, and the thin lemon tart, refreshingly intense and acidic on a buttery pâte brisée, is one of the best of its kind—it is the "must" dessert here. Reservations are vital during peak hours (7 p.m. to 10 p.m.) and on weekends; dress is casual-chic. Dinner averages $90 per couple, with a modest wine.

12/20 Erminia
250 E. 83rd St.
(Second & Third Aves.)
879-4284
ITALIAN
Open Mon.-Sat. 5 p.m.-11 p.m. Cards: AE.

When it comes to charm, it's hard to beat this place. The smell of a wood fire in this tiny, candlelit room, with its walls of exposed brick or thick-planked wood, makes for a setting that is romantic, rustic and warm without seeming calculated. Apparently, a lot of people are satisfied eating up the charm. The food at this popular restaurant doesn't inspire even culinary infatuation, but you won't go home hungry. The Lattanzi family, which also owns Trastevere and Lattanzi (in the theater district), owns this place and has named it after mama. She deserves better.

Erminia specializes in pastas and grilled foods. But even if you stick to those options—which is advisable—dinner is still a hit-or-miss proposition. Nothing is bad; most, however, is just average. What is billed as smoked carpaccio, for example, is a bland, utterly standard piece of meat, with a handful of capers and a couple of shards of Parmesan tossed on, almost as an afterthought. Artichokes Jewish-style spend a long time cooking in olive oil.

Tasty, to be sure, but nothing like the traditional version, in which the leaves crisp up and fan out like deliciously charred flower petals (the family manages to meet the standard down at Lattanzi, so why not here?). The best dish on the menu proves to be the orecchiette, with a savory mix of sausage and broccoli. Vermicelli pizzaiola displays full flavors of garlic, capers, tomato and olives. (Puttanesca, anyone?) It benefits from a generous sprinkling of Parmesan (which must be requested). Various grilled skewers (meat, poultry, shellfish) tend to be overcooked, and taste mostly of having been grilled over wood. There is a very restricted wine list. For people in need of a sugar fix, the ever-so-sweet ice cream concoctions will do the trick. Otherwise, there's also a chocolate mousse. More appealing are the deep-fried apples, with or without an avalanche of confectionary snow. Jackets are required. Dinner easily costs $100 per couple, with wine.

Ferrier

29 E. 65th St.
(Park & Madison Aves.)
772-9000

FRENCH

Open Sun.-Thurs. noon-midnight, Fri.-Sat. noon-1 a.m. Cards: AE, MC, V.

The local glitterati have bestowed the cherished Upper East Side stamp of approval upon this neighborhood bistro, opened in 1989, proving that simplicity appeals to those living the lifestyles of the rich and famished. Many French restaurants in this part of town command stellar prices for ordinary food, but popular Ferrier comes across kinder to the palate and gentler on the wallet. Some might regard its classic bistro menu as uninspired, but we welcome the tradition. One can grow tired of the multilingual, patchwork-quilt cuisine that many restaurants unsuccessfully attempt. Ferrier emphasizes substance over style, though it handles both well. The service is straightforward, not florid, and the tables crowded together seem intimate, not intimidating.

Here, they prepare familiar dishes with élan. We've enjoyed the cold leeks in a light vinaigrette, a subtly rich leek-and-potato soup, and a warm duck confit with arugula salad and green beans. For main courses, we like the bistro mainstay, steak frites, as well as salmon

in a mustard sauce and rack of lamb. At lunchtime, Park Avenue executives meet Madison Avenue shoppers over a menu of pasta, omelets and slight variations from the dinner choices. Let's hope Ferrier avoids the trappings of success. For an enjoyable diner, expect to spend about $90 per couple.

Fu's

1395 Second Ave. (72nd & 73rd Sts.)
517-9670

CHINESE

Open daily noon-midnight. All major cards.

Done up in a formal contemporary style, rather like a nightclub, popular Fu's participates in the uptown trend of Chinese dining. Unlike some downtown counterparts, where you feel lucky to get what you ordered, here, sincerely helpful captains and the hostess (executive director), Gloria Chu, will expound on any dish on the menu and help you put your meal together. While no one branch of Chinese cuisine could be said to dominate here (nor any one chef, as far as we can tell), the food comes with an appealing contemporary note—fresh and attractive, never mired in overly thick sauces. Appetizers include delicate steamed dumplings of shrimp, or pork with coriander and ginger, plus the crunchier, fried half-moon type, both with delicious dipping sauces. The succulent regular barbecued ribs, or the honey-glazed babies, little more than a mouthful on each, will disappear from your table in record time. We loved the calamari in black-bean sauce, with hot red and green peppers. You might like the currently trendy appetizer, that Chinese classic, Grand Marnier shrimp. Cold appetizers include sesame noodles (perhaps a little too heavy on the peanut butter) and good hot-and-sour cabbage.

Though we could complain about the many fried specialties (no matter how expertly done), Fu's version of spa cuisine, its "forgotten menu" of easy-to-eat, low-fat dishes, such as delicate steamed shrimp dumplings, or steamed shrimp or whole flounder in a blizzard of scallions, parsley and ginger, more than make up for it. Vegetarians will like mu shu vegetable, a crunchy and flavorful meatless version of the well-known pork dish.

The wait after appetizers for the main round of dishes can be considerable on crowded nights; nevertheless, Mrs. Chu runs a tight ship, and we rarely see service as deft as it is here; the Peking duck appears in its burnished entirety, magically prepared for eating almost instantaneously. Among other dishes we like are the crispy orange beef and the mango chicken, when available—otherwise, opt for the house special, lemon chicken. Also consider the home-style spicy chicken. We consider the shrimp with a garlic-and-scallion sauce outstanding, ditto the soft-shell crabs. For dessert, you should try ice cream, fresh fruit, the usual lychees and kumquats and unneccessary cheesecake. We think the wine list has improved, though it lacks sufficient Champagnes and the wines from Alsace that marry well with this cuisine, so you might simply opt for beer or tea (although they serve the latter, oddly, in demitasse cups and it is frequently cold—you may not pour tea yourself as you require it). About $75 for two.

The Gibbon
24 E. 80th St (Fifth & Madison Aves.)
861-4001
ECLECTIC/JAPANESE/FRENCH
Open Mon.-Fri. noon-2 p.m. & 6 p.m.-10 p.m., Sat. 6 p.m.-10 p.m. All major cards.

Perhaps catering more to style over substance, The Gibbon does a nice lunch business in the Metropolitan Museum area. When nouvelle cuisine chefs began applying the Japanese aesthetic to French food, The Gibbon chef, Ikuo Kamata, took an ambitious next step by frankly combining the salient features of both. We think the result intriguing and highly pleasing aesthetically, if not always uniformly exciting. You enter the elegant townhouse just off Fifth Avenue, through a small, cozy bar area with a brick fireplace. You may go through to the snug downstairs dining room, or ascend to the more formal parlor floor, with its antique Japanese and Chinese screens and paintings, and deep carpeting.

We believe the best starters those purely, or nearly, Japanese in origin—beautifully presented sashimi of moist, fresh tuna, yellowtail and fluke, especially pleasant to eat here without the usual sushi bar hubbub; taffeta-crisp tempura; or plump, steamed New Zealand mussels in a supernal garlic and bean-paste broth. We like, among the entrées, sautéed sea scallops, briny and flavorsome in a lemon garlic butter. Ditto the sakura-mushi, slices of salmon rolled around green buckwheat noo-

dles, served hot or cold with a vibrant ginger-and-scallion sauce. Some clients adore negimaki, asparagus and spring onions rolled in thin slices of beef, a tasty and pretty notion as long as the meat is charred, rather than steamed. Kamata at his best produces items like baby soft-shell crabs, delicately sautéed with soy, shallots and ginger. We delight in the presentation of all dishes, exquisite and imaginative, but regret that a consistent level of flavor excitement somehow never appears. For example, we found the graceful, edible wild-rice-flour cup has more flavor than does the tasteless grass it holds, and certainly more than the unimaginative string beans it accompanies. Yet The Gibbon has a solid following among well-heeled Upper East Siders. The pleasant and attentive staff will assist you in choosing from the selection of French and California wines, well-chosen to accompany this food. Lunch averages $70 per couple, dinner $110 for two.

Huberts
575 Park Ave. (63rd St.)
826-5911
ECLECTIC
Open Mon.-Fri. noon-2:30 p.m. & 6 p.m.-10:30 p.m., Sat. 6 p.m.-10 p.m. All major cards.

If we could turn back the clock, we'd keep Huberts in its warm Gramercy Park digs. Probably Karen Hubert and her husband, chef Len Allison, who have been satisfying diners with good, imaginatively rendered food and excellent wines since their Brooklyn restaurant days in the '70s, have had the same thought more than once. In early 1988, they moved their restaurant uptown to the old Perigord Park space. Adam Tihany designed a large and tasteful Americana room with beautiful cherrywood and mahogany tones, handsome furniture and American arts-and-crafts touches, such as Vermont pottery. There's a large sitting room and small bar near the entrance and a back dining room with a low ceiling we dub "Siberia." No one wants to be assigned to eat there, but no doubt the covers it represents are essential to pay the Park Avenue rent. Late in 1989, the prices at Huberts were cut a stunning 25 percent, which of course wouldn't have been the case if business were booming and the reservation book filled. We still don't see that back dining room in demand.

The food is an evolving fusion cuisine, capitalizing on the market, and on the vitality and ethnic variety that is New York City. On the one hand, Len Allison has rethought many standard regional American recipes; he has also embraced Japanese and other cuisines as well. We enjoyed in the past such items as grilled tuna appetizer surrounded by an exotic symphony of sauce, the Roquefort soufflé, grilled red snapper with potato sticks, grilled squid with black-olive vinaigrette, and shrimp appetizer served over crushed cucumbers. The grilled rabbit sausages with herbs served with mole sauce has been a satisfying opener here for years. We also liked pan-blackened salmon with a white horseradish sauce and the pan-fried duck. They present grilled tuna engagingly here with an endive ragoût. We found the venison with carrot noodles only so-so, but the rack of lamb with goat-cheese lasagne and spinach excellent. Chops and medallions come to the table pink and tender here, the contrasting lasagne creamy and luxuriant. The house treats vegetables, in general, as more than afterthoughts—yellow squash, sugarsnap peas, carrots, wild rice, onions, zucchini, asparagus and sweet-potato purée all enliven the plate to the eye and to the palate. We liked the bread and almost all of the desserts, from almond brittle ice cream or red currant sherbert, to plum or lemon tarts or a chocolate-fudge cake with whiskey sauce. The award-winning wine list, with 250 offerings (mostly California and French, with a few Italian selections), we feel a model of good taste, knowledge and reasonable pricing. It is constantly updated by efficient Oliver Von Brikenwaldau. We appreciate the service, earnest, friendly and generally effective. For dinner, expect to pay $130 per couple, and more if you want to sample a second bottle of wine.

12/20 Hulot's

1007 Lexington Ave.
(72nd & 73rd Sts.)
794-9800

FRENCH
Open Mon.-Fri. noon-2:30 p.m. & 6 p.m.-10:30 p.m., Sat. 6 p.m.-10:30 p.m. All major cards.

The ever-increasing bistro competition around town may have upped the ante and passed 4-year-old Hulot's by. Our most recent meal here wasn't up to the food that is turned out routinely at, say, Quatorze or Chez Louis or a number of the newer entries in the race. Still, this French bistro in a neighborhood full of nannies pushing imported strollers by day and blond professionals scouting out places to eat by night, has its devoted followers. At Hulot's, well-dressed people sit on chintz banquettes and imported bistro chairs and get served French workers' food. Narrow as an arrow, with a compact open kitchen at center right, the simple decor consists of posters advertising Jacques Tati's film *M. Hulot*, for which the restaurant is named. Try to sit up front, near the window, or in the rear; the twofers opposite the kitchen can feel a bit frenetic. Small cavils aside, eating here is quite enjoyable, so long as you understand the all-French menu without unpleasant surprises.

On a sweltering summer's day, the cold tomato soup with basil hits the spot, and the salmon carpaccio with fresh mint cools and refreshes as an opener. On a blustery fall or winter's day, the market sensitive menu may include a cosseting carrot soup, or curried purée of zucchini. For lunch in May, a marvelous vichyssoise appears. Simple, satisfying lunches include a good omelet basquaise, firm outside, properly runny within, with a garniture of the zesty tomato, green pepper and onion filling; croque monsieur (a gentleman's ham-and-cheese sandwich, served on wonderfully crusty bread) garnished with salad; fresh chicken salad dressed with a mustard mayonnaise; and unusual skate wings with pesto. Start dinner with a wedge of first-rate leek tart—sweet red peppers felicitously combined with a stuffing of mild goat cheese—or a simple salad of lentils, or cucumbers with savory eggplant purée. Chickens with herbs, grilled tuna, sautéed salmon (French home cooking?) all work fine as main courses. Fans of calf's liver will delight in Hulot's quickly sautéed version with shallots, simply dressed in a reduction of pan juices and sherry vinegar. Thin, moistly pink slices of leg of lamb, garnished with dauphinoise potatoes, is always a good choice at dinner. A variety of vegetable garnishes are especially tasty, always giving an extra interest to the main course. Service is bistro fine. (There's something very considerate about the way they take your order: "And you will have. . . ?" they say, and wait until you're sure you've made the right choice.) There's a competent pastry chef somewhere in the wings—Hulot's fruit tarts, which run from raspberry or apple to fine astringent lemon, are an effective finish. The tender, buttery tarte tatin is sinful. The house red, a Duboeuf Beaujolais, complements the food nicely, as does the house white, also Duboeuf's. The wine list as a whole is limited and undistinguished. Lunch averages $60 per couple, dinner $80 for two.

11/20 Hyotan-Nippon
119 E. 59th St.
(Park & Lexington Aves.)
751-7690
JAPANESE
Open Mon.-Thurs. noon-2:30 p.m. & 5:30 p.m.-10 p.m., Fri. noon-2:30 p.m. & 5:30 p.m.-10:30 p.m., Sat. 5:30 p.m.-10:30 p.m. All major cards.

Nobuyshi Kuraoka opened his second restaurant (he owns the Nippon) to cater to American tastes and increasing acceptance of Japanese fare. Calorie-counting, natural foods, broiled dishes and the drama of chefs doing their thing in front of the diners all figure in this concept. Even Hyotan's decor reflects "energized" Japanese cuisine. An enormous, amoeba-shaped wooden counter dominates the dining room, along with a large tank of frolicking lobsters. Chefs are always busy cooking, broiling, tempura-frying or preparing sashimi, like Kabuki actors in the throes of a colorful dance.

The menu is long. Salads are uneventful variations on iceberg with Japanese dressing. For dieters, there are many sautéed vegetables, and for vegetarians, a special Zen (what else?) lunch. Appetizers will perk you up; a very good one is aigamo-hasamiyaki, perfectly broiled seasoned duck. Just be sure that the sauce is served on the side, as it is overly sweet. Among the usual meat dishes of teriyaki, sukiyaki and yakitori, the only one worth serious consideration is veal à la Hyotan, tender pieces of veal sautéed with fresh shiitake mushrooms. Fish and seafood dishes are surprisingly well-prepared. Hirame kara-age, gently fried flounder served with soy sauce, has an honest taste, and the broiled eel served with a piquant sauce is tangy and satisfying. Bento meals, the best bet at this restaurant, are served in beautiful lacquered boxes, with compartments filled with delightful cold dishes such as sashimi, sushi, salad, vegetables, pickles and a surprise. The desserts are the usual fare: melon, ice cream and yokan. Average price per couple, with a drink, is $60.

12/20 Island
1305 Madison Ave.
(92nd & 93rd Sts.)
996-1200
ECLECTIC
Open Mon.-Sat. noon-3 p.m. & 6 p.m.-midnight, Sun. noon-4 p.m. & 6 p.m.-midnight. Cards: AE.

They are drowning in hipness at Island, a year-round version of the Hamptons summer scene. What does Island mean? An island of noise, as opposed to calm? An island in the stream of uptown traffic? A treasure island for the owners? The proprietors explain that the name describes the style of cooking (Mediterranean, including the off-shore islands) as well as where the clientele spends the winter. Nothing about the look or feel of the place, however, suggests any kind of island. Not Capri. Not Anguilla. Not Shelter or Block. This is a long, narrowish room divided into a bar area (with a half dozen or so tables) and a main dining room. The walls are a creamy off-white and are dotted with mirrors. There are marble-topped tables and bistro chairs. Neutral good taste, like the clothes of the clientele.

The menu is eclectic, offering a little of everything fashionable, but most resembling Provençal bistro. Grilled vegetables, grilled chèvre, grilled fish, grilled meat, radicchio, mâche, pasta and the top of the pops in desserts—crème brûlée, tarte tatin, tiramisu. Some monikers are confusing. There's no point asking about individual items. The music is too loud and the waiter is too busy, and he thinks questions are occasions for comedy, anyway. Explaining the pasta of the day—orecchiette—he smirks, "little ears," and wiggles his index finger under his flop of curls. Well, the little ears of pasta are just fine—with plum tomatoes, potatoes and wilted arugula—just add a hefty dose of Parmesan. And the grilled rabbit, brushed with mustard and fresh basil, is both tasty and spa-like; it feeds fashionably and keeps customers in size sixes. The wine list is consistent with everything else; there are some good selections, but they are hard to find. As the juggernaut of gentrification rolls inexorably uptown, it will deposit a thousand formula-hip Islands along the way. This one hasn't yet distinguished itself gastronomically from the pack. Dinner averages $100 per couple.

Jane's Bar & Grill
208 E. 60th St. (Third Ave.)
935-3481

AMERICAN

Open Mon.-Fri. noon-2:30 p.m. & 6 p.m.-11 p.m., Sat. 6 p.m.-11 p.m. All major cards.

You have to look pretty hard to find the entrance to Jane's if you approach it from Third Avenue and Bloomies. Its sign and awning get lost by the preeminence of its next door neighbor, Arizona 206. You'll find Jane's worth looking for, however, and indeed, the proof that more and more people have found this American café, opened in 1989, and have chosen to return to it, came in January 1990. During this traditionally slow restaurant period, Jane's was packed nightly and reservations were *de rigueur*—the envy of many an upstart restaurant. The chameleon crowd wears suits, ties and business garb during the week and more casual, on-display trendy threads on weekends. Same picture at lunch, plus shopping bags.

The term "bar and grill" misleads, the place being a bit more upscale, and less of a bar than the name suggests. In fact, there's only a small bar in the front of the long, rectangular room with white walls, black wainscoting, black chairs and banquettes. The starkness is offset only modestly by lovely flowers, mirrors and framed photographs and an occasional splash of red. The food can be very good, though we've also found it inconsistent. Take the choice entrée of grilled tuna in a gazpacho sauce with fried leeks. One time, we received the fish cooked to pink and moist perfection, another time, it came exceedingly dry. One time, we found the leeks crisp, light and sweet, the next, heavy and not nearly as good. We like the curious vegetable tart appetizer. It regularly comes almost as high as wide, looking like an open-face hamburger, but filled with eggplant, mushroom, tomato and zucchini moistened with olive oil. Sometimes, a timid hand does the seasoning, and then we haven't liked it so much. We adored the duck sausages (more a patty), but the accompanying lentils need work. The pattern of one excellent item on a plate, marred by a second item not up to the first's standard, continues

with the fish entrée of lotte with lobster risotto. We found the lotte excellent, the risotto simply standard rice. A grilled tomato renders the plate neutral. On another occasion, the risotto with bits of porcini and a garlicky sauce won out over the okay squab that nests upon it. Still, you eat well, and engagingly, in a relaxed atmosphere.

We liked for a dessert the "symphony" of three chocolates—sherbet, mousse and terrine follows the pattern. We'll leave it to you to spot the weak link. We like the slightly spicy apple tart when it comes, all-American, with vanilla ice cream. The list of perhaps 35 French/American/Italian wines is very well chosen and priced, with most costing in the $20 range, and only Champagnes requiring you to pay more than $40. Dinner will run about $90 to $100 per couple.

Lusardi's
1494 Second Ave. (77th & 78th Sts.)
249-2020

ITALIAN

Open daily noon-3 p.m. & 5 p.m.-midnight. Cards: AE, DC, V.

The Lusardi brothers' trattoria has lost some of its chic trendiness since opening in 1982, but has matured into a comfortable and reliable neighborhood eatery, frequented by a casual, but well-dressed, coterie and a smattering of celebs of one ilk or another.

Among the openers, try the seafood salad, the beef carpaccio with arugula and buffalo mozzarella, or grilled peppers. We like the fusilli with pesto, or any of the pasta specials, such as angel hair with tomatoes and basil. The waiters will tout the green tortellini with four cheeses. Nothing special, nothing to be sorry for it you order it. Try the good risotto with porcini mushrooms. We've had mixed results with the bruschetta, which can suffer from being made with pallid, unripe winter tomatoes, and while well conceived, it should not be served when true tomatoes are unavailable. Lusardi's gets first ranking for its pollo abruzzese (sautéed with tomato, rosemary mushrooms and white wine) as a main course. We adored the faultless veal chop valdostana, butterflied and thinly layered with prosciutto and a melt of Fontina cheese. Among other main courses we like are the veal chop with fresh sage and the swordfish sautéed with olives, garlic, celery and tomato.

The wine list is impressive for this genre of restaurant, and you'll want to try one of a nice assortment of luscious Italian dessert wines and firelike grappas. For dessert, we loved berries in season, but you can forget the commercial tartufo, chocolate cake, fruit tart and a highly touted tiramisu, served in a huge stemmed glass. Either Mauro or Luigi, who are hard to tell apart, is always on hand to keep an eye on things, and the staff is gracious and professional—none of those Italian restaurant theatrics, thank you. Dinner averages $96 per couple.

Malvasia
108 E. 60th St.
(Park & Lexington Aves.)
223-4790

ITALIAN
Open Mon.-Sat. noon-3 p.m. & 6 p.m.-11:30 p.m. All major cards.

Malvasia is yet another of New York's chic, uptown bistros/trattorias. The large, duplex dining room, designed by ultra-fashionable Adam Tihany, features banquettes upholstered with a southwestern motif and a ceiling adorned with what might be taken as symbolic waves—perhaps a reminder of the coastal Sicilian origins of chef and part-owner Gennaro Picone, or the island off the coast of Sicily that gives the restaurant its name. An enormous wood chandelier hangs over the tiny bar in an anteroom, where patrons wait for their tables and, in effect, their assigned companions for the evenings, the tables being so absurdly close together. From the second story balcony, you can gaze down at the other diners seated amid deafening noise.

First courses on chef Picone's elegant and simple menu include a well-seasoned squab salad (a trendy addition) and succulent, homemade warm mozzarella di bufala served with a delicate, yet spicy, roast pepper salad. We thought even more inviting a seafood salad of tender shrimp, lobster and scallops tossed with a lemony sauce and paired with a salad of white beans and potatoes fragrant with balsamic vinegar. A white-bean soup reaches perfection—simple, velvety, with just the right touch of herbs and an ethereal, smoky aftertaste. Pasta at Malvasia is no less than superb. We loved translucent pappardelle, topped with a hearty tomato sauce combined with slices of seared, rare tuna. Firm, tasty rigatoni carries a sauce of rich garlicky eggplant and ricotta. We thought the pick of the pastas Gennaro's spaghetti tossed with fresh sardines and infused with wild fennel.

Among the entrées, we liked the buttery duck breast, pink slices steeped in Malvasia wine and studded with sliced fresh dates and green olives; the flavors of this unusual dish blend beautifully. The thick, yet tender, veal chops would be bland if not napped with a heady porcini sauce and topped with velvety, tender porcini slices. We consider the grilled tuna with arugula served with oregano sauce very good, if unimaginative. Among Malvasia's few desserts are some better-than-average Italian pastries. If you love cheesecake, the Sicilian cheesecake, dotted with preserved fruit and tucked between two layers of genoise, will strike you as rich and lemony; unfortunately, the genoise comes overdoused with sweet liqueur. For a more refreshing choice, ask for the fresh fruit plate, which contains, in season, cactus pears and fresh berries; its accompaniment—several homemade almond cookies—might be addictive. Ask for a glass of sweet Malvasia wine to end the meal. The wine list provides no great surprises. Espresso, both regular and decaf, rounds out a perfect meal. Dinner for two comes to about $130, with a bottle of wine.

Maxim's
680 Madison Ave. (61st St.)
751-5111

FRENCH
Open Tues.-Sat. 6 p.m.-11:30 p.m. All major cards.

"What's in a name?" Shakespeare asked. In the restaurant and extended high-society world, Maxim's is a great name. Its Paris original set the modern standard for haute cuisine and high-society dining. Throw in the moniker of Pierre Cardin, the fashion impresario and owner of Maxim's in Paris and the hotel/restaurant in New York, and you've got more name recognition and money. So, you'd think Maxim's Restaurant in New York would be a shoe-in for success. Wrong. Opened in 1985, this place still hasn't developed much of a local reputation or following. In 1989, dancing to a live, five-piece orchestra was added, making this a good tourist spot or special occasion (say Valentine's Day) destination. All this fits with the Belle Epoque look of the New York clone of the original Paris restaurant and nightclub, which dates from 1893 and which has been frequented by *le tout* Paris for over three-quarters of a century. Your in-laws will like the look of the place, its name done in dancing red letters in joie-de-vivre upper case, plus a glorious array of flowers and vases, gleaming silver railings, glowing wood and art-nouveau-style glass.

Food takes second billing to the room and the band, but it can be very good (and expensive). Chef David Ruggerio has been playing around with those pricey products synonymous with Maxim's—caviar, foie gras, oysters and lobster. To start, try a little Russian beluga caviar, costing a king's ransom for a moundlet, or the quail eggs and caviar tarts, topped with a thumbnail-sized bit of sour cream and chives. We thought more contemporary the marriage of marinated raw tuna with caviar accompanied by an asparagus salad, as was the crab salad with caviar (maybe Pierre Cardin owns shares in a caviar import/export firm). We usually like a plate of ravioli for a more rewarding and frugal first course. If you skip the foie gras as an appetizer, you can enjoy it grilled and served as an accompaniment to roast baby chicken with vegetables as a main course. Did we mention truffles? How about sea scallops with black truffles on sautéed spinach and arugula with shallots? Or, the crépinette of sole with truffles and potatoes and celery? We prefer the simple braised red snapper with fennel and tomatoes. We liked the duck breast, too, and the veal chop served with eggplant and couscous. Salade Maxim's, in case you're interested, is an assemblage of roast breast of pigeon, lobster, scallops and foie gras over lettuce with a vinaigrette.

We thought the desserts a little more lyrical, headed by a parfait with citronella and a coulis of red berries. You can always dance off the desserts to Maxim's orchestra, so long as you're properly dressed. You can also order decent wines, but why do so when you can order bottle after bottle of Champagne, which goes so well with the restaurant's food ingredients and certainly with its nostalgic ambience? Two can eat here for about $130, but if you indulge in caviar and bubbly, add another couple of hundred.

La Métairie

1442 Third Ave. (81st & 82nd Sts.)
988-1800

FRENCH

Open daily noon-3 p.m. & 6 p.m.-midnight. Cards: AE. MC, V.

The country French food here has more than straightened out in owner Sylvain Fareri's upscale version of his cozy Greenwich Village farm (see page 51). The restaurant's name, taken from medieval French, refers to the sweet country farms of the old days, where fat ducks waddled past haystacks and doves cooed from the trees. Uptown, there's white linen and crystal on the tables, but chefs Joel Huchet and Patrice Boëly offer the earthy, traditional coq au vin, boeuf bourguignon, cassoulet, pot au feu, blanquette de veau and bouillabaisse.

Among the only slightly less classic items, we like the sweetbread pâté with foie gras and port wine as an appetizer, along with seafood ravioli, and especially the garlic mousse with sautéed wild mushroooms. Grilling over *feu de bois* is something of a specialty here, so consider a salmon grilled over the fire or a loup de mer grilled with fennel and, for meat, the cut of Black Angus beef that is meant to serve two. On one visit, our friends liked, for entrées, the braised baby bass with candied sweet peppers and onions and the rabbit cooked in white wine and mustard that's served with fresh noodles. We found just okay the bistro desserts and the classic French/American wine list. They'll cancel your dinner reservations if you don't reconfirm before 2 p.m. Dinner should run about $116 per couple, plus tax and tip, and about $70 for two at lunch.

Mezzaluna

1295 Third Ave. (74th & 75th Sts.)
535-9600

ITALIAN

Open Mon.-Fri. noon-3 p.m. & 6 p.m.-1 a.m., Sat. & Sun. noon-4 p.m. & 6:30 p.m.-1 a.m. No cards.

Mezzaluna is no longer as "in," or quite as good, as this casual Upper East Side Italian restaurant was in the first few years after its 1984 opening. Nevertheless, much of the neighborhood's well-heeled populace, including young upscale Italians, line up here (overcrowding begins around 7:45 p.m.) and wait, wait, wait, because Mezzaluna takes no reservations for the 46 seats squeezed around its marble-topped tables. (It's not so crowded at lunch, and the food is just as good.) We find the waiting easier because of the engaging look and feel of this up-to-the-minute trattoria. It has a narrow storefront with a split-level dining area, one wall completely obscured by 77 drawings, paintings and collages from students in a Florentine art school who'd been asked to create a "work" exploring the theme of Mezzaluna, referring to both the crescent-shaped vegetable cutter as well as the moon at half-cycle. The other wall is dominated by a breakfront filled with handmade, hand-painted Italian ceramics, a long bar, and—at the rear—a wood-fired pizza oven that stokes up at lunchtime and again at 10:30 p.m.

The fashionable pizzas—four cheeses, for example, or primavera (assorted vegetables)—are good bets, as are any of the pastas. Skip the appetizers, unless you go for something tame like the grilled mixed vegetables, the bufula mozzarella and tomato (be sure tomatoes are in season) or the Mezzaluna salad. Carpaccio with arugula and Parmesan is not better than at most places these days. We found the homey, delicious pastas far more satisfying, from the pansotti (dumplings stuffed with a blend of ricotta and light pesto and sauced with butter, Parmesan, and fried fresh sage leaves), or orecchiette (with diced potatoes, arugula and light tomato sauce), to "designer" pasta such as black linguine (the color comes from cuttlefish ink) with a feisty arrabbiata sauce—a dish that is as beautiful as it is toothsome. Do also note, specially, the whole wheat fettucine with pecorino and leeks. For dessert, we liked tiramisu or fresh fruit tart. The wine list is short and serviceable. Expect to pay $70 per couple, with wine, plus tax and tip.

10/20 Mortimer's

1057 Lexington Ave. (75th St.)
517-6400
CONTINENTAL
Open Sun.-Mon. noon-midnight, Tues.-Sat. noon-2 a.m. Closed first two weeks in August. All major cards.

We're glad there are restaurants such as Mortimer's—well, at least a couple. We critics continue to bash the food and service, and the regulars (a mix of Upper East Side society, Hamptons residents, and country-club denizens) clamor for more. The main room of this society bistro may be a sea of empty tables when you enter, but unless you are known through friendship or fame to the proprietor, don't expect to be given one; those without rank automatically go to the side room. Though the official policy is "no reservations" except for parties of five or more, Mr. Glenn Bernbaum, the owner, makes no bones about choosing to hold tables for his personal friends, making Mortimer's a de facto private club that fills extra tables with walk-ins.

At lunch, the regulars love the smoked salmon crêpe, the gravlax (with mustard-dill sauce), and then the paillard of chicken with tarragon, or one of several good salads, or perhaps a hamburger or omelet. By and large, the food at lunch and dinner is predictable, designed to be eaten without interrupting conversation beyond a quaff of Perrier (its withdrawal a veritable crisis for the restaurant early in 1990) to wash down the overcooked calf's liver or the dry twinburgers. (We speculate that the regulars must have learned to eat—and maybe even to enjoy—Mortimer's version of all-too-often poorly prepared food at boarding schools.) Main courses at dinner that we can recommend are the crabcakes, the grilled poussin, the Dover sole (if you take it the way they want to serve it) and the baby lamb chops (the best dish in the place). Crème brûlée is excellent, and you won't mind the pecan chocolate pie or the dense cheesecake. To record the disappointing and failed dishes (and thus our rating) would double or triple the length of this review. Rule number two here is keep it simple and keep your gastronomic expectations low. Rule number one: Go with someone who is known. The short and mundane wine list is, nevertheless, very satisfying, with some of the lowest prices in town. The room has its charm, lots of wood and mirrors, and well-spaced tables to allow gossiping eavesdrop-free. Sunday brunch is an important event. Figure on spending an average of $80 per couple for dinner with wine, plus tax and tip.

Pamir

1437 Second Ave. (74th & 75th Sts.)
734-3791
AFGHAN
Open Tues.-Sun. 5 p.m.-11 p.m. Cards: MC, V.

Walking into Pamir is like walking into a Kabulian bric-à-brac shop: the lights are dim and the walls covered with shawls and rugs from Afghanistan and Pakistan. You sit down at one of the closely spaced tables and a sweet mosaic of aromas—sharp spices, a tease of mint—dances over to greet you. This enchanting little oasis, created by the Bayat brothers, teems with activity every night and has earned much respect for its cuisine and professional style.

Afghan cooking is earthier than its Indian counterpart. Of the appetizers, sambosa goushti—deep-fried dumplings of ground beef and chickpeas, served with an "Afghan sauce" that tastes as if it were spicy ketchup—stands out. The best deal is the Pamir combination. Though you're offered a choice of three appetizers, they often give you all four: a scallion turnover with yogurt (bulanee gandana), a ground beef and potato turnover (bulanee kachalou), scallion dumplings (aushak), and the sambosa goushti. If you want a single appetizer, choose the latter (sambosa goushti)—stuffed, deep fried pastries of ground beef with chickpeas and spices served with an Afghan sauce. This group comes with a salad, however, that's as disappointing as it is inevitable—the supermarket lettuce and tomatoes come with all the main dishes as well.

We think best such entrées as the marinated kebabs—kofta (chicken), and Pamir, an assortment of four different meats (lamb chunks, lamb chops, ground beef and chicken). Our favorite vegetarian dishes are chalaw sabsi, a spinach stew with spicy sauce, and chalaw bedenjan, sautéed eggplant with yogurt. We also like the orange palaw (seasoned lamb under a mound of saffron rice, topped with almonds, pistachios, orange strips, rosewater and cardamom), or the quabilli palaw (here the lamb is under brown rice and topped with almonds, pistachios, carrot strips and raisins). Stick with Afghani tea for a finisher—the three regularly offered desserts are heavy and strange, dominated by pistachios and too much sugar. Figure on $70 or so per couple, plus tax and tip.

12/20 Panda Garden

1606 Second Ave. (83rd St.)
288-0400
CHINESE
Open Sun.-Thurs. noon-11 p.m., Fri.-Sat. noon-12:30 a.m. Cards: AE, MC, V.

In a spacious and unassuming room the size of a banquet hall, with a wall made up entirely of lace-curtain windows and vigorous plants jungling up the corners, Hunan and Szechuan specialties are cooked with a verve and skill unusual for an Upper East Side Chinese restaurant this size. While there's no reason to get overly excited by the cuisine here, there's good reason—say the existence of a couple of thousand pretty dreadful Chinese eat-ins and -outs sprinkled throughout the city—to take special note of this address.

The best appetizers are the steamed dumplings, served in a blazingly hot oil sauce; shredded pieces of fresh Chinese cabbage with a red oil sauce; fried crispy shrimp balls, a little greasy (which is sometimes nice); and paper-wrapped chicken. The hot-and-sour soup is a veritable song of flavors. The house special soup is a light broth filled with chunks of chicken, shrimp, and vegetables and is a meal in itself.

The best entrées are listed under "Chef's Specialties." Try the orange beef (chunks of high-class steak sautéed with an orange sauce) or the house special beef, which is a spicy mixture of steak and hot-pepper sauce, served with crisp, cool watercress. General Tso's chicken, a common dish at better-quality places, is excellent. Crispy prawns with walnuts, again with a tangy sauce, is also good. But the dish that's the most fun to eat here is the neptunes in bird's nest: noodles are moulded into a basket and fried until they're stiff, then the middle is filled with seafood. By the time you get through the seafood, the heat and moisture have softened the noodles, and they're a delicious way to finish. Among the nonspecials, which are almost as good, if a bit less elaborate, are the scallops with black-bean sauce, which taste better than the shrimps served with the same sauce. An often abused common dish, cold noodles in sesame sauce, is unusually notable: the sauce is creamy and full of nutty bite, the wheat noodles cooked al dente and served with a proper abundance of scallion greens. On a slow day, it feels like the waiting room of Grand Central Station here; portions are enormous. Average price per couple, for a full meal, is $40.

Paola's Restaurant
347 E. 85th St. (First & Second Aves.)
794-1890
ITALIAN
Open daily 5 p.m.-11 p.m. Cards: AE.

The civilized folk who live on East End Avenue and who started coming to small, romantic Paola's when it opened in 1983 are still coming in the 1990s. There's not much more chef/owner Paola Marracino can ask. WASPy women in elegant clothes and inherited jewelry, and men who were born into Brooks Brothers suits (and look like they run the company that owns the company you work for) sit quietly while the waiters work up and down the narrow aisle with oversize plates. Everyone seems to feel at home and to enjoy the simple, authentic Italian food, prepared here very well. The walls are covered with lots of little mirrors, a design which makes the place look bigger, and affords the bric-à-brac (candles, porcelain, flowers) a little breathing room.

Start with the mozzarella fresca (homemade, and served with vegetables), the brodetto di cozze e vongole (steamed mussels and clams with white wine and tomatoes), or the crostino (toasted bread with prosciutto, mushrooms, mozzarella and peas). Pastas can be ordered as an appetizer or main course—the popular choices, which, like most of the dishes, go back to the restaurant's beginnings, include the full-flavored, assertive fettucine puttanesca (homemade fettucine with tomatoes, olives, capers and anchovies) and the paglia e fieno all'aragosta (green and yellow noodles with lobster, shrimp and cream). For the second course, you might stay away from the lamb chops and, instead, try the veal chop or veal scaloppine, either pizzaiola (with olives and red peppers), or al Marsala (with mushrooms and Marsala wine). Or, ask for the fish of the day, which is usually prepared perfectly. Desserts change regularly, and the wines off the short Italian list are sound—for economy, go for the Pinot Grigio Santa Margherita, which comes in a full or half bottle ($28 or $14) and for red, the Rubesco of Lungarotti ($18). Dinner averages $76 to $90 per couple, plus tax and tip.

Parioli Romanissimo
24 E. 81st St. (Fifth & Madison Aves.)
288-2391
ITALIAN
Open Tues.-Sat. 6:00 p.m.-11:30 p.m. Closed July-Aug. Cards: AE, DC, CB.

Parioli, an elegant neighborhood in Rome, houses families from the upper-middle class, and bears a distinct sense of security and discreet power in its tree-lined streets. The New York restaurant that bears its name tries hard to give the same impression. Housed in a town house, the main dining room resembles a rich Italian banker's salon. A smaller dining room in a glass-enclosed courtyard features a gurgling fountain and a street lantern to give the illusion of a charming Italian piazza. Most of the tables on a given night are occupied by businessmen discussing the latest market crisis, fashionably-dressed divorcees, in groups of two or three, chatting over a large salad and stockbrokers trying to impress their dates with their knowledge of Italian. The confident maitre d', an Edward G. Robinson look-alike, and the suave waiters attempt to translate the names of the pastas offered on the menu through thick Italian accents. The serious staff functions quietly on a level one usually finds only in the better European restaurants—no flash, no tableside dazzle, just unobtrusive, good service.

Traditional appetizers include mozzarella with roasted peppers, arugula salad and ordinary sautéed shrimps; we found a more interesting alternative a succulent, barely-seared baby lamb filet served with delicious glazed shallots, though it was almost ruined by a red-pepper-cream sauce. Try also the lamb (instead of beef or tuna these days) carpaccio with red pepper cream and a cold sea bass with watercress sauce. We thought the pasta dishes well-prepared, but the sauces uninspiring, except for the fresh white truffles topping al dente spaghettini or perhaps the ravioli with porcini mushrooms in a light cream sauce. Price of the pastas create a problem for many people; some find it hard not to let the eighteen-carat cost negatively affect their tastebuds throughout the meal. We love the risotti, especially one cooked with porcini and a touch of curry. Among the entrées, we liked the Dover sole, fresh tasting, with just a hint of garlic. The baked sea bass has a sweet fennel flavor, but its tarragon sauce overpowers the delicate fish. A 21-day-old chicken (do they really count?) tasted as if it had been cooked for 21 days, and the black truffle slices, used as garnish, do nothing for its taste. Veal is prepared in several different ways, from paper-thin scaloppine with anchovies, capers and mushrooms to a chop so thick that it is difficult to cut into; again, a sea of tarragon sauce drowns out the flavor. We've also enjoyed the marinated grilled rack of baby lamb with candied fruit mustard. The restaurant does an excellent job with seasonal game. Be warned that most main courses come absolutely unadorned, and you must be prepared to raise your already hefty bill by the cost of one or more à la carte vegetables.

We found the desserts uninspiring, except for a very light, moist Italian cheesecake. Choose, instead, a selection of cheese from the staggering display—arguably the finest and most extensive (about 40 varieties) in New York—followed by a superb espresso. Parioli's wine list is extensive; you can pay as much or as little as you want. This place aims at an elegant, elaborate dining experience and generally succeeds; however, luxe has its price. Dinner for two will run about $200, with wine.

11/20 **Petaluma**
        1356 First Ave. (73rd St.)
        772-8800

ITALIAN

Open Mon.-Sat. 11:30 a.m.-3 p.m. & 5 p.m.-midnight, Sun. 11:30 a.m.-3 p.m. & 5 p.m.-11 p.m. Cards: AE, V.

A theatrical, pastel Californian-Southwestern, oceanliner-style architectural hybrid, Petaluma's spacious interior attracts one of the most diverse crowds you'll see in a Manhattan eatery—young and social singles, female and male duos, the retirement crowd, families who like a place where the varying taste of individual members can all be satisfied. The crowds are down since the mid-eighties, but this place still has its fans and devotees who come for the scene and decent eats. The brainchild of Elio Guaitolini of sister restaurant Elio's, Petaluma is sort of a modern-day Left Bank café, into which you can fall at almost any hour; the elegant bar has been brilliantly positioned so as to cater to the singles crowd without interfering with diners.

Likewise, the exposed kitchen does not intrude on the privacy of the raised dining area.

Petaluma's menu is a moderately priced, diversified grazing food list, bolstered with a small, but good, assortment of more substantial fare. It's designed to attract yuppies who'd rather snack, and oldsters who prefer to eat lightly or taste several dishes at once. At lunch, you can get a burger and fries, grilled tuna or duck breast salad, good Maryland crab cakes or various pastas or pizzas. Mozzarella in carozza, small batter-dipped mozzarella and Italian bread sandwiches, are ravishing to look at under a tangle of skinny fried zucchini around a pool of tomato sauce, but are too salty and capered. Mushroom salad and mixed antipasti are better starters. There are a number of pastas, all acceptable, none brilliant. The green gnocchi served in a sauce aurora is one of the better preparations; ditto for bucatini amatriciana with tomato sauce, onions and pancetta. Salmon and swordfish are treated impeccably, as is a free-range chicken, grilled or sautéed with peppers. Many people go for the individual dinner-plate-size pizzas available on both menus, pizzas with the kind of crispy thin crust characteristic of a wood-burning oven. The Margharita with mozzarella, tomato sauce and basil, and the Four Seasons with prosciutto, artichokes and mushrooms are two of the best, though the toppings are skimpy. The vanilla cheesecake for dessert is underwhelming; the chocolate cake

---

DANDY SALADS

If a recent trend persists, dandelions soon will earn their rightful place of honor, alongside nasturtiums, in the Unusual Salad Greens Hall of Fame. In New York, a growing number of restaurants, including Le Cirque, Lutèce and "21," have dandelions on their menus. During the 1980s, sales of commercially grown dandelions tripled, but as with any food fad, we predict its demise later in the nineties. Meanwhile, watch for small golden flowers in your food.

good, but too rich an ending. Service ranges from professional to inept. Reasonably priced Italian wines effectively wash the food down, but the listings are too often inaccurate; you might just stick to the good inexpensive house offerings or one of the terrific selection of beers. About $56 per couple at lunch, $76 for two at dinner. If you just want a pizza and a glass of wine, however, you might get by with $40 or so for two.

12/20 Pig Heaven
1540 Second Ave. (80th & 81st Sts.)
744-4887
CHINESE
Open Mon.-Thurs. noon-midnight, Fri.-Sat. noon-1 a.m., Sun. noon-11:30 p.m. Cards: AE, DC.

Pig Heaven, one of the restaurants in David Keh's camp, is the haunt for uptown chic crowds and kids who prefer pseudo-Chinese glitter to an away-from-home-turf experience in Chinatown. Sam Lopata, David's architect, surrounds us with the pink walls of a nursery barnyard—150 little, pink, dancing pigs overlooking a large yellow moon and a neon cartoon of a tipsy pig presiding over a white tiled bar. Roast ducks, chickens and suckling pigs (the restaurant's specialties) peer at you from behind a glass-enclosed barbecue grill. The menu reads authentically, that is, you'll recognize the big name traditional dishes, and Keh's chefs (there are several) do not get too fancy. The spicy, tangy shredded pigs' ears make a crunchy, excellent appetizer, followed by an array of dim sum, steamed and fried dumplings and scallion pancakes. The small dumplings steamed in a bamboo basket are exquisitely light, as are the unusual turnip cakes. If pork is not your cup of tea, the vegetarian rolls are as good as in Chinatown (which may be damning with faint praise).

As its name implies, Pig Heaven serves up great Cantonese-style suckling pig and roast pork. Tender and sweet, with crackling skin, both dishes will have you licking your fingers gleefully. The menu also features several Szechuan dishes, such as pork with pickled vegetables or with garlic sauce, and braised pigs' feet. Unfortunately, these dishes are not consistently good. Stick to three-glass chicken, lightly sautéed with fresh ginger, garlic, wine, soy sauce and vinegar, or a whole braised carp with hot bean sauce. Just beware

of the hundreds of fish bones! Double-fried bean curd, crisp outside and light as air inside, is the best nonmeat dish. The mussels in casserole with transparent mung beans is also a hit. The French and American desserts are strictly Upper East Side, and are not recommended. The restaurant serves wine, and on Saturdays and Sundays, Pig Heaven offers a Chinese breakfast of dumplings, congee (rice soup with pork and pickles), and suckling pig. Prices are uptown, not Chinatown. About $60 per couple.

12/20 Pinnochio
170 E. 81st St.
(Second & Third Aves.)
650-1513
ITALIAN
Open Mon.-Sat. 5 p.m.-11 p.m. Closed July-Aug. Cards: AE, DC.

Peeking their noses through the heavy curtains in the front windows of this tenement storefront restaurant to greet you are various antique, wooden Pinnochios. Welcome to a first-name kind of appealing family restaurant that keeps expanding its dining rooms. Obviously, people are ready to buy the extra seats and enjoy the kitchen's simple charms. The dining rooms have their romantic kind of charms as well—dark, spare, elegant and real, no frou-frou or pretense, save some Venetian chandeliers and artwork and taped opera music dampening the sounds and bustle of staff and guests.

The changing, handwritten menu offers, at its best, a solid, well-wrought example of northern Italian cooking, with stately sauces and lively meats. Start off with stuffed mushrooms or the special crostini nostri: muscular cheese melted over roasted peppers and strong anchovies, layered onto a good slice of crusty bread. Or try the carpaccio; the pâté of veal, artichoke, bacon and brandy; the hot Genoa salami served under grated cheese; or the sautéed and stuffed mushroom caps, which, with their fragrant mushroom and herb stuffing and gratinéed tops, are so good you'll want many more than the allotted two. Pinnochio's pastas are best for what's in them: the ardent veal and indefatigable ham in the green and white paglia e fieno; the tart capers and bacon pieces in the (sometimes too rich) cream sauce, spiked with a whiff of sharp cheese, in the penne palermitana. Other recommended pastas are the fettucine ai porcini, and the penne puttanesca. For entrées, you might order a special fish dish, since that's the only way you can sample the otherwise unlisted trout poached in red wine and butter sauce, or any of the salmon dishes. The liver torinese is stellar, and there are good lamb chops milanese and veal piccata.

Italian desserts can be delightful or fall flat (we're thinking of some rather pallid versions of cheesecake), and here you'd better stick with the best. Zabaglione is served cold over ripe berries, or it's slid into a glass and laced with hot espresso in caffè nonno. Budino al caffè is mocha mousse and dark, bittersweet-chocolate bits; a macaroon soaked in mocha lurks like a seductress in the bottom of the sundae glass. Something magic is done to the espresso here to make it strong, yet never bitter; its cap of amber froth has its own staying power. Dinner runs about $84 per couple.

 ### The Polo

Westbury Hotel,
948 Madison Ave. (69th & 70th Sts.)
535-9141

AMERICAN

Open daily noon-2:30 p.m. & 6:30-10:30 p.m. All major cards.

The restaurant of the Westbury Hotel, The Polo, has retained its solemn, stodgy, wood-paneled, English club decor despite completely revamping its menu in a style far from such things. Here, uptown and suburban matrons, hair pushed into place with black headbands, seem to feel unthreatened by the horsey atmosphere, the plush banquettes and the weighty leather furniture. At least, the elegant clusters of pink tulips in the foyer and the little bouquets on each table echo the new cuisine. The new menu is the work of Terrence Breenan, who has moved on, and is executed by former *sous*-chef Joseph Guerra.

The seasonally changing menu reflects new trends in American nouvelle cuisine, better known as New American. To begin a meal, we like the black-buck antelope tartare, laced with a pear-chutney sauce and crowning a bed of wild rice and barley: spicy and tart with a delicate, yet gamey, flavor. We also like the warm goat cheese ravioli and the smoked quail and yellowfin tuna and potato salad. Brennan clearly has been influenced by the Japanese, a

fact reflected in tender slices of tuna sashimi in a flat tart of crisp roast onion and bell pepper, served with a fennel salad. It needs a squirt of lemon or a touch of wasabe (Japanese horseradish), however, to give the tuna a lift. The velvety oyster soup, flavorful and creamy, studded with smoked salmon and topped with salmon "cracklings," we thought enchanting. Brennan and crew have a light touch with root vegetables. Barely cooked sea scallops are served, for example, with an airy and delicious celery root purée. Other main course choices include roasted squab, and a just-seared Atlantic salmon filet enclosed in a crust of horseradish that's sweet and piquant. We thought the drab sautéed cucumber slices an unfortunate addition to an otherwise excellent dish. Tournedos of smoked lobster tied with a thick slice of bacon sit in an exquisite blend of lentils, turnips, beets and parsnips. This exuberant composition leaves one a tad perplexed, but pleased.

The desserts menu similarly has been improved, and its offerings, too, come handsomely presented on sparkling Villeroy-Bosch china. We liked the light walnut chocolate soufflé, served with espresso ice cream. The kitchen's new masterpiece seems to be a startling blood orange napoleon: two thin and crusty wafers enclose a light and frothy orange mousse, studded with preserved kumquats and floating on a bed of tart cranberry and pomegranate coulis. A very light, barely sweet pear soufflé comes served with creamy, homemade caramel ice cream and enclosed in a golden nest of spun sugar. We think the black-tie service effective, but bearing a European-American indifference. The wine list (75 percent French and 25 percent other) hasn't changed much; it lacks some depth and interest. Dinner for two à la carte, with wine, will cost a hefty $180 or so.

 ### Primavera

1578 First Ave. (82nd St.)
861-8608

ITALIAN

Open daily 5:30 p.m.-midnight. All major cards.

Primavera, which opened in 1978, was one of the first uptown restaurants to abandon tomato sauce and to serve pricey northern Italian cuisine in a romantic setting. An unabashed, fancy Italian restaurant with a solid following of a fashionable crowd that gets dressed up to come here ("and keep the limo waiting outside"), Primavera is one of those restaurants synonymous with one man: in this case, proprietor Nicola Civetta. The quality and good service has remained constant due to his instincts and watchful eye, and the woman behind the man, his wife, who keeps an eye on the kitchen. We think the hors d'oeuvres fairly predictable, but people like the salmon carpaccio and the scallops. You can get a good spiedino alla romana (mozzarella with bread, fried with anchovy sauce) or simple clams on the half shell or a seafood salad. You would probably do better to start with a half-portion of pasta, or just let Nicola Civetta order for you. We like the tortellini with ham and peas, agnolloti, angel-hair pasta primavera, penne all' arrabbiata or linguine studded with fresh vegetable morsels in a sauce brought nicely together with a bit of cream and Parmesan. We thought the baked clams pasty, ditto the stuffed mushrooms.

Primavera customers can be fairly evenly divided between people who go to see and be seen, and those who go because they are addicted to the roasted, marinated kid that started out as a sometime special and developed a passionate following. It's like lamb, but better and sweeter, occasionally a bit tough, but mostly bone-gnawingly succulent and redolent of rosemary. We loved other dishes, too, such as the veal sautéed with peas, mushrooms and truffles, and the thinly sliced beef with rosemary and arugula. Nicola's fresh fruit plate, which he himself used to carve into fanciful and delightful shapes as a "gift" to special patrons, also became so popular it is now a staple. Other restaurants should take note. Service is professional and attentive, though occasionally you have to wait a long time for the main course. The wine list impresses, but great Bordeaux may not be entirely appropriate to the food. Stick to some of the excellent red wines from Italy or perhaps a California white to start. In 1989, they opened up and expanded the wine cellar to seat 40 or 50 for dinner. Men must wear a jacket and tie. Dinner will run between $110 and $120 per couple, plus tax and tip.

Primola

1226 Second Ave. (64th & 65th Sts.)
758-1775

ITALIAN

Open Mon.-Fri. noon-2:30 p.m. & 5 p.m.-midnight, Sat.-Sun. 5 p.m.-midnight. Cards: AE.

Bustling at night with enthusiastic regulars, Primola is enough off the beaten path to offer a deliciously tranquil lunch. Co-owner and maître d' Giuliano Zuliani, who has an encyclopedic memory for names and faces, seems to be everywhere, welcoming, seating, keeping an eye on dishes as they are served. Decor is spare, that is to say, nonexistent: there's a natural wood floor, some inoffensive posters and watercolors, a welcoming bar (which can be a bit raucous on crowded nights), and an appealing display of hors d'oeuvres and desserts. Chef Franco Iacoviello prepares the food skilfully. He's the same chef who opened the restaurant in 1986, and though his menu has not changed much since then, a steadiness, consistency and a respect for seasonal produce has settled in here that more than satisfies the hungry customers.

Besides listed items on the ambitious menu, we like some of the numerous specials, such as fried ricotta with fresh blended tomato, homemade pasta and tender eggplant in a vivid tomato sauce, or homemade ravioli filled with a flavorsome, well-seasoned spinach ricotta mixture in a fresh tomato-basil sauce. Our friends liked for other good starters such items as the toothsome sautéed sliced artichokes or salmon marinated with fennel. Excellent quality veal appears as scaloppine, piccata or with wild mushrooms. We loved the pink, moist charcoal-grilled lamb chops, too. They handle seafood skillfully, as well, at Primola. The fish of the day depends on the market and comes done as you like it—the grilled baby snapper sauced with a reduction of balsamic vinegar is simple and perfect. They don't treat the vegetable accompaniments as mere afterthoughts here: the grilled fennel and endive accompanying the fish arrive first-rate. We also liked the quail with polenta and sausage. Desserts include pleasant homemade ice creams, berry tarts, the ubiquitous ricotta cheesecake and crème brûlée. The simple Italian wine list could use more producers' names and some vintage dates. Lunch runs around $50 per couple, dinner about $90 for two.

12/20 Quaglino by Tino Fontana

Sherry-Netherland Hotel,
781 Fifth Ave. (59th & 60th Sts.)
759-9020

ITALIAN

Open daily 7 a.m.-10:30 a.m., noon-3 p.m. &
5:30 p.m.-9:45 p.m. All major cards.

It's disconcerting to walk by this restaurant. It's sad to see restaurants without people. At 10 p.m. on a Friday night, this place is dead. When the cosmopolitan restaurateur Harry Cipriani ran the show here, the place was just warming up. In a 1987 coup that made the front pages of *The New York Times* as well as Italian dailies, that celebrated Arrigo (Harry) Cipriani and his son, Giuseppe, of Harry's Bar in Venice and recently Bellini in New York, were ousted with military suddenness from their two-year-old restaurant by the management of Trusthouse Forte, the international hotel chain that financed the restaurant. Tino Fontana—restaurateur, caterer and consultant from Northern Italy—was brought in to take charge. Consultants don't have much success in New York. What next? Quagliano's days are either numbered, or the hotel is willing simply to run the place at a loss as a convenience to guests and the neighborhood crowd who drop in for lunch. Curiously, Trusthouse Forte's other New York hotels, the Plaza Athénée and the Westbury, have excellent restaurants.

Perhaps because the kitchen does not have to cope with a press of diners, the food is a notch better than it was under Cipriani. Still, $18-to-$25 plates of pasta don't beckon off-the-street drop-ins. The pasta is good, notably a plate of rectangular, flat noodle stracci served with an asparagus-cream sauce. With the recent influx of contemporary northern Italian restaurants in New York, risotto has taken on new meaning and life. Now it is a staple of New York Italian restaurants, and the native versions offered up at Quaglino are good. Desserts are rich, creamy and heavy. If you don't feel like sorbet or fruit, stick to the authentic espresso or finish your good, but high-priced, bottle of Italian wine. The hotel and condominium residents are no doubt pleased with the breakfast hours and room service; nevertheless, one can not help wondering about Quaglino's future. Expect to pay top prices here, $100 to $150 per couple for dinner, and only slightly less for lunch.

12/20 Rao's

455 E. 114th St. (Pleasant Ave.)
534-9625

ITALIAN

Open Mon.-Fri. 6 p.m.-10 p.m. No cards.

That one of the city's toughest reservations to come by is at Rao's is one of those crazy phenomena that makes New York extraordinary. The wait for one of the eight tables in this reverse-chic, old-time bar-and-grill of a restaurant averages two to three months, and that's only because reservations generally aren't taken any further in advance. "For my own sister, I had to wait three months for a table," the barman of thirteen years said with a straight face. Now in its second century, Rao's looks like it belongs in a 1930s movie, and some of the types who frequent it could get parts as extras in a minute. The singular and often big-name cast—politicians, reputed underworld figures, entertainers, power moguls and moglettes (with long legs)—which frequents this cozy corner restaurant in East Harlem, eye Vincent Rao as soon as they enter. The kitchen has been turning out good, home-style southern Italian/American food for decades. Able Frank Pellegrino is the host and manages the place.

Frankie pulls up a chair to your table and takes your order: "Everything is good," he says and provides engaging rhapsodic descriptions of dishes when prompted. A more apt broad description of the offerings is, "There's nothing bad." For starters, the seafood salad is more than not bad, it's cool, lush, chewy and flavorful. Lobster, crabmeat, rings of squid, octopus bits, conch meat, scungilli are tossed with celery, lemon juice, olive oil and parsley. Roast-red-pepper salad, with or without anchovies, is another good starter. Among the pastas, the garlicky linguine with clam sauce is recommended, as is the macaroni tossed with broccoli. For a main course, try the "famous" lemon chicken or the he-man dish of pork chops. There are veal, beef or pork pizzaiolas and many familiar preparations. Desserts are weak, and when you ask the engaging bartender for the wine list, he replies, "I'm the wine list." The half-dozen white and half-dozen red wines he recites belong in a pizzeria, but he'll steer you to the one or two best bottles. Everyone under the low black ceiling or behind the bar with the year-round Christmas decorations will steer you well. And you can even steer yourself well to Rao's and park your car safely outside. Frankie has everything under control. Prices, as well, are under control, and run about $80 to $90 per couple.

Le Refuge
166 E. 82nd St.
(Lexington & Third Aves.)
861-4505

FRENCH

Open daily noon-3 p.m. & 5:30 p.m.-11:30 p.m. No cards.

Over the years, Le Refuge has built a solid reputation as a neighborhood restaurant with good, simple French home cooking. Its neighborhood is a wealthy one, and over time, the food has been gussied up some to meet neighborhood expectations and the high prices the dressy clients are more than willing to pay. With its three small dining rooms, wooden beams, provincial armoires, small oil paintings of the French countryside and seventeenth-century French tapestries, the joint is rustic in an Upper East Side, inn-in-the-city sort of way. It's pleasant, and the food is pretty good, improved some in the last couple of years.

You'll find no culinary pyrotechnics on the small menu, but you'll enjoy the mussels Provençal or the quail salad as an appetizer. The chef/owner, Pierre St. Denis, offers a good millefeuille of salmon with potatoes as an entrée. We think a highlight of the menu the shellfish bouillabaisse with its terrific rouille. For dessert, try fruit sherbet, a good little chocolate charlotte, nice fruits with mint, and a recommended dacquoise if you go for rich cakes. Le Refuge is particularly pleasant at lunch, a good address to keep in mind if

---

Note that average prices given in this chapter do not include tax (which is a whopping 8.25 percent in New York) or gratuity. You can figure, then, on adding roughly 25 percent to each of the prices quoted here, for your final bill.

---

you're doing the Metropolitan Museum or uptown galleries. The French wines cover a broad and expensive range, though most of the Bordeaux, which Pierre selects, represent good values, even if the tab is $100 or $180. Lunch will run about $60 per couple, dinner $96 for two.

Le Régence
Hotel Plaza Athénée, 37 E. 64th St.
(Madison & Park Aves.)
606-4647, 734-9100

FRENCH

Open daily 7 a.m.-10 a.m., noon-2:30 p.m. & 6 p.m.-9:30 p.m. All major cards.

This very good hotel restaurant has something of a reputation for bringing in talented, young French chefs, who then move on to bigger and better things. Lately, the waltz of the chefs has slowed down. Consultants Jo, Michel and Philippe Rostang (father and two sons), owners of highly esteemed restaurants on the Riviera and in Paris, have been nominally running the show through the late 1980s into the '90s, but their latest executive chef on premise, Jean-Robert de Cavel, is talented, and has settled in after a couple of years, delivering consistently fine food. The restaurant is majestic (as in Versailles) and its dining room makes a strong and longer-lasting impression. The room would make a fine movie set for some courtly period piece out of Hollywood—sea-foam colors, gleaming crystal chandeliers, wall sconces, ceiling painted with clouds, smashing flowers and posh, leather-cushioned Louis XV chairs, so solid that it takes a waiter to help petit diners adjust their seats. The room has hours going for it as well. It's available for a power breakfast, or a Sunday lunch or dinner, which can't be said for other restaurants of its class.

The seasonal menu changes, but continues nicely all the same, with balanced offerings adapted to American produce. Lovely lobster ravioli with red butter sauce vies with tiny soft-shelled crabs (when available) as a top appetizer, followed up closely by a simple galette of smoked salmon with corn pancakes. We loved crispy veal sweetbreads with green lentils and the warm lobster salad with baby carrots and basil. Also, we adore pricey caviar or foie gras to start. We choose as favorite entrées the grilled red snapper with soya butter or veal crepinette (sausage) with Boston lettuce, julienne of vegetables and spaghetti in sesame oil. In the past, we've enjoyed the roasted squab dish accompanied by a light garlic flan. The squab (baby pigeon), coppery, with its skin lacquered with vinegar and honey, comes quartered, moist and medium rare (unless you stipulate otherwise). Wine to go along with all this will set you back some; there's a full-time sommelier and over 550 selections, ranging from $20 to $600 or so. The desserts won't divert your attention from the posh surroundings or the monied old folks nearby, but they're reasonably inviting, especially the cold chestnut soufflé with praline sauce and caramelized hazelnuts. We loved the pineapple pithiviers with raspberry coulis—it tastes better than it might sound. Figure on $90 a couple for lunch, $150 for two at dinner.

12/20 Le Relais

712 Madison Ave. (63rd & 64th Sts.)
751-5108

FRENCH

Open Mon.-Fri.noon-3 p.m. & 6:30 p.m.-11 p.m., Sat. noon-3:30 p.m. & 7 p.m.-11 p.m., Sun. 12:30 p.m.-3:30 p.m. & 7 p.m.-11 p.m. Cards: AE, MC, V.

People watching vies with picking at your food at this rare Upper East Side place with sidewalk seating (six, count 'em, six tables, ever in demand). A generally appealing restaurant decorated with mirrors and old engravings, Le Relais is the neighborhood headquarters for well-heeled youth at play. At almost any hour, you can see pretty young things clustered around the bar or relaxing at the miniscule tables outside. This is also one of the few places where at, off hours, you can sit down with coffee and the paper and not be looked at askance. Though it can be uncomfortably noisy when full (the wooden floor is uncarpeted), the animated crowd that frequents Le Relais doesn't seem to mind. The cuisine, while quite adequate, is unremarkable, the menu featuring the kind of bistro standbys that have made a comeback recently.

For openers at lunch, there is lentil salad with a zesty cold ravigote sauce, pâté and celery root rémoulade in season. Main courses include a pasta (pasta au pistou is hot), leg of lamb classically paired with flageolets, trout with almonds and Le Relais' ever-popular salade Eleonore, a good, moist, chunky chicken salad. Other recommended appetizers on the simple, short menu include the salmon marinated in basil and the wild mushrooms en croûte. Other items we've enjoyed in the past at dinner include the duck steak with grapefruit, a simple veal with mushrooms, steak au poivre and roast chicken with herbs. Desserts include crème caramel, oeufs à la neige, chocolate mousse and a good lemon tart. Service can be uppity. Average tab at dinner runs $90 per couple; at lunch, $60 for two, plus tax and tip.

11/20 Sam's Café

1406 Third Ave. (80th St.)
988-5300

AMERICAN

Open Mon.-Sat. 6 p.m.-midnight, Sun. 5:30 p.m.-10 p.m.. Closed Sun. in summer. All major cards.

The action is hot and heavy at the glittering bar, where the young crowd is almost as attractive as the restaurant's star-owner, Mariel Hemingway (who rarely, if ever, makes an appearance). Its two dining rooms are pleasant, each in a different way. The front room, on Third Avenue, seems to be reserved for the younger crowd, while the back room is for those adventurous oldies who want to experience a good meal. The latter clientele will enjoy the skylight, gabled ceiling and quilts adorning the walls, all lending a country feeling to the place, and aided by the friendly service. The food has deteriorated some, having regressed to a burger, grilled meat and fish, and fries place. Nevertheless, the escargots and scallops in a spirited garlic sauce, and the thick slice of foie gras on a bed of wild mushrooms in port wine are two excellent appetizers we've enjoyed. The fresh salad with barely-broiled goat cheese is an authentic version of a usually tired dish. Smoked salmon with fried capers has a lovely tang. Among the entrées we've enjoyed in the past are the grilled duck breast with Chinese vegetables, pungent and light. The grilled tuna is the best fish on the menu—rare in the center, charcoal broiled on the outside, and served with an excellent hoisin sauce. In season, the soft shell crabs with rice sausage is superb. When dinner is over and it is time for dessert, you'll be surprised by the coconut pineapple tart, made without dairy products or sugar. Its wonderful refreshing taste will happily conclude the evening. The wine list is extensive, with some excellent California wines. Prices are in the medium range. Dinner per couple, with drinks, runs $76.

12/20 Sant Ambroeus

1000 Madison Ave.
(77th & 78th Sts.)
570-2211

ITALIAN

Open Mon.-Sat. 9:30 a.m.-11:30 a.m., noon-3:30 p.m. & 6 p.m.-10:30 p.m., Sun. 10:30 a.m.-6 p.m.; tea daily 3:30 p.m.-6 p.m. All major cards.

The sleek but unassuming front of Sant Ambroeus is a pastry-and-gelato shop that might possibly make you think you're in Milan. Walk past the stunning pastries and appealing salads to the back, and you will see well-dressed East Siders eating in great style, nestled in a little jewel-box of a dining spot, the unusual ceiling draped in white like a boudoir. Sant Ambroeus is a pricey, but pleasing, spot to breakfast, lunch, have tea, dine or just relax after you've done the nearby gallery circuit. The antipasti hold no surprises, but are all good: air-dried bresaola, prosciutto with melon, vitello tonnato; only the sea food salad is curiously bland. The pastas are uniformly good, especially trenette al pesto (white gnocchi swathed in a pesto tomato sauce) and spaghetti bolognese. The buttery risotto is first-rate. Any of these, with the house salad, makes a perfect light meal at any time. (You may have a half-portion of pasta, but you'll be charged $2 extra.) Filet of sole, veal picatta and lamb chops with rosemary are all faultless. There is a simple list of Italian wines, but most people just order the good house red or white.

Save some room for the desserts, which are culled from the excellent gelati and pastries for which Sant Ambroeus is renowned, notably colibri, a delectable sorbet and fresh fruit combination, and the rich chestnut delizia. The coffee and capuccino are wonderful. This goodness and chic-ness is dear: expect to pay about $60 per couple at lunch, $90 for two at dinner.

The Sign of the Dove

1110 Third Ave. (65th St.)
861-8080

AMERICAN

Open Mon.-Sat. noon-2:30 p.m. & 6 p.m.-11:30 p.m., Sun. 11:30 a.m.-2:15 p.m. & 6 p.m.-11:30 p.m. All major cards.

Since the arrival of chef Andrew D'Amico in 1985, and some fresh paint and house cleaning at this landmark three-story building on Third Avenue, The Sign of the Dove has become one of the city's most comfortable, pleasant and genteel dining rooms, with ever-satisfying new American cuisine and fine wines. The flowers are beautiful, the tables well spaced, the conservatory dining room with its sliding roof and garden-like setting spectacular. Recently, the Music room has been redesigned to give it a new personality, as well as a resident pianist and violinist.

The diner menu is prix fixe at $60 and changes with the seasons, although some dishes can be had all year round. The menu continues to be French-influenced American, with occasional Asian or Italian overtones. A la carte lunch and brunch menus seem more-or-less scaled down, but with some inventive variations of the grand dinner offerings that are in tune with its spirit.We adore the summer beet ravioli, as well as the ravioli stuffed with duck confit and shiitake, topped with a fricassée of wild mushrooms; the tender duck is not masked by the transparent buttery cream sauce. We've enjoyed the seared tuna appetizer with white bean salad and the casserole of oysters and lobster (and its variation, substituting fava beans for the lobster). Another standout appetizer must be the ragoût of lentils and Sardinian pasta. We like, among the salads, one of the best, when available, warm roasted quail on a bed of tender-leafed raw baby spinach, artichoke hearts and a poached quail egg sprinkled with a tart vinaigrette.

Among the fish entrées, the caramelized bass with crisp and braised leeks stands out, as does grilled salmon marinated in charmoula. The chef demonstrates the originality of the menu in a simple dish of tenderloin of beef poached in its own broth and served with vegetables and coarse sea salt mixed with chopped scallions. He also has a wonderful touch in mixing tastes and textures, such as aïoli with red pepper purée, veal with sweet garlic custard, and venison with polenta. Our current favorite, the braised beef filet with zucchini vermicelli, vies with the roasted lamb loin with mustard seeds for our attention. We liked, among desserts, the lime miroir with strawberry coulis and the chocolate cake with raspberries. The wine list is impressive, with first-class wines from all over the world, and is constantly updated to include new and unusual wines, as well as "classical" selections. We consider the prices reasonable when you consider the quality. We adore the service, excellent, informed and unobtrusive. Lunch à la carte will cost you about $90 per couple, with a modest wine. For dinner, figure $150 for two, plus tax and tip.

Sistina
1555 Second Ave. (80th & 81st Sts.)
861-7660

ITALIAN

Open daily noon-3 p.m. & 5 p.m.-midnight. Closed Sun. July-Aug. Cards: AE.

The Bruno brothers (Antonio, Gerardo and Giuseppe) have evolved their place to the head of the class of the inexhaustible number of Upper East Side polished, expensive Italian restaurants. Sistina is packed every night. The blond wood facade, the bentwood chairs, the central casting Italian waiters (who swoop gracefully to relieve you of your wine bottle in mid-pour and who describe each dish as "Fantastico!," kissing their finger tips in the mere contemplation of such deliciousness), come across favorably. And it's just fine, because the food, for the most part, is as satisfying as the waiters lead you to expect. This is the case, in spite of the fact that much of your time is taken up in deciphering the menu, with its opaque titles for dishes such as Pollo alla Sisto IV and Scampi Sopresa. You'll never go hungry, however.

The very good bruschetta (chopped tomatoes and chopped basil on toast) and tiny slivers of fried zucchini, which appear immediately, whet your appetite for a fine pasta such as tagliatelle del capo cuoco (thin strands of noodle tossed with porcini mushrooms in a light, creamy tomato sauce) or pappardelle with porcini, arugula and prosciutto. We think these better starters than the seafood salad and the palatable grilled buffalo-milk mozzarella which, after the bruschetta, seems redundant

with its topping of chopped tomatoes, basil and extra virgin olive oil. Consider grilled endive and radicchio as an appetizer, or a more filling polenta with porcini mushrooms. We choose risotto with asparagus for a good main course. For all the pomposity of the title, Pollo alla Sisto IV turns out to be game hen, split and grilled with rosemary. It's on the dry side, but tasty all the same. We thought the Mediterranean seafood stew flavor packed. In our opinion, the somewhat less complex, but equally satisfying veal or chicken scallop with sun-dried tomatoes, white wine and puréed eggplant, should be essayed. Expect to pay $100 per couple for dinner, with a bottle of good wine from a mostly Italian list.

12/20 The Stanhope Dining Room
Stanhope Hotel,
995 Fifth Ave. (81st St.)
288-5800; Fax 517-0088

CONTINENTAL

Open daily 7 a.m.-11 p.m. All major cards.

The restaurant still looks good after its 1985 zillion-dollar face-lift, but in the kitchen, they're working with yet another round of changes and chef. This place still hasn't found itself, and we're waiting for the other shoe to drop, now that the Japanese brought the hotel in 1989. Maybe they should bring in a chef from Japan, or at least someone to crack the whip at the unionized waiters. So far, all the new owners have done is bring in a retired French chef as a consultant. That's a stop-gap move at best.

The dining room is elegant and tranquil, exquisitely appointed, yet low-key and comfortable, with pale wood paneling, chandeliers in the grand hotel manner and tables set well apart—the perfect place for a moneyed or amorous exchange. This is definitely a place where women can wear hats; gentlemen are required to wear ties and jackets. Waiters wear tuxedoes and deliver their commissions under silver serving domes.

The menu is extensive, the wine list exceptional (leave it to a hotel to be able to afford a showy list, and probably a very good consultant or a food and beverage manager with time and inclination to put it together). You might begin your meal with a good soup of sea urchins and oysters or perhaps a satisfying terrine of rabbit and foie gras. You can also play it safe with oysters on the half shell or with unadorned caviar. The pasta appetizer, which changes daily, is risky. Stripped bass steamed in a fumet of saffron and fennel is the top fish entrée and the roasted squab with red currants another top main course. You are in New York, so you can always get a good prime sirloin steak, though we could skip the wine sauce provided here. The chocolate cake and the nougat ice cream with pecans are the top desserts. Once the Lucullan contents are consumed, a busboy, oblivious to the tone of the rooms, stacks dirty plates on his arm like a waitress in a diner. Lunch (which requires an $18 minimum) averages $90 per couple, including a glass of wine; dinner is at least $150 per couple, with a modest bottle, plus tax and tip.

10/20 **Sylvia's**
   328 Lenox Ave. (126th & 127th Sts.)
   996-0660
AMERICAN/SOUL FOOD
Open Mon.-Sat. 7:30 a.m.-10:30 p.m., Sun. 1 p.m.-7 p.m. No cards.

Leave it to the Japanese. They descend upon Sylvia's in waves of chartered buses to eat real, rib-sticking soul food in Harlem, thereby joining hungry New Yorkers who go up to Harlem for breakfast or a main meal with a down-home Southern touch. Sylvia is Sylvia Woods, from South Carolina, and Mrs. Woods and her family tend to the local politicians, celebrities, the curious and, of course, the Japanese, who fill the long counter for a quick meal or the tables in the dining room, where waitresses are apt to call everyone "honey." (What's the Japanese word for honey?) Imagine eggs, sunny side up or down, with thick slices of sausage redolent of rosemary and thyme, and smooth grits served with fried chicken or pork chops. The best is yet to come: plump hot cakes with butter and syrup, always served with a side order of hot sausages, bacon or that same fried chicken. Sylvia's specialties include smothered chicken, greasy and spicy, with some of the best home fries in Manhattan, and short ribs of beef in brown gravy (the meat falls off the bone) with onions and green peppers, accompanied by a hot biscuit to soak up the sauce. You may need an Alka Seltzer later, but the pain is worth it! Sweet-potato pie is the mandatory dessert, or at least it ought to be. There is a full bar with beer, hard liquor and wine by the glass. Lunch or dinner per couple will cost around $40.

 Trastevere
   309 E. 83rd St. (Second Ave.)
   734-6343
ITALIAN
Open daily 5 p.m.-11 p.m.; closed Sun. in summer. Cards: AE.

The Lattanzi family seems to specialize in adorable little restaurants, the size of shoe-repair shops, that turn out some of the most garlic-infused Italian homecooking in town. Trastevere, named after the economically poor, but trattoria-rich, section of Rome, was the first of the family's restaurants, opening in 1980. Now there is Trastevere II, around the corner on 84th St., Erminia, Lattanzi and Trastevere (III), the latter in Forest Hills, Queens. One wonders whether the food might not be even better were the family to lease a larger space and concentrate their culinary skills in a single kitchen. The food here does not quite live up to its early repute, or to the charm of the minuscule room, with its brick walls, huge oil paintings and taped top-of-the-pops of Italian opera.

The menu is short—too short, in fact, even though amplified by several specials, to offer an appetizing variety of tastes. Too many of the sauces sound the same, and even when they don't *sound* the same, they end up *tasting* the same. That aside, this is a good restaurant, and many of the dishes make for satisfying eating. Garlic, as noted, is the preferred flavoring, and it is displayed to very good effect in a mixed vegetable appetizer with artichoke hearts, roasted red peppers, broccoli vinaigrette and mushrooms. It's even more pronounced in a fine capellini puttanesca, which also boasts the vivid flavors of capers, black olives and plum tomatoes. We think the linguine with white-clam sauce a little too al dente and a soupy rendition. When the mussels are fresh, we like the appetizer of a dozen or so of these mollusks, served in a buttery tomato sauce packed with garlic. We found chicken alla romana too salty, its sauce too reminiscent of the puttanesca; though it adds rosemary, red and yellow peppers and onions, the theme remains, really, garlic and capers. We choose for dessert the tartufo (chocolate studded ice cream at the heart of a good whipped cream outershell). The wine list is even shorter than the menu—just stick to the Pinot Grigio for white and Antinori's Chianti for red, and you'll wash the garlic down. With a bottle of one of those, dinner will cost about $96 per couple, plus tax and tip.

11/20 Il Valletto
133 E. 61st St.
(Lexington & Park Aves.)
838-3939
ITALIAN
Open Mon.-Fri. noon-3 p.m. & 5: 30 p.m.-midnight, Sat. 5:30 p.m.-midnight. All major cards.

Nanni is back from his retirement, and so are his devoted cronies in the dining room. When he's in the room, forget about a menu—Nanni whisks it away and orders for you. When he's not there, however, it seems you get the bum's rush. The large dining room, once plush, now seems a bit seedy. Its lighting is especially in need of a serious overhaul—bright, naked, candle bulbs went out long ago. If possible, stake out a table in the contrastingly elegant little dining room just beyond the bar; it's cozy and pleasant there. The bruschetta is irresistible, fresh toasted bread piled with garlicky diced tomatoes, basil and herbs, but you may not get it unless you ask. Baked stuffed clams are moist, flavorful and tender. The eggplant alla siciliana, with its delicate ricotta and spinach stuffing under a blanket of mozzarella-and-tomato sauce, is delicious. The popular special, bow-tie pasta tossed with diced tomatoes, zucchini, eggplant and fresh basil, is still tasty, but overly rich and soupy. Lemony seafood salad with tender rings of calamari and shrimp is good and fresh, but unremarkable. Linguine with garlicky white clam sauce is a winner, properly al dente, the clams fresh and tender. Chicken scarpariello, usually sautéed nuggets of chicken in a garlicky wine sauce, consists of too-large pieces of chicken, cooked too long, and though it looks pretty, it is short on sauce. Osso buco, a special, lacks that melting quality that characterizes its best readings. Steamed/sautéed zucchini accompanies main courses and is first-rate. Desserts? A nice baked pear, fresh fruit salad, berries in season, zabaglione. The okay Antinori Chianti classico is, at $30, one of the least expensive wines available. About $110 per couple for dinner, $78 for two at lunch.

11/20 Le Veau d'Or
129 E. 60th St.
(Park & Lexington Aves.)
838-8133
FRENCH
Open Mon.-Sat. noon-3 p.m. & 5:30 p.m.-10:15 p.m. Cards: AE.

Let food fashions come and go. This outpost of Paris, opened in 1946, changeth not. It has, instead, become an institution, attracting a broad generational mix of well-heeled New Yorkers, many who arrive with most of the family in tow. What attracts are reasonable prices, stability and ineffable charm. Le Veau d'Or is a small restaurant, a complex of alcoves in which every centimeter counts. Tables are wedged together in front of red leather banquettes. Walls are obscured under a clutter of a French ephemera: street signs, travel posters of the great châteaux, black-and-white glossies of flower markets, meat markets and Frenchmen eating French bread. The glory that is France is celebrated in maps, castles and cattle embossed in gold on large mirrors—all bracketing the portrait of the restaurant's namesake, the golden calf, asleep under a fluffy quilt, *le veau dort*, a pun as whimsical and good-natured as the restaurant itself. (Le veau d'or, "the golden calf," and le veau dort, "the sleeping calf," are pronounced exactly the same way in French).

The current chef joined in 1970, and the food is pure culinary nostalgia—down-home Parisian cooking as it is writ in the texts, from crunchy céleri rémoulade and snails in garlic butter to sauté de veau niçoise (a homey stew of cubed meat, tomatoes and green olives) or squab cooked in a casserole with bacon, mushrooms and pearl onions. Top picks among the entreés are the cassoulet, the leg of lamb (just an eyelash above the rack of lamb with garden vegetables) and the duck with cherries. Textbook, too, are the desserts, including a somewhat chalky chocolate mousse, and vanilla ice cream-filled profiteroles. French and American wines are reasonably priced, including sound choices in the teens and twenties that are agreeably potable. Dinner for two, with wine, costs $76 to $90, lunch less.

Wilkinson's Seafood Café
1573 York Ave. (83rd & 84th Sts.)
535-5454
AMERICAN/SEAFOOD
Open daily 6 p.m.-10:30 p.m. All major cards.

With smoked-glass lamps, attractive brick walls, and handsome trompe l'oeil flower niches, and sporting a long mahogany bar, where casually well-dressed East Siders gather nightly, Wilkinson's is a fine and stylish bistro-style eatery featuring some of the best and freshest seafood on the Upper East Side. The tone is definitely conservative and friendly; no mad singles scene here.

We like the tender, greaseless calamari fritti, served with a silken tomato sauce redolent of tarragon and garnished with fried parsley, a sophisticated new reading of this old Italian standby. When in season, soft-shelled crabs, deftly sautéed and dressed in lime butter, make a good appetizer or main course. For a salad, try the baby lettuces with stilton cheese and a lime vinaigrette. We loved poached red snapper in a saké sauce dotted with fermented black-bean sauce. We found the grilled marinated swordfish moist and tender, simply glazed with butter and lemon. Ditto the roast lobster with wild mushrooms. If someone in your party doesn't feel like seafood, have him or her try a grilled veal chop in a mustard sauce and/or a straightforward chicken or steak.

Study carefully the medium-size wine list (of about 60 items, counting the attractive reserve list), with French and American offerings ranging from about $15 up into the $50 range, plus a handful of higher priced bottles. The added selection of ports and brandies you'll find impressive. We thought the desserts irresistible, especially the oven-warmed chocolate mousse cake with raspberry purée. Cost will be about $98 per couple, with wine.

UPPER WEST SIDE

Alcalá
349 Amsterdam Ave.
(W. 76th & W. 77th Sts.)
769-9600
SPANISH
Open Mon.-Thurs. 5:30 p.m.-11 p.m., Fri.-Sat. 5:30 p.m.-midnight, Sun. 2 p.m.-10 p.m. All major cards.

To call this one of the more highly regarded Spanish restaurants in town sadly emphasizes a New York weakness. Apart from Harlequin in the Village, contemporary Spain and Spanish cuisine are represented woefully in New York. Okay, we think the tapas here pretty good and authentic, being served at the long bar up front of this long restaurant with exposed brick walls and a raised dining area in the rear. We get the impression, though, that the people at the bar seem more intent on picking up each other than the tasty morsels.

Meanwhile, back in the dining room, we order a wine from the attractive list and the waiter comes back and says it is out of stock. We ignore his recommendation a second time and choose another highly regarded Spanish wine. He returns with his regrets, so we drink what he tells us to. Perhaps that is the lesson: do what the waiter says, and don't be fussy. He will probably recommend the gambas al ajillo (shrimps in garlic sauce) for starters, which we find better than the grilled sardines, when they are available. As a main course, we like the bacalao (salt cod) with garlic confit and tomato, nicely spiced, or the suckling pig with crackling, probably the pick of the menu. If you insist on paella, the seafood variety with lobster, clams and shrimps bests the chicken version with rabbit and sausages. For dessert, its fans love the crema catalana, though we find it sweet and overly spiced, with nutmeg and the expected vanilla. You might just decide to load up on tapas. The waiters won't notice; they hardly notice anything. Figure $80 a couple.

> *We're always interested to hear about your discoveries, and to receive your comments on ours. Please feel free to write to us, and do state clearly exactly what you liked or disliked.*

Andiamo

1991 Broadway
(W. 67th & W. 68th Sts.)
362-3315

ITALIAN

Open Mon.-Fri. noon-2:30 p.m. & 5:30 p.m.-11:30 p.m., Sat. 5:30 p.m.-11:30 p.m., Sun. 4:30 p.m.-10 p.m. Cards. AE, MC, V.

It doesn't take too much to move to the front ranks of restaurants in the Lincoln Center area, and Andiamo did just that as soon as it opened in 1988. A big, slick, casually elegant restaurant, this place offers a short and safe menu of the nuova cucina sect. You actually enter an arcade behind the Café Bel Canto (an outpost of the restaurant) and walk down a corridor and into a dramatic modern, bi-level restaurant. Pieces from co-owner Lew Futterman's art collection give the space an even more contemporary feel.

Chef Francis Crispo has talent, and generally doesn't miss the mark, or at least not by much, even though he's turning 300 covers a night. We loved the lamb carpaccio, with cucumber, tomato and provolone with a sherry vinegar, a good and atypical version of this trendy appetizer. You're offered salads at the beginning of the meal here, rather than the end. Pasta can be had as an appetizer or main course. We liked the crabmeat tortelli in a carrot-butter sauce, and angel hair pasta with seafood in a light saffron. We believe the penne puttanesca rates sub par. Grilled salmon with tomato, basil and olive oil or sautéed veal chops with white wine, fresh thyme and veal juice get the nod for main courses. For dessert, fill up on the excellent sorbetti and the chocolate hazelnut dacquoise in vanilla sauce. Among the 225 or so wines offered with representation from Italy, France, California and Australia, we found good quality at reasonable prices, especially from Italy. As there are many lesser-known producers, you may have to rely on guesswork or the waiter when making a decision. We were undecided about a final rating for this restaurant, and could have gone a point higher. You will have a pleasant dining experience here, but the ambience ultimately contributes heavily to that; take the food to a humble trattoria and it earns the rating we've awarded it. With so many covers, that's still a feat. Things are pointing upward here. Figure $80 per couple.

12/20 Baci

412 Amsterdam Ave.
(79th & 80th Sts.)
496-1550

ITALIAN

Open Mon.-Fri. noon-3 p.m. & 5:30 p.m.-11 p.m., Sat. noon-3 p.m. & 5:30 p.m.-midnight, Sun. noon-3 p.m. & 5 p.m-11 p.m. No cards.

The clientele at Baci is casual, young, trendy Upper West Side, the menu is inviting, and service is friendly. If only the same attention was paid to the food.

A flavorful caponata is a good opener, and goes well with the crusty bread that's brought direct to your table. Though pasta is the centerpiece here, a standout is hard to find. Penne in a vodka sauce seemed promising, but the dish looked hastily assembled and the sauce lacked consistency and flavor. Ring-shaped anieletti con carne appeared confused in its mixture of beef, tomato sauce, pinoli nuts and raisins. Pasta con le sarde makes better use of similar ingredients, blending fresh sardines and fennel with the pinoli nuts and raisins. A well-made main course is chicken paillard, simply presented with lemon and basil. Orange zabaglione with strawberries is a pleasant dessert. Though it makes a worthy effort, Baci doesn't live up to its potential. You won't go hungry here, but neither will you leave completely satisfied. Expect to spend around $140 per couple for dinner.

10/20 Blue Nile

103 W. 77th St. (Columbus Ave.)
580-3232

ETHIOPIAN

Open Mon.-Fri. 5 p.m.-midnight, Sat.-Sun. noon-midnight. Cards: AE.

Who would figure that this ersatz African restaurant, where you eat with your fingers and sit on three-legged stools, would settle in as an Upper West Side oasis, but it has. Opened in 1985, there's no drought of customers. An intriguing, intimate restaurant that caters to a youthful clientele, the Blue Nile features authentic Ethiopian cuisine. The dining room, located below ground on a quiet Upper West Side street, is windowless but folksy, with its woven straw tables low to the ground and its various artifacts from the Nile delta adorning the walls. The waitresses are colorfully costumed, but slow on the uptake—you may have to call out several times for a beer, which is the recommended drink for this spicy food (try the imported beer from Ghana). Ethiopian food should certainly be sampled and savored, but for many, once is enough. The dishes, most in stew form, are arranged on metal platters lined with the national staple, a flavorless, spongy white flour pancake (injera). Additional, folded sheets of injera are provided in lieu of Western utensils. Eating here can be a fun, messy, exotic business. Dishes to try are headed by a spicy beef tartare (kitfo). There's also tibs wot, beef stewed in a hot sauce. The more people you are with, the more dishes you'll be able to order and dip into, literally. Consider the kale and potatoes with spices (yegomen wot), the hottest chicken in town (doro wot), or a chickpea purée (shuro wot). Avoid the Western desserts. The management also runs a sister restaurant in SoHo—Abyssinia. It's a toss-up between them, though some feel the food is better uptown. A meal here will run $30 for lunch per couple, and $50 for dinner for two.

12/20 La Boîte en Bois

75 W. 68th St.
(Central Park West & Columbus Ave.)
874-2705
FRENCH
Open Mon.-Sat. 5:30 p.m.-11:30 p.m., Sun. 5 p.m.-10 p.m. No cards.

The name of this modest French provincial restaurant means "wooden box," and that's what you get—a cozy (crowded), tiny room with wood on the walls. Within, the cooking is like it was before superstar chefs and nouvelle cuisine. On entering, you step down into a lace-curtained anteroom that houses the coat check, and then into a dining room that's not much larger, decorated with gladiolas. There, you're greeted by the patron, Jean-Claude Coutable—a delicate little man in a dark gray suit and a blue tie. Old-world charm and authenticity bear repeating, and among the clientele are Upper West Side regulars, for whom this is an elevator ride away.

The food is honest and substantial. Start with the cold smoked salmon and trout mousse, the snails in a Provence herb sauce or, perhaps, a fish soup done Marseille style. For an entrée, try the Norwegian salmon with watercress sauce, the baby chicken with

bacon, onions and mushrooms or the stewed lamb in a red-wine sauce. Crème caramel à l'orange is your best bet for dessert. A modest Burgundy or Rhône wine (several are available for about $28) will serve this fare nicely. Dinner will run about $100 for two.

Café des Artistes

1 W. 67th St.
(Central Park West & Columbus Ave.)
877-3500
FRENCH
Open Mon.-Fri. noon-3 p.m. & 5:30 p.m.-12:30 a.m., Sat. noon-3 p.m. (brunch) & 5:30 p.m.-12:30 a.m., Sun. 10 a.m.-4 p.m. (brunch) & 5 p.m.-11 p.m. All major cards.

We find Café des Artistes is still one of the prettiest spots in town, especially at lunch, when the sun streams in and highlights the opulent window plantings. The exquisite Howard Chandler Christie murals have been carefully restored and are as lush as ever (is it those nude nymphs that give the Café its reputation as a romantic spot?). Near ABC headquarters and Lincoln Center, celebrities—say, Peter Jennings, Paul Newman, Joanne Woodward, LeRoy Neiman, Itzhak Perlman, Leonard Bernstein, et al.—frequent the dining room and admire the old-fashioned three-level buffet table and the never-out-of-fashion profusion of flowers tended by the Café's own gardener.

Chef André Guillou has been tending to the kitchen since 1955, so despite some trendy names and plates, the staples are as they have been for decades. Just recently, though, the kitchen has seen some new life, and food and preparation are better than in past years. We liked the gravlax and found the charcuterie assortment superior. For openers, we loved the salmon four ways (smoked, poached, dill-marinated and tartare). And what's not to like about fresh oysters? On the other hand, the curried mussels were chilled to the point of unpalatable coldness and served with a cloying sauce. The house presents its salads very handsomely. Repeated tries of the soft-shell crabs blanketed with almond slivers, very dated, convinces us to opt for the crabs simply sautéed with lemon. When we see the word Provençale on the menu, we zero in, so when the scallops Provençale appeared as scallops in a fresh tomato sauce (fit for spaghetti in a good cafeteria), we were disappointed. Where was that spicy and aromatic light and loose sauce, redolent of tomatoes? The menu changes regularly with the market and season. In asparagus season, look for a separate menu for the stalks, which are offered vinaigrette, with eggs and so forth. What does owner George Lang recommend for a main course? Fresh sturgeon scaloppine or the roast baby chicken stuffed with fettucine.

We like the desserts here, including a delicious sour cream apple pie with walnuts, a pleasant Key lime pie, and some refreshing fruit sherbets. Of course, don't forget the Austro-Hungarian tortes and tarts, at least a dozen different types prepared daily on the premises. The house flourless Ilona torte will please chocolate addicts. We've even eaten through the chocolatissimo grand dessert plate, a guaranteed overdose. We like the short wine list, but think the house special offering of Champagne by the carafe absurd. Because of the restaurant's popularity (it's always filled), you must reserve well in advance. The management recommends booking one week in advance for dinner before or after a Lincoln Center event, two weeks for dinner on Friday or Saturday. Average dinner cost per couple is $98; for lunch, about $70.

 Café Luxembourg
200 W. 70th St.
(Amsterdam & West End Aves.)
873-7411
AMERICAN/FRENCH
Open Mon.-Thurs. 5:30 p.m.- 12:30 a.m., Fri.-Sat. 5:30 p.m.-1:30 a.m., Sun. 11 a.m.-3 p.m. & 6 p.m.-12:30 a.m. All major cards.

The kitchen of this trendy, frentic, noisy, good bistro-style restaurant has gained stability with a well-established team. Tony Chek has been the chef since 1987, and before that was the sous-chef under Patrick Clark; Joe Fontecchio has been the sous-chef since 1987 and Diana Van Buren the pastry chef since 1985. The setting, which attempts to recreate the charms of an art-deco bistro in 1930s Paris, hasn't changed since the 1983 opening, and continues to please. Perhaps most pleasing is the restaurant's promiximity to Lincoln Center.

You can always order the foolproof country salad of chicory, Roquefort, lardons, garlic croutons and mustard vinaigrette, or good steak and pommes frites. Those who admired the cassoulet in the past probably will like it still. We find the duck terrine a safe opening; it can be followed by a nice loin of rabbit (with sautéed Savoy cabbage, shiitake mushroooms and a mustard sauce) or a simply roasted chicken (with steamed spinach and garlic mashed potatoes). The pasta changes daily, and when available, we adore the ravioli stuffed with a duxelle of shiitake mushrooms, garnished with grilled whole shiitake mushrooms and sliced duck breast, and served on a sauce of mushroom juice reduction.

The warm chocolate soufflé cake with homemade ice cream tops our interest among the desserts. A relatively short wine list with reasonable markups and international breadth makes for easy drinking. The pretheater menu (served between 5:30 p.m. and 6:30 p.m.) draws a literate, prosperous crowd. The group that comes after eight is worth the price of a show—a mix of sleek New Yorkers from either side of Central Park and funky downtowners. Dinner costs about $120 a couple, with wine.

 Cavaliere
108 W. 73rd St.
(Amsterdam & Columbus Aves.)
799-8282
ITALIAN
Open Mon. 5 p.m.-midnight, Tues.-Sun. noon-midnight. All major cards.

Always high on appearance, Cavaliere's menu has taken a high road without changing much since David Silver (formerly at Sign of the Dove) joined as chef in May 1989. On the ground level of a house in a pleasant block of West Side brownstones, Cavaliere is a series of discoveries. The well-designed entry room, locus of the bar and small dining area, opens into the handsome, mirrored-ceiling main dining room, airy but intimate, with the single rose spotlighted on the mantle enigmatically revealing the origin of the restaurant's name. In back you'll find another ravishingly pretty, small, skylit room, used only on weekends (a perfect place for a party). Cool, sleek, blond-wood chairs, pale gray tweed banquettes, attractive flower arrangements add to the cosseting, festive feeling. The waiters, in formal dress softened with jaunty bow ties, can be a crackerjack professional team or antsy.

Fried squid, on every Italian menu in town, here are rescued from banality, first by the impeccable frying and secondly, by a tooth-some pesto-marinara sauce. We liked the hair-thin sesame-fried zucchini and the mussels with leeks, tomatoes, white wine and cream. Even ubiquitous tortellini are royally reborn when served up with mushrooms in a delicious Marsala-cream sauce. We found the garlic bread awash with pesto and Parmesan sauce tasty, but too rich for an appetizer, and the homemade mozzarella, rolled with red peppers and olive paste, a visual dud. Friends raved about the simple arugula endive salad in a marvelous balsamic vinaigrette with a sweet garlicky note. For an appetizer, try the melted, roasted baby eggplant slices and sweet red pepper with a tomato-garlic sauce, or enjoy them in a gorgeous main dish of grilled shrimp, their tails aloft. We also liked the veal chop with roasted shallot, a red-wine sauce and roasted garlic potatoes. Both grilled swordfish on a bed of fresh tomatoes with a minty overtone and the grilled salmon with a lemon-pepper aïoli on a bed of grilled zucchini merit raves, even though the grilled tuna served on a bed of arugula and endives with an olive-and-tomato sauce gets the waiters' most enthusiastic endorsement. Ditto the veal scaloppine with spinach and mushrooms. We also liked the roast chicken with rosemary butter and a warm potato-and-caper salad.

The wine list features many well chosen and well priced wines, mostly Italian, but with good French and Califorian offerings. Save room for dessert, because, among the rather ordinary offerings on the slightly silly trolley, you'll want to try the chocolate amaretto torte, topped with a dollop of espresso mousse, that gives sin new meaning. Otherwise, go for the fresh fruit tart. Because of its Lincoln Center location, the prix fixe theater dinner from 5 p.m. to 6:30 p.m. is popular

---

Note that average prices given in this chapter do not include tax (which is a whopping 8.25 percent in New York) or gratuity. You can figure, then, on adding roughly 25 percent to each of the prices quoted here, for your final bill.

(and includes many of the items here recommended). Dinner averages about $90 per couple, with a modest wine, plus tax and tip.

Coastal
300 Amsterdam Ave. (74th St.)
769-3988

AMERICAN

Open Mon.-Thurs. 6 p.m.-11 p.m., Fri.-Sat. 6 p.m.-11:30 p.m., Sun. 11:45 a.m.-2:45 p.m. & 5:30 p.m.-10 p.m. Cards: AE.

The word "yuppie" may be out, but not here. The prototypes are in Coastal. When the noise of the honking taxis and grunting buses on Amsterdam Avenue vies with the clatter of plates and chatter of diners, and when tables "turn" once an hour, you know you're not in for a Lucullan experience. Coastal—brought to you by the boys who gave you Memphis and 107 West—is a formula restaurant, but it gives as good as it gets. A lot of expense evidently has been spared on its decor, which is minimal, stark and high-tech track lights, blond wood, lots of floor-to-ceiling windows, turquoise trim and vague outlines (in gray, white and turquoise) of portions of the American coast. But when it comes to food, the ingredients are fresh and good, their integrity is respected in the cooking, and the prices are reasonable. We found the grilled fish and pastas almost always satisfying, so who can ask for anything more? Satisfying appetizers include house-made wild mushroom ravioli with wholewheat pasta in a light sage-and-rosemary-cream sauce, a yuppie shrimp cocktail in which Gulf shrimp and Bell River crawfish are served chilled in the shell with remoulade sauce, and grilled tuna medallions, served chilled and medium rare over blackeye pea vegetable succotash with grilled tortillas. The kitchen gets those appetizers ready early. Grilled fish selections always include mahi mahi, yellowfin tuna, salmon, swordfish, grouper, red snapper and specials. To accompany the simply cooked fish, you may choose one of eight sauces served in small ramekins: béarnaise; honey-mustard beurre blanc; wild-mushroom beurre blanc; spicy tomatillo-mango salsa; pear-papaya-and-tomato salsa; roasted red pepper ginger coulis; Italian olives, capers and tomato; and plum tomato, scallion and basil concassé of tomato. The waiters believe "one flavor fits all" and will recommend any sauce with any fish. Be forewarned, however, that some of the fish are brushed with a sweet teriyaki sauce before grilling. It's fine, it's tasty, but it wars against the "side" sauces. We also liked the grilled redfish fajita and, among the pastas, the angel hair primavera with shrimp.

You might want to try the frozen lemon ribbon pie for dessert, but homemade ice cream such as chocolate with Grand Marnier, amaretto and "sin" (coffee and Marsala) comes across as well as what you'll find in the designer ice cream outposts along nearby Columbus Avenue. Eating them here will spare you a second long line— those who arrive after 8 p.m. have to wait for a table. Dinner, with a modest wine, runs about $70 per couple.

Memphis
329 Columbus Ave.
(W. 75th & 76th Sts.)
496-1840
AMERICAN/CAJUN
Open Mon-Wed. 6 p.m.-11 p.m., Thurs.-Sat. 6 p.m.-1:30 a.m., Sun. 6 p.m.-10 p.m. All major cards.

Here, finally, is proof, indeed, that you are what you eat. Nightly in this chic Upper West Side icon, a blackened piece of fresh fish is served to someone attired in trendy, ubiquitous black. And the fish is the better looking of the two. As it's said, life is short, art is long. Which is undoubtedly what moves the owners of Memphis, for the restaurant's design reflects the famous school of architecture and not the Tennessee birthplace of rock-and-roll. Memphis attracts a material crowd that hasn't quite yet shrugged off the 1980s, but that's also true at Memphis's siblings: the hip, nearby Coastal and the less-expensive, far-flung 107 West.

Americans had their fling with Cajun several years ago, so it's a tribute to Memphis that people throng for it here. Fortunately, the adventuresome, crafted menu does offer occasional diversions from the delicately spiced New Orleans cooking. Memphis even plays with Japanese and Italian influences, including a rich fettucine laced with chicken and goat cheese. We also liked pan-seared tuna sprinkled with black peppercorns, served in a Cognac-cream sauce and accompanied with a scoop of couscous. For the real thing, try the mesquite fried chicken with baby back spareribs and served with a hefty portion of delicious sweet potato french fries. Dinner will cost about $80 a couple, with wine.

11/20 La Mirabelle
333 W. 86th St.
(Riverside Dr. & West End Ave.)
496-0458
FRENCH
Open Mon.-Thurs. 6 p.m.-10 p.m., Fri.-Sat. 5:30 p.m.-10:30 p.m. All major cards.

This place is as unpretentious as can be. Located on the ground floor of a residential hotel, La Mirabelle consists of four connecting dining rooms with pink walls trimmed in white, small tables with crisp linen, waitresses direct from the French provinces and bistro classics from coquille St. Jacques to entrecôte bercy and crème caramel. La Mirabelle could be a real charmer, but when it comes right down to it, the food's pretty standard. You will enjoy your meal, but don't expect an epiphany. The menu (pink and laminated) hasn't changed since at least 1987, when Georges Miquel took over as chef. (Annick Le Douaron is now the sole owner.) When available, the fresh asparagus are thick as carrots— albeit nicely cooked, and served with a creditable vinaigrette; the escargots bourguignon and the soft-shell crabs Provençale are no better, nor worse, than those served in a thousand other places. The loin of venison (in winter), the cassoulet, the bouillabaisse and the rack of lamb all have their neighborhood devotees. Crème brûlée is the recommended dessert. The place is full of lawyers talking cases and career changes, and aging actors still discussing showcases in third-floor walk-up acting studios. They don't mind the food. A modest place, with modest ambitions, La Mirabelle charges, by today's standards, modest prices. Dinner, with an inexpensive Mâcon or Beaujolais, comes to about $60 per couple.

Poiret
474 Columbus Ave. (83rd St.)
724-6880
FRENCH
Open Mon.-Thurs. 6 p.m.-11:30 p.m; Fri.-Sat. 6 p.m.-12:30 a.m.; Sun. 11:30 a.m.-4 p.m.(brunch) & 6 p.m.-11:30 p.m. All major cards.

The owners of this attractive little restaurant had the recipe right when they chose to locate in an unremarkable part of the Upper West Side, a quiet, upscale area without much culinary competition. Poiret's owners, however, are not a charming French couple, but, rather, a large restaurant corporation that counts terminally trendy Manhattan hotspots such as Ernie's and America in its stable. Poiret is its welcome departure, though in the first hectic months, it was nearly impossible to carry conversation above the crushing noise, made worse by high ceilings and bare floors. A soft carpet now covers the bright room and, thankfully, gives the restaurant more intimacy.

We like the bistro-style food, but some mainstays don't always match the lengthy list of creative nightly specials. We thought the mixed green salad pleasant, yet a salmon and arugula salad with tomatoes in a light Dijon mustard dressing, outstanding, was not on the regular menu. We believed the Mediterranean fish soup à la Marseillaise tasted thin, despite its rich-looking brown color and the nice added touch of a singular jumbo shrimp. You might want to try a salad alternative, the crab and grapefruit salad on endive with a mint vinaigrette. Perhaps too many specials accompany an already extensive menu. Among the dishes that are standard bistro fare, we liked a deliciously simple, tender roast chicken with french fries, steak au poivre and grilled lamb chops with garlic and herbs. The kitchen shows style by serving some entreés with a pilaf of couscous, fresh baby carrots and green beans. Again, a basic dish like duck ragoût was lost in an overpowering mushroom sauce that masked the bird's flavor. We think the desserts here worth the wait, and the best includes a tarte aux pommes à la maison and, yet another special, a homemade heart-shaped shortbread with strawberries smothered in crème anglaise. The wine list has been given careful attention. Expect to spend about $110 for dinner for two, with a bottle of wine.

11/20 **Santa Fe**
72 W. 69th St.
(Central Park West & Columbus Ave.)
724-0822
MEXICAN/AMERICAN
Open Sun.-Thurs. noon-midnight, Fri.-Sat. noon-12:30 a.m. Cards: AE, MC, V.

The best of the West, that's what Sante Fe is...the best of the Tex-Mex joints west of

Central Park and this side of the River, that is. This attractive, renovated town house on a side street off Columbus will satisfy the strongest yuppie love for Southwest chic. You'll find the requisite salmon-pink walls, Indian artifacts, handsome chairs and candles on each table that allow you (barely) to read the menu while flattering your complexions; all this may make you forget that the food here is straightforward, and nothing to get too excited about. You might as well fill yourself up with nachos (here, crisp tortillas served with chopped beef, onions and hot peppers) while drinking a fairly good margarita or a Mexican beer. The place has a strong following, but we've found the guacamole insipid, and the ceviche, while fresh, lacking punch. Avoid the special combinations—they are heaped on a plate and you can only guess at what you're eating. Among the specialties, the red snapper is acceptable, as is the salmon filet with avocado cream. The fish dishes in general are okay. The tacos al carbón turns out to be overcooked roast beef rolled in a soft floured tortilla and topped with what looks like cheese, but doesn't taste so appealing. Still, the place may fill your gastronomic urge for Tex-Mex. Desserts are not homemade. Dinner per couple will run about $70, with beer.

 Sfuzzi
58 W. 65th St.
(Central Park West & Columbus Ave.)
873-3700
ITALIAN
Open Mon.-Sat. 11:30 a.m.-3 p.m. & 5:30 p.m.-11:30 p.m., Sun. 11:30 a.m.-3 p.m. & 5 p.m.-11:30 p.m. All major cards.

A city with 16,000 restaurants needed one more; this one—a big, loud, hot spot across the way from Lincoln Center, where people can (and do) meet for drinks or a straightforward meal, before and after the show, and enjoy a setting seemingly off the stage of the Metropolitan Opera. The multilevel room, with its pseudo ancient walls, columns, moldings—trompe l'oeil ancient Rome—makes one part of an urban opera in, say, the Baths of Caracalla or the Imperial Forums.

You can eat well here, but with all the bustle, some dishes get a fast shuffle, and so the results arrive uneven. Don't get your expectation up at this crazy place, and you'll walk away satisfied. We consider the menu conventional Italian—so be prepared. Pastas and pizzas can be split as appetizers, and we love the grilled smoked salmon pizza with pancetta and basil pesto, though it can come a bit soggy. For pasta, try the fusilli with grilled shrimp, tomato and basil or perhaps the fettuccine with prosciutto, sweet peas and Parmesan cream. The warm pine nut crusted goat cheese salad with field greens and whole-grain mustard sauce works well as a starter or for a supper. Among the daily specials, ask for grilled fish or meat—say salmon or swordfish or pork loin with Dijon-honey sauce and oven roasted potatoes. For a rich dessert, go for the chocolate mousse or the ricotta gelato. The young, friendly and welltrained staff members have to keep moving. The wine list, half Italian and half French, has lots of good bottles in the teens, twenties and thirties, pricewise. For a white, try the Soave Classico Anselmi (in full or half bottle), and for a red, consider the Carmignano Capezzano 1983 ($25), especially nice with the heartier pizzas or grilled meats. Dinner costs can vary widely, but for a full course meal, with a bottle of wine, count $80 to $100 for two, plus tax and tip.

11/20 Sidewalkers

12 W. 72nd St. (Central Park West)
799-6070
AMERICAN/SEAFOOD
Open Mon.-Thurs. 5 p.m.-11 p.m., Fri.-Sat. 5 p.m.-11:30 p.m., Sun. 4 p.m.-10 p.m. All major cards.

This is the place to hail a crab. And now that Japanese businessmen and tourists have discovered it, Sidewalkers should sell stock in itself. Its three dining rooms (seating 25, 60 and 125, respectively) are filled with diners at paper-covered tables, wearing the ubiquitous bibs and cracking crabs to their hearts' delight. Not bad for a restaurant in its second decade. No restaurant on Earth sounds like this one. People are quiet while they concentrate on tap, tap, tapping open their hard crabs with a wooden mallet. Tap tap tap tap.

Maryland crab cakes can be had as appetizers, and Maryland spiced or garlic crabs are among the standout entrées. You can get a decent broiled or steamed lobster (which maintain the standard of messy eating) and the usual side stuff—cole slaw, french fries, onion

rings. The menu at Sidewalkers is extensive. Steamers (for two) makes a good alternative appetizer (or steamed mussels, and steamed spiced shrimp a good entrée). Seafood, including fresh fish, is prepared over a mesquite grill; try the Texas barbecued shrimp. Desserts are sound and substantial, and the mostly American and French wines are moderately priced. Dinner averages a modest $60 per couple, with wine.

11/20 Tavern on the Green

Central Park West & 67th St.
873-3200
ECLECTIC
Open Mon.-Fri. 11:30 a.m.-4 p.m. & 5:30 p.m.-1 a.m., Sat. 10 a.m.-4 p.m. & 5:30 p.m.-1 a.m., Sun. 10 a.m.-4 p.m. & 5 p.m.-1 a.m. All major cards.

A nasty front-page labor dispute did no harm to Tavern on the Green's position as the city's top special occasion and tourist destination restaurant. Manhattan's biggest dining extravaganza still serves food one step up from airplane grub, and even to manage that requires Georges Masratt, a talented and hardworking executive chef. They serve armies in here. The glitz is played down somewhat now since its heyday—confined to the Tiffany lamps, the rococo ceiling and the Venetian chandeliers of the Crystal Room, and the 350,000 twinkle lights that make every evening a Christmas fairyland. The disgruntled and seemingly underpaid serving staff that was among the hundreds out on strike may treat you grandly or ignore you. And though orders are written on a computerized form, you may or may not get what you asked for. It also seems few on the staff can speak knowledgeably about the food. When you book (reservations are recommended, but walk-in seating is often available), specify the cozier Chestnut room or the more glittery Crystal Room. In fine weather, dining on the terrace can be lovely, when the wind does not carry souvenirs from the nearby carriage horses in your direction.

The menus have been put together with great care, and range from simple to elaborate, trendy to traditional, hearty French to grazing food, hot and cold dishes, fish and shellfish, pastas, grills, sandwiches and salads. It would be the rare diner who could not find something appealing here. The $19.50 pretheater menu gets raves. The cheese ravioli with basil-and-tomato sauce is a good appetizer, as are the escargots tortellini in a garlic-butter sauce. Maine lobster and spring vegetable mosaic also makes for good eating early in the meal. Entrées include a crisp sautéed red snapper with mint tabouli and tomato salsa, and grilled Long Island duck breast with black mission figs. Naturally, there is salmon, which generally is served with asparagus.

Sweets lovers will adore the mouthwatering dessert selection: there's a dark chocolate cake; crème brûlée; a red, sweet, cold and crisp confection (raspberries and strawberries in folds of paper-thin pastry, served with vanilla ice cream); and all kinds of ice cream sundaes and fresh fruit sorbets. The huge, and excellent, wine list runs the gamut from a modest DuBoeuf Beaujolais to a $1,000 Lafite. The neat, little, prix-fixe pretheater menu features New England clam chowder, seafood sausage, mozzarella with tomato and basil for appetizers, followed by such entreés as roast baby chicken, steak and sautéed shrimp. Average lunch price is about $50 for two, dinner about $100 per couple (though the many tantalizing wines can easily run that price far above $100).

Terrace Restaurant

Columbia University, Butler Hall,
400 W. 119th St. (Morningside Dr.)
666-9490

FRENCH

Open Tues.-Fri. noon-3:30 p.m. & 6 p.m.-10 p.m., Sat. 6 p.m.-10 p.m. Closed July 15-Aug. 15. Cards: AE, MC, V.

This makes the city's top ten list of overrated restaurants, which means it has a big, but undeserved, reputation for good food, service and ambience. To us, the food is on par with a good room-service meal in a major hotel, though on a very pretentious scale. The Terrace sits atop a Columbia University building, affording a breathtaking view of Manhattan, both rivers included. One downer, however—to get to the restaurant, you enter a decaying college apartment building lobby, replete with caged-in guards. Meant to be elegant, romantic (read deep-red velvet, see a single

rose on the table and hear live harp music), intimate and softly-lit, the room has low ceilings and low lighting to the point where you can't read the menu. Chefs keep doing a dance here (though the elderly and suburban crowd aren't the sort to notice), and thus the restaurant has had more than its share of ups and downs since opening in 1974.

Among the appetizers, we found the recommended grilled quail with marinated leeks poor—the quail simply bad and the leeks unharmonious. We liked the poached Blue Point oysters in a Champagne sauce, simple and safe, and the roasted eggplant, tomato and pepper terrine. In the past, we have enjoyed the mousse de truite fumée, a delicious light mousse of smoked trout with a cream sauce, and the salade de foie gras gourmande, thin slices of American foie gras on top of a tepid salad of very thin French string beans, tossed in a honey vinaigrette. There are special entrées every night, although the à la carte menu has some very tempting dishes. We found the grilled tuna okay, ditto the grilled red snapper, done Adriatic sytle. Consider sliced breast and confit of Muscovy duck, roasted guinea hen with Savoy cabbage cake or toasted loin of rabbit with orzo and chanterelles. The bread is reminiscent of a bad college dining hall.

For a finish, you may choose from assorted domestic and imported cheeses with seasonal fresh fruit. The numerous desserts from the wagon include a scrumptious chocolate cake, fruit tarts made with transparent flaky pastry (the blueberry and lemon marriage on a custard base is recommended), and a sinfully rich, deeply satisfying chocolate mousse. The extensive wine list of American, French and Australian wines contains no half bottles. However, wine service, and service in general, is lamentable. One time, it took ten minutes for a bottle of wine to arrive, which was after the pre-prepared appetizers were delivered, and we had to repour our wine ourselves several times. There's free valet parking, which you need in this neighborhood, but beware of unreliability here as well: one time, after we had waited fifteen minutes to retrieve our car, the tardy parking attendant explained, "I fell asleep." A dinner will run about $150 per couple, including wine.

OTHER BOROUGHS

Adele
501 Eleventh St.
(Seventh & Eighth Aves.),
Brooklyn
(718) 788-4980
AMERICAN
Open Wed.-Sat. 6 p.m.-10:30 p.m., Sun 11:30 a.m.-3 p.m. & 5 p.m.-9 p.m. Cards: AE, MC, V.

Located in a converted town house on a quiet street in Brooklyn's Park Slope section, Adele is a romantic gem of a restaurant for those who like to think of all five boroughs as their home. Jim Dozmati, co-owner and maître d', purchased the building a couple of years ago, gutted the ground floor, and created a duplex dining room with a tin ceiling, quaint lighting, Oriental rugs and dark floral wall paper. If it weren't for the lively fireplace lit in one corner of the room, the atmosphere would be decidedly gloomy, like an old aunt's house untouched for 50 years. However, the mahogany tables shine under country-style china and unmatched silverware, and the din emanating from Brooklyn yuppies and an occasional adventurous Manhattanite couple seems cheerful.

The chef, Melicia Phillips, who trained at Chanterelle, has devised a short, but interesting, menu. Among the appetizers, try the tender slices of squab breast, served with an unusual salad of butternut squash and tart Granny Smith apples. We liked the vegetable consommé with lemon, speckled with a bit of turnip, though we thought it a bit too salty. We loved the wild mushroom canelloni, floating in a dark, woodsy mushroom broth. The menu changes every couple of weeks. Friends recommended the chicken consommé with corn and chives and the oyster fritters with ravigote sauce. We think you should try, for an entrée, the filet of skate with a crisp crust and moist interior, adorned with a blend of chopped hazelnuts and bacon, though again heavy on the salt. Its accompaniment of softly braised cabbage, infused with a touch of ginger, creates a pleasing culinary harmony. We adored a superb veal tenderloin, pink and buttery, bathed in a delicious roast-garlic

sauce and served with a successful timbale of broccoli. The duck with apple cider lacks complexity, but we liked the tuna with ginger, sesame and scallions. Forget most of the desserts, heavy and forgettable, even the tempting profiterole filled with dry fig ice cream. The pastry we found just too thick and pasty. We think the best bet is a sorbet—the pomegranate sparkles like a jewel and is refreshing. The medium-size wine list, emphasizing French and American wines, seems well balanced and very reasonably priced, with plenty of choices in and around the $20 range, such as a chardonnay from Dry Creek in Sonoma for $22. Nevertheless, dinner for two runs a hefty $130 or so, with wine; a 16 1/2 percent mandatory tip is included, à la française.

Amerigo's
3587 E. Tremont Ave.,
(Lafayette Ave.),
The Bronx
792-3600
ITALIAN
Open Tues.-Thurs. noon-11 p.m., Fri.-Sat. noon-midnight, Sun. noon-11 p.m. Closed 1st 3 weeks in July. All major cards.

Because owners Tony and Anna Cortese are devoted to good food and to their customers, their restaurant (which opened in 1934 and has been owned by them since 1981) gets better every year. Easily the best restaurant in the Bronx, Amerigo's operates to a suburban rather than Manhattan standard. The Corteses know rightly that a chi-chi Manhattan-style Italian *ristorante* or trattoria wouldn't make it in their nice neighborhood near the Throg's Neck Bridge. Anyway, their customers are people who come from all over the metropolitan area. If you are in the Bronx already, by all means make a little detour and try to get a table (reservations are needed on weekends). Parking, you'll be able to get. Since our last report, they've added an outdoor canopy and spruced up the ladies room; otherwise, the place looks the same: two big dining rooms, one slightly more "elegant" than the other, but with your basic, fancy Italian restaurant decor and waiters (male and female) in black tie. The less formal room usually contains families and casually-dressed regulars who think nothing about introducing a two-year-old to Amerigo's. They've probably been stuffing themselves here since they were two.

Enormous portions come after you order from the menu, which has everything on it: appetizers, soups, 31 pastas, fish, meats (including fourteen veal preparations), and, of course, the daily specials. You can easily split the good, hot antipasto to begin. Ditto the spedini alla Romana. You can't order a half portion of one of the excellent pastas as an appetizer, though two people can split a regular portion. We love the paglia e fieno alla molisana—green and white fettucine noodles in a savory cream-and-cheese sauce—and stellar capellini (angel hair pasta) alla provinciale (olives, onions and capers), a house specialty. A rich fettucine Alfredo or verdant seasonal spaghetti al pesto earn a place on the table, as do gnocchi and most of the other hearty and flavorful pasta dishes. The armies that get fed here appear very well nourished on steaks, chops (wonderful pork chops) and lobster. Order mussles marinara, and you get three dozen mussels in a flavorful tomato sauce. We like, also, the veal scaloppine alla Amerigo, big and tasty, with a layer of eggplant over the veal and a layer of not-so-impressive cheese over the eggplant; everything is bathed in a pure tomato sauce. We have found the breaded veal cutlet alla milanese too dry for our taste. Another house specialty is osso buco—a big shin of veal stewed in wine, herbs, tomatoes, onions, carrots and garlic—with meat that properly falls away from the shank. We have discovered that side vegetables tend to be overcooked and overspiced with garlic. Ninety-five percent of the roughly 150 wines offered are Italian, and run from pizzeria wines to distinguished offerings of top producers from all over Italy. You'll find good prices, even some special values to be found. Try the standard Livio Felluga Pinot Grigio ($24) as a white or the Ruffino Reserva Ducale Gold Label ($30) for a red. You'll wind up pouring your own refills. We learned that most desserts are not made on the premises. By the time you even think of dessert, however, it's doubtful you'll have room or the psychic energy for a sweet. The Italian cheesecake is homemade, but a bit dry. Espresso comes with the obligatory lemon peel and a pouring-capped bottle of anisette. It's that kind of place. About $76 per couple, with a modest wine.

10/20 Dominick's
2335 Arthur Ave.
(186th & 187th Sts.),
The Bronx
733-2807
ITALIAN
Open Mon.-Thurs. & Sat. noon-10 p.m., Fri. noon-11 p.m., Sun 1 p.m.-9 p.m. No cards.

This place remains wildly popular, which we have to attribute more to the experience of eating here than to what one actually puts in the mouth. The legendary waiting line every night and Sunday at midday (no reservations are taken) continues to be long, and is a veritable rite of passage. People still champion Dominick's lusty Southern Italian cooking, gargantuan portions and yesteryear prices. It has a remarkable and very satisfied following, who sit elbow to elbow between imitation wood paneled walls (the tiny place has increased in size by about a third—say five or six more communal tables than in years past). There is no menu, and if this is your first time here, don't be intimidated by the waiter, who will try to get rid of you as soon as possible. He won't be rude; he'll just treat you like one of a big, chaotic family. Ask questions. The steaks are the best, charcoal broiled. The pastas are the worst; watery, overcooked, with a basic red sauce that is underspiced—sad, because this is one of the last of the old guard of basic pasta houses. You'll probably order pasta anyway, so try one of the exceptions, the usually tasty homemade fettucine with fresh mushrooms in a cream sauce. The cold antipasto is not worth ordering, as it consists of iceberg lettuce, domestic Parmigiano or provolone, two slices of salami and, if you're lucky, some anchovies. The grilled pork chops are dry, but braised, they are not too tough. The fish soup is good, but be sure you ask for it very hot. Go for the home-baked bread—it's excellent; forget the desserts, they all weigh a ton. Order a Sicilian wine; as you might expect, Corvo is available in red or white. This place is a real scene! Price per couple, about $56.

Gage & Tollner

372 Fulton St. (Smith St.),
Brooklyn
(718) 875-5181

AMERICAN

*Open Mon.-Thurs. noon-3 p.m. & 5 p.m.-10
p.m., Fri.-Sat. noon-3 p.m. & 5 p.m.-11 p.m.,
Sun. noon-4 p.m. & 5 p.m.-9 p.m. All major
cards.*

Brooklynites have passed by its brave Victorian front countless times, glancing briefly at the graceful beige columns and delicate cornices that mark the oldest continuously operated restaurant in New York City. Resting on its laurels, Gage & Tollner forgot to innovate over the years, and lost many a client with rubbery shrimps and bland chicken. Now, with a change in mangement, this landmark seafood-and-chop house offers a more eclectic mix of old and new on its revamped menu. It's easy to forget the commercial buzz of the pedestrian downtown shopping street in this sanctuary lit by brass chandeliers, padded with red velvet and furnished with Thonet chairs and darkened oak tables. A striking mix of diners fills those chairs: from the courthouse crowd, loosening their ties as they pick at broiled clam bellies and sip Kentucky bourbon, or the Brooklyn Heights couple out for an early supper of fried oysters away from the kids, to the art patrons waiting for the opening night concert at BAM and feasting perfectly on poached lemon sole.

Gage & Tollner has many more years ahead of it because of Edna Lewis' cooking. The tall, black chef from South Carolina added an extra menu of her own, featuring highly seasoned and authentic Southern specialities, such as tender crabcakes, a complex catfish stew, pan-fried quail served with airy spoon bread and fresh fish ordered "any way you like." Despite the sophistication of the cuisine, its presentation is cafeteria-style: heavy, oval white stoneware, ice cream scoops of red rice, metal cups holding a lively tart sauce. Dessert time brings Edna's homemade wonders: peach cobbler, pecan pie and a sensuous chocolate soufflé drizzled with bittersweet-chocolate sauce and buried in freshly whipped cream. If you choose the $21.95 fixed-price menu, you've made a shrewd decision. Begin with Edna's Charleston she-crab soup and follow with a smooth, not-too-salty Smithfield ham, served with a mellow corn pudding and fresh string beans redolent of onions. Even the spareribs here have a fresh snap, thanks to Edna Lewis's special spicy sauce. Unfortunately, the wine list is mediocre and overpriced, and as for the service, you'd think the waiters, decorated army-style with emblems (gold eagle, gold star and gold bar) indicating their years of service, owned the place.

Manducati's

13-27 Jackson Ave. (47th Ave.),
Long Island City, Queens
(718) 729-4602

ITALIAN

*Open Mon.-Fri. noon-3 p.m. & 5 p.m.-10 p.m.,
Sat. 5 p.m.-11 p.m. Closed in Aug. No cards.*

There's a menu, but speak to gentle Vincenzo. He and wife, Ida, who cooks the nouvelle New York-Neapolitan fare that has made their restaurant a perennial discovery since it opened in 1978, "rely mostly upon imagination and availabity of seasonal ingrediants that allows for a constant variety of dishes that change regularly." It's the truth. So, let Vincenzo suggest something for you, including wine—he's a great wine maven, and a smile will come to his face when you agree to a special selection, whether it be a low-price "new" Italian wine or a 1968 Taurasi or a 1978 Gaya Barbaresco (each about $100).

Behind the pool-hall facade and a bar up front, with locals eating meatball heros, is an uninspiring (or downright ugly) back dining room of orange brickface, dimestore chandeliers with electric "candles" and vaguely obscene food posters. Featured are grade "C" Italian bread and grated Parmesan (probably not Parmigiano) in glass shakers. We like, however, homemade fettucine with Ida's hearty but subtle bolognese sauce (gently simmered ground beef with tomatoes, pine nuts and carrots), homemade spaghetti with sun-dried tomatoes, and Ida's ricotta gnocchi (which needs Parmesan to give it zip). Ida's pasta has been enticing Manhattanites to schlep to this blighted intersection in Queens on "the other side" of the Midtown Tunnel for some time, now. "Manducatis" is the second person plural of the Latin verb "to eat." And when you come to Manducati's, you eat cheaply, copiously and well. And not just pasta. There's also greaseless, crunchy fried seppia ("like large calamari"); sparkling

161

scungilli salad full of garlic, oregano and parsley; swordfish Manducati's (breadcrumbs, scallions and mushrooms); gutsy eggplant rollatini; and garlicky, room temperature broccoli, not a second overcooked. Though some of the fare is humdrum, there's enough plain good eating here to make the place a magnet for hungry Manhattanites and droves of gold-chained locals and suburbanites, as well as for prowling oenophiles. Dinner, with wine, costs about $60 to $70 per couple.

12/20 Nightfalls
7612 Third Ave. (76th & 77th Sts.),
Bay Ridge, Brooklyn
(718) 748-8700

AMERICAN

Open daily noon-midnight. All major cards.

This enterprising establishment added some elegance and sophistication to Bay Ridge's restaurant row when it opened in the early 1980s, and has carried on well with luncheons, dinners, brunches, grand buffets and classic dining ever since. In the shadow of the Verrazano Bridge, and thus easily accessible from Staten Island and New Jersey (as well as from Manhattan and neighboring Brooklyn), the two joined brownstones that comprise the restaurant have been redone in an attractive postmodern style. A handsome outside brick terrace garden dining room features a 36-foot wall of falling water, a terra-cotta interior, Roman villa columns and an exciting upstairs bar atrium.

The regional American cuisine does not quite measure up to the setting, but executive chef Maria Pirozzi is steady, and although the food can be inconsistent at very slow or fast times (reservations are a must on weekends), it is usually fine and intriguing. This is a great place for Sunday brunch ($13.95) and a steal at lunch (still $7.95 prix-fixe). For appetizers (yes, plural), consider beer-batter coconut shrimp or the eggplant filled with three cheeses (with a plum-tomato sauce) or a "for the health of it" tossed salad (the restaurant has a "fit for life" diet program). Among the handful of pasta offerings, the pick is the angel hair with lobster, in a light basil-garlic sauce. Fish and seafood are done well. Sautéed jumbo shrimp and bay scallops in a lobster-cream sauce ($16.95) is a worthy and popular offering. Also touted is the filet of veal,

stuffed with black peppered ham and fresh mozzarella with two sauces. The menu is ambitious, but it hasn't changed significantly in a few years, so the kitchen has it down well. You can always get a "sizzling" charcoal-grilled T-bone steak. Desserts are okay, especially if you like chocolate mousse. We're just not fans of white and bittersweet chocolate mousse with strawberry sauce in an almond tuile. How about an Oreo cookie crust, filled with coffee ice cream and covered with chocolate fudge and whipped cream? The wines are more than okay; there are about 125 European and American selections, reasonably priced, from $10 to $250 per bottle. Prices have not risen much here in years. Dinner is about $70 per couple, and lunch and brunch cost half that.

Peter Luger

178 Broadway (Driggs Ave.),
Brooklyn
(718) 387-7400

STEAKHOUSE

Open Mon.-Thurs. 11:45 a.m.-9:45 p.m., Fri.-Sat. 11:45 a.m.-10:45 p.m., Sun. 1 p.m.-10:45 p.m. No cards.

New Yorkers (and their out-of-town guests) love this landmark restaurant in the shadow of the Williamsburg bridge, and have since last century (before the bridge was built). One wonders if the Wall Streeters and lawyers of those days traveled by ferry—unlike their counterparts today, who travel by limousine—to pack this place at lunch and to gorge themselves on excellent quality, humongous steaks, large orders of french fries or hash browns, overcooked spinach and cheesecake. In the evening, some of these same businessmen, this time casually dressed, reappear with their families to eat more steak, served with thick slices of tomatoes and onions. The two-story restaurant (try to reserve a table in the downstairs dining room) sports well-worn oak tabletops, wood-handled knives and forks and waiters who have worked in this restaurant for years. The excellent steaks (well selected and aged), basted with butter and tender and juicy, are always cooked rare—if you order medium or well done, you will be frowned upon, and service will be terrible. Order one steak for two people and a steak for two for three. Seriously. The "Famous T-Bone Steak" is, in fact, listed for two persons at $49.50. The menu also offers two-inches-thick loin lamb chops and thick slabs of roast prime rib of beef, both of which are as good as the steaks. A doggie bag is provided if you cannot quite wipe your plate clean.

For dessert (of course, consider the cheesecake), the strudel, pecan pie and chocolate mousse all come with unlimited, freshly made "Schlag" (whipped cream, in this case). A limited but reasonably priced wine list offers mostly red wines from California, with some French and Italian offerings. You'll be fine with a Robert Mondavi cabernet ($28) or a Château Simard St. Emilion ($21). Many people partake, however, of the good selection of imported and domestic beers. Reserve a few days ahead for popular dining times. A word of caution: don't park you car on the street in this run-down area, park it in the adjacent lot or ask the doorman to park it for you. Taxis back to Manhattan are also available. Dinner for two runs about $95, plus tax and tip.

The River Café

1 Water Street (under pediment of the Brooklyn Bridge), Brooklyn
(718) 522-5200
AMERICAN
Open Mon.-Sat. noon-2 p.m. & 6 p.m.-11 p.m., Sun. 11:30 a.m.-2:30 p.m. & 6 p.m.-11 p.m. All major cards.

With its drop-dead view of the Manhattan skyline, the ambience of this place doesn't disappoint, but what's on the plate sometimes does. The view tends to make the River Café an "occasion" restaurant, a place for New Yorkers to observe significant birthdays and anniversaries. The deliberately understated decor of the dining room directs all eyes to the sweeping vista across the Hudson, of boats plying the waters from the Statue of Liberty up to the Citicorp Building. A piano player tinkles Porter and Gershwin. A bar crowd toasts the sunset. The Japanese tourists and businessmen take photographs. The River Café may seem to be trying to be too many things to too many people, in the overeager fashion of a restaurant "in the boondocks," yet it works, because the kitchen, too, remains ambitious. Probably too much so. We return and return, hoping for a breakthrough. We

enjoy watching the tide change, but too often shake our head because of overly elaborate, failed dishes.

David Burke, the former sous-chef who spent time training in France with Gaston Lenôtre, Georges Blanc and Marc Meneau, commands the kitchen. He learned the art of presentation in France, so the food here looks good. Curiously, we find you do better ordering off the regular menu than sampling one of Burke's overreaching tasting menus ($75). As of late, his food seems to edge toward the fish and seafood side. Try the carpaccio of yellowfin tuna, with its scoop of salmon tartare on top and vegetables filling and decorating the plate. We loved the swordfish carpaccio, with bits of shrimps, mâche (lettuce), sautéed mushrooms, chives and curry with olive oil and lovely, crisp potato strips. Ditto the pastrami-cured salmon, served with lush mashed potatoes and artichoke sections (or sometimes rye potato toast and mustard oil). Some of us liked, also, long-playing popular items from previous menus, such as the Black Angus sirloin, grilled over fruitwood. Consider some of the smoked appetizers—the smoked shrimp and red snapper chili or the cinnamon-smoked quail and foie gras dumplings. Popular fish dishes take your mind away from the East River: grilled yellowfin tuna and sweetwater prawns, and yet more salmon, this time seared with ginger and pepper, and served with Burgundy butter and lotus chips. Burke tries to build layers of flavor, but his failed dishes, though displaying a consistent inventiveness, lack cohesion. The banana-and-chocolate parfait heads our list of desserts, followed by a soufflé-like chocolate pudding. They try hard at this place; the service is more than competent, and the wine list is very good (it offers a broad spectrum, with attractive options in all price ranges, and it's notable for old California wines). Our problems with wines have been finding the right ones to marry with some of Burke's complex dishes. Prices, in general, invite criticism. The fixed price for dinner is $55 per person, and an à la carte lunch will run about the same, plus wine, tax and tips, so with anything but the minimum, you've got a $200-plus tab for two.

Tommasso's
1464 86th St. (14th & 15th Aves.),
Brooklyn
(718) 236-9883

ITALIAN

*Open Mon.-Fri. noon-3 p.m. & 4 p.m.-11 p.m.,
Sat. noon-midnight, Sun. 1 p.m.-10 p.m. All
major cards.*

Tommasso's is a favorite with New York food-and-wine writers. Tommasso, who is proprietor Thomas Verdillo, an engaging and flamboyant character who loves food, wine and opera singing, shares his ideas and achievements relating these topics freely. You'll find him always delighting in some regional Italian special of the day or in some choice from his Italian wine list and range of grappas, carefully selected and priced ever so reasonably. Filled with large parties of local Italian-Americans, this Bensonhurst eatery is a place for Manhattanites to eat copiously and raid the wine cellar. The two dining rooms tend to the glitzy.

Indulge in the lovely antipasti. We have dived more than once into Tommasso's fresh homemade mozzarella, accompanied by piles of roasted red peppers, bathed in olive oil and garlic. We have feasted well on the same mozzarella, this time in carrozza, and topped with a sauce spiked with chopped gaeta olives and capers. And thousands of succulent clams oreganato must have, in Oscar Hammerstein's words, galloped down ours and other satisfied gullets. Among the pastas, which are only okay, we champion pasta e fagioli ("Fazool!" Tommasso corrects). Friends also liked linguine with red clam sauce and light potato gnocchi. We found the chicken with a piquant olive, parsley, garlic and white-wine sauce a bit overcooked, ditto the breaded veal cutlet with a fine caper sauce. But when Tommasso insists that you make room for his Marsala-rich zabaglione, just whisked up in copper bowls, all seems right with the world. You'll notice the upright piano. There's a ready accompanist, and you can often hear opera being sung on weekends, sometimes by Tommaso himself. (He is always ready to tell you about his relatively recent—and only?—experience on stage, singing a lead in a small Manhattan opera production of *Tosca*.) You can eat and drink yourself into stupefaction for $40 per couple for lunch, $80 to $100 per couple for dinner, with a good wine.

Water's Edge
44th Dr. & the East River,
Long Island City, Queens
(718) 482-0033

CONTINENTAL/SEAFOOD

Mon.-Fri. noon-3 p.m & 6 p.m.-11 p.m., Sat. 6 p.m.-11 p.m. All major cards.

The free ferry service at night (in good weather), from Manhattan to this barge moored on the Long Island City side of the East River, is a hook to pull you in. The bigger hook is the magical view you can enjoy while dining. The jeweled towers of Manhattan illuminated at night make you feel you're in another world, especially if you arrive at the restaurant in time to see the sun set behind the sparkling Citicorp building. They designed the dining room at the Water's Edge, clean, refurbished, and all mahogany, with touches of suburban art nouveau, to direct your attention to the river. And there are the extras: a piano player, flowers on the bar and, on each table, small lights, whose reflections on the windows upstage the view. The cuisine under chef Mark French (a native of England), who joined in 1989, has shifted the emphasis somewhat (rightly so) to seafood and Continental fare. The new simplicity on the plate makes for safe, if somewhat straightforward, dining.

Queens couples celebrating a special occasion and adventurous Manhattanites will do well starting with a gravlax with a dilled cucumber salad or a seared foie gras presented with citrus fruits. The sesame linguine with sautéed shrimp and sweet peppers makes for a filling, and at times overcooked, starter. We like for a main course the Dover sole—fresh, and with a mustard-and-shallot sauce—or the peppered swordfish. The seasonal soft-shelled crabs were a disappointment, sautéed almondine style to the death. We also enjoyed the veal chop—thick, moist, and in a light sherry sauce with thyme and tomato. The elaborately presented desserts arrive by trolley, a treat (too sweet) for the eyes and palate. The prune clafouti gets the top vote, though the best dessert is still the view, enjoyed while sipping a good espresso. Rutherford Hill Chardonnay ($24) marries with much of the menu. Figure $116 per couple for dinner, less for lunch.

QUICK BITES

BETWEEN ACTS

You've got a yen to nosh? Boy, are you ever in the right town. There's such an enormous variety of snacking material, you may never want to eat an honest meal again. Native New Yorkers know their way around a corned-beef sandwich or a slice of pizza. They're also pretty good with a toasted bagel and cream cheese, a thick plate of ribs or a hot dog from a pushcart vendor on any midtown corner. How they do it and still have a hand free to hail a cab is one of those unsolved urban mysteries.

Word of mouth is one sure way to find some of the favorite haunts of the city's gourmands: absolutely everyone in town has a favorite obscure place that they swear nobody else knows. Another sure-fire method is to pick out a hungry-looking native on the street at lunchtime and follow him to wherever he's headed. Finally, you can simply take our advice on these pages. The latter will save you time and possible embarrassment, but the choice is yours. Keep in mind that the prices we give for an average snack or meal *do not* include New York's 8.25-percent tax, or gratuity.

BARBECUE

Dallas B-B-Q
27 W. 72nd St. (Central Park West & Columbus Ave.)
873-2004
Open Sun.-Thurs. noon-midnight, Fri.-Sat. noon-1 a.m. All major cards.
If you don't mind eating cattle-car style with a few hundred other diners who nightly pack this mammoth-sized eatery, you can share in one of the best food bargains in town. The decor is strictly old-warehouse style, with towering ceilings and tightly packed vinyl tables. Dallas's early-bird special makes all the confusion worthwhile: two people for dinner before 6:30 p.m. Monday through Saturday, or before 5 p.m. on Sunday, can each feast on chicken soup, half a barbecued chicken, cornbread and potatoes for just $6.95—for both. If you come later, the prices are just a couple of dollars more for the same menu. Or, choose tender baby back ribs, beef ribs the size of an elephant's midsection or an oversize load of fried onion rings (skip the soggy vegetable tempura). Don't expect real barbecue in this place—the sauce is too mild and the "country" singer is probably from Hoboken, but the prices are right and the waiters are good-natured. You can also order food to go. There's another location at 21 University

Place (674-4450). Dinner (after the early-bird-special hours) is about $25, with beer.

Wylie's Ribs & Co.
891 First Ave. (50th St.)
751-0700
Open daily noon-midnight. All major cards.
You say your out-of-town friend plays nose tackle for the Dallas Cowboys and he's hungry? No problem—join the crowd of bright young singles and healthy-looking families who spill out onto the sidewalk outside this no-nonsense rib house. And it's worth the wait, too, for meltingly tender baby back ribs, hefty beef ribs and barbecued chicken that's moist and juicy. The large pitcher on your table isn't sangría—it's extra barbecue sauce, and regulars even drizzle some on top of Wylie's much-touted "brick" of fried onion rings. Forgettable steak fries and coleslaw accompany your entrée. There's another location called Wylie's 2, at 59 W. 56th Street (757-7910), open daily from 11:30 a.m. to midnight. Here, you'll find an airy outdoor café for summer dining, along with gorgeous slabs of prime rib, meaty short ribs, and an oil-soaked aberration known as fried zucchini loaf that only a vegetarian could love. About $30 for a hefty dinner for two.

CAFES

Aglio & Olio
145 W. 55th St. (Sixth & Seventh Aves.)
582-9589
Open Mon.-Fri. noon-3 p.m. & 5 p.m.-9 p.m., Sat. 5 p.m. -9 p.m. All major cards.

This handsome café, with its elegant, indoor garden-style dining room, serves more substantial American fare than you'll find at its sister salad-and-sandwich bistro on the East Side (at 141 E. 56th Street). Adjacent to its own take-out muffin bakery, this popular lunch spot attracts a crowd ordered straight from central casting—handsome L.A. show-biz types, publishing executives and well-dressed businesspeople. They stop by regularly for such marvelous dishes as chicken pot pie with a tender shortbread crust and perfectly grilled fresh salmon over fettuccine with champagne sauce; a superb array of salads; and desserts such as crumbly oatmeal-pecan tart. The muffins have a citywide reputation, and many customers walk next door after their meal to pick up a few of the bran or cranberry-walnut treats for the next day's breakfast. For interesting, well-prepared food with a tab that won't burst your purse strings, this charming restaurant should not be missed. About $15 per person, with cappucinos (note that there is a $15 minimum at tables).

All State Café
250 W. 72nd St. (Broadway & West End Ave.)
874-1883
Open daily 11:30 a.m.-1 a.m. No cards.

Brick walls, a lively jukebox and a roaring fire in winter are some of the many modest charms that make this café a perennial favorite for hungry Upper West Siders. Actors and literary types conduct serious conversations at the bar, then sit down at one of the small wood-topped tables for a hearty and inexpensive meal. The food is filling and tasty, and you can't beat the $5.75 tab for a luncheon special that includes a bowl of soup or salad followed by sautéed calf's liver, grilled bluefish, or a scallion-and-Cheddar-cheese omelet. A plentiful weekend brunch with a complimentary Bloody Mary runs a humble $13 for two.

American Festival Café
20 W. 50th St. (at Rockefeller Center)
246-6699
Open Mon.-Fri. 7:30 a.m.-10:30 p.m., Sat.-Sun. 9 a.m.- 10:30 p.m. All major cards.

The regal beauty of Rockefeller Center and its guardian, the statue of Prometheus, are noteworthy surroundings for the American Festival Café, one of New York's most beloved traditions. In winter, diners gaze out through the glass walls onto a Currier & Ives vision of ice skaters on the surrounding rink; in summer, the rink turns into a colorful patio of umbrellas and tables for outdoor dining. The view is the real star—the American cuisine is acceptable, but don't expect any showstoppers. For breakfast, homemade muffins, tender ham steaks, pancakes, waffles and buttery french toast are always good choices. Lunch and dinner offer specialties like Thomas Jefferson's chicken hash, Maine-lobster gazpacho, skewers of (overcooked) seafood doused in herbs, free-range chicken with mustard, and a treacherous array of limp pasta dishes. Bring the kids at Christmastime for breakfast with Santa, and you'll understand what the magic of this place is all about. About $20 for two at breakfast. Lunch averages $40 for two, with wine; dinner averages $60, plus tax and tip.

Arizona 206 Café
206 E. 60th St. (Second & Third Aves.)
838-0440
Open Mon.-Sat. noon-midnight. All major cards.

This charming café shimmers with the same glow that young chef Marilyn Frobuccino creates at her stellar Arizona 206 Restaurant next door (See Restaurants chapter, page 120). The atmosphere is casual and contemporary, with bleached wooden tables, warm lighting and a vast, open grill that emits luscious aromas of seared meat and poultry, plus an attractive crowd of trendy diners who always seem to be having a great time. And no wonder, for chef Frobuccino's innovative, Southwestern-style fare is some of the most provocative and mouthwatering food in town. The menu consists of an ever-changing variety of marinated, grilled and smoked foods accompanied by tantalizing chutneys and homemade preserves; the items are served in small portions that range from $6 to $14 per plate, so you can choose as little or as much as you like to make a full meal. Sample the juicy grilled squab, or the seafood nuzzled with fruit and an incendiary dollop of chile oil, marvelously spicy skirt-steak tortillas or barbecued oyster tacos. For dessert, try the cooling cactus-pear sorbet, outrageously rich ice-cream cake made with mango-and-coconut ice cream, or the dark and deadly baked chocolate-mousse cake. If this is really what they eat in Arizona, we should all be Phoenix-bound.

Beach Café

1326 Second Ave. (70th St.)
988-7299
Open Sun.-Thurs. 11:30 a.m.-1 a.m., Fri.-Sat. 11:30 a.m.-2 a.m. Cards: AE

This relaxing café/gallery is a soothing spot in which to linger over lunch, drinks or a casual supper. Bright seascapes adorn the brick walls; wood paneling and classical music soften the mood; and an efficient staff serves generally well-prepared, if unimaginative, food. At lunch there's the usual roster of hamburgers, quiches, omelets, main-dish salads, and a few Italian dishes. At night the menu offers more Italian, with some passable pasta selections such as tortellini with tomato-cream sauce and angel-hair pasta with a choice of sauces. Lunch for two, with wine, comes in at about $24.

Beggar's Banquet

125 W. 43rd St. (Sixth & Seventh Aves.)
997-0959
Open Mon.-Sat. 11:30 a.m.-9 p.m. Cards: AE, DC.

This popular midtown eatery is a good choice for lunch or pre-theater supper. Friendly service and a casual, publike atmosphere attract regulars from the business district, who come for simple, well-prepared fare in a relaxed setting. A basket of whole-wheat bread and a jar of homemade honey accompany lusty bowls of chili, stew or soup—Italian lentil, cold cucumber-and-beet or pistou (a rich Provençal vegetable soup topped with crushed basil and garlic). The menu also features superior quiches, such as Provençal or one with ham, broccoli and Cheddar, plus a worthy assortment of salads and good sandwiches. Desserts are delicious (try the Scotch chocolate cake or the New Orleans rum pudding with hard sauce). For dinner, the kitchen produces platters of shrimp stuffed with crab meat, and a perfectly acceptable, if uninspired, rendering of chicken piccata. Lunch for two, with a glass of wine, is about $20; dinner for two, with wine, comes in under $40.

Caffè Dante

79-81 MacDougal St. (W. Houston & Bleecker Sts.)
982-5275
Open Sun.-Thurs. 10 a.m.-2 a.m., Fri.-Sat. 10 a.m.-3 a.m. No cards.

Espresso aficionados make the Dante part of their daily routine for some of the most bracing, well-made demitasse this side of the Trastevere. Capuccino, hot chocolate, iced drinks and a good selection of teas and pastries are also available. In summer, you can sit outside at tiny tables and people-watch for hours. Even if you're not hungry, you'll want to try one of the lovely sandwiches, made with crisp rolls and top-quality imported Italian cold meats and cheeses.

Caffè della Pace

48 E. 7th St. (First & Second Aves.)
529-8024
Open Mon.-Thurs. 10 a.m.-1 a.m, Fri.-Sat. 10 a.m.-2 a.m., Sun. 10 a.m.-1 a.m. No cards.

The East Village neighborhood is unpredictable, but the neighborhood regulars know exactly what they're getting at this small, unpretentious Italian restaurant with an excellent kitchen and wonderfully low prices. One of the more remarkable dishes is a savory antipasto with hunks of mozzarella, thinly sliced prosciutto, roasted red peppers and luscious tomatoes. Presented with a loaf of delicious Italian bread, the large order is a meal in itself. Pasta specials change daily, and though none stands out, all are good. Desserts, cappuccinos and Italian sodas round out a satisfying meal. Bring your own wine or beer and expect to spend $35 on dinner for two.

Café La Fortuna
69 W. 71st St. (Central Park West &
Columbus Ave.)
724-5846
*Open Mon.-Thurs. 1 p.m.-1 a.m., Fri. 1 p.m.-2
a.m., Sat. noon-2 a.m., Sun. noon-1 a.m. No
cards.*

Within a few blocks of Lincoln Center, this
cozy subterranean nook attracts a nightly
crowd of locals, who come for the best
espresso on the Upper West Side. There's a
soothing pace here, enhanced by the decor of
vintage opera records and yellowed photos of
Tristans and Aidas peering sadly from the
walls. A better-than-decent selection of pastries are on hand—anise cookies, chocolate
cakes, and rum-scented zuppa inglese—all at
remarkably low prices ($2.50 for a wedge of
velvety Italian cheesecake). For sipping, you
can choose from fragrant teas, fruit drinks and
frothy hot chocolate. In summer, the garden
terrace is open, and it's worth the half-hour
wait in line to relax over iced cappuccino
topped with a scoop of excellent homemade
gelato. About $10 for espressos and pastries
for two.

Café Madeleine
403 W. 43rd St. (Ninth Ave.)
246-2993
Open daily noon-midnight. Cards: AE, MC, V.

You'll find your favorite columnist, along
with much of the *New York Times* staff, lunch-
ing at this charming petit café with its lacy
white curtains and immaculate country decor.
In warm weather, the patio garden is a serene
spot in which to linger over a pleasing slice of
country pâté, a bowlful of herb-flecked mussels marinière or pistou. The salads are perky
and generously studded with nuggets of
Roquefort cheese and walnuts, or various crisp
vegetable combinations. Simple grilled fish
and roast duck are good choices for heartier
appetites. About $30 for two, with wine.

Café Mortimer
1057 Lexington Ave. (75th St.)
517-6400
*Open Mon.-Fri. noon-3:30 p.m. & 6 p.m.-mid-
night, Sat.-Sun. 12:15 p.m.-4:30 p.m. & 6 p.m.-
midnight. All major cards.*

It's hard to believe that this cheery café is
the offspring of New York's most disdainfully
exclusive dining salon, Mortimer's. The stun-

ning walnut bar, handsome beige tiled walls
and a soothing menu of good sandwiches,
individual pizzas and soups make this a popular spot, where tired shoppers repair for a light
luncheon or an afternoon coffee break. The
appetizers and desserts are from Mortimer's,
which has never been big on culinary inspiration; stick with simple items like artichokes in
vinaigrette or gravlax for appetizers, and the
satiny crème brûlée to polish off the meal.
About $15 per person for lunch.

Café Reggio
119 MacDougal St. (W. 3rd & Bleecker
Sts.)
475-9557
*Open Sun.-Thurs. 10 a.m.-2 a.m., Fri.-Sat. 10
a.m.-4 a.m. No cards.*

The Cavallacci family opened this shrine to
coffee and companionship in 1927, and the
place has been going strong on both counts
ever since. Plaster busts of Verdi and Wagner
nestle in the niches of the smoke-darkened
walls, and the faintly seedy air is vintage
Fellini. Sip a satiny-rich cup of espresso, frothy
cappuccino, or a devastating hot chocolate
whirled with whipped cream while you study
what passes for bohemia these days in the tame
Village streets. Try the tasty prosciutto-and-
cheese sandwiches and Italian pastries. Avoid
Rome by Night, which is a rather dull combination of yogurt and fresh fruits.

Café Un Deux Trois
123 W. 44th St. (Sixth Ave. & Broadway)
354-4148
*Open Mon.-Fri. noon-midnight, Sat.-Sun. 11
a.m.- midnight. Cards: AE, MC, V.*

This brasserie resembles a Parisian railway
station more than is probably intended, with
its ponderous chandeliers, neo-Gothic colon-
nades, and food that falls short of what a good
snack bar can do. Too bad, because with just
a little effort the owners could have a first-rate
theater-district eatery to be proud of, instead
of an ordinary people-watching mob scene.
The stunning Tiffany-glass-paneled bar is always popular, the service cheerfully efficient,
and you're provided with crayons to doodle
on the paper tablecloth while you wait. Be
prepared for disappointment: incredibly overcooked and sandy mussels, tough cubes of
skewered beef with a bland peanut sauce, oily
fried chicken strips and an eminently mediocre

cassoulet. On the plus side, there's a fair pepper steak served with some of the best pommes frites in New York, passable duck breast stuffed with spinach, good vinaigrette over crispy salad greens and perfect calf's liver with a rosy pink center. Stay away from the charlottes and much-touted profiteroles. Instead, try the poached pear with ice cream and chocolate sauce. About $40 per person for dinner, with house wine.

Cloister Café
238 E. 9th St. (Second & Third Aves.)
777-9128
Open Sun.-Thurs. 11 a.m.-12:30 a.m., Fri.-Sat. 11 a.m -1:30 a.m. No cards.

Artists, writers and a steady clientele of East Village regulars come here daily for the atmosphere and frothy café au lait served in bowl-sized china cups. In winter there's a cozy fire blazing, and in summer everybody moves outdoors to the brick courtyard that boasts a pretty fountain and fish pond without fish. The food falls into the standard omelet/burger/chicken category, but at $6.95 for the dinner specials, no one complains too loudly. Still, the desserts are of a good quality, and the setting makes this café a worthy spot to tarry for a while. Two will spend about $9 for dessert and coffee.

Cottonwood Café
415 Bleecker St. (Eighth Ave.)
924-6271
Open Mon.-Fri. 11 a.m.-3 p.m. & 5 p.m.-11:45 p.m., Sat. 10 a.m.-3 p.m. & 5 p.m.-11:45 p.m., Sun. 10 a.m.-4 p.m. & 5 p.m.-11 p.m. No cards.

This will never be mistaken for a roadhouse in Galveston, but the Tex-Mex specialties here are authentic, abundant and easy on the wallet. Cowboy posters and Lone Star memorabilia adorn the walls; music and good, friendly service more than compensate for the tiny tables jammed with neighborhood regulars. Start with wonderfully tender fried chicken livers or fiery chili. When you're ready to get down to serious eating, try the saucy ribs smoked over mesquite, or half a barbecued chicken, honest-to-goodness homemade mashed potatoes and crunchy fried okra. Avoid the overdone chicken-fried steak with pasty gravy and the underseasoned pork chops. The bar fixes a great frozen margarita to wash it all down, and with a couple of these

with dinner, you and a friend will go home well-fed for less than $25.

Cupping Room Café
359 W. Broadway (Broome St.)
925-2898
Open Mon. 7:30 a.m.-midnight, Tues.-Thurs. 7:30 a.m.-1 a.m., Fri. 7:30 a.m.-2 a.m., Sat. 8 a.m.-2 a.m., Sun. 8 a.m.-midnight. All major cards.

What can be better than a stylish SoHo eatery that serves great food at good prices and doesn't take itself too seriously? Such a restaurant almost restores one's faith in the beyond-hip, Eurotrash-flavored art-gallery scene that bludgeons the neighborhood. Yes, the downtown yuppies seem determined to bring their trendiness inside, but they clash with the cozy, wooden tables that give the restaurant a homey feel. As the Cupping Room is usually crowded, expect a wait. Weekend brunches demand particular patience. On those crazed Saturdays and Sundays, you can whittle away time at the bar sipping a California-like champagne-and-orange-juice creation called a mimosa, which could also be the adopted name of the blond on your right. The food makes everything right again. At the table, be sure to order the rich date-nut bread with cream cheese, the homemade muffins, a fluffy omelette or a stack of thick pancakes.

Danal
290 E. 10th St. (Third & Fourth Aves.)
982-6930
Open Tues.-Fri. 8 a.m.-6:30 p.m., Sat.-Sun. 11:30 a.m.-5:30 p.m. No cards.

Walk too quickly down this quiet sidestreet and you may miss Danal, which would be regrettable. Look for the wooden sign above a charming storefront and venture a few steps down. At first you'll think you're in a Laura Ashley warehouse, with the potpourri of quaint, flowery, country kitchenware that's for sale. But in the back are neatly arranged tables and a small kitchen that produces ample and adequate lunches, brunches and precious afternoon teas. If you enjoy café au lait on a bright morning, treat youself to a soup-sized Italian-style bowl of rich, creamy brew. Danal's small, gravel-strewn courtyard is an idyllic spot on sunny days to sip an iced cappuccino and linger over a simple turkey, lettuce and tomato sandwich served on a croissant. The only mar on an otherwise perfect setting is the house rule that requires you to order a complete meal on weekends and at lunchtime; it's not possible to sit idly with a croissant and coffee.

DDL Bistro
Trump Tower,
725 Fifth Ave. (56th & 57th Sts.)
832-1555
Open Mon.-Fri. 11:30 a.m.-4 p.m., Sat. 11:30 a.m.-4:30 p.m., Sun. noon-4 p.m. All major cards.

Ignore the tiers of unaffordable boutiques, the slack-jawed tourists, and the ennui-stricken pianist serenading passers-by in the foyer of this gilt-and-glitz shopping mall. Head for the lower level, where you'll encounter the cozy but pricey DDL Bistro (named for owner Dino De Laurentiis), with comfy redleather banquettes and chairs and marble-topped tables, plus a handsome crew of bow-tie clad waiters standing by to pamper a colorful, Eurochic clientele. The food is appetizing, freshly prepared and bright, with seasonal ingredients: fusilli nourished with juicy ripe tomatoes and basil, assorted antipasti, an excellent salad of roasted goat cheese with polenta, and superbly light gnocchi in a to-mato-and-Gorgonzola sauce. For dessert, gianduja mousse cake is a heavenly mixture of chocolate and hazelnuts. Lunch for two will run a whopping $70 for bistro fare—this is big-spender turf with a vengeance.

Elephant and Castle
183 Prince St. (Sullivan St.)
260-3600
Open Mon.-Thurs. 8 a.m.-midnight, Fri. 8 a.m.-1 a.m., Sat. 10 a.m.-1 a.m., Sun. 10 a.m.-midnight. All major cards.

Trendy SoHo restaurants come in and go out with the wind, but this comfortable spot is always crowded with local artists, actors and svelte uptowners stopping in during their ritual shopping sprees. Ceiling fans, small wooden tables and white-paneled windows add grandmotherly touches of friendly warmth, and the service is efficient and cheery. The interesting menu ranges from day to night choices: for breakfast there's creamy oatmeal with golden raisins and hazelnuts, scrambled eggs with curried sour cream, and crisp Indian bread as well as twenty ome-lettes—goat cheese with fresh and sun-dried

tomatoes is lavishly cheesy. The Elephantbur-ger for a pricey $7.25 is worth the money for this charcoal-grilled beauty that's topped with curried sour cream, bacon, cheddar, tomato, and scallions; more spartan tongues will enjoy the terrific Caesar salad. Desserts are a big draw and tend toward the rich and gooey: towering sundaes like the Kaffee Klatsch or Magnificent Obsession, satiny Indian pudding or dessert crêpes filled with ice cream and hot fudge. Dinner for two with a glass of wine and dessert will cost $30.

Gianni's
South Street Seaport,
15 Fulton St. (Water St.)
608-7300
Open Mon.-Thurs. 11:30 a.m.-11 p.m., Fri.-Sat. noon-midnight, Sun. noon-11 p.m. All major cards.

If you enjoy people-watching, you'll be in spectator's heaven at this teeming sidewalk café where pin-striped Wall Streeters rub elbows with tourists in running shorts. The vaguely northern Italian menu will fill but not thrill you: tangy garlic bread steeped in a creamy Gorgonzola pesto; an array of seafood salads; overcooked pasta dishes such as fettuc-ine in a bland lobster-cream sauce. Better choices are the snappy fresh-fish entrées, including grilled tuna and swordfish. For dessert, the smooth tiramisu of ladyfingers, mascarpone mousse and amaretto is one of New York's finest examples of this trendy dessert. On Friday and Saturday nights a Gatsby-esque crowd of well-heeled singles shows up for dancing. About $40 per person for dinner, with wine.

Hard Rock Café
221 W. 57th St. (Seventh Ave. & Broadway)
489-6565
Open daily 11:30 a.m.-2:30 a.m. Cards: AE, MC, V.

Only preteens, or adults with a passion for Torquemada's tortures, would come here a second time. Pass beneath the fins of a 1950s vintage Cadillac plastered against the building and you'll enter a rock-and-roll theme park gone mad. Beatles tickets and Elvis memora-bilia on the walls, a guitar-shaped bar, and waitresses "slam dancing" to music played to the screech level of a departing Concord jet are just part of the fun in store after a three-hour wait outdoors. The great surprise is that the food is pretty decent—if your waitress can hear your order—mammoth burgers in sesame buns, Pig Sandwiches made with juicy roast pork, and fresh salads, all to be washed down with a creamy milkshake or float. While you're tripping down memory lane with the Everly Brothers on tape, you can overload on a fudge-laced ice-cream sundae or any of several other rich, gooey desserts. Hopefully it will sweeten your mood before your teenager hits you up for a sweatshirt or other expensive must-have in the conveniently located gift shop near the exit.

Jim McMullen
1341 Third Ave. (76th & 77th Sts.)
861-4700
Open daily 11:30 a.m.-1:30 a.m. Cards: AE.

Few people are indifferent to this quintessential Upper East Side boîte where the cashmere-and-pearl-set shows up nightly. The atmosphere is modish but intimate, with pretty lace curtains, wood paneling, flowers on each table, and an impeccably groomed crowd that comes for the preppy singles scene that has always marked this cliquish establishment. As for the cuisine, it's as whitewashed and limp as the surroundings—omelets, good sandwiches, overdone seafood dishes, tender but tasteless calf's liver and a lovely chicken pot pie. Come here when you're in the mood for a country-club-style dinner. About $15 per person for lunch, with a glass of wine.

Kleine Konditorei
234 E. 86th St. (Second & Third Aves.)
737-7130
Open Sun.-Thurs. 10 a.m.-midnight, Fri.-Sat. 10 a.m.-1 a.m. Cards: AE, DC.

Once an Eastern European enclave, this area of New York known as Yorkville has lost nearly all of its ethnic trappings. Happily, Kleine is still going strong as a dear relic of Germanic gusto. Beef roulade, schnitzel, Sauerbraten, goulash, herring, and other rich specialties saturated in butter and heavy cream sauces will drive you willingly back to salad and yogurt for a few days. A better time to visit is during afternoon coffee break, when you can indulge your Teutonic fancy in such toothsome confections as chocolate-and-whipped-cream Black Forest cake, Gulgelhupf

(an Austrian version of Kugelhopf: cake flavored with currants and brandy and strewn with almonds), marzipan-cherry cake, Sachertorte, apple strudel and cups of marvelous Viennese coffee. A complete dinner for two costs less than $40.

O'Neal's Baloon
48 W. 63rd St. (Columbus Ave.)
581-3770
Open daily 7 a.m.-midnight. All major cards.

The fatty hamburgers and soggy French fries here somehow continue to draw diners. Perhaps it's O'Neal's convenient location across the street from Lincoln Center. The before- and after-curtain scene here is rowdy, animated and a great place to people-watch. Some excellent beers on tap; they'll mellow the blow delivered to your appetite by weak salads and club sandwiches, gravy-soaked chicken pot pies and lasagne that pleads a new recipe. A simple dinner for two with beer will run $25.

Penguin Café
581 Hudson St. (Bank St.)
627-7277
Open Mon.-Thurs. 8 a.m.-2 a.m., Fri.-Sat. 8 a.m.-4 a.m., Sunday noon-2 a.m.

On the spot of the original Trattoria da Alfredo, this funky, nostalgic café hangout serves up good omelets, burgers and delicious grilled chickens as well as a few more ambitious items and some standout desserts. Wines, beers, teas and coffees keep the West Villagers happy at all hours during the week, and they're joined by friends and out-of-towners on weekends. A pleasant spot, but the wrong choice for a weekend brunch unless you want an omelet or a true lunch. Don't miss the daily quote (or the penguin) in the window. About $20 for two.

Popover Café
551 Amsterdam Ave. (87th St.)
595-8555
Open Mon.-Fri. 8:30 a.m.-11 p.m., Sat. 10 a.m.-11 p.m., Sun. 10 a.m.-10 p.m. Cards: AE.

Don't let the Salvation Army decor and health-food trappings fool you. This Upper West Side eatery serves truck-stop breakfasts and luscious overstuffed sandwiches. Start your meal by noshing on a popover—a gigantic golden-crusted balloon made of eggs and flour. The extensive breakfast offerings include puffy omelets filled with fresh mushrooms, Cheddar, horseradish and other tasty tidbits; "cappuccino eggs," steamed under the cappuccino jet to clouds of yellow fluff; and perfectly made cheese grits. At other times of the day you can join all the hungry young actors and dancers who frequent the place for hefty eight-ounce burgers made of beef and veal, mammoth main-dish salads and tasty combination sandwiches. There is a good range of coffees and herbal teas for sipping, but someone in the kitchen should learn how to make an espresso that doesn't taste like dishwater. About $12 per person for lunch, with beer.

SoHo Kitchen and Bar
103 Greene St. (Prince & Spring Sts.)
925-1866
Open Mon.-Thurs. 11:30 a.m.-9:45 p.m., Fri.-Sat. 11:30 a.m.-4 a.m., Sun. until 10 p.m. Cards: AE, V, MC.

This large, multilevel restaurant with its rambling 120-foot bar boasts a wealth of both space and culinary talent. Dramatic lighting, attention-getting artwork, a black-as-midnight ceiling and rock music loud enough to shatter cement are a few of the more dubious charms of SoHo Kitchen. Just shrug them off and concentrate instead on the food: crackling-crisp french fries, chicken wings, ho-hum pastas and savory pizzas generously garnished with sausage, sun-dried tomatoes and cheese. Along with these snacks comes one of the most inspired wine selections in New York: over 110 different selections (including fourteen Champagnes) are available daily by the glass for sipping and comparative tasting among the many budding young oenophiles who frequent this notable SoHo place. After 10:30 p.m. there is a 25-percent discount on all Champagnes. About $20 per person for a light supper with wine.

Spring Street Natural
62 Spring St. (Lafayette St.)
966-0290
Open daily 11:30 a.m.-2 a.m. All major cards.

They said it couldn't be done, but here, in the gritty concrete jungle of Manhattan, an organic vegetarian nirvana has succeeded. The eclectic menu is extensive, creative and fairly priced. Soups are thick and delicious; salads are large and full of fresh vegetables; and sandwiches are big enough for any ravenous yoga teacher. The Asian-influenced vegetables and brown-rice dishes are less-enlightened. A spacious, wood-paneled interior is pleasant, and on warm days you can sit outside.

Success La Côte Basque
1032 Lexington Ave. (73rd & 74th Sts.)
535-3311
Open daily 7:30 a.m.-6 p.m., Sun. in summer 7:30 a.m.-3 p.m. Cards: AE, DC.

Superb French pastries and a pleasant, countrified ambience make this Lexington Avenue café an inviting spot at any time of day. For breakfast, there are wonderfully flaky croissants, ethereal Danish pastries and bitter French coffee. The luncheon menu offers a good selection of pâtés, salads, soups and quiches. The chocolate ganache cake (filled with dark-chocolate cream) and coupe Swan Lake (a frothy confection of meringue, ice cream and fresh fruit) will revive the spirits of even the most bone-weary uptown shopper. About $12 per person for lunch with dessert.

West Side Storey
700 Columbus Ave. (95th St.)
749-1900
Open Mon.-Sat. 7 a.m.-11 p.m., Sun. 8 a.m.-11 p.m. No cards.

Depending upon who's cooking the food on a particular day at this inviting neighborhood restaurant, it will be flavored with an American, Thai or French character, but in all cases the results are superb. Situated on the trendy Upper West Side, this neighborhood eatery offers interesting food, efficient service and a relaxed atmosphere for both families and the friendly neighborhood yuppies. Try to arrive before 8 p.m. unless you don't mind waiting for up to an hour in line. Saffron chicken broth punctuated with smoked chicken and tortellini is a good way to begin a meal. For entrées, try spicy chicken gai yang with a potent Thai hot sauce, crispy whole sea bass with black-bean sauce or excellent homemade raviolis; also, don't miss the interesting salads and vegetarian dishes. A lovely dinner in a cordial setting will run about $45 for two, with wine and espresso.

DELIS

Carnegie Delicatessen
854 Seventh Ave. (54th & 55th Sts.)
757-2245
Open daily 6:30 a.m.-3:30 a.m. No cards.

Ever since Woody Allen filmed *Broadway Danny Rose* in this hallowed New York landmark just off the theater district, the question running through every serious nosher's mind has been, "But is the pastrami still lean?" We're happy to report that it is—and the corned beef is still a fine specimen of cured meat. Despite its wisecracking waiters, cramped tables and cigar smoke, everyone still loves the place, even if the overstuffed sandwiches are overpriced and the chicken in a pot lacks some of its former luster. A deli lunch will cost between $10 and $12 per person.

Second Avenue Deli
156 Second Ave. (10th St.)
677-0606
Open daily 8 a.m.-11:30 p.m. No cards.

Got a craving for chicken in a pot, or the most mouthwatering stuffed cabbage this side of Moscow? Just head over to the East Village (once called the Lower East Side), where you'll find New York's best kosher deli. Owner Abe Lebewohl has perfectly captured the frantic hustle and bustle of a turn-of-the-century eatery with delicious kosher food; the nostalgic atmosphere comes complete with cramped booths and pickles at every table, and motherly waitresses ordering you to finish every spoonful of the divine chicken-and-matzo-ball soup. There are also zesty mush-room-and-barley soup, kasha, kishka (stuffed beef intestine), kugel (noodle pudding), silky-smooth chopped liver and cholent (a casserole of beef, potatoes, beans and barley). Each year at Passover Abe sells more than 3,000 pieces of his excellent gefilte fish. If you ask him for the recipe, he'll hold you spellbound as he passionately discourses on whether to use whitefish or carp. It doesn't matter to us; just bring it over. About $25 for a sumptuous deli feast for two.

Stage Deli
834 Seventh Ave. (54th St.)
245-7850
Open daily 6 a.m.-2 a.m. No cards.

Some cities are ravaged by partisan guerilla wars; New York has deli wars. It's a bizarre noshers' version of West Side Story: Carnegie versus the Stage. Each accuses the other of atrocities such as steaming its corned beef with water from—gasp!—New Jersey. But really, who cares? What's important is that the Stage and Carnegie have entirely different atmospheres. The Stage is more modern and less Brooklyn; it has window seats where you can watch people go by on Seventh Avenue, and a full bar. Both delis are expensive. The Stage's food is a matter of taste: its piles of lean, juicy corned beef between two pieces of doughy rye bread give the sandwich—and New York delis—a good name. The pastrami, however, while ample and tasty, loses to Carnegie by a nose. But surely this is not the definitive argument; we love them both.

FAST FOOD

The Big Kitchen
World Trade Center, Concourse Level
938-1153
Open Mon.-Fri. 7 a.m.-7 p.m., Sat. 9 a.m.-5 p.m. All major cards.

When this complex of restaurants first opened on the concourse level of the Twin Towers, it was hailed as a culinary triumph: eight marvelous stands serving fairly priced, wholesome and tasty food in a relaxed setting. Wall Streeters were bullish about it, tourists loved it and soon even uptowners who rarely ventured below 59th Street were trekking down to the Big Kitchen for lunch. Sadly, the quality of the food has plummeted in the last couple of years. While it is still possible to find a few decent items among the many disasters, you have to sift through soggy tacos, woebegone barbecued chicken, fatty ribs, mediocre deli sandwiches and greasy Chinese cooking.

Dosanko
135 E. 45th St. (Third & Lexington Aves.)
697-2967
Mon.-Fri. 11 a.m.-9:30 p.m., Sat.-Sun. noon-8 p.m. No cards.

Every workday at lunchtime scores of New Yorkers graze happily on gyozas (juicy pork or shrimp dumplings) at one of the many Dosanko branches scattered around midtown. These popular Japanese fast-food establishments are strictly no-frills in the design department, with garish Formica tables and too-bright lighting, but a tidbit from Dosanko's kitchen can be as delicate as a cherry blossom. Besides the light and tasty dumplings, there is superb fried chicken for less than $5 a basket, great noodle dishes, and aromatic soups laden with bright green vegetables and bits of meat. You can sip Japanese wines or beers, tea or coffee with your meal. Takeout service available at several locations. Check the telephone book for the nearest location. About $12 per couple for lunch or dinner.

ICE CREAM

Dimitri's Café
156 Spring St. (W. Broadway)
226-9157
Open daily 8 a.m.-9 p.m. No cards.

This tiny gray-and-white café is a popular spot for SoHo shoppers who come to revive their flagging spirits with a calorie-loaded treat. Ben & Jerry's ice cream from Vermont is the main attraction here, and you can choose from such flavors as Cherry Garcia (chocolate with cherries), Heath Bar Crunch or Oreo-Mint. There are good espressos and some worthy pastries on hand as well, such as densely nutty pecan pie or feather-light cheesecake.

Le Glacier
1022A Madison Ave. (78th & 79th Sts.)
772-3870
Open Mon.-Sat. 11 a.m.-7 p.m., Sun. noon-7 p.m. No cards.

A wide assortment of frozen products are on hand at this inviting spot to appease every kind of sweet tooth from the dieter's to the splurger's. Choose from low-calorie glacés made of fresh fruit, bean-curd-based Tofutti and sixteen flavors of Sedutto's ice cream, plus outstanding frozen yogurt that comes in vanilla, raspberry, peach and strawberry. Join the school kids and Madison Avenue shoppers who flock here for some delightfully sweet licks.

Minter's Ice Cream Kitchen
South Street Seaport, Pier 17
608-2037
Open Sun.-Thurs. 10 a.m.-midnight, Fri.-Sat. 10 a.m.-1:30 a.m. No cards.

After an endless journey through the maze of pricey tourist shops at South Street Seaport, you deserve something luscious and creamy, even if the calories will destroy a month of diet lunches. Walk up to the third level of Pier 17 and follow the sweet smell of vanilla, chocolate and coffee—it should lead you directly to Minter's. This attractive ice cream stand offers super-rich homemade ice cream made directly on the premises in sixteen tantalizing flavors, including Kahlúa-and-cream and triple chocolate. There's a wide range of goodies on hand for mixing into your cone—brownies, crumbled Heath Bars, fresh strawberries—as well as enormous crispy waffles filled with ice cream, then dipped in chocolate and nuts for a double dose of decadence.

Old-Fashioned Mr. Jennings
12 W. 55th St. (Fifth & Sixth Aves.)
582-2238
Open Mon.-Sat. 11 a.m.-7 p.m. Cards: AE

This is a deliciously prim ice-cream parlor that has been frequented for years by women of an elderly stature (the blue-rinse set). It serves the same purpose the neighborhood saloon does for their husbands. Mr. Jennings himself always hovers around like a good bartender, to lend a sympathetic ear and help settle such important questions as whether to choose the chicken salad or stick with the tuna on whole-wheat, and doesn't this nasty weather call for a butterscotch sundae? Most of Mr. Jennings's customers do have a sweet tooth, and he obliges them with a roster of lovely old-fashioned ice cream treats such as extra-thick shakes, sodas, banana splits topped with hand-whipped cream and creamy hot fudge, or fruits in season. Freshly made salads and sandwiches round out the menu.

Peppermint Park
1225 First Ave. (66th St.)
288-5054
Open Mon.-Thurs. 10 a.m.-midnight, Fri. 10 a.m.-1 a.m., Sat. 10 a.m.-2 a.m., Sun. 11 a.m.-midnight. Cards: AE, DC.

Homemade ice cream and chocolates, along with sandwiches, crêpes and salads form the menu at this attractive, modern ice-cream parlor decked out in crisp peppermint green. The ice cream comes in 50 flavors—big as far as the imagination goes, but definitely on the mediocre side as far as quality and taste are concerned. Forget about such abominations as strawberry cheese or Dutch-apple ice cream. Other locations on Fifth Avenue in the Tishman Building, and on 666 Fifth Street, in Penn Station.

Sant Ambroeus
1000 Madison Ave. (77th & 78th Sts.)
570-2211
Open Mon.-Sat. 9:30 a.m.-10:30 p.m., Sun. 10:30 a.m.-6 p.m. Cards: AE, DC.

Everything at this New York branch of a famed Milanese pastry shop is precious, ex-pensive and ostentatiously baroque—from the ornate dining room (see Restaurants chapter, page 146) to the jewel-like pastries, beribboned and decorated like June brides, to the well-heeled European clientele hobnobbing at the espresso bar over crusty panini sandwiches of ham and mozzarella. If you're dressed for all this pretense, have a seat at a table; if not, take out a serving of truly superb gelato in such magnificent flavors as hazelnut, zabaglione or cappuccino. On the lighter side, there are sparkling fresh fruit sorbets that vary according to the season. The price for a fashionably petite serving of gelato or sorbet is $1.50.

Serendipity 3
225 E. 60th St. (Second & Third Aves.)
838-3531
Open Mon.-Thurs. 11:30 a.m.-12:30 p.m., Fri. 11:30 a.m.-1:30 a.m., Sat. 11:30 a.m.-2 a.m., Sun. 11:30 a.m.-midnight. All major cards.

As its name implies, Serendipity is a charming hodgepodge—expensive toy boutique, ice-cream parlor, casual restaurant and, for more than two decades, New York's favorite dessert hangout after the movies. The young waiters are scrubbed fresh, all bright eyes and smiles, and the white-on-white decor with its marble tables and wire chairs add to the sensation that you've just entered a Victorian sugarplum fantasy. As for the menu, there are better-than-average burgers, omelets and salads, but most regulars come here for the colossal sundaes and banana splits made with excellent ice cream and butter-rich toppings, especially the incomparable hot-fudge sauce. There are some great iced drinks ("frozen hot chocolate," frozen espresso), plus a few good pastries for the inevitable heretic.

LATE NIGHT

Brasserie
100 E. 53rd St. (Park & Lexington Aves.)
751-4840
Open daily 24 hours. All major cards.

Busy as an airport lounge during Christmas, the Brasserie is filled into the dead of night with show-biz types, middle-aged night owls and all breeds of loyal customers who think it's normal to eat slabs of steak and platefuls of fries at 5 in the morning. The 24-hour menu is slightly French in the simple tradition of omelets, quiches, grilled meats, onion soup gratinée, crisp Monte Cristo sandwiches and a decent choucroute that is hearty enough to chase away the most persistent midnight hunger pangs. Another plus is that this place never closes. About $12 per person for a light meal without wine.

Corner Bistro

331 W. 4th St. (Jane St.)
242-9502
*Open Mon.-Sat. 11:30 a.m.-4 a.m., Sun. noon-4
a.m. No cards.*

Your basic bar/burger joint with a well-de-
served reputation, the Corner Bistro is always
crowded with a mix of people who live or work
in the West Village. The vintage jukebox is
well-stocked, the tables scarred with graffiti,
and nobody minds squeezing into the hard
wooden booths for beer, Irish coffee and
macho bowls of chili or "bistro burgers" made
with good beef, cheese, bacon, onion, lettuce
and tomato wedged between the two halves
of a toasted bun. About $7 per person.

Empire Diner

210 Tenth Ave. (22nd St.)
243-2736
Open daily 24 hours. Cards: AE.

At 4 a.m. on a Friday or Saturday night, this
art deco railway car radiates with megavolt
energy as the city's most rabid club-hoppers
stop by for breakfast. The menu offers glorified diner dishes—omelets, club sandwiches,
chili, burgers, brownies, hot fudge sundaes.
Much of the food is only passable and
wouldn't cut the mustard in a regular restaurant. But lots of leggy models love the place;
some stockbroker types think it's wild; and for
a saving grace, Miss Bea plays a mean piano
from 11 a.m. to 3 p.m. (other pianists entertain during dinner and until 4 a.m. on Saturday nights). About $10 per person.

Florent

69 Gansevoort St. (Greenwich &
Washington Sts.)
989-5779
Open daily 24 hours. No cards.

Smack in the middle of the city's meat-
packing district, this place was a ramshackle
diner until an adventuresome Frenchman
rashly decided to convert it into a bistro.
Thank goodness for his astute idea, for ever
since opening day, Florent has been good
news for New Yorkers of all incomes, ages and
tastes. The noise level is deafening, the small
wooden tables are placed too close together
and you'll probably end up squashed on a
stool at the long Formica counter—but it's all
great fun. Between 3 a.m. and 5 a.m., the

crowd is a mix of modishly dressed club crawl-
ers and Hulk-sized butchers wearing aprons.
There are three different menus for breakfast,
lunch and dinner. The food is essentially
Franco-diner cuisine: simple, hearty choices
such as grilled chicken, boudin, steak and
pommes frites, escargot in garlic sauce,
steamed mussels in wine. At 2:30 a.m., breakfast begins, and there's a good assortment of
eggs, omelets, breakfast steaks, burgers and
wonderfully light pancakes ($3.50 for a gen-
erous stack) that are close to crêpes in texture.
You can bring your toddler here for dinner,
or your date for late night supper; either way,
it's good idea to make reservations. About
$40 per couple for dinner, $12 for breakfast.

Kiev

117 Second Ave. (7th St.)
674-4040
Open daily 24 hours. No cards.

Where else would you satisfy a craving for
stuffed cabbage at 5 a.m. but Kiev? This fam-
ily-operated, East European coffee shop attracts a large local following who come for the
blintzes, soft potato dumplings called pirogi,
mushroom-barley soup, and delicious slabs of
french toast made with challah bread. The
portions are generous and prices are low,
which makes this place a popular student
hangout. About $14 for two.

Lox Around the Clock

676 Ave. of the Americas (21st St.)
691-3535
*Open Sun.-Wed. 7 a.m.-4 a.m., Thurs.-Sat. open
24 hours. Cards: AE.*

This punk deli has a decor that fashion
pundits call "demolition chic," and which
suggests homage to a junkyard. Conveniently
located near some of the major clubs—Limelight, Private Eyes and the Palladium—LATC
boasts a 35-foot bar, a video jukebox with
seven monitors and a 24-hour menu that
includes such basic Jewish standards as stuffed
cabbage, bagels, blintzes and, of course, lox
(and it's good lox!). For dinner, there are
fresh-fish plates and a few boring chicken
dishes, which will make you wish you had
ordered the chopped liver instead. About $14
per person, with a glass of wine.

Market Diner
572 Eleventh Ave. (43rd St.)
244-6033
Open daily 24 hours. Cards: MC, V.

This classic diner, decorated in Formica and aluminum, is first on the list of good, cheap eating for taxi drivers, police officers, truck drivers and anyone in the mood for old-fashioned home cooking. The robust menu includes a breakfast of ham and eggs with a stack of pancakes, and Yankee pot roast, chicken pot pie and meatloaf for dinner. If that's not enough, the parking is free, something as rare in New York as the $10-per-person tab you'll pay here for dinner.

103 Second Avenue
103 Second Ave. (6th St.)
533-0769
Open daily 24 hours. No cards.

At about 3 a.m. on any given morning, this bright and cheerful East Village spot is hot with fashion-industry types, clubgoers, musicians and various other night owls in rakish attendance. The jukebox is tremendous; the dress is outlandish; and on weekends there's a long wait for a seat at one of the butcher-block tables. All this results in a bright, friendly atmosphere, and the service is good, to boot. The menu offers round-the-clock basics, including sandwiches, burgers, omelets, vegetarian casseroles and an assortment of decent pies and cakes. The daily dinner specials usually include some zingy Mexican platters, such as carne asada or cheese-crisp tacos. About $15 per person, for dinner with wine or beer.

Restaurant
63 Carmine St. (Seventh Ave. South)
675-3312
Open Sun.-Thurs. noon-midnight, Fri.-Sat. noon-1 a.m. Closed Sun. in summer. Cards: AE.

Restaurant is a devastatingly "in" place that deliberately has no sign outside—the idea is that either you know, or you shouldn't know. This place is fashion-victim prison: designers, models, assorted artists, decorators and a few stray yuppies. The walls are painted with multicolored maps of the world, and the ceiling is a constellation of stars. Restaurant, of course, is at the apex of it. The food consists of cliché Californian-cuisine specialties: calamari with green tomatillo sauce, grilled tuna with mango, shrimp with artichoke, salmon sashimi. But everything is fresh and made with the proper light touch, so nobody's hourglass figure will be shattered. The kitchen closes at 12:30 a.m. About $30 per person, for dinner with wine.

Silver Star Restaurant
1238 Second Ave. (65th St.)
249-4250
Open daily 24 hours. All major cards.

More than just another Greek coffee shop, the Silver Star is well-known in the neighborhood to eagle-eyed bargain-hunters who drop in regularly for tasty, fresh seafood at moderate prices. Conveniently located near the major first-run movie houses on the East Side, the decor is vaguely nautical, and there's an enclosed outdoor area that's almost always full. The food ranges from such Greek specialties as pastitsio and moussaka to live lobsters, soft-shell crabs and a fish of the day. In addition, there are burgers, sandwiches, omelets, grilled steaks and chops, salads and most other basic food groups available on the menu. The full bar includes all the basics, as well as ouzo and retsina. If you must order dessert, go for the fruit salad instead of all those elaborate cakes and pastries that taste like styrofoam topped with artificial cream. About $11 per person for dinner.

Texarkana
64 W. 10th St. (Sixth Ave.)
254-5800
Open daily 6 p.m.-midnight. All major cards.

A few years ago, this West Village spot was hotter than a chili pepper and well-respected among food mavens for its snappy Creole and Cajun cookery. Today, the heat has dimmed to a dull glow as the kitchen suffers from a midlife crisis and the service gets even slower, if that's possible. It's best to come here late at night when the mood is more intimate and friendly people mill around the bar. For food, charred barbecued pork, dirty rice, blackened redfish, fried chicken, pickled shrimp, gumbo and a variety of Southern specialties are available. The walls are a light salmon color, interspersed with Western artifacts. The crowd likes to dress in the latest Calvin Klein, and the tab for this gussied-up roadhouse fare is heftier than a steer ready for market. About $30 per person.

MEXICAN

Arriba Arriba
762 Ninth Ave. (51st St.)
489-0810
Open daily noon-midnight. All major cards.

Many New Yorkers simply aren't used to Mexican food. To some, South of the Border means New Jersey. Arriba Arriba offers a new definition. Don't miss the delicious chicken with a rich, chocolatey mole sauce, or the greaseless tacos and savory enchiladas. The decor is simple and the work of local artists is featured on the walls. The excellent margaritas come in three sizes: the large "papa" is discipline enough but the enormous "mama" will ground you for a weekend. But you'll be back soon enough with $15 to spend on dinner and drinks. Arriba Arriba also has a small take-out restaurant on the Upper West Side, at 440 Amsterdam Avenue at 81st Street (580-8206).

Benny's Burritos
113 Greenwich Ave. (51st St.)
633-9210
Open Mon.-Thurs. 11:30 a.m.-midnight. Fri. 11:30 a.m.-1 a.m., Sat.-Sun. 11 a.m.-midnight.

One of the best things about Benny's Burritos is that, in addition to this quaint Greenwich Village–neighborhood branch, there is another branch in the East Village at Avenue A and 6th Street, for those who don't want to make the trek west. Another positive mark for Benny's is that the food and atmosphere are terrific, a sort of downtown-hip meets black beans, rice and tortillas. It's rightfully crowded at all hours. Enjoy a Mission Burrito, a $4.50 bargain filled with Monterey Jack cheese, guacamole and sour cream with lettuce and tomato on the side—although the kitchen could occasionally offer more guacamole. Benny's Bay Burrito is the identical creation with beef or chicken. The owners boast proudly, "Ours are bigger than yours." A good variety of Mexican beers is also available at a reasonable $2.50 a bottle. Two people can float out for about $20, for a satisfying dinner and a couple of Chihuahuas.

Cantina
221 Columbus Ave. (70th St.)
873-2606
Open daily 11:30 a.m.-1 a.m. Cards: AE, MC, V.

Imagine yourself being served Mexican food in a hospital—bland, soggy and precisely what you'll find at the Cantina. In summer, tourists at the sidewalk tables linger over passable nachos and decent margaritas before they resume exploration of the avenue's trendy boutiques. The taco and enchilada combination plates are filling, but mediocre at best. More exotic specialties, such as Mexican-style shrimp and red snapper, arrive cold and overcooked. Around 6 p.m. on weeknights, the bar starts to pulse with yuppies, who come for the friendly atmosphere and efficient service. The portions are enormous and the prices excessive, but Cantina provides one of city's best ringside seats to the Columbus Avenue scene. Dinner for two, with margaritas, is about $45.

Mary Ann's
116 Eighth Ave. (16th St.)
633-0877
500 E. 5th St. (Second Ave.)
475-5939
Open Mon.-Tues. noon-10:30 p.m., Wed.-Thurs. noon-10:45 p.m., Fri.-Sat. noon-11:15 p.m., Sun. noon-10 p.m. No cards.

Anyone who has scoured Manhattan in vain for Mexican food that has even a trace of authenticity can end the search here. Mary Ann's serves what is arguably the city's best Mexican food, and at better-than-reasonable prices; even Los Angelenos will be impressed. A big basket of homemade tortilla chips and tangy salsa arrives immediately when you sit down. Then comes the real eating, and what wonderful eating it is! In the true test of a Mexican restaurant, Mary Ann's tacos are not made out of the tasteless prefabricated shells served elsewhere in New York. Try the Azteca, a combination of a tender white-meat-chicken enchilada in a green sauce with a cheese chile relleno plus a soft taco stuffed with thick and tasty guacamole. Also recommended is pollo borracho ("drunken chicken" in Spanish): juicy chicken in a chocolatey mole sauce, with rice and beans. You can't go wrong for $7.95. There's also a wide selection of frosty Mexican beers and good margaritas. Dinner and a couple of beers for two costs $25.

Tortilla Flats
767 Washington St. (W. 12th St.)
243-1658
Open Sun.-Fri. noon-midnight, Fri.-Sat. noon-1 a.m. No cards.

The tabloid headline printed on each menu is the first clue to expect the unexpected: ELVIS IS ALIVE, it screams. If he were, he would probably hang out at this raucous West Village haunt of artists, clubgoers and locals. The King would love the tacky Christmas decorations and the old Mexican movie posters that dominate the decor. Elvis would command one of the coveted outside tables and dig into a well-prepared plate of chicken enchiladas with a tangy green sauce, carnitas burritos in a spicy red sauce or beef tacos with black beans and rice. He would marvel at the vat of margaritas atop the bar; the drinks are delivered in passable form by the glass or the pitcher, but he'd probably do the hip thing and order a satisfying Mexican beer like Bohemia. Sometimes, when the waitress engages an eerie yellow strobe light, Elvis might even stand up and do his famed gyrations to the jukebox sound of "Boogie Nights." Exhausted, he'd toss down $30 for two to cover dinner and beers, and stagger home to the Heartbreak Hotel.

PIZZA

American Pie
434 Amsterdam Ave. (81st St.)
877-6740
Open Mon.-Thurs. 5 p.m.-10:30 p.m, Fri. 5 p.m.-midnight, Sat. noon-midnight, Sun. noon-10:30 p.m. Cards: AE.

A couple of years ago, the Mantone family was contentedly serving zesty stuffed pizzas from a humble West Side take-out shop. Now they've moved and revamped their place into a postmodernist *nuova pizzeria* that's all glitter and no taste. Ignore, if you can, the jello-colored decor and uncomfortable plastic banquettes and take in deep draughts of the tomato-and-cheese-filled aromas that announce there's still good fare to be found among these precious environs. Plump calzones, piping hot lasagne and a stupefying selection of pizzas, made with either whole-wheat or white crusts plus impeccably fresh ingredients, are the main attractions. Pizza fillings range from such tried-and-true favorites as tomato with mozzarella and sausage to such outlandish offerings as Cajun pizza, made with poultry or seafood and hot spices. For more high-calorie fun, there are fudgey banana splits, sundaes, and a batch of nasty-tasting sweet pies for dessert. Prices range from $4.50 for a four-inch individual pie to about $20 for a ten-inch version with "the works" that will feed two.

Famous Ray's Pizza
465 Ave. of the Americas (11th St.)
243-2253
Open Sun.-Thurs. 11 a.m.-2 a.m., Fri.-Sat. 11 a.m.-3 a.m. No cards.

Despite many pretenders to the throne, this is the one, the only, the original Ray's Pizza, and it consistently rates as one of the best pizzerias in the city. Try a hefty slice for $1.50, or indulge in one of Ray's eighteen-inch whoppers that begin at a modest $11.50 for a basic pie.

John's
278 Bleecker St. (Seventh Ave.)
408 E. 64th St.
243-1680
Open Mon.-Sat. 11:30 a.m.-11:30 p.m., Sun. noon-11:30 p.m. No cards.

After more than a half century in the same spot in Greenwich Village, New York's best-loved pizzeria just keeps getting better. Maybe it's the coal-fired oven that deliciously chars the thin crust, the mounds of fragrant fresh garlic that top off every piece, or the first-rate ingredients like crumbly sweet Italian sausage, green peppers, and fresh mushrooms. Most likely, it's the combination of all of those things that makes for a truly excellent rendering of pizza at its basic best. Prices start at $7.25 for a basic fourteen-inch pie.

PizzaPiazza
785 Broadway (10th St.)
505-0977
Open Sun.-Thurs. 11:45 a.m.-11:30 p.m., Fri.-Sat. 11:45 a.m.-12:30 a.m. Cards: AE, MC, V.

This pretty-in-pink-and-green Village restaurant is a popular gathering spot for local businesspeople, neighborhood regulars and weekend shoppers. The food doesn't taste like what Mama used to make, but the place doesn't look like hers either. Soft-sculpture cacti and checked pastel tablecloths give the place a light, modern feeling, and the staff is courteous and efficient. Individual deep-dish pizzas on crispy whole-wheat crust in combinations that range from the bountiful to the outrageous are the attraction here, from the "all-white," with its savory topping of four cheeses and onions, to such rare birds as chicken mexicano, topped with tortilla chips. Burgers, main-dish salads, pastas and soups are also available. The bargain $5.95 luncheon special on weekdays features a choice of a small pizza or pasta, a choice of soup or salad and a beverage. The excellent double-fudge chocolate cake for dessert is a must.

Pizzeria Uno
391 Ave. of the Americas (8th St.)
242-5230
Open Mon.-Thurs. 11:30 a.m.-1 a.m., Fri.-Sat. 11:30 a.m.-2 a.m., Sun. noon-1 a.m. Cards: MC, V.

This marvelous pizzeria offers hefty Chicago-style deep-dish pies in three different sizes. A handsome, young crowd frequents this pretty eatery with its dark-green banquettes, chandeliers and black-and-white tiled floors. The pizzas are baked on a conveyor belt in a three-story oven and arrive at your table steaming with generous pools of melted cheese and tasty toppings. Try the "Uno," with extra cheese, sausage, pepperoni, mushrooms, onions and green peppers. There's sangría by the pitcher to wash it all down, and a nice assortment of beers as well. There's also a worthwhile $3.95 luncheon special on weekdays, which includes an individual pizza, plus soup or salad. Pizzas can be taken out fully or partially baked, or frozen.

Trattoria Pino
981 Third Ave. (58th & 59th Sts.)
759-1220
Open Mon.-Sat. 11 a.m.-11 p.m., Sun. noon-11 p.m. All major cards.

Cozily ensconced near Bloomingdale's and a string of first-run movie theaters, this cheery trattoria serves a good variety of pizzas deliciously charred with the flavor of a genuine wood-burning oven. The setting is standard issue—Tiffany lamps, brick walls and hanging plants—but relaxing, particularly if you ask for a table in the back away from the roar of Third Avenue. In addition to pizzas, there are well-made pasta dishes featuring a choice of six sauces, including perky tomato with eggplant and a redolent seafood sauce. About $20 for two, for a pizza dinner with a glass of wine.

SANDWICHES

Between the Bread
141 E. 56th St. (Lexington & Third Aves.)
888-0449
Open Mon.-Fri. 7:30 a.m.-7 p.m., Sat. 8 a.m.-3 p.m. All major cards.

This self-service eatery offers some of Manhattan's most imaginative and sumptuous sandwiches. Step up confidently to the sparkling glass counter and order a tasty lunch or casual supper. Choose from clunky white bowls overflowing with salads, baskets of irresistible fresh-baked muffins and all good things for sandwich fixings: applewood-smoked chicken, roast lamb with herb butter on black bread, smoked mozzarella and roasted red peppers on Italian bread, plus cheeses and imported hams galore to suit every taste. Desserts are worth every devastating calorie, from dark, luscious brownies to Southern pecan pie. Sandwiches range from $5.20 to $10.20. For more ambitious fare plus elegant ambience, visit Aglio & Olio, 145 W. 55th Street (583-9589); (see "Cafés" section, page 167).

Jackson Hole Burger Shop

232 E. 64th St. (Second & Third Aves.)
371-7187
Open Mon.-Sat. 10:30 a.m.-1:30 a.m., Sun. noon-midnight. No cards.

Remember when it wasn't a social crime to love red meat? This no-frills eatery will bring tears of joy to your eyes with its gutsy, eight-ounce burgers that are as juicy as they are huge. While purists will opt for just a slice of onion on top, you can add your choice of mozzarella, Swiss or blue cheese, along with bacon, ham or even mushrooms for some tasty counterpoint to the excellent quality beef. The french fries are the standard frozen sticks and the onion rings soggy, but you won't walk away unhappy. Two will spend between $12 and $25 for burgers, fries and sodas.

Manganaro's Hero Boy Restaurant

492 Ninth Ave. (38th St.)
947-7325
Open Mon.-Sat. 6:30 a.m.-7:30 p.m. Cards: AE, DC.

Call them heros, subs or grinders, but under any guise these torpedo-sized monsters, over-stuffed with hearty Italian cold cuts, are some of New York's best sandwiches. The environment is somewhat run-down and the roster of hot Italian dishes that fill out the menu is pretty lackluster, but the aroma of imported cheeses, fresh bread and olives is as intoxicating as a summer picnic in Florence. Sandwiches range from individual heros to order-in-advance specialties like the six-foot "champion," which feeds up to 40 hungry people at a single chomp. (See also Manganaros in Restaurants chapter, page 68.)

Mangia

54 W. 56th St. (Fifth & Sixth Aves.)
582-3061
Open Mon.-Fri. 7:30 a.m.-6:30 p.m., Sat. 9 a.m.-5 p.m., closed Sat. in summer. Cards: AE, DC (only with a $50 minimum).

This handsome take-out sandwich shop and coffee bar serves what are arguably the most intriguing and well-prepared sandwiches in the city, along with a cornucopia of excellent breads and pastries. Baskets laden with muffins and changing still-lifes of fruit and vegetables beckon from the large storefront window as the usual lunchtime throng of junior clerks lines up for take-out food. For sandwich fixings, there are more than 60 different cheeses to choose from (including Mangia's own homemade mozzarella), along with tasty hams, salamis, perfectly rare roast beef, roasted chicken, turkey and smoky roasted eggplant with tomato. To accompany these dishes, there are potatoes, pastas, and some colorful vegetable salads which are always tempting and freshly made. Even a high-minded stoic would find the marvelous selection of muffins, intensely rich brownies, pound cakes and crumbly scones irresistible (cleverly positioned as they are, right next to the cash register). Count on spending about $8 per person for lunch. Delivery service available.

Nathan's Famous

1482 Broadway, Times Square (43rd St.)
382-0620
Open Mon.-Thurs. 7 a.m.-2 a.m., Fri.-Sun. 7 a.m.-4 a.m. No cards.

At the turn of the century, long before golden arches and Whoppers became the dominant icons of the fast-food business, Nathan Handwerker was stuffing ground beef into sausage casings at his tiny snack bar on Coney Island, and selling them quicker than you could say "wiener." His customers liked these so-called "Coneys" so much that, in a few years, Nathan's hot dogs had become as much a New York institution as the Brooklyn Dodgers. Happily, the legend survives today at several Nathan's outposts in the metropolitan area. At the sprawling Times Square location, these plump, fragrantly spiced links sell for $1.49 apiece—steep when you consider the original price was a nickel, but still a bargain for these pedigreed all-beef hot dogs. In addition, there are hamburgers, pizza, corn-on-the-cob, chili, fried chicken, seafood, raw clams on the half shell and terrific french fries, as well as domestic beers and soft drinks. Times Square isn't Coney Island, but Coney Island isn't Times Square, either (Nathan would understand). Everything is self-service, with table seating as well as stand-up counters. Meats, sandwiches and, of course, franks can all be taken out.

Nyborg Nelson
Citicorp Center,
153 E. 53rd St. (Third & Lexington Aves.)
223-0700
Open Mon.-Fri. 11:30 a.m.-9 p.m., Sat. noon-7 p.m., Sun. noon-6 p.m. All major cards.

This inviting sandwich and take-out shop excels at Scandinavian delicacies. Choose from smoked fish (herring, salmon, trout), creamy Scandinavian cheeses, dainty open-face sandwiches and a deliciously cured gravlax. Meatlovers will opt for the well-made beef hash or maybe something from the good assortment of hams and cold cuts available. For an afternoon kaffee klatsch, there is a tempting array of Viennese pastries and desserts. Take-out service available. A Scandinavian sandwich and a glass of wine will cost about $8.

TEA ROOMS/PATISSERIES

Les Délices Guy Pascal
939 First Ave. (51st & 52nd Sts.)
1231 Madison Ave.
371-4144
Open Mon.-Fri. 8 a.m.-6 p.m., Sat.-Sun. 9 a.m.-6 p.m.; closed Sun. in summer. Cards: AE, DC.

When Guy Pascal, the former pastry chef and part-owner of La Côte Basque, decided to venture out on his own, he opened this cheery, thimble-sized café and stocked it with some of the most exquisite pastries this side of Provence. The tables are covered with pretty French-country fabric, the waitresses know mousse from crème Chantilly, and the glass cases are artfully arranged with gorgeous cakes, glistening fruit tarts, cups of chocolate mousse and exquisite little cookies. Come in the morning for a breakfast of a fragrant apple turnover, brioche, Danish, pecan roll or almond crescent, with a steaming café au lait. For lunch and a light supper, there are soups, salads, quiches, pâtés and saucissons en croûtes. The justly popular Délices cake is $2.75 for a single serving, and is a splendid construction of layers of almond meringue, chocolate mousse, whipped cream, and mocha-butter cream sprinkled with toasted almonds. About $10 per person, for a light lunch and pastry.

Note that average prices given in this chapter do not include tax (a whopping 8.25 percent in New York) or gratuity. Figure on adding roughly 25 percent for your final bill.

Eclair
141 W. 72nd St.
(Columbus & Amsterdam Aves.)
873-7700
Open daily 8 a.m.-midnight. No cards.

Wander into Eclair any time of the day and you'll find elderly Middle Europeans talking politics over slices of Opera torte and prune-filled Danish. This Upper West Side bakery and restaurant is well-known among diehard dessert lovers for its authentic Austro-Hungarian-style pastries. Steer clear of the obligatory croissants and artificial-tasting pound cake, and order like a regular: Sachertorte with a mound of whipped cream, Black Forest or Grand Marnier cake, chocolate-mousse-filled Princesse torte, and the buttery Danish that comes with assorted fillings. Although Eclair offers a full menu from breakfast to dinner, the desserts have remained the real lure for more than a quarter of a century. About $5 per person, for a confection and a cappuccino.

Helmsley Palace
455 Madison Ave. (50th & 51st Sts.)
888-7000
Tea daily 2 p.m.-4:30 p.m. All major cards.

The beaux-arts grandeur of the Gold Room may not be your cup of tea if you want a simple, unassuming place to relax. This opulent salon, with its ornate arched ceiling, painted friezes, and golden-tufted settees, was once the music room of financier Henry Vuillard, and it is every bit as elegant now as it was in its turn-of-the-century heyday. The tea service here is formal. Individual courses are served in sequence, beginning with an excellent array of Fortnum & Mason teas, followed by so-so sandwiches, scones with cream and fruit preserves and ending with slices of excellent fruitcake and moist choco-late-fudge cake. Tea is also served on Satur-days in the bright and cheery Madison Room. About $18.50 per person.

The Mayfair Lounge
Mayfair Regent Hotel,
Park Ave. & 65th St.
288-0800
Tea daily 3 p.m.-5:30 p.m. All major cards.

With its handsome floral centerpieces, gleaming oval tea tables, sunken court and warm gold-and-burgundy color scheme, the Mayfair Lounge offers its tea service with a grace and elegance unmatched in the city. Seven different varieties of Indian, Chinese and herbal teas are served in delicate china pots, each one covered with a pretty tea cozy. Simple but delicious finger sandwiches are on hand for discreet nibbling, along with feather-light scones served with cream and preserves, ladylike cakes, cookies and assorted ice-cream desserts. This is a charming place to linger all afternoon, over a wonderfully scented brew and cozy conversation. A worthwhile $13 per person.

Palm Court
Plaza Hotel,
Fifth Ave. & 59th St.
759-3000
Tea daily 4 p.m.-6 p.m. All major cards.

An hour into tea at the Palm Court, you begin hoping that Plaza Hotel owner Donald Trump will appear and start telling people to lighten up, the china's paid for. But it is not to be. Potted palms in every corner, green and floral chintz seats, fragile china teacups, plus a piano and violin duet playing waltz tunes—the entire effect is a pompous recreation of a Viennese coffeehouse. An inviting assortment of tea foods are well-prepared and attractively presented: freshly baked scones served with Devonshire cream; open-face sandwiches studded with smoked salmon, pâtés, hams or cold meats; dainty pastries; and ice cream. It's all very enchanting, though a bit too con-trived. About $15 per person.

Pâtisserie Lanciani
271 W. 4th St.
929-0739
Open Sun. & Mon. 9 a.m.-10 p.m., Tues.-Thurs. 9 a.m.-11 p.m., Fri.-Sat. 9 a.m.-midnight. Cards: AE.

Locals line up here early for breakfast crois-sants, pain au chocolat and danish pastries. The pastry cases hold a rapturous array of sweets: velvety chocolate mousse, wafer-thin crusted fruit tarts, nut tortes, fruit-laden pies. About $6 per person.

Rumplemayer's
46 Central Park South (59th St.)
755-5800
Open daily 7 a.m.-12:30 a.m. All major cards.

This marshmallow-fluff tea room decked out in pink may remind you of those saccha-rine-sweet soda fountains in fifties movies where teenagers Annette and Frankie smooched over malts. The decor is rife with fake marble, cute stuffed animals and enor-mous mirrors in which you can ogle yourself dribbling hot-fudge sauce. It's a good place to take children for a treat, for hot chocolate with real whipped cream, and shakes, sodas and sundaes of all kinds. There are also soups, salads and sandwiches. About $14 per person.

Le Salon
Stanhope Hotel,
Fifth Ave. & 81st St.
288-5800
Tea daily 2 p.m.-5:30 p.m. All major cards.

At last, this old doyenne of the horsey set has received a much-needed facelift, and she looks positively charming. The new tea salon is a light and gracefully spacious room with green-and-white striped wallpaper, French impressionist paintings, and small tables cov-ered with Spanish lace tablecloths. Afternoon tea served on lovely Limoges china is, unfor-tunately, a lot more show than substance. The $15-per-person prix-fixe includes a choice of sixteen different teas, bland finger sandwiches, scones with strawberry jam and a variety of fruit tarts and pastries that even a vending machine would reject as insipid. This is the place to come after a shopping frenzy, when you're too exhausted to know what you're eating.

HOTELS

INTRODUCTION

GRACIOUS HOSPITALITY

Renovation, renovation, renovation. That's all we hear and see, and that's what we read on our returned hotel questionnaires. Add to all these renovations a host of top-quality hotel openings in the past few years, and what you come up with is a city with a thoroughly upgraded hotel industry. New York is both a crossroads and a mecca, and its hoteliers are at last delivering, albeit at a price—a higher price than in the past, but one in line with those in the world's other great cities.

Amid all the frenzied activity of never-ending urban renewal projects and the perpetual turmoil of the Big Apple, New York hotels intelligently have adopted the role of serene, welcoming oases in the storm. Well staffed and well maintained, Manhattan lodgings are, in general, more attractive and appealing now than ever before, venerable grandes dames and brash newcomers alike. A European style of personalized attention, including 24-hour concierge service, is the direction for many luxury and first-class hotels. With visitors increasing both in numbers and in sophistication—more conventioneers are flocking to the new Jacob Javits Convention Center, and the ranks of business travelers and cultured tourists from Europe and Asia are swelling—occupancy rates are up, competition is keen and more and more travelers expect to be satisfied.

At the moderate/economy end of the spectrum (admittedly a limited area in New York City), our advice is to select with care, and insist on viewing the accommodations before accepting the room. Also, remember the valuable real-estate adage: what's important are three things—location, location and location. Saving a few dollars may take you away from where you wish to be and also result in higher transportation costs and inconvenience.

The prices listed herein do not include taxes. *Buyer Beware:* taxes add up. New York City has all sorts of room and sales taxes, so you must figure on adding about 16 percent to the prices we cite. One way to beat the high cost of lodging is to explore weekend packages, for which even some of the finest hotels slash prices to fill rooms that are booked by business travelers during the week. These package deals often include such amenities as theater tickets, champagne, dinner, brunch and sight-seeing tours.

SYMBOLS & ABBREVIATIONS

Our subjective reviews of many of New York's noteworthy hotels reflect our opinion of each hotel's quality, charm, appeal, personality, warmth, comfort and value, and are expressed in the ranking system outlined on the following page:

Very luxurious

Luxurious

Very comfortable

Comfortable

Keep in mind that these evaluations are relative and, thus, a place that is luxurious, but which we regard as overly expensive and overrated, might be ranked the same as a delightful and much less expensive "find."

Credit Cards
AE: American Express and/or Optima
DC: Diners Club and/or Carte Blanche
MC: MasterCard
V: VISA

DOWNTOWN
(Below 42nd Street)

 Bedford
118 E. 40th St., 10016
(Lexington & Park Aves.)
697-4800, (800) 221-6881;
Fax 697-1093
An agreeable, European-style hotel in the middle of the garment district, the Bedford is a decent home away from home for buyers and fashion-industry moguls. The 200 large rooms are pleasantly decorated, and equipped with kitchen facilities. A concierge is on hand, in-house laundry service is available and the staff is friendly and helpful—all this plus sensible rates, too.
Singles: $149-$169; doubles: $169-$199; suites: $199-$300. Weekend packages available. All major cards.

 Chelsea Hotel
222 W. 23rd St., 10011
(Seventh & Eighth Aves.)
243-3700; Fax 243-3700 ext. 2171
A stay at the Chelsea is like a pilgrimage to the Poet's Corner at Westminster Abbey—dark, dreary and haunted by the spirits of dearly departed literary and artistic luminaries. Dylan Thomas, Arthur Miller, Brendan Behan, Mark Twain and, lest we forget, Sid Vicious, all hung their hats here at one time or another. Likewise, today's clientele consists mainly of artists, writers and creative souls from the world over. The rooms are comfortable and have recently been supplied with new carpets and some new furniture. What they otherwise lack in decor, they make up in size,

soundproof walls and, in many rooms, woodburning fireplaces and/or kitchens.

Singles: $75-$105; doubles: $85-$135; suites: $165-$210. Cards: AE, MC, V..

Comfort Inn Murray Hill
42 W. 35th St., 10001
(Fifth & Sixth Aves.)
947-0200; No fax

When the Quality International hotel group recently spent $4.5 million refurbishing the premises, they transformed the old Murray Hill Hotel into a nice, European-style lodging with excellent amenities at affordable rates. Close to Jacob Javits Convention Center, the hotel's 115 rooms are decorated in soft pastels and contemporary furnishings, along with color TVs, newly added VCR equipment and air conditioning. Complimentary coffee and danish rolls for breakfast are nice eye-openers. The staff is crackerjack efficient and eager to please.

Singles: $97-$125; doubles: $112-$150. Weekend packages available. All major cards.

Doral Park Avenue Hotel
70 Park Ave., 10016 (38th St.)
687-7050; Fax 808-9029

This gracious hotel with a large percentage of European guests winningly combines big city sophistication with the intimate charm of a small provincial hotel in the French countryside. The renovation of the lobby, meeting rooms and restaurant will be completed before the end of 1990. This augments the cozy decor of the 203 newly redecorated rooms, with their pretty pastel tones and contemporary furnishings (including blow-dryers, shaving mirrors, marble baths and, yes, refrigerators). The handsome dining room and friendly bar are frequented by the well-dressed, privacy-seeking clientele who are the hotel's stock-in-trade. Business services are aptly handled, and complimentary use of the fitness center includes workout clothes.

Singles: $165-$175; doubles: $185-$195; suites: $350-$850. Weekend packages available. All major cards.

Doral Tuscany
120 E. 39th St., 10016
(Lexington & Park Aves.)
686-1600, (800) 847-4078;
Fax 779-7822

In contrast with the impersonal treatment endemic to today's sprawling contemporary hotels, the Doral Tuscany offers the civilized, tranquil charms of a gentler age. One of many small hotels located south of Grand Central Terminal, this establishment has a steadfast, international clientele who are loyal to this "biggest little hotel" in New York. Major refurnishing in 1988 improved the Doral's appearance considerably. The lobby now sports an airy, pastel decor, and the 150 rooms (all equipped with refrigerators) are attractively furnished in a variety of tasteful motifs. A new bar and restaurant complement the many amenities this pleasant hotel has been providing for years.

Singles: $195; doubles: $220; suites: $350-$700. Weekend and honeymoon packages available. All major cards.

Kitano
66 Park Ave., 10016 (38th St.)
685-0022; Fax 532-5615

The gracious welcome of a Japanese host is a unique experience for even a seasoned traveler. A stay at the Kitano is not simply another night at a hotel, but an experience as soothing and restful as a languorous bath. The simple furnishings and lovely, subdued decor in the lobby and 95 rooms create a mood of unruffled calm, which is furthered by the professionalism of the staff. There are two Japanese suites with tatami (straw-matted) sitting rooms, as well as traditional bathtubs and decor. Try Hakubei, the Kitano's Japanese restaurant, for sushi and other authentically prepared specialties. The hotel is, understandably, extremely popular with Japanese tourists, so don't be surprised if you find yourself in the midst of a large group of them!

Singles: $120-$165; doubles: $155-$180; suites: $250-$400. No packages or discount rates. Cards: AE, MC, V.

Madison Towers Hotel

22 E. 38th St., 10016 (Madison Ave.)
685-3700, (800) 225-4340;
Fax 689-0290

In the serene Murray Hill section of town, the Madison Towers offers a charming and unpretentious welcome. This small, intimate hotel combines old-world, European ambience and personal attention with prices as sensible as a sturdy pair of walking shoes. The rooms are cozy and prettily decorated; the coffee shop makes a decent breakfast; and the Whaler Bar boasts a roaring fireplace in winter and a good piano player all year round. There's a health club and a spanking new lobby.

Singles: $115-$150; doubles: $150-$170; suites: $200-$400. Weekend packages available. All major cards.

Morgans

237 Madison Ave., 10016 (38th St.)
686-0300, (800) 334-3408;
Fax 779-8352

One of New York's most willfully eccentric hotels, the former Executive Hotel is, in this incarnation, intimate and dramatically furnished: stereo cassette systems gleam in high-tech splendor in the essentially tiny, cramped rooms. Morgans approaches the hostelry business with humor and boldness: there is no lobby to speak of (let's just say it's extremely minimalist); the bathroom sinks are made of stainless steel; and the trademark Putnam decor used throughout the hotel (19 stories, 154 rooms) is a severe palette of gray, black and white—spare and chic. Who stays at Morgans? A star-studded clientele that includes Cher and Margaux Hemingway and a host of sunglasses-at-night people, along with world-weary international types who find the congenial, casual staff and the offbeat touches a fresh and welcome approach. Staying at Morgans is like having a share in a house in the Hamptons—fashionable and loaded with pretty young things. It's not for everybody (more conservative travelers find it overstyled and a little heavy on attitude), but this place works. The staff will do or get anything—just ask. The Morgan is usually booked solid, so reserve well in advance, unless you're a regular.

Singles: $195; doubles: $215; suites: $275-$380. Weekend packages available. All major cards.

New York Penta Hotel

Seventh Ave. & 33rd St., 10001
(across from Penn. Station)
736-5000, (800) 223-8585;
Fax 502-8798

The Penta is a most welcome artistic artifact, designed by Stanford White in 1904 and immortalized by Glen Miller when it was the Statler—remember "Pennsylvania 6-5 Oh-Oh-Oh"? It's the closest hotel (five blocks) to the Jacob Javits Center, and a recent major refurbishment of the premises has added a worthy trove of facilities geared to the business executive (floors two through six are completely renovated, and the sixth floor boasts a self-contained conference center). The 1,705 rooms are pleasantly decorated in a contemporary motif; the lobby sports a peaches-and-cream complexion; and there are pluses such as a health club, transportation desk and secretarial services. A bit of history, efficiency and a helpful staff—you can't ask for much more, especially in the Penn Station area.

Singles: $125-$175 (a few tiny rooms for $75); doubles: $150-$200; suites: $250-$1000. Weekend packages available. All major cards.

Sheraton Park Avenue

45 Park Ave., 10016 (37th St.)
685-7676; Fax 481-3265

Who would ever expect a Sheraton Hotel to have as much grace and personality as this lovely charmer? A 1987 refurbishment rendered the premises dashing. The rooms have been handsomely furnished in a traditional European decor, and many have fireplaces. You can count on warm, personal service around the clock in this Murray Hill–area. Don't hesitate to inquire about the hotel's own health club.

Singles: $195-$240; doubles: $225-$270; suites: $395-$650. Weekend packages available. All major cards.

Vista Hilton International Hotel

3 World Trade Center, 10048
(West & Liberty Sts.)
938-9100, (800) HILTONS;
Fax 321-2107

You'll find more briefcases in the lobby of the Vista than at Mark Cross, for this is a hotel catering to business executives bound for Wall Street, as well as tourists who enjoy vacationing off the beaten track. Located in the heart of the financial district, the Vista is a contemporary glass-and-chrome monolith that pulsates with efficiency and offers a score of modern amenities geared to fast-track guests. The rooms are comfortable and handsomely furnished, with many affording spectacular views of Lower Manhattan and New York Harbor. As of January, 1990, all are being renovated? There are free guided tours of nearby points of interest, such as SoHo and Chinatown, along with such creature comforts as an executive fitness center equipped with sauna and massage, heated indoor pool, jogging track and tennis and racquetball courts. Conference and meeting rooms are available, and the business service center offers market and secretarial help. Free shuttle bus to midtown. The American Harvest and Greenhouse Restaurant, which features American cuisine, has a steady and satisfied clientele, in addition to the hotel's guests.

Singles: $190-$255; doubles: $215-$280; suites: $525-$1,245. Weekend packages available. All major cards.

MIDTOWN
(42nd Street to 59th Street)

 Algonquin Hotel

59 W. 44th St., 10036
(Fifth & Sixth Aves.)
840-6800; Fax 944-1419

The conversations you'll overhear in the lobby may not be as scintillating as in the days of Dorothy Parker and the Round Table, but the Algonquin is still one of the most popular gathering spots for visiting artists, writers and other creative types. The atmosphere in the handsome lobby, with its traditional furnishings and unhurried, civilized pace, is more that of a private club than a hotel. At lunch, publishers and editors congregate in the dining rooms for cafeteria-quality food at haute-cuisine prices—no one complains, though, because the literary scene is what attracts them, not expectations of a grand meal. Most travelers find the hominess of the conservative, tastefully furnished rooms a welcome relief from the banality of many newer hotels. In the past couple of years, all the rooms and public spaces have been restored and refreshed. At night, the Oak Room turns into a cabaret, featuring a changing roster of some of the most spellbinding lyricists in the country.

Singles: $165-$175; doubles: $175-$195; suites: $330-$350. Weekend packages available. All major cards.

 Beverly Hotel

125 E. 50th St., 10022
(Lexington Ave.)
753-2700, (800) 223-0945;
Fax 753-2700 ext. 48

This genteel, family-owned establishment is a fine choice for travelers who crave serenity and personalized care, thanks in large part to the services of the resident concierge. The clientele is a mixture of business executives, families and, when the General Assembly is in session, U.N. delegates. Most of the attractively furnished rooms (197) are suites or junior suites, both featuring fully equipped kitchenettes. One noticeable flaw: the outside noise level can be outrageous, so ask for a room on one of the upper floors, or turn up the volume on your Walkman. A notably good value across the street from the colossal Waldorf-Astoria hotel.

Singles: $149-$159; doubles: $159-$169;

suites: $180-$450. Weekend packages available. Cards: AE, DC, MC, V.

The Box Tree

250-252 E. 49th St., 10017
(Second Ave.)
758-8320; Fax 308-3899

There's just nothing else like this in Manhattan—a luxurious inn comprised of twelve suites (two are penthouses) in two adjacent three-story townhouses in midtown. The suites (which are smallish L-shaped rooms in the guesthouse tradition) are plush, individually and elaborately decorated in a wonderfully eccentric style. Some are decorated in a French manner, others in English, Egyptian, Chinese or Japanese style. What could be a nightmare is a dream. The Box Tree restaurant offers fine French cuisine, and rooms come with a $100 credit toward dinner!

Rooms: $230-$300. Cards: AE.

Century Paramount

235 W. 46th St., 10036
(Broadway & Eighth Ave.)
764-5500; Fax 354-5237

For relatively low rates and safe, clean lodgings in the theater district, the Century Paramount is a good bet. The 600 rooms are cramped and rather stuffy, and the combination of thin walls and old windows make for a noisy setting at best. However, the rooms are well-maintained, with private baths and color televisions in each unit. A coffee shop is conveniently located adjacent to the lobby.

Singles: $110-$170; doubles: $130-$190. Weekend packages available. Cards: AE, DC, MC, V.

Doral Inn

541 Lexington Ave., 10022 (49th St.)
755-1200, (800) 223-5823;
Fax 319-8344

Some "inn" this is, with 700 rooms! Nevertheless, the Doral is a friendly and comfortable establishment, whose welcoming ambience is matched by attractive accommodations. All of the guest rooms at the Doral have been renovated in a clean, contemporary style. There is a floor of "Executive Suites," plus a new fitness center with squash courts and saunas, and a self-service laundry, coffee shop and restaurant. The staff is proficiently multilingual. One warning: The inn's popular location (across the street from the Waldorf-Astoria Hotel) draws large tour groups, so be prepared for long lines at the registration desk and overcrowded elevators. A 24-hour restaurant, the Equinox Café, is a recent addition supplementing Mormondo's Restaurant and Lounge.

Singles: $130-$150; doubles: $140-$160; suites: $250-$550. Weekend packages available. All major cards.

Dorset

30 W. 54th St., 10019
(Fifth & Sixth Aves.)
247-7300, (800) 227-2348;
Fax 581-0153

Although the staid Dorset may never win any hostelry awards, it does offer agreeable accommodations and a superb location, just off Fifth Avenue by the Museum of Modern Art. Current renovations should add some welcome crispness. The wood-paneled lobby and pastel rooms are somber but quietly elegant, as are many of the mostly middle-aged guests who enjoy the Dorset's serenity and moderate prices. Service is good, and executed with style. A dining room and café/bar are on the premises.

Singles: $155-$215; doubles: $175-$235; suites: $275-$475. Weekend packages available. All major cards.

Drake Swisôtel

440 Park Ave., 10022 (56th St.)
421-0900, (800) 5222-5455;
Fax 371-4190

Today's Drake is an attractive and gracious establishment. The lobby invites you to linger—to luxuriate among its warm woods, brass and pretty etched glass, to dip into the Swisôtel's signature gold fish bowl, brimming with heavenly Swiss chocolates. The lobby's dominant symbol—a huge, four-faced Swiss clock—reminds you that this jewel is part of the first-class Swisôtel chain. Its ample rooms are pleasant and pretty, with European and Asian touches, as well as refrigerators for more practical sensibilities. The sophisticated customers include business executives, jet-setters and entertainers. The Restaurant Lafayette is one of the city's finest dining salons (see Restaurants chapter, page 92). The

Drake's service is impeccable and its staff friendly, courteous and always willing to help; it's a pleasing combination of civility, intimacy and discreet luxury—that's why, in general, you'll need reservations well in advance.

Singles: $210-$240; doubles: $235-$265; suites: $405-$480. Weekend packages available. All major cards.

Edison
228 W. 47th St., 10036
(Broadway & Eighth Ave.)
840-5000, (800) 223-1900;
Fax 719-9541

The sprawling Edison is an accommodation worth considering if you want to stay in the Times Square district. Its 1,000 rooms are large and spotless, with good-size closets, color TVs and quiet air conditioners, and are continually refurbished at the rate of five floors per year. The hotel's café, cocktail lounge and lobby bustle with tourists sporting vinyl suitcases and "I Love the Big Apple" buttons.

Singles: $90-$108; doubles: $100-$120; suites: $130-$150. All major cards.

Elysée
60 E. 54th St., 10022
(Park & Madison Aves.)
753-1066; Fax 980-9278

The Elysée attracts the kind of clientele whose individual members look as if each wrote mystery stories for a living—tweed-suited, slightly eccentric in mannerisms and in search of privacy amid big-city chaos. This small and gracious midtown hotel (98 rooms) offers both serenity and amiable service at reasonable rates. The rooms are comfortable, and their formerly neon hues have recently given way to more soothing colors—though still welcomely individualized, which is a rarity today. The Elysée doesn't ignore modern comforts: the up-to-date marble bathrooms come with hair dryers, and VCRs accompany the new color TVs. The Monkey Bar, which dates from 1936 (the hotel from 1927), contains enough primate imagery to make even Tarzan feel at home. Count this hotel as unique.

Singles: $145-$200; doubles: $160-$215; suites: $275-$500. All major cards.

Essex House
160 Central Park South, 10019
(Sixth & Seventh Aves.)
247-0300; Fax 315-1839

This handsome hotel with a superb Central Park location is undergoing a major face-lift, and will not reopen again until the spring of 1991. On our last visit to the Essex House in its former incarnation, we found the staff to be efficient and friendly, the rooms spacious and well maintained. Despite its large size, the Essex has always run a very tight ship, and our stays here have been comfortable and always first-rate. As part of the renovation, the hotel is adding a health club (naturally); there's already a business center. We can only look forward to rating the new, improved Essex House: the rooms, when renovated, should be able compete with the best. The location already does.

Singles: $190-$250; doubles: $215-$275; suites: $275-$750. Weekend packages available.

Grand Hyatt
Park Ave. at Grand Central, 10017
883-1234; Fax 697-3772

As in the other hotels in the Hyatt chain, the decor is chilly and austere, in a style mistakenly called contemporary—meaning, of course, loads of glass, marble and chrome. Baseball and other sports teams stay here, along with business travelers and tourists who want efficiency, not personality, in their lodgings. The lobby features a splashing waterfall, delicate blooming trees and a jungleland of tropical flora. The rooms are airy and comfortable, but hardly memorable. In all, this is the kind of smoothly run, antiseptic, modern hotel that you forget about the moment you leave, excepting its grand size: 30 stories with 1,407 rooms.

Singles: $190-$245; doubles: $220-$285; suites: $350-$1,900. Weekend packages available. All major cards.

Halloran House
525 Lexington Ave., 10017 (49th St.)
755-4000, (800) 223-0939;
Fax 751-3440

The Halloran House offers a worthy combination of modern amenities and traditional charm. The lobby has the look of a private club, with its handsome leather furniture and oak paneling. The 652 oversize rooms combine old-fashioned spaciousness with such up-to-date features as closet safes, color TVs (with remote controls) and extension telephones in the bathrooms.

Singles: $160-$190; doubles: $175-$205; suites: $350-$575. Weekend packages available. All major cards.

Helmsley Middletowne
148 E. 48th St., 10017
(Lexington & Third Aves.)
755-3000, (800) 221-4982;
Fax 832-0261

Formerly an apartment house, the Helmsley Middletowne still has a residential quality that can be calming to frazzled nerves. The 192 rooms, spread over seventeen floors, were refurbished and redecorated in 1988 and 1989 in the inimitable style of Leona Helmsley, the "Queen"; all come with refrigerators, some with kitchenettes and still others with terraces. Like most New York City hotels with a critical mass, the hotel offers minibus service to major airports, a beauty salon and a friendly, professional staff who will make your stay pleasant, even if you aren't attached to the nearby United Nations. We recommend the Bukhara for dinner (see Restaurants chapter, page 75).

Singles: $135-$175; doubles: $145-$175; suites: $195-$380. Weekend packages available. Cards: AE, DC, MC, V.

Helmsley Palace
455 Madison Ave., 10022 (50th St.)
888-7000, (800) 221-4982;
Fax 888-1074

Texas oil barons stay here. Hollywood types thrive here. Post-debs take tea here. But you'll barely ever find a truly sophisticated American or European traveler here. The Palace is "Queen" Leona Helmsley's supreme indulgence, a gold and marble testimonial to the fact that money cannot buy good taste. The rooms are gilt-edged and lavishly ornate in a style that can only be categorized as Leona baroque. Once the private home of financier Henry Vuillard, the hotel has become, of late, as much of a tourist attraction as that other monument to materialism, Trump Tower.

Still, aside from the bad press coverage and worse decor, a large, experienced and courteous staff is available at all hours, and certainly the location is perfect—should your limo break down, it's an easy walk to midtown boutiques and businesses and Rockefeller Center.

Singles: $230-$295; doubles: $255-$320; suites: $395-$950. Weekend packages available. All major cards.

Helmsley Park Lane
36 Central Park South, 10019
(Fifth & Sixth Aves.)
371-4000, (800) 221-4982;
Fax 319-9065

The aura of new money and impersonality that wafts through the Park Lane seems to attract business guests, globe-trotting travelers and honeymooners who can easily hide out in complete privacy amidst the large-scale glitter and plush. The rooms are pleasantly furnished in a range of old-world styles, all recently refreshed and refurbished; at the top levels, the suites provide sweeping vistas of Central Park below. The experienced, multilingual staff is polite and courteous, and will help you find your way through the marbled-and-chandeliered confusion of the lobby.

Singles: $195-$265; doubles: $215-$285; suites: $350-$990. Weekend packages available. All major cards.

Helmsley Windsor
100 W. 58th St., 10019 (Sixth Ave.)
265-2100, (800) 221-4982;
Fax 315-0371

Recently redecorated, the Helmsley Windsor rooms are thankfully rid of early Leona's signature flowered bedspreads and billowing curtains. Now you get soothing pastel walls and pretty, contemporary decor, along with a staff whose fear of the "Queen" makes them efficient, if not particularly cheery. The location is convenient to Central Park and Carnegie Hall. For the neighborhood, the prices and quality are unusually attractive.

Singles: $135-$145; doubles: $145-$155; suites: $215-$325. Weekend packages available. Cards: AE, DC, MC, V.

Hotel Inter-Continental
111 E. 48th St., 10017
(Park & Lexington Aves.)
755-5900, (800) 332-4246;
Fax 664-0079

If Old World refinement combined with super-efficient amenities is what makes a good hotel, the Inter-Continental deserves a Distinguished Service Award. Typical of the Inter-Continental chain, this establishment prides itself on its genteel luxury and understated elegance, along with service that is keenly professional and friendly. The rooms are comfortable, spacious and furnished in excellent taste. In fact, good taste seems to be the modus operandi for everything here—the recently refurbished Barclay and Terrace restaurants, the attractive lobby and outstanding, professional, personalized service that makes a stay here as refreshing as a week on the Aegean. The long list of services includes a new health club; hair salon; 24-hour concierge and room service; secretarial, translation and interpretation services; wheel chairs and other amenities for the handicapped; a men's clothing shop; and last, but not least, a branch of Caswell-Massey, where you can buy everything from cucumber soap to black-tar chewing gum.

Singles: $215-$255; doubles: $235-$275; suites: $300-$3,000. Weekend packages available. All major cards.

 Lexington
511 Lexington Ave., 10017 (48th St.)
755-4400, (800) 448-4471;
Fax 751-4091

Conveniently located in midtown and staffed by a friendly, multilingual group, this establishment is popular with United Nations visitors and airline crew members. The lobby, restaurant and bar and four floors of rooms (of 27 floors, 800 rooms) were recently renovated. The new decor combines soothing pink and green pastels; the rooms are still small (although many come with refrigerators).

Singles: $145-$180; doubles: $160-$210; suites: $325-$450. All major cards.

 Loews Summit
569 Lexington Ave., 10022 (51st St.)
752-7000; Fax 758-6311

Short on style, long on efficiency—sometimes you can't have everything. The Loews Summit (721 rooms, twenty floors) is one of an increasing number of lodgings geared to corporate executives (the luxury level contains 135 rooms and 49 suites). The decor is what passes for contemporary these days, meaning lots of boring earth tones. But if you can ignore this, you'll enjoy such amenities as mini-refrigerators and extra telephones in the rooms, as well as an up-to-date health club with Nautilus equipment, a Jacuzzi and a sauna. Indeed, a major remodeling of the rooms was completed late in 1989. The staff is dedicated and conscientious in the brisk, impersonal style of everything you'll encounter here. Steer clear of the even-numbered rooms—they face the roaring confusion of the street below.

Singles: $149-$179; doubles: $164-$199; suites: $219-$578. Weekend packages available. All major cards.

 Lombardy
111 E. 56th St., 10022
(Park & Lexington Aves.)
753-8600, (800) 223-5254;
Fax 754-5683

The big plus of the Lombardy is its location—a hop, skip and a jump away from Tiffany's and other midtown shops. The studio-apartment rooms are pleasant, and come equipped with kitchen facilities. The multilingual staff provides friendly and helpful service. All in all, this is an acceptable, if uninspired, place to stay. The lobby (and more) has been renovated recently.

Singles: $150; doubles: $165; suites: $300-$450. No discount rates or packages. All major cards.

 Marriott Marquis
1535 Broadway, 10036 (45th St.)
398-1900; Fax 704-8930

This gargantuan hotel, with 1,877 rooms spread over 50 floors, is impressive, not just because of its size, but because it has everything and runs efficiently. Increasingly the place of choice for colossal dinners and events, the Marriott Marquis is one of those brazen new buildings that have sprung up all over the theater district as part of the recent Times Square gentrification project. The eighth-floor atrium lobby is a chrome and glass amusement park replete with Marriott-theme tropical flora and fauna; taking a ride in one of the tubular glass-enclosed elevators, straight from the set of *High Anxiety*, is one of the many distractions available. The over-size rooms are smart and expensively furnished, with two telephones per room. When you're ready to leave, you can take advantage of the video-checkout service. The View, the hotel's revolving rooftop restaurant and lounge, will remind you of all the other rotating dining rooms you've endured on business trips. Still, if you can't connect with anyone else here, you can always work on yourself. A well-equipped health club has all the goodies—sauna, whirlpool and exercise gear. And this is the only New York hotel with a theater (The Marriott) on the premises; its highly polished productions divert the resident conventioneer crowd.

Singles: $149-$270; doubles: $149-$280; suites: $425-$3,500. Weekend packages available. All major cards.

 ### Milford Plaza
270 W. 45th St., 10036 (Eighth Ave.)
869-3600, (800) 221-2690;
Fax 944-8357

If an action-packed lobby sounds like fun, park your suitcases at the Best Western Milford Plaza. Enjoy the roar in the glitzy lobby, crowded with airline flight crews, senior-citizen groups and gawking tourists. The rooms are cramped and a tad dull, although new bathrooms and carpeting have helped brighten the decor. The staff can be surly at times (who wouldn't be, in all this bedlam?), but the moderate rates and the convenient Times Square location make it more than a bearable choice—you could do much worse. Considering its location, the security system is reliable.

Singles: $95-$135; doubles: $110-$150; suites: $245-$480. Weekend packages available. All major cards.

 ### New York Helmsley
212 E. 42nd St., 10017
(Second & Third Aves.)
490-8900, (800) 221-4982;
Fax 986-4792

It's easy to mistake the Helmsley for an expensive-car dealership. The U-shaped driveway is perpetually clogged with Jaguars; the lobby is all stainless-steel columns and brass; and the staff follows you around as if they were magnetically attached to you. Formerly the New York Harley, this is now the high-level-executive link in the Helmsley chain, and the indomitable "Queen" Leona has made sure that every aspect of this establishment is efficient and modern in a nondescript, contemporary fashion. The rooms are spacious and airy, filled with loads of free toiletries, as well as magnifying mirrors and bathroom scales to assess the latest New York culinary damages. The rooms and suites in this 800-room, 41-story hotel are constantly being upgraded—wallpaper, carpet, upholstering, painting and such being fussed over. The scene in the lobby bar is a mixture of singles on the make and businessmen with happy-face nametags.

Singles: $180-$230; doubles: $205-$255; suites: $390. Weekend packages available. All major cards.

 ### New York Hilton
1335 Ave. of the Americas, 10023
(53rd & 54th Sts.)
586-7000, (800) HILTONS;
Fax 757-7423

With more than 2,121 rooms and amenities galore, this establishment that seems to function as a city unto itself fits into the category of Sprawling, Nondescript Megahotel. The rooms are airy and spacious—particularly in the Executive Towers, where a 24-hour concierge, private lounge, complimentary hors d'oeuvres and continental breakfast are among the perks of the day. Grays, mauves and blues decorate the rooms, and soft furnishings provide a feeling of comfort for guests, the majority of whom are staying on business. You name it and this hotel has it: two floors of nonsmoking rooms, accommodations for handicapped guests, bars, lounges, a disco, a coffee shop, a dining salon, a beauty salon, a multilingual staff, a *Wall Street Journal* business station offering dictation, typewriters and Dow Jones averages—all insure that your stay will be comfortable and that you will be pampered well.

Singles: $175-$235; doubles: $200-$260; suites: $400-$575. Weekend packages available. All major cards.

Novotel

226 W. 52nd St., 10019 (Broadway)
315-0100; Fax 765-5369

Built piggyback-style atop a pre-existing storehouse, the Novotel has a look you know well—glass, brass, chrome and stainless steel, and all the signature antiseptic comforts of a contemporary big-city hotel. The seventh-floor lobby is nearly always thronged with corporate types and well-dressed tourists about to venture out to oh-so-close Broadway and matinees. On the floors above (there are 33 stories with 470 rooms), the guest rooms are spacious and airy, with bright furnishings, and many offer fine views of the Hudson River and cityscape. Other creature comforts include a rather ordinary gift shop, a booth for theater tickets, a brasserie and a wine bar, to indulge your oenological passions with tastings of Champagnes and wines by the glass.

Singles: $129-$179; doubles: $159-$189; suites: $425-$700. Weekend packages available. All major cards.

Omni Berkshire Place

21 E. 52nd St., 10022
(Madison Ave.)
753-5800, (800) THE-OMNI;
Fax 355-7646

What a pleasure to linger in the atrium lobby of the Berkshire, with its stunning floral arrangements, pastel-hued decor and smart contemporary furniture. Conveniently located in midtown near major shops and businesses, this quietly elegant hotel offers personalized and impeccable service combined with an air of subdued luxury that most travelers will find enchanting. The rooms are spacious, airy and comfortable; complimentary coffee and newspapers await all guests, and to work off the excesses of New York dining, the hotel provides an off-premises health club.

Singles: $210-$245; doubles: $235-$270; suites: $300-$1,700. Weekend packages available. Cards: AE, DC, MC, V..

Omni Park Central

870 Seventh Ave., 10019 (56th St.)
247-8000, (800) THE-OMNI;
Fax 484-3374

Another member of the Omni-vorous hotel chain, this is a good place to stay when you don't need much more than a clean and comfortable place to hang your hat. This enormous hotel is filled wall-to-wall with guests at any hour of the day—flight crews, conventioneers and sightseers from the Great Plains. The 1,450 rooms have been recently redecorated; any one of them may put you in mind of your doctor's office. There's a new bar/lounge and a French "bistro" that's about as authentic as the occasional ethnic dish you're served on an airplane.

Singles: $135-$175; doubles: $155-$195; suites: $240-$450. Weekend packages available. All major cards.

Parc Fifty One

Equitable Center,
152 W. 51st St., 10019
(Seventh Ave.)
765-1900, (800) 237-0990;
Fax 541-6604

This European-style, 178-room luxury hotel opened in 1987 as the Grand Bay hotel, on new turf for upscale clientele. A completely new building in a gradually reviving neighborhood of Midtown West, Parc Fifty One boasts some of the city's highest room rates. Someone must pay for the imported marble, eighteenth- and nineteenth-century art and period furnishings, carved panels and doors, art deco details, sleek lacquered furniture and spa-sized marble baths. The rooms and the hotel staff offer all the pampering amenities you can ask for, from complimentary flowers to health-club privileges, even to an unpacking service at no charge. No two rooms are alike. The New York staff lacks the European charm and tradition of truly outstanding hotel service, so this posh addition to the city's lineup hasn't yet earned a distinctive profile among the highest-ranked hotels. Possibly the hotel's new owner, Park Lane Hotels International, will change that.

Singles: $255-$285; doubles: $275-$305; suites: $305-$925. Weekend packages available. All major cards (but only AE or DC to guarantee a reservation).

Parker Meridien
118 W. 56th St., 10019
(Sixth & Seventh Aves.)
245-5000; Fax 247-4698

The lobby of the Parker Meridien will have you convinced you're in Hollywood, with flashy California entertainers and moguls checking in at all hours of the day. A French-owned and -influenced hotel, the phone here is answered with a *bonjour*. This place is geared to the nouveau riche, and the pace here is fast, efficient and noticeably extravagant. That includes everything from the Aubusson tapestries and travertine-marble floors of the foyer to the lavish penthouse health club, where every conceivable form of modern exercise equipment is available—along with a running track, racquetball courts and heated swimming pool for all those bikini-clad starlets. The not-so-large contemporary-style rooms and suites provide excellent views of Central Park, and the hotel is conveniently located near the Fifth Avenue shopping arena. Its once highly touted dining room, the Maurice, closed in the summer of 1990.

Singles: $195-$235; doubles: $220-$260; suites: $275-$1500. Weekend packages available. All major cards.

Peninsula New York
700 Fifth Ave., 10019 (55th St.)
247-2200, (800) 262-9467

After an extensive renovation, the former Gotham Hotel reopened under new ownership and management in 1987 as Hotel Maxim's de Paris. Late in 1988, the hotel was sold to the esteemed Peninsula hotel group of Hong Kong and reopened in 1989 under the group's name and management. You can't get much better than that. Nor can you find a better location in New York City. This dignified, turn-of-the-century landmark with its sweeping entry stairway is now running smoothly as a top-drawer establishment with excellent service and a distinguished clientele. Despite its size—23 stories, 250 rooms—the Peninsula has the feel of a relatively small,

personalized hotel. As in many of the old New York hotels, the rooms are not huge, but some have been combined and are very comfortable. A few even boast views of St. Patrick's Cathedral on Fifth Avenue. All are functionally yet sumptuously furnished, and the new bathrooms shine. The hotel's trilevel, glass-enclosed health club offers an indoor swimming pool, exercise equipment and a full range of pampering for the face and body. The Gotham Lounge is a nice place to meet for drinks. Le Bistro and the upscale Adrienne restaurants are fine.

Singles & doubles: $210-$325, executive suites: $325-$800 (and a presidential suite at $2,500). Weekend packages available. Cards: AE, DC, MC, V.

Pickwick Arms
230 E. 51st St., 10022
(Second & Third Aves.)
355-0300; Fax 755-5029

Savvy budget-minded travelers have patronized the Pickwick Arms for years, with good reason—the prices are rock bottom, the rooms are clean and equipped with air conditioning and cable television, and the location, on a pretty midtown street on the East Side, is quite good. The accommodations range from rooms without baths to large studios with kitchenettes, and you'll find the service efficient and friendly. Daily payment required in advance.

Singles: $42-$55; doubles: $75-$85. Cards: AE, DC, MC, V.

The Plaza
768 Fifth Ave., 10019 (59th St.)
759-3000; Fax 759-3167

New York without The Plaza is as unthinkable as Rogers without Hammerstein. New York's most famous hotel, with an incredible location, is virtually an island unto itself, directly facing Fifth Avenue and 59th Street on one side and Central Park on the other. Though it has lost some of its glamor and status in recent years, that's a story from the past. When super-promoter Donald Trump purchased the hotel (he *had* to have it) for close to $400 million in 1988, he began a total "upgrade" to remake it into "the most luxurious hotel in the world." He put wife Ivana in charge (at the now infamous salary of "$1 per year and all the dresses she can wear"). She's as hard-nosed about business as he is, and the place is beginning to shine. Mrs. Trump has hired and fired staff, always aiming for the best. She's tyrannical about the quality of the restoration work. The public rooms have been restored to their early-twentieth-century splendor; the cobblestones out front have been relaid; the gold-leaf moldings glitter. Even venerable Trader Vic's restaurant has gotten the boot—too tacky for the city's, nay Trump's, most luxurious hotel. Some of the smallish rooms have been combined into suites, and all the rooms have been refurnished with crystal and antiques. Bathrooms have been refitted with black onyx and, on the ceilings, floral murals. Society's hotel has almost made its comeback, and so have its restaurants, the Oak and Edwardian rooms.

Singles: $200-$450; doubles: $250-$485; suites: $850-$5,000. Weekend packages available. All major cards.

Ramada Inn
790 Eighth Ave., 10019 (48th St.)
581-7000, (800) 272-6232;
Fax 976-0291

Ramada Inns are the fast-food chains of the hotel business. Don't expect any sophisticated touches just because this one happens to be located in New York. What you will get is a clean room (they were all refurbished in 1989), a location near the theater district, and, in summer, an outdoor rooftop swimming pool where you can cool off.

Singles: $108-$138; doubles: $120-$150. All major cards.

Ritz Carlton
112 Central Park South, 10019
(Sixth & Seventh Aves.)
757-1900; Fax 757-9620

Imagine a sojourn in an impeccably maintained English-country manor house, and you'll have a good impression of what it's like to stay at the Ritz. Self-assured, clubby and always very chic, this establishment attracts a sophisticated international clientele. The hotel's somewhat tarnished tiara should once again sparkle following a recent change in management and a 1990 renovation. The handsome lobby and rooms are decorated with English antiques graced with touches of

chintz, and pretty seasonal flowers add a fresh, cheery accent. The dignified Jockey Club Bar is well known as one of those elite watering holes where power brokers wheel and deal over Campari-and-sodas. Poised, self-confident and excellently staffed, the Ritz may again become one of the city's hotel jewels.

Singles: $180-$340; doubles: $210-$370; suites: $450-$1150. Weekend packages available. Cards: AE, DC, MC, V.

Royalton
44 W. 44th St., 10036 (Fifth Ave.)
869-4400; Fax 869-8965

Style layered upon style: that's the new and trendy Royalton, and if you like the style, you're in for an exhilarating experience. The architecturally stimulating elongated cavern of a lobby strikes some as stark and cold, but it has become a hangout for beautiful young American and European with-its; everyone looks as if he or she were a model. The lobby restaurant is very good, and the bar, which also serves light meals, is always bustling. The ultramodern decor carries over into the rooms, which, apart from zero views, lack nothing. In architect Philippe Starck's design scheme, all the rooms share the same colors and design elements, from grayish green curtains and rugs to mahogany cabinets to blue-velvet armchairs and gray-and-green bathrooms. (For review of the Royalton's "44," see Restaurants chapter, page 106.)

Singles: $210-$325; doubles: $235-$350; suites: $350-$1,400. All major cards.

St. Moritz on the Park
50 Central Park South, 10019
(Sixth Ave.)
755-5800; Fax 751-2952

The St. Moritz is like the expensive suit you've relegated to the back of your closet: too good to throw away, but hopelessly out of fashion. The small but well-maintained rooms (773 of them) are frumpy in that deadly dull style known to seasoned travelers as "hotel antique." You can count its "Continental" atmosphere as a plus. In warm weather, you can escape to the outdoor café and gaze at Central Park across the street. Off the lobby, wander into the bubble-gum-pink room known as Rumplemeyer's: this vintage ice-cream parlor, replete with stuffed animals, ice cream sodas and little girls in white dresses, will make you weep for the nostalgia of it all (see Quick Bites chapter, page 184).

Singles, doubles & weekend packages: $135-$175; suites: $189-$250. All major cards.

Salisbury
123 W. 57th St., 10019
(Sixth & Seventh Aves.)
246-1300; Fax 977-7752

Cozy and pleasant, the Salisbury is a welcome find, with its friendly ambience, proximity to Carnegie Hall and sensible prices. The 320 rooms are adequately sized, cheery and full of light. The coffee shop off the lobby serves better-than-average food at lower-than-average prices.

Singles: $98-$108; doubles: $108-$118; suites: $175-$310. Weekend packages available. Cards: AE, MC, V.

Sheraton Centre
52nd St. & Seventh Ave., 10019
581-1000, (800) 223-6550;
Fax 262-4410

The Sheraton Centre is one of New York's most popular convention and tourist hotels—a central-casting crew couldn't have filled the lobby with more predictable types. The 1,835 rooms (for guests and their pets) are comfortable and spacious; the top five floors, known as the Sheraton Towers, are tonier and more elegant, with butler service available. The buffet lunch at Caffè Fontana is stupefying in its variety, if not in its quality. Guests have swimming-pool privileges at the sister Sheraton City Squire across the street.

Singles: $170-$210; doubles: $200-$240; suites: $410-$645. Weekend packages available. All major cards.

Sheraton City Squire Hotel
790 Seventh Ave., 10019 (51st St.)
581-3300, (800) 325-3535;
Fax 262-4410

The City Squire has successfully risen from its lowly origins as a motel to become an agreeable place to stay in the theater district. The rooms are well-maintained and pleasant (some have skyline views) and on the premises are a beauty salon/barber shop, restaurant and coffee shop. Minibus service provided to all city airports. For a final worthy touch,

there's a glass-enclosed swimming pool, open year-round.

Singles: $155-$200; doubles: $185-$230; suites: $300-$450. Weekend packages available. All major cards.

Sherry Netherland
781 Fifth Ave., 10022 (59th St.)
355-2800; Fax 319-4306

The hauteur of the Sherry Netherland would give even a Sherpa guide respiratory problems, but if you're seeking the rarified elegance of the past, this is the place to come. The rooms are spacious and handsomely furnished with subtle good taste. Service is always courteous and personalized, for both overnight travelers and the hotel's many permanent residents. The excellent location and civilized, courtly ambience attract a loyal following of people who would never stay anywhere else.

Singles & doubles: $185-$250; suites: $300-$450. Cards: AE.

Shoreham
33 W. 55th St., 10019
(Fifth & Sixth Aves.)
247-6700; No fax

A new marble lobby can't disguise the fact that the Shoreham is for spartan tastes only. Well-situated a few steps away from Fifth Avenue, this establishment offers clean, modern rooms (all equipped with pantry units) at moderate prices. Caution: bring earplugs. The noise level from the street below, combined with the roar of ancient air-conditioning units, will make an insomniac of even the soundest of sleepers.

Singles: $90-$110; doubles: $100-$120; suites: $130-$150. Weekend packages available. All major cards.

United Nations Plaza Hotel
1 U.N. Plaza, 10017 (44th St.)
355-3400; Fax 702-5051

This handsome contemporary hotel built by the noted architect Kevin Roche has been garnering architectural awards ever since it opened more than a decade ago. And no wonder, for the United Nations Plaza Hotel is not only visually impressive, but also is one of New York's most vibrant and sophisticated hotels. You'll find scores of ambassadors and diplomats here with their entourages, as well as wealthy travelers who like this hotel's get-away-from-it-all location across from the East River. The lavishly appointed rooms don't begin until the 28th floor (offices occupy the first 27 floors), and these lofty heights offer stunning views of the Manhattan skyline. The lobby is all green Italian marble, chrome and mirrors. The total effect is that of a millionaire's fun house, but the guests find it chic. The top floors house tennis courts, an indoor swimming pool and an exercise center where any day of the week you just might encounter a foreign diplomat pumping iron. To keep up with the times, the hotel's owners invested $13 million in 1989, in remodeling the bathrooms (Italian marble, to be sure), installing sprinklers and increasing the number of suites. The Ambassador Grill serves an ambitious menu of modern American cuisine complemented by the rugged country cooking of Gascony. This is a place where power and privilege hold court with politics to create an aura that is at once luxurious and high-pressure and, for many, fascinating.

Singles: $195-$240; doubles: $215-$260; suites: $325-$1,100. Weekend packages available. All major cards.

 Waldorf-Astoria
301 Park Ave., 10022
(49th & 50th Sts.)
355-3000, (800) HILTONS;
Fax 758-9209

The Waldorf is finally learning how to age gracefully, rather than plummeting headlong into disarray, as it was doing a few years back. An ongoing restoration (costing more than $150 million) of the original art deco design has brought back a great deal of the glamour and beauty that this great hotel displayed in its heyday. The lobby is still choked with gawking tourists, business executives and travelers who honeymooned here 40 years ago, but the staff works valiantly and the service is smooth, if slow. The 1,692 rooms vary considerably, from ones resembling large closets to rambling suites with Texas-size bathrooms. Tucked away from the frantic crowd that is madly shopping and eating on the lobby level, the chic Waldorf Towers has its own entrance and an Old World elegance undiminished by time.

Singles: $190-$250; doubles: $215-$275; suites: $345-$3000. Weekend packages available. All major cards.

 Waldorf Towers
100 E. 50th St., 10022 (Park Ave.)
355-3100, (800) HILTONS;
Fax 758-9209

The Waldorf Towers would make a great location for a whodunit movie, with its private elevators and driveways, brusque security guards and privacy-seeking clientele—a head of state, this year's biggest rock star, eccentric nobility and every U.S. president since Hoover. The style here could be called "dowager elegance." Most of the rooms are one-of-a-kind suites outfitted with ornate wallpaper, period antiques, dimly lit chandeliers and lots of gilt and plush velvet. Butler and maid services are available for your private dining room, and the excellent staff provides the kind of perfectly executed service that would make Jeeves green with envy.

Singles: $260-$290; doubles: $280-$310; suites: $400-$3,000 (for the four-bedroom Presidential suite). All major cards.

 Warwick
65 W. 54th St., 10019
(Ave. of the Americas)
247-2700, (800) 223-4099;
Fax 957-8915

Once upon a time, the Beatles stayed here when they were in town, and we've had a fondness for the place ever since. The lads' zaniness clearly did not preclude a fondness for the creature comforts. The Warwick, built in 1927 by William Randolph Hearst, has always been carefully maintained, tastefully furnished and courteously staffed. It is showing its age these days, despite a recent face-lift given to both the public space and more than 100 rooms; but the Warwick is a relative bargain in midtown. Each of the 500 large rooms has spacious closets and double windows to filter out the street noise. The Sir Walter Raleigh Restaurant, hair salon and same-day laundry and valet services are good; and the Sixth Avenue location is convenient for executives and Fifth Avenue–shopping tourists alike.

Singles: $160-$180; doubles: $185-$205; suites: $225-$425. Weekend packages available. All major cards.

Wellington
Seventh Ave. & 55th St., 10019
247-3900; Fax 581-1719

The Wellington is a generic-brand hotel— low rates and mediocre quality—but it does get the job done. The rooms are clean and well-maintained, with ample closet space. Tour groups and clothing-buyers lugging their sample suitcases choke the lobby day and night, so checkout can be a nightmare. The upper level "tower rooms" offer better amenities at higher rates.

Singles: $94-$99; doubles: $104-$109; suites: $140. All major cards.

Wentworth
59 W. 46th St., 10036
(Fifth & Sixth Aves.)
719-2300, (800) 223-1900;
Fax 768-3477

The Wentworth's proximity to the fashion district makes this lodging a natural stopping place for buyers from all over the world—

there's even a jewelry exchange in the lobby, so you can buy your diamonds along with the morning paper. The 195 large rooms are well-kept and decorated with pretty floral bedspreads and curtains. With its high housekeeping standards and courteous, prompt service, this hotel is a good choice for any cost-conscious traveler.

Singles: $70-$85; doubles: $80-$95; suites: $100-$150. All major cards.

Wyndham
42 W. 58th St., 10019
(Fifth & Sixth Aves.)
753-3500; Fax 754-5638

The Wyndham lobby, with its comfortable sofas, greenery and earth-toned furnishings, is a most agreeable nook. Choose from 200 spacious and attractive rooms, some with pantries. Close to Central Park and Fifth Avenue shops, this intimate lodging is a jewel, prized by loyal clients who relish privacy, smooth service and a friendly, dedicated staff. And at these prices, you have to smile.

Singles: $105-$115; doubles: $120-$130; suites: $165-$195. All major cards.

UPTOWN
(Above 59th Street)

Barbizon Hotel
140 E. 63rd St., 10021
(Lexington Ave.)
838-5700; Fax 753-0360

The Barbizon is a delightful secret, closely kept (but not from us) by a steady roster of selective clients. Formerly a residential hotel for women, it has been renovated with charming results. Warm pastel walls, pink marble floors and lots of fresh flowers give the lobby a younger-than-springtime look. Most rooms are on the small side, but are adequate and pleasantly furnished; twelve tower apartments offer more luxurious living, plus terraces with superb views of the cityscape. Downstairs, the restaurant, café and bar do a brisk business with guests and exhausted shoppers from Bloomingdale's, located just a few blocks away.

Singles: $120-$175; doubles: $170-$270; suites: $275-$650. Weekend packages available. Cards: AE, DC, MC, V.

Carlyle
35 E. 76th St., 10021 (Madison Ave.)
744-1600; Fax 717-4682

As discreet as a Swiss bank, and generally regarded as New York's top hotel of the moment, the Carlyle exudes an atmosphere of privilege, good breeding and elegance that will make you feel as if you had arrived for high mass. Dowagers resplendent in heirloom jewelry, old-money gentry and millionaire chief executives frequent this unremittingly posh oasis for service that is as silken and polished as the dialogue of a Noël Coward play. The rooms are gracious and luxuriously furnished with one-of-a-kind accessories and antiques in every chamber. The Carlyle has undergone a complete redecoration of late, the kind you welcome but hardly notice, except for all the electronic additions such as a fax machine in every room. In the Café Carlyle, Bobby Short still performs his ineffable piano magic as if this world of noblesse oblige will go on forever . . . perhaps it will (see Nightlife chapter, page 223).

Singles: $240-$300; doubles: $265-$325; suites: $475-$1,100. Cards: AE, DC, MC, V.

 Esplanade

305 West End Ave., 10023 (74th St.) 874-5000, (800) 367-0367; Fax 496-0367

A stone's throw from pretty Riverside Park and close to Lincoln Center, the gracefully aging Esplanade is appealing for its old-fashioned courtesy as well as its very reasonable rates. A two-and-a-half year renovation and refurbishing, completed late in 1989, resulted in new windows, new wallpaper, recarpeted hallways and freshened rooms and suites. The spacious, pleasantly decorated rooms all have kitchenettes, air conditioners and cable TV. The hotel features many suites among its 200 rooms, and is a good choice for week-long or month-long stays. Also, the conscientious staff will cater to your every whim—eventually.

Singles: $79-$99; doubles: $89-$109; suites: $119-$209. Cards: AE, MC, V.

 Lowell Hotel

28 E. 63rd St., 10021 (Park & Madison Aves.) 838-1400; Fax 319-4230

It is impossible not to fall in love with the Lowell. Intimate, cozy and fashionable in the manner of an impeccably tailored couturier suit, this establishment caters to many English guests as well as independent-minded Americans who seek elegance, discretion and highly personalized service. Many rooms—we should say suites, as there are 60 suites but only eight double rooms—feature wood-burning fireplaces and kitchenettes. Needless to say, the furnishings are impeccable and distinctive. This is a hotel with personality. The Pembroke Room serves cinnamon toast

and watercress sandwiches on bone china at its afternoon tea service. And where else but in this bastion of civility would you find a library for all those *veddy* literate guests?

Singles: $240, doubles: $290; suites: $390-$1,200. Weekend packages available. All major cards.

 The Mark

25 E. 77th St., 10021 (Madison Ave.) 744-4300; Fax 744-2749

Once the Hyde Park hotel, then the Madison Avenue Hotel, this chameleon has now entered its newest and choicest, most luxurious incarnation, The Mark. Mark it down as a very good hostelry if you are looking for service, style and comfort in the heart of the Madison Avenue shopping, gallery and museum area. The Mark is part of a growing trend toward smaller lodgings that offer individualized service and decor that is not standard hotel-issue. Not all the rooms (notably the smaller ones) are a class above average, but some of the suites, especially the five with terraces, are lovely and oh-so-nouvelle in their decor. Rooms on the top floors afford striking views. Adjacent to the lobby, the Sant Ambroeus restaurant and tea room offers elegant Italian pastries, gelati and espressos to a gorgeous St. Tropez–tanned crowd (see Restaurants chapter, page 146, and Quick Bites, page 176).

Singles & doubles: $195-$285; suites: $350-$900. Weekend packages available. All major cards.

 Mayfair Regent

610 Park Ave., 10021 (65th St.) 288-0800; Fax 737-0538

The quintessence of civility, this most European of New York's hotels takes pride in a style of hospitality that is gracious and imperturbable. The establishment is small (199 rooms and 119 suites) and exclusive, and its loyal following a heady mixture of diplomats, fur-clad socialites and wealthy jet-setters who come for the highly individualized attention and soothing, relaxed atmosphere. Antiques abound, tastefully of course: in the lovely lobby, in the salon lounge where breakfast, lunch and cocktails are served amid flowers and swaying palms, in the pretty rooms that overlook Park Avenue. Always luxurious, never showy, this is a place of caviar days and Champagne nights.

Singles: $255; doubles: $275-$320; suites: $405-$1,700. Weekend package available. All major cards.

Mayflower

15 Central Park West, 10023
(61st St.)
265-0060, (800) 223-4164;
Fax 265-5098

An affable, easy-going oasis in the midst of the nouveau-riche bustle of the Upper West Side, the Mayflower is so close to Lincoln Center that if you open your window, you may just hear a violin playing. Attractive rooms (ask for one with a park view) and a friendly staff make this a good choice. At the over-priced Conservatory Restaurant, you'll dine with marathon runners, clarinetists and other performing artists who frequent this hotel. The weekend package includes breakfast.

Singles: $135-$155; doubles: $155-$180; suites: $235-$275. Weekend packages available. All major cards.

Pierre

2 E. 61st St., 10021 (Fifth Ave.)
838-8000; Fax 940-8109

Most of the members of the Pierre's predominantly European clientele look like passengers on the Orient Express—eccentric, old-money tycoons and their dowager wives dressed in good, solid tweeds and feather hats. This small, clubby establishment (204 available rooms spread over 42 floors) is home to many permanent residents, which may account for its calm, cozily elegant pace and almost dreamy atmosphere—time doesn't march, but rather waltzes by regally at the Pierre. The service, however, is crackerjack efficient, as if each guest were served by life-long family retainers. The rooms and lobby wear the subdued elegance of traditional European antiques and gleaming mahogany. Perhaps not as fresh and luxurious as some of the city's flashier upscale establishments, the Pierre feels and fits like one's most comfortable old suit. The Rotunda room serves tea, and for those daring couples who wish to indulge in a discreet two-step or fox trot, the

Pierre Lounge offers piano music nightly.

Singles: $265-$355; doubles: $295-$385; suites: $525-$1,650. Weekend packages available. All major cards.

Plaza Athénée

37 E. 64th St., 10021
(Madison & Park Aves.)
734-9100; Fax 772-0958

The grand opulence and elegance of the Plaza Athénée would make it a perfect site for the next royal wedding. For us mere commoners, this relatively new hotel strives for, and superbly achieves, an extremely high level of performance. The lobby is a crystal-and-marble fantasy, with massive floral arrangements, potted palms and Louis XVI furniture. The multilingual staff includes three concierges as well as an excellently trained corps well-versed in the vagaries of its *très soignés*, predominately European guests. Rooms are luxurious; several come equipped with kitchens. In the expert hands of the world-renowned chef Jo Rostand and his sons (all of whom are consulting chefs), the dining room, Le Régence, serves excellent French haute cuisine (see review in the Restaurants chapter, page 144). Like its sister hotel in Paris, this magnificent establishment, owned and managed by Trusthouse Forte, is a lustrous addition to city life at its elegant best.

Singles: $235-$345; doubles: $265-$375; suites: $590-$1,950. Weekend packages available. All major cards.

Regency

540 Park Ave., 10021
(60th & 61st Sts.)
759-4100; Fax 688-8898

At the Regency, you'll find leather-clad rock stars squeezing into the elevator alongside hordes of elderly matrons who look amazingly like Miss Marple. Eccentric, doddering, jet-setting, flamboyant, corporate stuffed-shirt—just name any type of well-heeled traveler and, sooner or later, you'll encounter the species wandering through this gilt-and-velvet playground. The rooms are furnished in regency decor with pretty green and salmon accents, while the lobby contains enough marble and gilt accessories almost to redecorate Versailles. As an antidote to all this fuss, the service is warm and extremely efficient. The

540 Park Avenue restaurant originated the concept of the Power Breakfast; on any weekday morning, you'll find members of New York's business community swapping fortunes over kippered herring and eggs. There's a health club to help you work off those closing-the-deal calories.

Singles: $205-$255; doubles: $230-$280; suites: $350-$1,050. Weekend packages available. All major cards.

 Stanhope
995 Fifth Ave., 10028 (81st St.)
288-5800; Fax 517-0088

Just about every aspect of this hotel has changed (including its name, formerly the American Stanhope), as the result of a series of major renovations and reburbishings. The latest change, in 1989, is new Japanese ownership. The new look is elegant, austere and very French, with sparkling Baccarat chandeliers and European antiques in the lobby, impressionist art on the walls and gratis Chanel toiletries in every bathroom. The rooms are ornately furnished, with masses of heavy drapery and Louis XVI furniture; and a Mercedes limousine is available to chauffeur guests around town. You can count on all the latest electronic gadgets as well, even laser-disc players. Located directly across the avenue from the Metropolitan Museum, the Stanhope has thankfully retained its pretty-as-a-picture outdoor café, Le Salon, one of New York's most popular and delightful settings for people-watching (see Quick Bites chapter, page 184. For review of Stanhope Dining Room, see Restaurants chapter, page 147).

Singles & doubles: $250-$325; suites: $400-$4,000. Weekend packages available. All major cards.

 Surrey Hotel
20 E. 76th St., 10021 (Madison Ave.)
288-3700; Fax 628-1549

Quiet good taste is the motto of the Surrey, from its *soignée* location on a tree-lined street near the Whitney Museum, to its pleasant, large rooms (all come with kitchenettes), to the tranquil gentility which permeates this small, established hotel. The recent renovations (new kitchens, baths, elevators, decoration) have added a fresh sparkle to the surroundings, but the attentive, old-world courtesy of the staff remains as reliable and welcome as ever.

Singles: $175-$195; doubles: $195-$215; suites: $265-$500. Weekend packages available. Cards: AE, DC, MC, V.

 Wales
1295 Madison Ave., 10128
(92nd St.)
876-6000; Fax 860-7000

Built in 1900, the tiny Wales is one of New York's oldest ongoing hotels, and many loyal clients would never stay anywhere else. The new owners (as of September 1988) have returned the hotel to its original elegance. All woodwork and marble have been restored. All rooms have been redone with cherrywood furniture, brass lighting fixtures and new carpeting, and windows and doors have been brought back to their original oak finish. Since it's off the beaten track of most hotels, you'll find the rates extremely reasonable at this Carnegie Hill European-style boutique hotel. Sarabeth's Kitchen, adjacent to the lobby, serves some of the finest breakfasts and pastries in town.

Singles: $95-$125; doubles: $95-$125; suites: $145-$175. Cards: AE, DC, MC, V.

 Westbury
15 E. 69th St., 10021 (Madison Ave.)
535-2000; Fax 535-5058

You need only pass a few hours in the lobby of the Westbury to get a bird's-eye view of what is *au courant* in the world of fashion and glamour. This Trusthouse Forte property caters primarily to a clientele of sophisticated Europeans, international celebrities who know precisely what they want from a hotel and others who, perhaps, can't get a room at its sister hotel, the Plaza Athénée. The Westbury services the demands of these experienced travelers with grace, refinement and poise. The rooms are well-furnished and were refurbished in 1989. The Westbury Lounge, with its dark mahogany bar and paisley seats, is a haven for beautifully dressed women and their dapper escorts. The hotel's restaurant, the Polo, looks decidedly British, but serves delicious New American cuisine.

Singles: $210-$260; doubles: $235-$285; suites: $375-$2,000. Weekend packages available. All major cards.

NIGHTLIFE

BRING ON THE NIGHT

By day, New York is a serious place with a fast-paced, relentless energy on its streets and in its high-rise office towers. But at night, the city transforms and becomes its own escape. Tonight is the night to be "in" with your particular crowd, whatever its pleasures. Those searching for the quiet intimacy of a secluded bar can easily find it, and those who want to continue an unbridled race from club to club, never stopping until the early morning hours, are also quickly accommodated. That New York has such a versatile nightlife is practically cliché. Rest assured that you'll never starve for entertainment and, if you want, you'll never rest.

New York at night is lit up and ready to dance. The Upper East and West sides are bar-hoppers' heaven for a certain young professional set, while downtown venues attract a more artistic, avant-garde clientele. Even itinerant locals find it hard to keep up with what's hot and what's not, although you can't steer wrong if you follow the crowds. If there's a line outside a doorway on a weeknight, especially on a Sunday, Monday or Thursday, you've found the current happening spot.

Supposing the latest 3 a.m. nightclub scene isn't on your dance card, New York offers more sophisticated indulgences, from serene piano bars to hip, swinging jazz clubs. Or, step into one of New York's headline comedy clubs and humor yourself; expect top-quality talent and you won't be disappointed. No matter how you spend evenings in New York, it's probably just the tonic you need to bustle through another day.

BARS

Acme Bar & Grill
9 Great Jones St. (Broadway)
420-1934
Open Sun.-Thurs. 11:30 a.m.-midnight, Fri.-Sat. 11:30 a.m.-1 a.m. Cards: AE.

The Acme holds the unofficial world's record for the largest collection of hot-sauce bottles, each poised precariously on a long shelf above a group of tables (the mind boggles at what the world's record *really* is). The regulars at this no-frills establishment are out for a good time, which the Acme gleefully provides with a menu of passable Tex-Mex food and a wide selection of beer and other refreshments. Rolling Stones fans probably already know that Keith Richards favors this place, but likely he's downstairs in a part of the Acme not open to the public, shooting pool.

Algonquin Hotel
59 W. 44th St. (Fifth & Sixth Aves.)
840-6800
Bar open Mon.-Sat. noon-1 a.m., Sun. noon-midnight. All major cards.

Years ago, a group of literary types met regularly at a meeting of the minds called the Algonquin Round Table. Today, they'd probably converse via video conference. Still, the Algonquin is a popular draw for modern-day artists, writers, actors and others of a creative bent. The attractive lobby retains the congeniality and tranquil pace of a private club. Most nights, the Oak Room features a top singer or entertainer. An intimate spot is the dimly lit Blue Bar adjoining the lobby, where more than a little history has taken place. Renovation of the bar should be completed by the spring of 1990, but call first to make sure.

Automatic Slim's

733 Washington St. (Bank St.)
645-8660
*Open Mon.-Sat. 5 p.m.-4 a.m., Sun. noon-4 a.m.
No cards.*

The West Village's daytime peace is shattered most nights when a young downtown crowd lights up a lineup of hip local bars and cafés. The informed set heads to this small, isolated watering hole that's just steps from the Hudson River. Here, they pass the hours against a wall of sound offering a popular assortment of jazz, blues and reggae hits. On weekday evenings, Automatic Slim's is mostly a neighborhood hangout. On weekends, it's strictly first come, first served as the homeyness transforms into a popular gathering ground for those in pursuit of a future in music, acting or art. Bottled beer is stiff at $3 a pop, but, then, not too many places serve Red Stripe, a smooth Jamaican brew. A reasonably priced menu includes the standard hamburgers, french fries and chicken wings, but also offers surprising specials like blackened swordfish. Tuesday through Saturday nights, tables command a $7.50 food minimum.

Beach Café

1326 Second Ave. (70th St.)
988-7299
Open daily 11:30 a.m.-4 a.m. Cards: AE.

When sharply dressed Wall Street junior executives mix with smartly attired young advertising executives at this upscale uptown meeting spot, the chemical result resembles a Chiquita Bulldog, a potent banana drink that's regularly poured here. By the way, that conversation you're overhearing isn't inside information about the stock market, it's just someone talking about a recent date.

Bowlmoor Lanes

110 University Pl. (12th St.)
255-8188
Open Sun.-Thurs. 10 a.m.-1 a.m., Fri.-Sat. 10 a.m.-4 a.m. No cards.

Bowling is one of those great suburban American sports, like miniature golf, that becomes chic when it's brought to young urbanites in a way they can understand. In this case, it's with trendy liquors, popular music, and high adrenaline and decibel levels maintained by 44 lanes split between two floors. All this makes the bowling just a spare. The strike is the chance to mingle with the beautiful people and other celebrity types who frequent this dimly lit Village scene. But bowling, as has been said, is fun for the whole family, and at least the older brothers and sisters are making an effort. It's hard to keep an eye on both the ball and the bottle, so alternate.

Cadillac Bar

15 W. 21st St. (Fifth & Sixth Aves.)
645-7220
Open Mon-Thurs. noon-midnight, Fri.-Sat. noon-2 a.m. All major cards.

The subways are supposedly free of spray-painted graffiti, and one look at the Cadillac gives you a clue as to where all the guerrilla artists went. It's as if the Cadillac's owners had invited them over and given away free cans of Krylon. In fact, the largely yuppie clientele *was* once handed spray paint and told to go wild. The result isn't so much postmodernism as it is postworkaday: no one's going to mistake that blob of black goo for Jasper Johns. The margaritas, thankfully, are genuine, but the Tex-Mex food could use a bit more artistic flair.

Café Iguana

235 Park Ave. South (19th St.)
529-4770
Open Mon.-Thurs. 11:30 a.m.-2:30 a.m., Fri. 11:30 a.m.-3 a.m., Sat. 5 p.m.-3:30 a.m., Sun. noon-2:30 a.m. All major cards.

On any weekend night, this part of lower Manhattan is full of well-dressed, fun-loving junior yuppies. But why? Possibly because this cavernous, pretentious club is a wall of handsome flesh. Its owners claim inspiration from the classic play and film *Night of the Iguana*, but they can't do better than a bar that serves silly concoctions such as "Sex on the Beach" and the "Woo Woo." With invitations like that, it's deflating to see a sign that says NO DANCING. Not that there's room to move anyway. Other signs bark orders: NO JEANS, NO TANK-TOPS, NO PHOTOGRAPHS. Please. The café serves "vacation cuisine," also known as Mexican food, but the aging disco music is too loud for more than a few sentences of uninterrupted conversation. If you really want to remember this place, T-shirts, coffee mugs and caps are sold in the upstairs Inca Lounge. You pay in $25 or $50 blocks of "Iguana Currency." Is it mere coincidence that over the bar hangs a giant artificial crystal iguana? We think not.

Café Society
915 Broadway (21st St.)
529-8282
Open Mon.-Thurs. 6 p.m.-1 a.m., Fri.-Sat. 6 p.m.-4 a.m. All major cards.

If you believe in a Manhattan with sophistication and flair, Café Society is your dream come true. The trendy, elegant art-deco interior, spread over two-levels, is a magnificent sight. Also easy on the eye is a fine-looking and well-heeled clientele of models and investment bankers, many of them available. Café Society moves with a certain self-confidence and ease, steering just clear of self-importance. The restaurant serves an Italian menu and, for those inclined, there's a small dance floor featuring ballroom dancing. Downstairs is the stylish Society Billiards, one of the many upscale, liquor-free pool halls that have attracted young urban professionals to the budding Flatiron and Chelsea districts of lower Manhattan.

Caramba!!
684 Broadway (W. 3rd St.)
420-9817
Open daily noon-midnight. All major cards.

Why the two exclamation points?? Perhaps it makes the gentrified young crowd here believe they're having more fun in this raucous place than they really are. Perhaps it helps them forget that the Mexican food is disappointing and the slushy margaritas are expensive, and, as we did, perhaps they'll forget that they had expectations of something better.

Chelsea Commons
242 Tenth Ave. (24th St.)
929-9424
Open daily noon-4 a.m. No cards.

On cold winter nights, a fireplace warms this old neighborhood standby. In late spring, summer and early fall, an enclosed backyard garden is a quiet and welcome retreat. And year round, the Commons can be counted on for reasonably priced drinks and better-than-average bar food. Tucked away behind the mammoth London Terrace apartment complex, the Commons avoids the clutches of the bar-hopping crowd and the noise and traffic of 23rd Street. Accordingly, it's rarely packed, always accommodating and refreshingly down to earth.

Chumley's
86 Bedford St. (Barrow St.)
675-4449
Open Sun.-Thurs. 5 p.m.-1 a.m., Sat.-Sun. 2 p.m.-4 a.m. Cards: AE.

This former speakeasy has been going strong in the West Village for more than 60 years. Yoy may fall in love with this casual, irreverent place—if you can find it. There's no sign out front, and printed on the matchbooks is the bar's motto: "You Can't Get Here From There." Two entrances, one on Bedford Street and another on Barrow Street, are testimony to the 1920s Prohibition era that outlawed liquor and popularized Chumley's. If the police came to one door, the regulars would hustle out the other. Today, both doors are open to artists, executives and graduate students, among others. At its root, however, Chumley's has always been a writer's bar. Book jackets encased in glass along the dimly lit walls feature the works of some of its famous (and less-famous) patrons. A grand jukebox spills out old and new rock-and-roll.

Here's how to get there: the front entrance is on Bedford Street, just steps from the corner of Barrow Street. Find number 86 and walk in. The more challenging side door is at 58 Barrow Street, tucked away at the far end of a small courtyard. Walk through to an imposing wooden door that looks locked; it isn't.

City Lights Bar
One World Trade Center, 107th Fl.
938-1111
Open Mon.-Sat. 3 p.m.-1 a.m., Sun. 4 p.m.-9 p.m. Cover charge varies. All major cards.

An old song said it best about taking Manhattan, the Bronx and Staten Island, too. You can have all that, plus a bit of New Jersey, in the view from this extraordinary bar atop one of the world's tallest buildings. The romantic music, comfortable surroundings, and the right companion just might elevate you a floor or two.

The Conservatory
Mayflower Hotel, 15 Central Park West
(61st & 62nd Sts.)
581-0896
Open daily 11:30 a.m.-12:30 a.m. All major cards.

Idyllic spots that don't cost a fortune are rarities in Manhattan. Congratulations to the charming Mayflower Hotel for providing one here, just across the street from Central Park and not far from midtown Manhattan, Lincoln Center and the Theater District. Softly lit, private and romantic, The Conservatory is a quiet meeting place for a mannered but unpretentious clientele of eclectic hotel guests, Upper West Side locals and theatergoers. The bartenders know how to mix a drink and carry a conversation, and the neighboring restaurant of the same name is good.

Costello's
225 E. 44th St. (Second & Third Aves.)
599-9614
Open Mon.-Fri. 10 a.m.-2 a.m. All major cards.

Time was when you could get a real drink in this town, instead of some fluffy milkshake with more pride than punch. Costello's, thankfully, remembers those days. It remains a serious drinking bar with a clientele to match. Among the regulars are newspaper types from the nearby *Daily News* building.

Ear Inn
326 Spring St.
(Greenwich & Washington Sts.)
226-9060
Open daily 11 a.m.-4 a.m. Cards: AE, DC.

If there was ever any reason to frequent such a deserted part of lower Manhattan, it's this user-friendly Hudson River hangout for local writers, poets and other unsung urban heroes. A crowd of regulars occupies the red stools that line the long wooden bar, drinking $3.50 pints of Guinness Stout and Bass Ale. In the background, the comforting ring of a cash register, so infrequently heard in this electronic age, thanks satisfied patrons. You can play backgammon or cribbage, listen to taped jazz and country music, doodle with the crayons on your table and sample some well-presented and tasty hamburgers, soups and salads. Occasionally the Ear Inn is the quiet setting for local poetry readings. Look for the trash dumpster outside that says EAR INN in large white letters; it's easier to spot than the red neon sign above the bar that simply says EAR. Be sure to read the back of the bar menu—it reveals how the place got its name.

Ernie's
2150 Broadway (76th St.)
496-1588
Open Mon.-Fri. noon-1 a.m., Sat.-Sun. 11:30 a.m.-1 a.m. All major cards.

You may ask, rightfully, what on earth an airplane hangar is doing in this part of town. Relax. Ernie's is a large, harmless space that's filled almost every night with hip Upper West Siders who brave the deafening noise to sample northern Italian pastas and pizzas or to lounge at the long bar. Outside tables are pleasant on sunny afternoons and warm nights.

Gold Bar
345 E. 9th St. (First & Second Aves.)
302-1144
Open nightly 6 p.m.-4 a.m.

Look closely above the door of this small, nondescript East Village space., and you'll see a faded sign that says WINES & LIQUORS. Now, it's a liquor store of a different sort. The drinks are good; the music is modern; and the appropriate clothing for the chic, young art crowd is basic black. A cliquish attitude prevails, but don't let that affect your enjoyment of one of downtown's most unique spots.

Gramercy Park Hotel Bar
2 Lexington Ave. (21st & 22nd Sts.)
475-4320
Open daily 11 a.m.-1:30 a.m. All major cards.

Near lovely Gramercy Park, this large, once-glamorous hotel nobly tries to retain its old charm, part of which lies in its intimate, lobby-level piano bar where locals and hotel guests gather nightly. These bartenders know how to pour a good drink, and the liquor bottles aren't equipped with those annoying devices that mete out measured amounts. Such a place, sadly, is a disappearing species.

Hard Rock Café
221 W. 57th St. (Seventh Ave. & Broadway)
489-6565
Open daily 11:30 a.m.-2 a.m. All major cards.

Look at that long line of kids on vacation with Mom and Dad. Say, isn't that a tour group behind them? Can all these people be waiting to get into the Hard Rock? Yes, and not only do they wait, they're downright civil about it. This is the New York version of the now-legendary London restaurant and bar, the winning format of which has been photo-copied in cities across the world. There's plenty to eat and drink, for a price, and a deafening sound system for experienced ears only. Squeeze yourself into a place at the guitar-shaped bar, or browse in the rock-and-roll memorabilia museum featuring 100 gold records and Chubby Checkers's boots, to boot.

Harvey's Chelsea Restaurant
108 W. 18th St. (Sixth Ave.)
243-5644
Open Sun.-Thurs. noon-midnight, Fri.-Sat. noon-1 a.m. Cards: AE.

Rich mahogany woodwork gives this re-stored Chelsea saloon the feel of a refined private club, and the etched glass behind the bar is a striking conversation piece. Advertising executives come to mix with the artists and photographers who also live and work in this trendy neighborhood. In addition to the bar, there's a back room serving good English and American pub fare.

Jim McMullen
1341 Third Ave. (76th & 77th Sts.)
861-4700
Open daily 11:30 a.m.-2 a.m. Cards: AE.

It's perplexing at this stage of civilization to encounter Jim McMullen. People don't come here for the drinks; the bartenders are nothing special; it can't be for the food. Yet this wel-come-looking place is always lively and packed with an uptown crowd. They're good-looking people, too, which is certainly a reason to come here if you have it in mind to meet a model, an athlete or someone of a similar gene pool. Still, though judgment has decreed this a place to see and be seen, New York is a big city, with plenty of attractive people in plenty of better locations.

Joe Allen
326 W. 46th St. (Eighth & Ninth Aves.)
581-6464
Open daily noon-1 a.m. Cards: AE, MC, V.

A casual manner is appropriate for this the-ater-district cornerstone, as are the theatrical

posters, gingham-topped tables, blackboard menus and the sound of Ethel Merman in her heyday. Women with glossy hair and men with embossed smiles gather to gossip about how they almost starred in the latest hit show and how they could have saved the one that bombed. The basic American menu is good, and the presence of a few celebrities will re-ward the diligent.

Johnny Rock'r
901 Broadway (20th St.)
533-1887
Open daily 11 a.m.-4 a.m. Cover charge $5 Fri.-Sat. after 9 p.m. No cards.

An oft-repeated pattern among the reso-lutely urban goes like this: a hot new club opens in some upcoming part of town, and people and limousines line up and stay awhile just to say they've been. But then, folks from the suburbs and uptown hear about it, and without ado, the chic set flocks elsewhere. You see it happen to established spots such as the Hard Rock Café, and our bet is that it soon will happen to Johnny Rock'r, if it hasn't already. The bar's clientele is predictably young and hip, or thinks it is. The lengthy wait to get in on any given night after 9 p.m. is more exciting than the loftlike bar inside, which features a now-tired concept of blaring rock music cutely combined with Three Stooges episodes and other trendy videos. On weekends, there's dancing downstairs. Johnny Rock'r also indulges in the obligatory, oversize, Freudian trend objects that all such places must boast. The Hard Rock displays a 1950s Cadillac bumper with vintage fins; at Johnny Rock'r, the centerpiece is a giant Gib-son guitar. Get the drift?

Landmark Tavern
626 Eleventh Ave. (46th St.)
757-8595
Open Mon.-Fri. noon-midnight, Fri.-Sat. noon-1 a.m. All major cards.

A classic Irish tavern delivering charm and good, hearty food, even if the neighborhood isn't quite as congenial. Built in 1868, it features a working fireplace, potbellied stove, mahogany bar and tin ceiling. The Irish oat-meal pancakes win over the Saturday and Sun-day brunch crowds. It's also popular with pre- and post-theatergoers.

Lion's Head

59 Christopher St. (Seventh Ave.)
929-0670
Open daily noon-4 a.m. Cards: AE, V.

Even though the New York literary scene itself is fragmented, several great writer's bars still exist, and this is one of them. The walls of its dark and suspect-looking interior are lined with book jackets, and a jukebox bursts out a high class of oldies. Traditional Village intellectuals discuss art, politics and other Big Questions of our day, and this is as good a place as any to ponder the answers. Beer on tap includes consciousness-raising McSorley's Ale and esteemed Guinness Stout. A back room features a grammatically correct, better-than-usual bar menu.

Live Bait

14 E. 23rd St. (Broadway)
353-2400
Open Mon. 11 a.m.-2 a.m., Tues. 11 a.m.-3 a.m., Wed.-Sat. 11 a.m.-4 a.m., Sun. noon-12:30 a.m. Cards: AE, V.

At Live Bait, be a model, or just look like one—you'll fit right in. This is a somewhat predictable pick-up scene, as the name would subtly imply. It's noisy, crowded and an established spot on the young downtowner's bar-hopping list. If the attractive clientele of fashion-industry types and stockbrokers gives you hunger pangs, explore the menu of Southern-style food.

Peter McManus

152 Seventh Ave. (19th St.)
463-7620
Open daily 11 a.m.-4 a.m. No cards.

This neighborhood tavern is nothing if not convenient. A subway-station entrance shares the corner with this quaint, sometimes-crowded bar. Although it's just up the avenue from the ultra-posh clothing store, Barney's, the crowd here is more downscale. So are the prices. Draught beers (seven on tap) are an inflation-fighting $2. There are tables and booths in the back, but the fun is up front. A good jukebox plays hits from Sinatra to Madonna. Check out the gold record from Rod McKuen's Amsterdam concert on the wall. The bartender will tell you why it's there, but it's probably best to use your imagination.

McGlade's Bar & Grill

154 Columbus Ave. (67th St.)
595-9130.
Open daily 8 a.m.-4 a.m. No cards.

Can this raucous place really be steps from Lincoln Center and Tavern on the Green? Tucked into one of McGlade's snug red booths, drinking a Rolling Rock beer and wading through a decent hamburger and french fries, you get a funny feeling that you're not in Manhattan any more. It's pleasant to join the comfortable, if unlikely, mix of professionals, serious beer drinkers and sports fans—and those who embody all three types—in this rare neighborhood spot.

McSorley's Old Ale House

15 E. 7th St. (Second & Third Aves.)
473-9148
Open daily 10 a.m.-midnight. All major cards.

Just getting a drink here often requires a long wait outside, but the college and otherwise downtown crowd knows a good thing when it lines up for it. McSorley's didn't allow women until 1970, but everything's equal now. It's authentic and fun, and features a roster of veteran bartenders and a matching lineup of beers, including the esteemed house brand, McSorley's.

Meriken

189 Seventh Ave. (21st St.)
620-9684
Open daily 6 p.m.-midnight. All major cards.

A young, trendy clientele frequents this Chelsea restaurant and bar, attracted by the traditional Japanese food, the suitably hip decor that features the work of local artists, and the comfort of finding kinfolk who are forever in fashion. The bar's specialty is called Windex: a biting, bright-blue potion made with Grand Marnier, vodka and Curaçao.

Odeon

145 W. Broadway (Thomas St.)
233-0507
Open Mon.-Fri. noon-3 a.m., Sat. 6:30 p.m.-3:30 a.m., Sun. noon-2:30 a.m. All major cards.

Take a deco-era decor, a hip downtown location and a trendy, well-heeled clientele and what do you have? Don't know yet? Here's another clue: a roomful of artists, art dealers, Wall Street types, fashion designers and others in appropriate dress. Come on, we're giving the answer away. Okay, last hint: vintage music plays in the background, you see white hanging gloves, a mural of New York, racks of newspapers and chrome chairs with plastic-covered cushions. Oh, just come see for yourself. You won't be disappointed.

Old Town Bar
45 E. 18th St. (Broadway & Park Ave.)
473-8874
Open daily 11:30 a.m.-12:30 a.m. No cards.

The street is quiet. Too quiet. You should be home, but you're not. A weathered neon sign halfway down the block catches your tired eyes. You move closer and see that it says OLD TOWN BAR. The place looks old. The entrance is covered with black wire screens. It seems closed, but you press on. A small doorway leads to some stairs. At the top is a bar: big, long and tall. The ceilings must be twenty feet high. You regard the tiled floor, the ornate pressed tin ceiling, the antiquated gas lamps that now run electric lights. You order a bottle of beer because there are no draughts. You eye the crowd of downtown regulars and figure this is what P.J. Clarke's would be like without yuppies. The bartender tells you the place opened for business in 1892. You decide it was a good year for bars.

Pete's Tavern
129 18th St. (Irving Pl.)
473-7676
Open Sun.-Thurs. 10:30 a.m.-midnight, Fri.-Sat. 10:30 a.m.-1 a.m. All major cards.

Pete's lays claim to being the oldest original tavern in New York, and also the lower Manhattan haunt of writer O. Henry. It has neighborhood charm and some fine beer on tap. The folks behind the long wooden bar know their jobs well, too. Sidewalk tables beckon in the warmer months, and the young professional crowd is friendly and chatty. All of which compensates for food that's nothing to cheer.

P.J. Clarke's
915 Third Ave. (55th St.)
355-8857
Open daily 11 a.m.-4 a.m. Cards: AE.

One of New York's last great saloons. Most days bring together an eclectic mix of bankers, advertising executives, artists and celebrities. Don't try to figure it out, just lean on the mahogany bar, keep the drinks simple and enjoy the fabulous, endless jukebox with the likes of Sinatra and Peggy Lee to chase all your cares away.

Prince Street Bar & Restaurant
125 Prince St. (Wooster St.)
228-8130
Open Sun.-Thurs. 11:30 a.m.-1 a.m., Fri.-Sat. 11:30 a.m.-2 a.m. No cards.

This must be the last spot in SoHo that doesn't have a designer label pasted across its menu. The food here is creative, with particular homage to Indonesian specialties; the atmosphere is what you make it. No one has taken a rubber stamp to the decor and given everyone inside an identical voice and walk. Such independence can be unsettling, but you'll get used to it.

The Saloon
1920 Broadway (64th St.)
874-1500
Open daily 11:30 a.m.-3 a.m. Cards: AE, MC, V.

Here is yet another place to sit at sidewalk tables and watch the Upper West Side's colorful foot traffic. The waiter/actors are friendly; so are the customers. The Saloon offers a wide menu of passable American fare and is conveniently located across the street from Lincoln Center. Expect a wait before and after a show.

Sam's 263
263 W. 45th St. (Broadway & Eighth Ave.)
719-5416
Open Sun. noon-9 p.m., Mon.-Sat. noon-1 a.m. All major cards.

An established Broadway-area watering hole, Sam's 263 draws a lively crowd of pre- and post-theater audiences, actors and impresarios. The comfortable decor includes wooden tables and nostalgic posters from your favorite Broadway shows. The bar serves a passable menu of American food staples, delivered in style by harried waiters.

Stan's Sports Bar
836 River Ave. (158th St.), Bronx
665-9521
Open daily 10 a.m.-midnight. No cards.

Two reasons to visit the Bronx are the courthouse and baseball's Yankee Stadium. If you're here for the latter, you'll want to visit Stan's. Directly across the street from The House that Ruth Built, Stan's is a generally congenial spot with a weathered wooden bar and bottles of cold American beer lying around for anyone with a few bills to spare. On game days and nights it packs a regular crowd of diehard Yankee supporters, whose mood depends on how well the Yankees are playing. And, leave your Boston Red Sox whoopee cushion at home.

Telephone Bar and Grill
149 Second Ave. (10th St.)
529-5000
Open Sun.-Thurs. 11:30 a.m.-2:30 a.m., Fri.-Sat. 11:30 a.m.-4 a.m. Cards: AE.

The three fire-engine-red London phone booths at the entrance really work, thanks to New York Telephone, but they don't make you want to toast the queen. The Telephone is an attractive East Village neighborhood meeting spot for young professionals, students and a very few local artist types, all of whom perch at a spectacular marbled bar, clutching $4 pints of Guinness Stout and Bass Ale. The menu offers common British fare, including Scotch eggs, shepherd's pie, and a lightly battered and flavorful fish-and-chips, in addition to sandwiches and a bland calamari salad. A limited wine list offers some pleasant French and Californian selections.

WCOU Bar
115 First Ave. (7th St.)
254-4317
Open daily 4:30 p.m.-4 a.m. No cards.

It's also known to locals as the "Clock Bar," because of the wall-mounted neon clock that says "WCOU." The bar is small, crowded and yet another stop for the oh-so-happening East Village art crowd that claims title to what's hip and avant-garde.

White Horse Tavern
567 Hudson St. (11th St.)
243-9260
Open Sun.-Thurs. 11 a.m.-2 a.m., Fri.-Sat. 11 a.m.-4 a.m. No cards.

Poet Dylan Thomas drank away his fortunes at this West Village institution, and the White Horse still offers refuge to local literati who rage against the dying of the light. The bar also draws its share of collegiates and yuppies who might consider Thomas's "Do not go gentle into that good night" a strange but unique pickup line. A standard menu fits the convivial atmosphere and antiquated wood interior, and picnic tables outside make for enjoyable warm-weather imbibing.

CABARETS & COMEDY

Asti
13 E. 12th St. (Fifth Ave. & University Pl.)
741-9105
Open Tues.-Sun. 5:30 p.m.-12:30 a.m. Closed July-Aug. No cover. All major cards.

The waiters sing opera classics and Broadway showtunes, and photographs of great divas and tenors adorn the walls. If you like, you can join in the music and become part of the entertainment. A sweet dose of nostalgia.

The Ballroom
253 W. 28th St. (Eighth Ave.)
244-3005
Shows Tues.-Thurs. 9 p.m., Fri.-Sat. 9 p.m. & 11 p.m. Cover $10-$15 plus two-drink minimum. All major cards.

This upscale cabaret is a fine venue for a regular lineup of the city's best comedians and singers. Now occupying larger quarters, The Ballroom features a well-placed stage and a two-tiered bar with an overhead rack of smoked hams and sausages.

Caroline's at the Seaport
89 South St. (South St. Seaport)
233-4900
Shows Sun.-Tues. 8 p.m.; Wed.-Thurs. 8 p.m. & 10 p.m.; Fri. 8 p.m. & 10:30 p.m.; Sat. 7 p.m., 9 p.m. & 11:30 p.m. Cover $7.50-$17.50 plus two-drink minimum. All major cards.

This glitzy room books some of the biggest headline acts in comedy. Some of these household names first started in the early 1980s at Caroline's' earlier incarnation on Eighth Avenue. The Seaport crowd is a predictable mix of locals and tourists; the jokes told here are urban and hip.

Catch a Rising Star

1487 First Ave. (77th & 78th Sts.)
794-1906
*Shows Wed.-Thurs. 9 p.m. & 1 a.m.; Fri. 8:30
p.m. & 11 p.m.; Sat. 7:30 p.m., 10 p.m. & 12:30
p.m. Cover $8-$12 plus two-drink minimum.
Cards: AE.*

On a lucky night, this place will live up to
its name. More often than not, it's a grab bag
of New York's best and most boisterous comedy. And, like some of the acts, the room is
dark and a bit dishevelled. But whaddya want,
Las Vegas?

Chippendales

1110 First Ave. (61st St.)
935-6060
Shows Wed.-Sat. 8 p.m. Cards: AE, MC, V.

Girls will be girls when boys are boys. The
boys here flash bursting biceps and perform a
sexy striptease to pulsating music, for a vocal
females-only clientele. To show appreciation
for the energetic young performers with
megawatt smiles, members of the audience
wantonly stuff dollar bills into the dancers'
tiny G-strings. The men thank them with
kisses, and the women respond with a fair
amount of, uh, manhandling. After the show,
the boys sell some interesting take-home souvenirs, including au-naturel playing cards.

The Comedy Cellar

117 MacDougal St.
(W. 3rd & Bleecker Sts.)
254-3630
*Shows Sun.-Thurs. 9 p.m.; Fri. 9 p.m. & 11:30
p.m.; Sat. 8 p.m., 10 p.m. & midnight. Cover
$5-$10 plus two-drink minimum Sun.-Thurs.,
$7 minimum Fri.-Sat. No cards.*

Tall people be forewarned: the name is no
joke. The low ceilings and dungeonlike atmosphere are reminiscent of most Manhattan
apartments. Fortunately, both the comics and
the drinks are usually good. If your sense of
humor isn't broadened by alcohol, you can
meet the minimum cover by ordering some
passable bar food.

Dangerfield's

1118 First Ave. (61st & 62nd Sts.)
593-1650
*Shows Sun.-Thurs. 9 p.m.; Fri. 9 p.m. & 11:30
p.m.; Sat. 8 p.m., 10:30 p.m. & 12:30 a.m. Cover
$10-$15 plus $7 minimum. All major cards.*

Rodney Dangerfield made a career out of
Getting No Respect. The aspiring comics who

stand up on stage each night at his namesake
club don't get any, either. The difference is,
they want it, and that's why they're in this
smoke-filled place trying to elicit laughs. Rodney himself doesn't perform here anymore,
except for an occasional cable-television special, so leave the autograph book at home.

The Duplex

55 Grove St.
(Seventh Ave. & Bleecker St.)
255-5438
*Shows Thurs.-Sat. 8 p.m. Cover $7-$11 plus
two-drink minimum. No cards.*

The Duplex is a legendary Greenwich Village showcase, where Woody Allen, Joan Rivers and Rodney Dangerfield got their starts.
On the weekend, the downstairs piano bar
packs a lively crowd of Manhattanites who
hope that the performer they see tonight will
be tomorrow's superstar.

Greene Street Café

101 Greene St.
925-2415
*Shows Sun. & Tues.-Thurs. 6:30 p.m., Fri.-Sat.
7 p.m. Cover $15 plus $10 minimum. All major
cards.*

This is your basic good-looking, upscale
SoHo restaurant and bar, with a clientele to
match. At night, Greene Street blossoms into
a multilevel, cavernous affair, with a pricey
restaurant on the ground floor and a comfortable nightclub upstairs. Music fills the entire
place, and the jazz combos and cabaret singers
are first rate.

Improvisation

358 W. 44th St. (Ninth Ave.)
765-8268
*Shows Sun.-Thurs. 9 p.m.; Fri. 9 p.m. & mid-
night; Sat. 8 p.m., 10:30 p.m. & 12:40 a.m.
Cover $8-$10.89 plus $8-$9 minimum. Cards:
AE.*

Billed as Manhattan's original comedy
showcase, the Improvisation offers an impressive parade of the comically talented and those
who just think they are. It's up to you and the
handful of talent scouts that make up a typical
audience to decide. At press time, the Improvisation was considering a move to an undis-
closed location, so telephone first.

Rainbow & Stars

30 Rockefeller Plaza
632-5000
Shows Tues.-Sat. 9 p.m. & 11:15 p.m. Cover $35. Cards: AE.

Situated atop the RCA Building, 65 stories above Manhattan, Rainbow & Stars is a cabaret dinner club that recalls a more refined and simpler past. The nightclub books some top-class talent and draws an enthusiastic crowd; reservations are best made far in advance. Similar advice goes for the accompanying Rainbow Room, an upscale restaurant that still remembers what a night on the town is supposed to be, complete with ballroom dancing.

Stand-Up New York

236 W. 78th St. (Broadway)
595-0850
Shows Sun.-Thurs. 9 p.m.; Fri. 8:30 p.m. & 11:30 p.m.; Sat. 8 p.m., 10 p.m. & 12:15 p.m. Cover $7-$12 plus two-drink minimum. Cards: AE, MC, V.

An established venue that draws some fairly prominent local and national acts. As the name implies, the comics stand up, microphone in hand, tell a few jokes and hopefully leave you in stitches. Like working for the Internal Revenue Service, comedy is not a profession for everyone. That's why you're sitting comfortably in the audience, joining a clean-cut Upper West Side crowd that has reason to like what it hears.

DANCING & NIGHTCLUBS

The Baja

246A Columbus Ave. (71st & 72nd Sts.)
724-8890
Open Tues.-Wed. 8 p.m.-2:30 a.m., Thurs.-Sat. 9:30 p.m.-4 a.m. Cover $5 Tues.-Wed., $10 Thurs.-Sat. Cards: AE, MC, V.

Junior-level Wall Street types go home to the Upper West Side, change from blue suits into blue jeans and head to this unpretentious, unintimidating club for a night that makes the stock exchange trading floor look tame. If you're at home in a college fraternity house, you'll love The Baja. The dance floor is huge; the music is heavy on sixties rock and Motown hits.

Au Bar

241 E. 58th St. (Madison & Park Aves.)
308-9455
Open nightly 9 p.m.-4 a.m. Cover $10 Sun.-Thurs., $15 Fri.-Sat.

Clubs are much like the beautiful people they attract; some have long, successful careers; others are never heard from again. Au Bar oozes white-hot Euro-chic, and moves with the subtlety of a rocket. Its upscale crowd rarely disappoints the models hunting for suitable partners. It's a good place to shop for the latest fashion ideas, and always a good address at which to be seen. Supper and breakfast are offered daily. Good luck getting a reservation.

Big Kahuna

622 Broadway (Bleecker & Houston Sts.)
460-9633
Open Tues.-Thurs. 5 p.m.-2 a.m., Fri.-Sat. 5 p.m.-4 a.m. Cover $7 after 8 p.m. Fri.-Sat. Cards: AE, MC.

You want your Wall Street buddies to call you "Big Kahuna" in the office from now on. The name is Hawaiian for "witch doctor," and you've decided it's what your parents should have named you. After all, with a pastel-colored tropical drink in one hand, a frisbee in the other, and two feet stomping on a picnic table to rhythmic music, you've got to be impressing somebody besides yourself. Those Bermuda shorts on your left, for instance.

The China Club

130 Broadway (75th St.)
877-1166
Open daily 10 p.m.-4 a.m. Cover $10 Sun.-Thurs., $15 Fri.-Sat. Cards: AE, MC, V.

Monday's the night to mix with the celebrities, athletes, musicians and models who press into this small Upper West Side club. If you look good, you'll get in. If you get in, you'll find an intimate space with hand-painted Asian murals, fish tanks and dragon sculptures. Other nights feature an appealing roster of rock-and-roll bands that makes this a popular hangout.

Club A

333 E. 60th St. (First & Second Aves.)
308-2333
Open Wed.-Sun. 9 p.m.-4 a.m. Cover $20 Wed.-
Thurs., $25 Fri.-Sat. Cards: AE, DC.

Several years ago, this Euro-chic meeting spot was a "must" on the self-respecting jet-set list. That special magic has since worn thin, downgrading Club A to at least an A-minus. The decor blends Greek and Roman statuary with burgundy banquettes. In between disco dances, be sure to sample cachaça, the national drink of Brazil. On "hot" nights, a few young Europeans mix with lots of locals. The food and live Brazilian music and the Brazilian Beat next door is good, and the club waives its cover charge if you dine. Take your own crowd for fun, and make an evening of it. Jacket and tie are required, except on Sundays.

Limelight

660 Ave. of the Americas (20th & 21st Sts.)
807-7850
Open daily 10 p.m.-4 a.m. Cover $15 Sun.-
Thurs., $18 Fri.-Sat. Cards: AE, MC, V

Since it's located in what was formerly an Episcopal church dating from the mid-nineteenth century, Limelight attracted notorious publicity and a suspect crowd when it opened a few years ago. Although Sunday nights draw a particularly hip crowd, the scene has cooled down quite a bit as the club has faded from the limelight. At many record stores and bars around Manhattan, it's possible to find free "membership" cards that offer discounted admission to the club—a sure sign of decline. Local personalities hold theme parties and fashion shows here during the week, with admission also by discounted public invitation. Inside, however, the old attraction remains. The holy trappings are intact, from the stained-glass windows to chapels that now are scheduled hideaways.

Mars

28 Tenth Ave. (12th & 13th Sts.)
691-6262
Open Sun. & Thurs. 9 p.m.-4 a.m., Fri. 10
p.m.-4 a.m., Sat. 9 p.m.-4 a.m. Cover $11 Thurs.
& Sun., $16 Fri.-Sat. Cards: AE.

In fact, it does seem as if it were another planet. The "in" crowd gives this unique place a gravity and orbit all its own. The club is dark, exciting, crowded and filled with the sound of first-class house music, with uninhibited dancing spread out across five levels and the roof.

Know what you're getting into. Mars is the moment's undisputed leader of selectivity. It accepts the famous and beautiful and dismisses the rest. Unless you dress or look exceptional, or you are somebody or know someone who is, it's difficult to gain admittance. Mars makes no claims otherwise, and that's why hundreds of people willingly face rejection on any given night. Go figure. Sunday is gay night, while Monday and Thursday nights in particular attract a crushing mix of models, celebrities, artists and other downtown fixtures. Weekends are just as relentless. Advice for regular folk: Make a scene climbing out of your taxi or limousine, so the people at the door with the two way radios will notice. Dress in high fashion or in black, or both. Stare at whomever judges people and act important. But if you're not tapped within ten minutes, you're probably out of luck.

If this scene is worth it, here's what awaits. A strobe-lighted basement blasts reggae music and features a half dozen video screens. The ground level and second floor offer unforgiving, nonstop dance tracks. A solid wall of terrific-looking people counters every move you make. The third level has isolated back tables but no dancing, and the top floor is a VIP lounge generally closed to all but a privileged few of the already privileged.

M. K.

204 Fifth Ave. (25th St.)
779-1340
Open nightly 10:30 p.m.-4 a.m. Cover $5 Sun.-
Thurs., $15 Fri.-Sat. All major cards (for din-
ner only).

This exclusive club was once a bank building, fitting because its undiminished popularity is making its owners a bundle. The confident crowd that frequents this high-fashion hangout just can't seem to shake that New York chic. It's infectious. Some of the clientele are likely featured in the trendy monthly magazine that's lying on your coffee table. The main floor features a spectacular bar that runs the length of the long room. The dance floor is in the bank vault downstairs and features a good selection of house music. Dinner is served in the upstairs restaurant, which offers an open view of the floor, at 7:30 p.m. nightly

(8 p.m. on Sunday). The top floor has a pool table and a VIP room. M. K.'s selective admission policy isn't as brutal as Mars's, but it's not painless, either.

Nell's
246 W. 14th St. (Seventh & Eighth Aves.)
675-1567
Open nightly 10 p.m.-4 a.m. Cover $5 Sun.-Thurs., $10 Fri.-Sat. Cards: AE (for dinner only).

Nell's has given the downtown set a good reason to travel west on 14th Street. It's an old-English-style club on two levels, with dark oil paintings, crystal chandeliers and an assortment of mirrors. Monday and Thursday nights in particular are crowded with an inner circle of Manhattan's beautiful people. If you get past the fickle doormen, notorious for having turned away Cher, or if you buy a $200 membership, you can join slender young women in leather miniskirts at a long wooden bar. In the back booths, folks like Bianca Jagger, Robert DeNiro and Sting enjoy a paparazzi-free dinner. Downstairs are two more bars, intimate couches and armchairs and an understated room for dancing. Avoid the overflow crowds on weekends.

The Palladium
126 E. 14th St. (Broadway)
473-7171
Open Thurs. 9 p.m.-3 a.m., Fri.-Sat. 8:30 p.m.-3:30 am. Cover varies.

Redesigned by leading Japanese architect Arata Isozaki, this huge theater is a visual extravaganza that features breathtaking large-scale murals and environmental installations by some of the city's hottest young artists, including Keith Haring and Jean-Michel Basquiat. Some of the club's original notoriety has worn off, but it still attracts a large sampling of New York lifestyles. The dance floor is huge, with blaring disco music and banks of video screens flashing fabulous images. Thursday nights feature Latin-flavored dance music, and occasionally the club books first-rate bands and solo acts. Like other spots that have seen more discriminating days, the Palladium offers discounted admission tickets, available at many record stores.

Peggy Sue's
University Pl. (13th St.)
260-4095
Open Mon.-Wed. 9 p.m.-3 a.m., Thurs.-Sat. 9 p.m.-4:30 a.m. Cover $5-$10. No cards (except AE at the bar, with a $25 minimum).

Nestled a floor above a Chinese restaurant, Peggy Sue's is unpretentious, intimate and devoted to dancing. This downtown hotspot is jammed with investment bankers, fashion models and local graduate students, especially Monday and weekend nights. Find your place at the small pool table, a cluster of tables in the back, the hip-looking bar with red plastic stools, or out on the dance floor with most everyone else.

Private Eyes
212 W. 21st St. (Fifth & Sixth Aves.)
206-7770
Open Sun. 6 p.m.-4 a.m. (men only); Mon. 10 p.m.-4 a.m. (women only); Wed. 5 p.m.-10 p.m. (women) & 10 p.m.-4 a.m. (men); Fri. 10 p.m.-4 a.m. (men); Sat. 9 p.m.-4 a.m. (women). Cover varies. Cards: AE.

This leading gay club is small, with a sleek, high-tech atmosphere highlighted by a giant tiled bar in the center of the room. It emphasizes videos, and two giant screens show seven or eight different movies or rock videos simultaneously. On private-party nights, you'll have to persuade the diligent doorman to let you into the exclusive festivity. If you're dressed right, you might get a chance to mingle with record producers and rock stars.

Pyramid Club
101 Ave. A (6th & 7th Sts.)
420-1590
Open daily 4 p.m.-4 a.m. Cover $10. No cards.

There aren't too many places in town where young East Village nonconformists dressed in uniform black can listen to garage bands, or where transvestites can dance on the bar. Yet the Pyramid has been a favorite too long for its popularity to be just novelty. Its winning formula includes good deejays, great house music and, on occasion, alternative local bands. By the way, the neighborhood isn't for senior citizens or frail types.

The Red Parrot
617 W. 57th St. (Eleventh & Twelfth Aves.)
581-4432
Open Wed.-Sat. 10 p.m.-4 a.m. Cover varies. No cards.

A dressy clientele frequents this city-block-long West Side club, so leave the jeans on your floor at home. On Friday and Saturday nights, a fifteen-piece orchestra plays classic melodies from the forties and fifties, with contemporary music played during the band's breaks. Spacious areas off the dance floor offer comfortable sofas arranged as conversation nooks, making the Red Parrot one of the easier clubs in which to socialize. It's worth a trip once, if only to see the striking red parrots watching the action from inside a large cage.

Red Zone
438 W. 54th St. (Ninth & Tenth Aves.)
582-2222
Open Wed.-Mon. 10 p.m.-4 a.m. Cover $10 weeknights, $15 Fri.-Sat. Cards: AE.

A younger-than-young crowd has popularized this immense and informal midtown dance space. Thursday is the night to be seen here, and you don't need a Chevy to cruise this pickup lot. On occasion, the Red Zone features a decent live rock performance.

Regine's
502 Park Ave. (59th St.)
826-0990
Open Mon.-Sat. 7:30 p.m.-4 a.m. Cover $15 weeknights, $25 Fri.-Sat. All major cards.

The glamour has faded from this famed French disco, where Queen of the Night Regine herself once charmed the rich and beautiful. The jet set has since moved on, leaving a clientele of mostly aging men with expense accounts and modelettes who smile just a mite too much. There are lots of mirrors, and a small neon dance floor. For $57.50, you get a prix-fixe dinner and admission to the disco.

Roseland
239 W. 52nd St. (Broadway)
247-0200
Open Thurs. & Sun. 2:30 p.m.-midnight, Fri. 10 p.m.-4 a.m., Sat. 2:30 p.m.-5 a.m. Cover varies. Cards: AE, V.

If you have a soft spot for the old soft shoe, this restored dancing legend is your place. The crowd nowadays is eclectic, from those who love to dance to ballroom and disco sounds to people who come to hear live contemporary bands. If all the dancing works up a hunger, there's a 700-seat restaurant and a bar to satisfy.

S.O.B.'s
204 Varick St. (W. Houston St.)
243-4940
Open Tues.-Thurs. 5 p.m.-2 a.m., Fri. 5 p.m.-4 a.m., Sat. 7 p.m.-4 a.m. Cover $15-$18 plus two-drink minimum at tables. All major cards.

A high-energy club featuring live bands from Brazil, Africa and the Caribbean. On Friday and Saturday nights, it becomes a Third World sweat house, packed with a casually dressed international crowd dancing wildly to beating drums. Try as you might to stand still, you can't fight the feeling.

Stringfellow's
35 E. 21st St. (Park Ave. South & Broadway)
254-2444
Open Tues.-Sat. 8 p.m.-4 a.m. Cover $15 Tues.-Thurs., $20 Fri., $25 Sat. All major cards.

Like its two successful sister clubs in London, this formal affair is owned by Peter Stringfellow, a trend-watcher who fancies extravagant clothes and a butterfly earring. A crowd with similar tastes flocks to his club, with its pink marble-topped bar, glorious flower arrangements, mirrors galore and waitresses in revealing chiffon wraps. It's a singles attraction (Wednesday is "ladies' night"), and a sprinkling of expense-account-driven men can be seen trying to impress bored, overdressed women by plying them with overpriced bottles of Champagne. At 11 p.m., to the fanfare of the "1812 Overture," a wall separating the disco from the restaurant rises and the place opens up to dancing.

Surf Club
415 E. 91st St. (First & York Aves.)
410-1360
Open Tues.-Sat. 9 p.m.-4 a.m. Cover $5. All major cards.

There's some strong neighborhood competition for the young investment bankers and otherwise well-to-do professionals who make up the Upper East Side club scene, but the

Surf Club remains an established attraction. This is very much a WASP nest—just a few steps from here to the country-club weekend.

Tramps

45 W. 21st St. (Fifth & Sixth Aves.)
254-2956
Open Mon.-Sat. 9 p.m. 4 a.m. Cover varies. No cards.

The old Tramps near Irving Place was a leading venue for the best in blues and jazz music. Now it's in a new, attractive location with a shiny wooden bar, a large dance floor and the requisite pool table in the front window. A different attitude for a different time. Tramps retains a casual atmosphere, and the upscale young crowd enjoys some top-flight live bands.

The Tunnel

220 Twelfth Ave. (entrance on 27th St.)
244-6444
Open nightly 9 p.m.-3 a.m. Cover varies. No cards.

What better use of 15,000 square feet in a desolate West Side building than to make it the home of one of Manhattan's trademark dance clubs? The decor is post–Judgement Day, with massive brick walls, exposed steel beams and arched chambers that lead into the darkness of abandoned railroad tracks. Small

rooms offer temporary relief from a deafening sound system and a sweaty dance floor. There's a serviceable bar; but don't get trapped into paying $1 for a cup of New York tap water. The Tunnel has an electric atmosphere and a self-conscious style. The patrons are young, some *very* young, and sport current good looks. The unwritten dress codes: for women, any combination of leather and lace; for men, any black, Italian-influenced threads.

Wetlands Preserve

161 Hudson St.
966-4225
Open Sun.-Fri. 5 p.m.-4 a.m., Sat. 9 pm..-4 a.m. Cover $4-$10. Cards: AE, MC, V.

That purple haze isn't the dawning of the Age of Aquarius, it's just the atmosphere at this self-described "eco-saloon" that features reggae, rock and neo-pyschedelic bands. The mantle of retro-chic has moved from the fifties to the sixties and seventies; look out. Between idealistic homage to the Grateful Dead and tie-dyed-T-shirt fashion, Wetlands has a serious message that the Earth is in trouble, and if you want to keep on drinking and dancing, you'd better do something to help. Unfortunately, some of the patrons here think you can preserve the Earth's environment while polluting your own.

JAZZ

Blue Note

131 W. 3rd St. (Ave. of the Americas)
475-8592
Shows Mon. 9 p.m., 11 p.m. & 1 a.m.; Tues.-Thurs. & Sun. 9 p.m. & 11:30 p.m.; Fri. 9 p.m., 11 p.m. & 1:30 a.m.; Sat. 3 p.m., 5 p.m., 9 p.m., 11 p.m. & 1:30 a.m. Cover $7.50-$22.50 plus $5 minimum. Cards: AE, MC, V.

This famed Greenwich Village jazz spot has a splendid art-deco interior and showcases seasoned musicions such as Joe Williams and Carmen McRae, proving that consistent talent at sensible prices really is possible. A refreshing spot for a true lover of jazz.

Bradley's

70 University Pl. (10th & 11th Sts.)
228-6440
Shows nightly 9:45 p.m., 11 p.m., 12:30 a.m. & 2 a.m. No cover; $8 minimum at tables. All major cards.

If your predilection is to spend an evening listening to some of the best jazz piano/bass duos in New York, head to this long, dark-paneled room to hear the likes of Tommy Flanagan and Kenny Barron perform for an enthusiastic crowd. Reasonably priced food is served in the back room until 12:30 in the morning, and the bar is lively.

Carlos I
432 Sixth Ave. (10th St.)
982-3260
Shows Sun.-Thurs. 9:30 p.m. & 11:30 p.m.; Fri.-Sat. 9:30 p.m., 11:30 p.m. & 1 a.m. Cover $10-$15 (no cover Mon.). All major cards.

The tiny stage at this supper club and bar in the Village is always filled with major established acts, and the audience appreciates and knows its music. Many nights find musicians taking the stand for an impromptu jam session.

Fat Tuesday's
190 Third Ave. (17th St.)
533-7902
Shows Sun.-Thurs. 8 p.m. & 10 p.m.; Fri.-Sat. 8 p.m., 10 p.m. & midnight. Cover $10-$15 plus $7.50 minimum. All major cards.

The bar and street-level restaurant are hangouts for singles who don't mind paying high prices. Down a flight of stairs is a comfortable space with excellent acoustics. On stage, well-known contemporary musicians play jazz music long and hard for an enthusiastic audience.

Indigo Blues
221 W. 46th St. (Eighth Ave.)
221-0033
Shows Mon. & Thurs.-Sun. 9 p.m. & 11 p.m., Tues. (comedy night) continuous show from 6 p.m. Cover $15 plus one-drink minimum. All major cards.

This midtown club takes its music seriously and gives the world's top artists an intimate and appreciative venue to showcase their talents. Those who frequent this deco-inspired room have been fortunate enough to hear the sounds of musicians such as legendary saxist Miles Davis, and the excellent Toshiko Akiyoshi Jazz Orchestra, featuring Lew Tabackin.

The Knitting Factory
47 E. Houston St. (Mott & Mulberry Sts.)
219-3055
Shows nightly 9 p.m. & 11 p.m. Cover $5-$15.

This plain downtown gathering ground favors an eclectic jazz and new-wave booking policy that has earned it a reputation as an informal, cutting-edge venue for new and established musicians. That's a source of pride for Michael Dorf and Bob Appel, the club's

two wholesome owners. Downstairs features a leisurely, unpretentious bar area with homemade quilted sweaters on the ceiling, quiet tables and good drinks. Upstairs is a narrow, dark space with a small stage, a slightly bigger dance floor, and another bar. Dress is basic jeans and T-shirts with the trendy designer-frame eyeglasses worn by the fashion-conscious SoHo tribe. But, remarkably, patrons don't bring phony attitudes here. If this is what the nineties will be like, count us in.

Michael's Pub
211 E. 55th St. (Second & Third Aves.)
758-2272
Shows Mon.-Sat. 9 p.m. & 11 p.m. Cover varies; two-drink minimum. All major cards.

Handsome Michael's Pub regularly treats a nostalgic, conservative middle-aged crowd to old-fashioned jazz. It's also where Woody Allen leads his New Orleans Funeral and Ragtime Orchestra most Monday nights, but management won't say if he's playing or not. At $25 a pop for a table, why should they? Still, locals and tourists line up on Monday evenings well before 9 p.m. If you only want to hear the band, Michael's bar area has the distinction of pouring some of Manhattan's most expensive drinks.

Mikell's
760 Columbus Ave. (97th St.)
864-8832
Open daily 4 p.m.-4 a.m. Shows 9 p.m., 11 p.m. & 1 a.m. Cover varies; $7 minimum. All major cards.

The jazz at this Upper West Side establishment is straightforward and pleasant. Such greats as Art Blakey have enthralled and entertained here, and a devoted band of jazz-loving neighborhood followers keep returning for more.

Red Blazer Too
349 W. 46th St. (Eighth & Ninth Aves.)
262-3112
Open Mon.-Tues. & Thurs.-Fri. 8:30 p.m.-12:30 a.m., Wed. 5:30 p.m.-1 a.m., Sat. 9 p.m.-2 a.m., Sun. 1 a.m.-9 p.m. No cover. All major cards.

The familiar strains of Dixieland rule this large, nostalgic and friendly venue that some

The Original X.O

X.O

COGNAC
Hennessy

say has singlehandedly revived whatever popularity the big-band sound has reclaimed. The club is always busy, with a mix of young professionals and an older crowd that wants to relive the days of Benny Goodman and Glenn Miller.

Spo-Dee-O-Dee

565 W. 23rd St. (Eleventh Ave.)
206-1990

Open nightly 5 p.m.-4 a.m. Shows 10:30 p.m. & midnight. Cover $5-$15. Cards: AE.

This new space has managed to ignite the sophisticated, looks-conscious downtown art crowd once again. Do these models, artists, photographers, writers, stockbrokers and film- and record-industry executives ever work? Or are deals and other creations simply made at this club's antique oak bar, or in one of its many overstuffed couches, or under the brass chandeliers? On the other side of green velvet curtains that separate the bar from the nightclub, you can listen to jazz, blues or swing blues that alternate with excellent house dance music. Also highly recommended is a game of pool upstairs, in the aptly named Great Expectations Room.

Sweet Basil

88 Seventh Ave. South (Bleecker St.)
242-1785

Open nightly 8 p.m.-2 a.m. Cover $12-$15 plus $6 minimum. All major cards.

One of the more attractive jazz clubs in town, with hanging plants, a glass facade and knotty pine walls. It offers a wide range of top jazz groups, from mainstream small combos to big bands and avant-garde artists such as South African jazz pianist Abdullah Ibrahim.

Sweetwater's

170 Amsterdam Ave. (68th St.)
873-4100

Shows Thurs. 9 p.m. & 11 p.m., Fri.-Sat. 9 p.m. & midnight Cover $10-$20 plus $10 minimum. All major cards.

Located near Lincoln Center, Sweetwater's is just fine as an after-theater spot, and many of its attractive, affluent-looking patrons have, indeed, just come from seeing a play. Sweetwater's features a top selection of today's leading jazz and pop musicians, who

find this striking, multilevel, mirrored cabaret a great place to play.

The Village Gate

160 Bleecker St. (Thompson St.)
475-5120

Shows nightly 9 p.m.-2 a.m. Cover varies; two-drink minimum. Cards: AE, MC, V

A music institution with a long history of presenting many top names from the jazz world, this popular club also has been presenting off-Broadway revues. One of the best is its "Salsa Meets Jazz" series every Monday night, when a top Latin band leader plays with a leading jazz soloist. The downstairs showroom is cavernous, with a dance floor in the back. The crowd is unpretentious and loves its music. For those who prefer their jazz as background, go upstairs to the terrace bar/café, where a pianist and bassist play for a crowd of Greenwich Villagers and tourists.

Village Vanguard

178 Seventh Ave. South (11th St.)
255-4037

Shows nightly 10 p.m., 11:30 p.m. & 1 a.m. Cover $12 plus $6 minimum. No cards.

This dark basement room has been a happening jazz scene for more than three decades. Great musicians such as Miles Davis, John Coltrane and Pharoah Sanders have graced its welcome stage, and the club still keeps step with the times. Those who play and those who pay appreciate the Vanguard's straightforward approach and its commitment to music. On any night, a performance can turn into a lively jam session. Monday night regulars Mel Lewis and the seventeen-piece Jazz Orchestra are becoming a Manhattan mainstay.

Zanzibar and Grill

550 Third Ave. (36th & 37th Sts.)
779-0606

Continuous shows Mon.-Sat. from 9 p.m., Sun. from 8 p.m. No cover; minimum varies. All major cards.

This new room features some promising bookings of local and international talent. The music can be eclectic; one evening you'll hear interesting sounds from Brazil and South Africa; another time, you might find yourself immersed in a evening of blues or enraptured by a guitar duo and the house Zanziband.

MUSIC

The Bottom Line
15 W. 4th St. (Mercer St.)
228-6300
Shows Sun.-Thurs. 8 p.m. & 11 p.m., Fri.-Sat. 8:30 p.m. & 11:30 p.m. Cover varies. No cards.

This consistently versatile, intimate club of national merit is often a last chance to see great music acts before their next album makes them big stars. Arguably the best venue of its kind in the city, The Bottom Line has presented everyone from Santana to Simply Red. The sound system is excellent, prices are sensible and the sight lines are good. Shows often sell out quickly.

The Cat Club
76 E. 13th St. (Broadway & Fourth Ave.)
505-0090
Shows Mon.-Thurs. 11 p.m. & midnight; Fri.-Sat. 10:30 p.m. & 1 a.m., Sun. 8 p.m. Cover varies; two-drink minimum. No cards.

Be sure of what day it is before you saunter over to The Cat Club. On Friday and Saturday nights, you'll enter a wild dance house filled with a strange brew of rockers, yuppies and black-clad downtown types. On Sunday nights—look out—the great sound system play 1930s and 1940s swing music, which attracts its own crowd altogether. Weeknights offer a range of live music in an intimate setting, from raw and raucous heavy-metal bands to pretty-boy popsters with guitars. Those nights attract a clan of black-haired shock-rockers, record-industry types and blonde girls and guys in tight jeans. The bands aren't bad to watch, either.

CBGB
315 Bowery St. (Bleecker St.)
982-4052
Shows Mon.-Thurs. 9:30 p.m., Fri.-Sat. 10:30 p.m. Cover varies. No cards.

It's hard to believe this temple of alternative music still exists, long after the bands that it fostered in the late seventies—such as Blondie and Talking Heads—have gone mainstream. CBGB's, in stark contrast, has no intention of cleaning up its act and marching to an establishment beat, and neither do the spiky-haired youngsters who come to hear fast-and-furious underground bands of local and national ill repute. In that sense, the club has lost its cutting edge for all but a certain fringe element of the music scene; its untamed attitude is certainly not for everyone. The club embodies the physical attributes of a nightmarish hangover; you can bet that the late-night leather crowd isn't missing choir practice.

Chelsea Place
147 Eighth Ave. (17th St.)
924-8413
Open nightly 5:30 p.m.-4 a.m. Cover $10 after 8 p.m. All major cards.

A touristy spot that can be smoky, crowded, noisy and friendly all at once. At first you think you're at the wrong address; the front room looks like an antique shop. Go past the swinging door into a world of flashing lights that features established pop music acts. More intimacy can be found upstairs at the sleek white bar.

Lone Star Café Roadhouse
240 W. 52nd St. (Broadway & Eighth Ave.)
245-2950
Shows nightly 9:30 p.m. & 11:30 p.m. Cover $7-$20. All major cards.

The Lone Star has moved uptown and a notch upscale, but it still attracts beer-drinking homesick Texans and those who just romanticize the idea. Fortunately, the booking policy hasn't changed, either. A huge stage features top soul, rock, country-and-western and rhythm-and-blues artists. Rhinestone cowboys can mosey over to a balcony table overlooking the stage or saddle up to a long bar on the main floor.

Maxwell's
1039 Washington St., Hoboken, N.J.
(201) 798-4064
Shows Thurs. 10 p.m., Fri.-Sat. 11 p.m. Cover $3-$10. No cards.

A small, unpretentious New Jersey landmark that put Hoboken on the map. It books an adventuresome mix of headline rock bands and struggling musicians who are often worth the Hudson River crossing. Record-industry executives come to check out promising acts, and the dress is anything from trademark postpunk black to collegiate-style blue jeans.

The New Ritz
254 54th St. (Broadway & Eighth Ave.)
5418900
Shows Mon.-Thurs. 9 p.m., Fri.-Sat. 11 p.m.
Cover $10-$25. No cards.

This established rock, rhythm-and-blues and new-wave venue is now at the former home of Studio 54. The acoustics and sight lines don't do justice to the excellent, nationally known musicians who take the stage on any given night, including Los Lobos, Living Colour, Todd Rundgren and The Coasters.

O'Lunney's
915 Second Ave. (48th & 49th Sts.)
751-5470
Open Mon.-Fri. 11 a.m.-7 a.m., Sat. 6 p.m.-4 a.m. Cover $3 weeknights, $5 weekends. All major cards.

All it takes to make you feel right at home with the loud young crowd that descends on this upscale Manhattan honky-tonk. is some old-fashioned live country music, a plateful of "citified" down-home cooking and a good cold brew.

PIANO BARS

Beekman Tower
3 Mitchell Pl. (First Ave. & 49th St.)
355-7300
Open Tues.-Sat. 9 p.m.-2 a.m. No cover. All major cards.

From the top of this vintage 1928 tower, the view unfolds to the north along the East River, and to the south past the U.N. building and the Empire State Building, all the way to downtown. Day turns to night before your eyes, sometimes with a mesmerizing sunset. Try to get a seat on the terrace—the pianist sounds just as good out there, and the view is spectacular.

Bemelmans Bar
Carlyle Hotel,
35 E. 76th St. (Madison Ave.)
744-1600
Open daily noon-12:30 a.m. Shows Mon.-Sat. 10 p.m. Cover $5. All major cards.

Named for Ludwig Bemelmans, the painter of classic murals and author of the beloved Madeleine books, this intimate bar attracts a relaxed crowd who enjoys first-class crooners.

Café Carlyle
Carlyle Hotel,
35 E. 76th St. (Madison Ave.)
744-1600
Music nightly 10 p.m. & midnight. Cover varies. All major cards.

For a taste of café society, spend an evening at Café Carlyle, listening to pianist-in-residence Bobby Short perform stylish renditions of Cole Porter, Gershwin and Hart. A Carlyle standby since 1968, Short has earned a large number of sophisticated admirers. Especially pleasant are the comfortable, cozy aqua banquettes next to the romantic pastel murals painted by Vertes. In Short's absence, such greats as George Shearing and Peter Niro perform.

Chez Josephine
414 W. 42nd St. (Ninth & Tenth Aves.)
594-1925
Open Mon.-Sat. 6 p.m.-midnight. Cards: AE, MC, V.

Named for Josephine Baker, the legendary singer of the 1920s, this bistro is owned by one of her many unofficially adopted sons. Jean Claude Baker has created a rococo atmosphere highlighted with red velvet curtains and banquettes, a brilliant blue-tin ceiling, a long zinc bar and posters and paintings showing Baker herself in various stages of scanty dress. On any given night, an eclectic crowd—including models, writers, a sprinkling of celebrities, international businesspeople and actors—fills the long, narrow restaurant. Be forewarned: You may enjoy the show so much that you decide to ditch your theater tickets and stay all evening. You can linger at the bar drinking Champagne and listening to show tunes hammered out by two sensational piano players.

The Hors d'Oeuvrerie
One World Trade Center, 107th Fl.
938-1111
Open daily 3 p.m.-1 a.m. Music Mon.-Sat. 7:30 p.m.-12:30 a.m., Sun. 4 p.m.-9 p.m. Cover charge $3.50 after 7:30 p.m. All major cards.

For a unique perspective of the city, the 107th floor of the World Trade Center offers this gorgeous, multilevel, internationally minded cocktail lounge. In between potent martinis, you can snack on fresh oysters, sushi and Spanish sausage. A mellow jazz trio alternates with a pianist, with dancing on a post-age-stamp-sized floor. Jackets are required but reservations are not, though there's often a wait for seats.

Knickerbocker Saloon
33 University Pl. (Fifth & Sixth Aves.)
228-8490
Music Sun.-Thurs. 9:30 p.m.-1:30 a.m., Fri.-Sat. 9:30 p.m.-4 a.m. Cover varies; $7 minimum at bar tables. Cards: AE, MC, V.

World War II posters and original Hirschfield drawings decorate the walls of this Village neighborhood bar and restaurant, where locals gather to enjoy fine jazz piano/bass combos. Such greats as Sir Roland Hanna and Ron Carter play in this upbeat atmosphere against a quiet backdrop of conversation.

One Fifth Avenue
One Fifth Ave. (8th St.)
260-3434
Open Wed.-Thurs. 9 a.m.-12:30 a.m., Fri.-Sat. 9 a.m.-1:30 a.m. All major cards.

A former watering hole of the madly stylish, this spot now attracts a noisy crowd of young singles and couples who hang out at the long bar or sit in the front toom listening to jazz trios and imagining that they're aboard an ocean liner (courtesy of the art-deco-style porthole photos of the sea).

One If By Land, Two If By Sea
17 Barrow St. (Seventh Ave.)
255-8649
Open Sun.-Mon. 5:30 p.m.-midnight, Tues.-Sat. 5:30 p.m.-2 a.m. No cover. All major cards.

A sophisticated crowd frequents this delightful carriage house for dinner and to listen to the show tunes played in the handsome bar. The front room is a relaxing amalgam of brick walls, rust-colored velvet banquettes and Spanish-American primitive paintings. Though the guests are super chic, casual dress is permitted. If you're lucky, you might catch Joseph Papp, Pat Kennedy Lawford or Diana Ross dining in the back.

Peacock Alley
Waldorf-Astoria Hotel, 49th St. & Park Ave.
355-3000
Music Sun.-Thurs. 8 p.m.-midnight, Fri.-Sat. 9 p.m.-1 a.m. No cover charge. All major cards.

A New York institution, Peacock Alley is located next to a two-ton, nine-foot-tall bronze clock that's topped with a miniature Statue of Liberty. An international crowd gathers around what was once Cole Porter's personal piano, to hear some fine music played with style by Jimmy Lyon; Lynn Richards sings after 10 p.m. and Penny Brook sits in on Sundays and Mondays.

Regency Lounge
Hotel Regency, 61st. St. & Park Ave.
759-4100
Music nightly 6 p.m.-1 a.m. No cover. All major cards.

The intimate Regency Lounge is an East Side citadel for men in Saville Row suits who speak four languages, and who have with them willowy beauties swathed in the latest fashion. The alternating pianists play second fiddle to the chic crowd.

The River Café
One Water St. (beneath the Brooklyn Bridge), Brooklyn
(718) 522-5200
Music nightly 6:30 p.m.-1 a.m. No cover. All major cards.

Poised below the Brooklyn Bridge, this barge restaurant with a piano bar and cocktail lounge offers a breathtaking view of lower Manhattan and the East River. This romantic rendezvous is elegantly simple: hardwood floors, fresh flowers and one wall made entirely of glass. Reserve well in advance if you're dining, and ask for a seat next to a window. A strict dress code requires jackets for men.

Village Corner

142 LaGuardia Pl.
473-9762

Music Sun.-Thurs. 9 p.m.-2 a.m., Fri.-Sat. 9 p.m.-3 a.m. No cover. No cards.

If you don't mind a seedy, if authentic, decor, you'll be rewarded with the fine playing of Lance Hayward. On Wednesday and Thursday nights, Jim Roberts plays lively 1930s music. There's beer by the mug, bottle or pitcher, and burgers, chili and cheesecake. Flashy young downtowners are regulars here.

The Village Green

531 Hudson St. (W. 10th & Charles Sts.)
255-1650

Music nightly 9 p.m.-3 a.m. No cover. Cards: AE, MC, V.

This stunning West Village townhouse features a dark, romantic restaurant downstairs and an upstairs lounge full of mirrors, fireplaces and flattering lighting. West Villagers and uptowners gather around the piano while Murray Grand sings his own songs and plays contemporary favorites.

CHANEL

CHANEL BOUTIQUE: N°5 EAST 57TH STREET,

NEW YORK CITY   (212) 355-5050

©T&CO. 1990

Seven ways to say three words.
Diamond, emerald, ruby
and sapphire rings from Tiffany.
Available at Tiffany & Co.,
Fifth Avenue and 57th Street, New York.
To inquire: 800-526-0649.

TIFFANY & CO.

SHOPS

WHAT'S YOUR PLEASURE?

To shop in New York is to know no limit, to choose among a wealth of treasures from every corner of the world. The discerning collector in search of an exotic Turkish spice, a rare out-of-print book or an antique bird cage; the gourmand in need of a fix of beluga caviar or a pound of Swiss Champagne-cream truffles; or the eccentric shopper for whom FAO Schwarz carries its $24,000 stuffed-moose family, will find their every whim catered to here. New York's shopkeepers pride themselves on satisfying the most demanding customer.

It's our intention to steer you to the best of the crop. Stroll along Fifth Avenue, Madison Avenue and across 57th Street to find New York's finest. Or cross through Central Park to the Upper West Side for the trendy boutiques on Columbus Avenue, and the ones beginning to sprout on Amsterdam Avenue. New York's 34th Street once epitomized midtown shopping, and Macy's still draws millions to its fortress. Those seeking funky fashions or artsy articles should trek downtown to both Greenwich Village and SoHo. Wherever your travels take you, New York's streets celebrate the passion for shopping.

ANTIQUES

The Manhattan Art & Antiques Center
1050 Second Ave. (55th St.)
355-4400
Open Mon.-Sat. 10:30 a.m.-6 p.m., Sun. noon-6 p.m.

One of New York City's richest shopping experiences. Collectors on the prowl for better-quality items at less-than-Madison-Avenue prices will fare well here. Fabergé, Tiffany, Lalique, Hummel, Cartier, Baccarat—all are casually displayed in one center. There are dealers offering English furniture, American quilts, Ming and Tung pottery and Satsuma pieces; in total over 100 dealers display their wares on three large floors. Look carefully: some of the best shops are hidden. The Center offers expert packing, crating and shipping.

Place des Antiquaires
125 E. 57th St. (Park & Lexington Aves.)
758-2900
Open Mon.-Sat. 11 a.m.-6 p.m.

Located in the heart of New York's poshest area, Place des Antiquaires houses more than 75 international art and antique galleries. Antique lovers cluster here, examining relics of yesteryear and exchanging anecdotes on col-lecting antiques. Included are European and American furniture, paintings, marble and bronze sculptures, period jewelry, ceramics, glass and even Russian works of art and icons.

ACCESSORIES & COLLECTIBLES

Bardith I
1015 Madison Ave. (79th St.)
737-6699
Open Mon.-Fri. 11 a.m.-5:30 p.m., Sat. 11 a.m.-5 p.m. Closed Sat. in summer.

This boutique's large selection of porcelain and china plates dazzles the eye and exemplifies the owner's good taste. Collectors flock here seeking eighteenth- and nineteenth-century English ware. Other locations at 31 E. 72nd Street and 901 Madison Avenue.

Charlotte Moss
131 E. 70th St. (Lexington & Park Aves.)
772-3320
Open Mon.-Thurs. 10 a.m.-5:30 p.m., Fri. 10 a.m.-5 p.m.

Anglophiles or purveyors of English country decor flock to Charlotte Moss. Her eclectic and unrivaled selection includes such finds as prints, bird cages, bows, tassels, boxes and candlesticks.

Funchies, Bunkers, Gaks & Gleeks
1050 Second Ave. (55th St.)
980-9418
Open Mon.-Sat. 10:30 a.m.-5:30 p.m., Sun. 1 p.m.-5:30 p.m.

Okay, the name sounds silly, but Funchies, Bunkers, Gaks & Gleeks is a delightful gallery with an authoritative collection of toys and nostalgia. Though the shop seems whimsical and its owner free as a breeze, beneath the apparent chaos is strong order. Items are organized by color, material or subject; ask to see the album that catalogs hundreds of patchwork quilts. The counters are covered with regiments of soldiers, windup toys, mechanical banks, chocolate molds and the like, and there's an impressive selection of duck and goose decoys.

Leo Kaplan Ltd.
967 Madison Ave. (75th & 76th Sts.)
249-6766
Open Mon.-Sat. 10 a.m.-5:30 p.m.

Specializing in four categories of accessories—art-nouveau glass, eighteenth-century English pottery and porcelain, antique and contemporary paperweights, and Fabergé and Russian works of art—this family-owned business has a grand reputation, and gives its patrons warm, personal attention.

Rita Ford Music Boxes
19 E. 65th St. (Madison & Fifth Aves.)
535-6717
Open Mon.-Sat. 9 a.m.-5 p.m.

This store is a world-renowned resource for automatic music boxes. Rita Ford stocks a large inventory of affordable, jeweled and intricately adorned antique and contemporary music boxes of all sizes and shapes. The most popular boxes are the antiques from Switzerland, Germany and France. Handcrafted carousels are also favorites. Both the shopper in search of unusual gifts and the collector will delight in the children's items, jewel boxes and gold-encrusted wonders. The prices range from pocket change to the stratospheric.

Rita Sacks
1050 Second Ave. (55th St.)
421-8132
Open Mon.-Sat. 10:30 a.m.-6:30 p.m., Sun. noon-6 p.m.

In this elegant, well-organized store, you'll find quality objects, including art nouveau, art deco, signed glass and twentieth-century costume jewelry. Rita is a cordial host who makes wonderful conversation while you browse among her valuables, especially when it concerns her special hobby, collecting fakes.

AMERICAN

American Hurrah Antiques
766 Madison Ave. (66th St.)
535-1930
Open Tues.-Sat. 11 a.m.-6 p.m. Closed Sat. in summer.

Americana is still in vogue, and American Hurrah is the place to find it. The family-owned and -operated business has a friendly atmosphere and authentic merchandise. For almost two decades, the owners have taken their penchant for collecting bits and pieces of America's history and built it into a business. They personally select, repair and restore each item. And double hurrahs for the selection of patchwork quilts, American Indian art, folk art and paintings.

Laura Fisher
1050 Second Ave., 1st concourse,
Gallery 57 (55th St.)
838-2596
Open Mon.-Sat. 11 a.m.-5:30 p.m.

Laura Fisher, the author of a reference book entitled *Quilts of Illusion,* is an authority on Americana. Her American gallery is a fantastic collection of baskets and such folk art as needlework, decoys, primitives, hooked rugs, quilts and coverlets. She arranges for quilt repair and restoration and searches for antique textiles. Many of her items are included in major corporate collections.

ART DECO & ART NOUVEAU

Artisan Antiques
81 University Pl.
751-5214
Open Mon.-Fri. 10 a.m.-6 p.m., Sun. noon-6 p.m.
This store houses the largest collection of French art-deco lighting in the world. Among the finds here are 1920s art-deco frosted-glass and metal chandeliers, wall sconces, lamps, period furniture, statues and bronzes. In the manner of Lalique, the lighting fixtures are beveled, shaped, etched and raised.

Delorenzo
958 Madison Ave. (75th & 76th Sts.)
249-7575
Open Mon.-Sat. 10 a.m.-6 p.m. Closed Sat. in summer.
Objects rare, unique and reflective of the French art-deco tradition are carefully displayed in this well-known Madison Avenue haunt. The handsome collection of art-deco sits side by side with more curvaceous European and art-nouveau designs. All attest to the refined taste of owner Delorenzo. For the serious collector of this genre, a visit to Delorenzo is a must.

Lillian Nassau Ltd.
220 E. 57th St. (Second & Third Aves.)
759-6062
Open Mon.-Fri. 10 a.m.-5 p.m., Sat. 10:30 a.m.-5 p.m. Closed Sat. in summer.
Carrying on the family tradition established years ago by his mother Lillian, Paul Nassau runs the store that's known to house one of the most extensive collections of Tiffany glass in the world. There are also beautiful bronzes, European art pottery and a broad range of art-nouveau and art-deco furniture.

Minna Rosenblatt Ltd.
844 Madison Ave. (69th St.)
288-0250
Open Mon.-Sat. 10 a.m.-5:30 p.m.
This tiny shop specializing in twentieth-century decorative arts boasts an impressive

choice of Tiffany lamps, art-nouveau glass, French Cameo, Daum and Gallé glass.

Philip Chasen Gallery
985 Madison Ave. (76th St.)
472-2200
Open Mon.-Sat. 10:30 a.m.-6:30 p.m.
This small shop beckons to passersby with a superb and colorful selection of art nouveau and art deco, including Tiffany, Gallé and Lalique. The owner and his associates are knowledgeable and friendly. Other works to note are the twentieth-century etchings.

Primavera
808 Madison Ave. (68th St.)
288-1569
Open Mon.-Sat. 11 a.m.-6 p.m.
Primavera was one of the first stores in New York to specialize in art deco; many of its items have been loaned or sold to major museums. Visitors will find pieces by leading deco designers on view. A fine collection of jewelry is combined with a judicious selection of furniture. Its SoHo gallery (at 133 Prince Street; 254-0137) specializes in 1950s decorations, postwar industrial design, and modern American jewelry.

ASIAN

Art Asia Inc.
1086 Madison Ave. (81st & 82nd Sts.)
249-7250
Open Mon.-Sat. 10 a.m.-6 p.m., Sun. noon-6 p.m.
Art Asia's many years in the business assure us that the collectibles found in this shop are chosen with a practiced eye. Jewelry from the Orient, Indian miniatures, fine chests and reasonably priced porcelains work well as room accents. The store's bounty is decorative and definitely mixable with items from different periods.

Doris Leslie Blau Inc.
15 E. 57th St. (Fifth & Madison Aves.)
759-3715
Open by appt. only.
The Blau gallery is stocked with Oriental and European tapestries and rugs of exem-

plary quality and distinction. For over seventeen years, the owner has specialized in rare rugs, carpets, and textiles from the seventeenth to the early twentieth centuries. Here one finds antique floor coverings of all types—Turkish, Caucasian, European, Indian, Chinese and Persian.

E & J Frankel Ltd.
1040 Madison Ave. (79th & 80th Sts.)
879-5733
Open Mon.-Sat. 10 a.m.-5:30 p.m.

A skilled eye for collecting, a wide range of items, and undisputed scholarship combine to create an unusually attractive Chinese and Japanese art gallery. There are splendid bronzes; delicate jewelry, furniture and paintings of excellent design and quality; and lovely robes, instruments and jade artifacts dating from the year 5000 B.C. to the present.

Flying Cranes Antiques
1050 Second Ave. (55th St.)
223-4600
Open Mon.-Sat. 10:30 a.m.-6 p.m.

Curator Clifford Schaefer regularly assisted *Metropolitan Home*'s Dr. Swatch with answers about Oriental art objects. Indeed, Japanese collectors familiar with his reputation regularly come from Japan to his New York gallery for fine eighteenth- and nineteenth-century Japanese furniture, ivories and silver.

Koreana Art & Antiques
963 Madison Ave. (75th & 76th Sts.)
249-0400
Open Mon.-Sat. 11 a.m.-6 p.m.

Displayed in homey room settings, Koreana's art and antiques are tastefully arranged. The owner, an artist and collector, has carried out authentic Korean designs in the displays. There is a wide selection of woods, paintings and ceramics dating from the eighteenth and nineteenth centuries.

AUCTION HOUSES

It's one thing to wander through an antique store, examining this and fingering that; it's quite another to feel the quickened pace of the auctioneer's cadence. Unlike retail stores, auction houses do not buy property for resale; they act as agents only. You'll find lively action and interesting antiques for sale—going once, going twice—at New York's handful of top-drawer auction houses.

Christie's
502 Park Ave. (59th St.)
546-1000
Open for business Mon.-Fri. 10 a.m.-5:30 p.m.; open for viewing Sat. 10 a.m.-5 p.m., Sun. 1 p.m.-5 p.m. Closed Sat.-Sun. in summer.

Christie's prides itself on auctioning anything: jewelry, furniture, stamps, wine, Russian art, toys, even movie memorabilia. Christie's has been selling fine art at auction for over 220 years. With offices worldwide, this venerable name in auctioneering holds sales several times a week. Even the doorman, Gil, has become a celebrity in his own right.

Christie's East
219 E. 67th St. (Second & Third Aves.)
606-0400
Open for business Mon.-Sat. 9:30 a.m.-5 p.m.; open for viewing Tues.-Sat. 10 a.m.-5 p.m., most Suns. 1 p.m.-5 p.m. Closed Sat.-Sun. in summer.

This Christie's subsidiary auctions off less expensive merchandise—furniture, art, glass, china and paintings. Like its parent company, it prints a catalog prior to the auction, and a sale here is equally exciting and interesting.

Phillips Fine Art Auctioneers
406 E. 79th St. (First & York Aves.)
570-4830
Open Mon.-Fri. 9 a.m.-5 p.m.

Located near the East River, this gallery has a substantial business worldwide. Offering a variety of auctions, it features mainly high-quality decorative arts, furniture and paintings.

Sotheby's
1334 York Ave. (72nd St.)
606-7000
Open Mon.-Sat. 10 a.m.-5 p.m., some Sundays.

A handsome building houses this important gallery, which is perhaps New York's most famous auction gallery in terms of gross sales; the media readily publicizes major purchases. Auctions are held frequently and by category—for instance, rugs, silver or furniture from a particular estate, country or period. The sales are always lively and brisk; buyers are fierce in their acquisitiveness and determination. Viewing the auction collector at work is a theatrical experience: go for the drama of it all.

Sotheby's Arcade Auctions
1334 York Ave. (72nd St.)
606-7147
Open Mon.-Sat. 10 a.m.-5 p.m., some Sundays.

In addition to Sotheby's' regularly scheduled specialized auctions, more than 30 Sotheby's Arcade Auctions are held during the year. These auctions, generally held every other week, are an excellent venue for buying and selling less expensive collector's items and estate property.

William Doyle Galleries
175 E. 87th St.
(Lexington & Third Aves.)
427-2730
Open Mon. 9 a.m.-7:30 p.m., Tues. 9 a.m.-5 p.m., Sat. 10 a.m.-5 p.m., Sun. noon-5 p.m.

Based on sales, Doyle, an American-owned firm, is the third-largest house in New York. For some reason, most likely the clientele, it can have some extraordinarily high prices. Watch for unusual estates that blend glamorous names with beautiful merchandise. Exhibitions are held on Mondays, Tuesdays, Wednesdays and Saturdays.

CLOCKS

Berger-Conklin Antique Clocks
29 E. 12th St. (University Pl. & Fifth Ave.)
929-1830
Open Tues.-Fri. noon-6 p.m., Sat. noon-4 p.m. or by appt.

You can purchase almost any kind of clock here, but the bulk of the business is in clock restoration and repair. Dealers, museums and private collectors attest to Mr. Berger's exper-

tise. Don't hesitate to entrust your cherished timepiece to his care.

Clock Hutt Ltd.
1050 Second Ave. (55th St.)
759-2395
Open Mon.-Sat. 10:30 a.m.-5:30 p.m., Sun. noon-5:30 p.m.

This sprawling gallery, housed in the Manhattan Art and Antiques Center, has over 1,200 square feet of space, yet its astonishing array of clocks spills onto the promenade. The Hutt family has been in this business for some 21 years, and is known for its meticulous repairs. Clock Hutt has the largest collection of eighteenth- and nineteenth-century European and American clocks in New York.

Oldies, Goldies & Moldies
1609 Second Ave. (83rd & 84th Sts.)
737-3935
Open Mon.-Fri. noon-8 p.m., Sat. 11 a.m.-7 p.m., Sun. 11 a.m.-6 p.m.

This store built its reputation on Victorian and turn-of-the-century objects, but now it specializes in clocks. You'll find all kinds of them—neon, radio, you name it. Ronald Reagan purchased one here in 1986. Wide variety and warm, personal attention are good reasons to shop here.

ENGLISH

Amdur Antiques
1193 Lexington Ave. (81st & 82nd Sts.)
879-0652

Judith Amdur Antiques
950 Lexington Ave. (69th & 70th Sts.)
472-2691
Open Mon.-Fri. 11 a.m.-5:30 p.m., Sat. noon-5 p.m.

There are no adjoining doors between these two Amdur shops, but they are definitely his-and-hers antique stores. Each one is filled with small English furniture and accessories, including trays, tables, candlesticks, vases—beautiful objects of a diverse nature.

Arthur Ackermann & Son Inc.
50 E. 57th St. (Park & Madison Aves.)
753-5292
Open Mon.-Fri. 9 a.m.-5 p.m., Sat. 9 a.m.-4 p.m. Closed Sat. in July & Aug.

Long established at this address between Park and Madison, Arthur Ackermann & Son has a reputation as the undisputed leader in resources for eighteenth-century English furniture. The gallery features extraordinary equestrian delights mingled with English accessories and fine furnishings. If you have trouble finding English antiques in England, come here.

Florian Papp Inc.
962 Madison Ave. (75th & 76th Sts.)
288-6770
Open Mon.-Fri. 9:30 a.m.-5:30 p.m., Sat. 10 a.m.-5 p.m. Closed Sat. in summer.

Serious eighteenth-century English furniture collectors should visit Florian Papp. This store was the first antique store of its kind to open in New York, and it remains one of the very best today. Since the start of the century, it has offered such quality decorative pieces as grandfather clocks and gleaming mirrors, plus a fine assortment of American Colonial and post-Revolutionary pieces.

Kentshire Galleries Ltd.
37 E. 12th St. (University Pl. & Broadway)
673-6644
Open Mon.-Fri. 9 a.m.-5 p.m., Sat. 10 a.m.-2 p.m. Closed Sat. in summer.

Kentshire is proud of its collector's gallery for antique collectibles in cut crystal, porcelain, silver, and tortoiseshell from the Georgian, Regency and later periods. The elegant larger gallery still boasts a big selection of magnificent wood furniture in excellent condition. Prices are high, but so is the quality.

Tiller & King Ltd.
1058 Madison Ave. (80th St.)
988-2861
Open Mon.-Sat. 10 a.m.-5:30 p.m. Closed Sat. in July & Aug.

For authentic eighteenth- and nineteenth-century English and American furniture, visit Tiller and King. Accessories of all types emphasize a deft collection of beautiful furnishings. Period lamps are the store's specialty.

EUROPEAN

Betty Jane Bart Antiques
1225 Madison Ave. (88th & 89th Sts.)
410-2702
Open Mon.-Fri. 11 a.m.-5 p.m., Sat. 10:30 a.m.-5 p.m. Closed Fri.-Sat. in summer.

Open less than a decade, this tiny shop, nestled inconspicuously among bigger shops along the avenue, deals in marvelous seventeenth- and eighteenth-century European antiques. Betty specializes in Italian and Spanish items, but also carries some French pieces. She favors furniture and things whimsical, such as puppets and amusing bird cages. Her painted furniture (with its original paint) is eminently collectible, as are her many decorative screens.

Kurt Gluckselig Antiques Inc.
1050 Second Ave. (55th St.)
758-1805
Open Mon.-Sat. 11 a.m.-5 p.m. Closed Sat. in summer.

This venerable old gallery was originally established in Austria. The owner, Kurt Gluckselig, currently sits on the board of directors of the Appraisers Association of America. His store specializes in sixteenth- to nineteenth-century porcelain, French furniture and paintings. Customers include the Metropolitan Museum of Art.

Linda Horn Antiques & Decorative Objects
1015 Madison Ave. (78th & 79th Sts.)
772-1122
Open Mon.-Sat. 10 a.m.-6 p.m. Closed Sat. in July & Aug.

Displayed in a fairy-tale setting, the antiques in this new location are romantically reminiscent of turn-of-the-century living. The previous New York store was painted to resemble the ruins of Pompeii; this one, full of trompe l'oeil by Russian artist Ilya Schevel, evokes the atmosphere of a garden. The store features dramatic selections favored by Linda Horn—a grouping of some 300 bulldogs atop a massive chest, and animal forms everywhere: including snakes, frogs, toads, even a bat sconce.

The Little Antique Shop
44 E. 11th St. (University Pl. & Broadway)
673-5173
Open Mon.-Fri. 9 a.m.-5 p.m.

Large, larger, and largely wonderful is a way to describe the highly unusual and decorative (and often highly priced) objects that are glamorously displayed throughout this "little antique shop." The name belies the truth, and the quality and unique aura of many of the pieces command attention. This is an eclectic collection of impressive quality, with outstanding Oriental pieces.

Pierre Deux
367 Bleecker St. (Charles St.)
243-7740
870 Madison Ave. (71st St.)
570-9343
Open Mon.-Sat. 10 a.m.-6 p.m. Closed Sat. in July & Aug.
Open Mon.-Sat. 10 a.m.-6 p.m., Sat. 10 a.m.-5 p.m.

Les deux Pierre Deux have long been famous for introducing America to the charms of rustic French provincial style. Its popularity was boosted by the festivities for and hoopla over the French Bicentennial. The downtown store carries antiques only, while the uptown location has Pierre Deux reproductions. Here you also will also find a potpourri of furniture, accessories and fabrics, all affordable.

REPAIRS

If it is expensive to buy antiques, so too is it to have them repaired. But many beautiful items are worth the cost, and we've found a few places for you to take your valuables without fear of their becoming further damaged.

CERAMICS

Hess Repairs
200 Park Ave. South, 15th Fl. (17th St.)
260-2255
Open Mon.-Fri. 10:30 a.m.-5 p.m.

Bernie Hirsch has spent over 40 years doing repairs, many for our city's museums. Jobs start at $20. This family of Russian immigrants works together closely on all projects.

Sano Studio
767 Lexington Ave., 4th Fl.
(60th & 61st Sts.)
759-6131
Open Mon.-Fri. 9:30 a.m.-5 p.m.

For over a decade, repairs have been skillfully done by owner Jadwiga Baran, who works on all types of ceramics for prices that range from $35 to $2,500 and up. Ask for a free estimate; for a fee of $50, she'll also provide insurance appraisals.

CHANDELIERS

Anthony Bazza Restorations
315 E. 62nd St. (First & Second Aves.)
755-1179
Open Mon.-Thurs. 8 a.m.-4 p.m., Fri. 8 a.m.-3:30 p.m.

Mr. Bazza will clean, refurbish and rewire such metals as iron, brass and tin, as well as crystal chandeliers. He can replace silver chandeliers and polish copper and brass; he also custom-makes chandeliers. All services have waiting lists several months long.

Gem Monogram
628 Broadway (Houston & Bleecker Sts.)
674-8960
Open Mon.-Fri. 9 a.m.-4:45 p.m.

Gem will clean crystal chandeliers in your home. It provides a full range of services for glass and metal fixtures, including replating brass, silver or gold, and the staff can replace broken metal ends. There's a wait for all work except cleaning.

FURNITURE

Sotheby's Restoration
440 E. 91st St. (First & York Aves.)
860-5446
Open Mon.-Fri. 8 a.m.-4 p.m.

This division of Sotheby's is a workshop for conservation and restoration of fine furniture, including a full-time metal foundry and a finishing center for japanning, lacquering, gilding and polishing. Your piece, whether furniture or a work of art, must be at least 100 years old. On-site work runs $450 for a half day and $650 for a full day; an estimate costs $75 to $150 and is deducted from the cost of the restoration.

BEAUTY & HEALTH

APOTHECARY

Bigelow Pharmacy
414 Ave. of the Americas (8th & 9th Sts.)
533-2700
Open Mon.-Fri. 7:30 a.m.-9 p.m., Sat. 8:30 a.m.-7 p.m., Sun. 8:30 a.m.-5:30 p.m.

This pharmacy has graced this location since 1838, which makes it one of the oldest apothecaries in the country—and an official New York landmark. No wonder—the fine oak showcases, light and gas fixtures, stained glass and mosaic floor are all original and lovely. The merchandise is far from archaic; in fact, the inventory changes constantly. In addition to reliable pharmaceuticals, makeup artists are available to do free makeovers with purchases of at least $30 worth of skin products.

Caswell-Massey
518 Lexington Ave. (48th St.)
755-2254
Open Mon.-Fri. 9 a.m.-7 p.m., Sat. 10 a.m.-6 p.m., Sun. noon-5 p.m.

Established in 1752, this midtown apothecary is both relic and revolutionary. With its cut-glass jars, mirrors and dark wood cases, the country's oldest chemist and perfume company still stocks scents that were worn by George and Martha Washington. Many of the exotic items come from all over the world, and all are of fine quality: oils, fragrances, potpourri, rice powder, face powder, huge sponges, loofahs, whale nail files and even assorted flavors of snuff. The selection of soaps is extensive, to say the least, and includes ones made with rainwater, seaweed, lettuce and tomatoes. The almond-cream soap and cucumber-based products are famous. The shop still stocks straight razors from France and pomander balls similar to those used in the seventeenth century. Several other locations around the city: Herald Center, 1 Herald Square (244-0411), 2 World Trade Center (945-2630) and South Street Seaport (608-5401).

Kiehl's Pharmacy Inc.
109 Third Ave. (13th & 14th Sts.)
677-3171
Open Mon.-Fri. 10 a.m.-6 p.m., Sat. 10 a.m.-4:30 p.m.

Museum or pharmacy? You decide. Amid a vast selection of home-brewed health products, you can survey snippets of the Kiehl family's history. Magical colored potions and powerfully scented dried flowers and herbs make this an exotic health-and-beauty wonderland. There are also rosewater *eau de toilette* with petals at the bottom, mystical henna and an incredible collection of homemade skin-care products to treat everything from dry skin to dandruff. White-aproned pharmacists will suggest and prepare a natural treatment for almost any beauty ailment. Prices are comparable to those of any department-store beauty-counter line, yet you get so much more.

BEAUTY & HAIR SALONS

Elizabeth Arden Salon
691 Fifth Ave. (54th St.)
546-0200
Open Mon.-Wed. & Fri.-Sat. 9:30 a.m.-5:15 p.m., Thurs. 9:30 a.m.-8 p.m.

A woman can leave this salon a different person. It is best known for its "Maine Chance" day, named after Elizabeth Arden's former resort in Maine—a six- to seven-hour experience in which you'll be remade from crown to toe, starting with an exercise class and continuing with a body massage, face treatment, hair styling, manicure, pedicure, light lunch and makeover. Total cost is over $200; you must book several months in advance for a Saturday. Or try a half-day package: Miracle Morning (massage, face treatment, hair and manicure) or Visible Difference (face treatment, hair, manicure and makeup lesson), each for over $150. Individual services are also available à la carte, including body waxing, makeup lessons and a deep

236

cleansing, non-depilatory paraffin bath. There are seven floors, five of service and two of merchandise that ranges from Arden's own makeup to quality sportswear and haute couture.

Astor Place Hair Designers
2 Astor Pl. (Broadway)
475-9854
Open Mon.-Sat. 8 a.m.-8 p.m., Sun. 9 a.m.-6 p.m.

No, people are not queuing for visas or a film debut. They're waiting for a haircut. Not just any haircut, either, but one of the infamous and cheap ($12) Astor Place cuts. Yuppies, punks, and grandparents alike all stop here. If you don't instruct the barbers, expect a generic cut. But the mere suggestion of freedom unleashes creative juices; crew cuts and mohawks are among the more mundane.

Bruno Le Salon
16 W. 57th St., 3rd Fl. (Fifth & Sixth Aves.)
581-2760
Open Mon. 9 a.m.-6 p.m., Tues.-Fri. 9 a.m.-7 p.m., Sat. 9 a.m. to early closing.

You are greeted by an electronic message board and a human receptionist behind the desk. Then you hear a name called over a loudspeaker, and a person arrives from nowhere to whisk you away to a private cubicle. This efficient and chic salon, very European in character, is run by the Italian master Bruno himself. The stylists don't impose their own styling ideas on you, but rather create a look that's free and manageable and, most important, one that you feel comfortable with.

Bruno Dessange
760 Madison Ave., 2nd Fl.
(65th & 66th Sts.)
517-9660
Open Mon.-Sat. 9:30 a.m.-6:30 p.m.

Walking into this above-street-level shop, you feel as though you've entered the Pearly Gates of hair heaven. Whiteness prevails on the walls, tiled floors, furniture, hair implements—even the hair stylists wear loose-fitting white robes with Bruno's name painted on one extremity or another. Bruno Dessange's signature is sleek and chic. Bruno himself shuttles between this shop and the one

he owns in Paris. The well-known stylist is also the creative director for the Jacques Dessange Group, which boasts over 200 salons stretching from France to Australia. At Bruno Dessange, a full package of pampering is possible for men and women: cutting, styling, permanents, coloring, highlighting, manicure and pedicure; and if your new "do" inspires you to give your face some attention, plan to visit the Institut de Beauté at the back. A haircut with Bruno costs $150 for women and $70 for men. Other stylists charge between $55 and $85.

Christine Valmy
767 Fifth Ave., Concourse Level
(58th & 59th Sts.)
752-0303
Open Mon.-Tues. & Fri. 10 a.m.-6 p.m., Wed. 10 a.m.-7 p.m., Thurs. 11 a.m.-7 p.m., Sat. 9 a.m.-5 p.m.

Below the hustle and bustle of Fifth Avenue lies this calm, small salon dedicated solely to skin care for both men and women. There's a wide range of facial treatments, including the patented skin-renewal treatments for teenagers and adults, which alternates between machines and the internationally renowned Valmy homeopathic skin-care products. After an in-depth skin analysis, a specialist will blend the Valmy products in the minilab on the premises, creating a home skin-care program that's tailored for you. Other services offered include body massages, manicures, pedicures and makeup lessons. An all-inclusive Valmy day (even lunch is served) is $200. Two other locations at 1 Rockefeller Plaza and 101 W. 57th Street, 2nd Floor.

Georgette Klinger
501 Madison Ave. (52nd & 53rd Sts.)
838-3200
Open Mon., Wed. & Fri. 9 a.m.-6 p.m., Tues. & Thurs. 9 a.m.-8 p.m., Sat. 9 a.m.-5 p.m.

Georgette Klinger offers pampering services that include facials, massages, hair and scalp treatments and makeovers. The facials are luxurious 90-minute treatments during which a specialist cleans and massages your face, prepares a steaming pot of chamomile and a potpourri of other therapeutic herbs, clears your face of blemishes, and finally treats you with two masks designed for your particular skin type. Klinger also offers manicures and pedicures as well as exercise and nutrition classes. Another location at 978 Madison Avenue (744-6900).

Il-Makiage
107 E. 60th St. (Park Ave.)
371-3992
Open Mon. 10 a.m-9 p.m., Tues.-Wed. 10 a.m.-6:30 p.m., Thurs. 10 a.m.-9 p.m., Fri. 9 a.m.-3 p.m., Sun. 11:30 a.m.-6 p.m.

You don't have to be a famous actress or fashion model to go to Il-Makiage, though celebrity faces are frequently seen here. Even though Ilana Harkavi, founder and president of the company, began her career in professional makeup and cosmetics, her salon benefits anyone interested in learning the art of beauty. Coming from the arts, Harvaki developed her own makeup line and innovative techniques for applying makeup, and created a new language with color. Il-Makiage is for those seeking an education in beauty techniques. The range of services includes skin treatments, facials, hand care, back treatment, makeup application, hair care and nail care.

Kenneth
19 E. 54th St. (Fifth & Madison Aves.)
752-1800
Open Mon.-Tues. & Thurs.-Fri. 9 a.m.-6 p.m., Wed. 9 a.m.-8 p.m.

Curious to find out how Jackie O. feels after a day of beauty treatment? This is the right address. The attention, pampering, and professionalism that Kenneth offers his clients is apparent from the moment the chauffeur picks you up and whisks you to the exquisitely decorated townhouse where the doorman and the rest of the staff will greet you by name. And all this before you've changed into a dressing gown and been escorted to your stylist. The four floors contain two main rooms where the stylists work, as well as numerous well-appointed private rooms. You may have your manicure where and when you choose, because the manicurist assigned to you can trail you from floor to floor. When you're all finished, you can be made up by one of two makeup artists using Kenneth's own line of cosmetics. There is a separate men's

salon on the main floor. All the services, except coloring, can be done in your home.

Make-Up Center
150 W. 55th St. (Sixth & Seventh Aves.)
977-9494
Open Mon.-Wed. & Fri. 10 a.m.-6 p.m., Thurs. 10 a.m.-8 p.m., Sat 10 a.m. to 5 p.m.

Enter this store and get a glimpse of Broadway. Located across the street from City Center and right near the theater district, the Make-Up Center is frequented by many artists who purchase this makeup for both professional and personal use. Well-known theatrical makeup by Bob Klein and Stein's can be found at affordable prices. A 15-percent discount is offered to those with a theatrical-union card. The affordable services include a makeover and lesson, a facial and eyelash dyeing, waxing, manicures and pedicures.

Mingus Salon
542 LaGuardia Pl.
(Bleecker & Houston Sts.)
777-0223
Open Mon. 11 a.m.-7 p.m., Tues.-Fri. 10 a.m.-7 p.m., Sat. 10 a.m.-5 p.m.

This sleek Village salon for men and women has been giving reliable contemporary cuts since 1971—first on Bleecker Street in the West Village and for the past few years just off Bleecker Street a few blocks south of Washington Square. A jazzy place with a jazzy name near many of the city's finest jazz spots, the cutters here blow cool and sing downtown prices. Owner Tony Cracchiola cuts lead and has a big repertoire. The salon also features Olga's Nails, where a first-rate Russian quartet does nail sculpture, manicure, pedicure, waxing and facials. Basic haircuts run $25 to $45 for men and $35 to $45 for women.

Suga
115 E. 57th St. (Park & Lexington Aves.)
421-4400
Open Mon.-Tues. & Thurs.-Sat. 9 a.m.-6 p.m., Wed. 9 a.m.-8 p.m.

This sleek, mirrored, white-and-gray salon, run by the renowned Japanese stylist Suga, concentrates only on hair and nails. A cut by Suga is $150 and others start at $50 (not including shampoo and blow-dry).

Vidal Sassoon

767 Fifth Ave. (58th & 59th Sts.)
535-9200
Open Mon.-Wed. & Fri.-Sat. 8:30 a.m.-5 p.m.,
Thurs. 8:30 a.m.-7 p.m.

This innovative hair salon for men and women continues to live up to its reputation as a source for excellent haircuts. Although its roots are in London, members of the team are also from Germany, Nicaragua and Spain, among other countries. High school students, children under 12 and airline stewardesses all receive a 30-percent discount. Others who are budget-conscious can have their hair done by closely supervised cutters-in-training for a fraction of the regular fee.

HEALTH CLUBS

Body by Jake New York

160 E. 56th St., 5th Fl.
(Lexington & Third Aves.)
759-5253
Open Mon.-Thurs. 6:30 a.m.-8:30 p.m., Fri.
6:30 a.m.-8 p.m., Sat. 8 a.m.-6 p.m., Sun. 8:30
a.m.-6:30 p.m.

Everything about this exercise studio exudes energy—from the lively hand-lettered signs announcing new classes to the bouncy, fit instructors wearing Body by Jake T-shirts. Although the trendy outfits of the clientele may indicate otherwise, this is not an aerobics studio. Instead, the focus is on nonimpact (your feet don't leave the floor), calisthenic, and isometric exercises that leave your body lean and mean. All classes are led by a trained instructor who is guaranteed to motivate (the loud music doesn't hurt either), as well as an assistant who walks around the studio correcting form. In addition to this workout, there are yoga and stretch classes that improve flexibility and a weight-room membership plan for just a small fee, with unlimited use of the studio's weights and exercise machines. Jake, by the way, is owner Jake Steinfeld, who spends most of his time in L.A., where he served as a personal trainer to such luminaries as Priscilla Presley, Steven Spielberg and Margot Kidder.

The Exercise Exchange

236 W. 78th St. (Broadway)
595-6475
Open Mon.-Fri. 7 a.m.-8:30 p.m., Sat. 9 a.m.-
4:30 p.m., Sun. 10 a.m.-3:30 p.m.

The guiding theory behind this studio is that all bodies are not created equal, and there is no single "right" regimen—so the aerobic, stretch-and-tone, workout and exercise classes incorporate the best from a variety of techniques, including yoga, Nickolaus, and Pilate. They teach exercise in such a way that you learn about and understand your body from the inside out. You'll learn correct positioning as well as your own limits and potential, enabling you to continue exercising correctly for the rest of your life. Jean-Paul Mustone, the director of this studio, has tried to eliminate as many of the excuses used for not exercising as possible. You won't be able to say you can't make the times, because he holds classes every day of the year except Christmas. Don't think you can afford to keep in shape? Think again! The prices are among the most reasonable in New York City, with discounts for college students and performing arts professionals. It costs $10 for a single class, $80 for ten, and $150 for twenty. Now, that's reasonable!

Exercise Plus

19 E. 48th St., 4th Fl.
(Fifth & Madison Aves.)
935-2677
Open Mon.-Thurs. 9:30 a.m.-7:30 p.m., Fri.
9:30 a.m.-3:30 p.m., Sat. 10:30 a.m.-1:30 p.m.
Closed Sat. in summer.

Don't expect to find lots of svelte women in shiny leotards jumping around the studio. Instead, you'll see women on their backs, carrying an extra load (a baby), working out in a low-key but vigorous fashion. Exercise Plus programs are designed to help women keep in shape at precisely the time they tend to feel most out of shape. Emphasis is on abdominal strength and proper breathing to complement Lamaze techniques. Classes are divided into prenatal and postpartum groups, and in addition to the training, they are an excellent, supportive meeting ground for women to share their feelings about pregnancy and motherhood. Free babysitting on the premises enables new mothers to enjoy a carefree hour of exercise and fun. One month (eight classes) is $95, six months (50 classes) is $470, and one year (100 classes) is $700.

Lotte Berk Method Ltd.

23 E. 67th St. (Fifth & Madison Aves.)
288-6613
Open Mon., Wed. & Fri. 6:30 a.m.-8:30 p.m., Tues. & Thurs. 7:30 a.m.-8:30 p.m., Sat. 8:30 a.m.-2:30 p.m., Sun. 9:30 a.m.-2:30 p.m.

Russian dancer Lotte Berk developed the method taught here for women only. It's based on strenuous movements to stretch and strengthen muscles, with particular attention on the abdominals. For women with lower-back or posture problems, or women who just want to tone their bodies, these safe exercises extract the best from ballet, modern dance, yoga and orthopedic theory. Individual classes or memberships available.

New York Health & Racquet Club

110 W. 56th St. (Sixth & Seventh Aves.)
541-7200
Open Mon.-Fri. 6:30 a.m.-10 p.m., Sat.-Sun. 9:30 a.m.-6 p.m.

Members of the NYH&RC can use any of the seven locations to take advantage of the plethora of facilities, services, and activities offered by this expansive, complete club. Among the basic facilities are a pool, whirlpool, steam rooms, sauna, tanning booths and tennis, racquetball, international racquetball and squash courts. The exercise equipment is equally varied, including Nautilus, Ergometers, Eagle Cybex, Kaiser-Cam, Lifecycles, Liferowers and old-fashioned free weights. Each member is prescribed an individualized exercise regime that is constantly updated. One-on-one training is also available. There are also ongoing classes in calisthenics, karate, aerobics, low-impact aerobics, and ballroom and tap dancing. You can also attend a nutrition class, a quit-smoking program or a weight-control seminar. Call the above number for other Manhattan locations.

Sports Training Institute

239 E. 49th St. (Second & Third Aves.)
752-7111
Open Mon.-Fri. 6 a.m.-8 p.m., Sat. 8 a.m.-1:45 p.m. Closed Sat. in summer.

The first thing you should know is that while STI is concerned with your health, it's not a club. The clients, mostly midtown business people, work one-on-one with personal trainers for 45-minute sessions, then shower and leave. No one hangs out; besides the exercise and locker rooms, there's no place to do it. STI is serious. To begin with, you can't be accepted without a physician's written clearance. Then you are evaluated by a staff member, 95 percent of whom have or are working toward a master's degree in exercise physiology. They compile your fitness profile and arrange a training schedule (three appointments a week are recommended) that emphasizes strength, endurance, power, flexibility and aerobic training.

The Vertical Club

330 E. 61st St. (First & Second Aves.)
355-5100
Open Mon.-Fri. 6 a.m.-10:30 p.m., Sat.-Sun. 9 a.m.-8:30 p.m.

The Vertical Club is one of the largest gyms in the United States, and certainly the largest facility in New York City. It has over 300 pieces of equipment, including Nautilus, Universal, Paramount, Kaiser, free weights, Lifecycles and Stair-Masters. In addition to the largest indoor track in the city, The Vertical Club offers a swimming pool, whirlpools, steam and sauna rooms, squash, racquetball, tennis, massage, aerobics, a sun deck, tanning facilities, a juice bar and a restaurant. Two types of memberships are available: executive, which includes everything, or a tennis membership exclusively for tennis players.

SCENTS

Crabtree & Evelyn

620 Fifth Ave. (49th & 50th Sts.)
581-5022
Open Mon.-Sat. 10 a.m.-6 p.m.

The Upper East Side is fortunate to have a source for wonderful Crabtree & Evelyn toiletries, which are delightfully perfumed with herbs, flowers and fruits. This boutique is crammed with powders, soaps, creams, toothpastes, hand-drawn brushes, tins and baskets. It also has a varied choice of comestibles, including jams, jellies, sauces (chutney, mustard), honey, spices, chocolates, cookies, biscuits, teas and other gourmet items from England and the rest of Europe.

Jean Laporte

870 Madison Ave. (70th & 71st Sts.)
517-8665
Open Mon.-Sat. 10 a.m.-6 p.m.

Let your nose guide you in this small, meticulously kept shop where you're treated to a wonderful blending of a French *parfumerie*'s best fragrances. Jean Laporte's inspiration comes from the scents of flowers, fruits, woods, and spices, which he carefully combines into novel, subtle fragrances, such as Eau d'Oranger (néroli oil, orange, jasmine), Orchidée Blanche (a bouquet of iris, ambergris, honey and vanilla) and Bois Epicés (spicy woods). Also sold are amber sachets, a unique terra-cotta amber ball, unusual contemporary jewelry, antique perfume bottles and burning oils. The *Livre des Senteurs* (Book of Scents), containing eight small bottles of different scents, serves as an olfactory bible.

BOOKS

Applause Theatre Books

211 W. 71st St.
(Broadway & West End Ave.)
496-7511
Open Mon.-Sat. 10 a.m.-8 p.m., Sun. noon-6 p.m.

This comfy, spacious bookstore is tucked away in a sunken plaza. It offers a complete stock of all theater titles and plays, criticism, biographies, how-to books and theater magazines. Applause Theatre publishes its own line of plays and books for the actor. Also worth a visit is its sister, Applause Cinema Books, at 100 W. 67th Street (787-8858).

Argosy Bookstore

116 E. 59th St. (Park & Lexington Aves.)
753-4455
Open Mon.-Fri. 9 a.m.-6 p.m., Sat. 10 a.m.-5 p.m. Closed Sat. May-Sept.

What a pleasure it is to leave the surrounding twentieth-century street scene for this store's Dickensian setting, exemplified by green lampshades, wood paneling and old leather bindings. The rare and used books are organized by subject, and there's virtually everything imaginable. By appointment only, you can also browse through the oodles of letters and signed photographs, and see the selection of choice modern first editions.

Barnes & Noble Book Store

105 Fifth Ave. (18th St.)
807-0099
Open Mon.-Fri. 9:30 a.m.-8 p.m., Sat. 9:30 a.m.-6:30 p.m., Sun. 11 a.m. -6 p.m.

Barnes & Noble is a great store for general book browsing, with its three million hardcovers, paperbacks, and new and used textbooks arranged in a huge space with lots of elbow room. Though Barnes & Noble's extensive medical and nursing department is famous, you'll also find engineering, business, reference and craft books; computer books and software; and high school and college outlines and study aids. The Sale Annex across the street contains thousands of bargains—best-sellers, current fiction and nonfiction, children's books, paperbacks, publishers' overstocks and more, at well below list price. Call the above number for other store locations in the city.

The Biography Bookshop

400 Bleecker St. (11th St.)
807-8655
Open Tues.-Fri. 1 p.m.-9 p.m., Sat. noon-10 p.m., Sun. noon-5:30 p.m.

This is the only bookstore in New York specializing in biographies, autobiographies, diaries, letters, journals and travelogues. All the well-known titles are stocked here, as are the smaller and more obscure presses, university presses and British and foreign-language imports.

Brentano's

597 Fifth Ave. (48th St.)
826-2450
Open Mon.-Sat. 10 a.m.-7 p.m.

A glorious shrine to books is the old Scribner Bookstore, saved (as a bookstore, anyway) from being turned into a Benetton outlet by Brentano's. The sales room, with its balconies and staircase, is protected by the Landmarks Preservation Commission. Excellent collections on many subjects, including travel and New York City books.

The Complete Traveller
199 Madison Ave. (35th St.)
685-9007
Open Mon.-Fri. 9 a.m.-7 p.m., Sat. 10 a.m.-6 p.m., Sun. noon-5 p.m.

Unless you have vacation time coming your way, browsing in this store may prove dangerous. An inexhaustable selection of books, arrayed logically in this small, crammed shop, beckons you to spend a delicious week or two browsing. Celebrating its eleventh year, The Complete Traveller is the oldest travel bookstore in the country, offering 29 complete travel series published both in the U.S. and abroad. It's also an excellent resource for maps, travel literature, foreign-language phrasebooks, dictionaries and cassettes, as well as old and rare travel books. If you want to chat about a destination or a particular travel book, you'll find that the salespeople are knowledgeable, hearty travelers.

Doubleday Book Shop
724 Fifth Ave. (57th St.)
397-0550
Open Mon.-Sat. 9 a.m.-midnight, Sun. noon-5 p.m.

What Doubleday lacks in character, it makes up for in breadth. The store is unquestionably a reader's paradise, whether you are looking for something in particular or just looking. This enormous store stocks a fine, broad selection. The paperback fiction section is especially appealing, as it manages to highlight both contemporary novels and the classics. Browsers can move around here; there's plenty of of space between shelves and a wide staircase that leads to the basement and second floor. The glass elevator is a nice touch, calling your attention to the store's well-lit and extensively stocked space. Call the above number for other store locations in the city.

Drama Bookstore
723 Seventh Ave. (48th St.)
496-7511
Open Mon.-Wed. & Fri. 9:30 a.m.-7 p.m., Thurs. 9:30 a.m.-8 p.m., Sat. 10:30 a.m.-5:30 p.m., Sun. noon-7 p.m.

One of the best places in the world to find books on the performing arts, especially theater, dance and film.

Forbidden Planet
821 Broadway (11th & 12th Sts.)
473-1576
227 E. 59th St. (Second & Third Aves.)
751-4386

Science fiction, from books to toys, games to comic books, is celebrated here—probably the largest store of its kind in the world (Earth, that is).
Broadway: open Mon.-Sat. 10 a.m.-7 p.m., Sun. noon-6 p.m. Uptown: open Mon.-Fri. 11:30 a.m.-8:30 p.m., Sat. 11:30 a.m.-9 p.m., Sun. noon-7 p.m.

Gotham Book Mart & Gallery
41 W. 47th St. (Fifth & Sixth Aves.)
719-4448
Open Mon.-Fri. 9:30 a.m.-6:30 p.m., Sat. 9:30 a.m.-6 p.m.

"Wise Men Fish Here" has been the motto of this bookstore for decades. Frances Steloff, who opened the store in 1925 with a $100 loan and a $100 Liberty Bond, was a legend in these parts. A strong opponent of censorship long before such opposition was fashionable, she helped launch the careers of such literary giants as D.H. Lawrence and Henry Miller by selling their books when no one else would. Unlike the modern-day bookstore, where titles are neatly categorized, Gotham Book Mart is often in a state of frenzy, but the staff knows its way around. Chances are if you request a title, they'll not only have it among their collection of a half million, but they'll be able to find it effortlessly. Rare first editions can also be retrieved here. The gallery, with changing exhibits, is upstairs.

Hacker Art Books
245 W. 57th St. (Fifth & Sixth Aves.)
757-1450
Open Mon.-Sat. 9:30 a.m.-6 p.m.

Here's heaven for lovers of art books. This long-established store is now just across the street from its former address.

J.N. Bartfield Books & Gallery
30 W. 57th St. (Fifth & Sixth Aves.)
245-8890
Open Mon.-Fri. 10 a.m.-5 p.m., Sat. 10 a.m.-2:30 p.m.

This fascinating book shop has an incredible variety of antiquarian books. Fine bindings, sets and singles of Dickens, Shakespeare and other famous authors vie for your attention. You'll find color-plate books, paintings, atlases, first editions and sporting books galore. The owners say they have the largest collection of "old worthwhile books"; we say it's worthwhile to make a trip here.

Kitchen Arts & Letters
1435 Lexington Ave. (93rd & 94th Sts.)
876-5550
Open Mon. 1 p.m.-6 p.m., Tues.-Fri. 10 a.m.-6:30 p.m., Sat. 11 a.m.-6 p.m.

Though this shop is far uptown, serious gourmets know it's worth the trek. There's even a kitchen in the back where authors sometimes hold demonstrations. The books are well organized by both subject (wine, pasta) and region. But it's more fun if you don't know what you're looking for; that way you're likely to come across the collection of old cookbooks and promotional recipe booklets, which should be savored for the illustrations alone. Don't forget to check the bulletin board on your way out for an update on cooking news, announcements and events.

Librairie de France-Librería Hispánica
610 Fifth Ave. (49th & 50th Sts.)
581-8810
Open Mon.-Fri. 9:30 a.m.-6:15 p.m., Sat. 10 a.m.-6:15 p.m.

What was once a meeting ground for French tourists now gives equal time to Spaniards and Latin Americans. Stocking roughly one million books in French, Spanish and other non-English languages, Librairie de France has one of the largest collections of foreign language books in the United States. It also carries dailies, periodicals, records and calendars, and has a second location at 115 Fifth Avenue (673-7400).

Madison Avenue Bookshop
833 Madison Ave. (69th & 70th Sts.)
535-6130
Open Mon.-Sat. 10 a.m.-6 p.m. Closed Sat. in summer.

This is a serious bookshop for devoted fans of the printed word. Current fiction and all that's new or important in art, poetry, philosophy and literary criticism can be found here. The staff is knowledgeable and goes out of its way to assist you, whether it's to select a gift or merely find something on the crowded second floor. The spindly spiral staircase is used to hold the overflow of books, making

the trip up or down a somewhat precarious venture. It's a book browser's delight; be prepared to dawdle.

McGraw-Hill Bookstore
1221 Ave. of the Americas (50th St.)
512-4100
Open Mon.-Sat. 10 a.m.-5:45 p.m.

With the company upstairs, as it were, this basement shop carries books from all publishers, despite its name and location (in the McGraw-Hill Building at Rockefeller Center). Many business-related books, including computer tomes and software.

The Military Bookman
29 E. 93rd St. (Fifth & Madison Aves.)
348-1280
Open Tues.-Sat. 10:30 a.m.-5:30 p.m.

Where can you find more than ten thousand titles covering every aspect of military, aviation and naval history? The Military Bookman, of course! This is the only bookstore in New York with books filed by war—from ancient battles right up through Vietnam. The Military Bookman also deals in rare and out-of-print books on such topics as strategy and tactics, armored vehicles and espionage.

Murder Inc.
271 W. 87th St.
(Broadway & West End Ave.)
362-8905
Open Wed. & Fri.-Sat. 1 p.m.-7 p.m., Thurs. 1 p.m.-10 p.m.

If you love "whodunits," you'll enjoy this shop devoted exclusively to mystery novels and their ilk.

The Mysterious Bookshop
129 W. 56th St. (Sixth & Seventh Aves.)
765-0900
Open Mon.-Sat. 11 a.m.-7 p.m.

New York is fortunate that there was somebody "who dunit." That mystery man was Otto Penzler, who, eleven years ago, had the guts to open a bookshop (on Friday 13, 1979, of course) exclusively devoted to mysteries, crime novels and detective fiction. Today, the store is a blood-curdling success, carrying an enormous selection of paperbacks and hardcovers, carefully preserved first editions, and out-of-print books, which are hunted down at no extra charge. If *Murder She Wrote* doesn't fulfill your suspense quota, grab your trench coat and flashlight and join the other diehard mystery fans at this favorite haunt.

New York Bound Bookshop

50 Rockefeller Plaza (50th & 51st Sts.)
245-8503
Open Mon.-Fri. 10 a.m.-6 p.m., Sat. 11 a.m.-5 p.m.

This comprehensive bookshop is paradise for "New Yorkophiles" and a perfect pit stop for the person who wants to know everything about New York, but wouldn't dare ask a native New Yorker. Seeming more like a library than a retail shop, New York Bound's ceiling-high shelves are filled with new and old books, prints, photographs, maps of the city as well as the state of New York, and other surprising memorabilia. When visiting, ask to meet co-owners Barbara Cohen and Judith Stonehill, both of whom are resident experts on New York.

The Rare Book Room

125 Greenwich Ave.
(Seventh & Eighth Aves.)
206-6766
Open Tues.-Sat. 1 p.m.-7 p.m.

Once upon a time, Greenwich Avenue was filled with rare-book stores. Today, Roger and Irvyne Richards' Rare Book Room is the only one left on the block, and one of the few left in the city. Contemporary and nineteenth-century novels are the specialty. Also evident is an astounding selection of signed celebrities' old photographs, the prize of which was a 1912 premovies photo of Charles Chaplin. Contemporary authors include Joseph Heller, Gore Vidal, Graham Greene, Tennessee Williams, Truman Capote, Gertrude Stein, Ernest Hemingway and more. There are a few copies of the first Webster Dictionary, dated 1828, that sell for thousands. The oldest work in the shop is a Shakespeare reader, dated approximately 1648, for $10,000. This store may soon be closed.

Rizzoli Bookstore

31 W. 57th St. (Fifth & Sixth Aves.)
759-2424
Open Mon.-Sat. 9:30 a.m.-10 p.m., Sun. noon-8 p.m.

You might want to put Rizzoli on your museum list. Plan to spend a lot of time in this sophisticated bookstore with its rich, wood-paneled walls, domed ceiling, chandeliers and perfect displays. If the ambience doesn't transport you, the art section will. You'll also find European newspapers and magazines, classical, jazz, and new-age records, and an exquisite section of Penguin paperbacks. Anything you purchase here, even if it can be found at a hundred other bookstores, will feel special. Large SoHo branch at 454 W. Broadway, 674-1616.

Samuel Weiser

132 E. 24th St. (Lexington & Park Aves.)
777-6363
Open Mon.-Wed. & Fri. 9 a.m.-6 p.m., Thurs. 10 a.m.-7 p.m., Sat. 9:30 a.m.-5 P.M., Sun. 11 a.m.-5:30 p.m.

New Age and other occult books are the specialties here, with wild items from everywhere, it seems. This store claims to stock more metaphysical books than any other store in the world.

Strand Book Store

828 Broadway (12th St.)
473-1452
Open Mon.-Fri. 9:30 a.m.-9:30 p.m., Sat. 9:30 a.m.-6:25 p.m., Sun. 11 a.m.-6 p.m.

Known for its eight miles (plus!) of books, this bibliophile's haven sells over one million used, new and rare books, and reviewers' copies in mint condition. Shipments of brand-new books arrive daily, so it makes sense to "know thine author," as a sign here warns. In the basement are stacks (and more stacks) of yesteryear's best-sellers. On the main floor, books are arranged by topic. The best deals are on the tables in front.

Zen Oriental Bookstore

521 Fifth Ave. (43rd & 44th Sts.)
697-0840
Open Mon.-Sat. 10 a.m.-7 p.m.

Don't be misled when you walk into this store and see that many of the books are in Japanese. Walk a little further, and you'll find books in English on just about every aspect of Japanese society, from gardening to etiquette, as well as translated works by major Japanese authors. In the back is a gift section with dolls, lamps, tea and saké sets, paintings and stationery.

CHILDREN

CLOTHES

Bébé Thompson
98 Thompson St. (Spring & Prince Sts.)
925-1122
Open daily noon-7 p.m.

You've come a long way, Bébé, considering that recently many of the other children's clothing stores in this trendy area have closed. Bébé Thompson is perhaps the choicest infants' store (sizes newborn to six) in the city, carrying a wide variety of adorable, original, top-quality clothes and accessories for the impeccably dressed infant. You can pick up a Panama hat, a cotton bonnet, or Maud Frizon shoes and baby boots. These treasures do not come cheap: the prices here are very SoHo.

Bellini
473 Columbus Ave. (82nd & 83rd Sts.)
362-3700
Open Mon.-Wed. & Fri.-Sat. 10 a.m.-6 p.m., Thurs. 10 a.m.-8 p.m., Sun. noon-5 p.m.

A fashionable one-stop resource for baby, Bellini carries an appealing array of merchandise. Young tots outfitted in Bellini's clothes will be right at home in the fashion parade that saunters up and down Columbus Avenue on weekends. But fashion doesn't stop with clothing. Everything for precious young ones, from European-crafted baby furniture to bedding and accessories, is available here. Prices are more reasonable than they are in some of Manhattan's more exclusive shops. The special touches and gift items make Bellini a fun shopping expedition for adults and children.

Au Chat Botté
903 Madison Ave. (72nd & 73rd Sts.)
772-7402
Open Mon.-Sat. 10 a.m.-6 p.m.

One of the most exclusive, tasteful, and ultra-expensive children's stores in the city, this is the place to buy that elegant, sophisticated, and very feminine dress your daughter needs for a party or, perhaps, dancing school. You won't find these classic styles in any department store—frilly smock dresses (many of them French, Italian and British imports) in cotton, silk and even taffeta. The clothes are definitely not suited for a romp through the playground. For newborns there's the exquisite Infants Room in the back—a perfect place to dress your up-and-coming debutante.

Citykids
130 Seventh Ave. (17th & 18th Sts.)
620-0120
Open Mon.-Sat. 10 a.m.-6 p.m.

This minute and absolutely meticulous store features upscale play and dress clothes for sophisticated little city slickers (sizes newborn to twelve) at hefty prices. The best imports and domestic lines are represented here, but come for the special items. A staff of in-house designers makes T-shirts, dyed cotton shorts, sweatshirts (with such New York City themes as yellow taxis and skyscrapers), wool collegiate jackets with leather sleeves, varsity sweaters and more, much of which features either the Citykids name or its skyline logo. Almost half of the store is devoted to a large selection of imaginative toys, knick-knacks and accessories.

Kids Kids Kids
436 Ave. of the Americas (9th & 10th Sts.)
533-3523
Open Mon.-Wed. & Fri. 11 a.m.-6:30 p.m., Thurs. 11 a.m.-7 p.m., Sat. 11 a.m.-6 p.m.

This small, new, fashionable and very funky Village clothing store for young kids (sizes infants to six-X) is as unpretentious as its owner, Carol Ray. "I'm the kissy monster," she coos as she makes funny faces while trying to find the best-fitting blue-and-white-striped baseball cap she can for an infant in his stroller (who isn't crazy about trying on hats). The clothing here is original and adorable, ranging from sophisticated European styling to a casual, funky look (a pair of black-and-mint-striped leggings with a matching black-and-mint pussycat T-shirt, handmade by a local artist). Nothing frilly or too fussy, and mostly reasonable prices.

Once Upon a Time
171 E. 92nd St. (Third & Lexington Aves.)
831-7619
Open Mon.-Sat. 10 a.m.-6 p.m.

This tiny store specializes in resale and antique clothing—but don't expect to find cheap, worn seconds here. Resale clothing for kids is a very good idea when it's properly done, and Ronnie Mann cleverly relies on a steady roster of mothers to bring her only the best names in infants' and children's clothing, all in good to excellent condition. She doesn't accept rips, stains or Health Tex. Some items do show their wear (usually just a year's worth), but these are top brands at reduced prices: baby items from Klimmers, Baby Dior, Marese, Sophie, Guess and Osh-Kosh, lots of adorable print and smock dresses, and such special items as Victorian christening gowns and a lovely assortment of antique quilts. New handmade crib quilts are sold here as well.

Wicker Garden
1327 Madison Ave. (93rd St.)
410-7001
Open Mon.-Sat. 10 a.m.-5:30 p.m.

A grand store full of classic clothing for babies and children to size ten. Owner Pamela Scurry loves beautiful things and has filled her store with them. On the main floor, you can sit on pretty white park benches while your child tries on shoes from a large selection (from Stride-Rite and Keds to their own line of dress and school shoes). Top-quality, mainly pastel infant layette clothing is found here, as are racks of frilly and very feminine party dresses. Even the playclothes are fine and delicate-looking—no jeans here. Climb the winding staircase and you'll find a fairly expensive boys' line (sizes two to ten) that includes sailor suits, cotton sweaters with nautical themes, and preppy dress clothes combining navy or Madras-print blazers with khaki pants, a Dior button-down and a tie by Grant or Cardin. Prices range from (believe it or not) the very reasonable to the ultra-expensive.

TOYS

Big City Kite
1201 Lexington Ave. (81st & 82nd Sts.)
472-2623
Open Mon.-Wed. & Sat. 10 a.m.-6 p.m., Thurs. 10 a.m.-7 p.m.

This store has the best selection of kites in Manhattan, from trendy stunt kites (two-string acrobatic kites from $15 to $200) to an entire wall of handmade nylon kites in the brightest, most playful designs, heralding anything from cuddly teddy bears to penguins relaxing under a beach umbrella. There are silk kites from China, paper kites from Japan and plastic kites for inexperienced flyers. The store carries about 200 different types in all, along with a full range of kite-flying accessories (bags, tails, wind socks, string winders and so on.). It also sponsors a kite-flying festival in Central Park each spring. The handmade and imported kites covering the walls and suspended from the ceiling are soothing, colorful and beautiful, and can be used for home decor.

Darrow's Fun Antiques
309 E. 61st St. (First & Second Aves.)
838-0730
Open Mon.-Fri. 11 a.m.-7 p.m., Sat. 11 a.m.-4 p.m.

Established in 1964, Darrow's claims to be the first antique and collectible toy store in the world. It certainly houses one of the most comprehensive selections of antique toys on the East Coast. Darrow Sr. spent his lifetime entertaining and explaining for rapt audiences about the world of toys. Now in a brand-new store, the second-generation Darrow carries on the legacy. Crowded aisles are lined with a constantly changing panorama of games and toys that muster up memories of childhood. The most popular items are jukeboxes and comic characters like Dick Tracy, Li'l Abner and Popeye. A nice variety of memorabilia.

Dollsanddreams
1421 Lexington Ave. (92nd & 93rd Sts.)
876-2434
Open Mon.-Fri. 10:30 a.m.-5:45 p.m., Sat. 11 a.m.-6 p.m.

A hand-picked selection of dolls, doll accessories and quality toys. You'll find treasures on every shelf of the store: expensive, one-of-a-kind collector dolls handmade in Europe, fine children's dolls from Gotz of Germany and even the popular La New Born from Spain—a soft, extremely lifelike baby doll (black or white) with newborn wrinkles, diaper, belly-button bandage, hospital tag and anatomically correct features. You can buy a sturdy, contemporary-style wood dollhouse and fill it with fabulous accessories. All the houses can be expanded with balconies and garages; you can even put a stable and a corral full of horses out back to increase your property value.

Dollhouse Antics

1308 Madison Ave. (92nd & 93rd Sts.)
876-2288
Open Mon.-Fri. 11 a.m.-5:30 p.m., Sat. 11 a.m.-5 p.m. Closed Sat.-Mon. in summer.

If you think you cannot afford to buy your dreamhouse in Manhattan, you may be pleasantly surprised when you visit this store. With dollhouses starting at $95, you'll have plenty left for custom interior design and furnishings. Among the custom products offered are miniature wallpapers, light fixtures and moldings. All merchandise, from ketchup bottles to couches, is on the scale of one inch to one foot, and all details are perfectly intact. For the do-it-yourselfer, dollhouse kits are also available.

The Enchanted Forest

85 Mercer St. (Spring & Broome Sts.)
925-6677
Open daily 11 a.m.-7 p.m.

Going on safari or a trip to the zoo are two ways to get close to the animal kingdom. The Enchanted Forest is the third. Set in a spooky medieval forest, a menagerie of animals (stuffed, we're told) lurk almost anywhere. Draped from the ceiling or hidden in a tree, each waits eagerly to be brought into domestication by a loving child or adult. If you want to talk to the animals, bring home a life-size panther for $245, or a burly gorilla, which for $360 comes with its own kitten playmate. In addition, books, folk arts, masks and puppets are available.

FAO Schwarz

767 Fifth Ave. (58th St.)
644-9400
Open Mon.-Wed. & Fri.-Sat. 10 a.m.-6 p.m., Thurs. 10 a.m.-8 p.m., Sun. noon-5 p.m.

If it's not in Santa's workshop, there's a good chance it's in FAO Schwarz. This wonderland for all ages has delighted even the most jaded New Yorkers since it first opened

in 1862, and a visit to the store's magical new home (just across from the old landmark site) is somewhat akin to a trip to Disneyland. There's an amazing 28-foot-high animal clock tower that welcomes you with a song (surrounded by such moving mechanical toys as the Little Engine That Could), and a cast of costumed characters (from Raggedy Ann to a clown) is on hand for both your entertainment and to direct you around this tremendous two-level store. Most of the new FAO Schwarz is divided into individual child-size boutiques, each with a clever name that reveals its special contents. Downstairs, you'll find the hugest kingdom of stuffed animals, from the reasonably priced traditional teddy bears to the incredible moose family, which includes father, mother and child ($24,000). Kids curious to try life in the fast lane, but who are too young for a driver's license, should check out the "Lamborghini" on the second floor (it'll hit 30 miles per hour and costs $14,500). On Little Madison Avenue, the Learning Center has the newest in high-tech laser and video toys, or you can buy plain old blocks by the pound. Schwarz loves to cater to out-of-towners—it'll arrange for a personal shopper or deliver anywhere in the world. There are fine toys for every "child" (at every price) in this fantasyland.

Forbidden Planet

821 Broadway (11th & 12th Sts.)
473-1576
Open Mon.-Thurs. & Sat. 10 a.m.-7 p.m., Fri. 10 a.m.-8 p.m., Sun. noon-6 p.m.

A science-fiction megastore. Kids of every age are sure to lose themselves in Forbidden Planet's vast selection (on two huge floors) of sci-fi comics, books, anthologies, magazines, toys, games, calendars, movie posters and more. Upstairs you'll find stacks of fantasy, horror and detective books, as well as hardcover and paperback science-fiction classics. Forbidden Planet is famous for having the largest selection of comic books in the city, and up here you'll find rack after rack of newly released comics, including Japanese and French comics and the currently in-vogue, book-length "graphic novels" (more for adults). Downstairs you'll find old and vintage comics, neatly arranged by title and edition date. The toy selection downstairs is superb if you're a devotee of science-fiction and fantasy toys; it contains all the hot, mass-market sci-fi toys, pet monsters and wonderfully frightening horror masks and wigs. Another location at 227 E. 59th Street (751-4386).

Iris Brown's Victorian Doll & Miniature Shop

253 E. 57th St. (Second & Third Aves.)
593-2882
Open Mon.-Fri. 11 a.m.-6 p.m., Sat. 12:30 p.m.-5:30 p.m.

Don't blink; you may miss it. This shop is tiny, but don't let the size fool you; it's a treasure chest filled with delicate porcelain Victorian dolls, child-scale furniture, dollhouses and accessories, all of which inspire fantasy in both adults and children. Though the store is really too small to accommodate browsers, Iris Brown, a renowned expert on rare and antique dolls, will happily answer any serious inquiries. Prices are high.

The Last Wound-Up

290 Columbus Ave. (73rd & 74th Sts.)
787-3388
Open Mon.-Thurs. 10 a.m.-8 p.m., Fri.-Sat. 10 a.m.-8 p.m., Sun. 10 a.m.-7 p.m.

The electronic age often has people yearning for days gone by, which explains in part the appeal of this place. If it can be wound up, it can be found here. The store's policy is to encourage you to live out childhood fantasies; there's a playpen where anyone is allowed to play on the premises. Whether it's a roving pair of eyes for $2.50, "phantom feet" that walk on their own for $2.95 or the "mini flik," a portable movie camera for $9.95, it'll wind up and take off here. Two other locations at 19th and Broadway and South Street Seaport.

The Laughing Giraffe at Monkeys Wedding

234 Court St., Brooklyn
(718) 852-3635
Open Mon.-Sat. 11 a.m.-6 p.m.

If you walk into this store and find adults on the floor playing with toys, don't be alarmed—it's probably the owner and friends testing out the merchandise. Susan Crowley, who taught for fourteen years, has a master's degree in education and really knows her stock, from both a practical and an academic standpoint. She sells everything from stuffed animals, board games and building sets to classic children's books, yo-yos and the unforgettable Etch-a-Sketch. The emphasis is on creative, intelligent toys for children from one to nine years of age.

The New York Doll Hospital

787 Lexington Ave., 2nd Fl.
(61st & 62nd Sts.)
838-7527
Open Mon.-Sat. 10 a.m.-6 p.m.

Owner Irving Chais, one of a long legacy of doll doctors (the business was started by his grandfather in 1900), is as friendly and charming as his shop. Here you can revive your tot's favorite doll or stuffed animal, whatever its condition. As Chais puts it, "We've never lost a patient yet." Ask to see his own collection.

Penny Whistle Toys

132 Spring St. (Wooster & Greene Sts.)
925-2088
Open Mon.-Sun. 11 a.m.-7 p.m.

Everything at Penny Whistle is carefully selected and meant to be "good for your child," but owner Meredith Brokaw's high standards don't take one bit of the fun out of these toys. There are neatly divided sections for science, robots, arts and crafts, construction toys, ride-ons, costumes, plush dolls and toys (from Madame Alexander to Gund and Steiff), dinosaurs, puzzles, games, magic tricks, pool toys (including a 23-foot-long sea-dragon raft), sporting equipment and more. You can get a knickknack for under a dollar or an entire Brio train set with accessories for about $425. You won't find any war toys here, but you will find a lot of imaginative, child-powered toys. There are other locations at 448 Columbus Avenue (873-9090) and 1283 Madison Avenue (369-3868).

We're always interested to hear about your discoveries, and to receive your comments on ours. Please feel free to write to us, and do state clearly exactly what you liked or disliked.

CLOTHES & JEWELRY

JEWELRY

COSTUME

Ciro of Bond Street Inc.
711 Fifth Ave. (56th St.)
752-0441
Open Mon.-Sat. 10 a.m.-6 p.m.
The designs here are fairly conservative—you won't find anything too big or too garish in this credible collection of costume jewelry. Simulated pearls are set simply and believably, and *faux* diamonds and gemstones are perfectly scaled. Fancy addresses mark the Manhattan Ciro stores (there are six other branches around the city)—proof that some of the high-profile people who appear to be dripping with the real thing are actually faking it.

QUALITY

A La Vieille Russie
781 Fifth Ave. (59th St.)
752-1727
Open Mon.-Fri. 10 a.m.-5:30 p.m., Sat. 10 a.m.-4 p.m. Closed Sat. in summer.
Located next to the Sherry Netherland hotel and diagonally across the street from the Plaza, this boutique is a monument to the wonders of Russian craftsmanship. Long a landmark at this special corner, A La Vieille Russie displays a magnificent array of jewel-encrusted icons, glass, jewelry and enamel that will dazzle your eye and dent your wallet. Go to see the beautiful pieces even if you're "just looking"—after all, a little dazzle never hurts.

Buccellati
Trump Tower, 725 Fifth Ave. (56th & 57th Sts.)
308-5533
Open Mon.-Sat. 10 a.m.-6 p.m. Closed Sat. in summer.
Buccellati's Trump Tower store screams money. The surprisingly stark interior reveals an ornate collection of Italian design, crafted to be works of art by themselves with perhaps less thought to how they look when worn. Big stones, thick chains, large pins—the look is expensive and showy, but undoubtedly elegant. There are some smaller pieces without the glitz and heavy price tags. Buccellati has a silver store at 46 E. 57th Street that features an exquisite collection of silver goods of more traditional design.

Bulgari
Hotel Pierre, 2 E. 61st St. (Fifth & Madison Aves.)
486-0086
Open Mon.-Sat. 10 a.m.-5:30 p.m. Closed Sat. in summer.
The house of Bulgari is one of the few privately owned family establishments that is as dedicated to important jewelry as it is to personal service. The New York branch of the Rome store is run by Nicola Bulgari, a grandson of the founder. From the moment you enter the brass-and-steel latticed doorway and are seated amid the recessed display cases, you are aware of the Bulgari difference. Bulgari's designs, originally inspired by the art deco movement, are today a skillful blend of the formal and the casual. Typical pieces are designed around antique coins or cameos, a Bulgari trademark. Also popular are the *trombini*, domed-shaped rings set with one or two precious stones.

Cartier
653 Fifth Ave. (52nd St.)
753-0111
Open Mon.-Sat. 10 a.m.-5:15 p.m.
The definition of good taste, Cartier is the only Fifth Avenue jeweler to openly display its wares—hence its windows are as much a tourist attraction as the Statue of Liberty. Browse freely through the gift collection of exquisitely simple fine jewelry and signature watches—all items are set in crystal-clear glass cases for easy viewing. In a separate room on the first floor, there are elegantly set tables proudly displaying Cartier's silver, china, glass, crystal and stemware. One can only dream about the lives of brides registered here. The store is immaculate, amazingly friendly and justifiably expensive.

Hans Appenzeller
820 Madison Ave. (68th & 69th Sts.)
570-0504
Open Mon.-Sat. 10:30 a.m.-5:30 p.m. Closed Sat. in Aug.

Beautiful modern jewelry by this Dutch designer is lovingly displayed in glass cases so the light hits the pieces just so. Appenzeller jewelry is flawlessly fluid and pleasingly graphic. There are made-to-order bracelets for stylish and daring wrists, hammered earrings, wire-mesh chokers and smooth, rounded rings twinkling with baby gemstones.

Harry Winston
718 Fifth Ave. (56th St.)
245-2000
Open Mon.-Fri. 10 a.m.-5 p.m.

Harry Winston is famous for its giant gems and the giant celebrities who buy them. Quality and size are the trademarks of the rocks found here. This is the real stuff, the big time. What other fine jewelry store is closed the day before Mother's Day?

WATCHES

Time Will Tell
962 Madison Ave. (75th & 76th Sts.)
861-2663
Open Mon.-Sat. 10 a.m.-6 p.m.

Although digital watches may be accurate, their excessive functionality has taken all the fashion out of wearing a watch. Re-enter the antique wristwatch. One of the most lovingly guarded collections of these timeless beauties can be found at Time Will Tell, a charming little shop that sells only antique watches. One of the knowledgeable staff will provide pertinent biographical data on whichever watch you're considering adopting. These little bits of history sell for $300 to over $30,000. You'll find names such as Patek Phillipe, Vacheron & Constantin, Hamilton and Paul Diteshem.

Tourneau Corner
500 Madison Ave. (52nd St.)
758-3265
Open Mon.-Fri. 10 a.m.-5:45 p.m., Sat. 10:30 a.m.-5:30 p.m.

A tall clock stands on the corner of Madison and 52nd Street. That's how you find Tourneau Corner, an established purveyor of Swiss watches. Step inside and you're met by helpful staff directing you to the right counter. Your sales help, well-mannered and resourceful, will walk you through the selections. Tourneau runs the spectrum, selling Rolex, Concord, Cartier, Patek Phillipe, Gucci and Piaget, though more moderately priced Movado and Longine too are on display. Prices start at $135 and can run up to $75,000. Down the street, at 488 Madison Avenue, Tourneau has a complete watch center that will take an entire watch apart or refit your watch with a new band.

Wempe
695 Fifth Ave. (54th & 55th Sts.)
751-4884
Open Mon.-Fri. 10 a.m.-6 p.m., Sat. 10 a.m.-5:30 p.m.

Wempe offers a complete selection of contemporary watches and clocks, as well as fine European jewelry in both classic and contemporary styles. The extremely professional staff will work with you while you choose one of the many designs, or they will help you select any combination of precious stones to be worked into your own design—you can choose from a complete selection of stones and diamonds.

MENSWEAR

DISCOUNT

BFO
149 Fifth Ave. (21st St.)
254-0059
Open Mon.-Wed. & Fri.-Sun. 10 a.m.-5:30 p.m., Thurs. 10 a.m.-6:45 p.m.

Ambience is not the purpose here; getting good prices on designer labels is. Rummage through bins and bins of shirts in all styles from all the top designers—Givenchy, Perry Ellis, Calvin Klein, Valentino, Ralph Lauren, Yves St. Laurent—sold for up to 50 percent off (and sometimes more) the average department-store price. A standard Oxford shirt, sold for $45 elsewhere, goes for $18. Silk ties by Ted Lapidus, Pierre Balmain and Fendi hang from the walls in many-colored splendor and sell for just $9.50. There is a small selection of sportswear (pullovers and cotton shirts) as well as belts, handkerchiefs, socks and underwear. American suits start at $195,

Italian suits average $295, and name rain-coats, sport-coats, and overcoats are priced about 60 percent below retail. Who shops here? Says one salesman, "All the best in-formed men, from Brooklyn to Argentina."

Moe Ginsburg
162 Fifth Ave. (21 St.)
982-5254
Open Mon.-Wed. & Fri. 9:30 a.m.-6 p.m., Thurs. 9:30 a.m.-8 p.m., Sat.-Sun. 9:30 a.m.-6 p.m.

A Fifth Avenue institution tucked away on the upper floors of an office building. The second-floor elevator doors open to a cigar-puffing, quick-talking old-timer. That's Moe, the man who's built a bargain empire known by savvy New Yorkers and people from all corners of the world. You'll find floor after floor of men's designer garments, ranging from suits and outerwear to boxer shorts. Unless you've done some serious weightlift-ing recently, you may have trouble sliding the clothes along the jam-packed racks. Fear not, an eager salesman is bound to find you, and will be reluctant to leave your side until you've found a suitable item.

N.B.O. (National Brands Outlet)
1965 Broadway (67th St.)
595-1550
Open Mon.-Sat. 10 a.m.-9 p.m., Sun. noon-8 p.m.

The natives here are eternally restless for a bargain, and when they go to N.B.O. they leave with nothing less. This colossal store specializes in European and American design-ers at considerably reduced prices.

Syms
45 Park Pl. (Church St. & Broadway)
791-1199
Open Mon.-Wed. 8 a.m.-6:30 p.m., Thurs.-Fri. 8 a.m.-7:30 p.m., Sat. 10 a.m.-6:30 p.m., Sun. 11:30 a.m.-5:30 p.m.

Syms is a bargain-hunter's dream and a service-needer's nightmare. This no-frills de-partment store sells highly discounted fashion for both men and women. There are designer suits, couture, famous-maker coats, shoes, un-derwear, ties, jackets, accessories and kids' clothes. Go if you have time to dig. The price of an item starts out low and is lowered at regular intervals based on its length of time in the store. No credit cards—cash, check or the Syms credit card only. The store is too big to seem crowded, but this City Hall location gets a little desolate on Saturdays.

READY-TO-WEAR & DESIGNER

Addison on Madison
698 Madison Ave. (62nd & 63rd St.)
308-2660
Open Mon.-Sat. 10 a.m.-6:30 p.m.

Addison on Madison is a little store with a catchy name that sells only shirts and related accessories. These shirts, 100-percent cotton and imported from France, come in only four variations: button-down, regular- or wide-collared and French-cuffed. In white, pastels or subtle prints, these shirts are good-quality staples for any wardrobe. Also in Trump Tower, as is Addison on Madison for Women.

Bijan Designer for Men
699 Fifth Ave. (54th & 55th Sts.)
758-7500
Open Mon.-Sat. 10 a.m.-6 p.m. by appt. only.

Tell your chauffeur to circle the block a few times—you might be a while. Bijan has cre-ated perhaps one of the finest retail establish-ments in the world. Greeted by the impeccably mannered doorman, you step into a world of beige and white (Bijan's favorite colors), with a Baccarat crystal chandelier and polished brass banisters on the double stair-cases leading upstairs. With typical Bijan verve, a simple workman's ladder is painted white and draped with a mink throw large enough to be a bedspread. The clothes are displayed like jewels behind heavy lead-crystal doors. Everything in the store, from suits, shoes and ties to wallets and luggage, is de-signed by Bijan himself, and all of his fabrics are exclusive.

Brooks Brothers
346 Madison Ave. (44th St.)
682-8800
Open Mon.-Wed. & Fri.-Sat. 8:30 a.m.-6 p.m., Thurs. 8:30 a.m.-7 p.m.

One doesn't chance into Brooks Brothers, one is born into it. This store is the definition of preppiness. Nothing's ever quite in style here, so nothing is ever out of style either. Classic suits, Oxford shirts, polos—everything one needs for the office or a fox hunt. Brooksgate starts boys off on the right preppy foot, and there is an ultra-conservative women's line in the same boxy styles. Prices are moderately high; quality and service are very high. Another location at 1 Liberty Plaza (267-2400), across from the World Trade Center.

Burberry's
9 E. 57th St. (Fifth & Madison Aves.)
371-5010
Open Mon.-Wed. & Fri. 9:30 a.m.-6 p.m., Thurs. 9:30 a.m.-7 p.m., Sat. 10 a.m.-6 p.m.

Burberry's classic trench coat offers just the right amount of status when the signature plaid lining peeks out as the coat is thrown casually over a blue-suited arm. Matching plaid accessories are available in scarves, umbrellas, bathrobes, even desk items. Burberry's carries complete, conservative lines for both men and women, all with the British flair for fine fabrics and exacting quality. Expect to pay for it.

The Custom Shop Shirtmakers
115 Broadway (Wall St.)
267-8535
Open Mon.-Fri. 8:30 a.m.-5:30 p.m.

A store in the old English tradition of London's Savile Row, the Custom Shop specializes in men's custom-made suits and shirts in a large variety of fabrics. The made-to-measure shirts start at $45, a price based on the cutting of four shirts. Suits start at $495. You can also purchase ties, suspenders, cuff links and ready-to-wear shirts.

D. Cenci
801 Madison Ave. (67th & 68th Sts.)
628-5910
Open June Mon.-Fri. 10 a.m.-6 p.m.; July-Aug. Mon.-Fri. 10:30 a.m. to 6 p.m.; Sept.-May Mon.-Wed. & Fri.-Sat. 10:30 a.m.-6:30 p.m., Thurs. 10:30 a.m.-7:30 p.m.

Che bello! D. Cenci can outfit the sophisticated man from shoes to shirts in its own line of Italian menswear. It's comfortable, although expensive, to shop here—the racks are full and the staff is friendly, a refreshing alternative to the snobby atmosphere prevalent on Madison Avenue. There's a nice selection of sweaters, as well as everything you can wear them with. Slimming, Italian-cut suits sell for $800 to $1,500.

Emporio Armani
110 Fifth Ave. (16th St.)
727-3240
Open Mon.-Wed. & Fri.-Sat. 11 a.m.-7 p.m., Thurs. 11 a.m.-7:30 p.m., Sun. noon-5 p.m.

Experimenting with his Emporio shop concept, Giorgio Armani opened his first U.S. store in New York. But the experiment didn't stop there. Rather than moving onto Madison Avenue next to the highly acclaimed couture clan, Armani set up shop in the up-and-coming Flatiron district, an area that began to metamorphose five years ago when advertising agencies, publishing companies, photographers and modeling studios were attracted to lower rents and bigger spaces. While Armani is not the lone fashion house, it is probably the biggest news in the neighborhood. The sprawling store, devoted mostly to classic menswear, highlights the timelessness of gentrified styling. There's also a section for women's items, with *faux* fur accented as the current rage.

F.R. Tripler & Co.
366 Madison Ave. (46th St.)
922-1090
Open Mon.-Wed. & Fri. 9 a.m.-5:45 p.m., Thurs. 9 a.m.-6:30 p.m., Sat. 9 a.m.-5:30 p.m.

Tripler is a favorite shop of the very affluent. Whether updated, traditional or formal, its men's clothing is of the highest quality. This is home to New York's largest assortment of both Hickey Freeman (suits, sport coats and topcoats) and Oxford (the finest hand-tailored suits available). Top-notch personal service is standard, and the shop's alterations department is perhaps the best in New York City.

Paul Smith
108 Fifth Ave. (16th St.)
627-9770
Open Mon.-Sat. 11 a.m.-7 p.m.

A trendy haunt for the well-heeled man who wants to look fashionable at work and at play. A full selection of beautifully tailored suits, dress shirts and up-to-the-minute fashion ties are housed in a small, intimate room. Next door, hi-tech and funky fashions give men the chance to dress daringly outside of the office. There's also a small selection of trendy home furnishings such as geometric clocks and picture frames.

Paul Stuart

Madison Ave. & 45th St.
682-0320
Open Mon.-Wed. & Fri. 8 a.m.-6 p.m., Thurs. 8 a.m.-7 p.m., Sat. 9 a.m.-6 p.m.

A staid, subdued atmosphere pervades the spacious interior at Paul Stuart, where shopping is unhurried and manageable. The store offers its male customers an American look that is updated, yet traditional and classic. The large staff gives plenty of assistance, and on hand is a coordinating consultant trained to create the look you're searching for. With its smart sportswear and dresses and elegant Japanese knits, Paul Stuart's tiny women's department caters to the woman who doesn't have to wear a suit (although suits are sold).

Yves St. Laurent Men's Boutique

859 Madison Ave. (71st St.)
517-7400
Open Mon.-Sat. 10 a.m.-6 p.m.

Yves St. Laurent's men's designs have a classic simplicity that befits the high prices. The store offers excellent service and plush surroundings to accommodate men who just can't be bothered to tackle crowds. The primary-colored casual wear and the elegant, traditional suitings make this the store of choice for an older, monied clientele.

TAILORS

Dunhill Tailors

65 E. 57th St. (Fifth & Madison Aves.)
355-0050
Open Mon.-Fri. 9:30 a.m.-6 p.m., Sat. 10 a.m.-5:30 p.m.

Dunhill presents custom men's clothing that exudes English style in suits, sportswear and formal wear. The shop's selection of polo shirts (in sea-island cotton and silk), cotton trousers and sweaters is both elegant and casual. Dunhill sells the definitive navy blue, gold-buttoned blazer, but you'll have to get past the lovely ties first.

Saint Laurie Ltd.

897 Broadway (20th St.)
473-0100
Open Mon.-Wed. & Fri.-Sat. 9:30 a.m.-6 p.m., Thurs. 9:30 a.m.-7:30 p.m., Sun. noon-5 p.m. Closed Sun. in summer.

Tired of mass-produced suits that seem to be programmed to lose their buttons the min-

ute you leave the store? Searching for hand-tailored suits, but can't afford the airfare to Savile Row or Hong Kong? Relax. Saint Laurie is a merchant tailor offering hand-tailored suits at less-than-mass-market prices. Selling directly to the public, they've eliminated the middleman's markup. For under $500, Saint Laurie sells traditionally styled suits in traditional fabrics for both men and women. Visit before 4 p.m. on any weekday and you can see the tailors in action.

TUXEDOS

A.T. Harris

47 E. 44th St., 2nd Fl. (Vanderbilt & Madison Aves.)
682-6325
Open Mon.-Wed. & Fri. 8:30 a.m.-6 p.m., Thurs. 8:30 a.m.-7 p.m., Sat. 10 a.m.-4 p.m. by appt. only.

This small, cluttered shop has been dressing men in traditional formal attire of the finest quality since 1892. In addition to tuxedos, dinner jackets and tails, you'll find all the elegant accessories necessary for a night on the town, including silk top hats, white kidskin gloves, spats, waistcoats and walking sticks (all for rent). Custom-tailored formal attire is also available. No wonder nine presidents have been outfitted here for weddings and inaugurations. Prices, luckily, are far from presidential: tuxedo rentals start at $95, which includes all accessories except shoes.

Zeller Tuxedos

201 E. 56th St., 2nd Fl. (Second & Third Aves.)
355-0707
Open Mon.-Fri. 9 a.m.-7:45 p.m., Sat. 10 a.m.-4:45 p.m.

A New York institution for rented formal wear, this showroom offers a unique salon atmosphere and a professional sales staff that can get you in and out in ten minutes. Of course, if you prefer, you can linger for a few hours until you find the perfect tuxedo by a designer such as Pierre Cardin, Luxiano Barbera, Windsor, or Padgett and Poole. All accessories are included in the price, which starts at $85; shoes are another $20. There is another location at 1010 Third Avenue (60th Street), 688-0100.

SHOES

Bally of Switzerland
645 Madison Ave. (59th & 60th Sts.)
832-7267
Open Mon.-Sat. 9:30 a.m.-6 p.m.

Bally makes the kind of shoes you might expect from the Swiss. Noted for its sedate loafers in a few limited styles with little variation, Bally relies on lightweight leather construction, not as sleekly styled as Italian footwear but not nearly as hard and clunky as English designs. Some people think Bally shoes are classy and comfortable, while others consider them to be stolid and dull, but few demean the materials or the workmanship. As for the store itself, it's as interesting as the shoes. Men's only at this location; call the above number for other stores in the city.

Billy Martin's
812 Madison Ave. (68th St.)
861-3100
Open Mon.-Fri. 10 a.m.-7 p.m., Sat. 10:30 a.m.-6 p.m., Sun. noon-5 p.m.

It may be an East Coast operation, but Billy Martin's exudes Western style. Long an American classic, it has an authenticity unparalleled in the city. Even cast members of *Dallas* have been known to shop here for exotic boots and accessories. There's an outstanding selection of boots priced according to the quality of the leather; expect to pay as much as $850 for a pair of ostrich boots (in black, chocolate, honey or chili) and as little as $250 for suede boots. You can also get Stetson and Cripple Creek hats. Everyone who walks in here walks out a dude.

Charles Jourdan
Trump Tower, 725 Fifth Ave. (56th & 57th Sts.)
644-3830
Open Mon.-Fri. 10 a.m.-7 p.m., Sat. 10 a.m.-6 p.m., Sun. noon-6 p.m.

Charles Jourdan's women's shoes and ready-to-wear clothing in sophisticated styles are never too dull or too daring, but always *très chic* in that particularly French way. Great men's shoes are found upstairs, and a small Seductra boutique on the garden level features a racier line of women's footwear. The staff is friendly, the store busy and bright and the prices almost reasonable.

Fratelli Rossetti
601 Madison Ave. (58th St.)
888-5107
Open Mon.-Fri. 10 a.m.-7 p.m., Sat. 10 a.m.-6 p.m., Sun. noon-6 p.m.

The irresistible look, smell and feel of beautifully crafted Italian leather shoes—that's what the discerning shopper finds under the Rossetti roof. Catering to both men and women, this international boutique excels at conservatively styled shoes. Soberly elegant loafers finished with stitching and tassels, or square-toed flats in autumn earth tones or summer pastels, combine fashion with classicism. The look is sporting, but rich. And the quality? It's what one would expect from a world-renowned shoe house.

Joan & David
816 Madison Ave. (68th & 69th Sts.)
772-3970
Open Mon.-Sat. 10 a.m.-6 p.m.

Joan & David's women's shoes combine fashion and affordability. From classic pumps and long, lean flats to '40s-style lace-up boots, the shoes are made with the finest leathers and the most attentive design. There are four other Manhattan locations, all tucked inside Ann Taylor stores. The Madison Avenue shop is the city's only freestanding Joan & David boutique, and it makes for a pleasanter experience—there is less of a mob scene and no wait at the register. If you're in the Hamptons, it's worth going the extra few miles to Amagansett to visit the Joan & David outlet there, where these pricey shoes can be purchased at a substantial discount.

Maud Frizon
49 E. 57th St. (Park & Madison Aves.)
980-1460
Open Mon.-Sat. 10 a.m. to 6 p.m.

Shoes as art, priceless and modern, is what you'll find at Maud Frizon: sky-high heels with exotic cut-outs, serpentine sandals, quilted flats. Textures, shapes, and colors are crafted into original designs that are as shocking as their prices. Some styles are truly outrageous, others more wearable, but all are interesting. If you can afford it, congratulations. If not, go to spectate.

Perry Ellis Shoes

1136 Madison Ave. (84th & 85th Sts.)
570-9311
Open Mon.-Sat. 10 a.m.-7 p.m., Sun. noon-6 p.m.

The collection of Perry Ellis shoes is tasteful and tempting. The trendy but not-at-all intimidating Madison Avenue boutique carries three lines: The Collection line, with prices ranging from $120 to $200; the Portfolio line, priced between $75 and $100; and a moderately priced American line, costing between $50 and $70. This shop holds strong appeal with the working woman who likes a particular style, and can buy one style in a few colors without having to mortgage her condominium. This shop also offers a smart selection of handbags, wallets, scarves and ties for the man in your life. Down the Avenue at 62nd Street, Perry Ellis has a second store that primarily carries the American line.

Peter Fox

105 Thompson (Prince & Spring Sts.)
431-6359
Open Mon.-Sat. 11 a.m.-8 p.m., Sun. noon-8 p.m.

This is your chance to feel like Cinderella. Peter Fox shoes are made for fairy tales, but work nicely for weddings, formal affairs or special occasions. A throwback to Victorian styling, Fox has a complete bridal line and a regular line. Practically unique, the shoes are made of delicate fabrics such as satin, lace, damask and moreen. And if you lose a slipper, no doubt Prince Charming will find your foot, because Fox's shoes are romantically distinctive. Another location on Amsterdam Avenue and 78th Street.

Susan Bennis Warren Edwards

440 Park Ave. (56th St.)
755-4197
Open Mon. 10 a.m.-7 p.m., Tues.-Wed. 10 a.m.-6:30 p.m.,Thurs. 10 a.m.-7 p.m., Fri. 10 a.m.-6:30 p.m., Sat. 10 a.m.-6 p.m.

Shopping for shoes at Bennis and Edwards is a luxury. The owners are also the designers, and, in typically autocratic style, they control every aspect of the production of their footwear. Both men's and women's styles come in classic and costly materials, such as alligator, ostrich, silk, satin and suede. Most importantly, the quality of workmanship and the

extraordinary details, colors and patterns set these shoes apart.

El Vaquero

908 Madison Ave. (72nd & 73rd Sts.)
737-8730
Open Mon.-Sat. 10 a.m.-6 p.m.

El Vaquero's window is a blaze of silver, white and gold, not to mention lizard, metal and jewels. Where else could you find gold, lizard-patterned, high-top sneakers, or even more outrageous silver-studded pumps? Made in Italy, these shoes are glitz galore.

WOMENSWEAR

DESIGNERS

Courrèges

520 Madison Ave. (53rd St.)
319-5766
Open Mon.-Wed. & Fri.-Sat. 10 a.m.-7 p.m., Thurs. 10 a.m.-8 p.m.

Courrèges's modern looks are brilliantly displayed in this airy Itokin Plaza collection of shops. The shops here cater to a youthful and glamorous crowd, and Courrèges is the most upscale of the bunch. Lots of primary colors, neatly spun knits and cool cottons make a perfect palette for these young, fashion-forward designs. It's a classic look made younger, bolder and freer than the uptown designers' styles.

Emanuel Ungaro

803 Madison Ave. (67th & 68th Sts.)
249-4090
Open Mon.-Wed. & Fri.-Sat. 9:30 a.m.-6:30 p.m., Thurs. 9:30 a.m.-7:30 p.m.

Ungaro is (relatively) unintimidating, and it has something to suit every woman's taste. Some of Ungaro's designs are perfectly styled—trendy and tailored in youthful cuts and classic fabrics. Other designs are strangely matronly and reminiscent of Miami—full-figured and boldly patterned in some less-than-pleasing florals and prints. The common elements are the Ungaro name and couture price tags. Try it—you might like it.

Givenchy

954 Madison Ave. (75th St.)
772-1040
Open Mon.-Sat. 10 a.m.-6 p.m.

Haute couture, attitude and phenomenal prices sum up this designer boutique. Everything—from show-stopping gowns to signature silk scarves—is lovely to look at, intimidating to touch and difficult to afford. Sit on a comfy chair while the staff displays a sampling of the wares, or browse through the stunning collection at your own leisure.

Gucci

685 Fifth Ave. (54th St.)
826-2600
Open Mon.-Wed. & Fri.-Sat. 9:30 a.m.-6 p.m., Thurs. 9:30 a.m.-7 p.m.

One of the oldest Italian retail establishments in the U.S. and now a household name, Gucci is a department store for those who never look at price tags. For the wealthy and/or status-conscious, Gucci offers a style all its own—those ubiquitous interlocking G's and red and green Gucci stripes. For extra-special customers, there's a key that allows access to a private showroom.

Hermès

11 E. 57th St. (Fifth & Madison Aves.)
751-3181
Open Mon.-Wed. & Fri.-Sat. 10 a.m.-6 p.m., Thurs. 10 a.m.-8 p.m.

Elegance abounds in this Paris-based fashion house; a grand escalier of cherry wood with an intricately forged brass railing, cherry-wood walls and rich cabinetry bring the flavor of French aristocracy to Madison Avenue. Hermès's fabled silk scarves create a vivid bouquet of color, while a complete line of accessories, including handbags, luggage and belts, is equally appealing. Even if you don't ride horses, visit the equestrian department, which stocks everything but the horse.

Jaeger

19 E. 57th St. (Fifth & Sixth Aves.)
794-0780
Open Mon.-Sat. 10 a.m.- 6 p.m.

Need a smart suit for an important executive meeting or a sharp outfit for next week's auction? Drop into Jaeger. Simple but smart is this designer's statement. The clothing, much of which is designed to mix and match,

appeals to anglicized tastes—it's tailored, and, while Jaeger is fashion-conscious, the colors never veer off to whimsical fads. Shopping at Jaeger's spacious stores is pleasant; the staff is more than gracious. You can buy quality garments here without having to rob a bank.

Koos van den Akker

795 Madison Ave. (67th & 68th Sts.)
249-5432
Open Mon.-Sat. 11 a.m.-6 p.m.

Remember the collages you made in elementary school? Well, this designer from the Netherlands has taken that idea one step further, creating both off-the-rack and customized clothing for men and women. His designs are wild, combining colors and fabrics in ways you never thought were possible. Tired of your old fur coat, or just can't decide which fur is right for you? Let Koos van den Akker create a new collaged fur coat for you.

Martha

475 Park Ave. (58th St.)
753-1511
Open Mon.-Sat. 10 a.m.-6 p.m.

Very few designer boutiques can beat Martha in the glamour department. Besides the luxurious salonlike setting, the old-money clientele, the attentive staff and the models prancing about in the latest evening wear, Martha is the home of the perfect party dress. Short and crinolined, satin and seductive, beaded and extravagant—they're all here, and they're all flawlessly executed. See some of these frocks, and you'll be tempted to conjure up an occasion to justify the extravagance. There's another store—models and all—at 725 Fifth in Trump Tower (826-8855).

Missoni

836 Madison Ave. (69th St.)
517-9339
Open Mon.-Sat. 10 a.m.-6 p.m. Closed Sat. in summer.

Missoni is known for richly textured sweaters in lush wools and colorful patterns. Color combinations you wouldn't dare to think of seem to work magic in Missoni's couture. While the sweaters are definitely the most popular items, this Italian designer also has a wonderful collection of suits and sportswear for both men and women.

Norma Kamali O.M.O.
11 W. 56th St. (Seventh Ave.)
957-9797
Open Mon.-Sat. 10 a.m.-6 p.m.

Step into this boutique and you'll realize that as Norma Kamali has grown up, she's gone through some serious attitude changes. Previously her designs tended toward the ridiculously sublime—lighthearted, fun fashion for the young at heart. But the long, rectangular shop is currently filled with a more sedate look—navy blues, glen plaids, white linens and basic black. There's still a hint of her old humor in this refreshing new look: a skirt is slightly oddly pleated, a navy dress dramatically shaped, a white shirt unusually tailored. Great lingerie and swimwear, too.

Sonia Rykiel
792 Madison Ave. (67th St.)
744-0880
Open Mon.-Wed. & Fri.-Sat. 9:30 a.m.-6:30 p.m., Thurs. 9:30 a.m.-7:30 p.m.

These signature knits are simple and distinctive, which gives Rykiel a most loyal following. This modern Madison Avenue boutique offers a wide selection of knitted day and evening wear, and the racks are packed full; a ruffled gown refuses to stay within the confines of the space allotted to it.

Yves St. Laurent Rive Gauche
855 Madison Ave. (71st St.)
988-3821
Open Mon.-Sat. 10 a.m.-6 p.m.

This archetypal designer's boutique is predictably elegant and surprisingly unintimidating. The daywear runs from the stylishly traditional to the downright matronly, but the evening clothes are pure glamour. It's all very expensive, but the clientele is devoted to the quality that is intrinsic to the St. Laurent name.

DISCOUNT

Bolton's
225 E. 57th St. (Second & Third Aves.)
755-2527
Open Mon.-Wed. & Fri.-Sat. 10 a.m.-7 p.m., Thurs. 10 a.m.-9 p.m., Sun. noon-5 p.m.

For some reason, a trip to Bolton's does not seem like shopping. Women come to this discount store so regularly that it becomes part of the weekly routine. There's no high fashion here, just standard wardrobe staples. With prices this low, it seems silly not to buy that extra blouse or cotton sweater. There's usually a decent collection of linen clothing in the warmer months, as well as great wool sweaters in winter. Sales are frequent and worthwhile. Call the above number for other store locations.

FURS

Forman's
78, 82 & 94 Orchard St. (Delancey & Grand Sts.)
228-2500
Open Sun.-Wed. 9 a.m.-6 p.m., Thurs. 9 a.m.-8 p.m., Fri. 9 a.m.-3:30 p.m.

Crossing Delancey has been a New York ritual for years. Scores of smart shoppers, in search of good buys, trek down to this seedy part of town to shop and haggle (the two go hand-in-hand on Orchard Street). Forman's has three shops: Large, regular and petite sizes. Inside, devout women, dressed in long smocks with covered heads even on the hottest summer day, will offer assistance immediately. Don't be fooled by their lack of pizazz; these women have been selling for years, and they're experts on fashion. Forman's has a broad selection of suits, separates, outerwear and some fancy dresses.

Fur Salon at Bergdorf Goodman
754 Fifth Ave. (57th St.)
872-8752
Open Mon.-Wed. & Fri.-Sat. 10:30 a.m.-6 p.m., Thurs. 10:30 a.m.-8 p.m.

Sit and be served at the Fur Salon at Bergdorf. Plush couches envelop you until the always-accommodating staff can bring you something delicious to slip on. As in the rest of the store, only the best and most fashionable is sold here. Be it Galanos, Fendi or Bergdorf's own line, the styles are either timeless or fresh off the runway. And in true Bergdorf tradition, no one who shops here cares if it can be found cheaper elsewhere.

The Fur Vault
581 Fifth Ave. (47th & 48th Sts.)
765-3877
Open Tues.-Wed. & Fri.-Sat. 10 a.m.-7 p.m.,
Thurs. 10 a.m.-8 p.m., Sun. noon-5 p.m.

At The Fur Vault you will not only find every fur, but fur everything. The choice of coats mixes original designs with many top designer labels, including Andrew Marc, Chloé, Giancarlo Ripa, Blackglama and Hudson Bay. Mink, sable, raccoon, fox, lynx, coyote, beaver and many other furs are offered in both classic and contemporary styles, and there's a complete salon of fur coats for men. The store also has hats, mufflers, flings, ear muffs, sweaters, shawls and other accessories made of or trimmed in fur.

Harry Kirshner & Son
307 Seventh Ave., 4th Fl. (27th & 28th Sts.)
243-4847
Open Mon.-Fri. 9 a.m.-6 p.m., Sat. 10 a.m.-5 p.m.

Making sure you are absolutely in love with your fur coat is the staff's primary concern here. Their mission is one of matchmaking, not selling. As a result, the shop is low-pressure, congenial and personalized without compromising style. Harry Kirshner & Son has developed an international reputation for workmanship over the years, and so can be trusted to alter, remodel, repair and custom-design. Look out for the yearly preseason sale, where you can find great discounts, along with furs from top designers: Lanvin, Dior, Carol Little, Valentino, Nina Ricci and Balenciaga.

Maximillian
20 W. 57th St., 3rd Fl. (Fifth & Sixth Aves.)
765-6290
Open Mon.-Fri. 10 a.m.-5:30 p.m.

You won't find the superb Maximillian furs anywhere but at its showroom. Maintaining one of the finest reputations for quality, style and service, Maximillian makes half its coats to order. Storage, repair, cleaning and remodeling services are also provided.

Revillon at Saks
611 Fifth Ave. (49th & 50th Sts.)
753-4000
Open Mon.-Wed. & Fri.-Sat. 10 a.m.-6:30 p.m.,
Thurs. 10 a.m.-8 p.m.

Surrounded with collections from all the high priests of designer fashion, the third-floor fur salon at Saks seems plain in comparison. The decor is bare and very brown—the furs, the carpet, even the petite couches for men to sit on while their wives or girlfriends model the exquisite furs. Most furs are Revillon's own label, but there are other big names available as well: Blass, Givenchy and the like. Note: it's all available much cheaper on Seventh Avenue, but here you can also find something fun to wear under your fur.

Ritz Thrift Shop
107 W. 57th St. (Sixth & Seventh Aves.)
265-4559
Open Mon.-Sat. 9 a.m.-6 p.m.

The Ritz Thrift Shop has made a reputation for itself the world over by selling almost-new fur coats for both men and women. They offer a wide selection of styles and skins at prices ranging from $500 to $15,000. All coats are cleaned and will be altered free of charge.

LINGERIE & HOSIERY

Leggiadro
700 Madison Ave. (62nd & 63rd Sts.)
753-5050
Open Mon.-Sat. 10 a.m.-6 p.m.

Young and not-so-serious, this stocking store has cubbyholes filled to the brim with legwear in parfait colors and a potpourri of designs, including stockings by Missoni, Cerruti, Elbeo, Hot Sox and Leggiadro's house line. Seams, textures, tassels and rhinestones enhance this youthful collection. Prices are reasonable and the selection is huge—you'll find it impossible to leave with just one pair.

La Lingerie
792 Madison Ave. (67th St.)
772-9797
Open Mon.-Wed. & Fri.-Sat. 10 a.m.-6:30 p.m.,
Thurs. 10 a.m.-7:30 p.m.

Enter La Lingerie and you could be in Jane Seymour's boudoir or on the set of an Anaïs Anaïs commercial. Sachets, dried flowers and wicker baskets create an air of ultimate femininity, setting the stage for silk-lined velvet bra, panties and garters, lacy teddies, satin tap pants and naughty nightwear—all ultra-romantic, ultra-luxurious and (naturally) expensive. Buying lingerie is fun; buying it here truly sets the mood in which it is meant to be worn.

Victoria's Secret

34 E. 57th St. (Park & Madison Aves.)
758-5592

Open Mon.-Wed. & Fri. 10 a.m.-7 p.m., Thurs. 10 a.m.-8 p.m., Sat. 10 a.m.-6 p.m., Sun. noon-5 p.m.

Once upon a time this lingerie shop was just a mail-order business associated with The Limited. Then it became a boutique attached to the store. With the new 57th Street location, it has branched out on its own. Victoria's Secret has one of the best (and definitely the least expensive) lingerie and loungewear collections in town. Lacy petticoats, racy garters, silk panties, flannel nightshirts, romantic teddies and cool cotton undershirts are all reasonably priced and meant to be worn. The professional staff will help hunt for those matching panties, search for the right size and gift wrap anything, no matter how small.

Wifemistress

1044 Lexington Ave. (74th & 75th Sts.)
570-9529

Open Mon.-Sat. 10 a.m.-6 p.m.

Buying lingerie doesn't have to mean choosing between cheap, tacky corsets and fabulously expensive, too-delicate-to-wear froufrou. Wifemistress falls squarely in the middle by catering to an above-average-income customer who wants very feminine, good-quality undergarments. Most of the bras, panties and silks are imported from France and Italy; many of the cottons are made in Switzerland and Germany. The shop also carries bathing suits.

READY-TO-WEAR

Ann Taylor

3 E. 57th St. (Fifth & Madison Aves.)
832-2010

Open Mon.-Sat. 10 a.m.-6 p.m., Thurs. 10 a.m.-8 p.m.

The flagship store on 57th Street carries not only Ann Taylor merchandise but also selections from other designers. The end result is a shop full of tailored, casual sportswear that is basic to the American lifestyle. Nothing is too fancy or frilly, and everything is stylish (versus preppy) and comfortable. Ann Taylor also carries Joan & David shoes, sensibly

priced (but not cheap) and chic. Call the above number for other Manhattan locations.

Betsey Johnson

130 Thompson St. (Houston & Prince Sts.)
420-0169

Open Mon.-Sat. noon-7 p.m., Sun. 1 p.m.-6 p.m.

Betsey Johnson's whimsical designs run the gamut from wild and outrageous to preppy conservatism: bubblegum-colored crinolines and bustiers, skin-tight stretchy dresses adorned with snaps, cheerful acrylic sweaters in silly patterns, floral print dresses cut long and boxy. It's kicky, odd, none-too-expensive and a lot of fun. There's a definite adventure to be found here, as the strange mix of clientele peep in and out of the barely curtained dressing rooms in various stages of Betsey dress (and undress). Call the above number for other store locations.

Charivari

441 Columbus Ave. (81st St.)
496-8700

Open Mon.-Wed. & Fri. 11 a.m.-8 p.m., Thurs. 11 a.m.-9 p.m., Sat. 11 a.m.-7 p.m., Sun. 12:30 p.m.-6 p.m.

Charivari is a French word meaning "hullaballoo," and, most appropriately, this six-store fashion empire has consistently turned the rules upside down. One of the first to lay claim in the then-unfashionable Upper West Side, Charivari now has six stores between W. 72nd and W. 85th streets; three of them appear on consecutive blocks. Charivari is what today's fashion is all about. Armani, Kamali, Gaultier, Williwear, Byblos and Kenzo, of course, are all featured now. But Charivari's success is based on the fact that it featured them *then*. It was one of the first retailers to venture into Japan, and those earlier discoveries are now fashion household names: Matsuda, Miyake, Yamamoto.

The Limited

691 Madison Ave. (62nd St.)
838-8787

Open Mon.-Fri. 10 a.m.-7 p.m., Sat. 10 a.m.-6 p.m., Sun. noon-5 p.m.

A massive multilevel store catering to a woman whose life has a number of dimensions: work, sport, leisure and evening engagements. Emulating Ralph Lauren's styling, The Limited's clothing plays on equestrian and country themes; prairie skirts and knitted vests are complemented with rugged sweaters or delicately patterned blouses. Traipsing from floor to floor, you'll be astonished by the extensive selection. The Limited's breadth of choice gives you the feeling you're in a department store.

Parachute
121 Wooster St. (Spring & Prince Sts.)
925-8630
Open Mon.-Fri. noon-8 p.m., Sat. noon-7 p.m., Sun. 1 p.m.-7 p.m.

Beware of a store with more empty space than merchandise—each item must be carrying more than its square-foot-share of New York City's sky-high rents. Alas, this is the case with Parachute. The expensive clothing has that baggy, unisex, unicolor look. It's all quite wearable, although it seems ridiculous to pay such prices to look like that. The staff and the price tags can be intimidating, but stick to your guns, try the stuff on and have some fun.

Polo/Ralph Lauren
867 Madison Ave. (72nd St.)
606-2100
Open Mon.-Wed. & Fri.-Sat. 10 a.m.-6 p.m., Thurs. 10 a.m.-8 p.m.

Ralph Lauren is not just a shopping experience; it's a way of life. Housed in a gorgeous French-Renaissance-style building, the shop excels in understated elegance and longstanding quality. Ralph Lauren brings the country to city folk. While Lauren's clothing and accessories for men, women and boys are available at several fine department stores, here you'll get the full scope. Special services include free alterations and made-to-measure gentlemen's clothing.

Victoria Falls
451 W. Broadway (Houston & Prince Sts.)
254-2433
Open Mon.-Sat. 11 a.m.-7 p.m., Sun 12:30 p.m.-6 p.m.

Former actress Rena Gill started this store after years of people begging her to sell them some of the antique hats she collected and displayed in her home on Thompson Street. She finally opened Victoria Falls and has since branched out into antique Victorian blouses and dresses, jewelry and her own line of day-into-evening wool, crepe and linen suits, plus lingerie and blouses. You'll find a fusion of the Victorian era through the 30's and up-to-the-minute styles. Many fashion designers, artists and actresses shop here for the wonderfully romantic (but not too fussy) clothes.

DEPARTMENT STORES

Barney's
106 Seventh Ave. (16th & 17th Sts.)
929-9000
Open Mon.-Fri. 10 a.m.-9 p.m., Sat. 10 a.m.-7 p.m., Sun. noon-6 p.m.

It's difficult to remember that Barney's is a full-scale department store—it's more like a large Charivari than a small Bloomingdale's. The young, chic, affluent crowd that shops here is in the know. They want to choose from only the best and expect to pay for the quality, service and designer names. It's all the top of the line, the cream of the crop—what's hot, what's in style and what's selling. Barney's is especially strong in menswear, with clothes for boys, too, in sizes four to twenty, but the smaller women's store is also exciting. Climb the spiraled stairs; each level offers the most forward-thinking fashion available today. Hot looks by Montana, Klein, Alaïa, Miyake, Gaultier, Yamamoto, Fendi, Rykiel, Ellis, Kenzo, Matsuda—you name it, it's here. Don't forget that Barney's also has home furnishings—silver, bedding, china, gifts, linens and even a bridal registry. If shopping helps you work up an appetite, try Barney's Cafe for lunch.

Bergdorf Goodman
754 Fifth Ave. (57th St.)
753-7300
Open Mon.-Wed. & Fri.-Sat. 10 a.m.-6 p.m., Thurs. 10 a.m.-8 p.m.

Welcome to the store for the rich and famous. In the same location since 1928, this grand store is always one step ahead of its neighbors. Shopping here is truly a royal experience, with marble floors, crystal chandeliers and the sound of water falling from a fountain that once flowed at the Long Island estate of the Vanderbilts. All the major names are here, innovative and conservative, including (among many others) Fendi, Angela Cummings, Barry Kieselstein-Cord, Issey Miyake, Azzedine Alaïa and Donna Karan. Many of these collections are created exclusively for Bergdorf's and can be found nowhere else in the United States. The windows offer a glimpse into the world of the "haves."

Bloomingdale's
1000 Third Ave. (59th St.)
705-2000
Open Mon. & Thurs. 10 a.m.-9 p.m., Tues.-Wed. & Fri.-Sat. 10 a.m.-6:30 p.m., Sun. noon-6 p.m.

Bloomingdale's is the place to see a slice of New York—wealthy women toting ribboned poodles, trendy art types sporting androgynous haircuts and up-to-speed yuppies all meander from floor to floor. The bazaarlike atmosphere of the main floor is enhanced by models and salespeople hawking perfumes, makeup and other specials to customers weaving their way through the Louvre of cosmetic and accessory counters. In addition to the usual carnival, Bloomingdale's transforms itself each spring into another country; recent festivals have featured France, Italy and the South Seas. Underneath all the glitz and showbiz, a veritable treasure trove of merchandise is to be uncovered by the stalwart shopper. Men are fortunate that their departments are relatively contained on the first and lower levels—women must roam the upper floors hoping to stumble on one of four to seven shoe shops (depending on the ever-changing layout of the store) or the boutiques of Yves St. Laurent, Missoni, Sonia Rykiel, Ralph Lauren and the current crop of Bloomie's young designer finds, plus furs and bridal ensembles. Then there are lots of objects, from furniture and home electronics to books and art supplies, along with all the attendant services, such as decorating, cleaning, repairing and engraving, and, finally, a travel bureau. If you wish to take something home for dinner, stop in at the delicacies shop, a madhouse of comestibles to match the madhouse of the upper floors. If all this sounds too much or too tiring, don't despair. Bloomingdale's has thoughtfully instituted a personal shopping service, so your whims may be indulged at moment's notice: just push

seven numbers on a phone (705-3375), and issue your commands to a willing servant.

Bonwit Teller
4 E. 57th St. (Fifth Ave.)
593-3333
Mon.-Wed. & Fri. 10 a.m.-7 p.m., Thurs. 10 a.m.-8 p.m., Sat. 10 a.m.-6 p.m., Sun. noon-5 p.m.

For years, Bonwit Teller has clung to its identity as a boutique-style department store for women. Always more middle-of-the-road than its competition, Bendel and Bergdorf, Bonwit has finally come into its own with the increasing numbers of working women who need tailored yet glamorous styles. Standard to the mix are Albert Nipon, Ralph Lauren, Anne Klein and Liz Claiborne. Following suit, the shoe department also emphasizes a blend of classic and comfortable styles. Bonwit's continues to be an excellent source for colorful, but not punky, accessories such as scarves, bags, belts and jewelry. But where the store has taken off in recent years is in its small boutique for men—look into it.

Henri Bendel
10 W. 57th St. (Fifth & Sixth Aves.)
247-1100
Open Mon.-Wed. & Fri.-Sat. 10 a.m.-6 p.m., Thurs. 10 a.m.-8 p.m., Sun. noon-5 p.m.

This is not a store for those lacking self-assurance. You must be able to move with Bendel's trend-setting clientele and know intimately the important names in fashion, accessories, cosmetics and gifts. You'll pay handsomely for anything you buy (especially clothes), but you'll no doubt be repaid extravagantly in compliments. Bendel's has nothing that is not clever and avant-garde, and that goes for the decor, too. Even if you haven't the funds, take the time to wander into this wonderland. The first floor boasts not departments but boutiques that wind in and out of each other. Not everything makes sense, but it doesn't have to: Henri Bendel is concerned only with the spontaneous and hip—very hip.

Macy's Herald Square
151 W. 34th St. & Sixth Ave.
736-5151
Open Mon. & Thurs.-Fri. 9:45 a.m.-8:30 p.m., Tues.-Wed. & Sat. 9:45 a.m.-6:45 p.m., Sun. 10 a.m.-6 p.m.

Macy's Herald Square is known everywhere as "the world's largest store"; it occupies nearly an entire city block. Serving the middle and upper-middle classes and resembling a zoo on Saturdays, Macy's is still the store for the basics, despite its occasional scuffed floors and painfully slow service. The show begins on the main floor, where a marble art-deco interior sets the mood for the fine jewelry, elegant leathers, bright scarves and chic cosmetics and fragrances. Climb a grand marble staircase up to the balconies and you'll find yourself browsing through two of Macy's most unusual boutiques: a branch of the Metropolitan Museum of Art Gift Shop, and an antique and estate gallery offering rare jewelry. Upstairs are the Little Shops, featuring for women the designs of Giorgio Armani, Anne Klein, Claude Montana, Calvin Klein and others. There are also several floors devoted to items and furnishings for the home: included are linens, china, crystal, furniture, state-of-the-art electronics and telephones; and the children's department is zippy and fun even for parents. Housewares and gourmet delicacies are available in the Cellar, which is one of Macy's highlights, and if your timing is right, you may find the likes of Julia Child or Paul Prudhomme conducting a seminar in the test kitchen. There's also a Glemby Hair Salon, a film-developing center, an American Express Travel Service and a full-service post office.

Saks Fifth Avenue
611 Fifth Ave. (49th & 50th Sts.)
753-4000
Open Mon.-Wed. & Fri.-Sat. 10 a.m.-6:30 p.m., Thurs. 10 a.m.-8 p.m.

For those who can afford to choose, there's no other choice but Saks Fifth Avenue. The store has become a byword for taste and elegance. This store does not aim to surprise its shoppers; it simply offers impeccable clothing and merchandise for those who seem to know what they want before they arrive. The emphasis is on designer fashions, with the majority of floors devoted to women's clothing of the more luxurious variety. But the menswear floor is also terrific, with a contemporary section that is evolving quite nicely. The cosmetics department on the first floor appears to be one of the most popular in the city, since it is bustling at the most unexpected hours. There are special boutiques (leather accessories, stationery and gifts) on 49th and 50th streets, a full-service beauty salon, a chocolate and food shop and, of course, the Revillon fur salon.

FLOWERS

Bouquets à la Carte Inc.
1110 Park Ave. (82nd St.)
289-8300
Open Mon.-Fri. 9 a.m.-6 p.m., Sat. 11 a.m.-5 p.m.

For over twenty years, Bouquets à la Carte has been helping New Yorkers celebrate every type of occasion with baskets and bouquets of flowers, as well as a stunning array of other gifts. Send a "Get Well Quick" message with chocolate and flowers; or a "Happy Birthday" basket, which includes a custom-decorated birthday cake, confetti, Moët & Chandon Champagne, and balloons. The store also features such select gift items as Moustier and Limoges porcelain; crystal; Belgian chocolates; British and Italian silver; and out-of-the-ordinary gifts, like a Lucite cowboy hat filled with chili fixings, barbecue sauce and down-home recipes.

Renny
159 E. 64th St. (Lexington & Third Aves.)
288-7000
Open Mon.-Sat. 9 a.m.-5 p.m.

Proceed past the huge orchid-covered antique marble table and you'll find yourself in one of New York's most enchanting flower shops. Understated opulence is the theme at Renny, which creates lush, overstuffed arrangements of exotic and specially imported flowers. You can find sweet peas in January, French tulips, and the most exquisite arrangements of flowers with Champagne or flowers with chocolates. Renny also designs for parties, whether for ten or 2,000. Arrangements start at $45.

Ronaldo Maia Flowers

27 E. 67th St. (Madison Ave.)
288-1049
Open Mon.-Fri 9:30 a.m.-6 p.m., Sat. 11 a.m.-5 p.m. Closed Sat. in summer.

Things are always changing in this shop—Mr. Maia is constantly in his upstairs studio designing new containers and baskets for flowers, along with glassware and candle and potpourri holders. Maia designs all the accessories to ensure a most exclusive look for his most select clientele. In addition to flower arrangements, which start at $50, the shop offers one-stop service for those planning a reception or special function. Maia will find you a space, a decorator, furniture, china and linen, and will also recommend a caterer. And if you want to visit the studio itself, just call and ask.

Twigs

381 Bleecker Street
620-8188
Open Mon.-Fri. 9 a.m.-6:30 p.m., Sat. 10 a.m.-5 p.m.

In some flower shops, flowers are flowers. At Twigs, flowers are art. The founder and owner of this Greenwich Village shop, Paul Bott, combines a passion for nature with a need to be creative; his renowned work ranges from romantic, luscious looks using buttery petals to avant-garde arrangements with starker plant life. A walk through Twigs takes us into Bott's imagination—swaths of flowers, both potted and cut, turn his shop into a garden. Twigs also creates arrangements for private parties and special occasions. A second store is in the World Financial Center in Battery Park City.

FOOD

BAKERIES

The Erotic Baker

582 Amsterdam Ave. (88th & 89th Sts.)
362-7557
Open Mon.-Thurs. 11 a.m.-7 p.m., Fri.-Sat. 11 a.m.-8 p.m.

The Erotic Baker offers the most notable expression of the sexual revolution in the field of confectionery. Though it will take on the occasional "nonerotic" project, this place specializes in graphic representations of sexuality in cake and cream. Whether or not you find them erotic is your business, but enough people do that the Erotic Baker suggests orders be placed a day or two in advance. Phone orders are accepted, and delivery is available.

Ess-A-Bagel

359 First Ave. (21st & 22nd Sts.)
260-2252
Open Mon.-Sat. 7:30 a.m.-10 p.m., Sun. 7:30 a.m.-5 p.m.

Bagels are a part of New York's heritage. If you want to try the best New York has to offer, this is the place. (One client reportedly packed two suitcases of Ess-A-Bagels for his Alaska trip.) The small, bustling shop bakes the bagels on the premises, virtually guaranteeing that you can always get a hot bagel of any of the ten varieties: pumpernickel, pumpernickel-raisin, cinnamon-raisin, sesame, plain, onion, whole-wheat, poppy-seed, garlic and salt. Recommended are the many cream cheeses (vegetable, salmon) and the various spreads, particularly the whitefish salad.

H & H Bagels

2239 Broadway (80th St.)
595-8000
Open daily 24 hours.

There's no doubt about where the bagels are baked here. Two monstrous rotating ovens pour out bagels like a volcano emits lava. A recent controversy over making bagels with a newer method makes H & H an invaluable find. This place believes in sticking to something that works. What does change is the growing choice of bagel flavors, which includes poppy-seed, onion, sesame, salt, garlic, sourdough, whole-wheat and pumpernickel. If your trips to H & H are few and far between, buy a baker's dozen and freeze the ones you don't eat immediately. Also, as New York still claims to be the bagel capital of the world, H & H will ship its holy treasures anywhere in the country.

Kathleen's Bake Shop
155 E. 84th St. (Third & Lexington Aves.)
570-1515
Open Mon.-Sat. 8 a.m.-7 p.m., Sun. 9 a.m.-5 p.m.

This small, sparkling-clean store proudly carries on a tradition that started when Kathleen King began selling cookies at her father's farm as a child. Kathleen is famous for her chocolate chip cookies (which are moist on the inside, crunchy on the outside and full of big chips) and her apple crumb pie. She also bakes, among other delights, fruit pies, a sour-cream coffee cake, and brownies, as well as her banana and zucchini breads and her famous Crutchley Cruller hearts. Prices are reasonable and the goodies delicious.

Lafayette Bakery
298 Bleecker St. (Seventh Ave.)
242-7580
Open Mon.-Sat. 6:45 a.m.-11 p.m., Sun. 6:45 a.m.-10 p.m.

A weather-worn neon sign flashes above the Lafayette Bakery. Amid the neighboring trendy Mexican restaurants and sleek clothing boutiques, a stranger might be inclined to keep his distance from this relic. Don't. This French bakery epitomizes the goodness of yesteryear. And the locals, who spill in at all hours of the day, are visible proof of this shop's following. Your nose will not tell a lie. The sweet aromas from fresh-baked pies, cookies, danishes and muffins will make your mouth water. Prices here are unbelievably low—in fact, they seem as antique as the tarnished cash register used to ring up sales.

Little Pie Company Ltd.
424 W. 43rd St. (Ninth 9th & Tenth Aves.)
736-4780
Open Mon.-Fri. 8 a.m.-7:30 p.m., Sat. 10 a.m.-6 p.m., Sun. noon-5 p.m.

Nothing is more American than apple pie, and this place believes in making it the way Mom did. From just one flawless apple-pie recipe, this store has built a business that sells an overwhelming variety of pies and cakes. The bakers use many varieties of apples, bake with only fresh ingredients and put tender, loving, homebaked care into all the goodies. Among the more popular items are apple-sauce-carrot cake and apple pie with a Cheddar-cheese crust, but the one to die for is the sour-cream-apple-walnut cake.

Pâtisserie Claude
187 W. 4th St.
(Sheridan Square & Sixth Ave.)
255-5911
Open daily 8 a.m.-8 p.m.

Parisians living in New York satisfy their cravings for croissants at this unpretentious and delightful small bakery that offers the best in French pastry. Besides sinfully buttery croissants, you can get brioche, éclairs, napoleons, fruit tarts and an incredibly rich dark-chocolate- and almond-layered square (all baked in the back). Claude also makes individual quiches with a light, flaky pastry and creamy cheese filling—if only they could set the standard for the rest of New York! The delicacies can be taken home or eaten at one of the few small marble-topped tables, where you can sit and watch the world go by or, perhaps, talk to Claude.

Zito's Bakery
259 Bleecker St. (Sixth & Seventh Aves.)
929-6139
Open Mon.-Sat. 6 a.m.-6 p.m., Sun. 6 a.m.-1 p.m.

If you were led in blindfolded, your taste buds and sense of smell would argue that you'd been carted off to Italy. This famous bakery (serving numerous restaurants) is the closest one can get to Italian baking without leaving the isle of Manhattan. Though often busy, the bakery offers a choice of Italian breads, including white, whole-wheat and Sicilian, with thick crusts and sesame seeds, all baked in coal ovens daily.

CANDY

Economy Candy
108 Rivington St. (Essex & Ludlow Sts.)
254-1531
Open daily 8 a.m.-5:30 p.m., Sat. 10 a.m.-5 p.m.

Catering to both the glutton and the gourmet, this store has a formidable selection of dried fruits, nuts, hand-dipped chocolates and candies. Many of the treats will take you down memory lane: chocolate babies and jawbreakers, to name a few. The selection is unprecedented, and the prices are 20 to 50 percent off suggested retail. The gourmet can also find coffees, spices and mustards at reduced prices.

Godiva Chocolatier
701 Fifth Ave. (54th & 55th Sts.)
593-2845
Open Mon.-Wed. & Fri.-Sat. 9:30 a.m.-6:30 p.m., Thurs. 9:30 a.m.-7 p.m., Sun. noon-6 p.m.
The recent entry of other European chocolatiers in the New York market has not affected the popularity of that old standby, Godiva, whose chocolates are still manna to a "chocoholic." Open oysters (milk chocolate filled with hazelnut cream) and truffles (pure, creamy chocolate in a variety of flavors dusted with cinnamon or cocoa) are the most popular single purchases, while a pound or more of selected chocolates cushioned in Godiva's famous jewel-like golden box is the most frequent selection for gift-giving. Other locations at 560 Lexington Avenue (593-2845) and 85 Broad Street (514-6240).

Li-lac Chocolates Inc.
120 Christopher St.
(Bleecker & Hudson Sts.)
242-7374
Open Sun.-Mon. noon-7:45 p.m., Tues.-Sat. 10 a.m.-7:45 p.m.
Since 1923, Li-lac has been hand dipping chocolates in the back of this small, pretty store—in a spacious, immaculate kitchen, complete with the original marble tabletops. You'll find all the basic sticks, squares, drops and slabs here, as well as a new, too-cute line of chocolate typewriters, computers and the like. Favorites are the French assortment (a one-pound, 50-piece selection for only $20) and the incredible truffles—rum, Champagne, mocha, caramel cream, Grand Marnier, amaretto and more. These treats are also sold at Barney's at 106 Seventh Avenue.

Teuscher Chocolates of Switzerland
620 Fifth Ave. (49th & 50th Sts.)
246-4416
Open Mon.-Wed. & Fri.-Sat. 10 a.m.-6 p.m., Thurs. 10 a.m.-7 p.m.
Truffles, truffles and more truffles made of renowned Swiss chocolate are flown in fresh from Zurich every week. The specialty of the house is Champagne—a delicious blend of fresh cream, butter and chocolate with a Champagne-cream center—and a dusting of confectioner's sugar. If you haven't already put this book down and run off to go buy one, let us add that you'll also find nougat, almond,

walnut, kirsch, orange, cocoa and solid milk-, dark-, and white-chocolate truffles. And if you still haven't left, you don't have to: you can order them by mail.

CAVIAR

Petrossian
182 W. 58th St. (Seventh Ave.)
245-2214
Open Mon.-Sat. 11 a.m.-8 p.m., Sun. 11 a.m.-6 a.m.
Are you one of the very, very picky gourmands who craves caviar of firm grain and delicate flavor, with a hint of sea spray, and no coloring or preservatives added? Don't book an airline to Russia just yet. Petrossian imports the finest Russian caviar—beluga, sevruga or osetra, whichever you prefer. The boutique, located off the restaurant in a beautifully restored landmark building, also offers a host of other well-known Petrossian products: smoked salmon, foie gras, cassoulet, smoked eel. In addition to the exclusive caviars and high-quality food products, Petrossian also sells exquisite caviar servers and spoons. There is a second boutique in Bloomingdale's ground-floor delicatessen shop at 59th Street and Lexington Avenue (355-5900).

CHEESE & PASTA

Cheese of All Nations
153 Chambers St. (Greenwich St.)
732-0752
Open Mon.-Sat. 8 a.m.-5:30 p.m.
An ideal venue for a mouse convention, this shop has every cheese you've ever wanted and then some, sold at reasonable prices. Saint-André is a bargain at $3.99 for a half pound, and there are daily reductions, such as Austrian Fontina for $2 a pound, or low-salt Edam for $2.50 a pound. Breads, crackers, oils and hors d'oeuvres are sold as well.

Ideal Cheese Shop
1205 Second Ave. (63rd & 64th Sts.)
688-7579
Open Mon.-Fri. 9 a.m.-6:30 p.m., Sat. 9 a.m.-6 p.m.
The name says it all. For many connoisseurs, this is New York's *only* cheese shop. There are hundreds of varieties, both domestic and im-

ported; the assortment of the latter is unsurpassed. Goat cheese, triple crème, Stilton, Livarot—be extravagant, and round out your selection with a pâté and crackers. The salespeople, friendly and extremely knowledgeable, will sometimes call your attention to a product for which you haven't asked, and this is a place where you should take their advice.

La Marca Cheese Shop
161 E. 22nd St. (Third Ave.)
673-7920
Open Mon.-Fri. 10 a.m.-6:45 p.m., Sat. 10:30 a.m.-5:30 p.m.
This tiny shop boasts more than 150 types of cheese. The owner, originally a partner in Dean & DeLuca, is a cheese connoisseur. All cheeses are aged on the premises. Customprepared trays are available, and a delectable pie, made from Gorgonzola and Mascarpone, is worth a try.

Pasta Place
247 10th St. (First Ave.)
460-8326
Open Mon.-Sat. noon-7 p.m.
Some New Yorkers take pasta as seriously as Italians do—and that's serious. This hole-in-the-wall is a staple store for anyone with a passion for pasta. Pastas change daily and include garden vermicelli, egg or spinach fettuccini, gnocchi, and spinach-and-cheese ravioli, starting at $2.50 per pound—the prices and quality can't be beat. Other goodies include homemade sauces by the pound, from marinara to pesto; freshly grated Parmesan cheese; and fresh homemade mozzarella.

COFFEE & TEA

McNulty's Tea & Coffee Co. Inc.
109 Christopher St.
(Bleecker & Hudson Sts.)
242-5351
Open Mon.-Sat. 11 a.m.-11 p.m., Sun. 1 p.m.-7:30 p.m.
The aroma of coffee beans and fresh tea wafting through this store is sufficient grounds to dissuade anyone from the "convenience" of instant coffee. The store's old-fashioned interior transports you back in time to the days before teas and coffees were sold in brightly labeled packages. The exotic origins of some of the merchandise will tear down

your resistance to these freshly roasted, caffeine-laden substances; places as far away as Timor and New Guinea are represented here. The selection of teas includes rare Darjeelings and extra-fancy jasmine.

Paprikas Weiss Importer
1546 Second Ave. (81st & 82nd Sts.)
288-6117
Open Mon.-Sat. 9 a.m.-6 p.m.
Right in front of this specialty food store are the items that gave this shop its start: seventeen varieties of coffee beans from Hungary, Colombia, Vienna, Turkey, Italy, Kenya and Guatemala, all freshly roasted and custom ground. Next to the coffees are eighteen types of loose tea as diverse as Russian Samovar and Prince of Wales.

Shapira Coffee Company
117 W. 10th St. (Sixth & Greenwich Aves.)
675-3733
Open Mon.-Fri. 9 a.m.-6:30 p.m., Sat. 9 a.m.-5:30 p.m.
The Shapira family, coffee-roasters and tea merchants in Greenwich Village since 1903, has been valued by New York patrons for its unrivaled selection of and resourcefulness with freshly roasted coffees and carefully selected teas. The Shapira Coffee Company exudes the ambience of an old-fashioned marketplace, with its bay windows, a coffee roaster at back and walls lined with green coffee sacks. Shelves strewn with tea bags and a tea chest remind the shopper that both tea and coffee are sold here, even though the coffee aromas are dominant. If you have questions about tea or coffee, this is the time to ask; the Shapiras have authored *The Book of Coffee & Tea*, a bible for those interested in the barks and tonics of the world.

GOURMET GROCERIES

Balducci's
424 Ave. of the Americas (9th & 10th Sts.)
673-2600
Open Mon.-Sun. 7 a.m.-8:30 p.m.
Balducci's has come a long way from the mom-and-pop stand it once was. Still family-owned, this large emporium is a gathering place in Greenwich Village, a neighborhood feast for the senses. As you walk into this European-style market you can see the quality

is topnotch. Balducci's is pleasantly crowded during weekday working hours; shoppers fill their carts with every imported goodie imaginable—English biscuits, fine Dijon mustards, the best Greek olive oils, mineral waters from around the world, German cookies and more. Customers chat with one another as they sample the fresh array of cheeses and decide whether to choose the homemade canneloni or the shrimp primavera. By 5:30 p.m. the pace quickens as devotees race in to pick up the main course before their dinner guests arrive. The produce section is like a burst of spring in winter; year-round mangos, asparagus and strawberries brighten any winter day. There are gift baskets and mail orders, too.

Bloomingdale's Delicacies
1000 Third Ave. (59th St.)
705-2958
Open Mon. & Thurs. 10 a.m.-9 p.m., Tues.-Wed. & Fri. 10 a.m.-6:30 p.m., Sat. noon-7 p.m., Sun. noon-5 p.m.

With an emphasis on name and display, Bloomingdale's Delicacies is a culinary boutique that stresses packaged samplers—Crabtree & Evelyn preserves, Petrossian bottled cassoulet, Mediterranean fish soup and so on. Unlike the unimpressive meat and cheese departments, the selection of prepared foods is extensive, though its tempting presentation does not justify the outrageous prices. There are seasonal and holiday displays, but much more fun, and the best reason for shopping here, are the in-store tastings.

Dean & DeLuca Inc.
560 Broadway (Prince & Spring Sts.)
431-1691
Open Mon.-Sat. 8 a.m.-8 p.m., Sun. 9 a.m.-7 p.m.

Since 1977, SoHo has been home to one of the finest specialty food stores in New York. Dean & DeLuca's quality does not rule out quantity—there's an in-depth selection in almost every food category. Breads, for example, come from twelve different bakeries around the city. There are about 200 cheeses in stock; selection depends on the season and availability from such countries as France, Spain, Belgium, Denmark, England and Canada. And Dean & DeLuca also carries 30 different varieties of coffee beans, including Sumatra, Mexican, Costa Rican and Kona, the only American coffee (from Hawaii). What-

ever you're buying, you can rest assured that owner Joel Dean has searched out the best for his Broadway store. You can phone and have your order delivered almost anywhere.

Fairway Market
2127 Broadway (74th & 75th Sts.)
595-1888
Open Mon.-Fri. 7 a.m.-midnight, Sat.-Sun. 7 a.m.-11 p.m.

Even if you don't live in the neighborhood, the abundance of fresh produce makes the trip worthwhile. About 45,000 customers each week will agree with us. Recently expanded, Fairway does such an incredible business that prices are extraordinarily cheap. There are stacks of kiwis, cherimoyas and cactus pears, as well as all sorts of cheeses. How to choose between the chèvres (beautifully displayed, on vine leaves, with charcoal), and the American camembert? Throughout the market are homemade signs indicating the how-tos of vegetable care and offering mouth-watering, foolproof recipes. There are also breads, grains, jams, vinegars, a deli and fresh fish.

Grace's Marketplace
1237 Third Ave. (71st St.)
737-0600
Open Mon.-Sat. 7 a.m.-8:30 p.m., Sun. 8 a.m.-7 p.m.

It's heaven to be in Grace's produce section; you never have to dig out the best vegetable from beneath an avalanche of rotten ones, because they are all of excellent quality. This high standard is evident in every area of the store: everything is fresh and fully stocked. Following the pattern of her parent store in the Village, Balducci's, Grace's has compact food "boutiques" with offerings of bread, cheese, deli items, produce and delicious desserts and European chocolates.

Jefferson Market
455 Sixth Avenue (10th & 11th Sts.)
675-2277
Open Mon.-Sat. 8 a.m.-9 p.m., Sun 9 a.m.-8 p.m.

It may look as if it's just another gourmet shop, but Jefferson Market has built a reputation for its exquisite selection of fresh fish and prime meats. Fussy New York shoppers come here because they're unwilling to compromise on quality. The knowledgeable staff will guide you to the right cuts or suggest cooking preparations. The prices are hefty, but the reward lands on your dinner plate.

The Silver Palate

274 Columbus Ave. (73rd St.)
799-6340
*Open Mon.-Fri. 7:30 a.m.-9 p.m., Sat.-Sun. 8
a.m.-7:30 p.m.*

This gourmet outlet has two kinds of customers: those who cook and those who don't. For those who do, The Silver Palate carries an impressive range of its own bottled sauces, relishes, nut oils and herb vinegars. For those who don't, this shop-in-miniature offers the famous Silver Palate cuisine already made. Created on the premises with the freshest ingredients and a bit of zip, the entrées (honey curried chicken, roast veal with lemon-caper mayonnaise, linguine with clam sauce) change daily. Portions can also be reserved by phone. The Silver Palate also vends homemade salads, breads and desserts and picnic baskets.

Zabar's

2245 Broadway (80th St.)
787-2000
*Open Mon.-Fri. 8 a.m.-7:30 p.m., Sat. 8 a.m.-
midnight, Sun. 9 a.m.-6 p.m.*

Zabar's isn't merely a food store—it's a sideshow as well, particularly behind the counter, where the lox men handle their knives with the skill of surgeons. Smoothly, they trim the smoked salmon, be it Scotch or Irish, Norwegian or Nova Scotian. Always pick a number first (different numbers are necessary for the cheese and prepared-meat departments), then browse while you're waiting. Zabar's carries everything you've ever heard of, and much that you haven't, at relatively low prices. The aisles are loaded with coffees, teas, spices, preserves, mustards, chocolates and breads. Climb to the second floor for an extensive selection of up-to-the-minute cookware and kitchen appliances. The store has the ambience of a subway car at rush hour, but to its regulars it's home.

HEALTH FOOD

Earth's Harvest Trading Co.

700 Columbus Ave. (95th St.)
864-1376
*Open Mon.-Fri. 9:30 a.m.-7:30 p.m., Sat.-Sun.
10 a.m.-6 p.m.*

This store prides itself on carrying only the finest and freshest of natural food products. It has a large grocery section with such everyday food items as juices, cereals, pasta and fresh bread, without the usual refined sugar or preservatives. It also sells bulk flour, grains, nuts and dried fruits, along with vitamins, a good selection of books and magazines and natural cosmetics (including the brands Weleda, Reviva and Kiss My Face). Over 200 herbs are sold in bulk for both cooking and medicinal purposes; an herbalist is on hand Monday through Friday to make recommendations.

The Health Nut

2611 Broadway (99th St.)
678-0054
*Open Mon.-Sat. 9:30 a.m.-7:45 p.m., Sun. noon-
7 p.m.*

This store's four well-placed locations eliminate many of the excuses made for not starting to eat more organically, with foods free of preservatives and refined sugar. East Side, West Side, uptown or midtown, there's a Health Nut near you. The stores are well stocked with organically grown produce, meat, poultry, nuts and seeds, as well as books and cosmetics. There is a special macrobiotic food section with all the necessary grains and seeds. Other locations: 1208 Second Avenue, 825 Second Avenue and 2141 Broadway.

Integral Yoga Natural Foods

229 W. 13th St. (Seventh & Eighth Aves.)
243-2642
*Open Mon.-Fri. 10 a.m.-9:30 p.m., Sat. 10 a.m.-
8:30 p.m., Sun. noon-6:30 p.m.*

Two things make this natural food store stand out from the others in New York City. First, it's affiliated with the Yoga Institute, and therefore can keep you up to date on the latest course offerings in yoga and Eastern religions. Second, it's a strictly vegetarian store—no meat, fish or eggs. What it does have is a large variety of bulk foods, from flour and rice to dried fruits and beans, with everything in between: vitamins, books, dairy products and a health-and-beauty section for natural shampoos, conditioners and toothpastes, as well as makeup. The highest standards are maintained. None of the products have sugar, fructose or preservatives.

SPICES

Pete's Spices
174 First Ave. (10th & 11th Sts.)
254-8773
Open Mon.-Sat. 10 a.m.-7:30 p.m., Sun. 12:30 p.m.-5 p.m.

A mecca for spices, this large store brims with bins, boxes and jars of every cooking ingredient from Wehani rice to calendula (marigold). It's safe to bet that the store will have the impossibly obscure ground seed you need for that Indian recipe. The store caters to caterers, restaurants and ethnic cooks. The sales staff is knowledgeable and glad to help you with an ingredient and explain its significance, as well as teach you how to bake a simple (or a complicated) bread. Spices are imported from all over the world—South America, Turkey, Spain, the West Indies—wherever the purest products are found. They also have a large selection of medicinal herbs, and such benevolent herbs, spices and teas as devil's claw, grains of paradise, and squaw vine, used in different countries for a variety of traditional, folkloric or superstitious purposes. Prices are low, especially in bulk.

GIFTS

Asprey
Trump Tower, 725 Fifth Ave.
(56th & 57th Sts.)
688-1811
Open Mon.-Sat. 10 a.m.-5:30 p.m.

Asprey is *the* place to find or create the perfect gift. In their own words, there is *nothing* that Asprey cannot do. You only need to visit the store to see the phenomenal collection of objects or talk with one of the enthusiastic, creative salespeople to see how wild the imagination can run. Among the items in New York's auxiliary to the 208-year-old London institution are desk sets, cigarette boxes, mother-of-pearl caviar servers, flatware, crystal, blankets, first editions of Mark Twain's *Tom Sawyer* and fine men's and women's antique jewelry. In addition, you can have anything made in solid gold, silver, leather or precious or semi-precious stones. You can have your favorite book bound—by their own bindery—in the finest leather and with exquisite end pages.

Fortunoff
681 Fifth Ave. (53rd & 54th Sts.)
758-6660
Open Mon.-Wed. & Fri.-Sat. 10 a.m.-6 p.m., Thurs. 10 a.m.-8 p.m.

Bold cylindrical columns and glass windows suggest an avant-garde mood, but Fortunoff is, in fact, a traditional "old faithful" for glassware, crystal gift items, sterling silver, flatware, hollowware, clocks, baby gifts and fine jewelry. Carrying a wide assortment of patterns from companies such as Waterford, Orrefors, Lalique, Reed & Barton, Oneida, Gorham and Christofle, to name a few, this mini-department store is perfect for engagement, shower or wedding gifts. There is a bridal registry here, and the salespeople are savvy about tableware and giftware.

Hammacher Schlemmer & Co.
147 E. 57th St. (Lexington & Third Aves.)
421-9000
Open Mon.-Sat. 10 a.m.-6 p.m.

Hammacher Schlemmer's retail policy may be eccentric, but at least it is clear: its merchandise must either be the best at what it does or the only product that does it. The Hammacher Schlemmer Institute tests all the products before they are stocked, including those brought to the company by many Edisons manqué. Where else can you find an electric ice cream scoop for all those hard-to-dig creamy flavors or a bicycle mower that allows you to exercise while you trim the lawn? The lengthy placard descriptions beside each item make browsing fun. As for the prices, there is a reason they are not displayed. Guess.

The Sharper Image
4 W. 57th St. (Fifth & Sixth Aves.)
265-2550
Open Mon.-Wed. & Fri. 10 a.m.-7 p.m., Thurs. 10 a.m.-8 p.m., Sat. 10 a.m.-6 p.m., Sun. noon-5 p.m.

This hi-tech wonderland is the place to find that gift for the person who thinks he has everything but didn't realize his life could be more complete with a Getaway Chair, for example, which massages you from head to toe. The price tag is $1,995. Or if music is a passion, a juke box might fit nicely in the den. A visit to The Sharper Image can be fun just for looking. No item falls within the realm of the ordinary, whether it's a desktop accessory or an electronic gizmo. Babbit would have thought this place was Nirvana. The Sharper Image also has a catalog, so you can ponder buying the $1,000 lion's head, the 1957 Coke machine at $4,500 or the temperature-controlled clock for $1,275.

Tuscany Galleries
1001 Second Ave. (53rd St.)
593-0728
Open Mon.-Fri. noon-7 p.m., Sat. 1 p.m.-6 p.m.

The unusual blend of objets d'art at this store means you can probably find the perfect present for the person who has everything. Whether it's a snow-filled glass paperweight, a goblet or a musical cigarette box, the store is a celebration of creativity. There's virtually no rhyme or reason to the eclectic display, so the shopper must be willing to rummage. The back of the store holds a gallery featuring the work of Joy Gush, a well-known local artist.

HOME

CRYSTAL

Baccarat
625 Madison Ave. (58th & 59th Sts.)
826-4100
Open Mon.-Sat. 10 a.m.-6 p.m.

Baccarat has been the world's preeminent manufacturer of fine crystal for more than two centuries, and its superiority shows scant signs of abating. Founded in 1764 under the aegis of Louis XV, Baccarat deals in both decorative and table glass. The store's chrome-and-steel étagères hold sculptured crystal statuary, often of animals, alongside fine glasses, stemware and decanters. In addition, the shop offers Christofle silverware, Caralene-Ravnaud china and Ruiforcat china and silver.

Hoya Crystal Gallery
450 Park Ave. (56th & 57th Sts.)
223-6335
Open Mon.-Sat. 10 a.m.-6 p.m.

Crystal that combines contemporary design, Japanese artistry and innovative technology is on display here. Fumio Sasa, Hoya's design leader, guides a staff of ten artists in producing an award-winning collection that has been exhibited in museums throughout the world. It includes crystal art sculptures ranging from $500 to $35,000, plus an extensive selection of functional crystal: stemware, vases, bowls, clocks and gifts ranging from

$60 to $500. Hoya's lead crystal is known for its purity, clarity and reflective brilliance.

Orrefors Crystal Gallery
58 E. 57th St. (Park & Madison Aves.)
753-3442
Open Mon.-Fri. 10 a.m.-6 p.m., Sat. 10:30 a.m.-5:30 p.m.

It feels more like a museum than a shop, but Orrefors's fine crystal art glass, tableware and accessories can be purchased for between $15 and $60,000. Once inside, you're enveloped by a stark Scandinavian elegance, personifed by the dimly lit gallery, marble floors, green-blue walls and a calculated order of space. Floating glass shelves house the Orrefors works; halogen lights reflect the craftsmanship and brilliance of each piece. At least four times a year, glass artists visit the gallery.

Steuben Glass
715 Fifth Ave. (56th St.)
752-1441
Open Mon.-Sat. 10 a.m.-6 p.m.

Steuben's beautiful, serene showroom is a museum as much as a retail store. At any time of day you'll find people admiring the remarkable design, quality and craftsmanship of the crystal and glass sculptures, vases and bowls that have made Steuben a household name internationally. Prices are far from cheap, but then again, when you buy a Steuben glass piece you join the ranks of royalty and foreign leaders: this glass has been chosen for gifts of state by every U.S. president since 1947.

FABRIC

Jerry Brown Imported Fabrics
37 W. 57th St. (Fifth & Sixth Aves.)
753-3626
Open Mon.-Sat. 9 a.m.-6 p.m.

It's hard not to get overwhelmed in this store—there are bolts and bolts of fabric in all colors, types and patterns. Here you'll find only natural fibers and European imports. The ground-floor showroom displays the more casual merchandise; the upstairs—for which you need a sales escort—is the locale for the more elaborate fabrics, such as sequined and beaded lace and gold lamé. Only fabrics are sold here, though; for patterns and accessories, you'll need to go elsewhere.

Laura Ashley
714 Madison Ave. (63rd St.)
735-5000
Open Mon.-Wed. & Fri.-Sat. 10 a.m.-6 p.m., Thurs. 10 a.m.-7 p.m.

Here's the place for quintessential English country prints in wallpaper and other fabrics for the home. Unlike most, Laura Ashley wallpaper is actually paper (with vinyl backing), because nothing here, not even the wallpaper, deviates from the delicate or the classic.

Marimekko
7 W. 56th St. (Fifth & Sixth Aves.)
581-9616
Open Mon.-Sat. 10 a.m.-6 p.m.

Don't mistake this establishment for a Japanese store. "Marimekko" is Finnish for "Mary's little dress." Those who are already au courant shop at Marimekko for unique, artistic leisure clothing and fabrics designed in Finland. Although the styles are understated, the colors range from subtle to brilliant. Also available are brightly colored and patterned pillows and other Finnish-style furnishings.

Paron Fabrics
60 W. 57th St. (Fifth & Sixth Aves.)
247-6451
Open Mon.-Sat. 9 a.m.-5:45 p.m., Sun. 11 a.m.-3 p.m.

A well-stocked, organized store with every type of fabric imaginable and plenty of salespeople ready to help. Each bolt of cloth is clearly labeled with the fiber content and price. A few doors down, on the fourth floor, is Paron II (56 W. 57th Street), where you'll find remnants of the same quality fabrics for 50 percent off the already reasonable prices.

FURNITURE & BEDDING

Conran's
Citicorp Center, 160 E. 54th St. (Third Ave.)
371-2225
Open Mon.-Fri. 10 a.m.-9 p.m., Sat. 10 a.m.-7 p.m., Sun. 11 a.m.-6 p.m.

Conran's is a department store for city living, jammed with solutions for cramped Manhattan apartments. Many a young professional can be seen filling up a cart with all the necessities to make a new apartment seem like home. This immense store carries all sorts of chairs, couches, drafting and coffee tables, bed frames and utility carts. An entire department has a complete collection of add-on shelving and closet organizers in primary colors. Then there are glasses in a million styles, inexpensive ceramics in a variety of mod pastels, vases, table settings, lighting, Marimekko fabrics, linens and duvet covers—plus toys, desk accessories, prints, cookware, tote bags and planters. Other locations at 2-8 Astor Place (505-1515) and 2248 Broadway (873-9250).

Kleinsleep
2569 Broadway (96th & 97th Sts.)
866-5300
Open Mon.-Fri. 10 a.m.-9 p.m., Sat. 10 a.m.-7 p.m., Sun. 11 a.m.-6 p.m.

Posturpedic, Maxipedic, Beautyrest, Correct Comfort, Perfect Sleeper—you'll find every kind of bed from all the name manufacturers at prices (especially during sales) that will let you sleep at night. Immediate delivery available.

KITCHENWARE

D.F. Sanders
952 Madison Ave. (75th & 76th Sts.)
879-6161
Open Mon.-Sat. 10 a.m.-6 p.m., Sun. noon-5 p.m.

Hi-tech housewares have been in vogue since the opening of MOMA's design collection. A lovely store filled with these functional objets d'art, D.F. Sanders has a good selection of well-designed pieces: everything is pleasantly graphic and completely practical. Also in SoHo, at 386 W. Broadway (925-9040).

Hoffritz for Cutlery
331 Madison Ave. (42nd & 43rd Sts.)
697-7344
Open Mon.- Fri. 8 a.m.-6 p.m.,
Sat. 9 a.m.-6 p.m.

Hoffritz made its reputation in cutlery, and you can still find an excellent selection of fine French, German and Swiss kitchen knives here, in addition to carving sets, hunting knives, pocket knives and literally hundreds of types of scissors. Indulge yourself in a pair especially designed for trimming beards, for instance, or ignore the implications and ask for the pair that cuts double-knit polyester. Hoffritz also carries some fine upscale gift items: gold-plated flasks, imported electric shavers, handmade shaving brushes and the like. Call the above number for other Manhattan locations.

Macy's The Cellar
Herald Square, 34th St. & Seventh Ave.
695-4400
Open Mon. & Thurs.-Fri. 9:45 a.m.-8:30 p.m.,
Tues.-Wed. 9:45 a.m.-6:45 p.m., Sat. 9 a.m.-6 p.m., Sun. 10 a.m.-6 p.m.

Macy's subterranean world of kitchenwares and housewares is unrivaled, both for its bountiful selection and its creative display. The selection of electric woks and waffle irons, for instance, is a marvel. From pots and pans to place settings, Macy's offers many good buys, especially during sales. Macy's carries most of the high-end brands, but don't be afraid to try The Cellar's own products: they're usually excellent.

Pottery Barn
117 E. 59th St. (Lexington & Park Aves.)
753-5424
Open Mon.-Wed. & Fri.-Sat. 10 a.m.-6:30 p.m.,
Thurs. 10 a.m.-8 p.m., Sun. noon-5 p.m.

The Pottery Barn offers a rainbow selection of color, from its pastel china to its two-toned stemware. Actually, some of the china is also two-toned and a bit wild, but most of the stock is simple and reasonably priced. The selection of glassware is excellent, and there are a half a dozen flatware styles from which to choose. As for plates, there is the aforemen-

tioned china, as well as a host of plastic alternatives. The Pottery Barn also carries such various and sundry household goods as flashy garbage cans, plastic picture frames, wicker baskets and folding chairs.

Williams-Sonoma
20 E. 60th St. (Park & Madison Aves.)
980-5155
Open Mon.-Fri. 10 a.m.-7 p.m., Sat. 10 a.m.-6 p.m., Sun. noon-5 p.m.

If cooking and entertaining are your pride and joy, you might wonder how you ever managed without Williams-Sonoma. This catalog and retail operation unveils the latest in kitchen technology. Cooks and gourmands cluster here to compare anodized, copper and cast-iron pots and pans. They mull over the latest cappuccino and espresso machines. But Williams-Sonoma also has built a reputation for its flair and accent with tabletop items. Appealing table settings mix floral ceramic ware with colored stemware, showing customers how to have fun entertaining. The best part of this store is that it's affordable.

Zabar's
2245 Broadway (80th St.)
787-2000
Open Mon.-Fri. 8 a.m.-7:30 p.m., Sat. 8 a.m.-midnight, Sun. 9 a.m.-6 p.m.

Legendary for its supply of foodstuffs, Zabar's has recently added an entire second floor of kitchenware, every bit as bracing as the first floor. One room is devoted entirely to pots and pans, from imported French copper to all-purpose aluminum, from fish poachers to woks. Another is filled with coffeemakers, food processors, electric potato peelers and portable meat slicers. A third houses even smaller gadgets: chopping boards, folding wooden dish racks, egg timers and the best garlic presses. All the items are very well priced, particularly the cutlery.

LIGHTING

Lee's Studio
211 W. 57th St. (Seventh Ave. & Broadway)
265-5670
Open Mon. & Wed.-Fri. 10 a.m.-6:30 p.m.,
Tues. & Sat. 10 a.m.-6 p.m.

If you're looking to light up your life—or desk, loft, bedroom or stage—then a visit to this store is a must. Be warned, though: the interior is just as crowded as the window display, and you should be careful if you're accompanied by an active youngster or a frisky pooch. The store has a warehouse feeling, with every available inch covered by lamps. But that means you're likely to find what you're looking for—besides lighting in all shapes, sizes, colors and styles, there are also wall and desk clocks, ceiling fans, sleek phones and Levolor shades. But first and foremost, both here and at the store at 1069 Third Avenue (371-1122), it's lamps, lamps and more lamps. It's also one of few Tizio distributors in New York City.

Let There Be Neon Inc.
38 White St. (Church & Broadway)
226-4883
Open by appt. only.

A vision of bright lights and big-city nights best describes this store, which claims to be the first and "by far the best" establishment to specialize in neon. It is known for artfully transforming customers' sketches, ideas and hand wavings into neon novelties. Owner Rudi Stern says, "People call up with neon dreams and need the images realized within 24 hours." All this and more is possible. Prices start at $200.

Lite-Elite II
150 Bowery (Broome St.)
226-3063
Open Mon.-Fri. 9 a.m.-5:30 p.m., Sat.-Sun. 9 a.m.-6 p.m.

This store is situated in what's known as New York's lighting district. Shop after shop devoted to lighting line this less-than-appealing street, but the choice and prices are unrivalled. Lite-Elite II, with six stores (some with different names), has a strong franchise in the area. Stepping inside this shop is like walking through a forest of lights—every feasible space is utilized. French-provincial brass and Bohemian crystal chandeliers hang from above, while floor lamps stand side by side like tall stalks of asparagus. This store has a good selection of contemporary halogen lighting, which is the hottest craze. Neoclassical fixtures, Etruscan vases and marble furniture are mixed among the seemingly endless choice. Try a bit of bargaining—most New Yorkers do.

LINENS

Anichini Gallery
150 Fifth Ave., Ste. 712 (20th St.)
633-0788
Open Mon.-Fri. 9:30 a.m.-5:30 p.m. by appt. only.

Operating almost as a salon, the Anichini Gallery offers antique linens, lace, crafts, poetry and drama readings, musicals and contemporary art exhibitions. A mixed bag, perhaps, yet the complete selection of hand-worked items provides unusual choices. There's a full range of bed and table linens from the nineteenth and early twentieth centuries, along with beautiful antique blouses, capes, dresses and shawls.

Descamps
723 Madison Ave. (63rd & 64th Sts.)
355-2522
Open Mon.-Sat. 10 a.m.-6 p.m.

These bed linens, towels and robes—all designed by Primrose Bordier and imported from France—deviate from a traditional look. Whether floral or geometric, the patterns border on the painterly, in the modern sense. Even the whites and solid pastels vibrate color. Descamps's baby linens are exquisite, though bolder than most. The terrycloth robes, sporty and vibrant, make wonderful gifts.

D. Porthault & Co.
18 E. 69th St. (Madison & Fifth Aves.)
688-1660
Open Mon.-Fri. 10 a.m.-6 p.m., Sat. 10 a.m.-5 p.m.

Recognized worldwide as the finest French manufacturer of bed linens, Porthault actually invented the printed sheet. Not surprisingly, its trademark is a large floral print available on sheets and terrycloth towels, robes and accessories. Although many items are in stock, custom orders are welcome on all the 100-percent-cotton, -linen and -silk merchandise.

Frette
799 Madison Ave. (67th & 68th Sts.)
794-8630
Open Mon.-Fri. 10 a.m.-6 p.m., Sat. 10 a.m.-5:30 p.m.

Indeed, this is the stuff that dreams and comfy nights are made of—a most uncompromising line of silk, linen and cotton sheets that will lull you to sleep in luxury. The prices are as lofty as the look, but you won't, if you choose carefully, be replacing these pieces soon. You'll also find towels, terrycloth robes and other items for the bath.

Jana Starr–Jean Hoffman Antiques
236 E. 80th St. (Second & Third Aves.)
861-8256
Open Mon.-Sat. noon-6 p.m., evenings by appt. only
Over the years, these two antique dealers have put together a huge inventory of fabulous table and bed linens. They are chosen from every imaginable country, and you'll marvel at the handmade lace and embroidery. The shawls, the jewelry, the hats, the canes and the charming white dresses are all quite outstanding. White is the key word here, and removing the few spots one finds is an art perfected by the owners. Known for their unusual materials, they sell a varied range of curtains, linens and things of yesteryear.

Pratesi
829 Madison Ave. (69th & 70th Sts.)
288-2315
Open Mon.-Sat. 10 a.m.-6 p.m.
Pratesi provides New Yorkers with an exclusive source for the world's finest Italian linens and lingerie. Although there are only two new collections a year, special orders are welcome. All sheets are 100-percent cotton and have a thread count of 320 per inch (by comparison, percale cotton, the best most department stores offer, is 220 per inch). Some of the most popular purchases include sheets, table linens, terrycloth robes, cashmere blankets, plush towels and baby items.

Scandia Down Shop
1011 Madison Ave. (78th St.)
734-8787
Open Mon.-Fri. 10 a.m.-6 p.m., Sat. 10 a.m.-5 p.m.
Before starting your annual hibernation, why not stop by this store and pick up a luxurious down comforter that's guaranteed to keep you warm? In more types and combinations of down and feather than you thought possible (white Balkan goose down, grey duck down, white goose feather, etc.), Scandia

Down's comforters are sold in sizes crib to king. In addition to down comforters, they sell down pillows and robes, lap blankets, European linens, potpourris and a small selection of imported beds. For a nominal fee, they also provide a washing and maintenance service (for Scandia Down comforters only). You'll pay more here than you will at a department store, but the quality is worth it; the store makes an extra effort to clean the down and reduce the feather content—leaving you with a comforter that will last a lifetime.

SILVER

Christofle Pavillion
680 Madison Ave. (62nd St.)
308-9390
Open Mon.-Fri. 10 a.m.-6 p.m., Sat. 10 a.m.-5 p.m.
A glittering buffet of fine tableware awaits cultured tastes. Christofle excels in sterling, silverplate, goldplate and stainless-steel flatware, holloware and gift items. Well-groomed salespeople will help you choose appropriate table combinations. Ask to see *les cloisonnés laque de chine*, a combination of silver plate and authentic Chinese lacquer in a cloisonné design.

James Robinson Inc.
15 E. 57th St. (Fifth & Madison Aves.)
752-6166
Open June-Aug. Mon.-Fri. 10 a.m.-4:30 p.m.; Sept-May Mon.-Fri. 10 a.m.-5 p.m., Sat. 10:30 a.m.-4:30 p.m.
Originally from London, the Robinsons give special attention to the acquisition and display of Georgian- to Victorian-era silver. There are more hallmarks here than you'd find in royal cabinets. Place settings of intricate, beautiful patterns form an interesting collection; these table settings can be completed by choosing antique china and porcelain dinnerware. Table accessories—crystal candlesticks and the like—are plentiful, and if your yen for silver goes beyond the table, take note of the silver jewelry.

Jean's Silversmiths
16 W. 45th St. (Fifth & Sixth Aves.)
575-0723
Open Mon.-Thurs. 9 a.m.-5 p.m., Fri. 9 a.m.-4 p.m.

Located in a sliver of a storefront somewhere between a nook and a cranny, Jean's has little choice but to stock its wares from floor to ceiling. As a result, this is not a store for browsing, nor should it be. Jean's specializes in American flatware. You've just inherited Grandmother's silver, and they haven't made that sort of salad fork since President Taft's time? Jean's probably has it, and at a reasonable price, too. Need a set of goblets, and a candelabra or a tea service as well? They're also available, as are an abundance of platters. Everything is somewhat tarnished, but that's the sign of a real bargain, right?

M. Raphael of London
1050 Second Ave. (55th St.)
838-0178
Open Mon.-Sat. 10:30 a.m.-5:30 p.m.

Established in London in 1911 and in New York in 1948, M. Raphael enjoys a solid reputation, and curator Henry Raphael is an internationally respected authority. The breadth of the shop's antique silver collection (English, Continental, American) is recognized on both sides of the Atlantic; many of the items date back to the seventeenth century. Excellent value here.

S. Wyler Inc.
941 Lexington Ave. (69th St.)
879-9848
Open Mon.-Sat. 10 a.m.-5:30 p.m.

If you're looking for silver or porcelain, or both, S. Wyler can offer you choice pieces, plus the expertise of the author of the definitive *The Book of Old Silver*. With a worldwide reputation built during 100 years in business, S. Wyler carries on the family tradition (via son Richard) of selling fine antique porcelain, silver and Victorian objets d'art.

Tiffany & Co.
727 Fifth Ave. (57th St.)
755-8000
Open Mon.-Sat. 10 a.m.-5:30 p.m.

If they ever did serve breakfast at Tiffany's, silverware wouldn't be a problem. Located on the second floor of this grande dame of gilt (known best for its luscious jewels), the silver department veritably gleams. Once you've seen the sterling omelet pan, for instance, it's hard to imagine why anyone who could afford it would use anything else. Strolling the aisles of glass display cases, one finds much that beckons, not the least of which are the museum-quality pieces interspersed with the retail items. The selection of flatware is handsome and costly, but after all, this is Tiffany's. Beyond silver, Tiffany is no slouch for crystal, tableware or its world renowned one-of-a-kind jewelry creations.

IMAGE & SOUND

CAMERAS & FILM

Duggal
9 W. 20th St. (Fifth & Sixth Aves.)
242-7000
Open Mon.-Fri. 7 a.m.-midnight, Sat.-Sun. 9 a.m.-5 p.m.

Widely acknowledged to be the top processing lab in the city, Duggal does professional work at professional prices, handling everything from Kodak processing to custom color printing. You can rent a studio, get slides duped and have your photos laminated and mounted.

47th Street Photo
67 W. 47th St. (Sixth & Seventh Aves.)
398-1410
Open Mon.-Thurs. 9 a.m.-6 p.m., Fri. 9 a.m.-2 p.m., Sun. 10 a.m.-5 p.m.

Walking up the narrow staircase at 47th Street Photo is like "Crossing Delancey." Bargains, yes, but if you don't know exactly what you want, stay away—service here can be as brisk as the sales. On the other hand, if you do know, and you're not interested in shopping around, this is probably your best one-stop. There are excellent prices on film, too. Another location at 115 W. 45th Street (at Broadway).

Ken Hansen Photographic
920 Broadway (21st & 22nd Sts.)
777-5900
Open Mon.-Fri. 9:30 a.m.-5:30 p.m.

If classic cameras—Nikons, Hasselblads, Rolleiflexes—make you drool, then make a pilgrimage to Ken Hansen, where you'll find an overwhelming selection. Think of it: 30 mint Leicas in a row. For Ansel Adams disciples there's an impressive large-format department, plus Hansen's peerless collection of bags and gadgets.

Lens & Repro
33 W. 17th St. (Fifth & Sixth Aves.)
675-1900
Open Mon.-Fri. 8:30 a.m.-5:30 p.m.

A family operation that deals exclusively in the most sophisticated professional equipment, Lens & Repro specializes in top-of-the-line studio fittings (strobes, tripods), which it rents as well as sells. As at Ken Hansen, you pay not only for product, but also for service. For instance, if you're on a shoot in Brazil and your equipment falls in the Amazon, you can trust Lens & Repro to have a replacement outfit sent in by helicopter.

Willoughby's Camera Store
110 W. 32nd St. (Sixth & Seventh Aves.)
564-1600
Open Mon.-Wed. & Fri. 9 a.m.-7 p.m., Thurs. 9 a.m.-8 p.m., Sat. 9 a.m.-6:30 p.m., Sun. 10:30 a.m.-5:30 p.m.

Willoughby's houses an astoundingly comprehensive camera collection, all under one roof. This shop draws photography buffs from all over the world. Surrounded by the latest in camera technology and a staff to explain it, both serious and amateur photographers can pore over zoom, wide-angle and telephoto lenses, filters and so on. Willoughby's has both a rental and service department, as well as a large and competitively priced computer and electronics section.

ELECTRONICS

The Audio Exchange
28 W. 8th St. (Fifth & Sixth Aves.)
982-7191
Open Mon.-Sat. 11:30 a.m.-7 p.m.

Probably the best place in the city to shop for used high-end stereo equipment, Audio Exchange is nothing if not thorough: it boasts an attentive staff, a well-appointed listening room and a service department that carefully inspects, then warrants, all the used components and even handles installations. You'll find good deals on everything from Carver to Tandberg, and on a wide range of peripherals, such as Grado cartridges, Sennheiser headphones and Monster cable.

Harvey Electronics
2 W. 45th St. (Fifth & Sixth Aves.)
575-5000
Open Mon.-Fri. 9:30 a.m.-6 p.m., Sat. 10 a.m.-6 p.m.

Though you can find a few medium-range components here, Harvey is basically high-end, both in image and inventory. While the discount houses have salesmen in sport shirts, Harvey's are in dress shirts and ties; the store's displays are no less neatly groomed. As for the equipment, all the big names are represented: Nakamichi, Bang & Olufsen, Yamaha, McIntosh. You see—and, more importantly, hear—everything before purchasing, unlike the electronics stores that display nothing and deliver your merchandise packed without your having inspected it. Regular prices are premium, but the sales are not bad. Harvey also maintains its merchandise with an in-house service department.

MUSIC

Bleecker Bob's Golden Oldies
118 W. 3rd St.
(MacDougal St. & Sixth Ave.)
475-9677
Open Sun.-Thurs. noon-1 a.m., Fri.-Sat. noon-3 a.m.

If Tower Records doesn't have the album you're looking for, Bleecker Bob's probably will, especially if it's an import single. Obscure albums, though, are still hard to find here, because the store's organization is somewhat eccentric: grouping is by genre rather than alphabetical order. Don't let the maze discourage you, because the people at the counter know the location of every album, and if you're just browsing, the ordered chaos might turn you on to a new band. Prices are consistently inconsistent, so search out the values (start with the clearance rack).

J & R Music World

23 Park Row (Ann & Beekman Sts.)
732-8600
Open Mon.-Sat. 9 a.m.-6:30 p.m.

Though it can be weak on independents and imports, J & R does carry a huge stock of back-catalog and reissue material, and it offers the best prices in town on current major releases. The main outlet at 23 Park Row houses rock, pop and folk, as well as the audio and video hardware departments. Affiliated stores nearby specialize in classical and jazz.

Record Mart

1470 Broadway (42nd St.)
840-0580
Open Mon.-Thurs. 9 a.m.-9 p.m., Fri. 9 a.m.-11 p.m., Sat. 10 a.m.-10 p.m., Sun. noon-8 p.m.

Calypso. Salsa. Samba. Reggae. Longing for these Latin and Caribbean beats, but can't afford the time or money to go to the exotic destinations that gave birth to these sounds? Look no further. Record Mart, located in the subway station in Times Square, offers one of the largest selections of Caribbean and Latin American music in the city.

Tower Records

692 Broadway (4th St.)
505-1500
Open daily 9 a.m.-midnight.

The 4th Street branch of Tower Records has more CDs and tapes under its roof than any other store in the city. It even carries most of the independent labels, a great reason to shop here. Come to take in the spectacle, too: in addition to the regular in-store band promos, the customers and the cashiers all model the latest East Village looks. As a result, the 4th Street Tower is where some of rock and roll's many contradictions come alive before your eyes: pink-haired fans of the Splat Cats ringing up Lionel Richie, Wayne Newton and the Chieftains at $7.99 a pop. The Tower Records at 66th Street and Broadway has a large selection as well, but boy, is it boring in comparison!

The Wiz

17 Union Square (15th St.)
741-9500
Open Mon.-Sat. 10 a.m.-8 p.m., Sun. 11 a.m.-6 p.m.

Music lovers (and electronics hunters) mill around this bustling shop fingering the latest selections of soul, rhythm and blues, disco or any other pulsating passion. Plan to spend a bit of time here, as it's a good trap for bargain hunting. For classical music buffs, this may not be the ideal shopping spot, but the vast choice will no doubt appeal to your other musical tastes. The Wiz is also a reputable outlet for discounted electronics. Call the above number for various locations around the city.

LEATHER

Andrew Marc

404 Columbus Ave. (79th & 80th Sts.)
769-2400
Open Mon.-Thurs. 11 a.m.-8 p.m., Fri. 11 a.m.-9 p.m., Sat.-Sun. 11 a.m.-7 p.m.

Spanning nearly half a street, Andrew Marc's first New York retail store draws in pedestrians sauntering down Columbus as well as those who know the breadth and quality of his merchandise. The store feels like a trendy downtown club with its hip staff and pulsating music. But the selection is eyepopping. Skirts and blazers, trousers, trench coats, bombers and this year's hot seller, shearlings, beg to be touched and modelled. Marc's styling is commendable and his prices are fair.

Beltrami

711 Fifth Ave. (55th & 56th Sts.)
838-4101
Open Mon.-Sat. 10 a.m.-6 p.m.

Italians produce exquisite leather goods with style, and Beltrami is the place to find them. Men and women can choose from leather and suede coats (with or without fur), suits and other clothes in glove-tanned leather. Beltrami also has shoes (most come with matching bags) and complete sets of matching luggage. About 80 percent of the merchandise is designed by Beltrami; the remainder consists of exclusives from other Italian manufacturers. The staff is very obliging; if, for example, you see a black coat but would prefer the style in yellow, they will gladly make it up for you.

Bottega Veneta Inc.
635 Madison Ave. (59th & 60th Sts.)
319-0303
Open Mon.-Wed. & Fri.-Sat. 10 a.m.-6 p.m., Thurs. 10 a.m.-7 p.m.

This Madison Avenue store looks as if it's the first floor of a department store, albeit an expensive one—umbrellas, hosiery and scarves, shoes and bags. The handbag collection is less formal and more colorful than other designer imports—woven leather is the trademark look, not repetitive initials. Some of the woven styles are available in interesting tricolor patterns—red, yellow and orange or blue, green and violet. The shoe department's selection is mixed—some styles are pretty and unusual, others dowdy and dull, but all are dazzingly expensive.

Lancel
690 Madison Ave. (62nd St.)
753-6918
Open Mon.-Sat. 10 a.m.-6 p.m.

Luxurious leather or practical polyurethane with at least one signature Lancel "L" on the bag is what you'll find here. The shapes are elegant—neatly rounded or starkly squared, all bags subtly yet securely fastened. The look is similar to Fendi, but the prices are slightly less. Lancel features a full line of handbags, luggage and accessories—from teeny wallets to large leather trunks.

Lederer
613 Madison Ave. (58th St.)
355-5515
Open Mon.-Sat. 9:30 a.m.-6 p.m.

The selection here is enormous—leather goods, handbags, luggage and accessories in an expansive array of styles—all executed flawlessly with proper attention to detail. Hermès and Chanel look-alikes sit next to exotic-skin treasures—alligator, lizard and crocodile bags, either classically plain or extravagantly fancy, with jeweled or cameo clasps. Also to be found are Hartmann luggage, a complete men's collection and a selection of authentic hunting

gear. There are no great bargains here, but prices are less than designer prices.

Louis Vuitton
51 E. 57th St. (Madison & Park Aves.)
371-6111
Open Mon.-Fri. 10 a.m.-5:30 p.m., Sat. 10 a.m.-5 p.m.

The famous LV initials on one of the world's most esteemed and durable luggage lines predates the days of ubiquitous manufacturer's initials. For more than a century, this Parisian firm has set a standard of craftsmanship and style that has made its trunks, luggage, handbags and leather goods the jet-set traveler's treasured companion. Today, with fanatically loyal customers willing to pay astronomical prices, LV is the ex-official status bag, suitcase, purse and so on, for the Japanese empire (and for a few of the rest of us as well). A second, more modern luggage line and an expanded range of products today complements the classic LV case.

Made in the USA
130 E. 59th St. (Park & Lexington Aves.)
838-5076
Open Mon.-Fri. 10 a.m.-7 p.m., Sun. 12:30 p.m.-6 p.m.

When shopping for women's leather clothing and outerwear, be sure to stop by here. This smallish store is teeming with racks of jackets, coats, pants and skirts in black or colored leathers and plain or adorned styles. Many of the same styles are found at comparable stores for one-third the price. The salespeople are very helpful and friendly, especially if they think you're buying, not browsing. Don't be bashful—if you don't see what you want, ask one of the salespeople to check in the back. There's a small selection of men's leather gear, too.

North Beach Leather
772 Madison Ave. (66th St.)
772-0707
Open Mon.-Fri. 10 a.m.-7 p.m., Sat. 10 a.m.-6 p.m., Sun 1 p.m.-6 p.m.

If you spot someone in a drop-dead leather outfit bought in this country, odds are it came from North Beach Leather. In this slick boutique that caters to hourglass figures, you'll find luxury leathers in ultra-high-fashion styles: bolero jackets, bandeaux, full-zippered minis, strapless dresses, trousers, blazers and jeans in jellybean colors or basic black. It's all so fashion-forward that most of the outfits seem as if they're next year's styles. Prices are predictable but not pretentious—in the $300-$500 range.

SPORTING GOODS

Athlete's Foot
16 W. 57th St. (Fifth & Sixth Aves.)
586-1936
Open Mon.-Fri. 10 a.m.-7 p.m., Sat. 10 a.m.-6 p.m., Sun. noon-6 p.m.

The Athlete's Foot has been around since the exercise craze was in its embryonic state. Today this establishment, the biggest of its kind, sports more than twenty different brands of sneakers. The variety of sizes and styles is unparalleled. There are several other shops around the city; call the above number for their locations.

Herman's Sporting Goods
135 W. 42nd St. (Sixth Ave. & Broadway)
730-7400
Open Mon.-Fri. 9:30 a.m.-7 p.m., Sat. 9:30 a.m.-6 p.m.

Herman's dabbles in most sports but is particularly strong in tennis, golf, exercise equipment and sportswear. The store carries all the name brands (Nike, Adidas, Reebok, New Balance), but itself is hardly chic—it looks more like an upscale Woolworth's. The two reasons to shop here are reasonable prices and convenience. The service, if you get any, is terrible; the salespeople are often so misinformed that they become misleading. Watch for the regular sales.

Horizontal
336 E. 61st St. (First & Second Aves.)
826-2992
Open Mon.-Fri. 10 a.m.-9 p.m., Sat. 10 a.m.-7 p.m., Sun. 11 a.m.-6 p.m.

The Horizontal, next door to the Vertical Club, appropriately offers the largest selection of bodywear in the city. The merchandise is divided into ten different departments that display the latest shoes, sports and active wear, tennis racquets, running gear and everything else, from headbands to socks.

Hudson's
97 Third Ave. (12th & 13th Sts.)
473-0981
Open Mon.-Thurs. 10 a.m.-8 p.m., Fri.-Sat. 10 a.m.-7 p.m., Sun. noon-6 p.m.

Ten years ago, Hudson's was known as one of the most complete outfitters in the city. Its slightly ratty surplus-store atmosphere befitted its seasoned, outdoorsy clientele. When the outdoors became "in," Hudson's remodeled and expanded to a full block of storefronts. Since that time, the clothing selection has ballooned, while the stock of equipment has actually receded (and the price of what remains has risen). But the selection of sweaters, anoraks, rainwear and long underwear can save you a phone call to L. L. Bean.

Paragon Athletics
867 Broadway (18th St.)
255-8036
Open Mon.-Fri. 10 a.m.-8 p.m., Sat. 10 a.m.-7 p.m., Sun. 11 a.m.-6 p.m.

Paragon lives up to its name. This establishment is simply the best sporting goods store around. No sport is too minor, no piece of equipment too superfluous for Paragon to stock it on one of its three sprawling floors. For every baseball glove at Herman's, Paragon carries four or five. And Paragon's excellence extends to its sales staff. Because the camping department is staffed (appropriately) with outdoorsy types, most of the salespeople have firsthand experience with the merchandise—you may end up comparing notes with one of them on your latest backpacking trip.

TOBACCONISTS

Famous Smoke Shop
55 W. 39th St. (Fifth & Sixth Aves.)
221-1408
Open Mon.-Fri. 8 a.m.-6 p.m., Sat. 8 a.m.-2 p.m.

This store has turned the selling of cigars into a smoothly run, very professional operation. The 1,000-square-foot humidor in the basement ensures that the cigars you carry home with you, priced at 30-percent to 50-percent off retail, are the freshest possible. The Famous Smoke Shop is a direct importer, which enables it to offer lower prices. Connoisseurs will find some of their favored brands: Macanudo, Don Diego, H. Upmann and Ramon Allones.

Pipeworks and Wilke
16 W. 55th St. (Fifth & Sixth Aves.)
956-4820
Open Mon.-Fri. 9:30 a.m.-5:45 p.m., Sat. 9:30 a.m.-4:45 p.m.

A specialty shop, Pipeworks and Wilke is New York's oldest pipe shop, first established in 1862. Handmade pipes are carved in a workshop in Shaftsbury, Vermont, and start at $65; machine-made start at $22.50. Antique pipes run up to $3,000. This shop blends its own tobacco and also carries a small selection of tinned tobacco, as well as pipe paraphernalia and books on smoking. The staff members here all smoke pipes themselves.

WHERE TO FIND/RENT . . .

A BABYSITTER

Avalon Nurse Registry & Child Service
250 W. 57th St., Rm. 723 (Broadway)
245-0250
Open Mon.-Fri. 8 a.m.-10 p.m., Sat.-Sun. 9 a.m.-7 p.m.

Avalon will send a reliable sitter to your house or hotel for a starting price of just $7 an hour, plus car fare, with a four-hour minimum (prices vary according to the age and number of children). In addition to babysitters, it can provide housekeepers, tutors, nurses, nannies, even hospital equipment. Whatever your predicament, this business will help you to have fewer worries.

Gilbert Child Care Agency Inc.
119 W. 57th St., Rm. 912
(Sixth & Seventh Aves.)
757-7900
Open Mon.-Fri. 9 a.m.-5 p.m.

Finding a babysitter you can trust is not as difficult as you may have thought. This company has been in business for over 40 years and has built its reputation by word of mouth. The sitters are carefully interviewed; references are checked thoroughly. And best of all, the rates are surprisingly affordable. (Inquire when you call; the rates vary depending upon the age of the child.)

A COSTUME

Allan Uniform Rental Service Inc.
112 E. 23rd St. (Lexington & Park Aves.)
529-4655
Open Mon.-Fri. 9 a.m.-5 p.m.

Fancy yourself as Scarlett O'Hara or Rhett Butler? Or maybe a 1920s flapper or gangster? These and 150 other costumes are waiting for you in this roomy loft on 23rd Street. Other favorites include Cleopatra, Zorro, clowns, the Easter bunny and, of course, Santa Claus. The shop is family-owned and -operated, reliable, and extremely accommodating. Most costumes come with all accessories (tommy guns, wigs, snakes, etc.) and there is makeup for sale. Prices are very reasonable ($30-$65 for 24 hours), and the stock is constantly being expanded.

Animal Outfits for People

2255 Broadway (81st St.)

877-5085

Open Mon.-Fri. noon-6 p.m. by appt. only.

Thought about becoming king of the jungle or would you prefer to monkey around? This store rents animal, and only animal, costumes for adults. Many of the animals you've seen on TV have come from this store: the six-foot lobster seen on the David Letterman show; the polar bear recently seen advertising a popular wine cooler. Keeping these two company in the store are reindeer, tigers, lions, alligators, the classic hairy gorilla and even an enormous cockroach or two (ubiquitous in New York). This store rents only original creations, so you won't find the likes of Big Bird or Kermit the Frog. The minimum price is $75 for two days.

Universal Costumes Co.

535 Eighth Ave., 21st Fl. (36th & 37th Sts.)

239-3222

Open Mon.-Fri. 9:30 a.m.-5:30 p.m.

Dread Halloween or costume parties? Fear no more. You'll surely find a costume to your liking in Manhattan's largest costume rental shop for adults. There are racks filled with period clothes, animals, futuristic ensembles and international garbs. What you don't see, they'll make in the workroom. Prices start at $50.

FURNITURE

Churchill Furniture Rental

44 E. 32nd St., 2nd Fl.

(Madison Ave. & Park Ave. South)

686-0444

Open Mon.-Thurs. 10 a.m.-7 p.m., Fri. 10 a.m.-5 p.m., Sun. 11 a.m.-5 p.m.

Here you can get one piece or an entire package for homes, apartments, or offices. Churchill also has complete accessories, including lamps, pictures, carpets, mirrors, draperies, televisions, bed linens, china and cookware. The huge selection includes styles that are contemporary, classic and traditional and children's furniture, too. Short- or long-term leases are available, as well as a purchase-option plan, immediate delivery and an interior design service.

A HELICOPTER

Island Helicopter

E. 34th St. & the East River

925-8807

Operates daily Jan.-Mar. 9 a.m.-6 p.m.; Apr.-Dec. 9 a.m.-9 p.m.

Island, in business for more than eighteen years, runs a large, diversified fleet of four- to fourteen-seat jet helicopters. It welcomes any kind of request, from airport runs to cinematography, personal and sightseeing charters. Corporations may lease the helicopters or use Island's own courier service.

A HOUSEKEEPER

Maid to Order

500 Park Ave. (59th St.)

223-4455

Open daily 6 a.m.-6 p.m.

If you've brought everything with you on your trip but your personal help, this agency may be exactly what you need. Maid to Order isn't just limited to maids; there are reliable and handy butlers, too. You can hire someone who will press your clothes, shine your shoes and drive your car; he or she can even serve as a translator. The entire on-call staff of 50 to 60 people is personally recommended, so you needn't worry about the character of the employees.

A LIMOUSINE

Bermuda Limousine Inc.

537 W. 20th St. (Tenth & Eleventh Aves.)

249-8400

Open daily 24 hours.

Absolutely classic and not flashy, Bermuda's Cadillac limousines have transported distinguished American and European families and members of clubs and corporations for more than 45 years. Reasonable hourly, daily, weekly and monthly rates. Both business and personal charge accounts are welcome.

Class Act Limousine
2315 Twelfth Ave. (32nd St.)
491-5300
Open daily 24 hours.

This ultimate limousine service considers the extraordinary to be normal. Standard features in each of the Mercedes, Lincoln and Cadillac stretch limousines are an open bar, fresh flowers, color TV, VCR with a choice of 200 movies, twelve-speaker stereo with a cassette library, fine crystal, solid and glass partitions, sensuous interiors and elaborate custom controls. Service 24 hours a day; trips to anywhere.

A SECRETARY

All-Language Services Inc.
545 Fifth Ave. (45th St.)
986-1688
Open daily 24 hours.

All-Language will translate and/or type your manuscript in any of 59 languages for a minimum of $40 per page.

Manhattan Wordprocessing
438 E. 75th (1st & York Aves.)
288-TYPE
Open Mon.-Fri. 9 a.m.-5:30 p.m.

"If we can read it or hear it, we'll type it," is this company's ambitious motto, and they will type anything—business letters, manuscripts, financial reports, résumés, directories and so on. Rates are $5.50 to $7 per page, with a $30 minimum.

A TUXEDO

A.T. Harris
47 E. 44th St., 2nd Fl.
(Vanderbilt & Madison Aves.)
682-6325
Open Mon.-Wed. & Fri. 8:30 a.m.-6 p.m., Thurs. 8:30 a.m.-7 p.m., Sat. 10 a.m.-4 p.m. by appt. only.

This small, cluttered shop has been dressing men in traditional formal attire of the finest quality since 1892. In addition to tuxedos, dinner jackets and tails, you'll find all the elegant accessories necessary for a night on the town, including silk top hats, white kidskin gloves, spats, waistcoats and walking sticks (all for rent). Custom-tailored formal attire is also available. No wonder nine presidents have been outfitted here for weddings and inaugurations. Prices, luckily, are far from presidential: tuxedo rentals start at $95, which includes all accessories except shoes.

Zeller Tuxedos
201 E. 56th St., 2nd Fl.
(Second & Third Aves.)
355-0707
Open Mon.-Fri. 9 a.m.-7:45 p.m., Sat. 10 a.m.-4:45 p.m.

A New York institution for rented formal wear, this showroom offers a unique salon atmosphere and a professional sales staff that can get you in and out in ten minutes. Of course, if you prefer, you can linger for a few hours until you find the perfect tuxedo by a designer such as Pierre Cardin, Luxiano Barbera, Windsor, or Padgett and Poole. All accessories are included in the price, which starts at $85; shoes are another $20. There is another location at 1010 Third Avenue (60th Street), 688-0100.

A TV/VCR

Columbus TV and Video Center
529 Columbus Ave. (86th St.)
496-2626; 496-2627
Open Mon.-Sat. 9:30 a.m.-8 p.m.

With stores such as this one, one need never buy another appliance again. You can rent a TV—small- or large-screen—a VCR, even an air conditioner for very reasonable fees. Many brands are available; prompt delivery and installation are free of charge and any broken item is replaced immediately. No minimum or maximum time limits, either.

A VIDEO

Cine Club Video
201 E. 42nd St. (Third Ave.)
818-1660
Open Mon.-Sat. 10:30 a.m.-6:45 p.m.

Becoming a member of Cine Club Video is more like subscribing to HBO than joining a video club. Membership fees are based on the number of tapes you wish to rent—$30 per month entitles you to three cassettes at all times. There are no late fees, no rewind charges, no time constraints and no hassles. Checkouts and returns are tracked by optical sensor for minimum waiting. There are over 7,600 titles to choose from, a computerized catalog, a monthly newsletter and even low-cost VCR rentals. This concept is definitely not for everyone, but it's perfect for diehard movie fans.

Rarebird Video
482 Broome St. (Wooster St.)
334-8150
Open Mon.-Thurs. 11:30 a.m.-10 p.m., Fri.-Sat. 11:30 a.m.-11 p.m., Sun. 11:30 a.m.-8:30 p.m.
"Our selection of video is the most esoteric in this city," boasts owner Jack Morris of his establishment. His selection is also one of the largest, housing over 7,000 titles in rentals and sales, with much variety in all genres: silent films range from slapstick comedy to Louise Brooks favorites, black-and-white classics from the original *Scrooge* to Bogie and Bacall flicks. There are also Disney films, animated features and the gamut of exercise tapes. Films in the foreign section are both subtitled and dubbed, and there are special divisions devoted to the careers of such masters as Fellini, Kurosawa, Buñuel and Bergman. Membership per year costs $49.95 ($35 to renew), and each video costs $3.25 per night. Periodically there are showings of neighborhood artists' work.

A YACHT

Manhattan Yacht Charters
233 E. 81st St. (Second & Third Aves.)
772-9430
Open Mon.-Fri. 9 a.m.-5 p.m.
This yacht charter company specializes in complete party planning for 2 to 600 people. An international boat brokerage firm with contacts all over the U.S. and the world, it'll put you in touch with a boat that suits your needs. That could mean a little red tugboat for a movie shoot or a luxury yacht for a once-in-a-lifetime wedding party. Menu planning, entertainment and decorations can be arranged.

Yacht Owners Association of New York
225 W. 34th St. (Seventh & Eighth Aves.)
736-6526
Open Mon.-Fri. 9 a.m.-5 p.m., weekends by appt. only.
Relief is in store for those unable to deny the sailor in them. This association acts as a broker for 400 licensed captains in the New York area who charter their boats, which can accommodate 2 to 400 people. Perfect for all occasions, from an intimate anniversary dinner to a glorious cruise to the Caribbean. Call them up for an appointment; they'll take you to inspect the boat that particularly impresses you. Then, mate, the rest is up to you.

AT CLUB MED, WE TAKE DINING SERIOUSLY.

Exquisite cuisine prepared by our specially-trained chefs, served to you in a sunny sea-side bistro, or under an evening sky blanketed by stars—that's dining, Club Med-style.

For breakfast, freshly-baked croissants, danish, and *pain au chocolat.* Eggs, any style, with sausage and bacon. Crepes and French toast. The ripest fruits.

For lunch, bottomless buffets. Dozens of salads, grilled meats and fish, savory local specialties, and the freshest vegetables and fruits.

For dinner, delicious appetizers from our salad buffets, and lavish main courses starring scrumptious fare from the four corners of the globe.

Did we mention the fresh-from-the-oven breads and rolls, baked right on the premises by our hand-picked *boulanger?* And the tempting assortment of pastries created daily by our own pastry chef? Or free-flowing wine and beer at lunch and dinner?

Between meals, there's every sport under the sun. From windsurfing and scuba diving to golf and tennis, complete with modern equipment and expert instruction. Laugh-out-loud games and activities like picnics, arts and crafts, boat rides, and classical music concerts on CD video discs. After dinner, there are Broadway-style extravaganzas, comedy shows, theme parties. In exotic, tropical settings as sumptuous as our cuisine.

Pre-paid and hassle-free. So you can enjoy your vacation, and your meals, without having to reach into your pockets.

If you now have a craving to sample a bit more of the Club Med vacation, simply call your travel agent or 1-800-CLUB MED.

CLUB MED®
The antidote for civilization.℠

CARTIER FOR THE TABLE

CARTIER, THE KING OF JEWELERS
BRINGS ITS ARTISTRY TO
THE TABLE AND PRESENTS
AN EXTRAORDINARY NEW
COLLECTION CALLED
"LES MAISONS DE CARTIER®".
CHINA, CRYSTAL, SILVER,
IN BRILLIANT DESIGNS
REFLECTING THE GREAT
CREATIVE PERIODS OF THE HOUSE
NEO-RENAISSANCE, ART NOUVEAU
ART DECO, CONTEMPORARY.
OBJECTS OF RARE BEAUTY
TO GRACE ANY TABLE.
AND EACH SIGNED CARTIER.
THE ART OF LIVING,
THE ART OF GIVING,
THE ART OF BEING UNIQUE.

les maisons de *Cartier*

Cartier

THE ART OF BEING UNIQUE

The Cartier Building, Fifth Avenue at 52nd Street (212) 753-0111
The Westbury Hotel, Madison Avenue at 70th Street (212) 249-3240
The Trump Tower, Fifth Avenue at 56th Street (212) 308-0840

ARTS

FILM

If you wander around the Washington Square area, you're bound to run into some earnest New York University students setting up a movie camera. Martin Scorcese, Oliver Stone, Spike Lee and many other directors trained in this city that has been called the most cinematically inspirational on Earth. If you're curious to visit the locations where your favorite movies were filmed, pick up *The Film Lover's Guide to New York*. If you'd just like to take in a movie, there are plenty of choices. In recent years, however, several major theater chains have bought up most of New York's small, independent movie houses. Fortunately, some quality theaters have managed to survive.

Foreign and American independent films can be seen at Film Forum (57 Watts Street, west of 6th Avenue; 431-1591) and Cinema Studio (1966 Broadway at 66th Street; 877-4040). The Paris (58th Street, west of 5th Avenue; 688-2013) and Lincoln Plaza Cinema (Broadway between 62nd & 63rd streets; 757-0359) show only first-run foreign films. Thalia SoHo (Vandam Street, west of 6th Avenue; 675-0498) and Theater 80 St. Marks (80 St. Marks Place; 254-7400) are best for foreign and domestic revivals. The Museum of Modern Art's Roy and Niuta Titus Theaters (11 W. 53rd Street; 708-9400) and the Public Theater (425 Lafayette Street; 598-7171) always have interesting programs that include foreign and domestic revivals, documentaries and first-run independents. Pick up a *Village Voice* for the most comprehensive film listings.

GALLERIES

57TH STREET

Blum/Helman
20 W. 57th St. (Fifth & Sixth Aves.)
245-2888
Open Tues.-Sat. 10 a.m.-6 p.m. Closed Aug.

Irving Blum, a man of great erudition and charm, opened his first gallery, Ferus, in Los Angeles; it became legendary, exhibiting the best from both the East and West coasts. Among some of the exhibitions were Andy Warhol's first show in the United States, early exhibitions of Jasper Johns, Robert Rauschenberg and Roy Lichtenstein, and an important but overlooked exhibition of the work of the late Joseph Cornell. Moving to New York some years ago, Blum formed a partnership with Joseph Helman and opened a now highly influential gallery of great international repute. Concentrating on contemporary "masters" (Ellsworth Kelly, Robert Moskowitz, Lichtenstein), Blum/Helman has also developed a stable of younger American artists, including Bryan Hunt and John Duff, whose work has had tremendous critical and popular success. The gallery therefore has a two-part function: promoting the new and giving added credence to the old. This serious, committed gallery always offers something of interest to gallery browser and collector alike.

Fitch-Febvrel Gallery
5 E. 57th St., 12th Fl.
(Fifth & Madison Aves.)
688-8522
Open Tues.-Sat. 11 a.m.-5:30 p.m.; Aug. by appt. only.

This small gallery, opened by Andrew Fitch and his wife, Dominique Febvrel, didn't take long to make its mark. It specializes in late-nineteenth-century master prints and drawings (mainly European, but also some American and Japanese). Here's where you'll find Redon, Bresdin, Max Klinger and Belle Epoque artists. A gallery to be watched.

Galérie St. Etienne

24 W. 57th St. (Fifth & Sixth Aves.)
245-6734
Open Tues.-Sat. 11 a.m.-5 p.m. Closed Sat. in summer.

Galérie St. Etienne's recent Fiftieth Anniversary Exhibition was a fascinating minitour through twentieth-century history. Letters from FDR, Orville Wright, Adolf Hitler, Albert Einstein and Rainer Maria Rilke hung next to paintings by Kokoschka, Kollwitz, Schiele and Klimt. The gallery reflects the interests of its founder, Otto Kallir, and specializes in both historical documents and fine art. The gallery staff is charming and helpful.

Kennedy Gallery

40 W. 57th St. (Broadway & Eighth Ave.)
541-9600
Open Tues.-Sat. 9:30 a.m.-5:30 p.m.; Summer Mon.-Fri. 9:30 a.m.-5:30 p.m.

This gallery is devoted entirely to American art, from the American Revolution up to the present. The work shown, including that of the moderns, is by nature extremely conservative. Painters such as Charles Demuth, Winslow Homer and John Marin are shown for their pictorial qualities, yet the work of tougher, more experimental artists, such as Morgan Russel, Marsden Hartley and Morton Schamberg, is not. The atmosphere is also decidedly conservative and restrained. A large gallery with rooms of hunting prints, naive oils, and the like, Kennedy—although one of the leaders in the field of indigenous American painting—is rather like a glorified antique shop. Nonetheless, it does show a group of important twentieth-century American painters, including Demuth, Edward Hopper, Georgia O'Keeffe, Walt Kuhn, John Sloan, and Charles Burchfield. Despite its limitations, the quiet, older, more institutionalized sensibility at Kennedy is endearing.

Marlborough Gallery

40 W. 57th St. (Broadway & Eighth Ave.)
541-4900
Open Mon.-Sat. 10 a.m.-5:30 p.m. Closed Sat. in summer.

Marlborough, at one time a veritable institution and one of the leading international galleries, has lost some of its glory in past years, simply because of age and competition. The gallery also suffered in no small part from its involvement in the improper handling of the estate of the late Mark Rothko. Aside from these concerns, Marlborough maintains a high profile, particularly in London, exhibiting the work of major American and European painters, sculptors and photographers, including Henry Moore, Francis Bacon, Kurt Schwitters, Barbara Hepworth, Oskar Kokoschka, Irving Penn, Brassai and Helmut Newton; also exhibited on occasion are works by Rodin, Degas and Renoir. Marlborough also represents a group of such contemporary names as Red Grooms, Reuben Nakian, Arnaldo Pomodoro and Fernando Botero, artists whose work can best be described as inconsequential and whose reputations, let alone prices, are ludicrously inflated. The gallery itself is enormous by midtown standards, and is the only gallery north of SoHo that boasts an outdoor sculpture terrace.

Pace

32 E. 57th St. (Second & Third Aves.)
421-3292
Open Tues.-Fri. 9:30 a.m.-5:30 p.m., Sat. 10 a.m.-6 p.m. Closed Sat. in summer.

Pace is one of the premier galleries in the world. Its vast collection of modern and contemporary works has secured the gallery its sizable reputation. Owner Arnold Glimscher has amassed an all-star list of major American and European artists, including Alexander Calder, John Chamberlain, Joseph Cornell, Jim Dine, Jean Dubuffet, Alfred Jensen, Saul Steinberg, Louise Nevelson, Lucas Samaras, Richard Serra, Agnes Martin, Robert Irwin, Isamu Noguchi, Chuck Close, Barry Flanagan and the estates of Picasso (in part), Mark Rothko and Ad Reinhardt. Pace caused quite a stir in the art world by snapping up Julian Schnabel from Mary Boone's gallery and adding the venerable English painter Malcolm Morley and the hot young American painter George Condo, to its already prestigious roster. Pace simply has the very best of just about everything and exhibits same with intelligence and panache.

Pierre Matisse Gallery

41 E. 57th St. (Second & Third Aves.)
355-6269
Open Tues.-Sat. 10 a.m.-5 p.m. Closed summer.

From 1932 until his death in 1989, Pierre Matisse, son of the great French painter,

Henri Matisse, was the sole U.S. dealer for such major historical figures as Balthus, Chagall, Calder, de Chirico, Dubuffet, Giacometti, Miró and Tanguy. M. Matisse's influence cannot be overestimated. During the late 1930s, when he first exhibited the likes of Chagall, Miró and Calder, the Museum of Modern Art was still a fledgling parochial institution. It was Pierre Matisse, along with such others as Sidney Janis and the late Julien Levy, who provided a forum for current trends in European painting and sculpture to be viewed firsthand, and made a case for modern European art when it was little known, let alone fashionable. Today, the gallery mounts less frequent exhibitions, yet every two years or so it puts on a true blockbuster, such as Miró's sculpture in 1987 or Jean-Paul Riopele in 1989.

Robert Miller
41 E. 57th St. (Second & Third Aves.)
980-5454
Open Tues.-Sat. 10 a.m.-5:30 p.m. Closed Aug.
 This is, by far, one of the most elegant galleries in New York, with an attention to detail bordering on the compulsive. Since opening his gallery in 1977, Miller has offered a consistently exciting program of exhibitions with a group of gallery artists that includes Lee Krasner (the estate), William Brice, Joan Nelson, Milton Resnick, Robert Graham, Louise Bourgeois and Alice Neel (the estate). The gallery also exhibits fine and rare photographs (including the estates of Robert Mapplethorpe and Diane Arbus), a selection of fine classical antiquities, and the work of such modern Americans as Martha Diamond, Marsden Hartley, Andy Warhol and Georgia O'Keeffe. Robert Miller's urbane yet open demeanor, the pleasantness of the surroundings, and the competence of the staff make a visit to this gallery a joy.

Sidney Janis Gallery
110 W. 57th St. (Sixth & Seventh Aves.)
586-0110
Open Mon.-Sat. 10 a.m.-5:30 p.m.
 Sidney Janis, one of the great deans of the New York art scene, has been in business for more than 40 years. The list of exhibitions at both his old locale and the gallery's new location reads like a "Who's Who" of modern art: Kandinsky (1948), Henri Rousseau (1951),

de Kooning (1952), Pollock (1952), Gorky (1953), Rothko (1955), Kline (1956), Guston (1959), Duchamp (1959) and Kelly (1965). In 1989, to celebrate its 40th anniversary, the gallery mounted an impressive exhibition of Giacometti, Mondrian, Arp and Léger. Other exhibitions have displayed an originality and concern for scholarship worthy of any museum—and indeed, many works shown at Janis over the years have ended up in museum collections, the most impressive being the Janis personal collection, now housed in the Museum of Modern Art. Janis, like Alfred Stieglitz, has sought to bring together the best of European and American art in a setting that offers a cohesive aesthetic, and his exhibitions both establish and break historical precedent.

UPTOWN

Acquavella Gallery
18 E. 79th St. (Fifth & Madison Aves.)
734-6300
Open Mon.-Fri. 10 a.m.-5 p.m.
 Acquavella occupies one of New York's most distinguished French neoclassical townhouses. Built in 1908 and modeled after an eighteenth-century Bordeaux residence, the building was once owned by Duveen Brothers, the celebrated art dealers who formed the greatest individually owned collections in the United States—those belonging to J. Pierpont Morgan, Henry Clay Frick, Andrew Mellon and John D. Rockefeller, Jr. The interior is noted for its rusticated stone, black-and-white tiled floors and monumental stairway. Acquavella, which acquired the building in 1967, exhibits nineteenth- and twentieth-century American and European painting and sculpture, with a strong emphasis on the impressionists. A recent major exhibition featured works from Delacroix and Corot to Picasso.

Barry Friedman
1117 Madison Ave. (83rd & 84th Sts.)
794-8950
Open Mon.-Sat. 10 a.m.-6 p.m.
 Barry Friedman's appetites are both voracious and catholic, to say the very least. His gallery is devoted to certain art movements of

the twentieth century, including art nouveau, French and German symbolism, and *Neue Sachlichkeit* (or, new realism of the twenties and thirties). Artists shown include Christian Schad and Tamara de Lempicka. Friedman also collects and exhibits the finest in furnishings and objects, featuring the work of both this and the last century's greatest designers: Hoffman, Rietveld, Bauhaus, Breuer, Moser, the Russian avant-garde, Mallet-Stevens and others. Highly recommended.

La Boetie Gallery
9 E. 82nd St. (Fifth & Madison Aves.)
535-4865
Open Tues.-Sat. 10 a.m.-5:30 p.m. Closed Aug.

Owned and directed by Helen Serger, La Boetie specializes in early-twentieth-century art, including Bauhaus, De Stijl, Dada, surrealism and futurism. These individual and for the most part unrelated movements had a profound influence upon modern society, for they attempted to change the very nature of everyday life through design, ideas or the potentially revolutionary act of applying paint to canvas. La Boetie mounts one or two major exhibitions yearly; the gallery's facsimile exhibition of the Nazis's "Degenerate Art Exhibition" of 1937, for example, was one of major historical importance, reproducing in great detail the works of Otto Dix, George Grosz, Max Beckmann and others condemned by the National Socialists. Pieces shown are primarily works on paper, but a few paintings and sculptures are also on view. La Boetie offers a wealth of important historical material from one of the richest and most influential periods in the history of art.

Colnaghi Gallery
21 E. 67th St. (Fifth & Madison Aves.)
772-2266
Open Mon.-Fri. 9:30 a.m.-5:30 p.m., Sat. 11 a.m.-4 p.m. during exhibitions; reduced summer hours.

Colnaghi is one of the most important galleries for and appraisers of old master English paintings and drawings; sculpture, furniture, and works of art from the sixteenth century to the nineteenth century; and European paintings and drawings from the sixteenth century to the twentieth century. It is indeed a marvel to walk into a commercial gallery and find paintings by the likes of Tintoretto, Bronzino,

Canaletto, Vermeer, Rembrandt, Van Eyck and Titian for sale—at enormous prices, no doubt, but nevertheless available. Steeped as it is in the grand European tradition of art dealing, Colnaghi's atmosphere is decidedly reserved and intended for the serious collector. Casual viewing or browsing is, of course, allowed, but certainly not encouraged to any degree, though the staff is gracious. Although Colnaghi focuses its attention primarily on the works of old masters, it also exhibits and places the works of such important nineteenth-century artists as Courbet, Corot and Rousseau. A gallery experience not to be missed.

David Tunick Gallery
12 E. 81st St. (Fifth & Madison Aves.)
570-0090
Open Mon.-Fri. 9 a.m.-6 p.m.; summer Mon.-Fri. 9:30 a.m.-5 p.m.

The preeminent print dealer in the world, David Tunick exhibits only the finest material in the most elegant surroundings. Walking into the gallery may be likened to entering the house of Dior in Paris for an exclusive, private showing. Located in a beautiful townhouse just off Central Park, Tunick is filled with period furniture, dark rugs, and mahogany-lined viewing rooms, all replete with old master prints and rare, limited modern prints that are second to none and include only first strikes. Among the old masters shown are Durer, Rembrandt, Tiepolo and Piranesi. The moderns include Beckmann, Kirchner, Picasso and Toulouse-Lautrec, as well as a strong American group including Whistler, Sloan, Marsh, and Stuart Davis. The inventory is extensive, as is the list of published material that accompanies exhibitions. Tunick is only for the serious collector; simple browsers are either frowned upon or merely ignored. We recommend calling ahead for an appointment.

Gagosian
980 Madison Ave., 6th Fl.
(76th & 77th Sts.)
744-2313
Open Tues.-Sat. 10 a.m.-6 p.m.

After closing a once-active and progressive gallery in Los Angeles, Larry Gagosian opened an impressive space in New York with a group of blockbuster exhibitions. In 1989, the gallery moved from its Chelsea location to a space uptown. The new gallery has mounted exhibitions of Walter De Maria, Yves Klein and Jasper Johns. Exhibitions are not always scheduled to immediately follow one another and they tend to run for different lengths of time; a phone call in advance is strongly advised. Although the gallery does not represent artists per se, one can usually find examples of work by such artists as Willem de Kooning, Andy Warhol and Cy Twombly. Gagosian recently added to his holdings a private collection of fifty-odd abstract-expressionist and Pop works, including those by Mark Rothko, Clyfford Still, Barnett Newman, Roy Lichtenstein and Warhol.

Hirschl and Adler
21 E. 70th St.
535-8810
Open Tues.-Fri. 9:30 a.m.-5:30 p.m., Sat. 9:30 a.m.-5 p.m.; June, July & Sept. Mon.-Fri. 9:30 a.m.-5 p.m. Closed Aug.

Hirschl and Adler's collection has expanded so quickly that within recent years it has taken over three gallery spaces. The first, Hirschl and Adler, exhibits eighteenth- and nineteenth-century European painting and American art from the late eighteenth century to the mid–twentieth century. The newer, smaller galleries are just across the street (851 Madison Avenue) and house Hirschl and Adler Modern and Hirschl and Adler Folk.

M. Knoedler and Co.
19 E. 70th St. (Fifth & Madison Aves.)
794-0550
Open Tues.-Fri. 9:30 a.m.-5:30 p.m., Sat. 10 a.m.-5:30 p.m.; summer Mon.-Fri. 9:30 a.m.-5:30 p.m.

Knoedler is an internationally established and recognized gallery housed in yet another imposing Upper East Side townhouse. The gallery specializes in abstract expressionism and represents such artists as David Smith, Frank Stella, Richard Diebenkorn, Robert Rauschenberg, Nancy Graves, Glenn Goldberg and Robert Motherwell.

Serge Sabarsky
58 E. 79th St. (Park & Madison Aves.)
628-6281
Open by appt. only.

Sabarsky is this country's major dealer and authority on German expressionism. A scholar of great repute, Sabarsky was instrumental in bringing the work of this period to the greater attention of the public at large, which, even as late as the fifties, regarded German expressionism with surprising disinterest. Many important names are featured here: Gustav Klimt, Franz Marc, Egon Schiele, Max Beckmann, Oskar Kokoschka, Paul Klee, Leon Kirchner, George Grosz and Otto Dix. Sabarsky no longer has exhibitions, which is a great loss for New York, since he was able to borrow the best examples of artists' work from museums, private collections and institutions.

Wildenstein
19 E. 64th St. (Fifth & Madison Aves.)
879-0500
Open Mon.-Fri. 9 a.m.-5:30 p.m.; summer Mon.-Fri. 9 a.m.-5 p.m.

Founded in Paris in 1877, Wildenstein is undoubtedly one of New York's poshest commercial art enterprises. Their forte has always been, and still is, French impressionist paintings. They either have or can get their hands on the best, and if you are willing to pay the price, they might be able to acquire your chosen painting for you. The owner, Daniel Wildenstein, produced a catalog on Claude Monet's paintings, an attestation to the gallery's longstanding commitment to scholarship, which today is represented by a wonderfully varied and select handful of historical exhibitions. The very definition of gentility and erudition, Wildenstein is not to be missed.

SOHO & VICINITY

DIA ART FOUNDATION

New York Earth Room
141 Wooster St. (Houston & Prince Sts.)
473-8072

The Broken Kilometer
393 W. Broadway (Spring & Broome Sts.)
473-8072

The Dia Art Foundation, a nonprofit foundation funded by the de Menil family, maintains four permanent exhibition spaces in the greater SoHo area. Works are commissioned or owned by the foundation and are exhibited in settings that are more akin to museum spaces than conventional commercial galleries. The spaces are well maintained and staffed, and comprehensive printed information is offered on each work.

The most striking of the four exhibits are the two installations by Walter de Maria, the first being the New York Earth Room—fourteen tons of dark, verdant earth filling a 3,600-square-foot gallery up to earth level. The leveled dirt is balanced against a typical SoHo gallery space: white walls, ceiling columns, track lights and so on. This extraordinary sight, coupled with its pungent odor of damp earth, is a wonderful study in contrast to the *ex natura* quality of most art galleries.

De Maria's Broken Kilometer comprises 500 highly polished solid brass rods arranged in five parallel rows of 100 rods each; the distance between each rod increases from the beginning of the row to the end, so that the last, barely visible rows of the rods seem to recede into nothingness. Housed in a large ground-floor gallery with high ceilings and diffuse natural light, this large piece (45 feet wide by 125 feet long) is lit by stadium lights, which activate the highly polished surface of the rods. The overall effect is one of precision, clarity and tranquility—a beautiful, if not stunning, achievement.

Recently Dia opened a spacious permanent exhibition space at 548 W. 22nd Street in the Chelsea area (989-5912). In a building located in a primarily industrial and warehouse neighborhood, the foundation mounts a few select, large-scale exhibitions. The first was a tripartite show of the work of Blinky Palermo, Imi Knoebel and Joseph Beuys. The facility also houses works from the foundation's extensive permanent collection.

Leo Castelli Gallery
420 W. Broadway (Prince & Spring Sts.)
431-5160
Open Tues.-Sat. 10 a.m.-6 p.m.

The most prestigious gallery for contemporary art in the world. For the past 30 years Leo Castelli has exhibited a group of primarily American artists who have become the acknowledged masters of our time. Jasper Johns, Robert Rauschenberg, Frank Stella, Andy Warhol, Roy Lichtenstein and many others had their beginnings at Castelli and

remain with him to this day. Castelli's influence on art since the end of World War II cannot be overestimated. What is shown here inevitably takes hold and is soon in the forefront of modern paintings and sculpture, beginning with such important movements as abstract expressionism, pop, minimalism and, more recently, the new wave of figurative painting. A landmark. Another gallery location and Castelli Graphics are at 578 Broadway (941-9855).

Mary Boone
417 W. Broadway (Spring & Prince Sts.)
431-1818
Open Tues.-Sat. 10 a.m.-6 p.m.; July-Aug. by appt. only.

If Castelli is the most prestigious contemporary art gallery in the world, Mary Boone is certainly the most fashionable, and hence the most visible to the public. The gallery became the focus of international attention in the early '80s via two of its American painters, the young, talented, outspoken and prodigious Julian Schnabel, and David Salle. Although Boone later lost Julian Schnabel to the Pace Gallery, she has since added to the luster of her stable by adding Brice Marden, Ross Bleckner, Gary Stephan, Moira Dryer and Eric Fischl, as well as art media darlings Sherrie Levine and Barbara Kruger. All styles are displayed here, elegantly and with great care. The gallery has also exhibited a variety of important European artists, originally shown in the Cologne gallery run by Michael Werner, Ms. Boone's husband (who now runs his own New York gallery). Two of these are Markus Lupertz and Sigmar Polke. The prestige and influence of this gallery cannot be overestimated, and though it has been severely criticized on occasion for fueling the already overstoked fires of art-world hype, Mary Boone has survived the blows very well indeed.

Pat Hearn Gallery
39 Wooster St. (Broome & Grand Sts.)
941-7055
Open Tues.-Sat., 10 a.m.-6 p.m..

The last of the important galleries left in what was once a thriving hotbed of activity in the art world (the East Village), Pat Hearn seems intent upon remaining in the daunting reaches of "Alphabet City," while her colleagues, such as Jay Gorney and Massimo Audiello, have moved westward. The gallery is beautifully done. All is clean and light, and the gallery's stable of artists, especially painter Philip Taaffe, is admirably chosen.

Sonnabend
420 W. Broadway, 3rd Fl.
(Prince & Spring Sts.)
966-6160
Open Tues.-Sat., 10 a.m.-6 p.m.

Illeana Sonnabend, former wife of Leo Castelli, has devoted herself to contemporary art with a zest equal to that of her ex-husband (and for as many years), and has a gallery whose reputation is near-equal to that of the Castelli gallery. Sonnabend represents some of the most talked-about and coveted young American artists working today, including Terry Winters, Carroll Dunham, Jeff Koons, Ashley Bickerton, Robert Morris, Peter Halley and Meyer Vaisman. Much of this work is very controversial—Sonnabend has never shied away from controversy and a certain aesthetic audacity, even when it was distinctly unfashionable. Certain artists long associated with the gallery, such as Barry LeVa, Mel Bochner and John Baldessari, once existed in comparative obscurity because their work is more conceptual and was therefore considered "difficult." This sort of work has enjoyed

a renaissance, due in part to changing trends, but also to Sonnabend's unflagging support for its creators. Other artists of note represented here include young American painter Robert Yarber and a number of important Europeans: Jannis Kounellis, Peter Fischl, David Weiss, Gilberto Zorio, Boyd Webb, Gilber & George and Bernd and Hilla Becher. Sonnabend's is definitely one of the most consistently engaging, provocative galleries in New York.

Sperone Westwater
142 Greene St. (Houston & Prince Sts.)
431-3685
Open Tues.-Sat., 10 a.m.-6 p.m.

Sperone Westwater boasts a high-powered, immensely successful group of American and European artists. Although somewhat small by SoHo standards, the gallery is an important one. Having achieved a great deal of attention in the early 1980s by hosting the very first U.S. exhibitions of "the three C's," Sandro Chia, Francesco Clemente and Enzo Cucchi. Other notable exhibitions have included those of Bruce Nauman, a true American genius, and Gerhard Richter, one of Germany's most outstanding and prolific postwar painters. Richard Long, Ray Smith, and Susan Rothenberg—the highly regarded painter of mysterious images—further add to the gallery's already substantial international presence.

MUSEUMS

Strolling along Fifth Avenue from 82nd Street to 103rd Street, you'll find the Metropolitan Museum of Art, the International Center of Photography, the Museum of the City of New York and the Guggenheim, Jewish and Cooper-Hewitt museums. A day spent in the Museum Mile is as obligatory on a trip to New York as a visit to Chinatown or the Statue of Liberty. But even if you cover every inch of this extraordinary stretch of museums, you'll still have the Frick Collection, the Museum of Modern Art, and the Whitney to exhaust. And once you've taken in New York's art, remember, the Big Apple also has museums for lovers of dollhouses, movies, television and dinosaurs.

MAJOR MUSEUMS

The Frick Collection

1 E. 70th St. (Fifth & Madison Aves.)
288-0700
Open Sun. 1 p.m.-6 p.m., Tues.-Sat. 10 a.m.-6 p.m.

The most exquisite small museum in New York, the tranquil Frick is an often-necessary alternative to the crowded Metropolitan. Occupying a single floor of the former mansion of steel industrialist Henry Clay Frick, the museum, nevertheless, holds an amazing number of masterpieces, most of which were part of Frick's private collection. From Duccio's *Temptation of Christ* to Renoir's *Mother and Children,* the museum offers the visitor a brief but satisfying survey of pre-twentieth-century Western painting. Whole rooms of the Louis XIV– and Louis XV–style mansion are devoted to Fragonard's *The Progress of Love* and Boucher's *The Four Seasons.* Bellini's *St. Francis in the Garden,* Rembrandt's *Polish Rider,* and Ingres's *Comtesse d'Haussonville* are all prominently displayed.

After exploring the museum, take time to linger in the mansion's lovely garden court. You'll see why a trip to the Frick is recommended for both art-lovers and museum-boycotters.

Guggenheim Museum

Fifth Ave. & 89th St.
360-3500
Open Tues. 11 a.m.-7:45 p.m., Wed.-Sun. 11 a.m.-4:45 p.m.

There is no museum experience comparable to that of the Guggenheim. Wedged between the staid buildings of Fifth Avenue's Museum Mile, Frank Lloyd Wright's masterpiece is almost as shocking and provocative as it was when it opened its doors 40 years ago. There is only one way to wander through the Guggenheim—from the top floor down. As you descend the long, reinforced-concrete spiral, artwork will appear not only before your eyes, but below your feet and above your head as well. The museum owns, and exhibits in rotation, some 5,000 modern paintings, sculptures and drawings. The collection, which is both high in quality and intelligently planned, is dominated by the collections of

Kandinsky (close to 180 canvasses); Mondrian's abstract work; cubist paintings by Juan Gris, Georges Braque and Picasso; works by Paul Klee, Marc Chagall, Picabia, Michaux, Max Ernst and more; as well as pieces by such important contemporary American artists as Jackson Pollock and Robert Rauschenberg. The Tannhauser collection, which became a part of the museum in 1965, is of an earlier period and includes 75 pieces (masterpieces, many of them) by Renoir, Cézanne, Van Gogh, Degas, Pissarro and Picasso (from his Blue Period).

It would be unfair not to single out the museum's cafeteria, situated on the ground floor. The food is not only attractively presented, it is actually edible, thus affording the establishment a unique position in the otherwise lugubrious landscape of New York museum restaurants.

Metropolitan Museum of Art

Fifth Ave. & 82nd St.
535-7710
Open Tues.-Thurs. & Sun. 9:30 a.m.-5:15 p.m., Fri.-Sat. 9:30 a.m.-9 p.m.

The greatest collection of art in the United States is also an exhilarating visual history lesson, a tour of 5,000 years of civilization. The Met does more than display art—it re-creates whole worlds. You can visit the Temple of Dendur in the Egyptian wing, the Ming scholar's garden in the Asian wing, or the salon of an eighteenth-century mansion in the European Decorative Arts wing.

If you've come to the museum only to look at paintings, you won't be disappointed. Go directly to the second floor and wander through room after room of European canvasses. The Met has Brueghel's *The Harvesters,* El Greco's *View of Toledo* and more Vermeers than any other museum in the world. The Andre Meyer Galleries are among the Met's most popular. Here are a remarkable number of nineteenth- and early twentieth-century European paintings. Unless you're planning a trip to Paris soon, don't miss the impressionist collection.

American paintings by Sargent, Homer, Eakins and others can be found in the American wing. This department's main attraction—an enormous courtyard with splendid examples of Tiffany glass—is not to be missed.

You will never be able to exhaust the Met's possibilities, but in case you'd like to try, there are marvelous galleries of Islamic, medieval, primitive, Greek and Roman art to explore. Spend some time visiting the Costume Institute or the musical instruments collection. Then sample some contemporary sculpture against the backdrop of the New York skyline on the Iris and B. Gerald Cantor Roof Garden. Of course, the Met also mounts the most impressive of special exhibitions. These are highly publicized and invariably crowded. If you have time for only one visit to the museum, explore the permanent collection. If you absolutely must see a temporary exhibition, be prepared to wait on long lines for tickets. Above all, don't visit the Met at the end of a day of sightseeing. Give yourself time to appreciate one of New York's most essential attractions.

Museum of Modern Art
11 W. 53rd St. (Fifth & Sixth Aves.)
708-9400
Open Mon.-Tues. & Fri.-Sun. 11 a.m.-6 p.m., Thurs. 11 a.m.-9 p.m.

After Franco's death, Picasso's masterpiece, *Guernica*, left MOMA to take up permanent residence in Spain. Although many New Yorkers may have mourned its loss, they could console themselves with such riches as the recently acquired Van Gogh portrait of Joseph Roulin and his *Starry Night*, Dali's *The Persistence of Memory*, Wyeth's *Christina's World*, Matisse's *Dance*, Boccioni's *Unique Forms of Continuity in Space* or Picasso's *Les Demoiselles d'Avignon*. It seems impossible that any one museum could contain as many masterpieces of late-nineteenth- and twentieth-century art, and probably no other museum in the world has a comparable collection. Founded in 1929 with only eight prints and one drawing, the museum now boasts over 100,000 works of art. These, in addition to paintings and sculpture, include a vast film archive and impressive photographs, prints and drawings, and architecture and design galleries. The museum mounts many excellent temporary exhibitions, most of which are jam-packed. If the crowds start to get to you, just duck into the outdoor sculpture garden where Rodin's *Monument to Balzac* presides.

A ticket to this extraordinary museum is not cheap—$6 for a nonmember—but this includes free admission to any of the two or three films shown daily in the Roy and Niuta Titus Theaters. Advance tickets are available only to members, so arrive early to ensure yourself a seat.

Whitney Museum of American Art
945 Madison Ave. (75th St.)
570-3676
Open Tues. 1 p.m.-8 p.m., Wed.-Sat. 1 p.m.-5 p.m., Sun. noon-6 p.m.

The Whitney's excellent collection of primarily contemporary American painting and sculpture contains over 6,000 works, with such artists as Edward Hopper, Georgia O'Keeffe, Robert Rauschenberg, Jasper Johns, Willem de Kooning and Andy Warhol well represented. Don't miss Calder's *Circus* in the lobby. The accompanying film is almost impossible to hear but great fun to watch. The Whitney's midtown branch is in the Phillip Morris headquarters on 42nd Street across from Grand Central Station, and there's a branch in the Equitable Center (see listing on page 297).

OUT OF MANHATTAN

American Museum of the Moving Image
35th Ave. & 36th St.,
Astoria, Long Island
(718) 784-0077
Open Wed.-Thurs. 1 p.m.-5 p.m., Fri. 1 p.m.-7:30 p.m., Sat. 11 a.m.-7:30 p.m., Sun. 11 a.m.-6 p.m.

Opened in 1988, the American Museum of the Moving Image has the potential to become a first-rate institution. It has not yet fulfilled that potential. Still, movie buffs and their children can have a marvelous time at this—the only museum in the U.S. devoted to the art, history and technology of motion pictures, television and video. The museum's core exhibition, "Behind the Screen: Producing, Promoting and Exhibiting Motion Pictures and Television," is its most successful. Here you can find everything from a full-scale movie set to Partridge Family lunch boxes. There are sound-editing machines to play with and film clips to view. One of the better displays shows how makeup was applied to the

Elephant Man (in the movie of the same name) and the aliens in *Cocoon*. Unfortunately, the museum's temporary exhibitions are not nearly as effective as "Behind the Screen." Recently, the museum reserved its entire third floor for an exhibition of (if you can believe it) video games. But the museum is still growing, and it plans to open a fourth floor in 1993.

Astoria is a safe, residential area, easily accessible by subway. The museum is part of the Astoria Studios complex, where Rudolph Valentino and Gloria Swanson made pictures in the twenties and Woody Allen does today. The $5 ticket includes admission to any one of the more than 700 films shown annually in the Riklis Theater.

Brooklyn Museum
Eastern Pkwy. (near Washington Ave.),
Brooklyn
(718) 638-5000
Open Mon. & Wed.-Sun. 10 a.m.-5 p.m.

This massive fin-de-siècle building (since enlarged) stands at the northeast entrance of a vast botanical garden, remarkable in particular for its reconstruction of a sixteenth-century Japanese garden. Though not a cheery place, it houses an excellent collection of African, Oceanic and Native American cultural artifacts, and if you're interested in Egyptian art, it's worth a trip. The Brooklyn Museum also houses an exquisite collection of sculptures, bas-reliefs, small bronzes, ceramics and jewelry dating from the predynastic period until Ptolemaic and Coptic times. Their temporary exhibits are usually interesting.

OTHER MUSEUMS

American Craft Museum
40 W. 53rd St. (Fifth & Sixth Aves.)
956-3535
Open Tues. 10 a.m.-8 p.m., Wed.-Sun. 10 a.m.-5 p.m.

This small, relatively new museum plans to add another floor to display more of its permanent collection of post–World War II American crafts. At the moment, very little of the permanent collection is ever on display and the museum relies on temporary exhibitions of everything from woodworking and ceramics to umbrella art and confectioneries objects to entice visitors.

American Museum of Natural History
Central Park West & 81st St.
769-5000
Open Mon.-Tues. 10 a.m.-5:45 p.m., Wed. & Fri.-Sat. 10 a.m.-9 p.m., Sun. 10 a.m.-5:45 p.m.

This immense, pompous hodgepodge is jammed on Sundays, with large families and Boy Scout troops. The miles of cabinets display global flora and fauna from prehistoric times on, including a 90-foot-long (Fiberglas) blue whale. The Gardner D. Stout rooms show off a vast ethnographical collection from Asia and the Middle East, but the museum would benefit from more rigorous organization.

The museum also offers free hour-long "Highlight Tours." Films on topics ranging from the Grand Canyon to the human body are shown daily at the Naturemax Theatre (adults $4, children $2). Also visit the Hayden Planetarium, where presentations on astronomy are given in the Guggenheim Space Theater.

The American Numismatic Society
Broadway & 155th St.
234-3130
Open Tues.-Sat. 9 a.m.-4:30 p.m., Sun. 1 p.m.-4 p.m.

What do Herodotus, George Washington and Caesar have in common? Their faces are all artfully engraved on various bronze, silver and gold discs, expertly displayed in the American Numismatic Society. Ring the doorbell and you will be ushered into vaulted rooms where currency spanning the period from its invention to the present can be seen. Two special exhibits trace the evolution of American currency and international medals and decorations.

The Asia Society
725 Park Ave. (70th St.)
288-6400
Galleries open Tues.-Sat. 11 a.m.-6 p.m., Sun. noon-5 p.m.

John D. Rockefeller III founded the Asia Society in 1956. Its galleries house his collection of Asian art and exhibit often-fascinating temporary shows of works from every corner of the East. The society takes an active interest in contemporary Asian affairs and sponsors many lectures, films, and performances. Its marvelous bookstore reflects the society's diverse interests.

The Cloisters
Fort Tryon Park (190th St. & Riverside Dr.)
923-3700
Mar.-Oct.: open Tues.-Sun. 9:30 a.m.-5:15 p.m.; Nov.-Feb.: open Tues.-Sun. 9:30 a.m.-4:45 p.m.
Overlooking the Hudson, beyond the Washington Bridge, lies this admirable collection of medieval art presented by the Metropolitan Museum, with the financial assistance of the Rockefeller family. Whole buildings are exhibited, and rooms from such monasteries as Saint-Guilhem-le-Désert have found sanctuary in the New World. These marvels, to which are added stained glass, tapestries and sculptures, are presented with great style. Even the gardens are works of beauty and scholarship.

Cooper-Hewitt Museum
Fifth Ave. & 91st St.
860-6898
Open Tues. 10 a.m.-9 p.m., Wed.-Sat. 10 a.m.-5 p.m., Sun. noon-5 p.m.
The Carnegie Mansion provides a sumptuous setting for this permanent collection of European furniture, wallpapers, porcelain, glassware, antique textiles of every possible origin, bronzes, wrought iron and silverware, along with a rich selection of drawings and architectural and decorative prints. This museum also presents excellent temporary exhibits. Asleep for years, the museum is currently experiencing a renaissance.

The Hispanic Society of America
Broadway & 155th St.
690-0743
Open Tues.-Sat. 10 a.m.-4:30 p.m., Sun. 1 p.m.-4 p.m.
This exhibit of Iberian (Spanish and Portuguese) painting, sculpture and decorative arts is located in the center of the Audubon Terrace. The interior courtyards and galleries contain items of art and archaeology from the earliest Spanish civilizations to the present (including colonial America), but the most

interesting art pieces are paintings by such masters as El Greco, Goya and Velázquez.

International Center for Photography
Fifth Ave. & 94th St.
860-1777
1133 6th Ave. (43rd St.)
768-4683
Open Tues. noon-8 p.m., Wed.-Fri. noon-5 p.m., Sat.-Sun. 11 a.m.-6 p.m.
Both branches of the ICP possess rich collections of works by the greatest photographers of the twentieth century. Their exhibitions are always of interest.

Jewish Museum
Fifth Ave. & 92nd St.
860-1888
Open Mon. & Wed.-Thurs. noon-5 p.m., Tues. noon-8 p.m., Sun. 11 a.m.-6 p.m.
This small, very active museum devoted to Jewish art and culture (manuscripts, coins, textiles, paintings, pottery and so on) often presents provocative exhibitions. The museum plans to close its building from November 1990 until late 1992, for renovation and the construction of a new wing; shows and programs will be held at the New York Historical Society (see listing below).

Museum of Broadcasting
1 E. 53rd St.
752-4690
Open Tues. noon-8 p.m., Wed.-Sat. noon-5 p.m.
This museum has over 40,000 radio and TV programs and is also putting together a collection of advertising commercials. The museum offers its collection for viewing by the public.

Museum of the City of New York
1220 Fifth Ave. (103rd St.)
534-1672, 534-1034
Open Tues.-Sat. 10 a.m.-5 p.m., Sun. & holidays 1 p.m.-5 p.m.
Located in a handsome neo-Georgian building, this museum contains remarkable models of New York's early development and of interiors throughout the centuries. On display are delightful collections of toys, puppets

and dollhouses and a perfect re-creation of John D. Rockefeller's bedroom; there's also an audio-visual show on the city's history.

New York Historical Society
Central Park West & 77th St.
873-3400
Open Tues.-Sat. 10 a.m.-5 p.m., Sun. 1 p.m.-5 p.m.

A visit to this museum agreeably rounds out a tour of the Museum of the City of New York (above). Here are superb collections of antique toys, nineteenth-century furniture and New York silverware from the eighteenth and nineteenth centuries, as well as portraits, carriages and 433 of John James Audubon's 435 original watercolors for *Birds of America*.

Whitney Museum at Equitable Center
787 Seventh Ave. (52nd St.)
554-1113
Open Mon.-Wed. & Fri. 11 a.m.-6 p.m., Thurs. 11 a.m.-7:30 p.m., Sat. noon-5 p.m.

This exhibition center has a sculpture court and a gallery of fine art, architecture and design. In addition to permanent galleries for full-scale traveling exhibitions, the Equitable has some of the most extraordinary public and corporate spaces in the city. These areas, including the restaurant Palio, contain artworks commissioned from such noted artists as Roy Lichtenstein, Sandro Chia, Scott Burton, Barry Flanagan, Thomas Hart Benton and Paul Manship. The auditorium also sponsors free dance performances.

MUSIC & DANCE

In the music and dance capital of the world, the real problem is not simply in deciding what to see, but in deciding what you can possibly afford to miss. Your choices may range from the debut of a young soloist at the acoustically spectacular Carnegie Hall to a sublime performance of George Balanchine's 1934 ballet *Serenade*, danced by the New York City Ballet at Lincoln Center's State Theater.

There is no height of the season on New York's cultural calendar, just changing seasons. In the fall and winter, Avery Fisher Hall houses the New York Philharmonic; come summer, it plays host to the breezy Mostly Mozart Festival. And, since 1988, the month of June (in 1990 and 1992) will bring the biannual New York International Festival of the Arts. Chamber music, modern dance, classic opera—from the established to the experimental—all have their forums in the city that is home to one of the largest populations of professional dancers and musicians in the world. Not surprisingly, most of them live within walking distance of Carnegie Hall and Lincoln Center; a performing artist can be identified easily as he or she walks by with turned-out feet or a pulled-back ballerina hairstyle or, perhaps, with a violin case and tuxedo.

For musicians, the New York debut is still a portentous event, the stage upon which international careers are launched—or cut short. Not only does New York introduce dozens of new faces each season, but it also gives audiences many occasions to welcome back the famous "old friends" they have come to know well over the years. Verdi, Wagner and Mozart are to be heard at the Metropolitan Opera House, and modern operas, with titles such as *Nixon in China,* are to be seen, heard and discussed at the Brooklyn Academy. Everyone—from former child prodigies such as Yehudi Menuhin and current prodigies such as the Japanese violinist Midori to contemporary and avant-garde composers—converges on New York, where, no matter how obscure or offbeat the production, there always seems to be a willing audience.

In finding your way through New York's dance world, it's important to know that the terms "downtown" and "uptown" apply more to orientation than geography. Uptown implies a more established artist and audience; downtown suggests that the art and audience are less restricted—anything goes. Or, as David White, experimental dance's chief producer, put it, "Uptown is learnable; downtown is ideas and inspiration, which are born instead of learned." New Yorkers pride themselves on discovering new artists, and the so-called downtown dance scene is a good place to go speculating—you'll have to wade through a lot of work that will forever be in progress, but when you do happen upon wonderful performers, you'll have the advantage of seeing them up close, at the start of their rising careers, and in an intimate setting. And you don't always have to go to a small theater to see a young choreographer's work: the big ballet companies are now inviting modern choreographers to create works for them. Japanese choreographers have also been drawing more focus in New York, and many have developed enthusiastic followings, particularly Natsu Nakajima and Michiyo Tanaka. If you prefer seeing dance in a different setting, check out the various dance events strutting about town that are sponsored by such groups as Dancin' in the Streets and the waterfront-based Art on the Beach.

TICKETS

Though you may be overwhelmed initially by the choices to be made, a careful glance at the listings and recommendations—some annotated by critics—in *The New York Times, Village Voice,* and *The New Yorker, 7 Days* and *New York* magazines will help you whittle down your selection. On Fridays, the major local papers list the weekend's goings-on in their entertainment sections, and the Friday and Sunday editions of *The New York Times* often give advance notice of significant concerts, so you may want to buy a copy a few months ahead of your visit to ensure getting tickets for popular concerts. Or write to the theater for a schedule of performances and then order by mail. Remember: the best seats for major companies and orchestras regularly sell out. In the city, tickets are available through most Ticketron (399-4444) and Telecharge (239-6200) outlets.

Although the prime seats for stellar dance and music events can be costly—at the Met they range from $40 to $85 for the parterre and $40 to $75 in the orchestra pit—inexpensive tickets are available if you're willing to stand or sit high up in the area dubbed "the Gods" (called so because you can just about touch the ceiling). Standing-room tickets, which go for about $6 in the family circle section or $9 in the orchestra, are available at 10 a.m. Saturdays for performances Saturday through Friday. You can also cut costs by buying an obstructed-view seat at the Met or State theaters. The best concerts, of course, are not always the most expensive; indeed, tickets to many of them can be had for a song (or a nominal fee) including those given by the Metropolitan Opera or the New York Philharmonic on Central Park's Great Lawn; in the elegant Frick Museum on Sunday afternoons in summer; or in the city's many churches. Also, try such small companies as the Light Opera Company of Manhattan, known as LOOM, which presents fine musicals and operettas at its small Playhouse 91 theater in Manhattan (LOOM was suffering financial problems in late 1989, but plans to commence business again in the summer of 1990; call 831-2000 for information).

Keep in mind that "sold out" rarely means unavailable, it just means you have to work a little harder. Your best bet is to go to the theater one hour before curtain time and look for anxious subscribers hoping to sell their extra tickets at the door. If you find yourself awaiting a late companion before the performance, simply leave the ticket at the box office in an envelope with the latecomer's name on it. The box office usually stays open for a half hour to an hour after the curtain goes up.

For half-price tickets to many performances, be sure to check out the Music and

Dance Booth in Bryant Park at 42nd Street and Sixth Avenue (382-2323). Tickets may include those for Lincoln Center and Carnegie Hall. Open daily, usually from noon to 7 p.m. (hours do vary, so call first).

LINCOLN CENTER

The central shrine of highbrow culture in New York, Lincoln Center is the country's largest performing-arts center, and certainly among its most flourishing. Located at 64th Street and Broadway, the imposing complex was built in the 1960s by several leading American architects, Philip Johnson among them, and has been responsible in large part for the revitalization of New York's Upper West Side (the area north of Columbus Circle). The major halls of the complex—the State Theater, the Metropolitan Opera House and Avery Fisher Hall—are rarely dark; flags above the Center's front steps announce the resident of each house, which may well range from the New York City Opera to the Bolshoi Ballet to the Kool Jazz Festival.

Despite its grandeur, Lincoln Center offers a number of free events throughout the year, including concerts at the cozy Bruno Walter Auditorium in the Library of the Performing Arts; at the Damrosch Park bandstand on the south side of the Met; and at the Juilliard School, where every Wednesday afternoon student prodigies give recitals. A guided one-hour tour is an excellent way to sample Lincoln Center's diversity. (Call 877-1800 ext. 516; tours run daily from 10 a.m. to 5 p.m.)

During the warmer months, you can dine at the outdoor café beside Avery Fisher Hall, grab an ice cream cone or cappuccino at the concession stand, or catch one of the many free performances in the plaza sponsored by Lincoln Center Out-of-Doors. The plaza's main fountain is not only a favored rendezvous point but a lovely brown-bag lunch spot and ideal vantage point for people-watching. For daily information, call the concert hotline at 877-2011 after 9 a.m. The Lincoln Center Park and Lock Garage has room for 750 cars and never closes. Enter on W. 62nd or W. 65th streets.

Alice Tully Hall

144 W. 66th St. (Broadway)
362-1911, 874-6770 (to charge)
Box office open Mon.-Sat. 11 a.m.-6 p.m. or showtime, Sun. noon-6 p.m. or showtime.

Snuggled in Lincoln Center's Juilliard School building, the intimate 1,096-seat Alice Tully hall is blessed with what are said to be the best acoustics in the complex. A wonderful setting for chamber music, it is home to the Chamber Music Society of Lincoln Center, which holds court here from October through May. In late September, the toney New York Film Festival screens the latest movies; call well in advance for tickets, as they are hard to come by. For a glimpse of tomorrow's musical fixtures, check out the Juilliard student orchestra, as well as the free Wednesday afternoon concerts at 1 p.m. given during the school year by fledgling virtuosos.

Avery Fisher Hall

111 Amsterdam Ave. (64th & 65th Sts.)
874-2424, 874-6770 (to charge)
Box office open Mon.-Sat. 10 a.m.-5:45 p.m., Sun. noon-5:45 p.m.

From mid-September to May, this 2,700-seat hall is home to The New York Philharmonic, the oldest symphony orchestra in the U.S. and one of the most vital. Originally called Philharmonic Hall, Avery Fisher was renamed to honor the patron who gave $10 million to redo the hall's poor acoustics, which were largely remedied in 1976 when the hall was considerably reconstructed. Tickets cost from $7.50 to $40, but you may want to sit in on one of the Philharmonic's 22 morning dress rehearsals open to the public (usually on Thursdays) throughout the season, for only $4. (All rehearsals begin at 9:45 a.m. Call for dates.) In June, the Kool Jazz Festival moves in, followed by the popular Mostly Mozart Festival, which offers exceptional programs at still-modest prices. Since its inception in 1966, the festival has presented scores of different chamber ensembles, as well as conductors and pianists, including Peter Serkin and Alicia de Larrocha.

Bruno Walter Auditorium

111 Amsterdam Ave. (64th & 65th Sts.)
870-1630
Hours vary.

Located in the center's library of the performing arts, this 212-seat hall has held free recitals, concerts and other performances for the past twenty years. Concerts are planned every weekday at 5 p.m. and on Saturdays at 2:30 p.m.

Guggenheim Bandshell
Damrosch Park
877-1800

Located on the southwest corner of Lincoln Center, the bandshell features free concerts in the summer, from rock music to opera. It also hosts frequent performances by the Guggenheim Band.

Juilliard School Concert Office
144 W. 66th St. (Broadway)
874-7515, 874-0465

One of the premier performing arts schools in the world, Juilliard has trained such exceptional talents as cellist YoYo Ma, violinist Itzhak Perlman, trumpeter Wynton Marsalis, singer Leontyne Price, dancer Paul Taylor, and actors Kevin Kline and William Hurt. During the school year, there are ample opportunities to see Juilliard's young artists perform at C. Michael Paul Hall or the Juilliard Theater. The School for American Ballet, which is the wellspring of the New York City Ballet, is also housed at the Juilliard School and holds its annual workshop production in late May or early June. If you're up for some of the finest dancing in town and a sneak preview of the next generation of ballet stars, put your bid in for tickets early; they go quickly. Call or write the School for American Ballet, 144 W. 66th Street, New York, New York 10023; 877-0600.

Metropolitan Opera House
W. 64th St. (Broadway & Columbus Ave.)
362-6000, 799-3100 (backstage)
Box office open Mon.-Sat. 10 a.m.-8 p.m., Sun. noon-6 p.m.

Plush and stately (some say gaudy), the Met remains the crown jewel of Lincoln Center. With 3,800 seats, it is the largest of Lincoln Center's three main halls. Signature Chagall tapestries hang in the lobby facing the plaza; red carpets cover the sweeping staircase; and crystal chandeliers inside the hall rise before each performance to a gold-leafed ceiling, never failing to evoke a gasp from the audience. Opening nights draw a decidedly well-heeled and expensively appointed crowd, though people like to dress up for any evening at the Met. Completed in 1966, it is home to the Metropolitan Opera and the luminous voices of the opera world. Beginning in May of each year, it welcomes the American Ballet Theater onto its stage. ABT's programs range from such tireless nineteenth-century classics as *Sleeping Beauty* to contemporary works by young choreographers. Come summertime, the Met Opera gives an occasional performance in the city's parks and the Opera House begins importing international ballet companies. In 1989, after a 25-year absence from New York, the Kirov Ballet performed. The Royal Ballet, the Royal Festival Ballet, the National Ballet of Canada and the Bolshoi appear more regularly. Ticket prices for opera and the big ballet companies rival those of Broadway shows. For a one-and-a-half-hour backstage tour of the Met, call the Metropolitan Opera Guild (582-7500).

New York Public Library at Lincoln Center
111 Amsterdam Ave. (64th & 65th Sts.)
870-1630
Hours vary.

If you consider yourself a dance-, music-, or theater-lover, be sure not to bypass this terrific library, certainly among the best performing-arts research centers in the world, and, in the case of its dance collection, the best. Chances are that the performance you've always lamented missing can be found on videotape in the third-floor dance library.

New York State Theater
W. 63rd St. (Columbus Ave.)
870-5570
New York City Ballet, 870-5570 (to charge)
New York City Opera, 307-7171 (to charge)
Box office open Mon. 10 a.m.-7:15 p.m., Tues.-Sat. 10 a.m.-8:15 p.m., Sun. 11:30 a.m.-7:15 p.m.

Home to the New York City Ballet and the New York City Opera, this 2,779-seat theater was designed by Philip Johnson and Richard Foster in 1964. Its recommendations were solicited from the late choreographer George Balanchine and Lincoln Kirstein, the co-founders of City Ballet, one of the world's great ballet companies. Since Balanchine's death in 1983, the company under his successors, Peter Martins and Jerome Robbins, has tried to uphold the legacy of the Balanchine repertory—celebrated for its plotless works and the speed and design of its choreography—and to extend its classical tradition. The company presents its winter season from November to February and its spring season from April to June. Just as it did under Balanchine, City Ballet bills itself as "starless," meaning no advance casting lists are published. Each season brings a new work by Robbins or Martins and, of course, those incomparable Balanchine classics. To appreciate the patterns of Balanchine's ballets, try the seats at the top of the house, which offer a particularly revealing vantage point. In December, City Ballet's performances of *The Nutcracker* remain an annual fixture and the hottest Christmas tickets in town.

From midsummer through the fall, the New York City Opera, led by Christopher Keene, offers opera at half the price of Met tickets, but certainly not at half the value. The company accents American singers. Keep in mind that there is no aisle down the middle of the orchestra, so get seats near the end of the row or in the upper rings if you don't want to climb over people.

OTHER CONCERT HALLS, DANCE & MUSIC SPACES

New York's many and diverse performances can be seen in countless different settings: auditoriums, concert halls and lofts come in every size imaginable; the smaller the theater, the more intimate the atmosphere and the lower the admission fee. At some of the fringe theaters, you may find yourself sitting in a hard-backed chair or on the floor, but such spartan amenities give these places their character. If it's jazz you're seeking, you'll find everything from the standards and the blues to fusion and beyond at any one of the city's numerous jazz clubs, ballrooms and lofts (see the Nightlife chapter). And in the dark, smoky nightclubs that gave them their start, you can still catch such jazz greats as Sarah Vaughan and Dizzy Gillespie. Check the *Village Voice* for weekly listings. The following is a sampling of New York's infinite variety of music and dance venues.

Brooklyn Academy of Music
30 Lafayette Ave., Brooklyn
(718) 636-4100

Although most Manhattanites deplore the thought of leaving the borough, a good many don't hesitate to make the trek to BAM, where some of the most innovative and unlikely programming in dance, music and theater is showcased. In the fall, the splashy Next Wave Festival pays tribute to the avant garde, with an eclectic array of solo and collaborative performances by emerging international artists; the roster in the past has included performance artist Laurie Anderson, choreographers Mark Morris and Pina Bausch and composer Philip Glass, whose 1972 opera *Einstein on the Beach* was given a full-blown revival here in 1985. Where else would Ingmar Bergman bring his Swedish *Hamlet?* Of its three theaters, the 2,100-seat Opera House is the largest and most elegant. During the intermission, you'll never be bored watching the parade of fashion-conscious patrons, whose costumes are often as colorful as those on stage. The oldest performing-arts institution in America (Anna Pavlova and Enrico Caruso stopped here), BAM also hosts the home concerts of the Brooklyn Philharmonic under the baton of Lukas Foss, as well as many local and touring dance companies, such as Twyla Tharp Dance and the Central Ballet of China. The Academy also owns the nearby, now completely refurbished Majestic Theater, which was reopened in 1987 with director Peter Brook's nine-hour epic, *The Mahabharata*. Don't go to BAM hungry; your choice of places to eat nearby is limited. BAM is a short subway ride to Brooklyn; take the IRT numbers 2, 3, 4 or 5 or the D, B, R, or N trains to the Atlantic Avenue stop. The less daring can always opt for a cab.

Carnegie Hall
Seventh Ave. & 57th St.
247-7800

An acoustical paradise, this 2,800-seat hall prompts rapturous praise. "It is a building built more by music than by man," declared Yehudi Menuhin. "It's the queen hall of New York," said Isaac Stern. For performers, a Carnegie Hall debut is the ultimate rite of passage, and sometimes a most unusual one: Yehudi Menuhin was 11 years old at his 1927 debut (the concertmaster had to tune the child's violin because his hands were too small). A year after his own debut, pianist Vladimir Horowitz said, "I played louder, faster and more notes than Tchaikovsky wrote." Tchaikovsky himself conducted on the hall's opening night on May 5, 1891; since then, the house that industrialist Andrew Carnegie built (in an area that was then a suburb) has surveyed several chapters of musical history. Those who have claimed its stage include Arturo Toscanini, Gustav Mahler, Duke Ellington, Billie Holiday, Judy Garland, and Isaac Stern and Jack Benny in their only known duet performance. The Beatles made their New York debut here, and even the funeral of the great impresario Sol Hurok was held in this hall. Many nonmusical greats have also left indelible impressions, including dancer Isadora Duncan, actress Sarah Bernhardt, and Statesman Winston Churchill, who lectured on the Boer War.

Carnegie Hall was scheduled for demolition in the early 1960s when the New York Philharmonic, its regular attraction, left it for the new Philharmonic Hall (now Avery Fisher). When violinist Isaac Stern led the fight to save it, the city took over, and a nonprofit corporation was set up to run it. In 1986, Carnegie Hall underwent a $50-million facelift to restore it to its original splendor, resulting in a revamped lobby and backstage area, mended masonry, new grand staircases, improved dressing rooms and plumbing, new seats, floors, and carpets, and a renovated recital hall, now called Weill Recital Hall.

There is a concert here practically every night of the week, ranging from a solo recital by Luciano Pavarotti to a Boston Symphony performance of Mahler's Ninth. A limited number of discounted student and senior-citizen tickets (about $5) go on sale in the lobby between 6 p.m. and 6:30 p.m. on the evening of the performance (between 1 p.m. and 1:30 p.m. for matinees).

Central Park Band Shell
Central Park, 72nd St. & Central Dr.
860-1335

Once one of the city's more neglected outdoor concert spaces, this bandshell was transformed into a showcase for contemporary performers by Summerstage, a two-month summer festival of free jazz, opera, dance and new music that began in 1987.

City Center Theater
131 W. 55th St. (Sixth & Seventh Aves.)
581-7907

Built in 1923 as a Shriner's temple, this Moorish-style Manhattan dance mecca underwent a major renovation in the early 1980s to improve its ground floor and sight lines. (Still, you should try to avoid the extreme side seats.) The first rows of the overreaching balcony are particularly good. Many of the leading national and foreign modern dance companies hold seasons here, including the Joffrey Ballet (which is also based in Los Angeles), the Alvin Ailey American Dance Theater, Dance Theater of Harlem and the troupes of Merce Cunningham, Paul Taylor, Lar Lubovitch and Trisha Brown.

Dance Theater Workshop
219 W. 19th St.
691-6500

A wonderful place to scope out the latest in new art, DTW has become the downtown dance world's center of incubation under the guidance of its director, David White. Many dancers and would-be choreographers, impatient with the long apprenticeships they may have to serve in the bigger companies, strike out on their own with a DTW debut, and some continue to return after they have moved on to bigger houses like BAM. The perimeters of the performing area change from show to show, and often the performers engage the audience in very direct ways. You may get glimpses of works in progress or see multi-media performances like a New-Wave puppet revue, in which an Ivory Snow bottle and baby shoes were meant to represent a schoolteacher and her pupils. You can expect the unexpected here.

Franklin Furnace
112 Franklin St.
(W. Broadway & Church St.)
925-4671

Franklin Furnace ranks high among the city's most popular purveyors of performance art. Established in 1976, it features monthly installations of mostly noncommercial art and also houses the country's largest collection of books made by artists. Laurie Anderson got her start here.

The Grace Rainey Rogers Auditorium
Metropolitan Museum of Art,
Fifth Ave. & 82nd St.
570-3949 (information)
Box office open one hour prior to showtime.
  Located in the galleries that house the Met's world-class Egyptian collection, the 700-seat Auditorium offers a number of concert series of vocal, chamber and early music. Several notable chamber ensembles play here, including the Beaux Arts Trio and the Guarneri Quartet. Lectures on art history, dance and music are given throughout the year by noted scholars.

The Joyce Theater
175 Eighth Ave. (19th St.)
242-0800
  The former Elgin movie theater in lively Chelsea has been redesigned to be a charming, 474-seat art-deco theater for smaller dance and regional theater companies. The American Theater Exchange is held here every summer; the rest of the year is devoted to seasons by the resident Feld Ballet, as well as to those by Karole Armitage, Lucinda Childs, Molissa Fenley and Garth Fagan. After the theater, sample one of the many funky restaurants in the neighborhood.

Kauffman Concert Hall
YM/YWHA
1395 Lexington Ave. (92nd St.)
415-5540 (information); 996-1100 (to charge)
  There is not a bad seat in this warm, burnished-wood-paneled theater tucked away inside the Young Men's/Young Women's Hebrew Association building. Kauffman features some of the most interesting programming in the city and draws a particularly eclectic and discerning audience. In a subdued, unpretentious atmosphere, you can savor first-rate performances of chamber and orchestral music as well as those by individual artists such as Yo Yo Ma and Sherrill Milnes. The Guarneri, Juilliard, and Tokyo String Quartet regularly perform here, as does the New York Chamber Symphony, the Y's resident group, which is conducted and directed by Gerard Schwartz. During the Christmas season, the Chamber Symphony performs Bach's *Brandenburg Concerti*, with a special champagne performance on New Year's Eve.

The Hall, however, is not only filled with music: throughout the year, its celebrated Poetry Center (established in 1939) offers readings by such literary lions as Isaac Bashevis Singer, Margaret Drabble, Nadine Gordimer and Milan Kundera. There are also lecture series by critics, composers, historians and policy makers.

The Kitchen
512 W. 19th St. (Tenth & Eleventh Aves.)
255-5793
  Founded in 1971 as a space for video art, The Kitchen quickly established itself as an important venue for major innovations in music, performance art and dance as well. Though it has moved several times, it's now housed in a former ice house and film studio on the far west side of Manhattan. Everything from new music from Japan to new theatrical performance pieces is showcased in The Kitchen's two large, open rooms. (It also boasts a video-viewing gallery.) "For many artists," says its director, Barbara Tsumagari, "we provide their first serious, well-produced performance opportunity in New York, in a context of interest in the art iself, not the audience." See for yourself.

La Mama E.T.C.
74 E. 4th St.
La Mama Annex
66 E. 4th St.
254-6468
  The seeds of this thriving hothouse of experimental theater, music and dance were sown more than 25 years ago by Ellen Stewart, the "mama" who is its namesake, and today, it's still as exciting as ever. The programming is eclectic and international in flavor.

Merkin Concert Hall
Abraham Goodman House,
129 W. 67th St.
(Broadway & Amsterdam Aves.)
362-8719
  One of the city's newest recital halls, the intimate Merkin seats 457 and offers varied concert series of chamber music, early music, Jewish music, original instruments and new music. The Mendelssohn String Quartet and the Boston Camerata are regular guests.

The Promenade
Battery Park City

Set along the shore of the Hudson River, the Promenade regularly features jazz and popular-music concerts during warmer weather.

P.S. 122
150 First Ave. (9th St.)
477-5288

This former public school (hence P.S.) in the East Village offers evenings of mixed, small-scale performances of dance, music, performance art, theater and comedy. Shows are held either on the second floor, in a long room complete with risers and chairs, that doubles as a rehearsal space, or in the downstairs gymnasium. Well-known New York artists who got their start here include Ethyl Eichelberger, known for his one-man rendition of *King Lear* with music, and playwright Eric Bogosian. Audiences are decidedly downtown and hip, and tickets are cheap: from $4 to $8.

Town Hall
123 W. 43rd St. (Sixth Ave. & Broadway)
840-2824

Here, you'll find a mixed bag of performances, with a focus on classical, jazz, folk and polycultural music events. The singers and comedians who have recently performed to sell-out audiences have hailed from places such as Brazil, Russia and Poland. Classical music ranges from concerts by the Philharmonia Virtuosi to a series featuring modern composers. A former drawing card was an all-male opera company that performed in drag.

Wintergarden
One World Financial Center,
200 Liberty St.
945-2600 (for information)

This 120-foot-high, glass-enclosed complex features performances by both emerging and established dance and music artists, from the Harlem Boys Choir to American Ballroom Theater. The space houses some of the only palm trees in New York (sixteen of them).

THEATER

To most people, theater in New York means Broadway, period. But Broadway is by no means the only show in town—nor is this theater-packed area off Times Square the only place to find first-rate actors and playwrights. If you fancy innovative American drama or something with an experimental bent, you can find it beyond Broadway, in the city's hundreds of smaller theaters. Since Broadway shows have become astronomically expensive to produce, prudence, rather than luck, has been the hallmark of the Broadway roster. Shows with state-of-the-art sets and wide box-office appeal prevail, though fine dramas occasionally get their due. In recent seasons, the trend has been toward Neil Simon plays, revivals of sure-fire hits, and blockbuster musicals, which are these days largely imported from London.

The theater is where most actors declare their hearts to be, and the Broadway—and Off-Broadway—stages are where you'll find some of the biggest names in film and television plying their trade. In seasons past, Dustin Hoffman took on Shylock in *The Merchant of Venice,* Vanessa Redgrave starred in *Orpheus Descending* and John Lithgow garnered rave reviews for his starring performance in *M. Butterfly.*

BROADWAY

The very mention of Broadway summons expectations of extravagance, spectacle and polish. These expectations are often dashed for the first-time visitor who stumbles upon porn shops, blinding neon signs and questionable street life surrounding New York's theater district (the area between 41st and 53rd streets, bounded by Sixth and Eighth avenues). Nevertheless, many of the 36 Broadway houses are elegantly appointed historical landmarks that are rich in theatrical lore. (When perusing your program, be sure to check the page devoted to the history of your particular theater.) And if it's theatrical history you want to sample, don't overlook Shubert Alley. The narrow walkway (between 44th and 45th streets, west of Broadway) was named for the three Shubert brothers, all of whom were producers and theater owners and who, in the early part of the century, founded the Shubert organization—still one of the two biggest theater owners on Broadway today (Nederlander is the other). You may also want to check out Sardi's, that celebrated thespian watering hole, where caricatures of both the famous and the near-forgotten paper the walls.

Before you start scurrying about for theater tickets, do a little homework. First, read a smattering of reviews to get a consensus of opinion on the show you want to see. *The New Yorker* is a good source for snappy capsule reviews and more expansive critiques of Broadway, as are the Friday and Sunday editions of *The New York Times, New York* magazine, and the weekly *Village Voice*. A good review, particularly in *The New York Times,* can set a show on a long-running course and cause an instant scramble for tickets; a pan, however, can leave a show shipwrecked overnight.

Broadway is very pricey, with seats generally running from $27.50 to $50. To secure seats in advance for hit shows, you can write to the theater, but make sure you enclose a certified check or money order for the proper amount, a list of alternate dates, and a stamped, self-addressed envelope. A simpler route is to call and charge your tickets to a major credit card; they will be waiting for you at the box office prior to the performance, but remember to bring your credit card for identification. (The credit-card services will charge you an extra $2.50 to $2.75 per ticket.) Try Telecharge 24 hours a day at 239-6200, or Chargit from 10 a.m. to 8 p.m. at (800) 223-1814 (in the city, dial 516-227-3600). You can also buy tickets at one of the many computerized Ticketron outlets in the city. For the most convenient location, call 399-4444. Remember that weekend performances are more expensive and more in demand.

STAGE NEWS

For news about the city's theater, dance and musical events, call NYC/On Stage. It's a 24-hour information service provided by the Theatre Development Fund, a nonprofit group that helps boost audience attendance. A recorded message will give you performance descriptions, locations, ticket prices, schedules and advice on how and where to purchase your tickets. In the city, call 587-1111; outside the city, call (800) 782-4369.

If you come up short at the box office, tickets for sold-out shows may be available at a commercial ticket agency, such as Golden & LeBlang's (1501 Broadway, between 43rd and 44th streets, Room 1814; 944-8910). Its commission is $2 plus a hefty 22 percent of the box-office price. The hours are 8 a.m. to 8 p.m. Monday through Saturday and 9 a.m. to 6 p.m. Sunday. If you're staying at a major hotel, chances are the concierge can whip up something for you at short notice, though at additional cost. If you're willing to join a (sometimes very long) queue and perhaps brave the elements, don't overlook the Times Square TKTS booth at Broadway and 47th Street, one of three kiosks run by the Theatre Development Fund. (Broadway celebrities announce the booths' various hours on a recorded message; dial 354-5800.) For a charge of $1.50 per ticket, half-price tickets to Broadway and Off-Broadway plays are available on the day of the performance *only*. Secure your place early if you want decent seats, and bring the current theater listings in case your first three choices sell out (a sign at the front of the booth tells you what shows are still available). The booth is open from 3 p.m. to 8 p.m. Monday through Saturday; from 10 a.m. to 2 p.m. Wednesday and Saturday for matinees; and from noon to 2 p.m. on Sunday. Traveler's checks and cash are the only methods of payment accepted. Shorter lines can be found at the TKTS satellite booth in the lobby of Two World Trade Center. For Broadway tickets, the hours are 11 a.m. to 5:30 p.m. Monday through Friday and 11:30 a.m. to 3:30 p.m. Saturday. Tickets to Off-Broadway evening performances are sold from 11 a.m. to 1 p.m. Monday through Saturday. For Wednesday, Saturday and Sunday matinees, tickets may be purchased the day before the performance from 11 a.m. to closing.

If stalking the streets hasn't worn you out, you may want to try standing-room tickets which are available for about $10 at some of the Broadway houses, either in advance or on the day of the performance. Another option is to hunt down "twofers"—tickets that entitle you to buy two seats for the price of one. Twofers are usually available for shows that are not packing them in every night, which means they are either in previews, in an extended run or not very good. If it's a long-running show, its unlikely you'll catch the original cast. To get these tickets, try the front desk at your hotel, the cashier's booth at many restaurants or the Visitors' Bureau, 2 Columbus Circle (59th Street and Eighth Avenue); 397-8222).

OFF-BROADWAY

Off-Broadway is not a geographical demarcation—it's an umbrella term that refers to the city's smaller, not-for-profit theaters where new plays are tested; classics are revived; promising talent is discovered; and some of the theater's finest actors, directors and playwrights converge. Many of the plays that eventually make it to Broadway are first performed Off-Broadway; in fact, Broadway often looks to the fringe for its future productions.

Among the many plays that started here and moved to Broadway are such Pulitzer Prize winners as *A Chorus Line, Sunday in the Park with George, Crimes of the Heart,* and *The Heidi Chronicles.* (If you see these shows early on, you'll have the luxury of seeing first-rate theater up close and at nearly half the price of

MIDSUMMER SHAKESPEARE

Come summertime, Joseph Papp's Public Theatre—or, the New York Shakespeare Festival—moves outdoors to Central Park's Delacorte Theatre (go to the the 81st Street entrance on the west side, or 79th Street on the east side, and walk straight to the center of the park). Free Shakespeare in the Park is presented most evenings through early September, usually one month per production, and is a summer ritual for many New Yorkers. Tickets are dispensed to those in line at 6 p.m., but it's wise to arrive at the Sheep's Meadow as early as 1 p.m. Bring a picnic and a book, and plan for a long but enjoyable wait. Call 598-7100 for more information.

Broadway.) Keep in mind, however, that not every show aspires to Broadway, and some are better experienced in intimate settings. Since productions here cost much less to mount, Off-Broadway is much more open to experimentation. Not only are the houses smaller, but the minimum wage for performers is lower than on Broadway, where performers work under an Equity (actors' union) contract. As a result, Off-Broadway gives new talent a venue—playwrights like Eugene O'Neill, Edward Albee, Samuel Beckett and Sam Shepard and once-struggling actors like Geraldine Page, Meryl Streep and Al Pacino all looked to Off-Broadway for their first important showcases.

There are several theaters and established repertory companies that can be counted on to produce significant work. Among them are some of the many repertory companies along Theater Row, the stretch of former porn-movie houses on 42nd Street, west of Ninth Avenue, that was converted in the late 1970s into a compound of theaters and restaurants. Here you'll find such companies as Playwrights Horizons (where the Stephen Sondheim musical *Sunday in the Park with George* was developed), the Harold Clurman Theater and the Samuel Beckett Theater. These theaters now have a common box office called Ticket Central, which is open from 1 p.m.-8 p.m. daily. Call 279-4200 for credit-card reservations.

Be sure to check the Circle Repertory Company (where Lanford Wilson's plays were first produced), The Roundabout, Provincetown Playhouse, the Negro Ensemble, the Manhattan Theatre Club, the Hudson Guild, the Lucille Lortel, Circle in the Square, the American Place Theatre and, of course, Joseph Papp's Public Theater. Papp is one of the city's leading producers, and his Public Theater, also known as the New York Shakespeare Festival, premieres some of the most vital theater in the city. Meryl Streep, Robert De Niro and Kevin Kline are among the actors who have shone in the Public's productions. You can get half-price tickets at the box office on the day of performance, but go early—lines can be long.

Don't overlook the two theaters at Lincoln Center, the Vivian Beaumont and the smaller Mitzi E. Newhouse, where Spalding Gray brought his one-man *Swimming to Cambodia*, Robin Williams and Steve Martin revived *Waiting for Godot* and Madonna made her theatrical debut in David Mamet's *Speed the Plow*. "Good Plays, Popular Prices" is their slogan—one that might be applied readily to Off-Broadway itself.

Since there are many more actors in New York than there are theaters (your young waiter is almost certain to be an aspiring Olivier) diverse showcases have sprung up around the city to display their wares. In the Village and TriBeCa, churches, lofts, and schools frequently play host to the fledgling star. Off-Off-Broadway is devoted to innovation, which means that just as you stand a good chance of happening upon something inspiring, so, also, may you endure something dreadful. Check the listings and keep your eyes out for posters announcing inventive theatrical experiences. The most reliable are to be found at the Performing Garage in SoHo, where you can see the wonderfully eclectic Wooster Group; La Mama E.T.C. (Experimental Theater Club), an avant-garde, international venue; and the Squat Theater, a repertory group that mixes the media of theater and film. Also, try St. Clement's Episcopal Church and the Minetta Lane. Bear in mind that imagination and a sense of adventure are helpful assets when combing the outer reaches of New York theater.

SIGHTS

DISCOVERING THE CITY

One of New York's great wonders—and frustrations—is its endless potential for exploration and entertainment: there's always something new to see and do. First-time visitors usually step off the plane and head straight for the Statue of Liberty, Rockefeller Center and the tallest buildings; this mini-tour gives you only a tentative nibble of the Big Apple. New York is a city of distinctive neighborhoods, each with its own flavor and character. It's also a place in which you can indulge all your interests—the arts, architecture, fashion, finance and even nature. And exploration shouldn't be solely the province of gawking-and-pointing tourists; native New Yorkers can always rediscover their own city. Take off on foot, guidebook in hand, on your own tour, or choose one of the packaged ones we've listed and visit some of New York's unique attractions. Don't be afraid to wander off the beaten path, and you'll experience this intriguing city on an intimate, human scale.

AMUSEMENTS

Bronx Zoo
Fordham Rd. & Bronx River Pkwy.,
the Bronx
367-1010
March-Oct.: open Mon.-Sat. 10 a.m.-5 p.m., Sun. 10 a.m.-5:30 p.m.; Nov.-Feb.: Mon.-Sat. 10 a.m.-5 p.m., Sun. 10 a.m.-4:30 p.m. March-Oct.: adults $4.75, children $2; Nov.-Feb.: adults $1.75, children 75 cents. (Tues.-Thurs. optional donation.) Parking $4.

Adults and kids alike will be fascinated by a visit to one of America's largest and most innovative zoos, home to more than 3,800 animals. With 265 acres to cover, it's a good idea to take one or more of the guided tours (available March through October). The Safari Tour train ride (adults $1, children 75 cents) and Skyfari tram (adults $1.25, children $1) provide good overviews of the park. The Bengali Express monorail (adults $1.50, children $1) winds through "Wild Asia," and gives visitors a fascinating glimpse at wildlife in its various natural habitats—look for gazelles, elephants, tigers, antelope. There's plenty to see on foot, as well: the World of Birds aviary, complete with a simulated jungle and rain forest; the World of Darkness nocturnal-animal exhibit; and, of course, the reptile and monkey houses (25 cents).

Coney Island
Surf Ave., Brooklyn

Its glory days are long past, but Coney Island still attracts up to one million visitors on summer weekends. The beach, though crowded in good weather, is wide and pretty, and a few attractions remain—the old Cyclone roller coaster, the original Nathan's hot dog stand, the boardwalk. Nearby are reminders of a more elegant time, including the skeleton of the 1939 World's Fair parachute jump.

Intrepid Sea-Air-Space Museum
Intrepid Square, Pier 86,
Twelfth Ave. & W. 46th St.
245-0072
Summer (Memorial Day-Labor Day): open daily 10 a.m.-5 p.m.; fall, winter & spring: open Wed.-Sun. 10 a.m.-5 p.m. Adults $6, children $3.25.

Here's an impressive look at military hardware in an authentic environment—the aircraft carrier U.S.S. *Intrepid*, veteran of World War II, Vietnam and NASA recovery missions. The museum portion features films (on the history of the *Intrepid* and the Medal of Honor) and a large collection of airplanes and weaponry, but just as interesting is exploration of the massive carrier itself.

310

New York Aquarium
Surf Ave. & W. 8th St., Brooklyn
(718) 265-3400
Open Mon.-Fri. 10 a.m.-4:45 p.m., Sat.-Sun. 10 a.m.-5:45 p.m. Adults $3.75, children $1.50.

Just east of the Coney Island boardwalk is a lively collection of 2,000 sea creatures, including sharks, whales, dolphins (on view only in the summer), seals, sea turtles, electric eels and—everyone's favorite—penguins. Watching them all at play and then strolling among the indoor tanks can't help but leave you feeling cool and relaxed.

South Street Seaport
Water St. (Peck Slip & John St.)

Yes, it's "touristy" in the manner of other urban commercial developments, but South Street Seaport is one of the classiest projects of this type, with dozens of fashionable shops, gourmet food stores, and restaurants housed in restored buildings. Similar to Boston's Fanueil Hall and Inner Harbor in Baltimore, South Street Seaport is another in the Rouse Corporation's series of landmark restorations—and it's long on the hard tourist sell and short on history. "Eat, drink and spend as much money as you can" seems to be the real theme of this attractive development at the tip of New York Harbor, and there are endless opportunities for doing so, from the tourist shops to the enclave of restaurants situated on the third floor of each of the main buildings. The food ranges from good to the worst abominations of so-called ethnic fare. Among the more notable snacks, you'll find frothy egg creams, succulent barbecued ribs, grits, garlicky falafel and great hot fudge sundaes. You can walk it all off as you stroll along the harborside. Visitors may explore a museum gallery and ships, including the square-rigger *Peking* (1911), the *Lightship Ambrose* (1908), and the fishing schooner *Lettie G. Howard* (1893). The museum is open daily year-round (call 669-9424 for the exact hours, as they vary; adults $5, seniors $4, children $2). From May to September, the schooner *Pioneer* is available for harbor sails (call 669-9416 or 669-9400).

Staten Island Ferry
Foot of Whitehall St., next to Battery Park
806-6941

At 50 cents, it's the cheapest ride in town, and one of the best, with gorgeous views of the Statue of Liberty, Ellis Island and the Manhattan skyline. The trip to Staten Island and back takes less than 25 minutes each way, and is a refreshing way to rest your feet and escape the crowds.

LANDMARKS

Brooklyn Bridge
From Frankfort St. & Park Row in Manhattan to Cadman Plaza, Brooklyn

The best loved and most famous bridge in New York is this graceful web of stone and steel. A marvel of engineering, its Gothic arches have inspired artists, poets and joketellers for more than a hundred years. If weather permits, take a walk across the wooden pedestrian path—the view of the city and the East River is unforgettable.

Cathedral Church of Saint John the Divine
Amsterdam Ave. & W. 112th St.
316-7540
Open Mon.-Sat. 7 a.m.-5 p.m., Sun. 7 a.m.-7:30 p.m.

Though only three-quarters finished, this massive Episcopalian church ranks as the world's largest Gothic cathedral, with a floor area greater than Notre Dame and Chartres combined. Upon completion, the church promises to be the largest of any kind in the world. Begun in 1892, the all-stone cathedral is actually a mixture of Byzantine/Romanesque (the apse, choir and crossing, built first) and French Gothic (the nave and western facade). World War II put a halt to construction, but efforts to complete the cathedral's 294-foot-high towers resumed in 1979. The work is slow, since each tower requires 12,000 stones, all carved with the same tools and methods employed on the great medieval cathedrals. Visitors can watch apprentice craftspeople, many of them local young people, at work in the cathedral's stone yard. There's also the "Biblical Garden" that is planted with herbs mentioned in the Bible.

Inside, a cluster of eight 130-ton granite columns frame the sanctuary opposite the 40-foot-wide rose window. The marble pulpit, the set of Barberini tapestries and the seven apsidal chapels are equally memorable.

The Chrysler Building
Lexington Ave. & 42nd St.

This art-deco monument symbolizes the romance of the city to many New Yorkers. And no wonder—the stainless-steel sunburst spire, which resembles the 1929 Chrysler radiator grill, gleams on sunny days and adds a distinctive sparkle to the skyline at night. Built into the facade are many automotive-inspired touches, most notably gargoyles fashioned after 1929 radiator caps. The lobby, decorated in African marble and chrome, is full of delightful surprises, including inlaid-wood-on-wood elevators and a painting of the building itself on the ceiling.

Ellis Island
New York Harbor
269-5755
Tentatively scheduled to reopen in Oct., 1990.

From 1892 to 1954, millions of immigrants passed through the halls of these neoclassical/Byzantine brick-and-iron buildings, currently being restored. Accessible by ferry (from Battery Park and Broadway), Ellis Island is especially meaningful to those whose ancestors arrived here, but the now-silent buildings are evocative to anyone interested in America's "melting pot" heritage.

Empire State Building
Fifth Ave. & 34th St.
736-3100
Observation deck open daily 9:30 a.m.-midnight. Adults $3.50, children $1.75.

It isn't the world's tallest building anymore, but the Empire State Building is still the most famous skyscraper ever built, and a potent symbol for New Yorkers—tall, elegant and exciting. A visit to its 86th-floor outdoor observatory and 102nd-floor enclosed viewing area should be one of your first stops in the city. The view (as far as 50 miles on a clear day) is dazzling, of course, and a good way to get your bearings. If possible, at night as well—the city glitters below like a romantic fairyland. The Empire State's five-story base blends in so well with surrounding buildings that passersby never feel overwhelmed by its height. The lobby contains a Guinness World Records exhibit hall that is especially popular with children (open daily 9 a.m.-10 p.m.; adults $4, children $2.75; 947-2335).

Flatiron Building
23rd St. & Fifth Ave.

This building on the triangle where Broadway crosses Fifth Avenue was supposed to be called the Fuller Building, but it looked so much like a flatiron that the name stuck. Built in 1902, the limestone-clad Flatiron was one of the city's first steel-frame buildings.

Fulton Fish Market
South St. between Fulton St. & Peck Slip
Open daily 4 a.m.-7:30 a.m.

When Sinatra sings about "the city that never sleeps," he could be referring to the Fulton Fish Market, where thousands of pounds of fresh seafood are bought and sold each day before the sun rises. It is truly a sight to see, with sellers loading icy boxes of fish and bags of oysters and clams onto vans headed for supermarkets, restaurants and fish stores in the metropolitan area. Early risers who come downtown to take in this fishy ambience can join the dealers for breakfast at Carmine's Bar and Grill at the corner of Front and Beekman streets.

Grand Central Terminal
42nd St. to 46th St. between Lexington & Vanderbilt Aves.

Most of the half-a-million people who pass through the concourse at Grand Central every day don't have time to look up and admire its 125-foot-high vaulted ceiling twinkling with the constellations of the zodiac. Lucky tourist. This Beaux Arts building will wow you architectually, and also tempt you to spend your spare change within its 60 shops.

Grant's Tomb
Riverside Dr. & 122nd St.
666-1640
Open Wed.-Sun. 9 a.m.-4:30 p.m. Admission free.

High above the Hudson sits the white granite mausoleum of Ulysses S. Grant, commander of the Union Army during the Civil War, and President from 1869 to 1877. In truth, Grant isn't *buried* here (as the old joke would have it). He lies *entombed* here—above ground—beside his wife, Julia, in a nine-ton black marble sarcophagus centered in an open crypt (modeled after Napoleon's tomb at the

Hôtel des Invalides in Paris). The interior rotunda and exterior terrace and stairs are all quite stately, but the best part of a visit to Grant's Tomb is relaxing on the colorful (actually, slightly garish) mosaic-tile benches surrounding three sides of the building. Designed by community residents in 1973, they're graced with a flowing, free-form series of city scenes, animals (look for Mickey Mouse), automobiles and more. The effect is refreshing and fun.

New York Public Library
Fifth Ave. & 42nd St.
340-0849
Open Mon.-Wed. 10 a.m.-9 p.m., Thurs.-Sat. 10 a.m.-6 p.m.

Eighty-eight miles of books are shelved in New York's beautiful Beaux Arts library, one of the five largest libraries in the country. Book-lovers will want to visit the huge reading room on the third floor; everyone else can lounge on the steps between those famous marble lions, Patience and Fortitude, and watch the throngs hurry by.

New York Stock Exchange
20 Broad St. (Wall St.)
656-5167
Open Mon.-Fri. 9:15 a.m.-4 p.m. Admission free.

Interested in money? If so, you'll be fascinated by this glimpse of capitalism in action, as 3,000 people scurry around the paper-covered floor of the Stock Exchange. Before entering the third floor viewing gallery, you can hear a short explanation of stock tables, the workings of the market and the activities of the frantic people on the trading floor. Don't expect to see ticker-tape machines—transactions are recorded electronically, and most of the hubbub takes place around TV screens.

Pierpont Morgan Library
29 E. 36th St. (Madison Ave.)
685-0610
Open Tues.-Sat. 10:30 a.m.-5 p.m., Sun. 1 p.m.-5 p.m. Closed last week in Aug. & 1st week in Sept.

Pierpont Morgan *père* actually lived in a separate building on this site, one that was demolished when the library was expanded. This structure was originally built to house his and his son's splendid collections. Lively exhibits and a wonderful gift shop lift the gloom and deep-seated ennui that sometimes sets in when visiting the place where some of the richest of the super-rich had fun indulging in their passion for rare books, incunabula, manuscripts (both literary and musical), drawings and so on. A favored item: the pair of lapis lazuli columns in the rotunda (ask a guard to point the way).

Riverside Church
Riverside Dr. & 122nd St.
222-5900
Church: open daily 10 a.m.-4:30 p.m. Tower: open Mon.-Sat. 11 a.m.-3 p.m., Sun. 12:30 p.m.-4 p.m. Admission to tower $1.

Some of the loveliest views of the city can be seen from atop the 21-story tower of Riverside Church, home of the world's largest carillon. You may even feel as if you're a character in a Hitchcock movie as you climb the final twisting steps among the 74 bells (the largest weighs almost 41,000 pounds; the smallest, about ten). A few of the carillon bells peal on the hour, but it's more fun to actually watch the instrument being played by expert carillonneurs, who sit in this small cabin in the sky and press wooden levers with their hands and feet. Concerts are given at noon on Saturday and at 3 p.m. on Sunday. The church itself was built by John D. Rockefeller, Jr. in 1930, from a design inspired by Chartres cathedral. From the outside, the nave is dwarfed by the 400-foot tower, which isn't surprising, considering the steel columns and beams required to support twenty floors of offices and 100 tons of carillon.

Rockefeller Center
48th St. to 51st St., between Fifth & Sixth Aves.

That distinctive "New York" feeling you'll get at Rockefeller Center does not just derive from the hordes of office workers and tourists surrounding you—it also comes from the wonderful mix of limestone-covered buildings, open spaces and acre upon acre of underground shops and restaurants. In fact, Rockefeller Center, built in the '30s by John D. Rockefeller, Jr. on land leased from Columbia University, may be America's most successful piece of urban architecture.

Begin your exploration of the area by strolling through the Channel Gardens, named for their location in the Promenade between the British Empire Building and La Maison Française (Fifth Avenue between 49th and

50th streets). You'll feel yourself drawn to the famous bronze–and–gold leaf statue of Prometheus, which presides over the equally famous skating rink in winter, and an outdoor cafe in summer.

Rising majestically above Prometheus is the 70-story RCA building, home of NBC-TV. The lobby of "30 Rock," as New Yorkers call it, is decorated with murals representing *American Progress*, by José Maria Sert. Guided tours of NBC's studios begin here (Monday through Saturday 9:30 a.m.-4:30 p.m.; no children under age 6; admission $7; 664-7174) and you can inquire about tickets for TV show tapings at the information desk in the center of 30 Rock. Tickets for *Saturday Night Live, Donahue* and *Late Night with David Letterman* must be ordered well in advance by writing to NBC Tickets, 30 Rockefeller Plaza, New York, New York, 10112; standby tickets may be available (664-3055).

Each of the thirteen original Rockefeller Center buildings contains art-deco touches, many have roof gardens and all are accessible through the vast underground passageways. Note especially the view of St. Patrick's Cathedral and the statue of Atlas as seen from the underground escalator in the International Building, Fifth Avenue (at 51st Street). Rockefeller Center's jewel is Radio City Music Hall, the art-deco showplace that seats almost 6,000 people. Everything is glamorous here: the grand staircase and chandeliers (among the largest in the world) in the foyer, the mural-covered restrooms downstairs, and, of course, the Rockettes, who perform precision dances and high kicks at Music Hall stage shows several times a year. Backstage tours are available (Monday through Friday; call 632-4041 for reservations and times; admission $6).

Statue of Liberty
The American Museum of Immigration,
Liberty Island, New York Harbor
269-5755 (ferry)
Open daily 9:15 a.m.-5 p.m. Ferry leaves from Battery Park. Year-round tours run every hour on the hour. Ferry admission: adults $3.25, children $1.50; statue admission free.

Even jaded New Yorkers feel a lump form in their throats at the sight of the most famous statue in the world's torch shining from 305 feet up in New York Harbor. You can get a good view of sculptor Frédéric Bartholdi's copper-clad masterwork from the Staten Island Ferry, as well as from the ferry that goes to Liberty Island (45 minutes one way). If time permits, do take an hour or so to explore the island—the statue's size is most apparent when you're standing at the base. An elevator (providing it's in working order) takes you to the top of the 154-foot pedestal, which houses the American Museum of Immigration; hardier souls can then climb 171 spiral-staircase steps (twelve stories) to the crown for a bird's-eye view of New York.

Trinity Church
Broadway & Wall St.
602-0800
Open Mon.-Fri. 7 a.m.-6 p.m.; Sat.-Sun. 8 a.m.-4 p.m.

An imposing presence at the base of Wall Street, the original Trinity Church was built in 1696. The current sooty black building, constructed in 1846 of dark-red sandstone, is actually the third Trinity Church to stand on this site. The adjoining cemetery dates back to 1681, and is filled with famous folks, including Alexander Hamilton, Robert Fulton and William Bradford. Workers in the financial district often sit in the coolness of the churchyard to enjoy a (relatively) quiet lunch.

Trump Tower
725 Fifth Ave. (E. 56th & E. 57th Sts.)

Even if you can't afford to shop at Bonwit Teller or Cartier, a trip to Trump Tower is worth your time. The 68-story tower is both the tallest residential building and the tallest concrete structure in New York. Its exterior facade of bronze glass and aluminum provides mirror images of the surrounding buildings. Wander around inside the tower's six-story atrium where an 80-foot waterfall cascades down marble walls past terraced walkways and hanging gardens.

United Nations
First Ave. between 42nd & 48th Sts.
963-7713 (tours)
Guided tours every 30 minutes daily 9:15 a.m.-4:45 p.m.; call for information on foreign-language tours. Adults $4.50, children $2.50; no children under 5.

The familiar modern buildings of the United Nations (1947–1953) still look impressive, especially as juxtaposed with the glass-covered U.N. Plaza across the street. A visit to the U.N. takes you (quite literally) out of the country, without leaving Manhattan—the complex lies in international territory. As proof, postcards mailed here will bear a U.N.—rather than a U.S.—postmark. The complex's designs were selected by an impressive group that included Le Corbusier, Oscar Neimeyer and Wallace K. Harrison. The U.N. tour is extremely popular, but you won't see much unless the General Assembly is in session (mid-September to December). Do take special note of the beautiful Léger murals on the Assembly Hall walls. On your own, you can walk through the carefully groomed U.N. gardens, see the Chagall stained-glass window, the *Apollo 14* moon rock, and the model of *Sputnik I* in the lobby of the General Assembly building. Free tickets to General Assembly sessions and meetings of the various U.N. councils are available on a first-come, first-served basis a half hour before that day's meeting (usually 10:30 a.m. and 3:30 p.m.) at the main information desk (963-1234). You'll be able to listen in with earphones—in English, French, Spanish, Chinese, Arabic or Russian, the official languages of the U.N. Have lunch with a view of the East River, in the delegates' dining room. It's open to the public (Monday through Friday 11:30 a.m. to 2:30 p.m.), but unless you're in a group, it's first-come, first-served. Wonderful souvenirs from around the world are on sale in the basement, tax-free, along with U.N. stamps.

World Trade Center
Two World Trade Center, 107th Fl.
466-7397
Open daily 9:30 a.m.-9:30 p.m. Adults $3.50, children $1.75.

Though the most recent King Kong seemed to be fond of these giant twin buildings, they aren't particularly interesting to look at. But the view from a quarter mile up is spectacular. Weather permitting, you can even go outside on the 110th-floor rooftop, the world's highest outdoor promenade, for a truly heart-stopping look at the Wall Street skyscrapers (they look so small!), the Statue of Liberty, New York Harbor and the rest of the city, even past the George Washington Bridge, uptown at W. 178th Street.

NEIGHBORHOODS

The following is by no means an all-encompassing list, just a taste of what's quintessentially New York.

Brooklyn Heights
Just across the Brooklyn Bridge, Brooklyn

The Brooklyn Heights Promenade offers a wonderfully romantic view of Lower Manhattan's skyscrapers, the Brooklyn Bridge and the Statue of Liberty. But a trip to the promenade is also a good excuse to explore the charming residential streets of Brooklyn Heights, popular since the nineteenth century for being close to—and yet removed from—the city. Some of America's best writers have called this neighborhood home: Walt Whitman, Herman Melville, Thomas Wolfe, Arthur Miller and Norman Mailer among them. From the Heights it's a long but pleasant walk to Prospect Park, the Botanic Garden, Park Slope and the Brooklyn Museum.

Chinatown
Mott & Pell Sts.

Arrive with a healthy appetite, because Chinatown means delicious, inexpensive eating (don't be put off by the hole-in-the-wall look of many of the restaurants). It's also fun to window-shop for fans, tea sets, jade, ivory and other souvenirs as you make your way down the narrow streets. You can visit the Eastern States Buddhist Temple of America at 64 Mott Street (daily 9 a.m. to 8 p.m.). When you're ready for dessert, walk north on Mott Street to Grand Street, and enjoy a pastry and cappuccino in Little Italy. There aren't any tourist attractions per se in the neighborhood, but there are plenty of sidewalk cafés where you can sit, talk, drink and be merry.

Greenwich Village
14th St. to Houston St.

Many New Yorkers feel so passionate about the Village that they claim they never feel comfortable north of 14th Street. Greenwich Village is, indeed, a world unto itself—a maze of streets so convoluted that W. 4th crosses W. 12th, where echoes of bohemia on MacDougal Street are just steps away from the modern buildings of New York University, and high-rises co-exist with quiet blocks of brick-and-stone row houses. Take time to explore this fascinating neighborhood, beginning at Stanford White's Washington Square Arch at the base of Fifth Avenue. Note the Greek Revival homes once occupied by Edith Wharton, Henry James, William Dean Howells and John Dos Passos on Washington Square North (the stables behind them are now MacDougal Alley and Washington Mews). Then walk south on MacDougal Street, past the historic Provincetown Playhouse and Minetta Tavern, to Bleecker Street. From there, go west and lose yourself in the web of streets lined with quaint shops, restaurants, antique dealers and every type of dwelling (especially picturesque: Grove, Gay, Morton and Jane streets). The East Village (east of Broadway), especially lower Second Avenue, has a funkier air; the hippies of the '60s have been replaced by young artists of the '80s. St. Marks Place is the best spot for people-watching, and St. Marks Bookstore is the best in Greenwich Village. The East Village is also one of the more ethnically interesting areas of the city. Here, you can eat authentic Ukrainian or Middle Eastern food, or the cheapest Indian cuisine in the city (Little India, E. 6th Street).

Lower East Side
Bowery to the East River

Craving kosher pickles, lox or knishes? Head for the Lower East Side. This traditionally Jewish neighborhood (now more ethnically mixed) is also one of the best areas of the city to bargain shop. Visit on Sunday when Orchard Street turns into a pedestrian mall specializing in men's and women's clothing, and be prepared to bargain. Check out Grand, Allen and Essex streets for more bargains and Jewish delicacies.

SoHo
Canal St. to W. Houston St.

Between Chinatown and Greenwich Village is the city's artist community, SoHo (for South of Houston—pronounced *HOWston*). It's an area of spooky-looking cast-iron architecture, originally built for industry but converted into studio lofts by artists in the '50s and '60s. Galleries, restaurants and trendy shops make the area a must for art-lovers; branching out from W. Broadway and Spring Street, you can visit some of SoHo's galleries (see listings in the Arts chapter), then pick up a chic outfit or some jewelry and spend the evening dining in the area. Southwest of SoHo is an even newer artistic neighborhood with yet another acronymic name, TriBeCa (derived from Triangle Below Canal Street).

Times Square
Broadway & Seventh Ave.,
42nd St. to 47th St.

By day, it looks seedy and uninviting; by night, there's plenty of excitement left on the Great White Way. Named for the newspaper that for years was headquartered on the southern end (*The New York Times* has since moved up to W. 43rd Street), Times Square—which is actually shaped more like an hourglass than a quadrangle—is the hub of the city's theater district as well as its X-rated entertainment scene. The giant Marriott Hotel at Broadway and 45th Street (since 1985) marked the beginning of a controversial movement toward redeveloping the area. A number of large office buildings and hotels have been proposed, but opponents fear that the special honky-tonk quality of the neighborhood could be lost.

Upper East Side
59th St. to 96th St., between Central Park & the East River

The skyline of this neighborhood—one of the richest in the world—is rapidly being taken over by some hideous high-rises, but the gorgeous Beaux Arts palaces and Neo-French chateaux of the Vanderbilts, Astors and Whitneys remain. Stroll along Fifth Avenue's Museum Mile or down East End Avenue along the river and Carl Schurz Park. You'll find that each avenue has its own particular flavor: Park is completely residential while nearby Madison is filled with expensive boutiques and galleries.

B&D de Vogüé

Escape to a Chateau in France . . .

Choose from:

- over 90 private Chateaux throughout Europe from $80/night
- 200 Villas and country house from $500/week
- 300 Private apartments in PARIS from $90/night
- Luxury barge cruising from $975/person with Barge About France/Quiztour

Complete color brochures on request or call toll-free:
USA 1-800-727-4748
Australia (008) 226014
1830 S. Mooney Blvd., Suite 103 • P.O. Box 1998 • Visalia, CA 93279 USA
Your specialists for private accommodations and tours in France.

Upper West Side

59th St. to 125th St. between Central Park & the Hudson River

More than any other area of the city, the Upper West Side defines gentrification. Back in the '60s and '70s, Broadway, Columbus and Amsterdam avenues were run-down and drug-infested. Today they are riddled with cafés, small expensive shops and yuppies. After exploring Lincoln Center and window-shopping on Columbus Avenue, get somewhat off the beaten path and walk over to Riverside Drive for some splendid architecture and a sweeping view of the Hudson River. If you're in the mood for a longer walk, follow Broadway to 110th Street. Rich in academic tradition, this area from 110th Street to 125th Street is called Morningside Heights and is home to Barnard College, Union Theological Seminary, the Jewish Theological Seminary, Bank Street College and Columbia University.

PARKS & GARDENS

Brooklyn Botanic Garden

1000 Washington Ave., Brooklyn

(718) 622-4433

Open Tues.-Fri. 8 a.m.-6 p.m. (8 a.m.-4:30 p.m. in winter), Sat.-Sun. 10 a.m.-6 p.m. (10 a.m.-4:30 p.m. in winter). Admission free, conservatory $2.

Though much smaller than its companion garden in the Bronx, the 50-acre Brooklyn Botanic Garden is well worth a visit for delights like its Japanese Garden (open April to October 11 a.m. to 4 p.m.), Shakespeare Garden, herb garden and America's oldest and probably largest collection of bonsai trees. In springtime, the blossoming cherry trees are just as pretty as Washington, D.C.'s; in June, the rose garden comes vividly to life. There's also a fragrance garden with Braille markers for the blind, and a conservatory.

Central Park

W. 59th St. to W. 110th St. between Fifth Ave. & Central Park West

Believe it or not, Central Park was once 843 acres of swampland. For more than a century, it has been the heart of the city, a truly democratic place where New Yorkers can escape their apartments and office cubicles to fly kites, jog, skate, play checkers, ride horses, go for a romantic row on the lake or simply stare at the sky in their own peaceful corner. The design, by Frederick Law Olmstead and Calvert Vaux, brilliantly combines open vistas, meadows and small bodies of water with woods, hills and thousands of trees. Remarkably, the maze of pedestrian paths, bridle paths, and crosstown roads only rarely intersect—a series of tunnels, arches, bridges and sunken roadways keep all forms of traffic moving yet separated.

Each visit to Central Park reveals new treasures, new views, new areas to explore. The latest is the newly renovated Central Park Zoo (Fifth Avenue at 64th Street). Don't come expecting the Bronx Zoo (Central Park's is one-fiftieth its size) but do expect to be entertained by the sea lions, polar bears, monkeys or any of the other 450 animals now residing in the heart of Manhattan. (Open every day of the year; April to October: open Monday through Friday 10 a.m. to 5 p.m. [Tuesday 10 a.m. to 8 p.m. from May to September], Saturday, Sunday and holidays from 10 a.m. to 5:30 p.m.; November to March: open daily 10 a.m.-4:30 p.m.; adults $1; children [ages 3 to 12] 25 cents, senior citizens 50 cents, children under 3 free. For more information call 861-6030.)

Other highlights: the charming Gothic Revival Dairy at 65th Street in the center of the park doesn't sell milk anymore; it's now the Visitor Information Center, a source of free maps, exhibits, slide shows and Ranger tours (call 397-3156 for information). Just below the Dairy is the refurbished Wollman Memorial ice skating rink (open in winter; call 517-4800 for information). To the west is every child's favorite attraction, an antique merry-go-round (open Monday to Friday 10:30 a.m. to 4:30 p.m., Saturday and Sunday 10:30 a.m. to 5:30 p.m.; in winter open Saturday and Sunday only, weather permitting; 879-0244 for information). Children will also love—and can climb—the statues of Alice in Wonderland and the Mad Hatter at the elliptical Conservatory Water, above the entrance at 72nd Street and Fifth Avenue. In the summer, children can hear stories every Saturday at 11 a.m. at the statue of Hans Christian Andersen.

On springtime Saturdays, model-yacht enthusiasts hold races in the water. To the west is the lovely Central Park Lake, where you can rent rowboats at the Loeb Boathouse ($6 an hour with $20 refundable deposit; daily 9 a.m. to dusk; 517-3697 for information) or simply watch the action from Bethesda Terrace, lovingly restored by landscape architects and stone craftspeople. With its majestic fountain, the terrace anchors the northern end of Central Park Mall, a formal promenade lined with giant elms and statues. Street performers vie for attention near the mall's large band shell, home to a variety of concerts in warm weather.

West of the lake, near Central Park West and 72nd Street, is Strawberry Fields, a two-and-one-half-acre garden dedicated to the memory of John Lennon, who lived in the Dakota apartment house across the street. Some 25,000 strawberry plants nestle among flowers, trees and exotic plants, many of them donated by other countries. Rising from the eastern bank of the lake is a heavily wooded section of the park known as the Ramble. Birdwatchers frequent this area because it is so overgrown and contains dozens of easy-to-get-lost-in paths. Don't explore alone here. Just behind the Metropolitan Museum of Art is the park's best picnic area, the Great Lawn. Hundreds of thousands of New Yorkers gather here on summer evenings to hear free concerts by the New York Philharmonic and the Metropolitan Opera, and rock fans have enjoyed performances in recent years by Simon & Garfunkel, Diana Ross and others. Theater-lovers gather on the great lawn every summer as well, lining up for free Shakespeare-in-the-Park performances at the Delacorte Theater (call 861-7277 for information). On the hill above the theater stands Belvedere Castle (built in 1869): once a weather station and now an educational center.

If you're a jogger, you might want to join the hordes who circle the reservoir located above 86th Street. As you clock your miles, you can discreetly watch for celebrity runners like Madonna and Jackie O. Bridle paths also ring the reservoir; experienced riders may rent a horse and English saddle from the Clare-mont Riding Academy (175 W. 89th Street; open weekdays 6:30 a.m. to 10 p.m., weekends 6:30 a.m. to 5 p.m.; $27 an hour; 724-5100). When exploring Central Park, unless you're attending an organized event, stay away after dark and *never* explore isolated areas alone. This includes using any of the isolated jogging paths.

Gramercy Park
Lexington Ave. between 20th & 21st Sts.

Though you can't stroll inside—Gramercy Park is the city's last surviving private park, for use by area residents, who have keys—you'll be charmed by this model of a nineteenth-century London square. The west side is composed of a lovely row of red-brick town houses with intricate ironwork porches. The south side includes the National Arts Club, once the home of New York governor Samuel Tilden, and the Players Club, founded by actor Edwin Booth in 1888. (A statue of Booth as Hamlet stands in the center of the park.)

New York Botanical Garden
Fordham Rd. & Bronx River Pkwy., Bronx 220-8700
Garden: open Tues.-Sun. 8 a.m.-dusk. Admission free; Conservatory: open 10 a.m.-4 p.m. Adults $3.50; children, students & senior citizens $1.25; free on Sat. 10 a.m.-noon.

For instant relaxation in a gorgeous natural setting, spend a few hours walking among the azaleas, magnolias and rhododendron in the famous Bronx Botanical Garden, located just north of the zoo. You'll see hundreds of flowers, trees and herbs from around the world, plus a 40-acre hemlock forest, rock garden and pine grove. The jewel of the 250-acre garden is the beautifully restored Enid A. Haupt Conservatory, a domed glass pavilion built in 1901. Inside are simulated deserts, a waterfall, an orangery, coconut palms, orchids and many more goodies to delight you.

Prospect Park
Grand Army Plaza, Brooklyn

One landscaping feat was not enough to satisfy the ambitious Olmstead-Vaux team that created Central Park. This Brooklyn landmark, another masterwork by the two, includes a large lake, meadows cut with paths and streams, a small zoo and a variety of arches, pavilions and bridges, all designed to follow the area's original landscape. In fact, because Olmstead and Vaux had a freer hand here than in Central Park, they were happier with the result. The entrance is at the impressive Grand Army Plaza, which includes a monument to John F. Kennedy and a triumphal arch dedicated to Union Army soldiers and sailors. On Saturdays and Sundays from 11 a.m. to 4:30 p.m. you can climb to the top for free, and have a view of Brooklyn rooftops and of the Manhattan skyline on clear days.

Riverside Park
Riverside Dr. to the Hudson River between 72nd & 145th Sts.

It isn't large enough to be a real oasis in the manner of Central Park, but Riverside Park provides a peaceful slice of green for West Siders. Notable along the park's three-plus miles are the 79th Street boat basin, where a

number of houseboats are parked (there's a short promenade for waterside strolling), and the Soldiers' and Sailors' Monument at W. 89th Street. Also interesting are the park's varying levels, from old railroad lines down to the Henry Hudson Parkway.

Washington Square Park
Base of Fifth Ave.

You'll see it all in this former potter's field—musicians and magicians, aging hippies, NYU students, elderly chess players, neighborhood kids and more than a few drug dealers. In good weather, all forms of humanity gather here at the center of the Village. There's nothing pastoral about it, but you'll see an interesting cross-section of New York life here.

SPORTS

The New York City Sports Commission (463-2004) puts together a day-to-day calendar of sporting events. Below is a partial listing of events that are of interest to both the athlete and the spectator.

BASEBALL

Mets
Shea Stadium, Queens
(718) 507-8499

Yankees
Yankee Stadium, Bronx
307-7171
Apr.-Oct.

BASKETBALL

Knicks
Madison Square Garden
563-8000

Nets
Brendan Byrne Arena, Meadowlands, N.J.
(201) 935-3900
Nov.-Apr.

BIKING

Five-Borough Bike Tour
Battery Park to Staten Island
Late Apr.

FOOTBALL

Giants
Giants Stadium
(201) 935-8111
Sept.-Feb.

Jets
Giants Stadium, Meadowlands, N.J.
421-6600

HOCKEY

Islanders
Nassau Coliseum, Long Island
(516) 794-4100

Rangers
Madison Square Garden
563-8000

Devils
Brendan Byrne Arena, Meadowlands, N.J.
(201) 935-3900
Oct.-Mar.

HORSE RACING

Belmont Stakes
Belmont Park, Queens
(718) 641-4700
Triple Crown, mid-June.

Thoroughbred racing
Aqueduct Racetrack, Queens
(718) 641-4700
Oct.-May.

RUNNING

L'Eggs Mini-Marathon
Central Park West at 66th St.
860-4455
Last weekend in May.

New York City Marathon
Staten Island to Central Park
860-4455
1st Sun. in Nov.

New York Road Runners Club
9 East 89th St.
860-4455
Holds more than 150 races throughout the year.

TENNIS

Nabisco Masters Tennis Championship
Madison Square Garden
563-8300
Late Nov.-early Dec.

U.S. Open Tennis Championship
Flushing Meadows, Queens
(718) 271-5100
Aug.-Sept.

Virginia Slims Women's Tennis Championship
Madison Square Garden
563-8300
Mid-Nov.

TOURS

BY AIR

Island Helicopter
Heliport at E. 34th St. & the East River
925-8807
Operates daily Jan.-Mar. 9 a.m.-6 p.m., Apr.-Dec. 9 a.m.-9 p.m.; $35-$144 (2-person minimum per flight).
Here's the most dramatic way to see the city, with a chance to come face to face with the Statue of Liberty and peek inside the top floors of the World Trade Center. Five choices of flights range in length from six minutes to 40 minutes. Best bets: the flight over the financial district to the Statue of Liberty ($45), or the same one, plus midtown and Central Park ($55). Photographers love it.

BY BOAT

Circle Line
Pier 83, W. 43rd St. & Twelfth Ave.
563-3200
Operates Mar.-Nov.; departure times change. Adults $15, children $7.50.
The Circle Line tour—a three-hour ride literally around Manhattan—is a terrific way to get a new perspective on the city. As you ride under the great bridges, note the differences in terrain (upper Manhattan looks almost rural!), and take in the great skyscrapers and luxury riverside apartment buildings. An experienced guide points out the major sights, shares bits of gossip and tells corny jokes. Most New Yorkers have never taken the Circle

Line, but it's their loss. You can save the Circle Line for a pretty afternoon when you're really exhausted or, in the summer, opt for a night-time cruise. Take a picnic basket and enjoy!

Hudson River Day Line
Pier 81, W. 41st St. & Twelfth Ave.
279-5151
Only 5 trips per year: May 29, June 17, July 14, Aug. 5, Sept. 4; departs 9 a.m., returns 6 p.m. Adults $15, children $7.50. Reservations suggested.

Our favorite time of year to take this all-day trip up the Hudson is in September, when the weather is cooling off a bit and the leaves are just about to start turning gold. You'll cruise north as far as Poughkeepsie, with stops at lovely Bear Mountain State Park and at the Military Academy at West Point. If you choose to stay on the boat to West Point, a sightseeing tour of the U.S.M.A. costs a few dollars extra; otherwise, you can spend four hours exploring, picknicking and swimming at Bear Mountain, then wait to be picked up on the boat's return trip.

The *Petrel*
Battery Park
825-1976
Operates April to Oct.; times vary. $8-20. Reservations suggested.

JFK used to charter the *Petrel* for private sails and this 35-passenger, 70-foot yawl provides an unusual, fun way to spend a lunch hour, happy hour, or, for romantics, a starry night. For lunch you'll need to bring your own, but you can buy sodas or drinks at the cash bar. Sails take you around the Upper Bay and last between 45 minutes and two hours; they'll take you around the Statue of Liberty as long as wind and weather permit.

The *Pioneer*
South Street Seaport, Pier 16 (off Fulton St.)
669-9400
Operates May-2nd week in Sept., Wed.-Sun.; times vary. $15 for a 2-hour ride, $22 for 3 hours. Reservations suggested.

This 102-foot schooner takes two- and three-hour cruises in warm weather. Charters are available as well (a mere $975 for three

hours, or $800 for two) and you can invite your friends for a ride.

World Yacht Cruises
Pier 62 W. 23rd St.
929-7090
If you're not up for packing your own picnic, you may want to opt for one of these cruises; for $64.50, you'll be treated to dinner, dancing and a table with a view. Reservations and proper dress required.

BY BUS

If time is short or you're not keen on walking everywhere, consider a bus tour of the city. You'll cover a lot of ground and learn more about New York from the multilingual tour guides than most of the natives know. The companies listed here offer a variety of tours, including lower Manhattan, uptown, all the major sights and some boat tours. Prices vary, so shop around and compare.

Campus Coach
545 Fifth Ave.
682-1050

Crossroads Sightseeing
150 W. 49th St.
581-2828

Gray Line Sightseeing
900 Eighth Ave.
397-2600

Manhattan Sightseeing Tours
150 W. 49th St.
869-5005

New York Big Apple Tours
22 W. 23rd St.
691-7866
Regular tours given in French, German, Spanish and Italian. Private tours for ten or more available in English.

Short Line Tours
166 W. 46th St.
354-5122

BY FOOT

Art Tours of Manhattan
76 Library Pl., Princeton, N.J.
(609) 921-2647; (609) 683-0881
Pre-arranged tours available. $25-$45.
Whether you're seriously interested in art or simply curious, take a private tour of artists' studios, galleries and museums with a Ph.D. as your guide. And if you're looking to buy that perfect piece for your home, an art-consulting service is available for an additional fee.

Municipal Art Society
457 Madison Ave.
935-3690
Tours April-Oct., Sat.-Sun.; times vary. Call for reservations. Members $8; nonmembers $12.
This preservation-minded civic group conducts tours of different neighborhoods around the city. Knowledgeable guides share a wealth of information about architecture, city planning and history. A free one-hour tour of Grand Central Station is given every Wednesday at 12:30 p.m. (call for meeting place).

Museum of the City of New York
1220 Fifth Ave. (103rd St.)
534-1672
Tours in spring (mid-March–May) & fall (late Sept.–mid-Nov.), some Suns. 11 a.m.-1 p.m. Members & seniors $10, nonmembers $15.
Take a four-hour exploration (with a lunch break) of a particular neighborhood's historical, cultural and sociological history, led by one of the museum's urban historians.

New York Walk-About
Lister Travel Service, 30 Rockefeller Plaza
582-2015 (weekdays);
(914) 834-5388 (evenings & weekends)
Operates Mar.-July & Sept.-Nov., Sun. 11 a.m. & 2 p.m., Sat. 9 p.m., 11 a.m. & 2 p.m. $8.
Most of the walkers on these informative tours are New Yorkers eager to learn more about the evolution of their city. About 25 different tours are offered (one or two per weekend), including "Millionaires' Row— New York's Gold Coast," "Greenwich Village—Echoes of the Past," and walks through the Lower East Side, Brooklyn Heights and Chinatown and Little Italy. Occasionally, there's a Saturday-afternoon tour of SoHo or a Saturday-evening tour (9 p.m. to midnight) entitled "Nocturnal New York."

92nd Street Y
1395 Lexington Ave.
415-5600
Open year-round; most tours on Sun. $8-25.
The Y has long been a leader in sponsoring unusual walking tours, often with celebrated guides like historian Kate Simon. Three or four tours are offered every weekend, with subjects as varied as Jewish Harlem, the East Village, a "mystery tour," a day in Irish New York and a tour of Coney Island.

SPECIALTIES

Backstage on Broadway
228 W. 47th St.
575-8065
Open Mon.-Sat. 10:30 a.m. Adults $7, students $6.
Theater buffs will be enthralled by a 60- to 90-minute tour of a current Broadway show. A theater "pro" takes you backstage to explain how the magic really happens. Early reservations are a must.

Doorway to Design
1441 Broadway, Ste. 338
221-1111; (718) 339-1542
Open by appt. only. $20-$25 for a half-day program; longer tours available.
A professional interior designer will give you a behind-the-scenes look at top furniture and fabric showrooms, antique dealers, artists' studios and private townhouses. A similar tour is offered for the fashion houses and design studios both on and off Seventh Avenue.

Federal Reserve Bank
33 Liberty St.
720-6130
Tours Mon.-Fri. 10 a.m., 11 a.m., 1 p.m. & 2 p.m. Free admission; reservations required a week in advance.
After you've visited the stock exchange, where fortunes are made and lost, drop by the

Federal Reserve Bank to see a real "piggy bank" and ogle at the $165 billion in the gold vault. Also included in the hour-long tour are the security and cash-counting departments.

Harlem Spirituals, Inc.

1457 Broadway, Ste. 1008
(41st & 42nd Sts.)
302-2594
Sun. and weekday tours leave from Short Line tour office, 166 W. 46th St.

Harlem's jazz age comes to life again in a fascinating nighttime tour every Thursday, Friday and Saturday. After a traditional soul-food dinner, you'll visit a cabaret and hear some good jazz or rhythm-and-blues (7 p.m. to midnight; $60 including dinner and cocktails; you'll be picked up afterward). If you prefer a daytime visit, consider a rousing "Spirituals and Gospel" tour held every Sunday from 8:45 a.m. to 12:45 p.m. ($25), which culminates at a Baptist church service. A more complete tour of this historic neighborhood is available on Thursday from 9 a.m. to 1:30 p.m. ($35), with a soul-food lunch included.

Horse-drawn Carriages

Central Park South & Fifth Ave.
$20 for 1st half hour, $35-$40 for longer ride.

For many visitors, a trip to New York wouldn't be complete without a romantic carriage ride through Central Park. Carriage rentals are available at the southeast corner of the park near the Plaza Hotel.

Inside New York

203 E. 72nd St.
861-0709
Times vary; tours by appt. only. Prices start at $20 (groups only).

For the clotheshorse in the crowd, there's a tour of the studios of famous designers and furriers, plus the chance to shop for designer fashions at wholesale prices. Multilingual guides cover the hottest spots on Seventh Avenue. Art tours around SoHo and the Lower East Side are also available.

Schapiro's Winery

126 Rivington St.
674-4404
Tours: Sept.-April, Sun. 11 a.m.-4 p.m. Tastings: year-round, Sun. 11 a.m.-5 p.m. Admission $1.

Find out how kosher wine is made and sample "The Wine You Can Almost Cut With A Knife," then browse through the food booths in the large Essex Street Market.

Singer's Tours

130 St. Edward's St., Brooklyn
(718) 875-9084
By appt. only. $25.

Lou Singer, also known as "Mr. Brooklyn," loves showing people around his city. Give him a call to reserve a place on one of his personalized tours of Brooklyn or Manhattan: "Waterfront Brooklyn," "Noshing on the Lower East Side," "Historic and Architectural Brooklyn," "Fabulous Flatbush," "Little Old New York" and many more.

BASICS

AT YOUR SERVICE

FOREIGN EXCHANGE

It's still difficult to walk into the average bank and get foreign money changed. Many banks require you to have an account with them before they'll exchange your dollars for drachmas. Not to worry, though—many international banks gladly provide this service, along with some companies that deal exclusively in foreign exchange. Of these, two of the best are Bank Leumi Trust Co. of New York at 535 Seventh Avenue, 392-4000; and Deak New York Inc., with five branches: 630 Fifth Avenue, 757-6915; 1 Herald Square, 736-9790; 41 E. 42nd Street, 883-0400; 875 3rd Avenue, 355-4500; and 29 Broadway, 820-2470.

SAFETY

Common sense is your best security in New York City. No matter what neighborhood you're in, it's safest to be aware of what's happening around you at all times. Wear your jewelry but don't flash it, and don't go onto the subway with it in full sight. If you take the subway at night (which many people do), wait for your train in a well-lit area near the token booth. The parks are beautiful, so stroll through them if you like, but never at night and never alone in isolated areas, no matter what the time. If you know where you're going and you behave as if you're sure of yourself, you can spend a wonderful, crime-free vacation in New York.

TELEPHONE NUMBERS

Airport Flight Information (for JFK, LaGuardia, Newark), (718) 656-4520

Emergencies (Ambulance/Fire/Police), 911

Library Information, 340-0849

Mayor's Office of Special Projects and Events, 566-4074

Telephone Directory Assistance, 411

Time, 976-1616

Transit Authority Travel Information Bureau, (718) 330-1234

U.S. Customs, 466-5550

Visitors Bureau, 397-8222

Weather, 976-1212

GETTING AROUND

AIRPORT

BUSES

Carey buses (718-632-0500) depart for Kennedy and LaGuardia from five Manhattan locations: 125 Park Avenue near Grand Central Station, Port Authority between Eighth and Ninth avenues at 42nd Street, the Hilton Hotel near Rockefeller Center at 53rd Street and Sixth Avenue, Sheraton City Squire at Seventh Avenue and 51st Street, and Marriott Marquis at Broadway and 45th Street. There's also an express bus from Grand Central to the Pan Am Shuttle at LaGuardia. Buses run each 30 minutes from the stations, from 6 a.m. to 1 a.m., every twenty minutes from the hotels, from 5:45 a.m. to 10:45 p.m. The price is $9.50 to JFK and $7.50 to LGA. Buses between JFK and LGA run for $8.50. Carey also has buses to Ashland Place and Hanson Place in Brooklyn ($6 from LGA, $8 from JFK) and Jamaica Station in Queens ($5 from either airport). Head to the latter for connections to the Long Island Rail Road. More convenient than a bus and much more reasonable than a taxi, Transport Limousine of Long Island offers door-to-door service from JFK and LGA. Check with Ground Transportation at the airport or call 1-800-832-5466. If you're operating on a strict budget, try the Transport of New Jersey buses from the Port Authority Bus Terminal (41st Street and Eighth Avenue, platform 39). You won't find a better price unless you walk or ride a bicycle. The 24-hour service is $5.

HELICOPTER

For an unparalleled view of Manhattan and the fastest trip possible to the airport, New York Helicopter's (800-645-3494) ten-minute ride to JFK can't be beat. Flights depart from 34th Street and the East River. The price is $65 one way, with departures every half hour from 2 p.m. to 7:30 p.m.

TAXIS

The cost for getting to the airports from the city by cab can be shocking, especially if you're leaving during rush hours. Allow yourself plenty of time to make your flight; the ride should take about one hour to Kennedy or Newark and 30 to 40 minutes to LaGuardia. Average prices, according to the New York Taxi Commission (869-4110) are: midtown to LaGuardia, $20, to JFK, $30, and to Newark, $40 plus a $10 base fee added to the meter fare. These prices include tips and tolls, which must be paid by the passenger. JFK to Newark averages $60 and JFK to LaGuardia $15.

AUTO RENTAL

If you're the kind who enjoys dodging—potholes, taxis, bicycles, jaywalkers, delivery trucks—then you may be the brave soul who'll want to rent a car in Manhattan. You'll find the rental companies at the airports as well as in the city. Summer weekends are the most difficult times to find a car, so reserve well in advance. The major companies are Avis, (800) 331-1212; Hertz, (800) 654-3131; and National, (800) 328-4567.

BUSES

Buses are a good, albeit slow, form of reasonable transportation around the city. If you ride them during non–rush hours, you'll get a seat and can enjoy sightseeing through Manhattan for just $1.15. Bus drivers accept only exact change and subway tokens. If you'll need to make a connection to another bus, ask for a transfer upon boarding. There are no transfers between the subway and buses. Call the Travel Information Bureau at (718) 330-1234 to find out about special cultural and shoppers' buses, and for information on the Port Authority Bus Terminal, call 564-8484.

FINDING STREETS

Manhattan is one of the simplest big cities in the world to navigate. North of the Village, most of the streets make up a logical criss-crossing grid, with numbered streets running east-west and avenues (Park, Madison, Fifth) running north-south. The higher the number of the avenue, the farther west it is. The higher the number of the street, the farther north it is. From the Village on down to Wall Street and Battery Park, however, you'll need help finding your way through the crooked maze of streets. Check with our map of downtown in this guide; page 333, and if you need more detailed information, pick up a Flashmaps guide—almost all bookstores carry them. Fifth Avenue divides the east and west sides of the city, and east-west blocks are about twice as long as north-south blocks. If you can, call your destination to find its cross street and, if necessary, directions.

LIMOUSINES

Limousines come in all sizes and colors, and all offer comparative services at competitive prices. Some of the best choices are Bermuda Chauffeured Limousine Service, 537 W. 20th Street, 249-8400; Class Act, 2315 Twelfth Avenue, 491-5300; Express Car and Limousine Service, 1729 First Avenue, 831-8900; Jerusalem Car and Limousine Service, 404 E. 88th Street, 996-6600; Sabra Car and Limousine Service, 171 E. 88th Street, 410-7600; and Carey Limousine, 517-7010.

SUBWAYS

If the tracks aren't being worked on or the trains being diverted to another route because of water-main problems, the subway is the fastest way to get around in the city and its boroughs. It is by no means luxurious traveling, but for the money ($1.15) you can't beat it. If you haven't been to New York for a while, you'll find that the subways have improved. Almost all trains are new and air-conditioned.

TAXIS

Taxis are a necessary evil in this city. They're expensive, often in ill repair, and sometimes downright uncomfortable, especially when the seat springs are broken and you're jouncing around on the potholed Manhattan streets. But on the up side, they're plentiful in most areas, except during rush hour and pre-theater hour, or when you really need them—say, when it's raining. Don't assume your driver speaks English or knows his way around the outer boroughs, and be sure any taxi you take is a licensed medallion cab; then, if you run into problems, you can contact the Taxi Commission at 869-4110. It'll cost you $1.50 just to enter the taxi plus 25 cents per one-fifth mile. If the traffic flows, you can expect to pay about $11, including tip, for a midtown-to-SoHo ride; about $6, plus tip, from midtown to the Upper East Side; and about $4, plus tip, for a simple crosstown ride.

RADIO TAXIS

There are many radio taxis from which to choose, and most will arrive ten to fifteen minutes after you've phoned. Some of our favorites are Skyline, (718) 482-8686; All City, 796-1111; Battery City Car and Limo Radio Group, 947-9696; Liberty 2 Way Limo, 334-9200; Last Radio Group, Inc.; and UTOG, 741-2000.

TRAINS

For information on train travel into and out of New York, call Amtrak, Penn Station, 582-6875; Long Island Railroad, Penn Station, (718) 454-5477; or Metro North, Grand Central Station, 532-4900.

GOINGS-ON

The following is a list of some of the major events that take place throughout the year. For more detailed and up-to-the-minute information, visit or call Visitors' Information at the New York Convention and Visitors' Bureau, Two Columbus Circle, 397-8222, or the Information Center at Times Square, on 42nd Street between Broadway and Seventh Avenue. They are both open Monday through Friday from 9 a.m. to 6 p.m. and weekends from 10 a.m. to 6 p.m. The best publications to consult for weekly or daily events are *The New York Times*, the *Village Voice*, *The New Yorker* and *New York* magazines.

JANUARY

- National Boat Show (mid-Jan.), Jacob Javits Center; 216-2000.
- Winter Antiques Show (mid- to late Jan.).
- Seventh Regiment Armory, Park Ave. at 67th St.
- Greater New York International Automobile Show (late Jan.), Jacob Javits Center; 216-2000.
- Ice Capades (mid-Jan.), Madison Square Garden; 563-8300.

FEBRUARY

- Westminster Kennel Club/Westminster Dog Show (mid-Feb.), Madison Square Garden; 563-8300.

MARCH

- St. Patrick's Day Parade (Mar. 17), Fifth Ave. from 44th St. to 86th St.; 397-8222.

APRIL

- Ringling Bros. and Barnum & Bailey Circus (April and May), Madison Square Garden; 563-8300.
- Easter Parade (Easter Sunday), Fifth Ave. from 49th St. to 59th St.; 397-8222.
- Cherry Blossom Festival (late April), Brooklyn Botanic Garden; (718) 622-4433.

MAY

- Washington Square Art Show (Memorial Day weekend and first two weekends in June), University Place; 982-6255.
- Rose and Orchid Show (late May), New York Botanic Garden, the Bronx; (718) 220-8777.
- City beaches open (late May).

JUNE

- Guggenheim Concerts (mid-June to early Aug.), Damrosch Park, Lincoln Center and Seaside Park in Brooklyn; 594-5151.
- Metropolitan Opera/New York Philharmonic free concerts (all month), city parks; 360-1333.
- Museum Mile (mid-June), Fifth Ave. from 82nd St. to 105th St.; 722-1313.
- JVC Jazz Festival (late June and July), locations vary; 877-1800, 787-2020.

JULY

- Shakespeare in the Park (July and Aug.), Delacorte Theater, Central Park; 598-7100.
- American Crafts Festival, Lincoln Center; 677-4627, (201) 746-0091.
- Mostly Mozart Concerts (July and Aug.), Lincoln Center; 874-2424.

AUGUST

- Lincoln Center Out-of-Doors Festival, Lincoln Center Plaza; 877-3860.

SEPTEMBER

- New York Philharmonic season opens, Avery Fisher Hall, Lincoln Center; 874-2424.
- Washington Square Outdoor Art Exhibit (first two weekends), University Place; 982-6255.
- New York Film Festival, Lincoln Center; 362-1900 ext. 484.
- Feast of San Gennaro (mid-Sept.), Little Italy, Mulberry St.; 226-9546.
- New York Is Book Country (mid-Sept.), Fifth Ave. from 47th St. to 57th St.; 593-3983, 661-6030.

OCTOBER

- Start of ice-skating season at Rockefeller Center; 757-5731.

NOVEMBER

- Macy's Thanksgiving Day Parade (last Thurs. of Nov.), Central Park West from 77th St. to 59th St., Broadway from 59th St. to 34th St.; 560-4495, 397-8222.

DECEMBER

- Christmas tree lighting at Rockefeller Center; 397-8222.
- Baroque crèche and Christmas tree display (throughout Dec. and into early Jan.), Metropolitan Museum of Art; 535-7710.
- Messiah Sing-Along, Avery Fisher Hall and local churches; 874-2424.

MAPS

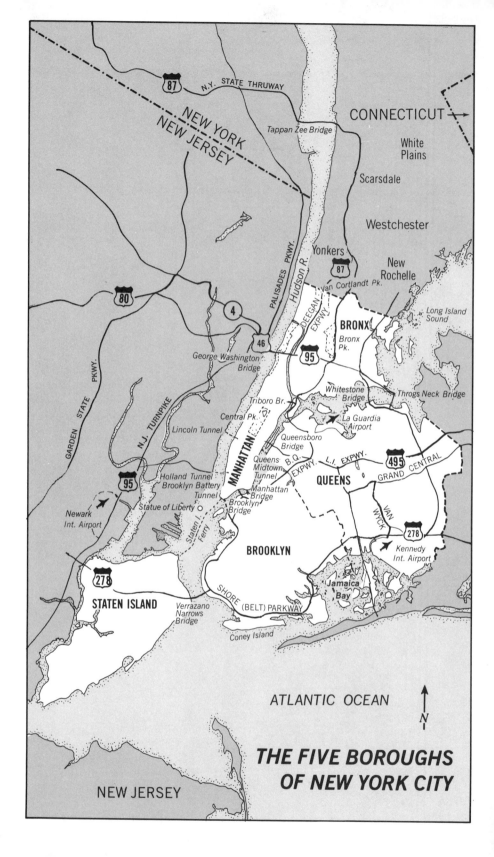

THE FIVE BOROUGHS
OF NEW YORK CITY

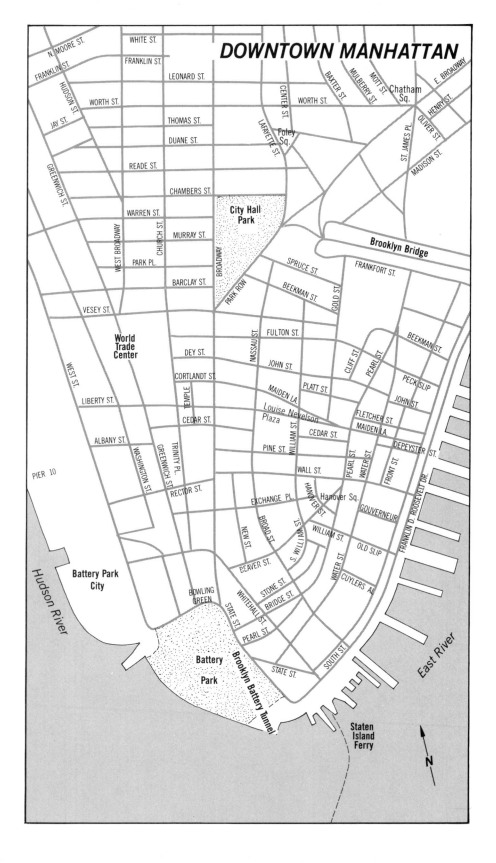

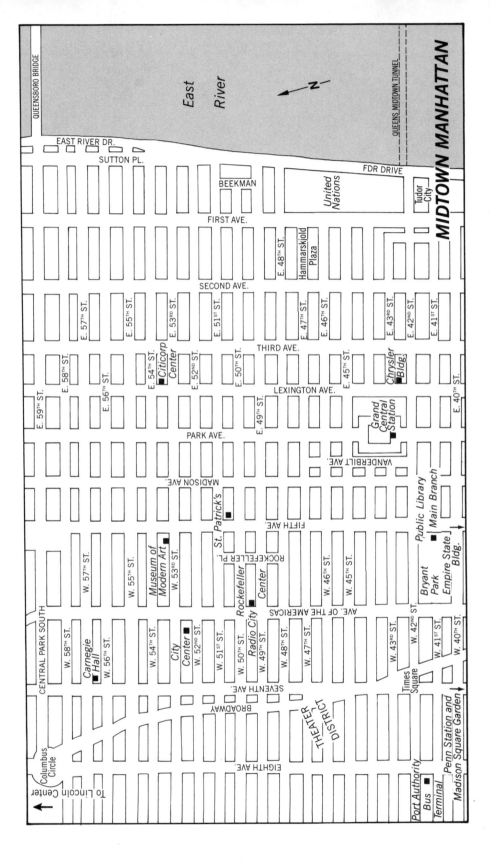

Upper Manhattan

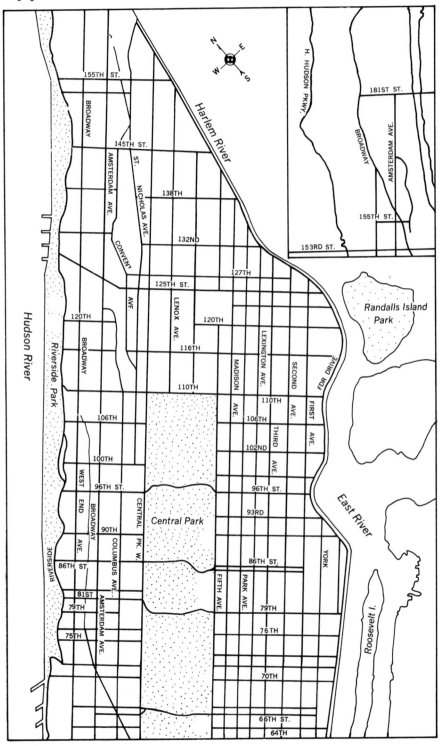

INDEX

MORE *GAULT MILLAU* GUIDES TO THE BEST

Now the guidebook series known throughout Europe for its wit and savvy reveals the best of major U.S., European and Asian destinations. **Gault Millau** books include full details on the best of everything that makes these places special: the restaurants, diversions, nightlife, hotels, shops and arts. The guides offer practical information on getting around and enjoying the area—perfect for visitors and residents alike.

Please send me the books checked below:

☐ The Best of Chicago $15.95
☐ The Best of London $16.95
☐ The Best of Los Angeles $15.95
☐ The Best of New England...$16.95
☐ The Best of New York $16.95
☐ The Best of Paris $16.95
☐ The Best of San Francisco $16.95
☐ The Best of Washington, D.C. $16.95
☐ The Best of France $16.95
☐ The Best of Italy...$16.95
☐ The Best of Hong Kong $16.95

PRENTICE HALL PRESS
Order Department—Travel Books
200 Old Tappan Road
Old Tappan, NJ 07675

In the U.S., include $2 (UPS shipping charge) for the first book, and $1 for each additional book. Outside the U.S., $3 and $1 respectively. Enclosed is my check or money order made out to **Prentice Hall Press**, for $ _____

NAME _____

ADDRESS _____

CITY_____ STATE _____

ZIP _____ COUNTRY_____

301/90

André Gayot's
TASTES
with the Best of Gault Millau

THE WORLD DINING & TRAVEL CONNECTION

P.O. Box 361144, Los Angeles, CA 90036

♦ All you'll ever need to know about the beds and tables (and under the tables) of the world.
♦ The best—and other—restaurants, hotels, nightlife, shopping, fashion.
♦ What's hot, lukewarm and cold from Hollywood to Hong Kong via Paris.

☐ **YES,** please enter/renew my subscription for 6 bimonthly issues at the rate of $30. (Outside U.S. and Canada, $35.)

Name_____

Address_____

City_____State _____

Zip_____Country _____

☐ **ALSO,** please send a gift subscription to: *

Name_____

Address_____

City_____State _____

Zip_____Country _____

Gift from_____
(We will notify recipient of your gift)

* With the purchase of a gift subscription or a second subscription, you will receive, **FREE,** the **Gault Millau guidebook of your choice**—a $17 value. (See preceding order form for a complete list of Gault Millau guides.)

☐ CHECK ENCLOSED FOR $ _____.
☐ PLEASE SEND ME, **FREE,** THE GAULT MILLAU GUIDE OF MY CHOICE: _____

301/90